The U.S. Supreme Court and Racial Minorities

ELGAR STUDIES IN LAW AND SOCIETY

Elgar Studies in Law and Society brings together critical and thought-provoking works by scholars from around the globe, on the most pressing topics and issues within the field of Law and Society. The books in this series reflect original, cutting-edge scholarship on aspects of the Law's role in modern society and its intersection with social structures and institutions, such as politics, gender, race, religion and ethics.

The U.S. Supreme Court and Racial Minorities

Two Centuries of Judicial Review on Trial

Leslie F. Goldstein

Judge Hugh M. Morris Professor Emerita, University of Delaware, USA

ELGAR STUDIES IN LAW AND SOCIETY

Edward Elgar
PUBLISHING

Cheltenham, UK • Northampton, MA, USA

Published by
Edward Elgar Publishing Limited
The Lypiatts
15 Lansdown Road
Cheltenham
Glos GL50 2JA
UK

Edward Elgar Publishing, Inc.
William Pratt House
9 Dewey Court
Northampton
Massachusetts 01060
USA

A catalogue record for this book
is available from the British Library

Library of Congress Control Number: 2017931778

This book is available electronically in the **Elgar**online
Law subject collection
DOI 10.4337/9781786438836

Printed on elemental chlorine free (ECF)
recycled paper containing 30% Post-Consumer Waste

ISBN 978 1 78643 882 9 (cased)
ISBN 978 1 78643 883 6 (eBook)

Typeset by Columns Design XML Ltd, Reading
Printed and bound in the USA

Contents

Tables and figures

Acknowledgments

For a slow worker like myself, a scholarly book takes so long to complete that one accumulates many, many helps along the way. Of course, all errors are my own, but without the kinds of support I acknowledge here, the book would have taken even longer to come to life.

First, I must thank the University of Delaware for the generous leave policy that it makes available to "named professors." This policy provided invaluable time for research and reflection.

I must also thank the *University of Maryland Law Review* for permission to use sections of two of my articles: "How Equal Protection Did and Did Not Come to the United States, and the Executive Branch Role Therein," *University of Maryland Law Review* 73 (December 2013): 190–226, and "Slavery and the Marshall Court," *University of Maryland Law Review* 67 (winter 2008): 166–199.

Next, I single out Michael Zuckert and Lee Epstein for very long ago having urged me to write a casebook on the civil rights of African-Americans; that task proved impossibly large so I wrote this instead. But without the nudge from each of them, perhaps not even this book would have come into being.

For feedback on my thoughts, for intellectual stimulation, for helpful suggestions, and in general, for making the life of an academic the pleasure that it is, I must gratefully acknowledge all of the following: Sanford Levinson, Mark Tushnet, Mark Graber, and Jack Balkin, each as individuals and also as organizers of the DC-Baltimore Schmooze; also all the participants in the many Schmoozes I attended and the several Liberty Fund meetings that I attended, whose names make too lengthy a list to itemize in full; also Pam Brandwein, Daniel Hoffman, Paul Finkelman, the late Kermit Hall, Jim Stoner, Peter Kolchin, Ann Boylan, Carole Marks, Paul Sracic, Daniel Guenther, Matthew Hall, Eric Segall, Marty Lederman, Jim Magee, Wayne Batchis, Sue Davis, Eileen McDonough, Howard Gillman, Ronny Kahn, and Carol Nackenoff.

I also thank Catherine Zuckert and the late David Ingersoll for praising my work, on occasion, in ways that deeply encouraged me. I thank my longtime colleague, Henry Reynolds for arguing with me consistently and capably against the institution of judicial review (I wonder if this book would change his mind). I thank my husband Phil for putting up with me all these years, serving as my techno guru in all things computer-related, and helping to keep me sane during my daily challenges at finding lost objects. I dedicate this book to my extended family members, Audrey, Chris, and Jackson, and to my good friend Alice Ba. To the extent that this book accomplishes anything toward improving life in America for the members of racial minorities, these are all people close to me who may reap some benefit.

Leslie F. Goldstein, Morris Professor Emerita of Political Science
University of Delaware

Table of cases

Introduction

For someone like myself who grew up in the middle of the last century, the image of the Supreme Court as the Supreme Defender of the constitutional rights of racial minorities is still vivid in memory. In the mid-1950s the Supreme Court declared an end to separate but equal in schools, parks, and all government-run facilities.[1] It was a shock to the South and was met with considerable resistance, including by governors, and even mob violence. To be sure, the Court then allowed for a turtle's pace rate of speed for correcting segregation, which pace it called "all deliberate speed."[2] Despite the Court's producing an opinion in 1958 signed by all nine justices (for the only time in Court history) that insisted that community opposition is never a valid reason for government to deny or postpone honoring someone's constitutional rights,[3] by1964 there had been hardly any actual school desegregation.

The assassination of President John F. Kennedy, however, supplemented by televised coverage of brutal treatment of peaceful black protesters led by Martin Luther King and his allies, created a wave of sympathy that enabled JFK's former Vice President Lyndon B. Johnson to push through Congress the pending 1964 Civil Rights Act (originally proposed by Kennedy), despite opposition from most of the southern Democrats. The majority of the votes for the 1964 Civil Rights Act came

---

[1] Public schools: *Brown v. Board of Education,* 347 U.S. 483 (1954); theater group performances in city park: *Muir v. Louisville Park Theatrical Assoc.*, 347 U.S. 971 (1954); state- and city-run bathhouses and beaches: *Mayor … of Baltimore City v. Dawson*, 350 U.S. 877 (1955); city-run golf courses: *Holmes v. Atlanta*, 350 U.S. 879 (1955) and *New Orleans City Park v. Ditiege*, 358 U.S. 54 (1958). Into the 1960s the Court continued to reaffirm these rulings and to throw out convictions of blacks charged with entering whites-only governmentally-run facilities: *Watson v. Memphis*, 373 U.S. 526 (1963) (ruling that cities may not maintain whites-only parks); *Wright v. Georgia*, 373 U.S. 284 (1963) (threw out conviction of blacks for using all-white park); *Johnson v. Virginia*, 373 U.S. 61 (1963) (reversed conviction of a black man for sitting in whites-only section of courtroom, and refusing judge's order to sit in black section). Davis and Graham 1995, 140–41.

[2] *Brown v. Board II*, 348 U.S. 294 (1955).

[3] *Cooper v. Aaron*, 358 U.S. 1, 16–17 (1958).

from Republicans. Then the debacle of Barry Goldwater's candidacy for President against Lyndon Johnson swept a historically large Democratic majority into Congress, and LBJ was able to use this to get Congress to pass the follow-up, 1965 Voting Rights Act, and the 1968 Open Housing Act. By the mid-1960s LBJ's efforts to persuade Congress received additional impetus from urban riots that were happening every summer for several years as well as immediately consequent to the assassination of Martin Luther King in April of 1968.

The 1964 Act had the crucially important feature of cutting off the new federal financial assistance to local public schools for any system that stayed segregated. This federal monetary assistance received a big boost in 1965 in the Elementary and Secondary Education Act. This money-based carrot-and-stick approach pushed the South to desegregate promptly.

The other main features of the 1964 Act were, first, the insistence on racially non-discriminatory access to privately owned public accommodations—hotels, restaurants, theaters, and gas stations—that affect interstate commerce. Secondly, the 1964 Act prohibited race-based, nationality-based, and gender-based discrimination in employment within interstate commerce.[4] This law eventually changed the face of America. Within a couple of decades, one saw faces of color where they had not been before—on television, as leads in movies, in mainstream commercials, as clerks in high end department stores, as bank tellers, and also as customers in hotels and restaurants throughout the country.

The Supreme Court continued in a leadership role by first, in 1964 and 1967 making clear that laws making it a crime to engage in sex across racial lines were unconstitutional. The Court struck down state laws forbidding interracial cohabitation[5] and interracial marriage.[6] In doing so, the Court deployed the "strict scrutiny test" that it had developed for dealing with anti-Japanese discrimination during World War II.[7]

On school desegregation, the Court also continued to lead, by insisting that schools formerly segregated by the force of laws now had to use laws to un-segregate. They could not just remove the labels "colored" and "white" from the schoolhouse door and pretend all was well. They had to

---

[4] For a more complete description of the Civil Rights Act of 1964, see below, Chapter 6, text at nn.205–9.

[5] *McLaughlin v. Florida*, 379 U.S. 184 (1964).

[6] *Loving v. Virginia*, 388 U.S. 1 (1967).

[7] Ibid., at 9–12.

actively mix together the kids whose racially-segregated school attendance habits the laws had been shaping for generations.[8] Available tools for this de-segregating included the option of busing, the Court said in 1971,[9] and these rules also applied to *northern* districts,[10] like the one in Boston that used laws surreptitiously rather than openly to push the races apart in district schools. Boston's reaction to court-ordered busing, as recently as 1974–75, showed that white mob violence against blacks, unfortunately, was not limited to the South.[11]

Even in the face of clear and strong popular opposition to "forced busing" all over the U.S., the Supreme Court continued in the posture of insisting on actual desegregation up through the late 1980s.[12] In 1989 for the first time it started applying the rule of strict scrutiny *against* race-based affirmative action programs, and around 1991 started declaring (as it had predicted it would back in 1971) that school districts were now effectively desegregated and did not need to continue further racial mixing.[13] Throughout the period of 1954–89 (for thirty-five years), the Court played a role of clear and strong moral leadership, upholding constitutional principles, first when Congress was unwilling to act and secondly, long after Congress had started to oppose what it called "forced busing."[14] Eventually, the Court (whose retirees are replaced by nominees

---

8 *Green v. New Kent County*, 391 U.S. 430 (1968).

9 *Swann v. Charlotte-Mecklenburg N.C.*, 402 U.S. 1, 29–31 (1971). The Court noted that the length of busrides should not be so excessive as to interfere with the learning process or children's health and well-being. Riding a bus to school was a well-entrenched practice in American public schooling by this time.

10 *Keyes v. School District ... Denver*, 413 U.S. 189 (1973).

11 Wolff 2014.

12 In addition to supporting busing orders, the Supreme Court aggressively enforced old civil rights laws that had lain dormant for a century. See *Jones v. Alfred Mayer,* 392 U.S. 409 (1968) and discussion of it and its sequelae in Rutherglen 2013, 137–8.

13 *Richmond v. Croson*, 488 U.S. 469 (1989) (strict scrutiny of state-level affirmative action); *Adarand v. Pena,* 515 U.S. 200 (1995) (strict scrutiny of federal level affirmative action); *Swann*, 402 U.S. at 31–2, "Neither school authorities nor district courts are constitutionally required to make year-by-year adjustments of the racial composition of student bodies once the affirmative duty to desegregate has been accomplished and racial discrimination through official action is eliminated from the system" (1971); *Oklahoma City v. Dowell*, 498 U.S. 237 (1991); *Freeman v. Pitts*, 503 U.S. 467 (1992).

14 "Congressional Anti-Busing Sentiment Mounts in 1972." Congress adopted the anti-busing measure S 659-PL 92-318 in 1972, but Supreme Court Justices Lewis Powell and William Rehnquist each ruled (in separate cases) that the law would not affect any actual judicial busing orders because of the way it

of elected presidents), one might say, was tamed into submission, and began exhibiting the uneasiness about affirmative action that majority sentiment seems to feel.

I told this tale many times in courses in American Government, but as a political scientist, had to wonder, How typical is this? Has the Court over the long haul been more supportive of the Constitutional rights of unpopular racial minorities than the other branches?

Alexander Hamilton, urging his fellow New Yorkers to ratify the pending U.S. Constitution in the summer of 1788, wrote that people need not fear the provision for lifetime tenure of Supreme Court justices. Such tenure, wrote he, would keep the justices independent from majoritarian political pressures, thereby enabling them to stand firm in defense of the constitutional rights of the individual, to "prevent oppressions of the minor party," and also to "mitigat[e] the severity" of "unjust and partial laws" that operate with harshness on "particular classes of citizens" but do not amount to an "infraction[] of the Constitution."[15]

Justice Joseph Story in his magisterial *Commentaries on the Constitution*, published while he served on the Court, similarly justified independence of the judiciary from electoral politics:

> There can be no security for the minority in a free government, except through the judicial department … .[I]n free governments, where the majority who obtain power for the moment, are supposed to represent the will of the people, persecution, especially of a political nature, becomes the cause of the community against one … . In free governments … the independence of the judiciary … is the only barrier against the oppressions of a dominant faction, armed for the moment with power, and abusing the influence, acquired under accidental excitements, to overthrow the institutions and liberties which have been the deliberate choice of the people.[16]

Surely both Hamilton and Story were conscious that majority oppression on the basis of race was a problem crying out for amelioration in the United States. Alexander Hamilton, himself, was concerned enough about the evils of slavery to have been one of the co-founders of the

---

was worded. (It banned busing for "racial balance" and the justices said that the judiciary was ordering busing for "desegregation" rather than "racial balance." Ibid.)

[15] *Federalist Papers* #78.

[16] *Commentaries on the Constitution of the United States* section 833 abr. (Section 1606 orig.) (Carolina Academic Press, 1987, repr. of 1833.) Thanks to William Ford for this reference.

Manumission Society of New York. Justice Story while on the Court participated in several important cases involving both slaves and Native Americans, quintessential examples of oppressed minorities. Outside of his judicial role he consistently expressed the view that slavery was an unjust and immoral institution, and that people of European descent were systematically treating the Indians with gross injustice. Within his judicial role he expressly condemned trade in slaves as unjust and immoral.[17]

The U.S. Supreme Court is both notorious for having (in 1857) issued the dictum that under the Constitution of this country, "[The black man] had no rights which the white man was bound to respect,"[18] and famous for having (in 1954) declared the unconstitutionality of *de jure* segregated public schools, a system that harmed black children because it "generates a feeling of inferiority as to their status in the community that may affect their hearts and minds in a way unlikely ever to be undone," thereby undermining their motivation to learn and producing unequal education.[19] These well-known judicial pronouncements show the Court first re-entrenching (indeed, arguably exacerbating) the majority's oppression of a racial minority, and the second, the Court fighting against it, as Hamilton and Story predicted the Court would. Which is the more apt, or more typical, picture of the Court's tendencies over the course of U.S. history? Has the judicial branch, staffed by lifetime appointees intended to be immune from political pressures, in fact as a general matter served to "prevent oppressions of the minor party" more typically than the elected branches have? That is the answer this book aims to uncover. And

---

[17] Cover 1975, 238–43; Roper 1969, 532. For instance, at a public meeting in Salem in 1819, Story insisted that the principles of the Declaration of Independence and the spirit of the Constitution demand that Congress ban slavery in the territories. Ibid. As to the slave trade, on circuit in *U.S. v. La Jeune Eugenie,* 26 F. Cas. 832 (1822), Story went on for page after page to condemn it as "breach[ing] all the maxims of justice, mercy and humanity," as involving "corruption, plunder and kidnapping" of "the young, the feeble, the defenceless and the innocent," as "desolate[ing] whole villages and provinces," as resulting in massive numbers of deaths in transit due to the "cold blood[ed]" and "inhuman" treatment of the captives, and as "incurably unjust and inhuman." 26 F.Cas., 845–8. While one of the Cherokee cases was pending in Congress, Story wrote his wife of the Cherokee, "I feel as an American, disgraced by our gross violation of the public faith toward them." Letter to Mrs. Joseph Story, Washington, Jan 13, 1832, in W.W. Story 1851, II, 79. Similar additional letters are cited in the discussion of the *Prigg v. Pennsylvania* case in chapter 2.

[18] *Dred Scott v. Sanford*, 60 U.S. 393, 407 (1857).

[19] *Brown et al. v. Board of Education et al.*, 347 U.S. 483, 494 (1954).

if Hamilton and Story were correct, or if they were mistaken, which aspects of U.S. institutions explain why?

***

White British settlers established the first British colony in North America at Jamestown, Virginia in 1607. They were preceded here by French to the north and Spaniards to the south, not to mention the Native Americans, who preceded all of the Europeans. By the time of the British landing, the European diseases to which indigenous people had been exposed for 100 years had already decimated perhaps as many as 90 percent of the natives, known as Indians to the Europeans.[20]

In 1619, black Africans were brought to Jamestown, and initially were treated as indentured servants, who were freed after their period of servitude. Only in the second half of the seventeenth century did laws begin to make sharper distinctions between indentured persons and slaves, and to link slavery specifically to persons of African descent.[21]

By the time of the U.S. Constitution, although several states in the northern U.S. had freed their slaves by legislation, and Massachusetts had done so by judicial interpretation of her state Constitution, slavery was firmly entrenched by law in the majority of states.[22] At some point or other, prior to the Civil War, every single state, along with the federal government, discriminated against blacks in some way. Some examples were white preferences for the militia, segregated schools, laws against miscegenation (interracial marriage), laws imposing on blacks stiffer property qualifications for voting, and laws requiring of blacks proof of freedom and a posted bond in order to enter the state (the latter went unenforced).[23]

Apart from U.S. law's specialized treatment of Native Americans, or Indians, the myriad of law-enforced discriminations in both the pre- and

---

[20] R.M. Smith 1997, 520, n.30. Historians previously estimated 50 percent, but the more recent consensus is toward 90 percent.

[21] Higginbotham 1978, 21–2; Finkelman 1986, 1; C. Harris 1993, 1716–21.

[22] Completing the post-Revolutionary-War trend of abolition in the states north of Delaware, New York in 1799 and New Jersey in 1804 adopted legislation that freed the slaves but did so quite gradually. Pennsylvania's Abolition Act of 1780 also had been quite gradual; it liberated only persons born after that Act and established indentured servitude until the age of 28 for all offspring of present slaves. By 1830, more than 3500 (elderly) blacks remained in slavery in the North, two-thirds of them in New Jersey. Litwack 1961, 3, 14. Harper 2003.

[23] Litwack, *passim*.

the post-Civil War U.S. between "white" and "other" people or between white and "colored," produced legal questions eventually over who counted as "white." Such cases involved not only east Asians, such as Chinese or Japanese people, but also simply darker complexioned people such as Mexican-Americans, people of India, Afghans, Filipinos, Syrians, Lebanese, and Armenians.[24]

This book explores the rights of racial minorities, as perceived by the Supreme Court, and also as protected or attacked by either of the elected political branches of the federal government. It compiles this history in order to judge whether the constitutional project of establishing judicial review to be exercised by judges with lifetime appointments as a preventive of "oppressions of the minor party" has succeeded, as weighed against the behavior of the more popularly accountable branches.

Of course, the case can be made that each of the branches to one degree or another is "undemocratic," but there can be no doubt that the federal judiciary is less accountable to the electorate than is either elected branch. All but the two top members of the executive bureaucracy are appointed rather than elected, but the two at the top wield significant hiring and firing power and do face election and re-election; moreover, the top layer of the executive bureaucracy is subjected to elected officials' judgment both as to nomination by the elected President and confirmation by the elected Senate. The Supreme Court justices, once in office never have to fear ouster by failing to get re-elected, nor has any ever been removed from office consequent to impeachment. Similarly, Congressional staff members, who are unelected, have great influence over the legislation of the land, but, again, at least their bosses who hire and fire them do have to stand for re-election.[25] Have these facts mattered in the way they were expected to? This book aims to uncover the answer.

---

[24] Lyman 1991.

[25] Granted, those elections take place in gerrymandered districts, with a large incumbency advantage, but there has never been a nationwide Congressional election in which no one gets voted out of office.

1. Minority rights up through the Marshall Court, 1789–1835

THE ELECTED BRANCHES AND AFRICAN-AMERICANS

One year after the Bill of Rights was ratified, the Congress of the United States adopted the Uniform Militia Act (1 Stat. 271), requiring that every free, able-bodied *white* male citizen between the ages of eighteen and forty-five enroll in the national militia and supply himself with a proper weapon and ammunition (emphasis added). Prior to this law many states had allowed blacks into their state militias (although some did not, a tradition dating to the colonial period), and the meritorious service of black soldiers during the Revolutionary War was still a relatively fresh memory. Even with the federal law in place, many states, North and South, ignored the racial restriction (if it was meant as a restriction, rather than simply as a minimum membership) and enrolled free blacks in their militias, especially during times of invasion.[1]

Militia discrimination was not the whole story. In 1790 Congress limited access to naturalization for U.S. citizenship to whites, a limit that it re-enacted in 1802 with the phrase "free white persons." Senator Charles Sumner after the Civil War failed in his attempt to have the word "white" removed from this statute. Instead Congress modified it in 1870 by adding to whites the permission for naturalization of "aliens of African nativity and to persons of African descent" (pointedly, albeit silently, excluding Chinese).[2]

In 1810 Congress forbade blacks to be postal carriers, and in 1820 authorized the *white* male citizens of the District of Columbia to create a municipal government and to adopt legal codes governing blacks and

1 Cottrol and Diamond 1991, 331–3.
2 Lyman 1991, 204; Nieman 1991, 20.

slaves.[3] Congress specifically authorized the District government to ban meetings of free blacks at night and to use whippings in the punishment of slaves.[4]

In most states (including in the South) free blacks had been allowed to vote in the late eighteenth century.[5] In the 1830s, as pro-slavery sentiment heated up (see below), a number of these states cut back on black suffrage rights, and the newly admitted states were not extending the vote to blacks (and Oregon added Chinese to the unenfranchised category).[6] By the time of the Civil War, the number of states allowing blacks to vote had fallen to five.[7]

Within the slave states, restrictions upon free blacks were particularly harsh, especially after the slave revolt led by Nat Turner in 1831. In the Georgia state code of 1860, for instance, a rape of a white woman by a black man carried a mandatory death sentence; an attempted rape, a potential death sentence. By contrast, rape by a white man of a black woman could be punished "by fine or imprisonment, at the discretion of the court."[8]

Some states even barred entry by free blacks, although these laws went unenforced.[9] On some occasions, but not on others, the Attorney General of the U.S. refused to grant U.S.-born, free blacks the right to passports or to apply for publicly available land, on the grounds that they were not U.S. "citizens" in the full legal sense.[10]

The judicial system in the country, too, was infected with racial subordination. Several northern states refused to allow blacks to testify against a white person, and only Massachusetts allowed blacks to serve on juries.[11]

As to unfree blacks, as the country was a mix of slave states and free states, the Constitution and pre-Civil War legislation show a mixed record. The Constitution omitted any explicit mention of slaves or

---

[3] R.M. Smith 1997, 175; Nieman 1991, 20.

[4] *Cohens v. Virginia*, 19 U.S. 264, 284 (1821).

[5] Blacks were "clearly prohibited" from voting, as of 1790, in only three states Virginia, Georgia, and South Carolina. (email from Paul Finkelman of Albany Law School, 11/11/2005).

[6] R.M. Smith 1997, 105–6 and 215; Nieman 1991, 28. New Jersey took the vote from blacks in 1807, and Connecticut did so in 1808.

[7] Litwack 1961, 91. These were Massachusetts, Rhode Island, Maine, New Hampshire, and Vermont.

[8] Fehrenbacher 1978, 31.

[9] Litwack 1961, 67–74.

[10] R.M. Smith 1997, 258; Graber 2006, 29, n.84.

[11] Litwack 1961, 93–4.

slavery, a stylistic choice that James Madison's notes claimed to reflect a deliberate effort to avoid entrenching the institution of slavery in the constitutive document of a free republic.[12] On the other hand, the Constitution notoriously contains serious compromises with the institution.

(1) The slave states were given a representation bonus by counting each slave as an extra three-fifths of a person, instead of as zero (as might have been appropriate, since they had zero say in who governed them). This fact meant that the voters in the southern slaveholding states were given a boost both in clout in the House of Representatives (moving their numbers to 46 percent of the total rather than the 41 percent it would have been) and in the Electoral College, whose numbers were pegged to Congressional membership.[13]
(2) Congress was forbidden to ban the international importation of slaves prior to 1808. Congress did enact the ban, to take effect right after midnight December 31, 1807.[14]
(3) Article IV, §2, cl.3 says: "No person held to service or labor in one state, under the laws thereof, escaping into another, shall in consequence of any law or regulation therein, be discharged from such service or labor, but shall be delivered up on claim of the party to whom such service or labor may be due."

(Incidentally, each of these clauses refers to slaves as "persons," never as "property," so if the Constitution were read literally, the Fifth Amendment due process clause would have freed all slaves in federal jurisdictions.)

Congress did re-enact the prohibition on slavery in the Northwest Territory (which had been in place under the Articles of Confederation) and in 1794 ban the export or international transport of slaves. In negotiating the Jay Treaty the executive branch did abandon the demand, desired by many slaveowners, that Britain pay reparations for slaves she had freed during the Revolutionary War. On the other hand, Congress permitted slavery in the District of Columbia and in the federal territory that later became Kentucky, Tennessee, Mississippi, and Alabama. In 1820 it extended the line straight westward that divided this southwest territory from the non-slave Northwest Territory, prohibiting slavery in

---

12 Farrand, *Records*, 2:417.
13 Nieman 1991, 11. See also Paul Finkelman 2002.
14 Kent 1826, I: 179–87.

westward territory above the line, and permitting it below the line. This division was the Missouri Compromise.

And in 1793 Congress enacted a Fugitive Slave Law. This law arranged for the recapture of slaves, even though the relevant constitutional clause said nothing of federal power, but simply prohibited state laws from releasing slaves and ordered nameless parties to "deliver up" such runaways "on claim" of a party to whom service was owed. This Fugitive Slave Clause appears in the article on interstate relations, not in any list of federal powers, and it mentions only state actions, not federal enforcement. The paradigm for the Clause was state extradition, not federal rendition, just as with criminals.[15] In short, in order to pass the Fugitive Slave Law Congress had to treat the constitutional commands to *states* as implying a *federal* enforcement power. The 1793 federal law ordered that "upon proof to the satisfaction of" any local or county or federal "judge or magistrate" in the area where a runaway who owed "labor or service" was seized by the claimant of that laborer or claimant's agent, when the claimant had presented evidence:

> either by oral testimony or affidavit taken before and certified by a magistrate of [the home] State or Territory, that the person so seized or arrested, doth, under the laws of the State or Territory from which he or she fled, owe service or labor to the person claiming him or her, it shall be the duty of such Judge or magistrate to give a certificate thereof to such claimant, his agent, or attorney, which shall be sufficient warrant for removing the said fugitive from labor to the State or Territory from which he or she fled.[16]

Under this federal law the black person accused as a slave had no right to testify or to be defended by an attorney against the claim of ownership.[17]

After 1830 sectional animosity over slavery intensified. Southerners became more intransigently pro-slavery.[18] This increase can be attributed both to the increased importance of cotton in the regional economy and

---

[15] The immediately preceding constitutional clause mandates state extradition of criminals "fleeing from justice."

[16] *Proceedings and Debates of the House of Representatives of the United States at the Second Session of the Second Congress, Begun at the City of Philadelphia, November 5, 1792, Annals of Congress*, 2nd Congress, 2nd Session (November 5, 1792 to March 2, 1793), pp. 1414–15. The law also made it unlawful for interfering with such recapture and imposed a five hundred dollar fine therefor, payable to the claimant of the escapee.

[17] R.M. Smith 1997, 142–3; Nieman 1991, 15–17.

[18] Rhetoric around slavery shifted in the 1830s from depictions of it as an economic necessity albeit one that was unfortunate and immoral, to a depiction of it as a positive good. Tillery 2009, 647.

to the slave revolts of Denmark Vesey (suppressed) in 1822 in South Carolina and of Nat Turner in 1831 in Virginia (the latter of which produced deaths of dozens of whites).

Meanwhile, abolitionist and anti-slavery sentiment grew more widespread and more intense in the north. The conflict over the Indian Removal Act of 1830, which committed the federal government to supporting removal of Indians to west of the Mississippi, supposedly by lawful treaties, in fact stimulated the abolitionist movement.[19] In the 1820s opponents of slavery had largely been colonizationists, encouraging a policy of offering a free return to the ancestral homeland for those freed slaves who desired it. When the Indian removal issue heated up, the parallels to colonization for blacks were too obvious to ignore, and many a colonizationist became an "immediatist," or abolitionist in today's terminology.[20] Thus was the abolitionist movement launched.

Southern states, in turn, reduced the legal rights of free blacks, going so far as to mandate that free blacks arriving as sailors be locked up while in Southern ports, so they would not have a subversive influence on slaves by mingling with them.[21] Southerners claimed that abolitionist essays might stimulate slave revolts (even though teaching a slave to read was a crime in most of the slave states[22]), and this argument convinced President Andrew Jackson to have the national postmaster authorize local postmasters (federal employees) to destroy anti-slavery tracts rather than allow them through the mails, in flagrant contravention of the First Amendment's freedom of press clause.[23]

Presidents with Senate confirmation appointed Supreme Courts that from the beginning contained a dominant presence of justices from the South—twenty of the thirty-five appointed prior to the Civil War came from slave states.[24] How these appointments played out in Court decisions from 1801 through 1835 is detailed in the section below.

---

[19] Indian Removal Act of May 28, 1830. U.S. Statutes at Large, Vol.IV, Ch.CXLVIII, 411–12, Twenty-first Congress, 1st Sess.

[20] Hershberger 1999, 35; Magliocca 2003, text at nn.179–198. See also, Kerber 1975; Portnoy 2005; Hershberger, 2006; Joy 2008.

[21] Hamer 1935.

[22] R.M. Smith 1997, 219; Kolchin 1993, 129.

[23] Nieman 1991, 16. President Jackson in 1835 attempted to have Congress criminalize the circulation of such material. Congress refused, but it did word the federal law in such a way that postmasters refusing to deliver material declared unlawful locally would not be violating federal rules. Curtis 2000, 155–75.

[24] Graber 2006, 116.

THE MARSHALL COURT AND SLAVERY

It is within this context of widespread anti-black sentiments formalized into law throughout the U.S. and the post-1820s intensified polarization of opinion on slavery that the Supreme Court decisions are best assessed. The racial discriminations (against free blacks) prevalent in state and federal law did not produce any Supreme Court cases from the Marshall Court, although they did produce two important circuit court decisions (penned by individual Supreme Court justices) in the early 1820s protective of the rights of Negro seamen in the South, decisions that southern states flagrantly ignored.[25]

The most prominent of the antebellum slavery cases concerned fugitive slaves, but these did not reach the Supreme Court until the chief justiceship of Roger Taney. By the 1820s, the absence of procedural protections for the accused in the 1793 (and also later in the 1850) Fugitive Slave Act angered many northerners. Several northern states began to intervene, both by legislating procedural protections for the accused runaway and ordering their own judges and sheriffs not to cooperate with the slave-chasing enterprise. These clashes between federal and state authority would eventually produce two well-known Supreme Court decisions in the two decades preceding the Civil War: *Prigg v. Pennsylvania* (1842), and *Ableman v. Booth* (1857). These are discussed in Chapter 2. Although slaves were mentioned in the Court's first important decision, *Chisholm v. Georgia* (1793) in the context of being the only persons in the U.S. who did not share in equal rights of citizenship,[26] the Supreme Court took no slavery cases as such until after 1801 (the same year that John Marshall became chief justice). Prior to the discussion of the slave cases, it is worth observing that this *Chisholm* decision did contain important dicta with relevance for the rights of *free* blacks. The statement is:

---

[25] See, *Elkison v. Deliesseline*, 8 F.Cas. 493 (1823) (Justice Johnson declaring unconstitutional on commerce clause grounds a South Carolina law that imprisoned free persons of color who worked on ships that landed in South Carolina for the duration of the ship's stay, and according to which, if the ship abandoned them there, they would be sold as slaves); and *The Wilson v. U.S.,* 30 F.Cas.239 (1820) (Justice Marshall declaring on rather tortured reasoning that the Virginia law meant to keep free Negro seamen imprisoned while docked, did not apply to the seamen "of color" in question). For discussion of the political importance of these decisions, see Hamer 1935; Schoeppner, 2010.

[26] *Chisholm v. Georgia*, 2 U.S. 419 (1793) at 471–2; *Dred Scott v. U.S.*, 60 U.S. 393, 407 (1857).

> [a]t the Revolution, the sovereignty devolved on the people; and they are truly the sovereigns of the country, but they are sovereigns without subjects (unless the African slaves among us may be so called) and have none to govern but themselves; the citizens of America are equal as fellow citizens …

The Court's implication here, that *free* blacks were equally free citizens, contrasts with Congress's untroubled assertion in 1820 that whites in DC were authorized to impose special restrictions on free blacks (See above, text at notes 3–4), as well as with the Court's notorious 1857 remark in *Dred Scott* to the effect that free blacks in the U.S. had no rights.

In the year 1801, Congress adopted the extant slave law of Virginia and Maryland for the parts of their territory that became the District of Columbia. In many of its earliest slave cases, the Supreme Court's role was that of highest appellate court applying the law of this territory. Prior to 1801, other than in *Chisholm*, the only mention of slaves in Supreme Court decisions occurred in lists of types of property. In these listings, slavery was not singled out as warranting special treatment (apart from the mandate regarding taxes in the three-fifths clause) nor was it presented as involving special moral issues.[27]

During the Marshall Court years issues concerning slavery arose in the following contexts:

(1) property disputes between white people over particular slaves, which the Court handled according to rules that would have applied to other chattel property;
(2) lawsuits by slaves claiming their freedom on one or another ground, and
(3) questions of criminal law once federal law banned the export[28] and import of slaves.

If one puts aside those cases where the Court was simply settling property disputes over who owned which chattel, and focuses on the

---

[27] *Hilton v. U.S.*, 3 U.S. 171 (1796); *Ware v. Hylton*, 3 U.S. 199 (1796); *Wiscart v. Duchy*, 3 U.S. 321 (1796). The decision by Marshall in 1803, *Hamilton v. Russell*, 5 U.S. 309, similarly, simply lists the slave as chattel along with "other personal property" that was in dispute. 5 U.S., at 315. Marshall continued this practice of dealing with slaves as it dealt with other property in various property disputes that came before him, e.g. *Ramsay v. Lee*, 8 U.S. 401 (1807); *Spiers v. Willison*, 8 U.S. 398 (1807).

[28] E.g., *Adams v. Woods*, 6 U.S. 336 (1805), dealt with the application of the federal statute of limitations (on criminal penalties) to someone accused of engaging in the forbidden export of slaves.

cases involving slavery as such (i.e., on the latter two categories), what comes into view is a picture of the Marshall Court as considerably less opposed to slavery, at least for the first sixteen years, than one might expect based on the public pronouncements of Justice Story or the privately expressed detestation of slavery of Chief Justice Marshall.[29] It is even more puzzling if one accepts the assessment of historian Donald Roper that in terms of private sentiments a majority of the (seven-member) Marshall Court opposed slavery: two, strongly (Story and McLean); and two (Marshall and Washington) at least, "tepidly," in the sense of "wish[ing] it would go away."[30] Whereas some biographers tend to single out various dicta or rulings where John Marshall's opinions helped slaves toward freedom,[31] in fact, as Table 1.1 below reveals, he or his Court rather often sealed the enslavement in question, *even* in cases that were reasonably contestable to the degree of:

(1) producing a non-unanimous vote on his own court;
(2) provoking a written dissent in the Supreme Court;
(3) overturning a circuit court reading to the contrary (in favor of freedom);
(4) presenting an argument of the (indirectly electorally accountable) U.S. Attorney General to the contrary; or
(5) involving a statute that if read literally would have freed the slave, but where the Court constructed a legal argument elaborate enough to produce an anti-freedom result. (These indicia of legal contestability are noted in bold in Table 1.1).

---

[29] E.g., "Nothing portends more calamity & mischief to the southern states than their slave population; Yet they seem to cherish the evil ..." 1826 letter to Thomas Pickering, cited in Rudko 2001, at 79–80. Marshall himself owned a small number of slaves throughout his life, and also bought them, and gave and received them as gifts. At the end of his life, he freed one in his will and bequeathed the others. He lobbied privately and publicly for a program of voluntary emancipation to be funded by the federal government which would then "colonize" (which he understood as repatriate) the freed slaves in Africa. Rudko 2001, 77–9.

[30] Roper 1969, 534. He does not say where the others fell. McLean did not join the Court until 1829. Justice Duvall (who joined in 1811) was sufficiently anti-slavery to argue in dissent that "the right to freedom is more important than the right of property." *Mima Queen v. Hepburn*, 11 U.S. 290, 299 (1813). Justice Johnson, who joined the Court in 1804, angered the southern public by insisting on due process for slaves charged in the Denmark Vesey uprising. Roper, 533–4.

[31] An example of this practice occurs in Jean Edward Smith 2000, 1123–1126.

Moreover, the Marshall Court was inconsistent in its fidelity to the relevant state common law when it came to applying the slave code of the District of Columbia adopted from the states of Maryland and Virginia, varying its approach so as both times to produce a pro-slavery result. Under the 1776 constitutions of Virginia and Maryland, judges were appointed to good behavior tenure (so were not "elected branches," as I have been using the term). In Maryland justices of the peace—county level magistrates—were elected; in Virginia, appointed.[32] In one instance the Marshall opinion for the Court, when interpreting the D.C. law on slavery that governed the formerly Maryland part of the District, substituted its own judgment as to prudent law rather than follow a particular common law rule of Maryland on hearsay, which common law rule had produced a decision freeing the slave.[33] (This Supreme Court opinion, returning the person to slavery, provoked Justice Duvall, of Maryland, to author the only dissenting opinion of his life).[34] Then, in a later decision where following the plain meaning of Virginia statutory law for the formerly Virginia part of the District had caused a jury to set free a slave, the Supreme Court announced itself relieved that it had discovered a Virginia (i.e., common law) precedent to follow (from 1818, seventeen years after Congress had adopted the Virginia law as part of the D.C. code) which resulted in reversing the judge's instruction to the jury and thereby the jury's decision; thereby, the Marshall Court effectively re-enslaved the litigant.[35] In light of this degree of available latitude at the edges in these cases, one must conclude that the Marshall Court in these cases saw itself as engaged in an effort to firm up property rights in the nascent republic, even when doing so conflicted with its common law obligation that statutes are in doubtful cases to be construed "*in favorem libertatis*" (in favor of liberty). And one must certainly question Kent Newmyer's 1969 explanation of this body of decisions: "The Marshall Court did not have substantial lawmaking discretion in the slavery cases."[36]

Other scholars, and Newmyer himself in a detailed reconsideration thirty years later,[37] have produced a variety of explanations for the degree

---

[32] Lewis 1976; Virginia Constitution 1776.
[33] *Mima Queen v. Hepburn*, 11 U.S. 290 (1813).
[34] Easterbrook 1983, 491.
[35] *Mason v. Matilda*, 25 U.S. 590, at 592 (1827).
[36] Newmyer 1969, 540–4.
[37] Newmyer 2001.

to which this Court, a majority of whose members opposed slavery "attitudinally" (as the contemporary jargon of political science would phrase it) produced so many pro-slavery decisions. Historian Donald Roper was the first to analyze the topic, and he concluded that internal division on the Court as to the morality of slavery, compounded by fear of antagonizing Congress into restricting its jurisdiction and by the Court's own strong commitment to property rights, caused the Court under Marshall to hide behind the posture that it was obliged to apply the objectively discovered law in favor of slavery, even in cases where the law on the subject was contestable and open to meliorative interpretation.[38] Newmyer, in a biography-length reconsideration of the subject revised his earlier critique of Roper far enough to acknowledge that there was some "indeterminacy in the common law of slavery" that would have permitted Marshall "to extend the area of freedom," and that he often chose not to.[39] Still, he insists (as anyone would grant) that political and legal forces did constrain the Court in terms of the big picture; the Court could not simply announce, "We believe that slavery is wrong and therefore will no longer uphold it." Therefore, one is discussing here amelioration at the edges: producing decisions that free particular slaves, that uphold and facilitate punishment of illegal traders in slaves, that facilitate judicial demonstration by one held in slavery that the situation is unlawful, or that facilitate voluntary manumission. In response to the query, "Why did the Marshall Court not do more in this direction?" the later Newmyer retreats to the view that the Court did feel bound both by commitment to property rights and to a federal system that left control of slaves to each state. He also flirts with the possibility that Marshall's very public involvement in the colonization movement (as president of his local chapter from 1823 until his death, and a lifetime member of, and big donor to, the American Colonization Society, beginning with attendance in December 1816, at its founding meeting) is more properly read as an expression of a racist desire to rid America of blacks than of Marshall's "intellectual opposition" to slavery.[40]

By contrast, law professor Frances Rudko aligns with Marshall biographer Jean Edward Smith in reading Marshall as one who genuinely "hated" the institution of slavery as a moral and social evil, and sees him

---

38 Roper 1969, 532–9.

39 Newmyer 2001, 426.

40 Ibid., 414–34; on colonization, 419–23. On Marshall's active involvement in colonization, Rudko 2001, 84 and Noonan 1977, 105.

as having believed the best approach to fighting it was by promoting Congressional financial support for colonization as the only realistic hope for creating incentives for voluntary manumission. Marshall believed that such a program could be effective at least in large portions of the upper South, and would be fair—Rudko depicts it as an early nineteenth century version of "forty acres and a mule." Thus she reads Marshall as basically temporizing in those decisions that strengthened slavery, while he worked diligently off the bench toward the goal of having Congress deliver the U.S. from this evil.[41]

Table 1.1 below, a systematic compilation of all the slavery cases that came before the Marshall Court, offers a chance to sort through these competing interpretations. The Table makes apparent two things. First, as already noted (and is indicated in bold type), most of these cases did present a legally respectable alternative to whichever holding ended up winning over the Court; and second, the Court observably changes direction between 1816 and 1817. Out of a total of thirty-three cases, eleven go in an anti-liberty direction. All but one of these occurs prior to 1817. It seems impossible to deny that, as a Court, prior to 1817 the Marshall Court was not only willing to treat slaves as property, but also in borderline situations showed a much stronger commitment to the property rights of the slaveholder than the liberty rights of the enslaved. Thirteen of the decisions move the law in a pro-liberty direction (eight produced mixed results; one presented no obvious direction regarding liberty). The pro-liberty decisions *all* occur in or after 1817.

It is true that none of these cases display the Court directly reversing itself, not even *sub silentio*, on a single re-litigated point of law. Nonetheless, a clear shift of policy inclination is observable. Something of the flavor of this shift can be seen by consideration of the following pair of contrasting cases. In a case where litigation at the Supreme Court continued from 1812 to 1816, the Marshall Court reversed the first of the circuit court holdings to rule that a prior judicial ruling that had established a woman as free on the grounds that she had been proven to be white could not operate to establish that her children were descended from a white woman and on that grounds legally free. By contrast, in 1834 in applying the will of a Tennessean that freed his slaves upon their reaching age twenty-one, the Supreme Court although acknowledging that under Tennessee law, offspring born of such a slave before she

---

[41] Rudko 2001.

reached twenty-one would remain slaves, nonetheless ruled that a lawsuit by heirs making a claim to such slave offspring had to be dismissed (and the offspring set free) because the description of the offspring was too "vague and uncertain."[42]

It is not obvious what causes this pro-liberty shift. One candidate for explanation is that the cases that begin in 1817, much more typically involve the slave trade, where Congressional sentiment has been clearly expressed. In 1807, Congress first outlawed the importing of slaves, with a law to take effect after December 31. It reiterated and refined this law in 1818. In 1819 it changed the law's disposition of captured slaves; instead of allowing states to sell them off, they had to be turned over to the President to be returned to Africa, and Congress appropriated $100,000 therefor. In 1820, Congress declared it piracy to seize or decoy any "negro or mulatto" from Africa into slavery or onto a boat intended for the slave trade and imposed the death penalty therefor.[43] Moreover, in the period from 1814–1820, a flurry of diplomatic activity in the maritime nations of Europe resulted in some restrictions on the slave trade by France (1817), Portugal (1818) and Spain (1820), preceded by Britain's total ban in 1807.[44] Thus, one might argue that as to the slave trade at least, legal proscription was beginning to look like the civilized thing to do.

Still, this explanation of the Court's simply following the elected branches on slave trade does not cover all the cases. Despite the 1794 law and follow-up legislation banning export, foreign transport or import of slaves on U.S. vessels and Attorney General prosecution under these laws, the Marshall Court in the early period did resist the political branches, treating the accused slave trader/importer leniently in 1805 and 1810. Also there are cases having no direct bearing on the slave trade—cases regarding the freeing of individual slaves in the 1817–1835 period—where the Court produces a pro-freedom decision, something it never did before 1817.

Another possibility is that because what is called "the" Marshall Court comprised several different sets of justices over time, it was the personnel change that produced the shift of decisions. Duvall joined the Court in

---

42 Compare *Wood v. Davis* (1812) and *Davis v. Wood* (1816) with *McCutcheon v. Marshall* (1834) in Table 1.1 below.

43 Kent 1826, I: 179–87. Slave Trade Act of March 3, 1819, U.S. Statutes At Large, Vol.III, Fifteenth Congress, Session II, Ch.101, pp. 532–4.

44 Kent, ibid.

1811 and Story in 1812. No-one joined between 1812 and 1823. Perhaps the post-1816 Court was a product of the fact that the seven personalities on the Court needed a few years to gel as a group around the new personnel mix, which now included the relatively ardently anti-slavery Justice Story.

Finally, there is the possibility—the one that appears most likely—that the shift has something to do with colonization policy. The American Colonization Society was founded in December, 1816. Frances Rudko dates Marshall's involvement in the society as "almost from its beginning," since he signed up for a lifetime membership in 1819 and become in 1823 local chapter president (which he remained throughout his life). But legal scholar (and now federal judge) John Noonan dates Marshall's involvement as literally from the beginning moment of the organization: Marshall attended that founding meeting in December of 1816. Justice Bushrod Washington was the founding president of the National ACS and remained president for many years. Noonan notes that "several justices" on the Court attended Colonization Society meetings. It is certainly conceivable that for the judicial votes of these two morally troubled slaveowners, Marshall and Washington, their being able to conceive of a way to set the slaves free without imposing millions of unlettered black people on Southern society was what freed up their consciences to rule in more pro-liberty ways from 1817 on.[45]

Whichever of these explanations eventually carries the day, it seems clear from this systematic look at the Marshall Court's slavery decisions that something definitely changed around 1816–1817. This something is worth further scholarly exploration. The core details of these rulings that raise these questions about the Marshall Court and slavery appear in Table 1.1.

[45] Noonan 1977, 91, 16, 105. Rudko 2001, 84.

Table 1.1 *Marshall Court slavery cases*

Date	Case	Ruling	Action	→
1805	Adams v. Woods, 6 U.S. 336	U.S. statute of limitations interpreted so as NOT to impose penalty on illegal exporter of slaves.	Answer to Q. from **divided Circuit panel**. **Against U.S. Att'y. Gen.**	–
1805	U.S. v. Schooner Sally, 6 U.S. 406	Ct. rejected plea of U.S. to decide case by stricter rules of the common law rather than maritime and admiralty law, and thus refused to reverse the acquittal for engaging in slave export contrary to U.S. law of 1794.	Affirmed district and circuit court decisions. **Against U.S. Att'y Gen.**	–
1806	Scott v. London, 7 U.S. 324	D.C. (originally VA.) statute requiring new residents to take oath within sixty days of intent to reside and not to import slaves, without which slaves of new residents would be set free after one year in the state, is relaxed to allow heir to take the oath after father neglected to but before one year had elapsed.	**Reverses** circuit court. **Opinion speaks for "Majority of the Court."** No recorded dissent.	–
1810	Scott v. Ben, 10 U.S. 1	Accepted that procedures listed in statute banning import of slaves to D.C. (originally MD.) for proving qualification under exceptions (for owner moving into state with own slaves) were not the exclusive means by which lawful importer of slaves could prove lawfulness of import.	**Reverses** circuit court.	–
1810	Brigantine Amiable Lucy v. U.S., 10 U.S.330	U.S. 1803 statute forbidding importation of slaves into any state that shall have banned such importation, and 1804 one extending this statute to the territory of LA., and forbidding importation of slaves into Orleans territory except by bonafide new residents for own use, interpreted to PERMIT importation of slaves into Orleans because territorial legislature created in 1805 had not acted to ban the import.	**Reverses** district court, **Against U.S. Att'y. Gen**.	–
1812	Wood v. Davis I, 11 U.S.271	Responded to suit for freedom by the offspring of Susan Davis. Suit claimed that previous judicial determination of Davis's freedom on the grounds that she was born of a white mother rendered her own offspring free. Wood argued that prior decision had settled the law only as to her freedom not as to her birth. Supreme Court sides with Wood.	**Reverses** circuit court.	–
1813	Mima Queen v. Hepburn, 11 U.S.290	Rejected common law rule that had prevailed in MD. (for D.C.) to allow hearsay of hearsay when facts at issue were so ancient that direct witnesses no longer alive to testify.	Upholds circuit court **5-1 against district court. (Duvall dissents.)**	–

Table 1.1 (continued)

Date	Case	Ruling	Action	→
1813	Brig Caroline v. U.S., 11 U.S.496	Reversed a sentence of forfeiture of the ship as a slave trader, because original version of the charge—the "libel"—was too vague to justify forfeiture but sent the case back to Circuit Court to allow the libel (formal charge) to be amended.	**Reversed circuit court** but remanded for amended charge.	+/–
1815	Brig Alberta v. Moran, 13 U.S.359	Slavetrading ship belonging to a Cuban Spanish national (for whom the slave trade was lawful) had been captured by a privateer commissioned in France, at war with Spain, and where slave trade was not lawful. Prior to the capture the capturing vessel had put in at New Orleans for repairs and had augmented its crew with U.S. residents. Because U.S. was neutral in the French-Spanish conflict, use of such augmented crew for a capture of "cargo" (i.e., cargo of 150 slaves) violated U.S. law and law of nations. (There was no likelihood, Court noted, that the French privateer planned to free rather than sell the slaves.) Court orders the slaves returned to their Cuban Spanish owner.	Affirmed circuit court. Opinion by Justice Washington; Justice Todd absent.	–
1816	Negress Sally Henry v. Ball, 14 U.S. 1	Ruled that D.C. (formerly MD) law banning importing out-of-state slaves but exempting bonafide new resident owners bringing own slaves and also owners on temporary sojourns, would also exempt someone who for a seven-month period employed a slave owned by a Virginian, Ball, but then repossessed by Ball, taken back to Virginia, and then brought anew into D.C.	Affirmed circuit court decision.	–
1816	Davis v. Wood II, 14 U.S. 6	(1) Reaffirms hearsay rule of Mima Queen. (2) Rules that prior judgment as to ancestor's freedom cannot be treated as evidence of offspring's freedom.	Affirmed circuit court.	–
1817	Beverly v. Brooke, 15 U.S.100	Master of ship who had hired three slaves, from whom slaves had escaped while docked in Liverpool, England (where slavery is unlawful), did not owe compensation for the escape to owner who had hired out the slaves, because the hiring contract implied such risks.	Affirmed circuit court.	+

Date	Case	Ruling	Action	→
1820	The Josefa Segunda 18 U.S. 338	Ruled that pursuant to U.S. law banning slave importation after 1807, ship and cargo including 175 slaves, captured by commissioned privateers of Venezuela from Spain (and therefore property of the privateer due to ongoing war between Venezuela and Spain) that had then unlawfully entered waters of Louisiana must be forfeited to U.S., with the slaves delivered to overseers of the poor in the port where ship confiscated or other persons appointed by state for this purpose.	Affirmed district court. Opinion by Justice Livingston.	+
1823	The Mary Ann 21 U.S. 380	Reversed decree ordering forfeiture of slave-transporting ship for violating federal law requiring documentation of all "Negroes, mulattoes and persons of color" on board, on grounds that the libel from the district attorney had neglected to charge that the ship weighed forty tons or more, but remanded to allow the decree to be so amended.	**Reversed** decision of district court. **Against U.S. Att'y. Gen.**	–/+
1824	The Emily and Brig Caroline, 22 U.S. 381	(1) Charge for violating U.S. law forbidding export or import of slaves (because under admiralty law) did not require the formality and technical precision of an indictment at common law. (2) The offense of preparing a ship for the slave trade can be proved before the ship is completely sea-ready, so long as the intent is clearly manifest. (3) Thus the two ships at issue were forfeited to the U.S.	Affirmed decrees of district and circuit court. By Justice Thompson.	+

Table 1.1 (continued)

Date	Case	Ruling	Action	→
1824	The Merino, The Constitution, and The Louisa, 22 U.S. 391	(1) As to The Merino and The Louisa (U.S. vessels attempting to transport Spanish slaves from one Spanish port to another), the charge against them is not supported by the evidence but the evidence shows that they did violate other sections of U.S. slave-trade laws, so decree is reversed and remitted so that the libel against them may be amended to accord with the evidence.[1] (2) The decree condemning and ordering forfeited the cargo and vessel of The Constitution (a similar boat and activity) is upheld except as to the eighty-four slaves on board. (3) The eighty-four slaves go back to their Spanish owners who held them lawfully in Spanish territory; had the boat capturing them been a commissioned vessel capturing a U.S. boat engaged in transporting slaves from one foreign place to another (as was true of The Merino and The Louisa), then the slaves would be forfeited to the U.S., along with the rest of the cargo. Since The Constitution was captured first by a non-commissioned boat, to be brought to court so the captain could sue to be awarded the slaves, but then while not engaged in the slave trade was captured by a U.S. revenue boat and only then (i.e., not while engaged in slave trade) taken to court, the owners may retake their slaves from The Constitution. Situation is governed by the 1800 law which forfeits the slaves only if their owners had an economic interest in the boat or the voyage.	**Reversed** and remitted for amended charges to **district court** on The Merino and Louisa libels (implying approval of amended charge with sentence of forfeiture of slaves, cargo and ships). Upheld decree as to forfeiture of ship and cargo **of The Constitution**, but **as to its slaves, reversed decree and returned those slaves to Spanish owners.** By Justice Washington. As to slaves on The Constitution, **against the U.S. Att'y. Gen. as to return of slaves.**	+/–
1824	The St. Jago, 22 U.S. 409	Court interpreted an imperfectly worded libel against a slave trader in such a way as to sustain the libel and agreed with Att'y. Gen. in refusing reimbursement for wages of seamen and for materials from suppliers on grounds that there was ample evidence that they knew boat was fitted out as a slaver.	**Reverses Circuit Court.** By Johnson.	+
1825 Mar. 14	The Plattsburgh, 23 U.S. 133	Slave-trading schooner seized by U.S. ship of war off coast of Africa must be forfeited to U.S. because, despite ruse of a purchase by Spaniards in Cuba in mid-voyage (where boat was fully equipped for slave trade), voyage originated in Baltimore with manifest intent to continue to Africa, and U.S. crew stayed on boat to Africa. These facts made voyage violate U.S. law.	Affirmed District and Circuit Court. By Justice Story.	+

Date	Case	Ruling	Action	→
1825 Mar.15	The Antelope, 23 U.S. 66	Spanish vessel (Antelope) that had been captured by a (piratical) U.S. crew from Spanish owners, and that held the surviving remnant of twenty-five Africans captured from a U.S. slaver, and of a total of 255 slaves from a Portuguese slaver and from the original Antelope crew, now having been captured by U.S. revenue cutter in U.S. coastal waters was in U.S. court for violation of U.S. law, with Spanish and Portuguese consuls in court demanding return of the slaves to their respective countries, and claiming that they were lawfully owned property under their laws. (Preceded by 1822 decision on circuit by Story, *La Jeune Eugenie*, where French consul had intervened re: captured French slaver, and U.S. President had also intervened in aid of French consul. Story had ruled that French slave trader vessel seized on high seas by U.S. commissioned vessel in peacetime would have been tortiously seized only if the vessel seized were not involved in piracy, but that slave trading must count as piracy since it was unlawful under laws of the country of the boat seized. Boat and cargo [including slaves] returned to France for adjudication. Additional dictum: slave trade is by now contrary to the law of nations and therefore always piracy UNLESS permitted by laws of particular sovereign governments; alleged slave trader has burden of proof to show this permission.) Rules slave trade NOT *contra* law of nations (rejecting Story's dictum), since so many states allowed it within modern times (even though the recent trend is outlawing it), but grants that it is *contra* the law of nature. Slave-trade vessel is engaged in piracy ONLY if ITS government so rules. Only such ships may be seized on high seas and if so will be turned over to own courts for trial. U.S. treaty requires return to Spain of [slave] property captured by U.S. pirates. Court says in this case, "The sacred rights of liberty and property come in conflict with each other." Court says since **it IS (equally) DIVIDED as to whether all these slaves should be returned**, it will follow principle set forth by the circuit court: viz., that slaves owned lawfully in another country whose owners did not violate U.S. laws be returned to owners. Spanish government claims 150 slaves were theirs but, Supreme Court adds, they bear the burden of proving not only how many of the 280 slaves were originally owned by Spaniards (for which they succeeded only as to the number ninety-three of the original 280, but also "The individuals who compose this number must be designated to the satisfaction of the Circuit Court.") In 1826, (24 U.S. 413) clarified that "designated" meant "proved." No proof of Portuguese owners had come forth in five years since capture. Supreme Court rules all except the proved Spanish surviving slaves are free. Hearings eventually reduced the returnable Spanish slaves to 20 percent of the surviving total. Court rules in 1827 (25 U.S. 546) that the proof as to the identities of the owned slaves was "reasonably satisfactory."	**U.S. Attorney General is arguing for freedom of all surviving slaves, c.200; circuit court had originally freed only sixteen, chosen by lot.** Todd absent. **Supreme Court frees eventually all but thirty-nine, and Circuit Court turns over to the Spanish government to distribute to the owners** these thirty-nine whose owner could clearly identify and prove ownership of them. **Partly against U.S.Att'y Gen., but not as much as Circuit Court was**. U.S. Att'y Gen argued at final case (1827) that the proof as to identity of slaves was not adequate and all should be freed. Freed slaves arrived in Africa in Dec. 1827.	+/–

Table 1.1 (continued)

Date	Case	Ruling	Action	→
1825	The Josefa Segunda II, 23 U.S. 312	Boat forfeited and sold as per the 1820 decision, had its slaves sold pursuant to Louisiana law adopted to carry out the U.S.1807 law against slave trade. Louisiana law gave half proceeds from the slave sale to the "commanding officer of the capturing vessel," and other half to a charitable hospital. Court read the ambiguous U.S. law as implying that (1) a federal district court had jurisdiction to decide who received the proceeds under state law; (2) under the state law the "commanding officer of the capturing vessel" had to be one who followed up on the seizure by prosecuting the case in federal court and also had to be an officer of U.S. "armed vessel or revenue cutter." (This decision was superseded by the re-worded 1818 (April 20) U.S. law, which awarded half the forfeiture proceeds to whomever prosecuted the ship as a slaver.)	**Circuit court** decision awarding one-half the proceeds of sale of slaves to man who prosecuted the libel was **overturned.** The money from ship and its contents remained with U.S. government. [Disposition of money from sale of slaves not clarified until 1830 decision, Segunda III.] By Justice Story (with U.S. Att'y. Gen.)	0
1827	Mason v. Matilda, 25 U.S. 590	D.C. (originally VA.) statute requiring new residents to take oath before a magistrate within sixty days of move to the state, declaring intent to reside and not to import slaves, without which slaves of new residents would be set free after one year in the state is here interpreted as NOT applying to set free slaves who had been held in VA. part of D.C. for more than twenty years without any evidence that owner had ever taken the required oath. Undoes decision of jury below that Matilda et al. are free. Rules that twenty years possession of a slave should be viewed as creating a "presumption" that the oath was taken, so judge's instruction to jury erred.	**Reverses decision of county court of D.C.** ; re-enslaves Matilda et al. , who had been declared free by the jury of that court, following judge's instructions as to meaning of the law. Opinion by Johnson.	-
1827	Lear v. Armstrong, 25 U.S. 169 [followed by 1833 Estho v. Lear, 32 U.S. 130; and by 1834 Armstrong v. Lear, 33 U.S. 52.]	Begins series of three Supreme Court cases reviewing competing claims against bequest by Polish republican activist Thaddeus Kosciuszko of a fund for the purchasing, vocational training and liberation of slaves of Thomas Jefferson. Each time, Court demands fuller documentation of relevant foreign laws and of the competing claims, one of which would take away the entire fund.[2]	1827 affirms Circuit Court; **1833 reverses Circuit Court; 1834 reverses Circuit Court.** 1827 by Story; 1833 by Marshall; 1834 by Story.	+/–

Date	Case	Ruling	Action	→
1827	U.S. v. Gooding, 25 U.S. 460 [future Justice Taney att'y for defense]	Federal criminal prosecution of slave trader challenged as to validity of the indictment. Supreme Court "**express[ed its] anxiety, least, by too great indulgence to the wishes of counsel, questions of this sort should be frequently brought before this Court, and thus, in effect, an appeal in criminal cases become an ordinary proceeding to the manifest obstruction of public justice, and against the plain intendment of the acts of Congress" [at 467-468],** and ruled unwarranted six of defense counsel's objections (1) to admissibility of testimony from the captain of the slaver vessel, (2) to admissibility of testimony from a mate the captain tried to hire, (3) to the indictment of the ship's owner for "aiding and a betting" slave trade on the basis of actions and testimony of the ship's captain without prior conviction of the captain, (4) to indictment for equipping a ship intended for the slave trade without proving that it had been fully equipped in the U.S. or (5) that the owner had been present during the equipping, and (6) to failure to specify detailed acts of equipping the boat instead of equipping it in general; and ruled two as valid ([1] sloppy wording on failure to say "intent to employ the ship in slave trade," and [2] charging as a crime the mere sending out from a U.S. port of a boat intended for slave trade, as distinguished from there equipping it as such—on this point Story admitted he had erred in two prior circuit court decisions—and noted that he was differing from the U.S. Att'y. Gen. but noted that the AG's position would [unintentionally] entail guilt for FOREIGN slavers who accidentally landed in a U.S. port and then sailed forth, and that this position followed from the literal words of earlier statutes but had been corrected by Congress in 1818.	Answered questions certified from **circuit court** due to a **division of opinion** there, prior to its decision. Result: three of the indictments fatally defective but four still valid. **Against argument of U.S. Attorney General** on convicting a ship for merely setting forth from U.S. port to engage in slave trade. Opinion by Story.	+/–
1828	Sundry Slaves v. Madrazo, (Madrazo I) 26 U.S. 110	Undid District and Circuit Court decisions that took twenty to thirty slaves from governor of state, who was planning pursuant to state law to give them to Colonization Society for delivery to Africa, and that rendered them to the proven Spanish owner (and that gave him the proceeds from additional slaves of his that had been stolen by U.S. pirates and then judicially forfeited and sold by Georgia). Reason: since State of Georgia was a party, jurisdiction was original in the U.S. Supreme Court. Case returned on original jurisdiction in 1833 as *Ex Parte Madrazzo* (Madrazo II), 32 U.S. 627.	**Reversed** District and Circuit Court decisions. **Johnson dissented**.	+

Table 1.1 (continued)

Date	Case	Ruling	Action	→
1829	Boyce v. Anderson, 27 U.S. 150	Rejected strict liability standard that applied to common carriers transporting *freight*—"most skilful and careful management"—in context of carelessness in loss of slaves transported by steamship company, and applied the more lenient standard used for transporting *persons*, namely, absence of negligence. In opting for the "persons" rule, Marshall avoided arguments made by counsel that the rule should apply because slaves were "intelligent beings" with "power and rights of locomotion and self-preservation." Instead he posed their difference from "inanimate matter" as lying in their having "volition" and "feelings": "In the nature of things, and in his character, he resembles a passenger, not a package of goods."	Affirmed Circuit Court.	+
1829	Le Grand v. Darnall, 27 U.S. 664 [Taney for appellant, urging simply that the law be settled.]	Friendly suit posed issue whether slaveboy of eleven [Darnall], freed by father's will could qualify as free (and thereby legally capable of selling real estate to Philadelphian) under Maryland law that allowed testamentary manumission of only those slaves able to earn a livelihood. In light of undisputed testimony that Darnall at eleven was able to maintain himself by such work as household servant, Court upheld circuit court ruling that he qualified under Maryland law, such that the sale was valid.	Affirmed Circuit Court. Opinion by Duvall.	+
1830	(Josefa Segunda III) U.S. v. Preston, 28 U.S. 57	**Att'y Gen. of LA. argued** that LA. deserved the proceeds from the sale of slaves on the Josefa Segunda, carried out pursuant to LA. law of 1818, adopted to carry out the U.S. law of 1807. Supreme Court ruled that U.S. law of 1819, adopted while appeals in the case still pending caused the slaves to be ordered rendered to the President for return to Africa. Money paid for them ($68,000) was to be returned to purported purchasers.	**Reversed decree of U.S. district court.** Opinion by Johnson (with U.S. Att'y Gen.)	+
1830	Lagrange v. Chouteau, 29 U.S. 287	Court refused to set free a slave owned in Missouri who alleged that eight days spent with his master in Illinois (after which he was brought back to and sold in Missouri) freed him under the Northwest Ordinance, in response to which allegation jury had been instructed that if they found he had been carried to Illinois "with a view to residence" there, they should declare him free. Court ruled this a correct construction of the Ordinance.	Affirmed Court instruction to jury, which allowed that a slave's owner who took him to a free state and resided there (unlike this case) and then returned to the slave state could be freed upon a lawsuit by the slave.	+/–

Date	Case	Ruling	Action	→
1831	Menard v. Aspasia, 30 U.S. 505	Because of prior treaty with France, 1787 Northwest Ordinance's ban on slavery in NW territory and its later re-enactments by Congress and in the IL. Constitution, had been treated as implicitly exempting the slaves owned by the French pre-1787 inhabitants of NW territory. Menard (of French descent in IL) claims that he therefore has right to own Aspasia as the offspring of such a slave. He tried to take her from MO. where they had resided from 1821–1827, back to IL., but she sued for her freedom in MO. and won there in both the local and state Supreme Court. U.S. Supreme Court denies that it has jurisdiction, since the Missouri decision did not "call into question" the Congressional re-enactment of the Northwest Ordinance, but simply honored its ban on slavery.	Court refuses to review pro-freedom decision of Missouri Supreme Court. Upshot is that post-1787offspring of former slaves still being held in IL. can now claim freedom. Opinion by McLean.	+
1833	*Ex Parte Madrazzo* (Madrazo II), 32 U.S. 627	Madrazo, lawful Spanish owner of twenty-seven to thirty slaves held by state of Georgia, awaiting the transfer of them to the American Colonization Society for shipment back to Africa and liberation, tried to sue Georgia for the slaves under the Supreme Court's admiralty jurisdiction. Supreme Court rejected jurisdiction on grounds that it was covered by Eleventh Amendment rather than admiralty.	Jurisdiction denied. Georgia retains the twenty-seven to thirty slaves and is free to follow through on its pledge to turn them over for liberation in Africa.	+
1834	Lee v. Lee, 33 U.S. 44	Court ruled that jury instructions below had erred in not allowing jury to consider whether hiring slaves out temporarily in one county of D.C before importing them into another had been a fraudulent attempt to evade the D.C (formerly MD) law against slave import, as modified in 1812 Act by Congress to allow moving slaves from one D.C county to another. Court divided in half on how strictly to interpret the 1812 act; half would have viewed the act as freeing the slaves in this context.	**Reversed Circuit Court decision and remanded** for new jury instructions. Did NOT free the slaves on point where **Supreme Court split 50-50**. Opinion by Thompson.	+/–
1834	McCutcheon v. Marshall, 33 U.S. 220	Court rejected claim of purported [out-of-state] heirs to slaves set free by will of Tennessean. Court ruled that Tennessee law was clear in permitting such freeing of slaves (contrary to allegation of heirs). Court ruled that offspring born after death of testator of two to-be-freed women slaves who had not yet reached twenty-one, the age at which these mothers were to become free, remained legally slaves under Tennessee law (although court might rule otherwise "if this were an open question"), but that description of these offspring in the lawsuit was "too vague and uncertain" for court action against their manumission, so lawsuit should be dismissed.	Affirmed decree of Circuit Court, dismissing the lawsuit, with costs. Opinion by Thompson.	+

Table 1.1 (continued)

Date	Case	Ruling	Action	→
1835	Fenwick v. Chapman, 34 U.S. 461	Court rules that executor of estate erred in allowing orphan's court to sell as slaves two persons who had already been set free under terms of will of deceased Marylander. Maryland law allowed such manumission as long as it was not "in prejudice to creditors." Sale of slaves was unlawful on two grounds: (1) "If an executor permits manumitted slaves to go … free from the death of the testator, it is an assent to the manumission, which he cannot recall any more than he can, after assenting to a legacy, withdraw that assent" [at 475]; and (2) when testator declares will to free slaves, other property, including real estate, must be used to satisfy debts—i.e., orphan's court had erred in attempting to preserve real estate of decedent above freedom of the named slaves.	Circuit Court judgment affirmed, with costs. Opinion by Wayne.	+

Notes:

Key to Table 1.1:
1) The direction (→) column (far right) uses a plus sign for pro-freedom rulings and a minus sign for anti-freedom rulings.
2) **Bold** indicates some element of contestability in Court ruling.
3) Where opinion author not noted, it is Chief Justice John Marshall.
4) Where case listed more than once (e.g., *Josefa Segundo*), later versions present new issues rather than merely clarifying earlier holding.

[1] 1824 *Merino* case: These slaves were brought to Alabama for trial. Under 1818 U.S. law, if vessels found in violation, slaves would be dealt with according to law "adopted hereafter" of state where slaves brought in, and slaves in this case had been so rendered to Alabama authorities. Alabama law of 1822 made such slaves labor for the state or else auctioned them to highest bidder. U.S. law changed in 1819 to order such captured slaves free and made U.S. President obliged to arrange transport back to Africa for them. Josefa Segundo III (U.S. v. Preston) made clear that the 1819 change of U.S. law (ordering the slaves to be sent to Africa and freed) took effect upon all decrees still pending in 1819 and thereafter.
[2] Eventually, long after John Marshall's death, the estate was settled. "Undergoing protracted litigation, the bequest to Jefferson remained legally blocked until 1852 when the U.S. Supreme Court awarded the American investments to relatives in Europe, thus frustrating Kosciusko's original intent. … [M]ost of the funds, which had grown several times in the intervening years, were embezzled by one of the administrators." Cizauskas 1986.

Marshall Court Assessment as to Black Americans

Apart from the role of the justices acting on circuit, where they judged unconstitutional (or else refused to apply) the harshly discriminatory Negro Seamen Acts in 1820 and 1823,[46] the only judgments the Marshall Court issued with respect to black Americans involved chattel slavery. On this matter, the judicial attitudes appear to have undergone a transition. Despite whatever doubts a majority of the justices harbored about a clash between moral or natural law and slavery, they systematically voted prior to 1817 to uphold slavery or go easy on slave traders, even in many cases where a legally respectable decision could have gone the other way. Beginning in 1817, the situation changed somewhat. The justices appeared to begin to pay much more attention to the common law principle of "in *favorem libertatis*" in the matter of individual slave petitions for freedom. Why this is so is not definitively discoverable. But that a marked shift took place is hard to dispute.

For a second conclusion, one can now reconsider the inquiry with which this book began. Did Hamilton's prediction about the tendency of judicial independence to "mitigate the severity of unjust and partial laws" and Story's confidence that the judicial department would provide "security for the minority" prove valid as to racial minorities for the federal judiciary up until 1835? One would have to answer that it varied across time.

In the time period from 1776 through 1791 (while the Supreme Court was just being established), legislatures and constitutional conventions (elected bodies), caught up in the fervor of the War for Independence, were exceptionally pro-liberty, freeing slaves, outlawing slavery in the Northwest Territory, writing a twenty-year limit on the import of slaves into the Constitution, and by silent omission permitting blacks into the electorate in most states.

The elected branches, however, shifted quickly: Congress adopted a Fugitive Slave Law by 1793 that appeared to be more anti-liberty than the Fugitive Slave Clause of the Constitution actually warranted, and imposed both slavery (in 1801) and racial hierarchy (in 1820) on the District of Columbia. On the other hand, Congress opposed the foreign slave trade consistently, outlawing it in 1807 (effective January 1, 1808), and toughening sanctions against it in 1818, 1819, and 1820. Importantly, in 1819 Congress stopped the practice of auctioning off slaves from

---

[46] See note 25 above.

captured slave traders and instead returned them to their home country to be freed (see note to 1824 *Merino* case in Table 1.1).

Until 1817 the U.S. Supreme Court undeniably supported the slavery system in its decisions, supported it *more* than law itself demanded, if one can assume that the lower federal courts and the U.S. Attorney General knew law as well as the justices did. On at least three occasions between 1801 and 1816, the executive branch, as represented by the Attorney General argued for pro-freedom legal conclusions that the Court *rejected* (twice in 1805 and once in 1810; see Table 1.1 above). In the 1817–1835 period, by contrast, the Court does not appear to have been noticeably less pro-freedom than the elected branches of the national government. Congress was repeatedly passing laws to get tougher on the foreign slave trade, and the Court generally either went along with the Attorney General in these cases or allowed the federal prosecution a second chance by allowing indictments that were technically flawed to be amended for a retrial at the Circuit Court level. Even in this period, though, one can argue that the elected branches were slightly ahead of the Court in moves to restrict the slave trade. The Attorney General under President John Quincy Adams, for instance, in the *Antelope* Case of 1825–26 argued for freeing thirty-nine more of the unlawfully traded slaves than the Supreme Court was willing to set free. And it was Congress, not the Court, that changed the rules in 1819 to end the practice of states' auctioning off captured slaves from the illegal foreign slave trade, instead requiring their return to Africa and freedom.

Around 1820, however, a gap did begin to widen between the Supreme Court and the state-level political branches' treatment of *free* blacks. Southern state legislatures cracked down on free black sailors, imprisoning them upon the docking of their ship, and insisted on banning free discussion of slavery. As to the U.S. postal system, the Jackson administration basically cooperated, and even Congress worded the law so as to permit these state-level discussion bans. In this period the federal judiciary did offer some resistance to this new southern mistreatment of free black sailors, although no freedom of the press case arose to challenge the ban on anti-slavery mailings. So from 1820–1835 one might conclude that the Marshall Court, while it did not distinguish itself on slavery, was in fact somewhat more the defender of free blacks than either Congress or the President. The difference was barely visible, however, because the justices were acting at the Circuit Court level and these cases did not reach the Supreme Court.

THE MARSHALL COURT AND NATIVE AMERICANS

In contrast to black Americans, Native Americans, or Indians as they were termed in the legal cases, did bring a number of important constitutional law cases to the Marshall Court. The earliest of these was *Johnson v. McIntosh*, 21 U.S. 543 (1823), but it was preceded by more than three centuries of colonial legal discourse about the conquest of indigenous people in America, discourse that itself had roots going back to the legitimation of the conquest of infidels by the Christian Crusaders during the Middle Ages.

Christopher Columbus wrote of the Caribbean natives whom he encountered on his first voyage that they went naked but bore no weapons, and had no religious creed and were not idolators. They did, however, "all believe that power and good are in the heavens." On this basis the Spanish monarch wrote to Pope Alexander VI (a corrupt member of the family of Cesare Borgia, as it happens), who obliged Spain by declaring on May 4, 1493 that America belonged to Spain, "with the proviso that these ... lands ... be not actually possessed by some other Christian king or prince." In this declaration the Pope described the American native peoples as living peacefully, going unclothed, and "not eating flesh." He concluded they were "well fitted to embrace the Catholic faith and be imbued with good morals." The Pope combined his talk of "bring[ing] them to the Catholic faith" with mention of gold and precious spices that had also been discovered in America.[47]

Forty years later, as Spanish involvement in the New World intensified (and with its hegemony there not yet seriously challenged by Britain), the Spanish king consulted Francisco de Vitoria, a prominent theologian, for guidance as to the rights and wrongs of Indian conquest. Vitoria replied that that the Indians were the true owners of the land and that therefore the doctrine of "title [for Europeans to Indian property] by discovery" could *not* apply, since that doctrine justified taking land only when the piece of property had no owner. As long as the Europeans had no provocation to launch a "just war" (which might happen if the Indians did not respect the Spaniards' natural rights to travel and trade among them), there could be no grounds to claim the Indian property by conquest. Therefore Europeans were obliged to obtain the voluntary consent of the Indians, through purchase via treaties, if they wanted land in America. Since at first only small settlements of Europeans were established, they needed the friendship of much more powerful Indian

---

[47] Getches, Wilkinson, and Williams 1993, 46–7.

tribes in order to survive, so the Spanish for a while took this doctrine seriously.[48]

As is well known, once the Europeans became far more numerous and powerful in the Americas, relations were marked by violent conquest and even enslavement, especially in South America. Nonetheless in North America, despite intermittent outbreaks of violence, treaty making became the dominant mode of legal and political relation between the Indians and the Europeans. Both the British and the Dutch followed the core tenets of Vitoria's guidelines. These rested on three premises: (1) each tribe acted as a sovereign in making treaties; (2) tribes as such possessed some sort of transferable title to the land; and (3) acquisition of Indian land was solely a governmental prerogative, in that it could happen only via formal agreement between two sovereigns.[49] On the other hand, these restraining principles were somewhat undercut by the belief among Euro-Americans, well-entrenched by the early 1600s, that those who farmed land, thereby making it productive, had moral authority to take it from people who merely hunted on it from time to time. Still, in the British colonies, prudence counseled the voluntaristic approach of treaty making.[50] When the colonies formed their own independent [con]federation, the United States began to take over this treaty practice. The U.S. government formed its first Indian treaty with the Delaware tribe in 1778. In the next century, more than 600 treaties were made between the national government and the native tribes and nations of North America.[51]

Johnson and Graham's Lessee v. McIntosh[52]

The first important Indian case to come to the U.S. Supreme Court concerned a challenge to the premises of this longstanding treaty practice. In 1754 Britain, in order to secure Indian assistance against the French, agreed to, and did, prohibit settlement by British subjects on any Indian land west of the eastern mountain ranges (e.g., the Appalachians). In the Peace Treaty of 1763, the French ceded its land claims between these mountain ranges and the Mississippi to Britain. The King of Britain then proclaimed in the same year that this territory was reserved for Indian tribes and that no British subjects could settle there. American

---

48 Deloria 1996, 124–5.

49 Getches, Wilkinson, and Williams 1993, 60–61.

50 Ibid., 58–60.

51 Deloria 1996, 125-6.

52 *Johnson and Graham's Lessee v. McIntosh,* 21 U.S. 543 (1823).

colonists widely regarded this proclamation as an unlawful interference with their individual freedom to acquire property and ignored it. In 1767, for example, George Washington instructed a business confederate by letter to survey on Washington's behalf 2,000 acres of land in the forbidden territory in order to "secure" it against claims of other investors. He noted just "between ourselves" that the king's proclamation was merely a "temporary expedient to quiet the minds of the Indians and must fall ... in a few years, especially when the Indians are consenting to our occupying the lands." Thus it was crucial, he wrote, that a prudent man not "neglect[] the present opportunity of hunting out good lands, and in some measure marking and distinguishing them for his own in order to keep others [of European descent] from settling it ..."[53]

A group of such prudent investors, one of whom was Thomas Johnson, purchased from the Illinois Indians for $24,000 two large tracts of land in 1773 and from the Wabash Indians a second two large tracts of land in 1775 for $31,000. By relying on a [mis]reading of a British legal opinion concerning the rights of the East India Company to acquire land in India, Johnson claimed that he had lawful authority to defy the 1763 proclamation. By 1823, two of Thomas Johnson's heirs to part of this land, his son Joshua Johnson and his grandson Thomas Graham, had in turn leased it to a third party, who wound up at the U.S. Supreme Court in a dispute over the title.

The U.S. Government in 1794 had defeated the tribes in the Battle of Fallen Timbers, which defeat resulted in a treaty by which the tribes ceded this land to the U.S. Government. The federal government then sold the land off in parcels to investors, one of which sales took place in 1818 to William McIntosh. McIntosh was an Illinois resident and Johnson and Graham were Maryland residents, so the land dispute went to the Supreme Court as a controversy between citizens of different states (see Article III, Sec.2).

The lead attorney for the Johnson and Graham Lessee was Daniel Webster. He argued that the initial tribal transfer should be honored because, since tribes can make treaties, they are sovereign entities, and if they are sovereign entities, they have the freedom to sell properties to individuals if they so choose. The attorneys for McIntosh argued in effect that the Indians never owned the land in the first place:

> [T]he practice of all civilized nations ... [and] the whole theory of their titles to lands in America, rests upon the hypothesis, that the Indians had no right of soil as sovereign, independent states. Discovery is the foundation of title, in

---

53 Getches, Wilkinson, and Williams 1993, 61–2.

> European nations, and this overlooks all proprietary rights in the natives. (21 U.S. 543, 567)

In deciding the case, *Johnson ... v. McIntosh*, John Marshall rejected each of these legal theories and carved out his own position on the subject, a position that then set the constitutional law of the respective powers of the federal government, the state governments, and individuals, when it came to purchases of Indian land. He proceeded in the mode of a common law judge, appearing to describe the legal practice as it has evolved through official acts, but at the same time, clarifying for the future what the prevailing rules will be.

Indians, Marshall noted, were in "the peculiar situation of in some respects ... a dependent, and in some respects ... a distinct people" [21 U.S. 543 at 596].[54] Marshall traced the diplomatic history of Europeans and North American Indians to conclude that while there was a sense in which discovery (by particular European peoples) gave "exclusive" right to lands in North America, this was so only in the sense that the discovery was exclusive of OTHER European powers. It did not mean that discovery excluded the Indians from their own land. Of the Indian claims he wrote:

> The potentates of the old world found no difficulty in convincing themselves that they made ample compensation to the inhabitants of the new, by bestowing on them civilization and Christianity, in exchange for unlimited independence ... . The exclusion of all other Europeans, necessarily gave to the nation making the discovery the sole right of acquiring the soil from the natives, and establishing settlements upon it ... . Those relations which were to exist between the discoverer and the natives, were to be regulated by themselves ... .
>
> In the establishment of these relations, the rights of the original inhabitants were, in no instance, entirely disregarded; but were necessarily, to a considerable extent, impaired. They were admitted to be the rightful occupants of the soil, with a legal as well as just claim to retain possession of it, and to use it according to their own discretion; but their rights to complete sovereignty, as independent nations, were necessarily diminished, and their power to dispose of the soil at their own will, to whomsoever they pleased [such as competing European powers], was denied by the original fundamental principle, that discovery gave exclusive title to those who made it.
>
> While the different nations of Europe respected the right of the natives, as occupants, they asserted the ultimate dominion to be in themselves; and

[54] The clauses of the Constitution that mention the Indians would seem to confirm this depiction: see Art. I, Sec. 8; cl. 18, and Art. I, Sec. 2; cl. 3.

> claimed and exercised, as a consequence of this ultimate dominion, a power to grant the soil, while yet in possession of the natives. These grants have been understood by all, to convey a title to the grantees, subject only to the Indian right of occupancy [21 U.S. 543, at pp. 573–4].

Thus while Marshall acknowledged tribal sovereignty with respect to the rights to use, possess and occupy their own soil, he admitted that the European peoples and Euro-American peoples did not treat Indian nations as fully sovereign in the sense of free to make treaties with any foreign power of their choice.

For purposes of settling the issues of this case Marshall traced the history of the right to acquire territory from the Indian tribes, starting with the British Crown (which obtained it by discovery) then to the British colonies by grants from the Crown, then to the American states via the War of Revolution and the peace treaty, and then to the government established by the 1787 U.S. Constitution, under which each state ceded its land claims to the U.S. The outcome he described as follows:

> The United States, then, have unequivocally acceded to that great and broad rule by which its civilized inhabitants now hold this country. They [the United States] hold, and assert in themselves, the title by which it was acquired. They maintain, as all others have maintained, that discovery gave an exclusive right to extinguish the Indian title of occupancy, either by purchase or by conquest; and gave also a right to such a degree of sovereignty, as the circumstances of the [Indian] people would allow them to exercise [21 U.S. 543 at p. 587].

The degree of sovereignty retained in the Indians, as Marshall described it, did not permit them to transfer title of their land to individuals, once the U.S. had acceded to that aspect of sovereignty. Only the U.S. Government could transfer the right to title of Indian lands, subject always to the Indians' right of occupancy. The latter right could be ended only by treaty or conquest, as with any foreign country. For this reason, Johnson's initial purchase from the Indians had never been valid, irrespective of what the law of individual states might say about it, and McIntosh's later purchase from the U.S. Government gave the valid title to the land.

Marshall went on to address certain broad principles of Euro-American–Indian relations. With respect to the facts on the ground, established by war, he confessed that courts had no power to intervene:

> We will not enter into the controversy, whether agriculturists, merchants, and manufacturers, have a right, on abstract principles, to expel hunters from the territory they possess, or to contract their limits. Conquest gives a title which

> the Courts of the conqueror cannot deny, whatever the private and speculative opinions of individuals may be, respecting the original justice of the claim which has been successfully asserted. The British government, which was then our government, and whose rights have passed to the United States, asserted a title to all the lands occupied by Indians, within the chartered limits of the British colonies. It asserted also a limited sovereignty over them, and the exclusive right of extinguishing the title which occupancy gave to them. These claims have been maintained and established as far west as the river Mississippi, by the sword. The title to a vast portion of the lands we now hold, originates in them. It is not for the Courts of this country to question the validity of this title, or to sustain one which is incompatible with it [21 U.S. 543 at pp. 588–9].

Marshall then broached a subject that was to bedevil Indian policy for the next two centuries. He described the typical conquest situation as one where it is best to let the conquered nation assimilate amidst the people of the conquerors, becoming eventually treated as equal members of the body politic and equally protected in their legal rights. But this approach, he claimed presented problems with respect to the Indians:

> But the tribes of Indians inhabiting this country were fierce savages, whose occupation was war, and whose subsistence was drawn chiefly from the forest. To leave them in possession of their country, was to leave the country a wilderness; to govern them as a distinct people, was impossible, because they were as brave and as high spirited as they were fierce, and were ready to repel by arms every attempt on their independence.
>
> What was the inevitable consequence of this state of things? The Europeans were under the necessity either of abandoning the country … or of enforcing those claims by the sword, and by the adoption of principles adapted to the condition of a people with whom it was impossible to mix, and who could not be governed as a distinct society, or of remaining in their neighbourhood, and exposing themselves and their families to the perpetual hazard of being massacred.
>
> Frequent and bloody wars, in which the whites were not always the aggressors, unavoidably ensued. European policy, numbers, and skill, prevailed. As the white population advanced, that of the Indians necessarily receded [21 U.S. 543 at p. 590].

He reiterated that courts sometimes must bow to deeply entrenched facts, even if those facts "perhaps" may not be rationally supportable:

> However extravagant the pretension of converting the discovery of an inhabited country into conquest may appear; if the principle has been asserted in the first instance, and afterwards sustained; if a country has been acquired and held under it; if the property of the great mass of the community originates in it, it becomes the law of the land, and cannot be questioned. So,

too, with respect to the concomitant principle, that the Indian inhabitants are to be considered merely as occupants, to be protected, indeed, while in peace, in the possession of their lands, but to be deemed incapable of transferring the absolute title to others. However this restriction may be opposed to natural right, and to the usages of civilized nations, yet, if it be indispensable to that system under which the country has been settled, and be adapted to the actual condition of the two people, it may, perhaps, be supported by reason, and certainly cannot be rejected by Courts of justice [21 U.S. 543 at p. 591].

The Cherokee Cases and Indian Removal

The U.S. Constitution plainly reserves treaty-making power to the federal government and (in Art.I, Sec 10) forbids it to the states. The administration of George Washington solidified the practice of dealing with Indian nations by the treaty process, just as was done with foreign nations.[55] Marshall's *Johnson … v. McIntosh* opinion noted that during the colonial period one important reason for generally reserving authority over Indian land to the central as contrasted with the more local government (i.e., the British monarch as contrasted with the colonies) was to enable that more distant, central government to prevent Indian wars "by restraining the encroachments of the whites" [21 U.S. 543 at p. 597]. (Marshall's understanding that distant central authority would be more protective of unpopular local minorities thus conforms to the expectation of James Madison's Federalist #10.) Not many years after the *McIntosh* case, conflict between state and federal authority over Indians came to a head in the state of Georgia where gold had recently been discovered on Indian lands. The need to "restrain the encroachment of whites" lay precisely at the center of this conflict.

In the background of this conflict lay increasingly tense relations between whites and Indians, which reached crisis proportions in the 1820s. The military dominance by whites by this time, along with their continuing population increase and a decline in Indian population created great political pressure to abandon treaties securing the Indian homelands on the eastern side of the Mississippi.[56]

Large swaths of land in Georgia were occupied by Cherokee and Creek tribes at the time the Constitution was ratified. In order to persuade

---

55 Michael Green 1996, 486.

56 Ibid., 510–16. Between 1810 and 1820, the white population of Indiana, Mississippi, Illinois, and Alabama (all new states) quadrupled. The white population of nearby older states with large swaths of Indian territory—Georgia, Tennessee, and Ohio—nearly doubled. Most of this population increase occurred between 1815 and 1820. Ibid., 498–501.

Georgia to give up its claims to land west of its own borders (in what became Alabama and Mississippi) President Jefferson in 1802 had signed a compact with the governor of Georgia agreeing to extinguish the Indian title to land within the boundaries of Georgia as soon as this could be done "peaceably" and "on reasonable terms."[57] This compact appeared to conflict with treaties the U.S. had made with the Creek and Cherokee as recently as 1791 and 1798, guaranteeing to them this very land.[58] It also appears to represent a change from President Washington's preferred policy, which had been to encourage gradual assimilation of the Indians out of tribal life and into the political community as U.S. citizens, each with his own plot of land carved out of the tribal holding.[59]

Once the Jefferson administration acquired the enormous land tract west of the Mississippi via the Louisiana Purchase of 1803, the dominant emphasis of federal government policy shifted from acculturation to removal.[60] Instead of pressuring the Indians to join Euro-American civilization as individuals, the federal government now tried to lure them by generous land grants to move west of the Mississippi in order to make more room for white settlement within the boundaries of already settled states. Some groups of Cherokee accepted these offers and moved westward in 1809 and 1819, but most refused, insisting on their treaty rights within Georgia. In 1827 the Cherokee in Georgia formed their own republic, claiming independence, with a Constitution modeled after that of the U.S.[61]

In the following two years the Georgia legislature, stimulated by the discovery of gold in Indian territory, enacted laws proclaiming that the Indian land now belonged to the various county governments (who then

---

57 Burke 1969, 593. Longaker 1956, 343.

58 Norgren 2004, 37.

59 Ibid., 36; Sturgis 2007, xiii.

60 Acculturation efforts did continue on an intermittent basis; in 1819 Congress pledged $10,000 per year to be devoted to teaching Indians "the habits and arts of civilization," and Presidents James Monroe, John Quincy Adams, and Ulysses S. Grant all actively promoted the use of this fund for educating and Christianizing efforts via missionary activity (in an era where local public schools routinely promoted Christianity). Congress continued appropriations for this fund until 1873. Federal funding in general of missionary educational and Christianizing activity on Indian reservations did not end until 1900, but churches continued to run schools on reservations using money from tribal trust funds and treaty funds, all derived from the federal government (via past treaties mostly for land cessions). Fisher 2002, 150–56; *Quick Bear v. Leupp*, 210 U.S. 50 (1908).

61 Norgren ibid., 36–8, 44–6. Burke 1969, 503.

began to expropriate the tribal gold mines) and that as of June 1, 1830 all Indian law in Georgia would be null and void. The law also reduced the Indians to second-class status by denying them the right to testify against a white person in court and criminalizing any attempt to keep an Indian from emigrating out of the state.

Newly elected President Andrew Jackson backed up the Georgians on Dec. 8, 1829. He condemned the Cherokee adoption of their own republican constitution, and said they would have to be ruled by Georgia law and give up any land that had not been (individually) "improved by their industry" unless they agreed to leave Georgia and Alabama to move to tribal land that could be set aside west of the Mississippi outside the bounds of any state. He proposed an Indian Removal Bill to accomplish this.

Congress then did enact legislation, providing western lands, and authorizing compensation to individual Indians for improvements made upon their land in the eastern states and appropriating funds to assist in Indian removal.[62] In contrast to President Jackson, however, Congress at this point did not *openly* turn its back on prior treaties by saying that Indians who stayed put would have to be ruled by state law; instead, the actual Indian Removal Act of May 28, 1830 maintained a veil of legitimacy by stating in section seven, "[N]othing in this act shall be construed as authorizing or directing the violation of any existing treaty between the United States and any Indian tribes."[63] Like many passages in statutes, this one obtained legislative support in part due to its ambiguity; Georgia's Senator Forsyth insisted on the Senate floor that Georgia's policies of imposing removal and second-class citizenship on Indians did not violate any existing treaties.[64] The Indian Removal Act applied not just to the Cherokee, but to the eastern U.S. as a whole.

As a general matter, the legislative power is authorized to adopt new laws that throw out old laws, on the grounds that democracies have the right to rule themselves and do not have to be ruled by the dead who came before them. In the U.S., the treaty power is the President plus two-thirds of the Senate, and the Constitution says nothing explicit about whether the legislative power (a majority of the House plus a majority of the Senate plus the President, or two-thirds of each chamber without the President) may override a previous treaty. Under general principles of

---

[62] Burke 1969, 503–6, 512. Norgren 2004, 81–6. Green 1996, 516.

[63] U.S. Statutes at Large, Vol.IV, Ch.CXLVIII, 411-412. Twenty-first Congress, 1st Sess., reprinted in Sturgis 2007, 98–100.

[64] Gales and Seaton's *Register*, Senate Journal, 21st Congress, 1st Sess., April 15, 1830, pp. 325–6.

international law, Congress is supposed to honor treaties made in the past, although there is a doctrine in international law that allows treaties to be abrogated unilaterally on the grounds that conditions have significantly changed.[65] A mere state within the U.S., however, cannot abrogate a treaty made by the national government. On this the Supremacy Clause of Art.VI is clear.[66]

The Cherokee conflict in Georgia produced four nationally publicized Supreme Court cases involving the Cherokee, only one of which eventuated in a decision on the merits. The first concerned George Tassels or Corn Tassels, a Cherokee accused of murdering another Cherokee on Cherokee land. Existing treaties acknowledging Cherokee control over Cherokee territory would have left this matter to Cherokee authorities. The Georgia government arrested (or abducted, depending on one's point of view) Tassels, tried him for murder and sentenced him to hang. William Wirt, an eminent attorney who had served as U.S. Attorney General for twelve years, (1817–1829) was hired by tribal leaders to fight Georgia's attack on their sovereignty. He appealed first in Georgia, where

---

[65] The Latin term for this doctrine is "*rebus non sic stantibus*." I am indebted to the late Gerard Mangone of the University of Delaware for this information. The U.S. Supreme Court treats the matter somewhat more cavalierly. It stated in the Chinese Exclusion Act Case of 1889:

> It must be conceded that the act of 1888 is in contravention of express stipulations of the treaty of 1868, and of the supplemental treaty of 1880, but it is not on that account invalid, or to be restricted in its enforcement. The treaties were of no greater legal obligation than the act of congress. By the constitution, laws made in pursuance thereof, and treaties made under the authority of the United States, are both declared to be the supreme law of the land, and no paramount authority is given to one over the other. A treaty, it is true, is in its nature a contract between nations, and is often merely promissory in its character, requiring legislation to carry its stipulations into effect. Such legislation will be open to future repeal or amendment. If the treaty operates by its own force, and relates to a subject within the power of congress, it can be deemed in that particular only the equivalent of a legislative act, to be repealed or modified at the pleasure of congress. In either case the last expression of the sovereign will must control.

Chae Chan Ping v. U.S. [The Chinese Exclusion Case], 130 U.S. 581 at p. 600 (1889). The Court has not overturned this longstanding rule.

[66] Art.VI, cl.2:

> This Constitution, and the laws of the United States which shall be made in pursuance thereof; and all treaties made, or which shall be made, under the authority of the United States, shall be the supreme law of the land; and the judges in every state shall be bound thereby, anything in the Constitution or laws of any State to the contrary notwithstanding.

his appeal lost in September 1830, and then to the U.S. Supreme Court for a writ of error (an order granting review of the case). Wirt's argument was that the Georgia laws violated existing treaty rights of the Indians, and under Article VI of the Constitution treaties are part of the supreme law of the land, which must be honored by states. The Marshall Court granted the writ, along with a stay of execution, pending the outcome of the appeal. In much-publicized open resistance, the Georgia government refused to appear at the U.S. Supreme Court, the Georgia legislature ordered government officials to ignore the U.S. Supreme Court's order, and the state executed Tassels on Christmas Eve, 1830.[67]

(Two years later another Cherokee, James Graves, was sentenced to hang for murder in similar circumstances, and again the case was appealed to the Marshall Court. Again Marshall issued a writ of error [and stay] to Georgia authorities. Again the state authorities pointedly ignored the Court and executed the prisoner in 1834.[68])

Cherokee v. Georgia (1831)

The first of the Cherokee cases for which the Marshall Court actually issued an opinion was *Cherokee v. Georgia*, 30 U.S. 1 (1831), and it resulted from a continuation of attorney William Wirt's efforts on behalf of the Cherokee to have the state laws that nullified Indian authority declared unconstitutional as violation of the law of U.S. treaties. Early in 1831 Wirt and his co-counsel John Sergeant petitioned the U.S. Supreme Court to grant an injunction blocking execution of the Georgia laws within Cherokee territory. They maintained that the Cherokee Nation was a "foreign state" in the sense of Article III, Sec.2, which granted the Court original jurisdiction for controversies between a state or its citizens and a foreign state. True to form, Georgia refused again to appear at the U.S. Supreme Court to argue its side of the case. After hearing Wirt and Sergeant's arguments, the Court ruled on March 18, 1831 that it did not have jurisdiction to decide the case on its merits. At first, all the public saw was the Marshall opinion for the Court and the opinion of two concurring justices (with the division 2-1-1 as to reasoning and one justice absent). Despite ruling against the Cherokee's jurisdictional claims, Marshall put his heart squarely on his sleeve in the second paragraph of his decision, which reads as follows:

---

67 Norgren 2004, 61–2, 95-98; McDonald, 104–105.
68 Longaker 1956, 344.

> If courts were permitted to indulge their sympathies, a case better calculated to excite them can scarcely be imagined. A people once numerous, powerful, and truly independent, found by our ancestors in the quiet and uncontrolled possession of an ample domain, gradually sinking beneath our superior policy, our arts and our arms, have yielded their lands by successive treaties, each of which contains a solemn guarantee of the residue, until they retain no more of their formerly extensive territory than is deemed necessary to their comfortable subsistence. To preserve this remnant, the present application is made. (30 U.S. 1, 15)

Despite his open sympathies, Marshall nonetheless rejected jurisdiction for this case. While noting that the Court majority did consider the Cherokee entity to amount to a "state," in that it was "a distinct political society, separated from others, capable of managing its own affairs and governing itself" (30 U.S. 1, 16), he had trouble concluding that they could properly be viewed as a "foreign state" for purposes of the U.S. Constitution. Because Indian territory was wholly within the bounds of the U.S., and because the Indians acknowledged themselves to be under U.S. protection and under U.S. control for purposes of external commerce and all other external relations, it did not really make sense to consider them foreign. (He suggested instead the descriptive term, "domestic dependent nations," 30 U.S. at 17.) The wording of the commerce clause, he noted, supported his conclusion in listing "Indian tribes" separately from "foreign nations" (30 U.S. at 18–20). Thus, the Supreme Court did not have original jurisdiction.

The two concurring opinions denied at length that an Indian tribe or nation could be thought of as a state at all: Indian tribes were not recognized by foreign governments, nor did they exercise sovereign powers. These two opinions got the bulk of attention from gleeful Jacksonian politicians and press. This reaction evidently upset Chief Justice Marshall, who then (in contrast to his usual effort to maintain an image of a unified court) encouraged Thompson and Story to make public their disagreement with his views by publishing a dissent, even though the Court session had already ended.[69] They did so and their dissent, authored by Thompson, became part of the official record.

This dissent insisted that the Indian tribes were both "states" and "foreign." They had been allowed to be self-ruling entities from the beginning. Our government had dealt with them from the beginning by treaty making (or conquest) just as one does with a foreign country, and they were not U.S. citizens. What else could they be but a "foreign

---

[69] Burke 1969, 516–19.

state"? In sum, although this decision denied jurisdiction, in the end it put five of the justices (Marshall and the two who concurred silently with him and the two in dissent: Thompson and Story) on record as favoring the view that Indian tribes were at least "states," which was to say, sovereign entities.

***Worcester v. Georgia* (1832)**

Although the dominant political forces at both the state and federal level supported the effort by white Georgians to drive the Cherokee from their homes, the Indians did have many white sympathizers. One of these, Samuel Worcester, was a missionary from Vermont who had lived among the Cherokee in Georgia for years. Worcester, along with ten other missionaries publicly defied the Georgia law that prohibited white adult males, except for agents of the federal government, from residing in Cherokee Territory without a license from the state after February of 1831. At first the Georgia judges tried to avoid creating a case appealable to federal court, by treating the missionaries as exempt from the law on the grounds that they received federal financial support, so could be construed to be federal agents. The Georgia governor, wanting to act against them, persuaded President Andrew Jackson to deny that the missionaries were federal employees and to fire Worcester from his extra job as the local federal postmaster. Georgia authorities then prosecuted him and ten others, and sentenced them to four years at hard labor. Most of these accepted the pardons that the governor immediately offered, but Worcester and Elizur Butler began to serve their sentences, in order to let the Cherokees' challenge against these laws go to the Supreme Court.[70]

In both courts, Worcester pleaded innocent on the grounds that Cherokee law, not Georgia law ruled in Cherokee territory. He lost in Georgia and the Supreme Court issued a writ of error to let his appeal be heard, and, as before, the Georgia authorities refused to appear at the U.S. Supreme Court to argue their case. Once again the case was argued by the team of Wirt and Sergeant, and Justice Story was later to report to his law students that he had observed Chief Justice John Marshall moved to tears by William Wirt's eloquent presentation.[71]

Marshall wrote the opinion for a unanimous court in *Worcester v. Georgia*, 31 U.S. 515 (1832). Since Worcester was presenting a claim that the Georgia law violated a treaty and thereby violated the supremacy

---

[70] Ibid., 519–20.

[71] Warren 1922, 216, n.1, citing *Life of Rutherford B. Hayes* (1914) by Charles R. Williams, I.

clause of Article VI of the U.S. Constitution, it was plain that the Court had jurisdiction under the Judiciary Act of 1789. Georgia's position was that treaties could not transgress a state's sovereign right to rule its own land and the people on it, and that this category included the Indians of Georgia.

Marshall began with the basics: As in *Johnson … v. McIntosh*, he acknowledged that in matters involving American Indians, judges could not just pose the abstract question of who was right or wrong according to the nature of things, or natural right, but instead judges had to bow to important facts on the ground.

> Did these [European] adventurers, by sailing along the coast, and occasionally landing on it, acquire for the several governments to whom they belonged, or by whom they were commissioned, a rightful property in the soil, from the Atlantic to the Pacific; or rightful dominion over the numerous people who occupied it? Or has nature, or the great Creator of all things, conferred these rights over hunters and fishermen, on agriculturists and manufacturers? [Treating these as rhetorical questions to which the obvious answer was "no," he continued as follows:]
>
> But power, war, conquest, give rights, which, after possession, are conceded by the world; and which can never be controverted by those on whom they descend. We proceed, then, to the actual state of things, having glanced at their origin; because holding it in our recollection might shed some light on existing pretensions (31 U.S. 515, p. 543).

Similarly, Marshall reiterated the principle from *Johnson v. McIntosh* that the "title" granted from the British monarch to American colonies over land in America entitled the colonists to exclude other European powers, not to rule over the Indians without their consent. What Georgia obtained simply "was the exclusive right of purchasing such lands as the natives [in tribal units] were willing to sell" [31 U.S. 515, at p. 545]. He admitted that the various colonial charters "contain passages showing one of their objects to be the civilization of the Indians, and their conversion to Christianity" but he immediately explained that these were "objects to be accomplished by conciliatory conduct and good example; not by extermination" [31 U.S. 515, at p. 546].

Marshall insisted that the sense of the power conferred in the colonial charters with respect to Indians, and then later transferred to the states and then to the U.S. Government needed to be understood by the model the British monarch had presented toward the Indians:

> The king purchased their lands when they were willing to sell, at a price they were willing to take; but never coerced a surrender of them. He also purchased their alliance and dependence by subsidies; but never intruded into

> the interior of their affairs, or interfered with their self -government, so far as respected themselves only [31 U.S. 515, at p. 547].

Then Marshall reviewed the sequence of federal treaties with the Cherokee and found them consistent in their basic premises. He summarized them as follows:

> This relation was that of a nation claiming and receiving the protection of one more powerful: not that of individuals abandoning their national character, and submitting as subjects to the laws of a master.
>
> ***
>
> [These treaties], thus explicitly recognizing the national character of the Cherokees, and their right of self government; thus guarantying their lands; assuming the duty of protection, and of course pledging the faith of the United States for that protection; has been frequently renewed, and is now in full force.
>
> To the general pledge of protection have been added several specific pledges, deemed valuable by the Indians. Some of these restrain the citizens of the United States from encroachments on the Cherokee country, and provide for the punishment of intruders.
>
> From the commencement of our government, congress has passed acts to regulate trade and intercourse with the Indians; which treat them as nations, respect their rights, and manifest a firm purpose to afford that protection which treaties stipulate. All these acts, and especially that of 1802, which is still in force, manifestly consider the several Indian nations as distinct political communities, having territorial boundaries, within which their authority is exclusive, and having a right to all the lands within those boundaries, which is not only acknowledged, but guarantied by the United States … .
>
> The treaties and laws of the United States contemplate the Indian territory as completely separated from that of the states; and provide that all intercourse with them shall be carried on exclusively by the government of the union [31 U.S. 515, at pp. 555–7].

Since the terms of the commerce clause (Art.I, Sec.8; Cl.3) plainly gave Congress authority to regulate commerce with Indian tribes, these laws were plainly constitutional. "Georgia, herself, has furnished conclusive evidence," noted Marshall, in the Compact of 1802 that:

> prove[s] her acquiescence in the universal conviction that the Indian nations possessed a full right to the lands they occupied, until that right should be extinguished by the United States, with their consent: that their territory was separated from that of any state within whose chartered limits they might reside, by a boundary line, established by treaties: that, within their boundary, they possessed rights with which no state could interfere: and that the whole

> power of regulating the intercourse with them, was vested in the United States [31 U.S. 515, at p. 560].

Georgia had not changed her position on tribal rights until 1828, but in the face of 200 years of precedent, that latter day shift could not be given legal force:

> The Cherokee nation, then, is a distinct community occupying its own territory, with boundaries accurately described, in which the laws of Georgia can have no force, and which the citizens of Georgia have no right to enter, but with the assent of the Cherokees themselves, or in conformity with treaties, and with the acts of congress. The whole intercourse between the United States and this nation, is, by our constitution and laws, vested in the government of the United States [31 U.S. 515, at p. 561].

The Georgia statutes and enforcement efforts of which Worcester complained were indeed unconstitutional and therefore void. The U.S. Supreme Court "reversed and annulled" the decision of the Supreme Court of Georgia.

Two days after handing down its decision, on March 5, 1832 the U.S. Supreme Court issued a mandate to the Georgia court to reverse itself and to release Worcester and Butler. The Court sent a messenger to Georgia, because the Court needed to receive an official document from Georgia indicating the refusal of the Georgia court to comply before the Supreme Court could order the U.S. marshal to free the two missionaries. The Court had power to do this under the Militia Act of 1795. Under the same Act, if the state used force to block the federal marshal, then the President could call out the militia in response. The U.S. Supreme Court ended its session before the messenger could get back to D.C., so the two missionaries ended up spending more time at hard labor. By January of 1833 the rise of a nullification movement in South Carolina moved Andrew Jackson to prevail on the Georgia governor to pardon the two missionaries, and this time their lawyers advised them to accept the pardons, so they finally went free.[72]

Indian removal

Meanwhile, marauders and fraudulent land dealers, aided and abetted by state legal systems, continued to harass the Cherokee, Choctaw, and Creek Indians of Georgia, Mississippi and Alabama. In the years 1827 through the early 1830s Alabama, Georgia, Mississippi, and Tennessee adopted laws extending state law (law that treated Indians as second-class

---

[72] Ibid., 524–30; Warren, vol.2, 205–37. See also Miles 1973.

citizens and did not allow them to testify against whites) to Indian territory within their boundaries, thereby purporting to negate the relevant federal treaties.[73]

In Alabama, despite the 1832 Treaty of Cusseta, which assured to Creeks their right to remain on their land until they chose to leave, whites rushed in as squatters. The treaty promised that federal authorities would remove white intruders. This time President Jackson did order federal troops to attack the squatters in August 1832, and then the state governor and legislature backed up the whites with new state laws and claims that the federal authorities were in the wrong. The result was rampant, unchecked looting of Indian property. A second clash occurred the following summer, and this time a county official, supportive of the squatters, was killed by the federal troops. General Winfield Scott advised Jackson's Secretary of War, Lewis Cass, that if the army continued to enforce this federal law, Georgia, Mississippi, Virginia and both Carolinas would rise up to join arms with the Alabamans. Eventually, Jackson ordered the federal troops to back off.[74]

In the end, the devastation wrought by the depredations by southern whites against Indian land and Indian possessions, assisted by the deliberate efforts of whites to keep the Indians intoxicated, by courts that would not let Indians testify, by treaties sometimes signed by unauthorized Indians, and by outright assault and murder on both sides, culminated in the use of federal troops to fight against the Creeks of Georgia in 1836, to fight against the Seminoles in Florida and to forcibly remove the Cherokee. By 1838 the Indians were driven out of Alabama, Mississippi, and Georgia (in the notorious Trail of Tears), and by 1842 most of the Seminole had been removed from Florida.[75]

The driving force behind Indian Removal was essentially rampant fraud (to take Indian land) backed up by local mob violence with the support of state law. Thousands of Indians died from starvation and from the cold and from illness, during Indian Removal, in addition to those killed in military conflicts.[76] Had the federal government been willing to commit the military personnel and money for adequately defending the bonafide Indian treaties that the Indian Removal Act said *would* be honored, treaties that the Supreme Court in *Worcester v. Georgia* said

---

[73] Green 1996, 517. Mississippi was an exception; it did allow Indians to testify and to serve on juries, but (like the other states listed) it barred them from voting. Hoxie 2007, 342.

[74] Jack 1916; Foreman 1953, 107–28; McDonald 1982, 109.

[75] Foreman 1953; Green 1996, 514–30; Saunt 2015.

[76] Foreman 1953.

should be honored, Indian Removal might not have proceeded. But the civil war as a war between the federal government and the southern states might have come simply thirty years sooner.

Indian removal in the North took place more peaceably (by and large) and more often by bonafide treaties.[77] This was because the southern tribes had become more acculturated to the Euro-American way of life, having established farms, factories, schools, and roads and relatively well-developed institutions of self-government; therefore they offered more resistance to removal.[78] By mid-century most American Indians had been pushed west of the Mississippi.

Assessment on Policy Toward Native Americans

In contrast to the situation of African-Americans, in the matter of Native Americans one can observe by 1835 a truly sharp contrast between the federal judiciary and the elected branches, as well as a mild contrast between the two federal elected branches. Congress in the Indian Removal Act of 1832 did moderate Andrew Jackson's proposals by insisting that no Indian removal take place in violation of the treaty rights of the tribes. Elected branches can include state judges, who are, in some states, appointed for fixed terms rather than life and who are either elected themselves or appointed by elected officials.[79] Native Americans repeatedly were subjected to violation of their treaty rights, typically in the form of violent land theft combined with state laws that disregarded their legal and political rights to group autonomy and state judges complicit in fraudulent takings of Indian land. At least verbally, the federal judiciary under John Marshall's leadership stood out alone among government branches as by far the most willing to defend rights of Native Americans and to condemn the wrongs against them. Unfortunately, without executive branch force, supported by the legislative power of the purse, there was little the Court could do on its own to stem massive mob violence at the state level and nothing it could do to block a combined federal legislative and executive determination to carry out Indian removal. On the rare occasions when Andrew Jackson committed federal troops to armed intervention against state authorities in order to protect Indian rights, the threat of civil war launched by

---

[77] Green 1996, 529–33; Foreman 1953, Preface (pp.unnumbered).

[78] Foreman, ibid.

[79] For instance, in Alabama, as of 1830, state judges were elected by the elected legislature and served six-year terms. "Judicial Selection in the States – History of Reform Efforts" 2016.

southern states ended his rights enforcement campaign. In short, without a determined national political will to protect the Native Americans, the Court could not do much more than issue moral/legal judgments and hope for the best.

John Marshall left the Supreme Court in 1835, and President Jackson appointed Roger Taney of Maryland to replace him as chief justice. Roger Taney had briefly (April–August, 1831) served as acting Secretary of War, directing the government's Indian removal efforts concerning the Choctaw of Mississippi. Under his tenure as chief justice the Supreme Court lost its preeminence as defender of the legal rights of the Native Americans.[80]

---

[80] R.M. Smith 1997, 240–42.

2. Minority rights in the Taney years, 1836–64

THE LEADERSHIP OF JUSTICE JOSEPH STORY

The most prominent of the justices on the Taney Court was Justice Joseph Story, a holdover from the Marshall Court whose tenure lasted until September 1845, and he authored the Court opinion for two of the three most significant slavery cases that preceded the Civil War, *U.S. v. The Amistad* (1841) and *Prigg v. Pennsylvania* (1842). (Throughout this volume, terms like the "Marshall Court" or the "Taney Court" basically serve as a shorthand to denote the Supreme Court of a specific historical period. Only rarely can one confidently say from opinion patterns that the Chief Justice exerted influence in a particular direction. It is safe to conclude that Justice Story was more inclined to protect the rights of blacks and Indians than Chief Justice Taney was. It is also safe to conclude that Chief Justice Hughes and Chief Justice Warren inclined toward protecting the rights of black Americans. Apart from those examples, the labeling of a Court by Chief Justice should be read as simply a convenient shorthand.)

The Court opinion for the third of these slavery cases, *Dred Scott v. Sanford* (1857), was authored by the Chief Justice himself, Roger Taney. Taney was also the author of a major Indian case opinion, *U.S. v. Rogers* (1846).

U.S. v. The Amistad (1841)

The *Amistad* case,[1] like the *Antelope* case before it (see Table 1.1 earlier), dealt with the international slave trade, rather than with constitutional issues as such. In contrast to the *Antelope* situation, in the *Amistad* case, clear proof was presented that the slaves in question had been taken in Africa in direct violation of the treaty law of Portugal (whose nationals had purchased and shipped them to Cuba) and of Spain, who was now

1 *U.S. v. Amistad*, 40 U.S. 518 (1841).

insisting on the right to have them for trial in its own courts since they had mutinied on a ship owned by residents of Cuba, a Spanish colony.

The Attorney General of President Van Buren (a northern Democrat anxious to stay on good terms with the southern wing of the party),[2] urged the Court to turn the slaves over to Spain as per the diplomatic request. Instead, Justice Story ruled for a unanimous court that all needed to be set free. They had been unlawfully kidnapped, and the mere demand of a government for a free person who had merely acted in self-defense (during the mutiny) was not grounds to hand over such person to the demanding government, certainly not in a country whose constitution enshrined the right of habeas corpus. Still, as the Supreme Court had done in the *Antelope* case, the lower courts in the *Amistad* case had agreed that as to the cabin boy on the ship, the one for whom there was clear proof that he had been lawfully held as slave in Cuba under Spanish law, he was to be remanded to Spain for delivery to his putative owners. By the time of the U.S. Supreme Court decision, none of the lawyers was disputing this aspect of the case.[3] (Outside the courtroom, this cabin boy, assisted by abolitionists escaped to freedom in New York.[4])

In the White House, after Martin Van Buren, four additional Presidents (Tyler, Polk, Pierce, and Buchanan), acceding to Spain's requests, attempted to have Congress authorize reparations to Spain for its lost "property" in these slaves. Since Congress never followed through, it is possible that these presidential gestures toward Spain were matters of diplomatic symbolism; one can speculate that the President may have been aware that they would not succeed.[5]

Groves v. Slaughter (1841) and *Prigg v. Pennsylvania* (1842)

Prigg v. Pennsylvania[6] (1842) did deal with constitutional issues regarding domestic slavery, and highly controversial ones. A year earlier, it was preceded by a far less consequential case, *Groves v. Slaughter*,[7] which

---

2 Maltz 2009, 29–31.

3 John Quincy Adams in his attorney role claimed that he would have disputed it if not or the fact that the boy himself wanted to go home to Cuba, even if that meant staying there as a slave. Linder 2000-A.

4 National Portrait Gallery, "The Amistad Case."

5 Fehrenbacher 1978, 39.

6 *Prigg v. Pennsylvania*, 41 U.S. 539 (1842).

7 *Groves v. Slaughter*, 40 U.S. 449 (1841).

provides a useful backdrop for understanding what the *Prigg* decision accomplished.

The issue in *Groves* was a Mississippi constitutional provision banning import into the state of slaves intended for resale. The recipient/purchasers of certain slaves were refusing to pay up on the grounds that this ban voided their contractual obligation. Senator/Secretary of State Daniel Webster,[8] and Senator Henry Clay argued in defense of the sellers, who wanted their payment. The Court settled the case by deciding on state law grounds that the ban had not taken legal effect by the time of the contract, so the payment was owed. Apart from the case result, these prominent lawyers' arguments on power to ban sale of slaves themselves provoked important position-taking on the Court.

The argument put forth by many abolitionists that Congress should use its exclusive commerce power to ban the interstate slave trade was very much in the air at this time.[9] Both Daniel Webster and Henry Clay, went out of their way to indicate that, although this power was exclusively federal, Congress was nonetheless constitutionally forbidden to exercise it to ban this species of commerce.[10] Since federal exclusivity precluded a state ban, by their arguments *no* government could ban interstate slave trade. If it prevailed, this rule would help maintain slavery in the states of the northern South, where changes in the agricultural market had made plantation-style slavery unprofitable, thereby creating economic pressures for slaveowners to sell their slaves southward.[11]

Clay and Webster were eminent compromiser nationalists and the position they staked out here can be viewed as a kind of national political median point on the slavery issue in 1841. Webster coined the phrase "liberty and Union, now and forever" and later would famously endorse the compromise of 1850 with its tough fugitive slave act in a speech on March 7, 1850, arguing that holding the union together warranted substantial compromise with slavery. Senator Clay, formerly Speaker of the House, was famously influential in putting together both the Missouri

[8] Webster resigned from the Senate in February of 1841 to serve as Secretary of State in the Harrison-Tyler administration. He argued *Groves* in February and it was decided in March.

[9] Wiecek 1978, 51–3.

[10] For Clay this was because Congress could foster but not ban commerce (in general), and for Webster it was because the Fugitive Slave Clause recognized slaves as property and therefore, "The protection of this right of property [in slaves] in the intercourse between the states became a duty [of Congress] under the Constitution." Clay: 40 U.S. 449, 488-9; Webster: 40 U.S., at 495.

[11] Marks 2009, *passim*.

Compromise of 1820 and the Compromise of 1850. Justice Story writes no opinion in this *Groves* case but his quiet vote in dissent suggests both a more directly anti-slavery position and less nationalist position than either of these prominent Whigs.

To read the opinions in *Groves v. Slaughter* is to realize why one might conclude that the U.S. had come to be a "house divided against itself." The justices' discussion of slavery reveals that they believed they lived under radically different constitutional orders. McLean agreed that the state ban had not yet taken effect but otherwise wrote something fairly described as an anti-slavery polemic: Under the Constitution freedom is national and slavery is local, permitted only if created by positive, state law: "The Constitution acts upon slaves as persons, and not as property."[12] Carried to its logical conclusion, as the political abolitionists like Gerrit Smith wanted it to be, this latter position meant that the federal courts were obliged by the due process clause to set free every slave in federal jurisdiction. On the specific issue of slave importation, McLean would permit the Mississippi ban (which, he agrees, had not yet taken effect), despite the exclusivity of the federal commerce power, because slavery presented many societal evils addressable under the state police power.

Baldwin and Taney, provoked by McLean's dicta, wrote dicta of their own. Baldwin's was virulently pro-slavery and Taney's was militantly pro-states'-rights. Baldwin insisted that slavery was a basic property right prior to the Constitution and therefore was secured by it, as against federal power, under the federal due process clause and, as against state power, by the Article IV privileges and immunities clause. This state rule discriminating between out-of-state and in-state sellers of this property was unconstitutional. Slavery was national and freedom local; slavery could be restricted only by state laws that specifically established liberty. These state laws could never abridge the national right of Americans from slave states to take their slave property with them [and, presumably, sell these slaves, as they could sell other property] wherever they wished.

For Taney, the power to regulate slave sales or any other aspect of slave ownership within their borders belonged exclusively to the states under the Constitution. Congress could not regulate it, period (despite the constitutional clause appearing to give Congress power to regulate all commerce "among the states").

Where does Justice Story align here? He and Justice McKinley both refrained from writing opinions in this volatile setting. But the two of

---

12 *Groves*, at 507.

them endorsed the only position that would have immediately had concrete, anti-slavery results: The Mississippi constitutional ban on slave importing was constitutional and did have legal effect. Thus, they affirm state power to limit interstate slave trade. (Implicitly, although McKinley probably disagreed, their position also renders questionable the ownership of three million dollars' worth of slaves brought in for resale from 1833–37.) To reach this anti-slavery result, Story rejects the nationalist exclusive power claim of Webster and Clay. He also avoided the provocative position-taking of McLean, Baldwin, and Taney, but would be moving the next year, in *Prigg*, to gather a Court majority around the abstract proposition of McLean's that freedom, under the Constitution, was the national default position, and that slavery existed only as a matter of positive law.

By the early 1840s, one can observe cross-cutting cleavages on the matter of slavery. Political sentiment divided sharply on state vs. federal power but also on pro- vs. anti-slavery.[13] Southerners tended to be for states' rights but sometimes the state power position cut against slavery, as happened here with the votes of McKinley and Story in favor of a state law banning slave trade. In 1841, only one justice, McLean, was willing to espouse the view that freedom was national and slavery preserved only within limited state borders as a matter of positive state law, entrenched by the positive recognition of such law in the federal Constitution.

By 1842, in *Prigg* Justice Story managed to corral a majority for what had been the most openly anti-slavery view (albeit an abstract one) espoused (by McLean) on the Court one year before. He wrote for the Court in *Prigg*:

> By the general law of nations, no nation is bound to recognise the state of slavery, as to foreign slaves found within its territorial dominions, when it is in opposition to its own policy and institutions, in favor of the subjects of other nations where slavery is recognised. If it does it, it is as a matter of comity, and not as a matter of international right. The state of slavery is

---

[13] The issue from *Groves v. Slaughter* returned to the Court after Story's death in *Rowan v. Runnels*, 46 U.S. 134 (1847). At this point the Mississippi Supreme Court had made plain its understanding that the state constitutional provision was self-executing (a point on which it had been less clear prior to the *Groves* decision). Nonetheless, the U.S. Supreme Court continued to assert that the Mississippi constitutional provision had *not* yet taken effect, which interpretive maneuver enabled the Court to avoid the ticklish question of whether the exclusive power of Congress prohibited state-based restrictions of the interstate slave trade, and if so whether Congress could ban such trades. Maltz 2009, 74–6, 149–50.

> deemed to be a mere municipal regulation, founded upon and limited to the range of the territorial laws. This was fully recognised in Somerset's Case, [*Somerset v Stewart* (1772) 98 ER 499] which was decided before the American revolution. It is manifest, from this consideration, that if the constitution had not contained this clause, every non-slave-holding state in the Union would have been at liberty to have declared free all runaway slaves coming within its limits, and to have given them entire immunity and protection against the claims of their masters; a course which would have created the most bitter animosities, and engendered perpetual strife between the different states.[14]

This rule localized slavery except as delineated in the fugitive slave rendition clause. This rule from the Court opinion in *Prigg* caused Justice Story to describe it repeatedly as a "triumph for freedom."[15] Fugitive slaves would have to be returned but other slaves brought into free states would be by law free (unless the receiving state explicitly said otherwise). This implication of *Prigg* did get cited in support of laws and rulings in northern states that set free slaves of travelers within the state, and also was to reverberate in the anti-slavery slogan, "Freedom national, slavery local."[16]

Although this legal import of *Prigg*—localizing slavery—was an aspect of the case of which Justice Story was particularly proud, it is not the whole story of the case. Indeed, whether the decision is pro-freedom or pro-slavery is a question that has been debated since it was handed down.[17] And it pleased neither side: Abolitionists condemned it because it upheld the Fugitive Slave Act of 1793 and slaveowners did so because its practical effect drastically undermined the effectiveness of that very law.

The case dealt with a clash between two statutes. First, was the federal Fugitive Slave Act of 1793. Congress had moved to adopt this law because of a dispute between Pennsylvania and Virginia over the latter's refusal to extradite to Pennsylvania a group of white men who kidnapped a free black there and sold him into slavery in Virginia.[18] Thus, the 1793 law adopted rules both for extraditing criminals and for reclamation of

---

[14] *Prigg v. Pennsylvania*, 41 U.S. 539, 611–612.

[15] Swisher 1974, 542–3, and Wiecek 1978, 46, n.47, both citing letter from Charles Sumner to Samuel Chase of March 12, 1847, Chase Papers, Library of Congress; Story 1851, 2: 292–3.

[16] Wiecek 1978, 56; *Lemmon v. The People*, 5 Sand. 681 (NY, 1852), cited in Maltz 2009, 166; 20 N.Y.562 (1860), cited in Wiecek at 57.

[17] For an overview of the debate see Goldstein 2011-A.

[18] *Prigg v. Pennsylvania*, 41 U.S. 539, 620 (Justice Story) and 666–7 (Justice McLean, concurring, 41 U.S. 539, at 658–74).

runaways who owed "service or labor," as described in Article IV, Section 2, clauses 2 and 3.[19] In the part of this law that referred to runaways from slavery, Congress included no protections to give the person accused as a runaway a chance to make the case that his or her capture was a matter of mistaken identity. The sworn word of the claimant of ownership, so long as it was detailed enough to become "proof to the satisfaction of" the judge where the captured slave was caught, became, in effect, the law.[20]

Then in 1826 Pennsylvania had responded to perceived abuses that took place under the guise of slave recapture by legislating procedural protections for persons accused of being runaway slaves from out of state. The law was cast in terms of preventing persons from using "force or fraud" to "take or carry away or seduce" any "negro or mulatto" out of Pennsylvania in order to sell or put that person into slavery. To do so was deemed a felony punishable by seven to twenty-one years at hard labor and a fine of $500 to $1,000 split evenly between the kidnap victim and the state. Similar punishments were announced for selling "a negro or mulatto" fraudulently into out-of-state slavery.[21]

The new procedures mandated that the person claiming ownership of a runaway, or that person's agent (by written authorization), had to swear or solemnly affirm before a "judge, justice of the peace or alderman" that the accused resident of Pennsylvania is a "fugitive … from his service." If it were an agent of the claimed owner, the agent had to present a sworn affidavit of ownership from the claimant certified by a justice of the peace of the claimant's home state (or territory) along with written certification of the authority of that justice of the peace signed by a clerk and authenticated by a seal from the court of record in that state. This

---

19 Located in Article IV, which describes interstate relations, in section 2, the clauses read as follows:

> A Person charged in any State with Treason, Felony, or other Crime, who shall flee from Justice, and be found in another State, shall on demand of the executive Authority of the State from which he fled, be delivered up, to be removed to the State having Jurisdiction of the Crime.
>
> No Person held to service or labor in one state, under the laws thereof, escaping into another, shall, in consequence of any law or regulation therein, be discharged from such service or labor, but shall be delivered up on claim of the party to whom such service or labor may be due.

20 "An Act respecting Fugitives from Justice, and Persons Escaping from the Service of Their Masters," *1 Stat. 302* (1793).

21 Facts here and below, unless otherwise indicated are taken from case records in the U.S. Supreme Court Reports, 41 U.S. 539–558.

affidavit had to provide the name, age, and description of the fugitive. Upon presentation of these documents, the Pennsylvania official was to issue an arrest warrant to a constable for bringing the accused to trial before a judge of the county where the alleged fugitive was found, at which trial "the truth of the matter [would] be inquired into." "[U]pon proof, to the satisfaction of such judge" that the accused in fact owed "service or labor" and had fled from it, the judge was to issue a certificate to the claimant that would serve as a warrant for removing the fugitive from Pennsylvania to the home state.

Significantly, the law mandated "that the oath of the owner or owners, or other person interested, shall in no case be received in evidence before the judge, on the hearing of the case." In other words, the state law excluded from evidence precisely the sworn testimony that the federal law established as decisive. The law provided for holding the accused in the local jail at the claimant's expense if either side needed a reasonable amount of time to prepare for the trial. Court costs were to be paid by the claimant.

In addition to these procedural protections, the Pennsylvania law took a plain swipe at the federal law of 1793. In direct contradiction to the words of the federal law, it prohibited all aldermen and justices of the peace of the Commonwealth of Pennsylvania from having jurisdiction to hear a case or issue any warrant under the federal act of 1793 concerning "persons escaping from the service of their masters" … "or under any other law, authority or act of the congress of the United States." A fine of $500 to $1,000 was to be imposed on any alderman or justice of the peace who defied this prohibition on cooperation with the federal government.[22]

What the federal law said, by contrast, was that the claimant of the fugitive or his agent was authorized simply to "seize" the suspected runaway, presumably by his own force, and drag the runaway before any federal judge (of which states often had only one unless a U.S. Supreme

[22] Both these sorts of interferences with the federal scheme for slave recapture were being enacted in a variety of Northern states in the period 1824–1859. These included Indiana, Massachusetts, Connecticut, Vermont, Rhode Island, Michigan, Ohio, Maine, Wisconsin, and Kansas. For details see Goldstein 2001-A, 165–171. Pennsylvania did anticipate that the two federal judges in the state would continue to carry out the federal law; it mandated that judges in the state who did issue a certificate under the federal law were obliged to make a detailed record of it, a certified copy of which was to be kept in specified local offices.

Court justice happened to reside there[23]) *or* before "any magistrate of a county, city or town" where the seizure took place. Under the federal law, the oath of the claimant slave-owner describing the missing slave, sworn before his home justice of the peace, so long as this affidavit amounted to "proof to the satisfaction" of the judge before whom the alleged runaway was taken, was all it took to get from this judge a certificate authorizing removal of the fugitive from the state or territory of the seizure, no matter how long the alleged fugitive may have resided there. The law did not specify any right of the accused black person to offer evidence in his or her own defense or have a lawyer do so. The federal law treated an accused runaway slave essentially the same as a runaway horse or cow.[24]

The facts by which these contending laws reached the Supreme Court, according to the jury's decision in the original trial, began with the "escape" of a black slave, Margaret Morgan from Harford County Maryland, over the state line into neighboring York County Pennsylvania in 1832.[25] In 1837, Margaret Ashmore of Maryland, claiming ownership of Morgan and Morgan's children, hired Edward Prigg and three other men to capture Margaret Morgan and bring her back into Maryland.[26] Edward Prigg went before a Pennsylvania justice of the peace, Thomas Henderson, and there swore an oath that Margaret Morgan was a slave of, and therefore owed labor to, Margaret Ashmore. Henderson then issued a warrant to the York County constable William McCleary to arrest

---

[23] *Prigg*, 41 U.S. 539, at 631 (Chief Justice Taney concurring and dissenting at 41 U.S. 539, 626–36). Pennsylvania itself had a total of two federal judges for the whole state, not counting the Supreme Court Justice obliged to "ride circuit" there from time to time. Swisher 1974, 536.

[24] See note 20 above.

[25] Margaret the slave had lived all her life with her parents on the property of John Ashmore, who died in 1824. Although legally enslaved, the family members had been permitted virtual (but not legally official) freedom by him. Margaret (the Ashmore slave) eventually married a free black man, Jerry Morgan, and in 1832 moved into his home in the next county, across the state line. This was the supposed "escape" of Margaret Morgan.

[26] The reason for the five-year time lapse, from the "escape" in 1832 to the capture in 1837, is unknown. It may be relevant that the year 1837 included a bank panic that set off five years of economic hardship. Margaret Ashmore, the widow of John and heiress since his death intestate in 1824, wished to claim Margaret Morgan and Morgan's children as part of her inheritance. For this she hired Prigg and three helpers. Prigg and two helpers were close neighbors and longtime friends of the Ashmore family and had a face-to-face acquaintance with Margaret Morgan. The third helper was Margaret Ashmore's son-in-law, who had long resided with his wife in the Ashmore household. Finkelman 1994, 274–6; Holden-Smith 1993, at nn.217–218, citing "The Great Slavery Case" 1842.

Margaret Morgan and her children, and to bring her to a justice of the peace court. Constable McCleary proceeded to do this, but once he brought them before the same justice of the peace Henderson, Henderson refused jurisdiction. The court records do not say why, but perhaps it was because Prigg could offer no further evidence than the oath he had already taken, and under the Pennsylvania law this was not admissible. At this point Prigg and his three helpers took the law into their own hands and took Margaret Morgan and her children by force (including one child born after Morgan had resided more than a year in Pennsylvania) back to slavery at the home of Margaret Ashmore in Maryland. There, in May of 1837 Margaret Morgan launched a suit for her freedom, which suit she lost in a two-day jury trial in August.[27]

Meanwhile back in Pennsylvania, Prigg was indicted for kidnapping. While the jury could agree as to the fact that Margaret was a slave "held to service" under the laws of Maryland and that Prigg had been duly authorized by the owner to recapture her, they were uncertain whether this combination of facts and laws made Edward Prigg and his accomplices guilty of the crime of kidnapping and they asked the court to guide them on this point. Outside the courtroom the politics of interstate conflict had shaped what transpired within. Pennsylvania's governor had demanded extradition, Maryland's governor had resisted, negotiations had ensued, both state legislatures got into the act, and an agreement had been reached whereby the trial would produce a result based on facts stipulated to by an agreement between the two states and guaranteed to reach the U.S. Supreme Court, which would then settle the legal issues.[28] The jury found Prigg guilty, the Pennsylvania Supreme Court affirmed, and the U.S. Supreme Court took the case on a writ of error.

Prigg v. Pennsylvania (1842) produced a highly splintered Supreme Court decision, wherein differing groups of justices combined to form majorities around separate pieces of Justice Story's "Court opinion." Seven justices wrote opinions, with only Justices Catron and McKinley concurring silently.

As to the specific result, the justices agreed unanimously to declare void the Pennsylvania law that had attempted to alter the procedures mandated by federal law to be used by Pennsylvania magistrates for issuing certificates allowing the transporting of a fugitive slave. But as to reasoning, even for this one result, they were all over the map.

---

27 Finkelman ibid., 278, n.123.
28 Ibid., nn.223–229.

Six justices (in the face of dissents from Chief Justice Taney and associate Justices Thompson and Daniel) concurred in the view of Justice Story that the power to legislate the method of recapture of runaway slaves rested *exclusively* in Congress; that is, that state governments were forbidden to legislate on this subject (41 U.S., at pp. 614–25). And even these six were not fully in accord: Justice Baldwin (as explained not by his own cryptic, two-sentence opinion [41 U.S., at 636] but by his colleague, Justice Wayne [41 U.S., at 637]), believed *neither* Congress nor the states were allowed to legislate on the subject (and that the claimant slaveowner would have to use simply self-help for reclaiming lost slaves, and that the Constitution authorized this), but Baldwin did agree that since the majority of his colleagues were upholding the federal law of 1793, state legislation on the same subject was certainly forbidden. This leaves a bare majority of five in support of this important aspect of Story's reasoning.

Among the three who argued that the states *could* legislate in aid of Congress for the recapture of slaves, only one of the three, Chief Justice Taney (forecasting his strongly pro-slavery views of the later Dred Scott decision) insisted (41 U.S., at 627) that all states *must* so legislate, in order to carry out the implicit command of the fugitive slave clause.[29]

As to a second concrete result of the Court holding, the justices were more unified; all but one concurred that the conviction of Edward Prigg and his associates for kidnapping had to be declared void, since the state courts of Pennsylvania admitted that the accused fugitive (along with her children)[30] was a slave under Maryland law. The lone dissenter on this point was Justice McLean. He insisted (941 U.S., at pp. 672–3) that states had a right to assure peaceful and orderly processes: thus, since state judge (Henderson) had refused to accept jurisdiction for a hearing to grant a certificate authorizing removal of the fugitive from the state, Prigg had been then obliged to take Margaret Morgan and her children before one of the two federal judges of Pennsylvania in order to obtain a lawful certificate of removal. Since he had not, he could be punished as a kidnapper.

---

[29] Justice Thompson limited his dissent to the federal preemption point. In his view if and only if there were, hypothetically, no federal statute on procedures for slave recapture would the states be free to create their own procedures.

[30] None of the judges in the various decisions addressed the situation of the baby conceived and born in Pennsylvania, who was legally free under Pennsylvania law and legally a slave under Maryland law.

On the question whether the states were free to insist by law (as Pennsylvania and some other northern states had done) that no state official, as a matter of official capacity, cooperate in the Congressionally mandated activity of returning fugitive slaves, surprisingly, only one justice explicitly dissented, Justice McLean. The rest, except for Chief Justice Taney, all appeared to align silently with the view expressed by Justice Story[31] that the federal government may not coerce state officialdom to do its bidding in carrying out federal law. While not explicitly on point, Chief Justice Taney's insistence that states must legislate in support of slave recapture would at least imply a state legislative obligation to cooperate in the federally legislated scheme.[32] By contrast, Justice McLean conceded that federal power to regulate the modes for capture and return of slaves was exclusive, but he insisted that the federal government could certainly order states to cooperate in the enterprise, just as it could order governors to extradite criminals. He embraced the paradoxical position (at pp. 665–6) that the federal government had authority to order state cooperation, but that if the states unconstitutionally resisted these orders, there was no way for the feds to coerce state compliance.

This combination of rulings in *Prigg* was immediately attacked in *both* abolitionist circles and proslavery areas.[33] Abolitionists attacked it, first, because it upheld the Fugitive Slave Act of 1793 (whereas Article IV's rendition clause made no mention of federal enforcement power) and, secondly, because it struck down state-based efforts to provide procedural protections for accused fugitives.

Southerners attacked it because it would render the Fugitive Slave Act a dead letter in two ways: It allowed states like Pennsylvania to refuse the federal command to help enforce the law; since there were only one or two federal judges per state, the expenses of recapture would become

---

31 Five justices on the modern Court agree as to state executive officers, but disagree with extending this rule to state judges as the Story majority was doing. See *Printz v. U.S.*, 521 U.S. 898 (1997).

32 Taney fleshes out his views in a related decision in 1861, *Kentucky v. Dennison*, 65 U.S. 66, handed down as the South was in the midst of seceding. Kentucky was demanding that the Ohio governor extradite an Ohioan for the crime of enticing a slave to run away, and was asking for a writ of mandamus from the Court directly ordering the recalcitrant governor to do so. Taney ruled (for a unanimous Supreme Court) that the governor did have a legal obligation to extradite but one that the federal government could *not* enforce. See discussion in Swisher 1974, 686–90.

33 For an overview of contemporary scholarship on the case, see Goldstein 2011-A.

prohibitive. Moreover, the federal exclusivity rule rendered void those Southern laws that purported to aid in fugitive recapture by locking up supposedly suspicious looking blacks as potential fugitives and holding them in jail while advertising for their potential owners to claim them. (If they went unclaimed these black people were then sold into slavery.[34])

That *Prigg* would produce the practical impossibility of most recaptures, was forecast in the dissents of both Chief Justice Taney and Justice Daniel, and was understood by Justice Story as well—he said so in a private correspondence written eight weeks after handing down the decision.[35]

In terms of the concerns of this book one might ask, did the decision show the unelected justices to be any more protective of blacks than elected branches were? It certainly did not free any slaves. But it did succeed in making slave recapture unfeasible in most of the North for an eight-year period until the Fugitive Slave Act of 1850 eventually plugged the hole ripped open by *Prigg*, by appointing federal commissioners for every county, specifically designated to decide fugitive slave cases. In terms of its practical import then, *Prigg* operated in the North for eight years as pro-freedom, in that it gave an explicit green light to Northern states for refusing to cooperate in slave recapture. *Prigg* basically insisted that whatever legislative solution was devised for the problem of fugitive slaves had to be a national level solution.

THE SLAVERY ISSUE, 1835–60

Outside the Court, 1835–52

The intensified anti-abolition sentiment in the South that began in the 1830s bore fruit in congressional policy. The House of Representatives from May, 1836 until December, 1844 observed a "gag rule" to forbid the reading aloud of, or discussing, petitions against slavery, despite the right "to petition government for redress of grievance" enshrined in the First Amendment. And in 1835–36, President Jackson arranged for Congress to legalize the refusal by Southern postmasters (federal employees) to refrain from delivering all criticism of slavery—

[34] Wilson 1994, 63–66.

[35] This letter and its import specifically for understanding Story's views on the connection between strengthening national authority and protecting racial minorities, both black and Indian, is discussed extensively in Goldstein 2011-B.

categorized in the federal law simply as material locally declared unlawful.[36]

Although anti-slavery forces in Congress did try to insert procedural protections for accused runaways into the 1850 Fugitive Slave Law,[37] it ended up treating accused slaves even more harshly than the 1793 version it superseded. Adopted as part of the Compromise of 1850, it was combined with barring slave sales in the District of Columbia and admitting California as a free state to the union. Under the 1850 Act, accused fugitives could neither testify as to their non-fugitive status nor engage defense attorneys, nor appeal an adverse finding as to their status, nor demand a writ of habeas corpus, and the newly created federal commissioners were in effect bribed—the government paid ten dollars for guilty findings but only five for finding mistaken identity.[38] The anti-slavery *New York Tribune*, declared the new law without moral authority and predicted widespread violation.[39]

The Fugitive Slave Act was a response to the moves by several northern states legislating to forbid their own judges to cooperate with the 1793 Fugitive Slave Act. The paucity of federal judges had been making slave recapture increasingly difficult, especially after *Prigg v. Pennsylvania* gave a stamp of approval to these state non-cooperation moves. The 1850 Act responded by creating hundreds of federal officials (commissioners) who would hear the claims of slave-owners in quest of runaways. If the owners showed a home-state-court-issued certificate of loss of a runaway slave, the commissioner was obliged to appoint marshals to help in the recapture and these could in turn demand assistance from bystanders (as a posse).[40] Once captured, the accused black person was subjected to the thoroughly rigged procedures described above, with no rights of appeal.

Strangely enough (in light of these policy developments), the House of Representatives was increasingly dominated by non-slave states by the

---

36 Nieman 1991, 16.

37 Maltz 2009, 138–40; Goldstein 2011.

38 Smith 1997, 259 and 262; Nieman 1991, 30; Ch. 60, 9 Stat. 462–465 (1850) (repealed 1864). The rationale for the pay disparity was that it took a commissioner additional time to issue a certificate of removal. Payment to magistrates on a fee-for-services basis was common in this period. Schmitt, 2011, 804–5 at nn.35–42.

39 Maltz 2009, 141. But cf. "The Fugitive Slave Case," *The Cincinnati Daily Times*, Aug. 18, 1853 ("The feeling among our citizens generally, is that in such cases the law should be obeyed, however much the system of slavery is to be deprecated," cited in Schmitt ibid., 816 at n.105.)

40 Maltz 2009, 140.

early 1840s. The decades of 1820–60 were a period of a rapidly shifting power balance with respect to slavery.[41] By the 1830s both the economic growth of the country and its population base had discernibly shifted from South to North.[42] The political impact of this shift was too plain to ignore: In 1790, Virginia had double the population of New York. By 1850, New York had triple the population and representation of Virginia. States of the former Northwest Territory, like Ohio and Wisconsin, now were larger than the original slave states. In 1790, the balance of slave (forty-nine) and free (fifty-seven) representation in the House was roughly equal; by 1820, free states had 123 to slave ninety; by 1850, the balance was 147 free to ninety slave. This shift, of course, affected the Electoral College, rendering the election of an anti-slavery President increasingly likely.[43] By 1850, the balance even in the Senate had shifted: Rather than the earlier predominance of slave states, the senators from free states now outnumbered those from slave states by two.

These developments, however, as of 1850, instead of producing more anti-slavery policies at the national level, paradoxically only made the southerners ever more insistent on protection for their "peculiar institution"—and more successfully so! During the decade of the 1840s, although the House twice adopted the Wilmot Proviso, in 1846 and 1847, the Senate twice defeated the measure. It would have banned slavery in all the new territory to be acquired from the Mexican War—territory from which Mexico had *already* outlawed slavery. This measure would have in practical effect blocked all spread of slavery westward. In the process of fighting the Proviso, Senator John C. Calhoun developed a full-blown constitutional theory defending the proposition that the Constitution obliged Congress to *protect* slavery in all federal territory (a theory that presaged the *Dred Scott* decision).[44] In fear that the Congress would adopt the Wilmot Proviso, a southern convention was called in Nashville "to devise and adopt some mode of resistance to [northern] … aggressions."[45] Prior to the convening of Congress in 1850, southern

---

41 Weinberg 2007, 108–12 (claiming, at 109, that by 1850 "it was reasonably foreseeable that no new slave state would ever be admitted again.")

42 Weinberg 2007, 103–8; Marks 2009, 137; Davis 2003, 58, 77–8.

43 Graber 2006, 126–8.

44 Fehrenbacher 1978, 136–45, 148. This was also the period in which Calhoun wrote his *Disquisition* (published only posthumously by the government of South Carolina in 1851), arguing that every minority interest group (e.g., slaveowners) affected by a government policy should be given a right to veto that policy.

45 Morris 1974, 130. Cited in Schmitt 2011, 800 at n. 9.

editorials, mass meetings, and congressmen widely warned of the possibility of disunion if the sectional issues were not resolved.[46] Meanwhile, now that Calhoun in the Congressional debates of 1847–48 had turned the territorial question into one of constitutional interpretation, the political momentum of the expectation that the Supreme Court would resolve the territorial question was set in motion.[47]

Supplementing the southern intransigence of the 1840s, some northerners also supported the institution of slavery because of the economic reliance of northern textile mills on cheap southern cotton. Such men were known as "Cotton Whigs."[48] Northern nationalist Whigs like Daniel Webster, along with northern Democrats, continued to advocate compromise, attempting to stave off secession threats from the southern states. In this setting, the 1850 Fugitive Slave Act was adopted.

Moore v. Illinois (1852), *Jones v. Van Zandt* (1847) and Political Branch Activity on Negro Seamen Laws

In the South, meanwhile, prior to the 1850 legislation, *Prigg*'s ban on states' using their own legislation to arrange the recapture of slaves was ignored. Once Story left the Court, under Taney's leadership it became more overtly pro-slavery,[49] and in 1852, in *Moore v. Illinois*, the Court undid *Prigg*'s ban on state laws designed to assist in the capture of fugitive slaves, claiming that *Prigg* had created no such ban.[50] Moore was punished by Illinois law for harboring a fugitive slave and the Supreme Court upheld the conviction. McLean argued in lone dissent that this state law punished a crime also already punished by federal law, thus creating unconstitutional double jeopardy. In the course of this decision, the Taney Court also stated, although the issue was not before it, that states had power under the Constitution to bar or "repel" *free*

---

[46] Potter 1976, 96. Cited in Schmitt ibid. at n.12.

[47] Fehrenbacher 1978, 146–7.

[48] Schmitt 2011, at n.109 (citing northern businessmen's effort to promote support for the Fugitive Slave Act of 1850 out of fears of secession by the South) and n.197 (using phrase "Cotton Whigs").

[49] Maltz 2009, 173.

[50] *Moore v. Illinois*, 55 U.S.13 (1852). Cf. Maltz ibid., 163, insisting that *Prigg* and *Moore* dealt with different issues (regulating recapture vs. punishing harborers of escapees), but acknowledging that the *National Era* at the time considered the *Prigg* and *Moore* grossly inconsistent as did Carl Swisher.

black persons from within their borders, on the grounds that such persons are "likely to become … paupers and criminals."[51]

In this latter dictum the Court was arguably by implication reversing the circuit court opinion written by U.S. Supreme Court Justice Johnson, *Elkison v. Deliesseline* (1823). That opinion had declared unconstitutional on commerce clause grounds a South Carolina law that imprisoned free persons of color who worked on ships that landed in South Carolina for the duration of the ship's stay, and according to which, if the ship abandoned them there, they would be sold as slaves.[52] These laws had proliferated in the South in the 1820s and 1830s. Neither diplomatic pressure (for the seamen were often foreigners) nor lobbying by northern commercial interests nor circuit court decisions moved the South to desist in these laws.[53]

While the federal judiciary had stood firm against these "Negro Seamen" laws in the 1820s, and at first was backed by the executive branch, in the form of an official opinion from Attorney General Wirt, the situation in the political branches shifted rapidly. By 1831, Andrew Jackson's Attorney General John Berrien issued an official opinion contrary to Wirt's.[54] Petitions opposing these southern laws from northern interests addressed to the Commerce Committee in the House of Representatives appeared to make progress at one point, but that, too, changed. This committee did produce a bipartisan report backed by seven of its nine members on Jan. 20, 1843 declaring such state laws to be in "direct, positive, and permanent conflict with the express provisions or fundamental principles of the national compact." Nonetheless, this committee report was then tabled in the House on March 2 in an 86-59 vote.[55]

---

[51] *Moore*, 55 U.S. 13, 18. Emphasis added. The Court majority had issued a similar dictum in the *Passenger Cases*, 48 U.S. 283 (1849), but there the decision had been deeply fragmented: Nine opinions were written; the majority holding was only five to four; and the leading dissent had specifically denied the validity of this dictum. Maltz ibid., 151–4. *Moore* by contrast was an eight to one decision.

[52] This reversal was a legal outcome that had been desired by Chief Justice Taney at least since he had written an unpublished legal opinion to this effect in 1832 while serving as Andrew Jackson's Attorney General. Maltz ibid., 34. On the other hand, one might argue that a right to ban or repel from the state is not as extreme as a right to imprison a free person once that person has entered the state for a temporary sojourn.

[53] Hamer 1935.

[54] Maltz 2009, 151.

[55] Hamer 1935, 21–2; Nieman 1991, 22–4.

In sum, while the post-Justice-Story Supreme Court was no friend of black Americans, slave or free, Congress, except for ending the slave trade in the District of Columbia, was not doing anything to protect them either in this period. Nor did the President offer assistance in the 1846–60 period.

The ruling tenor of the times was keyed to attempts to pacify the South, while, meanwhile, northern opponents of slavery grew increasingly frustrated and radicalized. An example can be seen in the case, *Jones v. Van Zandt*, 46 U.S. 134 (1847). John Van Zandt had given a ride in his covered wagon to some eight fugitive slaves, later captured with him. Prosecuted under the Fugitive Slave Act for "harboring" and "concealing" fugitive slaves, he appealed his conviction to the U.S. Supreme Court where it was argued by leading attorneys from the radical wing of the anti-slavery forces, Salmon Chase and William Seward. Among other things they argued that *Prigg*'s ruling the (1793) Fugitive Slave Act constitutional was mere erroneous dictum and need not be followed; the Act's procedures violated several Bill of Rights provisions; the Rendition Clause rightly interpreted would apply only to free persons owing service or labor under contract, not to persons forcibly enslaved; and that slavery could not be made lawful anywhere on earth because it violated natural human rights: "No legislature can make men, things; or things, men." Seward chimed in that slavery had "odious form and revolting features, and … dreadful pretensions for the present and for the future."[56]

Van Zandt, unsurprisingly, lost his case, but more telling is what happened to Chase's and Seward's argument. It was standard practice in this period that attorneys' briefs were published as prefaces to the U.S. Supreme Court opinions in the official reports of those opinions, and in those days the reports were compiled by an official court reporter and printed by a private company. In 1847, the reporter was Benjamin C. Howard, a former Maryland legislator.[57] The climate in the South was virulently hostile to allowing any public criticism of slavery. This sentiment was enforced both by state statutes and by mob law.[58] An Arkansas statute in 1850, for instance, imposed a one-year prison term for merely criticizing the right to own slaves.[59] As noted above, from the time of the Jackson administration the federal mails were keeping

56 Maltz 2009, 155–8. Both quotes on p. 158.
57 "Howard, Benjamin Chew" 2008.
58 Curtis 2009, 1385–6.
59 Fehrenbacher 1978, 35.

anti-slavery tracts out of the South.[60] Thus, Howard, the official Supreme Court reporter, omitted Seward's and Chase's briefs from the official reports.[61] Chase did privately publish the brief in order to help stimulate anti-slavery sentiment.[62]

Off-Court Developments, 1853–60

The mid-1850s then produced a series of developments that increasingly radicalized northern sentiment to the point that Abraham Lincoln could get elected by a 39.7 percent plurality and a majority in the Electoral College (in a climate where even advocating Republican Party platforms was treated as a crime in southern states).[63] His Republican party had garnered 33 percent of the national vote four years earlier (and 38 percent of the Electoral College), while splitting the non-Democrat vote with the Whigs, whose candidate Millard Fillmore took 22 percent. These elections represented an enormous shift in public sentiment as compared to the elections where the predecessor of the Republicans, the Free Soil Party had recently competed: it garnered only 5 percent of the popular vote in 1852 after 10 percent in the 1848 election.

The radicalizing events included, first, Congress's demonstrated willingness to pacify the South even further by adopting the Kansas-Nebraska Act of 1854, which undid the earlier barrier to the spread of slavery westward, north of the dividing line established by the 1820 Missouri Compromise, the latitude that ran along the southern border of slave state Missouri. The Kansas-Nebraska Act allowed the people of a territory to decide for themselves (via "popular sovereignty") whether to ban or permit slavery prior to statehood (removing the former absolute ban on the movement of slavery into the West, north of the 1820 line). The line of the Missouri Compromise had run just south of the pre-existing North-South, free-slave, division of the original thirteen

---

[60] Chapter 1 at n.23.

[61] Maltz 2009, 159. I am not clear on whether this was the Court Reporter's decision or the private printer's decisions, nor whether the former was employed as an executive branch official or a judicial branch official. Still, the omission is striking.

[62] Ibid.

[63] Leip 2008. His leading opponent, Stephen Douglas for the Democratic party took 29.5 percent but only two states. The second most electoral votes were garnered by Breckinridge, for the Southern Democrats; he basically swept the South, but his popular vote was only 18.2 percent (a figure that understates his total support, because South Carolina assigned its electoral votes based on a decision by the state legislature rather than a popular vote). Ibid.

states (below Virginia and Kentucky). This 1854 Act was viewed as a betrayal by anti-slavery forces and then led to violent conflict in the territory of Kansas (which became known as "bloody Kansas") as both slaveowners and anti-slavery settlers moved there, and from time to time violently tried to "cleanse" the state of each other. The Democratic President, Buchanan, then further exacerbated tensions by urging Congress to admit Kansas to statehood under a pro-slavery Constitution (the Lecompton Constitution) that had been *rejected* by the territory's voters in January 1858. Congress refused, setting a second referendum for 1859, where the Lecompton Constitution was again rejected (which rejection delayed statehood until 1861).

Meanwhile the executive branch under President Franklin Pierce acted to discourage free blacks from settling in the West: In the period from 1820–60, Congress had passed a series of laws granting to settlers on public lands in frontier areas the right to be the first purchasers of such land—in other words, the right to pre-empt other willing buyers. Then in 1856 the executive branch specifically excluded black persons from participating in this program of pre-emption.[64]

The core plank of the Republican Party was that no slavery would be allowed into the territories, and thus that there would be no additional slave states. While southerners realized that apart from Texas and the southern part of California, the land west of the Mississippi was not hospitable to plantation-style slavery, nonetheless they hoped that if slavery were at least legally permitted in western states, these states would side with the South in Congressional conflicts, keeping the South from becoming permanently marginalized in geo-economic policymaking.[65] By 1856 it was plain that the two major factions of the country were at loggerheads over the territories issue, and it was increasingly erupting into violence in Kansas.

Scott v. Sandford (1857)[66]

Into this cauldron, the Supreme Court plunged itself, by its handling of *Scott v. Sandford* in 1857. The case of Dred Scott has been the subject of volumes of scholarship, and the treatment here will not need to settle every fine point of disagreement.[67] On its surface the case presented a question of conflict of laws. Dred Scott, a slave, had been taken by his

64 Nelson 1995, 12; Fehrenbacher 1978, 64.
65 Weinberg 2007, 101–3.
66 *Scott v. Sandford*, 60 U.S. 393 (1857).
67 See e.g., Fehrenbacher 1978; Allen 2006; Graber 2006.

owner Emerson, an employee of the military, first to live in the free state of Illinois at Fort Armstrong, for two years, and next to live in the (also free) Wisconsin territory at Fort Snelling, for four years, from 1836–40 (interrupted by a brief sojourn in Louisiana for about six months in 1838).[68] Slavery was outlawed both by Illinois state law and, for the Wisconsin territory, by the federal Missouri Compromise. Dred Scott married in Wisconsin territory to a slave woman named Harriet and she eventually bore him two daughters. In 1840, Emerson moved his wife and the Scott "slaves" to St. Louis and headed off for a two-year stint in Florida, after which he rejoined them. He died in 1843. Three years later Dred Scott, after a failed effort to buy his and his family's freedom from the widow Emerson, sued in Missouri courts for his and his wife's and daughters' freedom, grounding his claims in the fact that they had resided in free territory (and for himself, that he had also resided in a free state).[69]

As of 1846 the law of Missouri, and indeed of all the slave states was clear on this matter. The legal consensus distinguished between a "sojourn," which was an intentionally temporary stay by master and slave of relatively short duration, and legal "domicile," which contemplated permanency. Permanent residence in a non-slave state would cause the slaves to become free. Northern states prior to 1830 honored southern property rights of travelers—that is, slaves traveling with their masters on "sojourn" retained their status as slaves. In fact, statutes on the subject in the states of Pennsylvania and New York specified concrete deadlines; in Pennsylvania, six months, and in New York, nine months, after which a slave kept there would become free.[70] And southern state courts, too, honored this consensus; according to Don Fehrenbacher, they "consistently ruled" that slaves taken to live in non-slave states or territory were thereby emancipated, and stayed emancipated even upon voluntary return to their home state.[71] In contrast, staying in the North for a temporary sojourn had no liberatory impact. After 1830, as abolitionist sentiment heated up, northern states withdrew from slaveowners the legal right of sojourn with their slaves, both by judicial decision (e.g., *Commonwealth v. Aves* [1836]) and by legislation.[72] In 1852, even the right of mere transit through the state with one's slave property intact was rejected by a

[68] Fehrenbacher ibid., 244–7.
[69] Ibid., 248–450.
[70] Ibid., 611, n.17.
[71] Ibid., 52–4.
[72] Ibid., 57; *Commonwealth v. Aves*, Mass. Sup.Ct., 35 Mass. 193 (1836).

New York court (decision upheld in *Lemmon v. The People* (1860).[73] These policy changes infuriated slaveowners.

Dred Scott launched the suits *Scott v. Emerson* and *Harriet v. Emerson* in 1846, but the trial did not occur until mid-1847. A variety of legal maneuvers ensued on both sides, until, in January of 1850, a trial court declared Dred and Harriet to be free. Attorneys on both sides signed a stipulation that whatever the outcome of Emerson's appeal to the Missouri Supreme Court, it would apply to both Dred and Harriet. Further legal maneuvers caused the state Supreme Court decision to be delayed until 1852.[74]

By this time the U.S. Supreme Court had decided an apparently unrelated case, *Strader v. Graham,* 51 U.S. 82 (1851). *Strader* dealt with a few slave musicians hired out by their owner for short, temporary work assignments in Ohio, who had then run off. The Supreme Court of Kentucky followed the usual rule about sojourns and declared that they were still slaves at the time of running off. The U.S. Supreme Court settled the appeal by denying its own jurisdiction in a situation where the governing state law was clear.[75] Attorneys arguing that the slaves had become free in Ohio resorted to the Supremacy Clause with the argument that the Northwest Ordinance prohibiting slavery made them free upon landing on Ohio soil, in a way that the mere state law of Kentucky could not undo. Chief Justice Taney dispensed with that argument by noting that Ohio's Constitution and laws had superseded the territorial ordinance. Taney went on to add that irrespective of whether Ohio law had freed persons merely sojourning in the state, Kentucky law, the law of the state to which the slaves had returned and where the suit was brought, ruled the decision. And *then in dictum,* he addressed the hypothetical situation, one not at issue in *Strader* but the one arguably faced by Dred Scott's wife Harriet: "The [federal] ordinance in question, if still in force, could have no more operation than the laws of Ohio in the State of Kentucky."[76]

Under this (unexceptional) precedent, Missouri law would determine the Scotts' fate. Suddenly, however, Missouri changed its law. Missouri

---

73 Fehrenbacher ibid., 60–61; *Lemmon v. The People,* 20 N.Y. 562 (N.Y. 1860).

74 Fehrenbacher ibid., 253–7.

75 *Strader v. Graham,* 51 U.S. 82 (1851). The Court did not always stick to this rule; see n.13 above.

76 Fehrenbacher 1978, 260–62. *Strader*, 51 U.S., at 94. That is, she would face it if her stay in Wisconsin were determined to be mere sojourn rather than legal domicile.

switched from appointed judges to elected judges in 1851, and the new state supreme court reflected the pro-slavery sentiment of the voters. The *Dred Scott v. Emerson* decision of 1852 openly rejected a clear line of Missouri precedent to declare the Scotts still slaves, despite their long-term domicile in non-slave areas, with no more explanation than, "Times have changed." Or in their words:

> Times are not now as they were when the former decisions on this subject were made. Since then, … [some] States have been possessed with a dark and fell spirit in relation to slavery, whose gratification is sought in the pursuit of measures, whose inevitable consequences must be the overthrow and destruction of our government. Under such circumstances it does not behoove the State of Missouri to … countenance any measure which might gratify this spirit.[77]

With this abrupt shift in Missouri law, Dred Scott's fate seemed to be sealed. The U.S. Supreme Court had ruled that Missouri law would prevail, and Missouri said its law went against the Scotts. And so the Court did rule. By a seven to two majority the U.S. Supreme Court ruled that the Scotts were still slaves. Chief Justice Taney's opinion of the Court reasoned that the U.S. Supreme Court did not have jurisdiction to decide the case, so the Missouri decision settled it.

The federal courts did not have jurisdiction for two reasons. Dred Scott was claiming diversity of citizenship jurisdiction for his federal appeal, because by this time Mrs Emerson had transferred their ownership to her brother, John Sanford, a New York resident.[78] Taney reasoned that Dred Scott could not bring a lawsuit into the federal courts, first, because as a Negro, he could not be a citizen of a state for purposes of federal diversity jurisdiction. Under the U.S. Constitution, the black man "had no rights which the white man was bound to respect."[79] Alternatively, even if this argument were unpersuasive, he could not bring the suit because under regnant law—the law of Missouri as pronounced by its Supreme Court in *Scott v. Emerson*—he was still a slave and therefore not a citizen, and therefore not entitled to claim diversity of citizenship jurisdiction.[80] The Court opinion went beyond these two rulings[81] to

---

[77] Ibid., 264–5, citing *Scott v. Emerson*, 15 Missouri 576, 582–587.

[78] Ibid., 270–74. The U.S. Reports spelled his name wrong.

[79] *Scott v. Sandford*, 60 U.S. 393, 407 (1857). This piece of the decision retained force only until November 1862, when Lincoln's Attorney General issued an "official opinion" that it did not have precedential force and that free men of color born in the U.S. were U.S. citizens. Fehrenbacher 1978, 576.

[80] Fehrenbacher ibid., 331–3.

insist (in dictum that McLean's dissent decried as lacking legal authority) that the Scotts' residence in Wisconsin territory (then ruled by the Missouri Compromise of 1820, which had since been superseded by the Kansas-Nebraska Act) could not have rendered them free (irrespective of Missouri law) because *Congress had no power to outlaw slavery in the territories*.

The reason presented for this was the Fifth Amendment due process clause, which forbade depriving persons of "life, liberty, or property without due process of law." Taney's reasoning both ignored the phrase "without due process of law," reading the clause as though it said, "No person shall be deprived of life, liberty or property," and read the word "property" but not the word "person" as applying to a slave (in contrast to the rest of the Constitution which everywhere uses the word "persons" to refer to slaves). Thus *any* federal ban on slavery "deprived" someone of property and would violate the Fifth Amendment. Restoring liberty to slave persons, which many abolitionists argued was demanded by the clause, instead would be forbidden by it. This decision, in judging Congress powerless to eliminate slavery from the territories it governed, rendered the *raison d'être* of the Republican Party unconstitutional.

The dissents of McLean and Curtis disputed the majority claims that blacks could not be citizens with constitutional rights, citing a variety of precedents and historic legal facts to the contrary, and they argued that the Missouri Supreme Court's abrupt departure from its own settled precedents in this case alone, because it was so idiosyncratic, need not be followed as the true law of Missouri. Anti-slavery forces took encouragement from their arguments, and Abraham Lincoln running in 1858 for Senate, asserted in his debates with Stephen Douglas that he would not be guided by the Taney opinion (except as settling the dispute between the specific litigants in the case), and would aim to appoint justices to overturn the decision as a rule of law.

In the interim between *Dred Scott* and Lincoln's winning the presidency in 1860, the case of *Ableman v. Booth* (1859) reached the Supreme Court from Wisconsin. *Scott v. Sandford* had dealt with the first of the two issues roiling the country—territories. *Ablemen v. Booth* dealt with the other—runaway slaves.

---

[81] Ibid., 366. Justice Nelson wrote an opinion reaching the same results without taking up the issue of the Missouri Compromise.

Ableman v. Booth (1859)[82]

The case of *Ableman v. Booth* (1859) is important not so much for what it decided as for the background political situation that it highlights. Scholars Earl Maltz and Jeffrey Schmitt both suggest that Northern acceptance of the 1850 Fugitive Slave Act, while grudging, did prevail until Stephen Douglas introduced the Kansas-Nebraska Act in Congress. Many northerners who had gone along with the 1850 Compromise now felt betrayed and said so. A prominent form of their resentment was a new willingness to engage in open, group defiance of the Fugitive Slave Act.[83]

On March 2, 1854 the House of Representatives (the North-dominated branch of Congress) passed the Kansas-Nebraska Act.[84] On March 11, newspaper editor, Sherman Booth and his Free Soiler allies distributed handbills and organized a mass rally to protest the recent jailing of an alleged fugitive slave (Joshua Glover) in Milwaukee. There several speakers challenged the Fugitive Slave Act as unconstitutional. The crowd rushed the jail with axes and a battering ram, and rescued Glover who fled to nearby Canada.[85]

On May 22, 1854, the Kansas-Nebraska Act passed the Senate. Anthony Burns, a Virginia slave who had fled to Boston and been captured and jailed on May 24, 1854 was the subject of an abolitionist rally in Faneuil Hall on the night of May 26. At the rally's end, some of its participants went to the jail and broke down the door but were then blocked by officials, one of whom was killed. The mayor called in local militia, and the U.S. marshal called in federal troops to protect the courthouse. President Fillmore ordered marines, cavalry and artillery to Boston as back-ups, and sent a federal revenue boat to stand by for delivery of Burns after his certificate of removal were issued. Hearings on the certificate lasted for four days, and then Burns was delivered to the boat before a crowd of 50,000 on June 2, three days after the Kansas-Nebraska Act had been signed into law. (In 1855 the free black community of Boston bought him his freedom.)[86]

While the Anthony Burns case wound up being handled outside the courtroom, Sherman Booth was arrested on March 15 for aiding and abetting the rescue of a fugitive slave. Booth's public account was that he

[82] *Ableman v. Booth*, 62 U.S. 506 (1859).
[83] Maltz 2009, 181; Schmitt 2007, 1322–3.
[84] *Congressional Globe*, 33rd Congress, 1st Sess., 531–2 (March 2, 1854).
[85] Schmitt 2007, 1330–35.
[86] Ibid., 1254 (May 22, 1854); Maltz 2009, 180–82.

objected to the Fugitive Slave Act on constitutional grounds: it violated due process of law and habeas corpus and the right to trial by jury. The newspaper that he edited published an editorial "regret[ting] the breaking into the jail to rescue Glover." Meanwhile, as his federal trial was pending and he was out on bail, he organized a public meeting where people quoted the Virginia and Kentucky Resolutions and insisted that each state as party to the compact that is the federal Constitution has the authority to interpret for itself the limits of federal power. Thus, any state that so believes can declare the Fugitive Slave Act of no force within its borders. On May 26, a justice of the Wisconsin Supreme Court issued a writ of habeas corpus to free Booth from federal custody, and later the whole court issued an opinion declaring the 1850 Act unconstitutional.[87] The Wisconsin Supreme Court distinguished *Prigg v. Pennsylvania* on two grounds: the 1793 law upheld by *Prigg* was enforced by regular Article III judges (who served for "good behavior"), not mere (temporarily appointed) commissioners; and, secondly, *Prigg* had not examined whether the absence of a requirement of trial by jury made the law unconstitutional.[88] (Prior to the U.S. Supreme Court hearing in *Prigg*, there had been two jury trials as to slave status, one in Pennsylvania and one in Maryland.) Nor had either *Moore v. Illinois* or *Jones v. Van Zandt* specifically examined the (Fifth, Sixth, and Seventh Amendment) jury issue.[89] Both on the grounds that the law was enforced by officials who were not proper Article III judges and that it failed to include trial by jury, the Wisconsin Supreme Court declared it unconstitutional.[90]

The federal government was undeterred. The U.S. Attorney had Booth indicted by a federal grand jury and re-arrested. Since this action was by proper officials rather than by a federal commissioner, the Wisconsin Supreme Court refused to issue a second writ of habeas corpus. The federal jury convicted Booth of aiding the escape of Joshua Glover (in violation of the 1850 Act), although the jury added a statement that they viewed Booth's action as "noble, benevolent and humane."[91] Booth was sentenced to thirty days in the county jail and a $1,000 fine. A few days later he succeeded in obtaining a writ of habeas corpus from the Wisconsin Supreme Court, by unanimous decision, and was released after having served only ten days of his sentence. The Pierce administration then appealed this decision to the U.S. Supreme Court.

---

87 Schmitt 2007, 1330–35; *In re Booth*, 3 Wis. 1 (1854).

88 *In re Booth*, 3 Wis., at 60–64.

89 Ibid., at 62–64.

90 Ibid., at 64–70.

91 Maltz 2009, 201–4.

The U.S. Supreme Court then reversed. As Georgia had done in the Cherokee cases, Wisconsin had refused to send an official record of the case to the U.S. Supreme Court so that the case could be reviewed on a writ of error. The Wisconsin Supreme Court had no wish to be overturned.[92] The U.S. Supreme Court proceeded without the officially conferred case record.[93] By the time the case was decided (March, 1859), secession of the South loomed large. Taney ruled for a unanimous court that state courts were not authorized to use a writ of habeas corpus to order someone released by federal officials. A state could issue the writ in order to have the matter of federal incarceration examined, but once offered a written explanation by federal authorities that the party is being held properly, the state has gone as far as it can. Taney also explained at length that the state court did wrong in failing to comply with the writ of error demanding a record of the case. And in one terse sentence, Taney insisted that the Fugitive Slave Act of 1850 was completely constitutional: "In the judgment of this court, the act of Congress commonly called the fugitive slave law is, in all of its provisions, fully authorized by the Constitution of the United States, … the commissioner had lawful authority to issue the warrant and commit the party, and … his proceedings were regular and conformable to law."[94] Once again, a federal fugitive slave act, deficient in the matter of trial by jury, was upheld by a Supreme Court that refrained from addressing this problem in a setting where the relevant parties had received a jury trial.

Back at the state level, one year after the U.S. Supreme Court decision, Booth was re-arrested to serve the rest of his thirty-day sentence, on orders of the federal district court judge, and confined to the federal customs house. When his sentence ended he refused to pay his fine and stayed imprisoned, writing widely published letters to continue agitation against the legal situation. An armed mob then broke him loose from prison on August 1, 1860. Armed crowds kept him free until a successful re-arrest on October 8, 1860. On the final day of his term of office, President Buchanan pardoned Booth.[95]

These two outbreaks of violent opposition to the Fugitive Slave Act were emblematic of northern behavior in the 1854–60 period. The *New York Times* described the situation in early 1859:

---

92 Schmitt 2007, 1341–2.
93 Maltz 2009, 208–9.
94 Ibid., 282; *Ableman v. Booth*, 62 U.S. 506, 526 (1859).
95 Maltz 2009, 284–5.

> It has come to be understood that the expense, trouble, odium, and risk of … endeavors [to recover escaped slaves] far outweigh the pecuniary value of the property … . Southern slave-owners have made up their minds … that they will make no effort to enforce the Fugitive Slave Law of 1850, in the Northern states.[96]

THE TANEY COURT AND NATIVE AMERICANS

Like Marshall before him, and perhaps even more so, Justice Story had enormous sympathy and respect for American Indians. As the 1835 Treaty of New Echota (for Cherokee removal) was pending ratification in the U.S. Senate, Story wrote to his son:

> The Europeans were always the aggressors of the natives in America, in all their contest … [T]he sins of all the murders and desolations on these shores are attributable to their baseness and avarice and detestable passions. I never think on the subject without bitter regret and undisguised indignation.[97]

Shortly after Story's death, in the case *U.S. v. Rogers* (1846), Chief Justice Taney had occasion to pronounce on the matter of the history of the treatment of Indians by the (Euro-American) government of the U.S. and the contrast to Story's view of the facts could not have been more stark:[98]

> [F]rom the very moment the general government came into existence to this time, it has exercised its power over this unfortunate race in the spirit of humanity and justice, and has endeavoured by every means in its power to enlighten their minds and increase their comforts, and to save them if possible from the consequences of their own vices.

Moreover, Taney claimed in this opinion that "European governments" had *never* "acknowledged or treated" native tribes as "independent nations" and that the Indians had been, first by European governments and then by the U.S. Government, "continually held to be, and treated as, subject to their dominion."[99] As Indian law scholar David Wilkins has noted, in light of the lengthy history of treaty negotiation between, first, European governments and Indian tribal governments and, then, between

---

[96] *New York Times*, April 9, March 4, 1859, cited in Maltz 2009, 285, 333.

[97] Letter to William W. Story, Washington, Feb. 21, 1836, W.W. Story 1851, 229.

[98] *U.S. v. Rogers*, 45 U.S. 567, at 572 (1846).

[99] Ibid., at 571.

the U.S. Government and tribal governments, this claim was both "astonishing" and "inaccurate."[100] The ruling in *U.S. v. Rogers* was unanimous. Rogers had been convicted in federal court of murdering another man, and both murderer and victim were originally white men who had in adulthood been formally adopted into tribal memberships. U.S. law at the time (per act of 1834) exempted from U.S. jurisdiction crimes committed by one Indian against another in Indian territory. Rogers
was claiming this exemption applied to him and should invalidate his conviction.

The Court ruled that tribal "adoption" operated within Indian law for the conferring of tribal privileges, but that it could not confer exemption from the reach of U.S. federal criminal law; the exemption in the law of 1834 applied to persons who were Indians as a matter of "race," not as a matter of conversion or adoption. The Court opinion acknowledged that the 1835 Treaty (of New Echota) with the Cherokee did in its terms extend tribal jurisdiction over persons who "have connected themselves with" the Cherokee but insisted (despite the apparently clear language) that Congress could not have meant for this phrase to cover "a white man, of the white race."[101]

The Court's misreading of treaty in the *Rogers* case had only limited impact. It would soon be reversed by the political branches in a new treaty. But the political branches in these years were having a far more devastating impact on Indian life than this particular Court decision could.

THE POLITICAL BRANCHES AND NATIVE AMERICANS, 1835–60

Because the sad story of Indian Removal Policy began during the years of the Marshall Court, it was already narrated in Chapter 1. To recap: The states of what was then the Southwest, Alabama, Mississippi, Georgia, and Tennessee, between 1827 and the early 1830s adopted laws that asserted their own control over Indian territory, purporting to negate federal treaties; rendering Indians second-class citizens with no right to testify in court against whites; and purporting to legalize white theft of Indian land. Whites fraudulently and/or violently took Indian land,

---

[100] Wilkins 1998, 528.
[101] Ibid., at 572–3.

assisted by crooked local level judges. Mob violence at the local level and retaliatory violence by Indians abetted this process. Congress adopted the Indian Removal Act of 1830 to authorize moving Indians to land west of the Mississippi, but to do so only in terms that comported with federal treaties. The Jackson Administration eventually found a group of Cherokee who claimed to speak for the tribe and signed the Treaty of New Echota in 1835 agreeing to move. Other Cherokee protested that this group lacked authorization.

In 1832 the Jackson Administration briefly (against its own pro-removal proclivities) sent troops to Alabama to *defend* Indians against local mob violence. The military backed off when threatened with militia action from neighboring states.

This situation then came to a head during the years of the Taney Court, as the level of local violence convinced the federal government to send troops to promote Indian removal. Federal troops fought the Creek in Georgia in 1836 and the Seminole in Florida between 1835 and 1842; the troops then operated the coercive removal of Cherokee from Georgia, Alabama, and Mississippi by 1838 in the notorious Trail of Tears, and the removal of most Seminole from Florida by 1842.[102] Once federal policy altered through new treaties and warfare, the Supreme Court had no role to play. Even if it had been motivated to intervene, no case was brought to it to block Indian Removal, and it would have been powerless to block the plenary power of the President and the Senate to sign new treaties abrogating old ones.

CONCLUSIONS

Between the time that John Marshall died and the time that Joseph Story died (in 1845), one can observe that the Court moved into a position slightly more protective of racial minorities, specifically, of black slaves, than the elected branches were. This was an era when Congress was enforcing the gag rule and President Jackson was letting the post office refuse to deliver anti-slavery essays. This judicial distance from the executive branch was plainly observable in the *Amistad* (1841) case (and contrasts with the *Antelope* case under Marshall, where the executive branch would have freed more slaves than the Court did free). As to *Prigg* (1842), the tendency was not so obvious, but in allowing that state officialdom was free to flout federal law to the degree of removing itself

[102] See Chapter 1, n.75.

from cooperation with its enforcement, the Court broke with Congress in a way that made slave recapture newly difficult. This difficulty endured for eight years until southerners were able to get the 1850 Fugitive Slave Act through Congress, thereby undoing the effect of the *Prigg* case that had made slave recapture impracticable.

Presidents sympathetic to, or eager to appease, the South had a strong enough influence over appointments to the Court that, after Story's departure, the Supreme Court in the 1846–60 period was *more* pro-slavery (i.e., more supportive of policies harmful to black people) than was the House of Representatives.[103] The House twice passed the Wilmot Proviso (a check on the expansion of slavery), while ten years later (1857) the Court ruled that Congress had no power to ban slavery in the territories, and had never had such power (despite Congress's having acted on this power from the beginning of the Constitution). On the other hand, the House did eventually vote to enact the Fugitive Slave Act of 1850, while the Court merely upheld it. And then the House and Senate, although both were dominated by non-slave states, voted to enact the Kansas-Nebraska Act. This act had not gone so far as the Court in *Dred Scott* (1857), for it still at least had authorized slavery to be banned in the territories, at the will of the settlers. (In fact the Democratic Party after the *Dred Scott* decision then split over whether a territorial legislature could enact such a ban prior to statehood, but the natural reading of the *Scott* decision and its conflict with the Kansas-Nebraska Act in this respect seem plain enough.)

The most useful conclusion about the period of 1846–60 is that during these years no branch of the federal government acted to protect rights of either blacks or Native Americans.[104] The Court with Story gone and under Taney's unchallenged leadership proved even worse than the elected branches in some respects. As to Indians, it interpreted a treaty developed and ratified by the elected branches as less protective of tribal

---

[103] There was one additional Taney Court decision relevant to slavery. *Kentucky v. Dennison,* 65 U.S. 66 (1861) posed a conflict between the governor of Ohio and the governor of Kentucky over Ohio's refusal to extradite someone charged in Kentucky for the crime of enticing a slave into escape. Kentucky asked the Court for a writ of mandamus commanding the extradition. Taney's unanimously supported opinion stuck strictly to the states' rights angle. Yes, Ohio was obliged to honor an extradition request from another state even for acts that its own government did not consider a crime, but, no, the federal courts could not issue a mandamus to a state official. Thus, the ruling left the status quo intact.

[104] The Wilmot Proviso, checking the spread of slavery after the Mexican War, had passed the House in both 1846 and 1847 but was killed in the Senate.

sovereignty than the words of the treaty said. On the other hand, with its power of the sword and of the purse, the elected part of the government by conquest and Indian Removal in the 1830s and 1840s harmed the Indians far more than any Court decision did.

As to slaves, the Supreme Court (in *Dred Scott*) opened up all federal territory to slaveholding, irrespective even of the "popular sovereignty" limitation that Congress had allowed in the Kansas-Nebraska Act. President Pierce's Administration exempted black Americans from the federally granted legal right to preempt other purchasers of land by settling on it (1856), and in 1858 President Buchanan went against the popular sovereignty check on the spread of slavery by (unsuccessfully) urging Congress to adopt the already-voted-down, proslavery Lecompton Constitution.

However, with the election of Lincoln, by the end of this period, it was starting to appear that Federalist Number Ten was going to prove more accurate (than Federalist Number 78) at predicting how minority rights would get protected in the U.S. As slavery became the dominant political issue and as the country grew by adding more land and more diverse immigrants, more and more the patterns of immigration shifted both population and political power to non-slave areas—i.e., to the North. In other words, as the country became even larger and even more diverse, the white political majority in the South, while strong enough to exert tyranny over slaves and free blacks *there*, and persuasive enough in Congress to postpone the day of reckoning until 1860, was nonetheless losing power at the national level. With the election of Abraham Lincoln, it became plain that the national level of government would now act to outlaw slavery in D.C. (which was surrounded by slave states, Maryland and Virginia), to prevent by law the expansion of slavery, and to check the interstate slave trade. Fearing even further attacks on slavery, which institution southerners perceived as essential to their way of life (but which northerners increasingly viewed as tyrannical), eleven states seceded.

3. Civil War and Reconstruction

INTRODUCTION

There is a sense in which the material in this chapter simply does not fit the framework of analysis of this book. The system of representative democracy set forth in the Constitution of 1787, with a lifetime appointed federal judiciary with (implied) power to protect minority rights against legislative majorities, fell apart after the election of Abraham Lincoln. Lincoln was elected by 39.7 percent of the voting population, but it was a segment that was heavily concentrated in, and comprised a sizable population majority of, the northern states with large numbers of Electoral College votes. Thus, even if his opposition had been united behind a single candidate, instead of divided among three contenders, he would have still taken a majority of the Electoral College vote and thus the presidency.[1]

His supporters were that minority of the population who considered the anti-slavery cause important enough to vote for him. White southerners were also a minority, and although as of 1860 only 26 percent of southern white families owned slaves,[2] enough of them believed in the way of life dominated by slavery that secession was popular in most parts of the South.[3] The Civil War pitted the Lincoln-supporting minority

---

[1] Extrapolating from the figures for popular vote and Electoral College vote at Wooley and Peters 1999–2017, I tabulate that he would have received 169 Electoral College votes and his hypothetical opposition 134.

[2] Kolchin 1993, 180. One can find a detailed state-by-state breakdown in "Results from the 1860 census," showing a range of 3 percent in Delaware to 49 percent in Mississippi.

[3] The mountainous regions formed pockets of resistance, mostly individual counties, but occasionally a whole region: The western part of Virginia seceded from that state in 1861 to form West Virginia and entered Congress as a non-slaveholding state in 1863. East Tennessee held a convention in 1861 that issued a call to secede from Tennessee and rejoin the union, but this never came to pass. Foner 1988, 1, 39. In part because of this significant segment of white unionists, Tennessee was the first state to undergo successful Reconstruction and re-enter the Union. It was also the home state of President Andrew Johnson.

against the pro-slavery white southern minority over the issue of what should be done about the black minority. Eight million whites lived in the South in 1860. There were about four million slaves and half a million free blacks, the latter of whose population divided in half as to north versus south. Twenty-seven million whites lived in the non-South, and of course a significant minority of these opposed the Republican insistence on hemming in the spread of slavery. The (white) South broke away from the North in order to uphold what it saw as its minority right to maintain slave property. Those Northerners who voted for Lincoln did so in part out of a belief in the right of the black minority to be free of slavery. Had it not been for secession, the dominance of the Republican Party at the federal level would have expressed the will of an electoral minority, enabled to rule because the U.S. has neither a system of proportional representation nor direct popular election of the President. But once the South seceded, the Republicans represented the will of a clear majority of what was left in the U.S. That electoral majority brought about enormous political change, indeed a constitutional revolution. Nonetheless, viewed from the perspective that considers the nation as a whole, circa, 1861, this revolution was produced by a minority party (Republicans) on behalf of a different minority (blacks). This fact goes a long way toward explaining what eventually became of Reconstruction.

THE CIVIL WAR AND EMANCIPATION

After South Carolina seceded, it asked federal authorities to vacate Fort Sumter. Their refusal and South Carolina's subsequent attack on April 12, 1861, began a Civil War[4] that endured until the spring of 1865, when the field generals of the Confederacy surrendered over the course of a few months, beginning with Robert E. Lee at Appomattox on April 9, 1865.[5] In the process of this war, not only were more Americans killed than in the total of all the other wars fought by the U.S., but also most of the slaves in the U.S. were freed.

They began by freeing themselves, running north to seek shelter with northern troops. For the first six months, while Lincoln was still seeking reconciliation with the South, official military policy was to respect slave ownership; slaves were either returned to their owners, or held in captivity as contraband of war.[6]

4 "Fort Sumter."
5 "The Surrender."
6 Smith 1997, 279; Foner 1988, 3–5.

Other conciliatory gestures promoted by Lincoln included an offer in his First Inaugural Address to have the Constitution be amended to say plainly that the federal government could not act to destroy slavery against the will of the states that wanted to have it, and even that this amendment could be made "irrevocable."[7] On the other hand, while conceding in the same Address that the Constitution plainly required the surrender of fugitive slaves to their masters, he sided with northern critics of the Fugitive Slave Act in his insistence that "all the safeguards of liberty known in civilized and humane jurisprudence [ought] to be introduced, so that a free man be not, in any case, surrendered as a slave," whether in federal or state laws on the subject.[8] And he implicitly sided with critics of the [state-level] southern Negro Seamen Acts by insisting that in enforcing the fugitive slave clause, Congress should act at the same time to "provide by law for the enforcement of that clause in the Constitution which guarantees that 'the citizen of each State shall be entitled to all privileges and immunities of citizens in the several States.'"[9] His speech did not succeed in postponing war. The South had no assurance that the slavery-protecting amendment would get ratified, and even if it did, they still would not have assurance that they could take their slaves wherever they wanted within the union, or that interstate slave trade would not someday be banned, or that the recapture of fugitive slaves would not be rendered utterly impractical by imposition of expensive procedural hurdles and widespread non-cooperation.

By August of 1861, as Union troop losses mounted, which losses increased hostility toward the South, Congress—i.e., Congress now emptied of the delegations from the seceded states—passed a Confiscation Act, authorizing federal seizure of the "property" of anyone employed by the Confederate military, and thus at least indirectly used to support the Confederate war effort. In March 1862, Congress forbade the U.S. Army to return any fugitive slaves into slavery. The changed legal environment stimulated thousands of slave escapes, especially with the masters away fighting the war and with friendly Union forces now nearby. In April, 1862, Congress ended slavery in D.C. (compensating masters $300 per slave), and in June prohibited it in all federal territory.[10] The last, of course, directly violated the ruling in *Dred Scott* (1857), which Congress simply ignored.

---

7 "Lincoln's First Inaugural Address March 4, 1861."

8 Ibid.; Nieman 1991, 54, 232 n.8.

9 Ibid.

10 Smith 1997, 279–80; Franklin and Moss 1994, 206–7.

In July, 1862, Congress expanded the Confiscation Act to cover the slave property of all persons who in any way aided or abetted the war effort. Half a million slaves fled to the North before the war ended. Congress in the same law authorized black enrollment in the military, and it reiterated this point in the Militia Act, passed on the same day.[11]

As is well known, the Emancipation Proclamation, issued September 22, 1862, announced that slaves in any states still in secession on January 1, 1863 would be freed as of that date. This left some still in the "border states"—e.g., 65,000 in Kentucky and 2,000 in Delaware at war's end. Maryland's elected officials (chosen in an election where pro-Union loyalty oaths were a precondition to voting) ended slavery (without compensation) there on November 1, 1864. Missouri followed the same path as Maryland, requiring loyalty oaths as a precondition to voting in the 1864 elections. This produced an electoral victory for emancipationists, who then not only freed the slaves of Missouri but also adopted a system of civil equality that instituted property rights for blacks and their capacity to testify in court.[12]

Although the Emancipation Proclamation outlawed slavery in the seceded South, the level of racist sentiment in the North in the war's early years became apparent on the days of July 12–16, 1863, when New York City whites rampaged in a riot ostensibly aimed against the national conscription (draft) act. This law enrolled all able-bodied men of suitable age in the Union army unless they could pay a $300 fee to hire a substitute. Although it was called a "draft riot," the rioters were working class whites who attacked individual black citizens along with businesses owned by, and orphanages serving, black Americans (and also attacked some offices of Republican newspapers and some wealthy individuals). More than ten people were killed before the U.S. Army could restore order.[13]

In December of 1863 Congress required the state of West Virginia (which had broken away from secessionist Virginia), to abolish slavery in order to join the Union. West Virginia voted to do so in a referendum three months later. In June 1864, Congress repealed the federal fugitive slave acts.[14]

Ruled by federal troops beginning in 1863, Tennessee under its military governor, Andrew Johnson, abolished slavery at the end of 1863. In February of 1865, under a referendum whose rules gave suffrage only

---

11 Ibid. [both sources]; Nieman 1991, 54; Hamilton 2004.

12 Foner 1988, 7, 37, 39–41, 41–3.

13 Smith 1997, 274.

14 Ibid., 279–80; Foner 1988, 38–9.

to white Unionists, the state abolished slavery by constitutional amendment. Tennessee retained these suffrage restrictions throughout the war. It ratified the Thirteenth Amendment in April 1865.[15] A year later, in July 1866 it ratified the Fourteenth Amendment, which had been proposed by Congress only a month earlier. This caused it to be granted Congressional representation in 1867, unlike other southern states, which refused to ratify that amendment.[16]

Arkansas, Louisiana, and Virginia similarly underwent militarily imposed Reconstruction with voting rights restricted to whites who supported the Union, and they similarly abolished slavery and were early ratifiers of the Thirteenth Amendment.[17] In contrast to Tennessee, however, they at first refused to ratify the Fourteenth Amendment and consequently were at first refused representation in Congress.

In addition to prompting the freeing of slaves, the war brought about a change in civil rights for free blacks at both federal and (northern) state levels. In 1862 Congress opened up the postal service to black mail carriers and in 1864 granted blacks legal capacity to testify against whites in federal court. In 1862 Oregon repealed its ban on black testimony against whites, and California did likewise in 1863. At first, however, many white northerners opposed the idea of having blacks serve in the armed forces; only in January of 1863 did Lincoln take advantage of the authority Congress had granted him six months earlier and ordered recruitment of significant numbers of black soldiers. Even then, they fought in separate regiments and under white officers and, until 1864, received less pay than white soldiers.[18]

In March of 1865 Congress, still without southern representation and with encouragement from President Lincoln (who would be assassinated a month later), established the Freedmen's Bureau, charged with helping former slaves adjust to free status and also with helping white war refugees make the transition to peace. Due to expire in 1866, the Act was renewed by Congress over the veto of (former southern Democrat) President Andrew Johnson. The Bureau operated schools and hospitals for freed slaves, helped with food, clothing, and fuel, for destitute white refugees and for freed persons, and continued in operation until 1872,

---

15 Foner 1988, 43–5; "The Thirteenth Amendment Ratification and Results."

16 "14th Amendment."

17 Foner 1988, 45 n.18, 45–50, 182, 196; "The Thirteenth Amendment."

18 Smith 1997, 279–80; Nieman 1991, 54; Franklin and Moss 1994, 203; "Civil Rights" 2012. Federal policy of maintaining separate black units commanded by white officers endured throughout the two world wars of the twentieth century. Staples 2016.

although its funds were cut significantly in 1869. For a brief period in a few locales, the Bureau also distributed plots of confiscated farm lands to freed slaves.[19]

The Thirteenth Amendment, officially proclaiming an end to "slavery or involuntary servitude" throughout the land, and granting Congress enforcement authority for the amendment was proposed by a two-thirds majority in the Senate as early as spring of 1864. Once Lincoln himself began to exert his political influence on behalf of the Amendment, the House, too, mustered enough votes; the amendment was officially proposed by Congress on January 31, 1865. Three-fourths of the state legislatures ratified before the year was out. Southern states were included among the ratifiers, and these were government bodies (elected by whites willing to swear an oath of future loyalty to the Union) that had been told by President Andrew Johnson, after he acceded to the presidency on April 14 (five days after the surrender at Appomattox), that ratification of the Thirteenth Amendment would be a condition of readmission into the union.[20]

CIVIL RIGHTS FOR BLACK AMERICANS, 1866–75

Still cleansed of Confederate representation, Congress (again over President Johnson's veto) adopted the Civil Rights Act of April 9, 1866, to protect the rights of the freed slaves against the postbellum black codes being adopted all over the South that were imposing slave-like status on all blacks. These black codes, now being federally outlawed, typically required blacks to be signed up for annual labor contracts at all times, and to have their employer's permission for travel away from the plantation. The codes made it a crime for anyone to attempt to entice a black employee away from his or her employer with an offer of a different job. They allowed corporal punishment of employees. South Carolina prohibited blacks from all employments except farmer or servant. Mississippi prohibited them from renting property in urban areas, where non-agricultural jobs might be available.[21]

The 1866 Civil Rights Act targeted such statutes by enacting the following:[22]

---

[19] Foner 1988, 69–70, 151–2, 158–64.
[20] Smith 1997, 282.
[21] Williams 1996, 3; Foner 1988, 199–201.
[22] 14 Stat. 27–30 (April 9, 1866).

> That all persons born in the United States and not subject to any foreign power, excluding Indians not taxed, are hereby declared to be citizens of the United States; and such citizens, of every race and color, without regard to any previous condition of slavery or involuntary servitude, except as a punishment for crime whereof the party shall have been duly convicted, shall have the same right, in every State and Territory in the United States, to make and enforce contracts, to sue, be parties, and give evidence, to inherit, purchase, lease, sell, hold, and convey real and personal property, and to full and equal benefit of all laws and proceedings for the security of person and property, as is enjoyed by white citizens, and shall be subject to like punishment, pains, and penalties, and to none other, any law, statute, ordinance, regulation, or custom, to the contrary notwithstanding.

In order to ensure, among other things, that this Act not be reversed by a future congress, the Thirty-ninth Congress in June of 1866 proposed the Fourteenth Amendment and sent it to the states for ratification. The first session of this Congress adjourned in July without having specified the terms by which southern states would be admitted back into the Congress.[23]

The second session of this Thirty-ninth Congress in January of 1867 (again over a Johnson veto) enfranchised black residents of D.C., and then did the same for U.S. territories. By March (again over Johnson's veto) this Congress adopted the Reconstruction Act of 1867. In order to get out from under military rule (imposed by the Act) and to receive Congressional representation, southern states would, under the terms of this Act, have to hold constitutional conventions chosen by universal manhood suffrage, include such suffrage in the new constitution, and ratify the Fourteenth Amendment.[24]

At first, many white southerners boycotted the state constitutional elections that were to enshrine black voting rights, even claiming that staying under federal military rule would be less onerous than being ruled by black citizens. (To take effect the new constitutions had to be ratified by a majority of eligible voters; so this tactic could thwart the acceptance of a new black-participation constitution. This abstinence strategy succeeded in Alabama in 1868, prompting Congress into loosening the rule of acceptability to a simple majority of those who voted, and under the new rule the Alabama Constitution got adopted.)[25] Numerous other southern whites were barred from voting or officeholding, on the grounds that as former officeholders they had taken oaths to uphold the U.S. Constitution and then

23 Foner 1988, 250–61.
24 Ibid., 273–80.
25 Email from Peter Kolchin, University of Delaware, January 18, 2016.

violated the oaths to support secession. Congress officially eliminated this disfranchisement by a general amnesty only in 1872.[26]

Because some whites continued for awhile to boycott southern elections in order to show disdain for black suffrage, it is difficult to ascertain the degree to which the 1868 and 1870 Congressional delegations accepted into Congress, fully represented the eligible electorate of the South. Thus, it is difficult to discern whether the Fifteenth Amendment and the 1870 and 1871 Enforcement Acts described below could have been adopted had southern whites participated fully in the electoral process.

In 1870, with the Fourteenth Amendment now also ratified, permanently enshrining citizenship for all born on U.S. soil,[27] along with equal protection of the laws and due process of law for all persons, Congress in §18 of the Enforcement Act of (May 31) 1870 stated that the Civil Rights Act of 1866 "is hereby re-enacted."[28] The re-enactment answered the challenge of persons like President Johnson who had questioned the constitutionality of the 1866 law, since it passed prior to the Fourteenth Amendment.

After the Civil War ended, even as the new state constitutions and the Fourteenth Amendment were being ratified, and the states admitted back into the union,[29] many white residents of the South at one point or another took up arms to intimidate blacks and white Republicans away from the polls. As a result of this violence, intimidation, and related fraud, again to a degree that is difficult to ascertain, the Congressional delegations from the "redeemed" southern states (i.e., the ones where the Democrats retook control from the Republicans) did not fully represent the black citizens of the South. The Redemption governments showed little interest in protecting the victims of this violence.[30] This problem was to continue until late in the twentieth century.

The southern states became "redeemed" in the following years: 1867—Maryland; 1870—West Virginia; 1869 and 1870—Virginia, Tennessee and Missouri; 1870 and 1871—Georgia; 1873–75—Texas, Arkansas and

---

26 Williams 1996, 7–9; Franklin and Moss 1994, 251.

27 Excluding, that is, persons not subject to U.S. jurisdiction—presumably reservation Indians and children of foreign diplomats.

28 16 Stat. 140 (1870).

29 The years of readmission to Congress were as follows: summer of 1866—Tennessee; summer of 1868—Arkansas, Florida, North Carolina, South Carolina, Louisiana, Alabama; summer of 1870—Virginia, Mississippi, Texas, Georgia. "Readmission to Representation in Congress."

30 This generalization is liable to particularized exceptions as to individual states or election years, but does describe the overall picture. For particular details see Foner 1988, 420–25; 442–4; 449–53; 508–11; 590–98; 600–601.

Alabama; 1870–76—North Carolina; 1875—Mississippi; 1874 and 1877—Florida; 1877—South Carolina and Louisiana.[31]

The recurrent waves of white violence prompted more corrective legislation from Congress, as well as many hundreds of federal prosecutions. The Enforcement Act of (May 31) 1870 forbade state officials to discriminate against voters on the basis of race and criminalized the use of terror, force or bribery to prevent people from voting because of their race.[32] The Ku Klux Klan Act of (April 20) 1871[33] went further, specifically targeting as criminal certain notorious practices of the KKK, such as "go[ing] in disguise upon the public highway or upon the premises of another for the purpose, either directly or indirectly, of depriving any person or any class of persons of the equal protection of the laws …"[34] It also allowed for prosecution directly by federal district attorneys and authorized, if necessary, suspension of the writ of habeas corpus and federal military intervention.

The Fifteenth Amendment itself came about as a kind of corrective legislation. In September, 1868, having earlier adopted a Reconstruction Constitution, Georgia's new legislature voted to oust all its black members therefrom. Congress intervened with the assistance of the Georgia Supreme Court to undo the legislation, but this development operated as a warning that the Reconstruction Act of 1867 could not prevent southern states in the future from legislating to take the vote away from blacks. Thus, in order to secure black suffrage against future legislative alteration, Congress sent the Fifteenth Amendment to the states in February 1869. Early in 1870, while ratification of the Amendment was pending, Congress restored Virginia, Mississippi, and Texas to Congressional representation under the "fundamental conditions" that they could not deprive blacks of voting rights or office holding. The Republicans themselves were deeply divided over these restrictions on the internal affairs of a state, and many expressed doubt as to their enforceability. The Fifteenth Amendment promised a more enduring solution.[35]

---

[31] Ibid.; Schlup and Ryan 2003; Franklin and Moss 1994, 251–4. Thus, the enforcement acts described in the following paragraph were adopted with the help of Congressional delegations from eight of the eleven Confederate states that had not yet been "redeemed" from Republican control.

[32] 16 Stat. 140 (1870).

[33] 17 Stat. 13 (1871).

[34] *Ibid.*, Section 2.

[35] Foner 1988, 347, 446, 452–4; Franklin and Moss 1994, 240. Only a handful of northern states allowed black suffrage as of the 1860s, but the vast majority of blacks lived in the South.

All-told, in this decade the Congressional Republicans gave the nation the Thirteenth, Fourteenth, and Fifteenth Amendments, the Civil Rights Act of 1866, the Reconstruction Acts of 1867–68, the Enforcement Act of (May 31) 1870, the Ku Klux Klan Act of (April 20) 1871,[36] and the Civil Rights Act of (March 1) 1875.[37] The last was pushed through a lame duck Congress—Congress having gone Democrat in the election of 1874—and was filibustered until its most controversial provision, desegregation of public schools, was dropped.[38]

The 1875 Act opened up public accommodations—inns, public carriers, theaters and places of public amusement—to all persons irrespective of race "subject only to the conditions and limitations established by law, and applicable alike to citizens of every race and color" (e.g., such as a rule of being well-behaved). It also prohibited racial discrimination in selection of jurors in state and local courts (as well as federal), so long as the juror was a "citizen possessing all other qualifications which are or may be prescribed by law." While this Act did squeak through the lame duck Republican House in the early months of 1875, its day (except for the jury provision) had already come and gone. It passed the House (162–99) only with the votes of *ninety* Republicans *who had just been ousted from office*.[39]

The political transition of 1868–74 proceeded unevenly. As the southern states first gained readmission to Congress and then rid their statehouses and Congressional delegations of Republicans, the size of the Democratic minority in Congress grew significantly, consequent to the elections of 1868 and 1870, but Grant's Presidential re-election of 1872 swept a two-thirds Republican majority into the House.[40] On the other hand, within the South, with southern Democrats returning to power, terrorism by Klan-like gangs functioned to keep blacks and white Republicans from the polls, so it is also difficult to discern whether, but for the terroristic violence in the South, the Congress would have been swept by Democrats in the election of 1874 quite as thoroughly as it in fact was.[41] Still, Ulysses

---

[36] 17 Stat. 13 (1871).

[37] 18 Stat. 335 (1875).

[38] Kelly 1959; Fairman 1987, VII: 176–84.

[39] Brandwein 2011, 68.

[40] Kernell and Jacobson 2000, 523.

[41] Foner 1988, 550–58, describes the 1874 election as particularly marred by violence in Alabama, Louisiana, and Mississippi. Still, due in considerable part to the Panic of 1873, the North, too, shifted massively to the Democrats in the 1874 election. Carson and Roberts 2011, 1–2.

S. Grant was elected to the Presidency in both 1868 and 1872, so one can conclude that the mainstream sense of the national electorate was, up through the year 1873, at least moderately Republican.

In the election of 1874 the American electorate basically turned its back on Reconstruction, changing the House of Representatives from a two-thirds Republican majority to a Democratic majority.[42] After the presidential election of 1876, a commission sorted through disputes over election numbers and gave Republican Rutherford B. Hayes the Electoral College by one vote, despite a clear popular vote majority for the Democrat, Samuel Tilden. The Democrats in 1876 retained a House majority and came within three of tying the Republican majority in the Senate. In the elections of 1878 they would be surpassing the Republicans in both houses. The national mood had plainly shifted by the time of the 1874 elections, and the shift endured long enough to let the Democrats control both houses of Congress by 1879.[43]

The executive branch shifted in a similar direction but far less abruptly. The President and his Justice Department and federal troops acted against the massive violent resistance in southern states by suspending the writ of habeas corpus in nine South Carolina counties in 1871,[44] bringing hundreds of prosecutions annually from 1871 through 1877, and then again during the Garfield-Arthur administration of 1881–85. See Figure 3.1 and Table 3.1 below.[45] The intensity with which the Democratic Party

---

[42] Democratic Governor-elect of New York, Samuel Tilden proclaimed of the election results that they had ended the "crusade preached every year against our erring but suffering and repenting fellow-citizens of the South" and promised the "redemption of free government" (Fairman 1987, VII, 180).

[43] Voting figures after 1872, until well into the twentieth century, cannot give a complete picture of national sentiment because of the role played by white violence [to keep blacks and their white sympathizers from the polls] and ballot fraud in the South once the Democrats had "redeemed" it.

[44] Foner 1988, 454–8; Williams 1996.

[45] Source for Figure 3.1: Wang 1997, 300, Appendix 7; data cited in Pamela Brandwein 2011, 129. The dip in prosecutions for 1878, President Hayes's first full calendar year in office, apparently reflects his effort to attempt to let southern officials provide "peace and security," as leaders such as Wade Hampton had promised they would if federal soldiers withdrew. By October of 1878, Hayes had received enough reports of electoral violence in South Carolina and Texas that he was moved to comment to his diary on the need for some sort of "firm statement" to the South. The next year his administration quadrupled the number of prosecutions, from 23 to 93. Logan 1997, 12–36; Wang 1997, 148, 161.

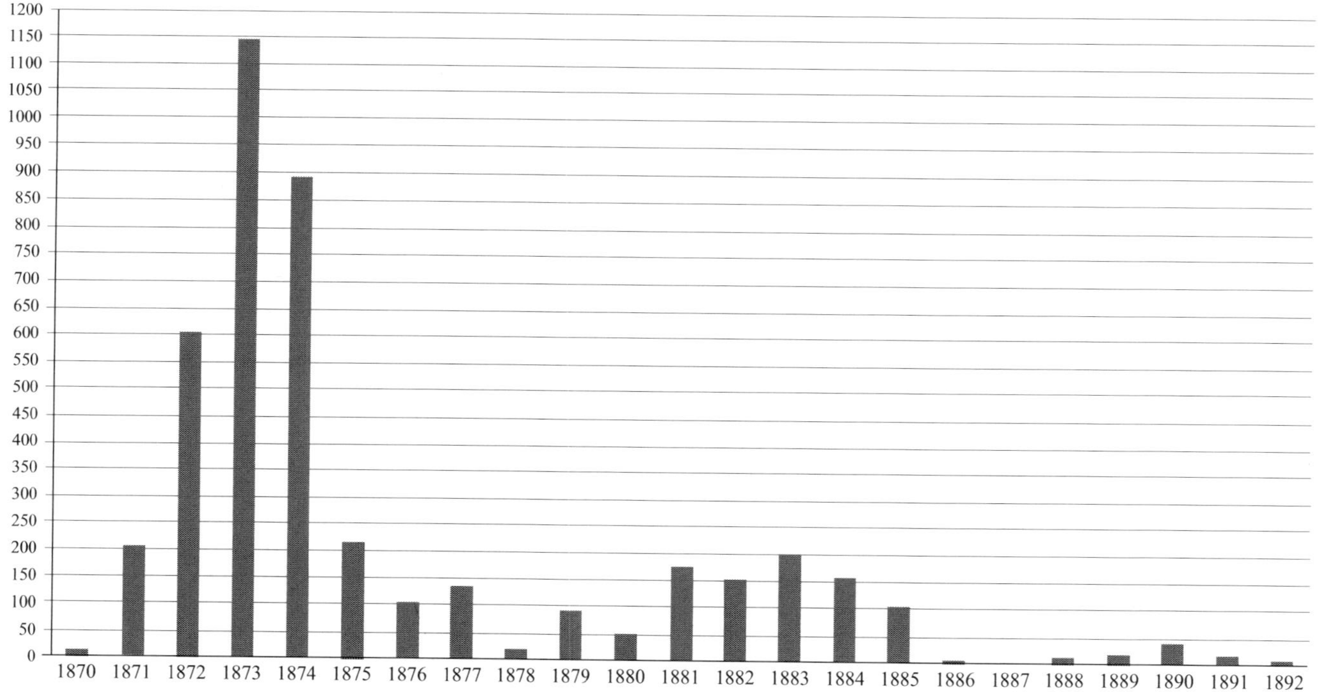

Figure 3.1 *Enforcement Act prosecutions (cases brought in the South) 1870–1892*

opposed these measures shows up in the low enforcement year of 1880, after the Democrats briefly took control of Congress. During the 1879–80 Congress, President Hayes vetoed no fewer than eight efforts (by Democrats) to repeal the voting rights enforcement laws.[46] Republican Presidents and their Justice Departments continued through most of the seventies and the first half of the eighties to act to uphold legal rights of blacks, after Congress's enthusiasm for civil rights cooled abruptly after March of 1875.

Table 3.1 Data for Figure 3.1—year followed by number of prosecutions

1870	16	1878	23	1886	8
1871	206	1879	93	1887	2
1872	603	1880	53	1888	14
1873	1148	1881	177	1889	22
1874	890	1882	154	1890	42
1875	216	1883	201	1891	19
1876	108	1884	160	1892	12
1877	133	1885	107		

ASIANS IN THE U.S., 1865–75

In the burst of enthusiasm for protecting racial minorities that swept the North in the several years following the Civil War, Asian-Americans, too, benefited to some degree. When Congress had adopted the Civil Rights Act of 1866, its phrasing had zeroed in on the creation and protection of civil rights of the former slaves. Section one of the law had "enacted:"

> That *all persons born in the United States and not subject to any foreign power, excluding Indians not taxed, are hereby declared to be citizens of the United States*; and such *citizens, of every race and color, without regard to any previous condition of slavery or involuntary servitude*, except as a punishment for crime whereof the party shall have been duly convicted, *shall have the same right*, in every State and Territory in the United States, to make and enforce contracts, to sue, be parties, and give evidence, to inherit, purchase, lease, sell, hold, and convey real and personal property, and to full and equal benefit of all laws and proceedings for the security of person and property, *as is enjoyed by white citizens*, and shall be subject to like

46 Logan 1997, 32; cf. Brandwein 2011, 141, who reports seven.

> punishment, pains, and penalties, and to none other, any law, statute, ordinance, regulation, or custom, to the contrary notwithstanding (emphasis added).[47]

Despite the evident focus on equalizing citizen rights as between former slaves or their descendants and white citizens, the members of Congress, both opponents and proponents of the bill, acknowledged in debate that the language of this Civil Rights Act would or should apply both to native-born Chinese and to off-reservation Indians, the "domesticated" ones who "live in civilized society."[48] Similarly, the birthright citizenship clause of the Fourteenth Amendment, sent to the states in 1866, was understood to apply to both groups.[49]

In this same spirit, in the immediate aftermath of the adoption of the Fourteenth Amendment, when Congress in § 18 of the Enforcement Act of (May 31) 1870 re-enacted the Civil Rights Act of 1866 (to assure its constitutionality), Congress made it a point to extend the reach of the 1870 law in other sections. Section 16 now extended almost all of the citizen rights enumerated in that Civil Rights Act to all "persons."[50] This

---

[47] 14 Stat. 27–30 (April 9, 1866).

[48] Greenfield and Kates 1975, 611 n.40; 673–4 nn.52-5, citing Cong.Globe 39th Cong. 1st Sess. 498 (re Chinese born in United States), 599 (re: "every person of color"), 498 (re: "domesticated" Indians who "live in civilized society"), 572 (re: "Indians not taxed"), 573 (discussion of coverage by 1866 Act of non-reservation Indians) (1866).

[49] Cf. *U.S. v. Wong Kim Ark*, 169 U.S. 649, 721 (1898) (Fuller dissenting: "[I]t is not open to reasonable doubt that the words 'subject to the jurisdiction thereof' in the [14th] amendment were used as synonymous with the words 'and not subject to any foreign power' of the [1866] act." (Fuller is claiming that both phrases mean to exclude all Chinese from citizenship, irrespective of whether parents are diplomats, but he does not look at evidence in the debate cited in n.48 above.)

[50] Section 16 of the Enforcement Act of May 31, 1870, 16 Stat.140, 144, read as follows:

> And be it further enacted, That *all persons within the jurisdiction of the United States shall have the same right in every State and Territory in the United States to make and enforce contracts, to sue, be parties, give evidence, and to the full and equal benefit of all laws and proceedings for the security of persons and property as is enjoyed by white citizens, and shall be subject to like punishment, pains, penalties, taxes, licenses, and exactions of every kind, and* none other, any law, statute, ordinance, regulation, or custom to the contrary notwithstanding. *No tax or charge shall be imposed or enforced by any State upon any person immigrating thereto from a foreign country which is not equally imposed and enforced upon every person immigrating to such*

alteration, along with the addition of an equal taxation clause in the section, responded directly to concerns raised in a meeting between a group of members of the U.S. Congress and a group of Chinese leaders in California in June 1869.[51] The Chinese residing in California had been particularly aggrieved by rules that did not allow them to testify against a white person, similarly to southern (and California) rules regarding blacks and Indians prior to Reconstruction, and by onerous taxes placed specifically on them.[52]

In addition to progress in the national legislative halls, Chinese residents had reason to be encouraged by diplomatic developments in the executive branch and Senate in this time period. On July 28, 1868, the U.S. signed the Burlingame Treaty, which provided that "Chinese subjects visiting or residing in the United States shall enjoy the same privileges, immunities and exemptions in respect to travel or residence, as may there be enjoyed by the citizens or subjects of the most favored nation."[53]

Although the amendments in the 1870 Civil Rights Act did directly address the racial injustices to which the Chinese in California were being subjected, and the Burlingame Treaty appeared to show a national government unified behind the goal of decent treatment for Chinese residents, even the relatively radical Republican federal government of 1870 did not fully remove the anti-Asian animus from U.S. law. The 1870 Naturalization Act permitted naturalization for citizenship to whites and (now, for the first time) Africans; it pointedly omitted mention of Asians.[54] The situation for Chinese residents was to begin to worsen in

---

> *State from any other foreign country; and any law of any State in conflict with this provision is hereby declared null and void* (emphasis added).

In §16 Congress did not include in this list of rights of "all persons" the right to buy, sell, or lease property, which it had assured to "all citizens" on the same basis as "white citizens" in the 1866 Civil Rights Act that was re-enacted in Section 18 of this 1870 Act.

[51] McClain 1999, 564–7. Present at the meeting were Senators Benjamin Wade and Roscoe Conkling and the members of the House Ways and Means Committee.

[52] Ibid.

[53] 16 Stat. 739 (1869–71). McClain 1999, 562–3. On the U.S. side, the person chiefly responsible for negotiating the treaty was Secretary of State William H. Seward. Hune 1982, 8.

[54] The omission was deliberate; it responded to concerns expressed by the members of Congress from western states who prevailed over the advocates of color-blind naturalization. Hull 1992, 404; Kim, 1992-B, 10; Greenfield and Kates 1975, 674 n.55, citing *Cong.Globe*, 41st Cong. 2d Sess. 5121–5, 5150–67,

the mid-1870s, but at this point the federal government to some degree was standing by them, upholding the principled commitment to equal rights at least as compared to other resident aliens. For the Chinese, the glass was half full.

By the end of 1874, this changed. Earlier in 1874, Justice Field of the Supreme Court wrote an opinion on circuit, striking down California's law that prohibited any vessels from bringing "lewd and debauched women" into California.[55] In this *In re: Ah Fong* case, Field reasoned that the law was applied only to Chinese women and therefore violated both the federal Burlingame Treaty and Civil Rights Act of 1870: It imposed on shipowners a bond for landing each such woman, and this amounted to an extra "charge" not imposed on immigrants (however lewd or debauched) who came into California by land. Justice Field said that if California wanted to change the immigration situation, help would have to come from Congress. Within months, likely moved in part by this court decision and the lobbying from Californians that it provoked, in his December 1874 address to Congress, President Grant suggested just such help.[56] He pointed to the evil of coerced labor that took the form of "head-men" bringing in groups of workers indentured to work for them for a fixed period of time (so-called "coolies") and of Chinese women brought to our shores against their will "for shameful purposes."[57]

On February 25, 1875, Congress re-affirmed in a statute its determination against allowing Chinese people to become naturalized citizens.[58] A week later, on the final day of the outgoing Congress, March 3, 1875, Congress obliged President Grant, with the Page Act, the first piece of Congressional legislation restricting foreign immigration by nationality or race.[59] Republican Congressman Page of California (the bill's author

---

5168–76 (1870). See also, *Cong.Globe*, 39th Cong., 1st Sess. 1120 for an 1866 effort to remove racial discrimination from naturalization laws. The 1870 national civil rights legislation did not take effect in California until 1873. McClain 1999, 567.

55 "An Act to prevent the kidnapping and importation of Mongolian, Chinese and Japanese females, for criminal or demoralizing Purposes," 230 *Cal. Stat.* 330-331 (1870); *In re Ah Fong*, 1 F. Cas. 213 (C.C.D. Cal. 1874) (No. 102).

56 3 *Cong. Rec.* 3 (1874).

57 Ibid., 3–4. Census reports claimed that 70 percent of Chinese women in California were prostitutes. A recent historical analysis put a more accurate figure at 50 percent. Being a prostitute was legal in California. Abrams 2005, 654 n.56.

58 Act of Feb. 18, 1875, ch. 80, § 300B, 18 Stat. 316, 318.

59 Forty-Third Congress. Sess. II. Ch. 141 (1875). Park 2004, 63; Henkin 1987, 855–6; Abrams 2005, 510. On the impact of the Page Law on prostitution

and promoter) had been (unsuccessfully) sponsoring Chinese exclusion bills for years, and was to be the lead sponsor of the eventually successful Chinese Exclusion Act of 1882.[60] Witnesses who testified on behalf of the Page Act included some of the same people who had presented losing testimony in the *Ah Fong* case. Indeed, written testimony that Page introduced from California's Commissioner of Immigration specifically complained that it was the *Ah Fong* decision that now left California helpless against the "moral and physical decay" being brought ashore by Chinese women.[61]

The Page Act in its terms singled out for exclusion from immigration those persons from "Oriental countr[ies]" who were perceived to be in coerced labor situations (which situations included either being in an indentured labor contract—or being a woman "imported for purposes of prostitution") or who were (coming from any country) serving a sentence for a non-political felony. Immigration by imported prostitutes or by felony convicts was itself forbidden across the boards, but special inspections were to be instituted for [seagoing] "vessels" that might be bringing in foreign prostitutes. No special inspections were instituted for migrants from Canada or Mexico. As an additional indicator of prevailing sentiment, in the Republican Party Platform of 1876, the party for the first time took a stand opposing the "immigration and importation of Mongolians."[62]

Although at least one scholar claims that the law had a drastic impact, figures in other scholarship indicate that long before the Act, male Chinese far outnumbered female Chinese immigrants, and this stayed true until after World War II. By 1907 the percent of female Chinese immigrants was above what it had been in 1870 (which was 7.1 percent), and it stayed above that thereafter.[63]

---

in California, see Chan 1994, 13–17. On the Page Law generally, see Abrams 2005. There was an 1862 law outlawing the Coolie Trade, understood as regulating commerce in Chinese quasi-slaves, which explicitly stated that it could not be construed to apply to free emigration by Chinese people. An Act to Prohibit the "Coolie Trade" by American Citizens in American Vessels, Ch.27 §§ 2158-64, 12 Stat. 340 (1862), codified at 8 U.S.C. §§ 332-4 (repealed by Act of Oct. 20, 1974).

[60] Abrams 2005, 690–91.

[61] Ibid., 693 at nn.329–330.

[62] Ibid., 690.

[63] Lee 2003, 115–19; cf. Abrams 2005, 700–701 (claiming a drastic impact). Decade by decade, total Chinese immigration to the U.S. was as follows: 1860s—64,301; 1870s—123,201; 1880s—61,711. "Nineteenth Century U.S. Immigration Statistics."

NATIVE AMERICANS, 1865–75

Just as the northern-state-filled Reconstruction Congress acted in the 1866 Civil Rights Act to undo Chief Justice Taney's pronouncement in *Dred Scott* denying citizenship and civil rights to American blacks, so, too, the elected branches acted in 1866 to undo Taney's denial in the (1846) *U.S. v. Rogers* case that decisions by tribal governments to adopt people into a tribe would extend tribal jurisdiction over them (and would thereby remove them from U.S. jurisdiction). The President, with consent of the Senate, accomplished this by forming a new treaty with the Cherokee, this time a treaty granting explicitly that courts of the Cherokee "shall be allowed to retain [!] exclusive jurisdiction in all civil and criminal cases arising within the [Cherokee] Country in which members of the Nation, *by nativity or adoption*, shall be the only parties."[64] This treaty also freed the not inconsiderable number of black slaves owned by Cherokee and granted to these freed persons and all their descendants "all the rights of native Cherokee."[65]

This early burst of support for the rights of Native Americans evidently reflected the pre-civil-war overlap between Abolitionists (many of whom now were Radical Republicans) and groups who had opposed the Indian Removal Policy of the 1830s and 1840s.[66] Reflecting the same sentiment, Congressional debate made clear that the Civil Rights Act of 1866 should extend citizen rights to Indians who were born within the U.S. but lived among whites, outside of reservations.[67] Similarly the Fourteenth Amendment, submitted to the states in 1866, expressed Congressional concern for Native American tribal sovereignty in the phrases excluding reservation Indians from the citizenship and representation clauses (which were limited to "Indians not taxed" or those "subject to the jurisdiction [of the United States].")[68]

This enthusiasm, however, was short-lived. It appears to have broken down by March 3, 1871 when the same Congress that adopted the 1870

---

[64] *Talton v. Mayes*, 163 U.S. 376, 380–381 (1896).

[65] *Alberty v. U S*, 162 U.S. 499, 500 (1896).

[66] Hershberger 1999, 16 n.2 and 22; Kerber 1975; Portnoy 2005; Hershberger 2006, 528–9; Joy 2008; Magliocca 2003.

[67] See references in n.48 above.

[68] Greenfield and Kates 1975, 663–4, n.9 (Fourteenth Amendment was meant at a minimum to constitutionalize the principles of the Civil Rights Act of 1866, so they could not be legislatively abandoned.)

Civil Rights Act, legislated the following as a rider to the Indian Appropriations Act:[69]

> hereafter no Indian nation or tribe within the territory of the United States shall be acknowledged or recognized as an independent nation, tribe, or power with whom the United States may contract by treaty: Provided further, That nothing herein contained shall be construed to invalidate or impair the obligation of any treaty heretofore lawfully made and ratified with any such Indian nation or tribe.

This shift of policy was prompted by two forces: (1) The House of Representatives had tired of its subordinate role in policy toward Native Americans, wherein the Senate alone would approve treaties negotiated by the executive branch, and then the House would be required to vote for the appropriations demanded by the treaty. The House wanted a co-equal role;[70] and (2) In the immediately preceding years, Commissioners of Indian Affairs, including in 1869 one Ely Parker, himself a Seneca Indian, had advocated shifting away from a system of formal treaties on the grounds that such treaties had become a "cruel farce," in that by now none of the tribes "have an organized government of such inherent strength as would secure a faithful obedience of its people in the observance of compacts of this character."[71]

At first, the announcement of an end to treaty-making amounted to a change of format rather than of substance: Congress continued to base policy on agreements negotiated between tribal leaders and the U.S. Government. But the symbolic pronouncement that the Indian tribes would no longer be dealt with as "independent nations," all too soon took on the concrete reality of producing Congressional policies toward Indians where no consent from tribal leaders, or even ostensible tribal leaders was sought.

The postbellum Congressional burst of enthusiasm for tribal sovereignty was accompanied by a similar (and similarly short-lived) burst of enthusiasm at the U.S. Supreme Court. In 1866 the Court handed down two unanimous decisions, one penned by Justice Davis and one by Justice Nelson, upholding tribal treaty rights to be immune from later state taxation in, respectively, *The Kansas Indians* case and *The New York Indians* case. Both returned to the doctrine enunciated by Chief Justice

---

69 16 Stat. 544, 566 (1971), cited in Getches et al. 1993, 179.

70 Getches et al. 1993.

71 Annual Report of the Commissioner of Indian Affairs, Dec. 23, 1869, reprinted in Getches et al. 1993, 177–8.

John Marshall, "The language used in treaties with the Indians shall never be construed to their prejudice … ."[72]

The movement in national policy away from respect for tribal sovereignty as expressed via treaties, and toward plenary federal control over the Indian tribes, showed up in a situation of executive interpretation supported by Supreme Court decision, very soon after Congress formally ended the treaty-making process with Indians. An 1868 federal law had expanded the tobacco tax to cover all tobacco products produced "anywhere within the exterior boundaries of the United States," but made no mention of Indians. The immediately prior Cherokee Treaty of 1866 expressly guaranteed that within the Cherokee nation Cherokee farmers could market their produce exempt from federal taxation. Two months after Congress's declaration of an end to Indian treaty-making, the U.S. Supreme Court, on May 1, 1871, issued a four-to-two decision of the *Cherokee Tobacco Case,* to the effect that the 1868 law implicitly abrogated the relevant piece of the 1866 treaty, and could stand as such.[73] Amos Akerman, the Attorney General, and Benjamin Bristow, the Solicitor General, both of whom were active pursuers of KKK malefactors in cases involving black civil rights,[74] argued for the government (against the tribes), and Justice Swayne, a firmly anti-slavery Republican wrote the opinion for the majority. Justice Bradley (joined by Justice Davis) dissented.

The majority relied simply on a plain meaning reading of the statute, noting that having the law cover Indian territory had the side benefit of preventing whites from disguising themselves as Indians in order to avoid the tax. Justice Bradley's dissent acknowledged that under the *lex posteriori* principle a later law might abrogate a treaty but insisted that it was inappropriate to read such abrogation into ordinary legislation when the legislation made no mention of the treaty or of a conscious intent to abrogate it. At this point, Congress could still honor its treaties with Indians, but would have to put such provisos explicitly into statutes, in order to avoid inadvertent clashes with its own prior tribal commitments.

The background to this seismic shift in policy toward the Indians is the following. By 1850, the vast bulk of the Native American population had been moved to west of the Mississippi, peacefully in the North, but with

---

[72] *The Kansas Indians*, 72 U.S. 737 (1866); *The New York Indians*, 72 U.S. 761 (1866). Quotation in *Kansas Indians* at 72 U.S. 737, 760, citing *Worcester v. Georgia* 31 U.S. 515, 582.

[73] Three justices were not present for the argument, so not participating. *Cherokee Tobacco Case,* 78 U.S. 616 (1871).

[74] Foner 1988.

much violence and suffering and the use of the U.S. military in the South via the so-called "Trail of Tears."[75] As detailed in Chapters 1 and 2, the trail of tears was preceded by two contra-legal developments in the 1830s and 1840s: (1) John Marshall's *Worcester v. Georgia* insistence that treaties with the Cherokee prevailed over contrary state law[76] was flouted in several southern states that had legislatively declared all their Indian lands open to white settlement and ownership (in effect, legalizing theft of Indian property); and (2) Congress's stipulation in the Indian Removal Act of 1830 that nothing in the Act should be read as contravening existing treaties with the Indians was evaded by executive branch officials, and complicit ratifiers in the Senate, who found rump groups of Indians with whom to sign treaties agreeing to removal (which the Senate then ratified), such as the Treaty of New Echota of December 1835 for Cherokee removal.

The Jackson administration and its successors had contemplated that once the Indians were beyond the Mississippi, in Indian Territory, peaceful relations could prevail. Criticism, however, soon arose against this policy of separation, by which tribes had agreed to exchange their aboriginal territory for the combination of expansive western tracts reserved for Indian control "forever" or "as long as rivers run," and of annuity payments to compensate for the value of the ceded lands. As early as 1858 the Annual Report of the Commissioner of Indian Affairs was defending a new policy that would induce the tribes to accept smaller tracts of land, "reservations," which could be more easily guarded by soldiers and in which they would be taught to farm and receive equipment and livestock, etc., in lieu of annuities. This report argued that both allowing the larger tracts of land and paying annuities to Indians was a mistake. The annuities fostered a culture of dependency, and:

> We have no longer distant and extensive sections of the country which we can assign them, abounding in game, from which they can derive a ready and

---

[75] Felix Cohen makes the sobering point that, for all its real horrors, Indian Removal involved purchase from Indian tribes of virtually every acre, in sharp contrast to the policies on treatment of indigenous property in South America, Canada, and Australia. The U.S., having paid Napoleon fifteen million dollars for the right to rule the Louisiana Territory, then turned around and paid the Native Americans 300 million dollars for that property (exclusive of the cessions the U.S. reserved to the tribes). Cohen 1947, 34–40. Through almost 400 treaties, the United States has purchased over two million square miles of land from Indian tribes at an estimated cost of at least 800 million dollars. Ibid.; Wilkinson 1987, 8.

[76] *Worcester v. Georgia*, 31 U.S. 515 (1832).

> comfortable support. [Because the buffalo supply has been severely depleted] they must, at times, be subjected to the pangs of hunger if not actual starvation, or obtain a subsistence by depredations upon our frontier settlements. ... It is impossible, in consequence of the very great extent of our frontier, and our limited military force, to adequately [prevent these attacks, and if it were practicable, it would] leave them to starve.[77]

Whites were attracted westward by the mineral wealth of the Rocky Mountains and by homestead opportunities for farming and ranching. The destruction of the buffalo intensified as the transcontinental railroad was completed in 1869. In the years 1872–75 alone, white hunters killed nine million buffalo, taking the skins for commercial use and leaving the bodies to rot.[78] This combination, of determination on the part of whites (and some blacks) to move westward (encouraged by open borders for immigration by Europeans and by Congressional homesteading subsidies[79]) and a literal threat of starvation facing Indians, provoked an intermittent series of flare-ups of warfare between U.S. soldiers and Indians in the period of 1866–90 that culminated in the slaughter of 300 Indians at Wounded Knee.[80]

Apart from the conflict over land, aggravated by the clash of contrasting approaches to land use between whites and Indians, another obvious source of conflict was the massive degree of fraud perpetrated against Indians. President Grant and later President Hayes attempted to mitigate this problem by attacking the corruption among Indian agents of the government. Beginning in 1869, Grant turned specifically toward two measures to clean up corruption and malfeasance by the Indian agents. A ten-member Board of Indian Commissioners was established, comprised of respected philanthropists, who would exercise oversight over the Indian agents and over political relations with the tribes. Secondly, all Indian agents would be replaced by individual missionaries selected by one or another Christian denomination.

The goal was to turn away from the separation policy, which kept producing outbreaks of warfare (costly in lives and treasure), toward a policy of Christianizing the Indians and teaching them how to survive through farming.[81] These two goals, broadly speaking, would remain the polestars of Indian education, at least through the 1920s. Despite funding from religious charities and from the Indian trust funds, the money

---

77 Getches et al. 1993, 167, 174.
78 Boyer et al. 2008, 503–4.
79 Ibid., 514.
80 Ibid., 505–510.
81 Wilkins 1997, 51–2; Hoxie 1984, 2–3.

supplied to the Indians was never adequate for such things as farming equipment for the adults or well-equipped schools for the children. The schools were plagued, moreover, by massive truancy and discipline problems, no doubt exacerbated by the anguish caused by their frontal assault on Indian culture.[82]

President Grant called this new approach his Peace Policy, and he depicted its unacceptable alternative as looking to the "extinction of a race," which policy would be appalling to "all Christendom."[83] As with Asian-Americans, the situation would worsen in the 1880s, but in this instance, Congress made its first fateful turn in 1871 with its abandonment of the treaty-making process.

U.S. SUPREME COURT, 1865–76

By way of overview of policies adopted by the elected branches, at this point one can say that at the national level (largely through the truncating of the electorate caused by secession) the commitment to racial equality toward black Americans on the part of the postbellum Republicans proved firm although not entirely efficacious, until they lost Congress consequent to the elections of 1874. After the winners of that election took office, the remaining Republicans in Congress could not avoid their awareness that American voters, by and large, were ready to abandon the Reconstruction program.[84]

Toward Asians, the (northern-states-dominated) Congressional commitment during the 1866–70 period proved somewhat helpful although not fully egalitarian. Congress by the 1870 Civil Rights Act blocked the hostile legislation toward them that Californians had been adopting since the 1860s, but refrained from allowing Asians to become naturalized citizens. Prodded by President Grant in December 1874, Congress took a sizable step toward limiting Chinese immigration in the 1875 Page Act that in its terms targeted both contracted coolies and women "imported for prostitution," but which instead was enforced to block the immigration of all Chinese females who could not demonstrate themselves to be the first wife (in a plural-marriage culture) of a man.[85] One week before

---

82 See Hoxie 1984, 189–210 (Ch.6); Bolt 1987, 209–51 (Chs.8–9).

83 Grant, State of Union Message, cited in Wilkins 1997, 52.

84 Foner 1888, 555–6; Fairman 1987, VII, 180.

85 Abrams 2005, 701.

the Page Act, Congress re-affirmed (by omission) that Asians could not become naturalized citizens.[86]

Toward Native Americans, the policy in the year 1866 was respectful of tribal sovereignty, as displayed by the new treaty with the Cherokee. This changed by 1871. In breaking away from the treaty process, and moving toward plenary control over the Indians, toward which Congress would move far more fully in the 1880s, Congress and the President were abandoning even the formal trappings, however hollow, of dealing with the tribal governments as co-equal sovereignties worthy of diplomatic processes.

Where in this picture should one place the U.S. Supreme Court, the branch whose life tenure was intended to give it the independence from political pressure that it would need to "prevent serious oppressions of the minor party," according to Alexander Hamilton in *Federalist* 78? The Court took no civil rights cases in the war years; during the years 1865–71, it underwent an especially tense relationship with Congress. The Reconstruction Republicans in Congress harbored lingering resentment over the *Dred Scott* decision (opposition to which had been one of the mobilizing events for the party); they manipulated the size of the Court between eight and ten in order to keep Democratic President Andrew Johnson from appointing any justices; they feared that after *Ex Parte Milligan* 71 U.S. 2 (1866) (which declared unconstitutional Lincoln's establishment of martial law in those northern areas that were not a theater of war) the Court would declare unconstitutional Congress's policy of having military governors over the South until it was reconstructed; and they stripped the Court of its jurisdiction after it had heard oral argument in a case, *Ex Parte McCardle,* 74 U.S. 506 (1869), the case that pundits speculated the Court would choose for striking down Reconstruction. Then the Supreme Court decided the first of the Legal Tender Cases, *Hepburn v. Griswold,* 75 U.S. 603, (1870), missing two justices, only to decide to reverse itself within fifteen months, in *Knox v. Lee,* 79 U.S. 457 (1871) after President Grant appointed two justices who favored the federal power to issue paper as legal tender. In the wake of *Knox,* the Court was treated as something of a laughingstock for having made itself look so obviously like a pawn of political forces.[87]

The national-level judicial picture as to racial minorities is as follows: In the first dozen years after the Civil War, as described above, the

---

[86] See Act of Feb. 18, 1875, ch. 80, § 300B, 18 Stat. 316, 318, cited in Abrams 2005 at 694, n.335.

[87] Friedman 2009, 111–60; Warren 1922, Vol.III, 140–254; Lasser 1988, 90–92.

Supreme Court showed no inclination to constrain *Congressional* policy toward Indians, but *did*, at least in 1866, echo Congress's respect for tribal sovereignty, following in the tradition of John Marshall by upholding federal treaty rights of the Indians with respect to conflicting *state-level* law. When, however, Congress turned in 1871 toward plenary control and away from respect for tribal sovereignty, so did the Court. As will be apparent in Chapter 4, this pattern of both Congressional and judicial abandonment of respect for tribal sovereignty worsened during the late 1880s.

As to Asians, the California statute that as applied restricted the entry of (suspected) Chinese prostitutes, which had been declared unconstitutional on circuit,[88] came before the Supreme Court in March of 1876, after it had been superseded by the Congressional Page Act of 1875. Chy Lung, excluded from landing in the same group of women as Ah Fong (who were then held in jail until the ship could take them on its return to China and who won their release at the circuit court on a writ of habeas corpus),[89] appealed to the U.S. Supreme Court on a writ of error to have the California statute declared unconstitutional nationwide. The U.S. Attorney General argued the case on her behalf but California sent no one to defend its statute. It had no reason to waste money doing so, because the federal Page Law accomplished all that its own law had attempted. Chy Lung won her case and a court order to release her from state custody, but the reasoning that she was able to elicit from the U.S. Supreme Court could have only an indirect impact on the Page Law, at best. The thrust of *Ah Fong* had been that the California law interfered with federal control over both foreign policy and civil rights and had to give way, which of course left it to Congress to decide whether to enact the Page Law. Plainly, if Justice Miller for the Court were simply to reiterate the argument of Justice Field on circuit, none of what he said would affect the Page Act, because Congress has authority to alter foreign policy. Justice Miller, instead of stressing the clash with national power, zeroed in on due process problems with the statute:

> The commissioner has but to go aboard a vessel filled with passengers ignorant of our language and our laws, and without trial or hearing or evidence, but from the external appearances of persons with whose former habits he is unfamiliar, to point with his finger to twenty, as in this case, or a

---

[88] See discussion above of *In re: Ah Fong* (1874), following n.55.

[89] *Chy Lung v. Freeman*, 92 U.S. 275, 276 (1876).

> hundred if he chooses, and say to the master, ... These are lewd ... [or] debauched women.[90]

For this he would be able to collect either a bond of $500 in gold for each person the shipmaster wanted to land, or to arrive at any agreed upon sum with the shipmaster, from which he would pocket 20 percent and give the rest to the state treasury.[91] This lack of due process protection in itself was enough to declare the statute unconstitutional, said Justice Miller, but in addition, he detailed international diplomatic problems that could easily result from allowing such unbridled discretion to a California official who had financial incentive to judge women "lewd" or "debauched" who might be distinguished persons in their own country.[92] By linking the clash between federal- and state-level authority to due process problems with administration of the statute, Justice Miller sent a signal to those implementing the Page Law. The federal judiciary could not control U.S. foreign policy, but it did have authority at the margins to protect persons already in America, such that their liberty not be deprived without due process of law. The *Chy Lung* decision thus foreshadowed a pattern that was to become more prevalent in the 1880s and 1890s and early 1900s, where the Supreme Court would focus its protective energies for Indians or Asians on low-level administrators to gain for these groups some modicum of due process protection.

The postbellum Court handed down two little-known cases regarding blacks prior to 1876, and then two major civil rights decisions and one minor one in 1876—just months prior to the agreement by President Hayes to remove federal troops from the role of elections supervisor in the South, in order to obtain the Presidency.[93]

The two Supreme Court cases that dealt with black rights prior to 1876 were *Railroad Co. v. Brown* (1873) and *Blyew v. U.S.* (1872).[94] The 1872 *Blyew* decision (which involved an exceptionally brutal murder by a white man of several members of a black family) required the Court to interpret a statutory phrase describing the category of cases to remove from state court to federal court in order to protect the civil rights of blacks. One version would remove to federal court from state court any

---

90 Ibid., at 278.

91 Ibid.

92 Ibid., at 279–81.

93 Boyer et al. 2008, 496.

94 *Railroad Co. v. Brown*, 84 U.S. 445 (1873); *Blyew v. U.S.*, 80 U.S. 581 (1872). The Court also in 1872 refused on technicalities to review two KKK prosecution cases. For details see Goldstein 2007.

case where a black was a material witness and was denied in state court the right to testify; the alternative reading would remove cases only where the black person being denied the right to testify was either the accused, the prosecutor, or one of the two opposing parties in a civil case. The Court majority opted for the latter, narrower interpretation, perhaps swayed by the attorney's argument that reading it the other way would have let all the accused criminals of Kentucky jam up the (only) two federal courts in the state by insisting that they needed to call a black witness.[95] This ruling did restrict black rights, but at the time (a time when the electoral public was still showing support for the Republicans) neither the Republican House, Senate, nor President made any effort to revise the law to counter the Court's interpretation of it.

In *Railroad Co. v. Brown* (in November) the following year, the Supreme Court took a pro-civil rights stance, interpreting a federal law of 1863 that governed a railroad running through the District of Columbia with the following rule: "no person shall be excluded from the cars on account of color." The Supreme Court upheld a $1,500 damages award to a woman who had been forced to sit in a car of identical quality to the car for whites but designated for non-whites (the cars literally rotated racial assignment). The Court explicitly *rejected* the "separate but equal" argument presented by the railroad company and linked railroad segregation to the era of black servitude (thereby implicating enforcement powers under the Thirteenth Amendment). Justice Davis wrote the opinion for a unanimous court.

While some scholars view the earlier (April) 1873 *Slaughterhouse* decision as having purposely cut back on civil rights for blacks, the Court there in fact made a point of indicating that any racial discrimination in state law would violate the Equal Protection Clause.[96] Thus, up until the realigning election of 1874, the Court stood with the electoral branches as moderately supportive of civil rights for black Americans.

Two (March) 1876 civil rights cases, *U.S. v. Cruikshank* and *U.S. v. Reese,* are a more troubling matter.[97] This was the year in which the voting majority would in November favor the Democratic candidate for President and again vote a Democratic majority into the House. The vast majority of scholars see the companion cases of *Cruikshank and Reese* as indicating a judicial turning away from protection for black Americans, or at least as a drastic constriction of the force of the Fourteenth

---

[95] Ibid., 139.

[96] Ibid., 139–40; *Slaughterhouse Cases*, 83 U.S. 36, 81 (1873).

[97] *U.S. v. Cruikshank*, 92 U.S. 542 (1876); *U.S. v. Reese*, 92 U.S. 214 (1876).

Amendment, by means of the state action doctrine, and of the force of the Fifteenth, by insisting on allegation and proof of racial motive for punishing interference with the vote. Two rare exceptions among these scholars are Pam Brandwein and Michael Les Benedict.[98] Benedict stresses the point that the language of the Fifteenth Amendment on its own would (like the Fourteenth Amendment) seem to restrain only governmental behavior, not private misbehavior, whereas the Court itself in these decisions *extends* Congressional power under the Fifteenth Amendment to cover private miscreancy.[99] Brandwein uncovers a legal doctrine in the thinking of Justice Bradley, utilized by the Court of this time, that explains why the Court engaged in this apparent expansion of Congressional power over black voting rights.[100]

In the reading of both these scholars (as well as my own) the *Cruikshank* decision actually expands Congress's power beyond that

---

[98] Brandwein 2011; Benedict 1978. See also Nieman 1991, 99.

[99] Fifteenth Amendment:

> "Section 1. The right of citizens of the United States to vote shall not be denied or abridged *by the United States or by any State* on account of race, color, or previous condition of servitude [emphasis added].
>
> Section 2. The Congress shall have power to enforce this article by appropriate legislation."

[100] This doctrine of Bradley's distinguishes between two kinds of rights: (1) Rights *created by* the national Constitution are rights the federal government may and must protect against any attack, private or governmental; (2) On the other hand, rights of natural or common law that the Constitution simply *secures* are rights concerning which the language doing the securing must be consulted, to determine whether the protection is against interference of all kinds (as in the Thirteenth Amendment freedom from slavery), or whether the protection covers only governmental interference—state action (as in the due process clause of the Fourteenth Amendment) (but including, for the equal protection clause, "interference" with the equal protection rule that takes the form of "state failure to protect" a single racial group). Because the right to be free from racial discrimination in voting is a right created by the national Constitution, Congress must protect it against all interference. On the other hand the right simply to vote (as distinguished from the right to be free of racial discrimination in voting) is a matter of state election law, created by states. On this the federal government has no authority, except as to elections for federal office, where it may exercise plenary corrective authority, under the "manner" provision of Art.I, Sec.4. Michael Kent Curtis explicated this theory of Bradley's two years before Brandwein's book independently described it, but he disagrees with Brandwein's claim (see n.104 below) that the Court was endorsing a "state neglect" or "state inaction" premise for invoking Congressional equal protection clause power. Curtis 2009, at 1420–23.

plainly given in the Fifteenth Amendment, because it removes the state action limit from the force of this Amendment. In contrast, the decision does insist that the federal government, in its policing of state-level elections, is limited to punishing racial discrimination, rather than all election-related misconduct. This fact is striking because Justice Miller himself in private letters of 1866–69 noted the problem of southerners' unrestrainedly violent expressions of "fiendish hatred for the Negro" by attacks on "the negro *and Union white man*" in such massacres as took place in Memphis and New Orleans in 1866 (emphasis added).[101]

The *U.S. v. Reese* decision of the same day is puzzling, because in it the Court declared unconstitutional two clauses of the 1870 Enforcement Act on grounds that make little sense. The majority, over a persuasive dissent by Justice Ward Hunt, complain that Sections Three and Four of the Act do not restrain themselves to interference with the right to vote on racial grounds, but punish all interference with voting rights. But in fact (as Hunt notes) these two sections contain the language "as aforesaid," plainly referring to the previous phrases in Sections One and Two, "on account of race, color, or previous condition of servitude." I have pointed out,[102] and Pam Brandwein has similarly argued, that the Court may have been swayed by the fact that between Reese's arrest and the Court's handing down the *Reese* decision, Congress had in 1873–74 recodified the U.S. Code, eliminating the "as aforesaid" language. Thus, the relevant new sections did read as the Court majority was pretending the old sections read. The Congress may have been trying to stretch the Fifteenth to protect white southern Republicans, and the Court may have been attempting to force Congress to rewrite the law so that it again targeted only racially-based election interference, at least at the *state* level; *Cruikshank* made clear that Congress could regulate *federal* elections as it wished under Article I. Congress got the message. *Reese* was handed down in March. By June 23 the Senate had voted to insert the words, "on account of race, color, or previous condition of servitude" in lieu of the vague "as aforesaid" in the relevant statutes.[103] Because the House of Representatives was now Democratic, the bill died.

In sum, neither *Cruikshank* nor *Reese* significantly cut back on federal authority for Reconstruction, in principle, although they did require more carefully designed prosecutions and clarifying additions to two voting rights enforcement laws. And they required stiff standards of proof in

[101] Goldstein 2007, 135.
[102] Ibid., 144, text for and n.64.
[103] Brandwein 2011, p. 126, n.187. 4 *Cong.Rec.* 4057–4075.

prosecutions under the equal protection clause, insisting that federal prosecutors, at a minimum, demonstrate that the state in question was neglecting to provide equal protection to one or another racial group.[104] Because these Supreme Court decisions did set free a flagrant violator of black voting rights and a couple of racially motivated murderers, immediate popular reaction in the South was that the Court had become an enemy of Reconstruction.[105] The Republican *Chicago Tribune*, by contrast saw correctly that the decision did necessitate "further and proper legislation" from Congress, and that such legislation was by no means precluded by the decision but merely required a renewal of Republican control of Congress.[106]

One month after handing down *Cruikshank*, the U.S. Supreme Court handed down *Walker v. Sauvinet*.[107] (By strange coincidence, Charles Sauvinet, the appellee, had played a role in the *Cruikshank* case, having been the grand jury foreman at the original hearing where Cruikshank was indicted for multiple murders.[108]) The Supreme Court decision in *Walker v. Sauvinet* built upon the *Slaughterhouse Cases* (1873) and *Cruikshank* precedents. As *Slaughterhouse* had essentially interpreted the Privileges or Immunities Clause to carry no legal force, and as *Cruikshank*, had rejected the claim that this Privileges or Immunities Clause incorporated the First Amendment right of peaceable assembly and the Second Amendment right to bear arms such that they applied against state governments,[109] so *Walker v. Sauvinet* rejected the same incorporation claim as to the Seventh Amendment right of jury trial in civil cases. But this rejection of incorporation by the Supreme Court could work *for* blacks as well as against them. As it worked against them in *Cruikshank*, it worked for them in *Walker v. Sauvinet*.[110]

---

[104] My claim here is controversial among Fourteenth Amendment scholars. Brandwein's excellent book (2011) amounts to an extended argument that the Waite Court applied a rights-friendly "state failure" or "state neglect" approach to the Fourteenth Amendment from the time of the adoption of the Amendment until the accession of Melville Fuller to the Chief Justiceship in 1888. I have made a similar, though less fully developed argument in print, Goldstein 2007.

[105] Warren 1922, III, 330.

[106] Ibid., 329.

[107] *Walker v. Sauvinet*, 92 U.S. 90 (1876).

[108] Fairman 1987, VII, 263; Goldman 2001, 50–51. I am indebted to Alan Sager (Political Science, University of Texas) for this point and these references.

[109] This claim is precisely what several speakers in Congress had said the Fourteenth Amendment would/should accomplish. Goldstein 2007.

[110] Curtis 1986, 170, 179.

Walker (a white man) owned a café where the bartender had refused, on racial grounds, to serve Sauvinet (a light-complexioned black man) as a customer, in violation of Louisiana law. As permitted in the Louisiana law, Sauvinet sued for damages and was awarded $1,000 by the judge. Walker then appealed, claiming that the Seventh Amendment right to trial by jury in civil cases concerning more than $20 now applied to the states because of the Privileges or Immunities Clause of the Fourteenth Amendment. The Supreme Court ruled (as it had in *Cruikshank*) that Bill of Rights provisions applied to the federal government rather than the state governments, and that the Fourteenth Amendment had not altered this fact. Therefore, Walker had to pay his fine to the black man, Sauvinet.[111]

The image presented here of the Supreme Court of these years, as moderately supportive of black civil rights—more so than claimed in most of the literature—is buttressed by Pam Brandwein's powerfully documented argument that despite intermittent electoral losses of Congress, the executive branch Justice Department correctly understood that the Supreme Court was not cutting off federal prosecution of white malefactors but was simply channeling it into more constitutionally defensible modes. And some lower federal courts did produce convictions under the new *Cruikshank/Reese* guidelines. The Justice Department continued to prosecute southern violators of the Enforcement Acts, although at a much reduced rate after 1885, until a combined Democratic President and Congress got rid of the key provisions of those Acts in February, 1894.[112] (See Figure 3.1 above.)

While it is not exactly the case that the Supreme Court "followed the election returns," it is the case that the Court took pains to show that it would not allow federal power to be used without clear demonstration of state failure to provide equal protection, except in the instance of racially motivated interference with the vote. In that situation, the Waite Court was willing to move ahead of the literal words of the Fifteenth Amendment to allow Congress to legislate directly against private crime. Had Congress been of the mindset that prevailed in the 1866–71 period, the Court was leaving room for more carefully drawn laws to enforce Reconstruction. In the 1872–76 period, the President and the Court were actively upholding rights of the black minority, and the Congress in 1874,

---

111 *Walker v. Sauvinet*, 92 U.S. 90 (1876); Fairman 1971, VI, 1374–7.

112 The repeal act is 28 Stat. 36 (1894). Smith 1997, 383; Brandwein 2011, 192–203.

took up the expanded Civil Rights Bill that would open public accommodations to blacks and desegregate all public schools. The bill passed in the Senate but hit a filibuster in the House of Representatives. There, the lame duck Republicans, having been voted out decisively in the 1874 elections, before leaving office proceeded to drop school desegregation from the bill and passed the 1875 Civil Rights Act to protect equal access to juries and to public accommodations.

CONCLUSIONS

In the decade prior to southern secession and Civil War, all three branches of the federal government appeared to be taking extreme measures to appease the slaveowners: Congress passed the Kansas-Nebraska Act in 1854, reneging on its pledge in the Missouri Compromise of 1820 to check any northward spread of slavery; President Buchanan interfered in bloody Kansas, urging Congressional adoption of the pro-slavery Lecompton Constitution despite its having been voted down by state residents in January of 1858; and the Supreme Court declared in the *Dred Scott* case that the black man had no rights that the white man was bound to respect.

The North reacted by voting Lincoln into office; the South seceded, as it had promised it would in that eventuality; and the nation went to war. During the War, what remained of Congress, i.e., the Representatives and Senators of only some of the people, with the leadership of President Lincoln freed the slaves (of seceded states) and sent the Thirteenth Amendment to the states for ratification. Then, against the opposition of President Andrew Johnson (who acceded to office from the Vice Presidency), Congress imposed black suffrage on the South and insisted on acceptance of the Thirteenth and Fourteenth Amendments as conditions of re-entry into the Union. Before white southerners could manage through force and fraud first to outvote and later to disenfranchise black voters, Congress passed several Civil Rights and Enforcement Acts to protect the freedmen, and even increased the legal rights of Chinese-descent persons and of off-reservation Indians, and strengthened treaty rights of the Cherokee. By 1868 (with the tobacco tax) in the case of Indians and by March, 1875 (with the Page Act) in the case of the Chinese, Congress turned toward restricting the rights of these groups.

The postbellum Supreme Court led from 1864–73 by Chief Justice Samuel Chase, an abolitionist, interpreted two clauses of federal civil rights legislation, one favorably to blacks and one not. In *Blyew v. U.S.* (1872), the Court interpreted narrowly the civil rights clause at issue, unfavorably to the black litigant, but apparently in accord with Congress's will, since no faction in Congress mobilized to overturn the decision. By contrast, in *Railroad v. Brown* (1873) the Court rejected a plausible argument from the railroad company that a "separate but equal" policy satisfied the civil rights clause in question, and insisted on immediate desegregation of the railroad cars. Again, Congress made no effort to overturn the interpretation legislatively.

Supportive of the railroad company's argument that Congress would have been satisfied with a "separate but equal" arrangement is the fact that Congress itself in 1864 had created and operated (with supportive legislation in 1866, 1868, and 1873) a separate but equal school system for the District of Columbia and Georgetown. White children were to attend schools separate from those for colored children and vice versa, but the schools were all to be funded by property taxes that would be allocated to each school on a per-pupil "proportionate" basis.[113] Therefore, the *Railroad v. Brown* (1873) decision shows the Supreme Court to be acting against the symbolically denigrating character of a separate-but-equal segregation system to a greater degree than was the Congress of the day.

In 1866 the Court upheld Indian treaty rights against interferences by two different state legislatures. By contrast, when the federal government itself chose to legislate in contravention of former treaties, (as in the Tobacco Tax Case of 1871) the Court felt lawfully obliged to uphold the most recent federal policy.

In 1875 the Court struck down a state-level variant of the anti-Chinese Page Act with reasoning that implicitly outlined the justices' future course; while they could not alter U.S. foreign policy, they could and would (at least sometimes) check administrative violations of due process rights of Chinese descent persons by low-level officials.

After the lame duck session of March, 1875, Congress (with the House now majority Democrat) stopped adopting meaningful civil rights legislation for nearly nine decades. The Supreme Court, now led by Chief Justice Waite continued to be moderately supportive of civil rights for blacks. The justices did reject incorporation of the Bill of Rights, but this rejection operated race-neutrally, sometimes helping (*Walker v. Sauvinet*) and sometimes hurting (*Cruikshank*) blacks. On the other hand, the Court indicated that in properly presented cases, it would uphold prosecutions of not only state officials but also private actors for violating Fifteenth Amendment rights (*Cruikshank*).

---

113 *U.S. Statutes at Large*, Vol.18, Pt.2 1875, 33–36 (§§ 281–85, 294–311).

In sum, the postwar period of 1865–76, was one of massive legal (including Constitutional) change to support civil rights of racial minorities, most of it brought about while the seceded states were excluded from Congress or in a way that forced the seceded states to support the changes. The Supreme Court in this period did generally operate, too, as a protector of racial minority rights. For Indians and Chinese, it did so against state level laws, and for blacks, it did so as the enforcer of federally adopted law against private parties in D.C. and, at least in principle, against parties, whether governmental *or* private, who might interfere with the voting rights of blacks qua blacks in the states, and against whom indictments had been properly worded. The executive branch too, continued to be supportive of civil rights of blacks, by bringing prosecutions through 1877 and again with a Republican administration in 1879–85. In terms of support for the rights of racial minorities, it was the peak period for the elected branches (albeit branches with highly distorted geographic representation) until the mid-1960s. The Supreme Court did not outdo the elected branches, but it also (contrary to much scholarly commentary) did not lag behind them.

4. After Reconstruction

INTRODUCTION

Conventionally historians date the end of Reconstruction at the presidential election of 1876, or at 1877, after a special commission looked into disputes over presidential ballot returns from several states and granted the Electoral College victory to Rutherford B. Hayes, who had lost the popular vote (by the official count), and who then bargained with Democrats in control of the House (which had to certify the election result) and agreed to pull federal troops away from their role of enforcing election results in the South. But the national legislative shift away from Reconstruction actually occurred consequent to the election of 1874 when the voters changed the House of Representatives from two-thirds Republican to majority Democratic. The Congress that took office in March of 1875 began an eighty-nine-year period of Congresses unwilling or unable (due to filibuster practice) to legislate meaningful support for civil rights of black Americans.

The 1875–1910 period also was a dismal one for the rights of Native Americans and Asian residents or would-be residents of the U.S. Because policy toward these two quasi-foreign or foreign groups is plainly lodged in the hands of the national elected branches, and because these two branches were unfavorably disposed toward the rights of these racial minorities during this period, the Supreme Court was often loath to intervene on their behalf, and when it did (for instance via a favorable treaty interpretation), the federal elected branches had the power to override the decision and typically did so. The policy areas where the Supreme Court could be helpful, and sometimes was, were interstitial: The Court could rein in administrators who interpreted laws and treaties overly harshly and it could rein in state law that violated federal treaties.

THE THREE BRANCHES AND BLACK AMERICANS, 1875–1910

In the entire period from March 1875 until 1889, there was really no two-year period when Republicans controlled both legislative chambers and the Presidency. For the Congress of 1881–82, they came close; they won the House and the Presidency in the 1880 election and tied for the Senate. When needed, they could call on their Vice-President to break a tie, but Democrats could easily filibuster controversial issues. As of (March) 1875, the postbellum era of civil rights legislation was over. Any remaining national protection for the civil rights of blacks in the nineteenth century would have to come from the executive or judicial branches. And for about a decade some did come.

As noted in Chapter 3, the presidential administrations of Grant (1869–77), Hayes (1877–81) and Garfield-Arthur (1881–85) did bring hundreds of prosecutions almost every year against the massive southern campaign of violent terrorism against black voting, to the degree that Congressional funding permitted. (See Figure 3.1 and Table 3.1; the exceptional year is 1878 when President Hayes himself temporarily cut back on prosecutions in reliance on the false promises of supposedly moderate southern leaders like Wade Hampton and L.Q.C. Lamar that if the federal government backed out of the South, white southerners would abate their racial violence.) During the 1879–80 years, when both legislative chambers were Democrat-controlled and refused to appropriate funds for prosecuting crimes of voter assault and murder, not only did President Hayes veto several efforts to repeal the voting rights enforcement legislation but also his Attorney General, Charles Devens ordered his federal marshals to keep working with no pay until funds could be appropriated.[1]

The Justice Department, for its part, adopted a policy beginning in September 1876 that focused enforcement efforts on federal elections, where the *Cruikshank* decision (of March 1876) had indicated that prosecutions would more easily be successful. Since Article 1, §4 allowed Congress to regulate the "manner" of federal elections, prosecutors attempting to prove violent interference with voting rights would not have to prove a racial motive. The Administration prepared for White League violence in the South for the 1876 elections by stationing

---

1 Brandwein 2011, 144; Logan 1997, 32.

338 federal marshals in South Carolina, 166 in North Carolina, 745 in Florida, and 840 in Louisiana.[2]

Waite Court and Blacks, 1877–88

The Supreme Court under Chief Justice Morrison Waite (1874–88) did trim Reconstruction at the edges, by requiring careful cases to be built for convictions (thereby setting loose on technicalities some truly vicious murderers of southern blacks). Except for Justices Clifford and Field (both Union Democrats, the latter appointed by Lincoln), the Court was entirely Republican until 1888. The voting public, however, by the election of 1874 was tiring of paying for military rule over the South,[3] and fearful of what seemed to be an ever-strengthening federal government. Thus when the Court assured people in the *Slaughterhouse* decision that it would not treat the three postbellum amendments as having revolutionized our federal system, but would read them only as designed to free and protect the former slaves, the decision was widely applauded.[4] Similarly, the 1876 *Cruikshank* and *Reese* decisions of the Waite Court (see Chapter 3) were generally well received as having been carefully reasoned. They did not strike the attentive audience of the time (except for the small minority who were still militantly pro-Reconstruction by 1876) as shockingly callous, i.e., as they read to twenty-first-century eyes. In short, the Waite Court did uphold the basic principles of the postbellum amendments, but did so in a cautious, middle way that avoided arousing serious political hostility. The post-1876 decisions on the civil rights of blacks that were handed down by the Waite Court can be grouped into three categories, those involving voting rights, those involving jury rights, and two 1883 decisions: one on (supposedly) racial violence, and one on the public accommodations clauses of the 1875 Civil Rights Act.[5]

---

2 Brandwein ibid., 130–31.

3 Friedman 2009, 148: "One low estimate put the cost of Reconstruction at a quarter of all federal spending."

4 Ibid., 137–57; Warren 1922, III, 255–83.

5 Also in 1883 the Supreme Court decided *Pace v. Alabama*, 106 U.S. 583 (1883), unanimously upholding the anti-miscegenation law of Alabama. The Court insisted that the law could not be judged a denial of equal protection since it punished white and Negro perpetrators exactly equally and indeed required in the definition of the crime that one party be of each race. Because there was no due process challenge, the Court said nothing about which aspect of the public interest this law furthered.

Waite Court voting rights decisions

Waite Court justices participated in three important voting rights cases, in the years 1877, 1880, and 1884. All three sustained indictments. The first was a circuit court decision written by Chief Justice Waite himself (serving on circuit), *U.S. v. Butler*. It concerned indictments of ten members of a white rifle club for their participation in what Pam Brandwein describes as an election campaign in which white mobs (numbering 300–400) in two South Carolina counties "marauded across a thirty-mile radius for over a week." In letters to his wife during the trials, Chief Justice Waite wrote that it was hard to "comprehend such a state of society. Negroes … shot down in cold blood without any cause or provocation." The circuit court sustained four of the five counts against claims of unconstitutionality, two involving racially discriminatory efforts to discourage voting and two involving violent interference with federal elections, and, in the process of the charge to the jury, gave a gruesomely detailed account of the mass shootings that took place. The account included numerous statements by the defendants that the plan was to kill leading Negroes or to kill leading Republican Negroes. And they killed many. The jury (of six whites and six blacks) split six–six, so there was no conviction. But there was now a published opinion of the Chief Justice, the same one who had written the *Cruikshank* opinion, demonstrating that it was possible to bring constitutionally sufficient indictments alleging private interference with Fifteenth Amendment rights.[6]

Ex Parte Siebold (1880) and *Ex Parte Yarborough* (1884) were both prosecutions that relied primarily on the federal power to run federal elections in an orderly manner.[7] Siebold and four other officials of Baltimore, Maryland were arrested by federal marshals for run-of-the-mill election fraud offenses, such as stuffing ballot boxes, destroying filled out ballots, etc. Since the election took place in Baltimore, racial issues were very likely implicated, but they are not mentioned in the reasoning. The officials were convicted of such charges as (§ 5515) being an official in a national election "who refuses to perform any duty in regard to such an election required of him by any law of the U.S." After conviction they applied for habeas corpus on the grounds that as state officials they could not be arrested by the federal government. Bradley based his rejection of their arguments in federal power that stemmed from Art. I, §4. While state government had concurrent power to regulate

---

6 Friedman 2009, 145–7; *U.S. v. Butler*, 25 F.Cas. 213 (C.C.D.S.C.) (1877). See also Nieman 1991, 99.

7 *Ex Parte Siebold*, 100 U.S. 372 (1880); *Ex Parte Yarborough*, 110 U.S. 651 (1884).

federal elections, federal authority was supreme and was free to enforce "ordinary duties" on election officials.[8]

Ex Parte Yarborough four years later upheld convictions of nine members of a Klan mob for brutally beating a black voter, on *two* counts: conspiracy to interfere by force or intimidation with voting or with giving "advocacy" in connection with national elections (§ 5520) *and* conspiracy to deprive of a Fifteenth Amendment right (§ 5508).[9] The men appealed their convictions arguing that the Fifteenth Amendment restricts only actions by state government or by federal government (as indeed its language suggests) and since they were private individuals, not acting on behalf of government, they could not be punished under any federal authority. Justice Miller's opinion for the unanimous Supreme Court rejected this argument.[10] This Fifteenth Amendment aspect of *Yarborough* is often overlooked by scholars: *The Supreme Court unanimously in 1884 upheld the convictions of private individuals for interference with Fifteenth Amendment voting rights.*[11]

In fact, it is quite fitting that Miller be the justice who wrote the *Yarborough* opinion, for he was the justice who in the *Slaughterhouse* majority opinion insisted that there was an important distinction to be made between the civil rights of state citizenship and the civil rights of national citizenship. The latter, said Miller's *Slaughterhouse* opinion, comprise the "privileges or immunities of citizens of the United States." They are the rights "which owe their existence to the Federal government, its national character, its Constitution, or its laws" (*Slaughterhouse,* at p. 79).[12] Here in *Yarborough* he is insisting that "when Congress undertakes to protect the citizen in the exercise of *rights conferred by the Constitution of the United States*, essential to the healthy organization of the government itself" (viz. the right to vote in elections for the personnel of that very government and the right to freedom from race-based discrimination in the opportunity to vote), the federal government is plainly obligated to secure those rights against *all* threats, whether they

---

[8] Friedman 2009, 147–8.

[9] *Ex Parte Yarborough*, 110 U.S., at 656–7 and 665–6.

[10] He also rejected the argument that only the state, not the federal government could police national elections.

[11] Brandwein 2011, 14–851. Nieman 1991, 99–100 (unlike most) does say the Miller opinion "strongly suggested" that the federal government could punish private violence in any election that aimed to keep blacks from voting.

[12] See also *Slaughterhouse* at 77: "rights [that] depended on the Federal government for their existence or protection."

come from state law or from private action.[13] Because both these rights would not exist but for the federal government and its Constitution, the federal government must have plenary authority to protect them over *any* threats, private or governmental.

Jury rights

The 1875 Civil Rights Act from the Republican lame-duck Congress explicitly permitted exactly the kind of qualifications of jurors that the U.S. Supreme Court has been criticized by some modern scholars for having permitted in its 1880–83 decisions; these were standards facially neutral as to race but later manipulated at the state level to exclude blacks.[14] Its Section Four reads as follows:[15]

> That no citizen *possessing all other qualifications which are or may be prescribed by law* shall be disqualified for service as grand or petit juror in any court of the United States, or of any State, on account of race, color, or previous condition of servitude; and any officer or other person charged with any duty in the selection or summoning of jurors who shall exclude or fail to summon any citizen for the cause aforesaid shall, on conviction thereof, be deemed guilty of a misdemeanor, and be fined not more than five thousand dollars (emphasis added).

Qualifications based on individual attainments such as education or property or virtues of character, any of which might be relevant to capacity, were acceptable, but the birth-based attribute of race was not. In a trio of 1880 decisions, the U.S. Supreme Court aligned itself with these civil rights principles. *Strauder v. W. Virginia*[16] ruled unconstitutional a law of West Virginia that limited jury service to white male adults. *Virginia v. Rives* ruled that while, as a matter of rights, the "colored man is entitled [to the rule] that, in the selection of jurors to pass upon his life, liberty, or property, there shall be no exclusion of his race and no

---

[13] See also n.100 of Chapter 3 above. Brandwein attributes this distinction (between nationally created rights and state-level rights) to Bradley, who had dissented in *Slaughterhouse*. In my view Bradley had, as of the time of his *Cruikshank* opinion on circuit, accepted this element of the *Slaughterhouse* precedent and was building upon it. Bradley completed his *Cruikshank* Circuit Court opinion in June, 1874 (Brandwein 2011, 93); *Slaughterhouse* had been decided in April, 1873.

[14] For instance, William Wiecek writes "In three 1880 cases, the justices drew lines that invited subterfuge … by white southern officials and resulted in all white juries" (1988, 102–3).

[15] 18 Stat. 335 (1875).

[16] *Strauder v. W. Virginia*, 100 U.S. 303 (1880).

discrimination against them because of his color," there was no rule that the composition of any particular jury had to contain persons of one or another race, as the defendant was demanding.[17] *Ex Parte Virginia*[18] upheld the arrest and conviction of a Virginia judicial officer for the federal crime of excluding blacks from jury lists on account of their race.

In *Neal v. Delaware* the U.S. Supreme Court noted the presence of 26,000 blacks in a total population of under 150,000, by way of rejecting as beyond credibility the assertion of the Chief Justice of this state that the state refrained from assigning any black person to a jury not because of race discrimination but because the legal requirement was that jurors be "sober and judicious persons." Justice Harlan quoted the Delaware Chief Justice's claim, "that none but white men were selected is in nowise remarkable in view of the fact—too notorious to be ignored—that the great body of black men residing in this State are utterly unqualified by want of intelligence, experience, or moral integrity to sit on juries," and, Harlan added, "'The exceptions,' he said, 'were rare.'"[19] Then speaking for a majority of seven, Harlan concluded that the acknowledged fact of zero blacks on jury lists in light of these population figures made out a prima facie case of racially based exclusion, and the state chief justice's remark revealed a "violent presumption" of racial unfitness for juries by the selection officers. The state court's refusal to correct the exclusion denied rights secured to blacks by the Constitution and laws.[20]

And, finally, in 1883, the same year when it would strike down the rest of the Civil Rights Act of 1875, the Court in *Bush v. Kentucky* threw out an indictment for murder by a black man of a white girl on grounds that blacks had been excluded from consideration for grand jury service, pursuant to [unconstitutionally discriminatory] state law in force at time of the indictment.[21]

At least through 1883, the Court's jury decisions followed in good faith the civil rights principles entrenched by Congress itself. There is no doubt that state courts continued *after* the 1880s to manipulate rules for

---

17 *Virginia v. Rives*, 100 U.S. 313, 320–23 (1880).

18 *Ex Parte Virginia*, 100 U.S. 339 (1880).

19 *Neal v. Delaware*, 103 U.S. 370, 393–4 (1881).

20 Ibid., at 397.

21 Despite the U.S. Supreme Court's reversal of the decision of the Court of Appeals of Kentucky, and its instruction that "the cause [be] remanded to that court, to be thence remanded to the Fayette Circuit Court, with directions to set aside the indictment," Kentucky went ahead and executed John Bush for murder without any further trial. *Bush v. Kentucky*, 107 U.S. 110, at 123 (1883). Reinette Jones & University of Kentucky Libraries. 2015.

jury service, but the post-1888 Fuller Court was noticeably less committed to policing racially discriminatory administration of laws than the Waite Court had been even as recently as 1886 in *Yick Wo v. Hopkins*.[22] This latter Waite Court decision had ruled that facially neutral laws administered with racial bias violate the anti-discrimination principle (and also had extended the anti-discrimination principle beyond blacks, to Chinese residents in the US).

The misunderstood cases (1883)

The Waite Court decided two additional cases in 1883 that have been widely misunderstood by scholars, the *Civil Rights Cases* and *U.S. v. Harris*.[23] In the first, the Court declared unconstitutional the public accommodations provisions of the Civil Rights Act of 1875, and in the second, it threw out § 5519 of the federal code, under which members of a lynch mob had been indicted. Brandwein's book documents her explosive discovery about *Harris*, namely, that (a) both the lynchers *and* the people being lynched were white—confounding the treatment of the case, as white-on-black violence, by numerous precedents and by generations of teachers, students and scholars[24]—and that (b) a sheriff and deputy sheriffs were listed among the indicted members of the lynch mob—showing that apparently unbeknownst to the U.S. Supreme Court, the case in fact involved a good deal of "state action."[25]

A few scholars[26] (including myself) agree with the claim in Pam Brandwein's recent book that both these decisions struck down the federal law at issue *not* on the grounds that the law punished private individuals rather than state officials for violating the Fourteenth Amendment and that the Amendment restricts Congressional enforcement to the checking of state officials acting pursuant to state law or to custom having the force of law. Most post-Reconstruction scholars affirm that these are precisely the Court's grounds, and that therefore the Supreme Court was making it impossible for the federal executive and judicial

---

22 *Yick Wo v. Hopkins*, 118 U.S. 356 (1886).

23 *Civil Rights Cases*, 109 U.S. 3 (1883); *U.S. v. Harris*, 106 U.S. 629 (1883).

24 E.g., Kelly, Harbison, and Belz 1983, 366: "In *United States v. Harris* (1883) the Supreme Court invalidated an indictment of whites for denial of Negro rights on the ground that the Ku Klux Klan Act of 1871, the basis of the indictment, failed to respect the state action limitation … ."

25 Brandwein 2011, 153–60.

26 Benedict 1978 and Frantz 1964, for two examples. No doubt there are others, but this group of scholars is a distinct minority.

branches to protect blacks from private white violence interfering with their civil rights. Instead Brandwein argues that the Court in both these cases was propounding a doctrine of "state neglect" for enforcing the Equal Protection Clause. That is, the federal government *could* enforce the clause against private behavior but would have to specify in the relevant laws that such enforcement can take place only where either the state laws themselves discriminate racially or the executive or judicial branch is systematically *neglecting* to provide equal enforcement or application of the state law (including common law) to protect a given racial group.

There is plain language to this effect in the opinions themselves, for instance: "Innkeepers and public carriers, by the laws of all the states, so far as we are aware, are bound, to the extent of their facilities, to furnish proper accommodation to all unobjectionable persons who in good faith apply for them."[27] In fact, one of the several Civil Rights Act cases being decided in 1883 came from Tennessee, which (apparently unbeknownst to the Supreme Court) three weeks after the 1875 Civil Rights Act was adopted, had deliberately flouted it with the following statute: "the rule of common law giving a right of action to any person excluded from any hotel or public means of transportation, or place of amusement, is hereby abrogated[; the right to exclude …] shall be as perfect and complete as that of any private person over his private house."[28] The Bradley opinion for the Court appears to be faulting the federal law for not requiring evidence of failure of a state to enforce these common law rights as predicate of the lawsuit.[29] The dissent in the *Civil Rights Cases* agrees with the majority on the claim that equal access to public accommodations, such as inns and public carriers for all persons of unobjectionable demeanor and behavior was a common law right. Notably, Congressional debate from both proponents and opponents of the law made the same point: Advocates of the law saw themselves as providing federal enforcement to what had long been viewed as a common law right but was going unenforced in the South.[30]

27 *Civil Rights Cases*, 109 U.S., at 24–5; see also *Civil Rights Cases*, 109 U.S. at 17. In *U.S. v. Harris*, e.g., the Court faulted the law specifically because, "It applies no matter how well the state may have performed its duty." 106 U.S., at 639–40.

28 Fairman 1987, 554–5, 559 n.13, citing Laws of Tennessee, 1875, 215.

29 109 U.S., 14–15, 24–25.

30 E.g. *Cong.Globe*, 42d Cong., 2d Sess.3189-3190 (Sen. Lyman Trumbull); *Cong.Record*, 43rd Cong.2d.Sess.940 (multiple speakers). See also Bogen 2007. These rights in fact remained unenforced by the U.S. Attorney General after

Brandwein documents that these Waite Court decisions were so understood not only by the court but also by contemporaries; had Congress wished to, it could have tightened the language and re-enacted the statutes.[31] But politically speaking, times had changed. In the wake of the 1883 decision, many northern states, in fact, did enact their own laws to enforce equal access to public accommodations, irrespective of race.[32] Congress, however, had lost the political will to force such laws on the South.

Political Transition to and during the Fuller Court

In 1884, for the first time since the Civil War, a Democrat, Grover Cleveland was elected to the White House and started appointing a different sort of Supreme Court justice. His first appointee, in 1888, was L.Q.C. Lamar, a southern Democrat, who had authored the Mississippi Ordinance of Secession and had served in the Confederate Congress (then later in the U.S. Congress and U.S. Senate from Mississippi).[33] His second, also in 1888, was Chief Justice Melville Fuller, a former campaign manager for Stephen Douglas, and a man who as an Illinois legislator introduced a bill endorsing a constitutional amendment to overturn the Emancipation Proclamation and guarantee slavery against federal intervention.[34] Democrat Grover Cleveland won the popular vote for the Presidency three times—in 1884, 1888, and 1892. (Republican Benjamin Harrison won the Electoral College in 1888.) The combination of Cleveland's judicial appointments and the public mood (which apparently also shaped Benjamin Harrison's appointments) made the Fuller Supreme Court (1888–1910) the worst Supreme Court for blacks from 1866 to the present.

In 1889, the Republicans for a two-year interlude came back into control of both Houses of Congress and the Presidency. Republicans Henry Cabot Lodge (Mass.) in the House and George Hoar (Mass.) in the

---

1875 (who repeatedly ignored requests for guidance from federal D.A.s and marshals, except with respect to travel interstate on railroads.) Fairman 1987, 553 n.6, citing John Hope Franklin paper "The Enforcement of the Civil Rights Act of 1875," and 555 n.9, quoting Attorney General Devens on the constitutional import of the fact that "the railroad is a channel of interstate commerce."

[31] I concur with Brandwein 2011, that the state neglect doctrine is being propounded, but where she differs from Frantz's analysis specifically of the *Civil Rights Cases*, I side with him. Cf. Brandwein, 178–80 and Frantz 1964.

[32] McBride 1986; Finkelman 2005, 981–986.

[33] Abraham 1992, 140–41.

[34] Kousser 1992, 135–76.

Senate struggled mightily to pass a bill that would create federal supervisors to observe voter registration and guard against fraud at the ballot box, to protect the endangered black voter. It passed the House. The Democratic Senate minority then used the following tactics to first stall and eventually, in the lame duck session, defeat it (the Republicans having lost the House again in the 1890 election): first a filibuster, then a mass Democratic walkout to prevent a quorum, and finally Democratic success (by a one-vote margin) at changing the subject. The thirty-five votes to change the subject included five Silverite Republicans (two each from Colorado and Nevada, and Washburn from Minnesota) and a business-oriented Republican, Senator Cameron of Pennsylvania, who was heavily involved in silver speculation.[35]

In 1891, House Republicans (now in a decided minority) abandoned their efforts to protect black voters. In November 1892 the national voting public chose to put Democrats in control of both Congressional houses and the presidency for the first time since the Civil War, marking the second and more decisive popular turning point away from Reconstruction.[36]

The Democrat-led Congress of 1893–94, supported by the Democrat President Cleveland, took advantage of its political dominance by actually rescinding almost all provisions of the Reconstruction voting rights enforcement acts in 1894.[37] The Republicans, having dropped the civil rights issue and become completely absorbed with protecting business interests against the rising labor and populism movements, did not even attempt a filibuster.[38]

An unremitting campaign of violence, fraud and intimidation kept many blacks in the South from voting in the fifty years following the Civil War, and cost many their lives. Racial violence in the 1880s shifted in emphasis to the format of lynchings. Between 1885 and 1900, 2,500 persons were lynched in the U.S., mostly in the South and the great majority of whom were black.[39] After the federal prosecutions of 1885,

---

[35] Brandwein 2011, 182–5. "James D. Cameron"; "William Drew Washburn"; *see also* "William D. Washburn."

[36] Brandwein 2011, 182–5. The first was the congressional election of 1874.

[37] 28 Stat. 36 (1894).

[38] Brandwein 2011, 185.

[39] Franklin and Moss 1994, 312. For acount from 1882–1911 that includes a racial breakdown see Table 5.1 in Chapter 5. The overall total of persons killed in mob violence between 1882 and 1968 was 4,743, of whom 3,446 were black. In the worst year, 1892, 230 lynchings took place, again mostly of blacks. "Senate Apologizes …" 2005. The NAACP reported that between 1889 and 1918, 3,224 African-Americans were lynched. NAACP.1919 (rprnt 2012).

in March of which Democratic President Grover Cleveland took office, the federal government stopped prosecuting violations of the civil rights of black Americans. Not until the Republican Administration of Teddy Roosevelt in 1901 would they begin again.

Even more effective in shaping election results, however, were the legislative and/or constitutional changes that spread across the South in a twenty-year period, starting with Florida and Tennessee in 1889 and Mississippi in 1890. After Mississippi, the next states were South Carolina, 1895; Louisiana, 1898; North Carolina, 1900; Alabama, 1901; Virginia, 1902. By 1910, all eleven Confederate states plus Oklahoma had legislated and/or constitutionalized restrictions producing black disenfranchisement. These eventually disenfranchised nearly all southern black voters.[40]

In the face of this massive black disenfranchisement, even though the Republicans regained control of Congress and the Presidency in the 1897–1911 period, neither branch made any effort to invoke Section 2 of the Fourteenth Amendment.[41] This provision mandates in the language of "shall be reduced" (rather than the permissive "may be" or "can be") the following:

> when the right to vote at any election for the choice of electors for President and Vice President of the United States, Representatives in Congress, the executive and judicial officers of a state, or the members of the legislature thereof, is denied to any of the male inhabitants of such state, being twenty-one years of age, and citizens of the United States, *or in any way abridged*, except for participation in rebellion, or other crime, the basis of representation therein shall be reduced in the proportion which the number of such male citizens shall bear to the whole number of male citizens twenty-one years of age in such state (emphasis added).

Prosecutorial efforts by President Teddy Roosevelt's Justice Department in 1901–1909 to bring to justice perpetrators of anti-black violence provided the only bright spot in this dismal picture of withdrawal by the President and Congress from the black civil rights arena in this twenty-year period of 1891–1910. Not only did President Roosevelt call upon Congress to adopt anti-lynching legislation in his State of the Union message of December 1906 (and had publicly condemned lynching as

---

[40] Kousser 1974; Logan 1997, 348; Nieman 1991, 107. In Mississippi and Alabama by 1910, fewer than 2 percent of blacks were registered to vote. Ibid. Cf. Klarman 2004, 82, "Blacks were mostly disfranchised … before legislatures had intervened." Kousser's data shows Klarman's claim to be a substantial error.

[41] Klarman 2004, 38–9.

early as 1902), but also his Justice Department brought successful prosecutions against lynch mobs: *Riggins v. U.S.* (1905), *United States v. Shipp (I)* (1906) and *U.S. v. Shipp (II)* (1909).[42] *U.S. v. Shipp II*, where members of a lynch mob were found guilty of criminal contempt of court (for proceeding with the lynching, with the cooperation of the sheriff and deputies, after being notified that the victim's appeal was to be heard by the U.S. Supreme Court), is the only case to date where the criminals were tried by the U.S. Supreme Court itself.[43] These lynch mob prosecutions marked the only occasions on which the Fuller Court upheld rights of black Americans (see Table 4.1 below).

The Department also prosecuted with some initial success individuals who forced black persons into "peonage" (compelled labor to pay off claim of a debt) and mobs that were terrorizing blacks into abandoning their jobs. The latter efforts, however, were to be thwarted by the Fuller Court in the cases *Clyatt v. U.S.* (1905), *Hodges v. U.S.* (1906) and *Boyett v. U.S.* (1907).[44] Details on these unfree labor cases are provided below.

Indeed, apart from sporadic efforts, largely unsuccessful, by the Teddy Roosevelt Administration (1901–1909) on behalf of all three groups, Asians, Native Americans, and blacks, the big picture is that the elected branches' treatment of all three deteriorated sharply, starting with Chinese Exclusion in 1882, the Major Crimes Act of 1885 restricting tribal sovereignty, and the 1886 cessation of federal prosecution of violent or fraudulent mistreatment of black Americans. The two national policy branches, abetted by the Fuller Court, probably influenced by prevalent ideas about racial social Darwinism, accepted a system of extreme racial injustice and showed deference to the nineteenth century ideas about state-level self-government that effectively dismantled Reconstruction by the 1890s.

Fuller Court on Blacks (1888–1910)

The first Fuller Court case concerning the rights of blacks made clear this Court's willingness to roll back principles set forth by the Chase or Waite Courts when black Americans were involved. The Waite Court in *Hall v. De Cuir* had declared unconstitutional in a close vote a law of Louisiana

---

42 *Riggins v. U.S.*, 199 U.S. 547 (1905), *United States v. Shipp* (I), 203 U.S. 563 (1906) and *U.S. v. Shipp* (II), 214 U.S. 386 (1909).

43 Linder 2000-C; Curriden 2009; Roosevelt 1906.

44 *Clyatt v. U.S.*, 197 U.S. 207 (1905); *Hodges v. United States*, 203 U.S. 1 (1906); *Boyett v. U.S.*, 207 U.S. 581 (1907) (per curiam); Fiss 1993, 379–84; "Hodges v. U.S." 2006; Karlan 2005; Hylton 1991, 320, n.21.

that prohibited racial discrimination by any licensed common carrier while within the state, including vessels on interstate journeys.[45] There Chief Justice Waite had opined for the Court that the statutory obligation to desegregate accommodations in Louisiana on a sailing vessel that traveled between New Orleans and Vicksburg, Mississippi imposed an unconstitutional "direct burden" on commerce among the states, since Congress had chosen not to impose such a regulation: "If the public good requires such legislation, it must come from Congress, and not from the states."[46] Justice Clifford (Democrat) wrote a concurrence that added to the majority reasoning a lengthy defense of the idea that "separate" can be "equal" in matters of race.[47] Noteworthy is the fact that no other justice from the Waite Court endorsed this idea by joining the concurrence. By the logic of Chief Justice Waite's opinion, only Congress, not the states could regulate the matter of segregation/desegregation in interstate commerce. Yet in the first Fuller Court decision on race, this Court in 1890 *upheld* a Mississippi law requiring racial segregation on common carriers traveling within the state (in a challenge brought by a railroad that traveled between Kentucky and Texas, via New Orleans).[48]

---

[45] Schmidt 1984, 751, n.67, citing C. Magrath, *Morrison R. Waite* (1963, 140), notes that Miller, Strong, and Hunt voted to uphold the desegregation law but chose not to dissent on record. Justice Harlan surely would have sided with them but did not participate. So the in-chambers vote was four–one (concurring in judgment) –three (dissenting).

[46] *Hall v. De Cuir*, 95 U.S. 485, 490 (1878).

[47] Ibid., at 499–500 (Clifford concurring):

> Irrespective of the decisions of the state court, it might well be doubted whether the state statute in question does prohibit a steamer carrying passengers from having and maintaining separate cabins and eating saloons for white and colored passengers, and whether the denial to a colored female of a passage in the cabin assigned to white female passengers is a denial of equal rights and privileges within the meaning of the state constitution or the first section of the state statute in question, provided the applicant was offered a passage in the lower cabin, with equally convenient accommodation.

See also 95 U.S., at 501–6 (defending the "separate but equal" rule for both public transport and public, government-operated schools). Clifford's concurrence went on for twenty-six pages of the U.S. Reports (491–517). Waite for the majority took up four pages (487–91).

[48] *Louisville, New Orleans, and Texas Ry. v. Mississippi*, 133 U.S. 587 (1890). See also *Chesapeake & Ohio Ry. v. Kentucky*, 179 U.S. 388 (1890) for a similar ruling based on a similar argument; and *Chiles v. Chesapeake and Ohio Ry.*, 218 U.S. 71 (1910) for a similar ruling based on the argument that interstate common carriers were free to insist on segregated cars (as a matter of company policy rather than as an obligation under state law) so long as Congress did not

Justice Harlan in dissent, joined by Justice Bradley, pointed out the obvious: the two lines of reasoning were mutually incompatible. If the desegregating law that operated only within state bounds on interstate vehicles amounted to an unconstitutional "direct burden" on interstate commerce, then so must the segregating law that operated only within state bounds on interstate vehicles.

Fuller Court on voting rights and jury rights

The extremist, anti-black tone of the Fuller Court is vividly illustrated by one of its lesser known decisions, *Mills v. Green* (1895).[49] At the trial level of this case, a federal circuit court judge, Nathan Goff, a West Virginia Republican, sitting on circuit for the South Carolina district issued an injunction blocking the election for a South Carolina constitutional convention in response to a claim that the registration system for this election violated the Fourteenth Amendment right to equal protection and the Fifteenth Amendment right to be free from a race-based denial of the right to vote.[50] Judge Goff observed that the voter eligibility laws created hurdles justly termed "vexatious" and "harassing"; that they effectively prevented all later registration by anyone who had been eligible to vote in May and June of 1882 but had not registered during those two months; for persons who came of age after June 1882, registration was permitted only during the eight months following annual election day and registration for participating to choose delegates to the upcoming 1895 constitutional convention was limited to ten specified days in March of 1895. The rules required not only that all voters be registered but also that at every election they present a certificate issued by a registrar attesting that they were registered, and for obtaining a certificate, they required detailed statements of voters' residential histories since 1882 or since the date of eligibility to register and that these be verified by "two respectable citizens" who were twenty-one years old on June 30, 1882 or when the applicant became eligible to vote.[51]

The *New York Times* reported rampant fraud by South Carolina registration officials, in conspiracy with the governor, to keep blacks from registering to vote by simply refusing to issue these certificates and

---

explicitly prohibit it, and that mandating racial segregation was "reasonable" since it conformed to community sentiment.

[49] *Mills v. Green*, 159 U.S. 651 (1895).

[50] "A Whole State Enjoined" 1895; "Nathan Goff, Jr."; *Mills v. Green*, 67 F. 818.

[51] *Green v. Mills*, 69 F. 852, at 860–61 (1895); *Mills v. Green*, 67 F. 818, 830–32 (1895).

by the governor's firing anyone who did issue them to black voters.[52] Judge Goff's decision did not mention testimony about this fraud but did say that the complexity and seemingly pointless rigidity of the requirements could produce only one conclusion:

> If we may judge of what the intention of the legislature was by the inevitable result of its enactment, as we are assured we can, then the one object that controlled the minds of those who formulated the enactment I have been considering was how to successfully destroy the greatest number of the ballots of the citizens of African descent, while at the same time to interfere with as few as possible of those of the white race. *The fact is that, with a candor that was as frank as it was amazing, this was virtually admitted during the argument of this case.* It is evident that the effect of this registration system is to fearfully impede the exercise of the right of suffrage by the colored voters of the state of South Carolina. It to a great extent defeats their constitutional right to vote, and it seems to be its leading—I must be permitted to say, its only—object, the effect being to so legislate as to apparently respect constitutional requirements, but at the same time to stab to the death the rights and immunities guaranteed by them (emphasis added).[53]

Judge Goff announced that he found the registration system of South Carolina unconstitutional and issued an injunction blocking the election. This announcement, according to the *New York Times* story, "A Whole State Enjoined," prompted Governor Evans of South Carolina to issue a formal statement, which the *Times* story quoted: "The people may rest assured…that white supremacy in South Carolina will be maintained."[54] South Carolina at the time was 60 percent black.[55]

Despite publicity like this, and despite the specific allegation in the complaint that Fifteenth Amendment rights were denied, Chief Justice Fuller sitting as an appellate judge on the Circuit Court of Appeals that next dealt with the case made the following astounding pronouncement in his ruling that lifted the injunction and allowed the election to proceed:

> To assume jurisdiction … to protect the purely political rights of individuals, would be to invade the domain of the other departments of government or of the courts of common law … [c]ourts of equity have no authority or jurisdiction to interpose for the protection of rights which are merely political, and where no civil or property right is involved. In all such cases the remedy, if there is one, must be sought in a court of law. The extraordinary jurisdiction

52 "A Whole State Enjoined" 1895.
53 67 F. 818, at 832–3.
54 "A Whole State Enjoined," 1895.
55 U.S. Census Bureau, "Table 55."

> of courts of chancery [i.e., ones that issue injunctions] cannot, therefore, be invoked to protect the right of a citizen to vote or to be voted for at an election, or his right to be a candidate for or to be elected to any office; nor can it be invoked for the purpose of restraining the holding of an election, or of directing or controlling the mode in which, or of determining the rules of law in pursuance of which, an election shall be held … This bill of complaint cannot be maintained, for it seeks on behalf of individuals to restrain the exercise of governmental powers, and asserts no threatened infringement of … civil rights, and no recognized ground of equity interposition.[56]

In the view of pro-slavery Democrat Chief Justice Fuller, despite the enactment of the Fifteenth Amendment, the rights to be free of race-based denial of the right to vote and to run for election and hold public office remained merely "political rights" and not yet "civil rights," protectable by court injunctions. Since the South Carolina voter registration system "on the face of the acts in question" did not mention race or previous servitude, Chief Justice Fuller said there was no denial of a civil right.[57] As to the claimed infringements by executive officials of what Fuller was now calling political rights, these he said could be addressed without injunctions, by lawsuits claiming damages.[58] When *Mills v. Green* did reach the Supreme Court after the election for the constitutional convention of South Carolina had taken place and the convention delegates had assembled (which convention was to adopt provisions that far more effectively kept blacks from voting), the Fuller Court simply washed its hands of the matter by saying the issues about the old registration laws were now moot, since the election was already over.[59] In fact the convention had not yet adjourned; it ran from September through December, with the U.S. Supreme Court dismissing the case as moot in November.[60] The Court might have declared the convention invalid on the grounds that its selection procedures had violated the U.S. Constitution. It chose not to do so, without even acknowledging the possibility.

This set of South Carolina voter registration decisions received national attention; the *New York Times* article on the second one referred to Chief Justice Fuller's decision as lifting "Judge Goff's famous injunction."[61] The set of decisions gave a pretty unmistakable signal to

---

56 *Green v. Mills*, 69 F. 852, at 858–9.

57 Ibid., at 859–60.

58 Ibid.

59 *Mills v. Green*, 159 U.S. 651 (1895).

60 Wallace 1896, 351.

61 "Judge Goff Is Overruled" 1895. In *Wiley v. Sinkler*, 179 U.S. 58 (1900) the Supreme Court continued its head in the sand approach, refusing to provide

other states in the South that the Supreme Court would look the other way when southern officials denied blacks the right to vote, so long as the laws "on their face" were race neutral.

A similar pattern soon emerged with respect to jury trials. In a series of twelve unanimous decisions extending from 1891 through 1909 the Supreme Court refused to accept or be convinced by claims from blacks (convicted of murder) that their jury selection process had systematically excluded eligible blacks.[62] The Fuller Court rejected many of these decisions on procedural technicalities but when it discussed the merits, it took the viewpoint that the adequacy of proof of racial exclusion from juries was a "question of fact" to be decided by *state* courts,[63] despite the plain evidence in *Neal v. Delaware* that southern state officials might tend not to judge black qualifications objectively. In an illustrative sample of a procedural rejection, *Gibson v. Mississippi* (1896), the Court ruled that systematic racial exclusion from the grand jury was not a proper grounds for a request for removal to federal court; the proper proceeding was a motion to quash the indictment (162 U.S., at p. 566). So the Court let stand Gibson's murder conviction despite Gibson's claim that the county list of "competent," grand jurors contained 7,000 "colored citizens" and 1,500 whites and that for "several years" only whites were selected. Similarly, only whites were selected for petit juries. In sum, the Fuller Court, despite a dozen opportunities over nearly twenty years, set free not a single black convicted of murder by all white juries.

One of these jury challenges turned on the issue of voting rights deprivation, *Williams v. Mississippi* (1898). Once blacks were excluded

---

damages for the denial of the vote in congressional elections to a South Carolinian who claimed that he was in every way legally qualified to vote, because he had neglected to claim that he was registered to vote. He needed to have specifically challenged a refusal by South Carolina to register him, before he could go to Court for damages.

[62] These are *In Re Wood*, 140 U.S. 278 (1891), *Andrews v. Swartz*, 156 U.S. 272 (1895); *Gibson v. Mississippi*, 162 U.S 565 (1896); *Smith v. Mississippi*, 162 U.S. 592 (1896); *Murray v. Louisiana*, 163 U.S. 101 (1896); *Williams v. Mississippi*, 170 U.S. 213 (1898); *Carter v. Texas*, 177 U.S. 442 (1900); *Tarrance v. Florida*, 188 U.S. 519 (1903); *Brownfield v. South Carolina*, 189 U.S. 426 (1903); *Rogers v. Alabama*, 192 U.S. 226 (1904); *Martin v. Texas*, 200 U.S. 316 (1906); *Thomas v. Texas*, 212 U.S. 278 (1909) [affirming 95 S.W. 1069 (1906)]. Fiss 1993, 373, n.76 cites ten of the cases. A number of them were written by Justice Harlan.

[63] In *Carter* and in *Rogers*, the Court acknowledged both procedural correctness and significant evidence of racially-based exclusion but then remanded back to the state courts to decide the evidentiary question. Fiss, ibid.

from voter lists, their names no longer showed up as eligible to be put on jury venires. The Fuller Court showed itself to be just as willfully blind to racist maladministration of voting laws as it was to racist maladministration of jury selection proceedings.[64]

The Congressional debates on the Fifteenth Amendment openly anticipated, and explicitly accepted, the kinds of qualifications on voters (and, implicitly, on jurors) that were later deployed to keep blacks, along with many poor and poorly educated whites, from voting in the South. Congress, after extensive debate, voted down wording that would have forbidden just such regulations. The anticipated regulations included literacy and property tests, the understanding clause, the poll tax, and complicated and/or deliberately confusing registration requirements.[65] In fact, the senator credited with having drafted the final version of the Fifteenth Amendment, Senator William Stewart of Nevada, personally persuaded the Nevada legislature to ratify by assuring them that they could adopt non-racial restrictions (such as native birth) so as to exclude Chinese-Americans from the vote.[66] The one exclusionary device not explicitly anticipated by this Congress was the *administrative* barrier, notorious during the post-bellum century in the South, of blatantly discriminatory manipulation of the rules with racist intent and effect.

Both the regulations on jury service and those on voting—had they been *administered* with racial neutrality, which in fact they were not—were compatible with the Congressional understanding of how the Fourteenth and Fifteenth Amendments should operate. The Waite Court opinion in *Yick Wo v. Hopkins* (1886) seems to have been a general invitation to bring lawsuits on the unequal administration of such laws. Had the federal government been motivated to do so, and had the Fuller Court stayed true to the Waite Court's promise in *Yick Wo* that it would oppose practices administering laws "with an evil eye and an unequal hand" as to race, southern practices in the late nineteenth century U.S.

---

64 In *Rogers v. Alabama* (1904), the allegation was that the voting scheme that the Court refused to undo in *Giles v. Harris,* 189 U.S. 475 (1903) (case discussed below at note 68) had caused racial exclusion of blacks from grand and petit juries. Rather than undo Rogers's murder conviction, the Court remanded to the Alabama Supreme Court so that it would consider whether his factual claim were correct (the Alabama court had earlier refused to consider his claim on the grounds that his motion including it was "prolix.")

65 Woodward 1966, 141.

66 "Black Voting Rights" 1998–2005.

would have come much closer to protecting the civil rights of racial minorities.[67]

But this is not how things turned out. Instead, in *Williams v. Mississippi* (1898) the Supreme Court continued down the trail it had blazed with *Mills v. Green* (1895), ruling that it could not declare unconstitutional the exclusionary voting system of Mississippi under the authority of *Yick Wo* because the challengers to the Mississippi scheme did not (yet) have a fact pattern similar enough to that in *Yick Wo* or *Neal v. Delaware*, such that: (a) the racial minority was utterly excluded from benefits; and (b) the benefitted majority race did not suffer at all from the challenged statute. Then in *Giles v. Harris* (1903), when the litigants really *could* demonstrate such a fact pattern as to the voting registration scheme of Alabama, the Supreme Court nonetheless refused to rectify the wrong.[68]

In the calendar year 1902 white citizens of Alabama had been allowed to register, for life, *en masse* and blacks had been refused *en masse*, and in January 1, 1903 strict new requirements took over, which, if evenhandedly administered, would exclude a very large fraction of both races from eligibility to register in the future. The 5,000 black litigants, led by fellow African-American Jackson Giles, who had voted in Alabama for the previous thirty years, 1871–1901, (and who was literate) were asking the Court to declare void the Alabama constitutional provisions setting up the scheme, as violations of the Fifteenth Amendment. The Court in a six–three opinion penned by Justice Oliver Wendell Holmes verbally threw up its hands and said this is a "political wrong" of a sort that judges as such cannot correct:[69]

> The bill imports that the great mass of the white population intends to keep the blacks from voting. To meet such an intent something more than ordering the plaintiff's name to be inscribed upon the lists of 1902 will be needed. If the conspiracy and the intent exist, a name on a piece of paper will not defeat them. Unless we are prepared to supervise the voting in that state by officers of the court, it seems to us that all that the plaintiff could get from equity would be an empty form. Apart from damages to the individual, relief from a great political wrong, if done, as alleged, by the people of a state and the state itself, must be given by them or by the legislative and political department of the government of the United States.

---

67 *Yick Wo v. Hopkins*, 118 U.S. 356, 373–4 (1886).
68 *Giles v. Harris*, 189 U.S. 475 (1903).
69 Ibid., at 488. Pildes 2000, 299.

Here the Court was saying that only the will of the electorally representative government was powerful enough to remediate such a massive wrong. But, in contrast to a similarly overpowered John Marshall deciding for the Cherokee in *Worcester v. Georgia*,[70] the Fuller Court would not even declare that *in principle* the blacks had the Constitution on their side. Moreover, when Giles went back to the Supreme Court the following year requesting the more traditional and familiar judicial remedies of damages for denial on racial grounds of the right to register to vote and a writ of mandamus compelling the board of registrars to let specified, qualified black citizens register to vote, the Fuller Court again turned a deaf ear.[71]

In 1904, a group of aggrieved black former voters in Virginia attempted to attain Supreme Court support for their Fifteenth Amendment rights by asking for nullification of the official results of the Congressional election of 1902, on the grounds that the Virginia Constitution of 1901–1902 and the election procedures it established violated the Fifteenth Amendment. Despite the fact that this involved specifically a federal election, and the fact that the publicly available minutes of the Convention contained several explicit remarks by speakers to the effect that the goal of reforming the state's constitutional provisions on voting would be to prevent blacks from voting by means of empowering election officials to manipulate registration procedures in ways that eliminated black votes,[72] nonetheless the Fuller Court in *Jones v. Montague* (1904) unanimously rejected the appeal from this group, purporting to follow its

---

70 *Worcester v. Georgia*, 31 U.S. 515 (1832).

71 *Giles v. Teasley*, 193 U.S. 146 (1904). The Court's "reasoning" truly is beyond credulity. Justice Brewer wrote, agreeing with the Alabama Supreme Court that if Giles were correct and the state constitutional provisions in question were unconstitutional violations of the Fifteenth Amendment, then the Board of Registrars had no legal power, so their denial of the franchise had no legal force, so no damages could be owed and no mandamus could issue to them because they had no legal power to act. Justice Harlan dissented without opinion.

72 E.g., Delegate Carter Glass speaking on behalf of the reform said, "This plan will eliminate the darkey as a political factor in this State in less than 5 years, so that in no single county … will there be the least concern felt for the complete supremacy of the white race in the affairs of government." https://acluva.org/6931/black-history-month-ii-felon-disenfranchisement-an-open-wound/ (downloaded July 24, 2013). The Minutes of this Convention are available still at The Library of Virginia, 800 East Broad Street, Richmond, Virginia 23219-8000.

Mills v. Green logic that the case was moot since the challenged Congressional delegation had already been seated by Congress.[73]

Fuller Court on school segregation

The Fuller Court's most famous anti-civil rights decision was *Plessy v. Ferguson* (1896), upholding the Louisiana law requiring "separate but equal" seating on public carriers within the state.[74] In contrast to the railway segregation law upheld earlier by the Fuller Court,[75] this law regulated not only officials of the public carriers but also passengers, who now faced criminal penalties of fine or imprisonment for refusing to sit in the proper, racially-designated section. Thus, the law was challenged as violating the (implicit) Thirteenth Amendment ban on "badges of servitude" and the Fourteenth Amendment guarantee of "equal protection of the law." These challenges, too, failed.

The cavalier attitude of the Fuller Court toward the "but equal" aspect of this ruling shows up in two school segregation cases brought to it in the early twentieth century. The first, *Cummings v. Richmond (Georgia) County Bd. of Education* (1899), unanimously sustained, against a Fourteenth Amendment challenge, the county's decision to close its public high school for blacks, while continuing to run a public high school for white girls and to subsidize a privately run high school for white boys. The county's rationale was that there were three private high schools (not subsidized by the county) open to blacks, and the public tax dollars were more needed for blacks in primary grades. The second, *Berea College v. Kentucky* (1908), upheld (eight–one) a Kentucky prohibition against even any *private* corporation's operating a school where white and "colored" children received instruction together in the same time and place.[76]

Free labor rights in the Fuller Court

In 1901 the U.S. Justice Department (under President Teddy Roosevelt) indicted a Floridean, Samuel Clyatt, under federal anti-peonage statutes dating from 1867.[77] These abolished any law that maintained "the

---

73 *Jones v. Montague*, 194 U.S. 147 (1904).

74 *Plessy v. Ferguson*, 163 U.S. 537 (1896).

75 See n.48 above.

76 *Cummings v. Richmond County Bd. of Education*, 175 U.S. 528 (1899), *Berea College v. Kentucky*, 211 U.S. 45 (1908).

77 Sections 1990 and 5526, Rev. Stat. The Justice Dept. oral argument was presented by Attorney General William Moody, one of only four that he argued at the Supreme Court in his two and a half year tenure, and he told the Court that

voluntary or involuntary service or labor of any persons as peons, in liquidation of any debt" and made it a federal crime to hold in, arrest for, or return to peonage anyone, or to aid and abet someone's doing so.[78] The Fuller Court upheld the federal law as constitutional under the Thirteenth Amendment but released the accused because the indictment had used the wrong phrasing; the evidence showed Clyatt had held two men in peonage (which did violate the law) but he had been indicted and convicted on the charge of "returning" them to peonage.[79] Over a dissent by Justice Harlan, the Court overturned the conviction and remanded to Florida for a new trial. The local prosecutor was now free to indict on the more correct charge but would be taking his chances with a new jury. The "notoriously" predominant pattern among southern juries was to refuse to return guilty charges for holding blacks in peonage, no matter how overwhelming the evidence.[80]

The Fuller Court again heard a peonage case in 1908 and again failed to act in a way that either helped the victims or punished the perpetrator. In this case Bailey (the debtor), imprisoned prior to trial in accord with Alabama's peonage statute, had requested a writ of habeas corpus on the grounds that the state law in question was unconstitutional under the Thirteenth Amendment. His plea had been denied by the trial court and then by the Supreme Court of Alabama. The statute in question treated as intentional larceny any failure to pay off a debt as specified in the debt contract, and subjected the debtor to compulsory labor to pay off both the debt and a fine. The Fuller Court allowed the Teddy Roosevelt Justice Department to file an *amicus* brief, which argued that the Alabama laws also violated the federal anti-peonage law of 1867. The Court then ruled seven–two that granting the writ would be premature, that Bailey was obliged to await his conviction for violation of the law and then would be able to appeal again on a writ of error. Harlan again wrote the dissent.[81]

As the Clyatt case was winding its way through the courts, the Teddy Roosevelt Administration in 1903 brought charges in two cases of white

---

the Administration had more than 100 peonage prosecutions pending since 1901. Roosevelt was to appoint him to the Supreme Court in 1906. Moody had to resign from the Court due to illness in the fall of 1910, before *Bailey II* was decided. Schmidt 1984, 31–2, 48, 838.

78 Ibid.

79 *Clyatt v. United States*, 197 U.S. 207 (1905).

80 Schmidt 1984, 831, quoting (for "notoriously") *Report of the Attorney General* of 1908 (at 6) and 1910 statement in *Anderson* [South Carolina] *Daily Mail, Apr.29.*

81 *Bailey v. Alabama,* 211 U.S. 452 (1908).

gang violence aimed at keeping blacks out of well-paying jobs. The first, *U.S. v. Morris,* charged eleven whites with intimidating black sharecroppers; the jury did not convict. The second, *U.S. v. Maples,* charged fifteen white men with intimidating eight black sawmill workers into leaving their jobs, and the jury convicted three. The charge was violation of §§ 1977 and 5508, Rev. Statutes, by conspiring to use violence and threats to deprive eight named black Americans of the Thirteenth Amendment right to contract freely to dispose of their labor. The appeal of this case became the 1906 Supreme Court case, *Hodges v. U.S.*[82]

The Thirteenth Amendment makes no mention of state action. Nonetheless, the Fuller Court invented a state action requirement to release the convicts in both *Hodges v. U.S.* and in a similar federal prosecution, *Boyett v. U.S.* (1907), which concerned white violence against black railroad workers.[83] In both, the Court ruled that efforts by private persons to intimidate blacks through violence into abandoning specific well-paying jobs could not be reached by Congress's Thirteenth Amendment enforcement power.

ASIANS IN THE POLITICAL AND JUDICIAL BRANCHES, 1876–1910

The brief postbellum good news for the Chinese in California, represented by the responsiveness to their concerns in the 1866 grant of birthright citizenship, in the Burlingame Treaty of 1868 and in the wording of Section 16 of the 1870 Enforcement Act (see Chapter 3 for details), quickly gave way to disappointing developments in Washington. After numerous California laws mistreating the Chinese were struck down by state and federal courts during the postbellum decade, anti-Chinese lobbyists and Congress members from California pressed within Congress and in solicitation at the State Department for changes to the Burlingame Treaty, and the pressure yielded results in both party conventions' platforms of 1876.[84] Anti-Chinese forces first struck paydirt in December 1874 in the carefully tailored request to Congress from President Grant that Congress restrict immigration by groups subject to coerced labor; these were understood to be Chinese males under indentured service contracts and Chinese females being imported by persons

---

[82] *Hodges v. U.S.,* 203 U.S. 1 (1906). Fiss 1993, 379–84; "*Hodges v. U.S*" 2006; Karlan 2005.

[83] 207 U.S. 581.

[84] Hune 1982, 8–10.

who controlled them, to work as prostitutes. The outgoing Congress complied with the request with the March, 1875 Page Act, which is detailed in Chapter 3.

Discriminatory local legislation was not the only mistreatment encountered by the Chinese in the western U.S. A major riot broke out in Los Angeles in 1871 that left nineteen Chinese dead. In the same year an attempt to burn down the Chinatown in Chico, California produced four Chinese deaths. Other anti-Chinese violence was sporadic around the West and reached epidemic proportions in the mid-1880s.[85]

Congressional commitment to honoring the Burlingame Treaty (which gave to Chinese "most favored nation" immigration status) was gone by 1879. The House and Senate (both Democratic) voted for a bill that would abrogate in part the Burlingame Treaty by limiting any vessel from bringing more than fifteen Chinese persons into the U.S. The Democrats heavily favored the bill and the Republicans slightly opposed it, in each house. President Hayes successfully vetoed it as a violation of his treaty obligations and against the national interest. In his diary he lamented America's disappointing past treatment of "other weaker races" as well, such as "Negroes and Indians."[86]

Anti-Chinese riots were becoming more numerous in the western states, and the Chinese Government responded by exerting diplomatic pressure for protection of their subjects and compensation for destroyed property. In this setting, the President's ability to stand on principle (or to prioritize diplomatic concerns over domestic electoral benefit) gradually weakened. Both parties again pledged in the 1880 election to do something about the Chinese "problem," as did the Greenback-Labor Party, and, this time, both Republican candidate James Garfield (the current Vice-President) and his Democratic opponent endorsed a restriction of immigration. In November 1880, the U.S. and China signed a modification of the Burlingame Treaty that permitted the U.S. to adopt "reasonable" regulation, limitation, or suspension of immigration by Chinese laborers when the U.S. Government considered such immigration or residence a threat to the national interest or to "good order." Present Chinese residents of the U.S. were to be protected. Garfield won

[85] McClain 1985, 352–8; Park 2004, 79. For one non-comprehensive list of such incidents, see the website of the Chinese in Northwest America Research Committee. http://www.cinarc.org/Violence.html#anchor_101 (downloaded May 5, 2011). Congress eventually, without admitting liability, appropriated a total of some $425,000 to compensate survivors of anti-Chinese pogroms. The Chinese consulate distributed the funds. McClain, ibid., 373.

[86] Hune 1982, 10–15.

the election and, like Hayes before him, did not mention the Chinese issue in his inaugural. He was assassinated some months later, and his successor Chester A. Arthur delivered an annual message in December of 1881 that was the first presidential message in forty years not to mention the South; it endorsed restricting Chinese immigration.[87]

Congressional legislation swiftly followed, to suspend immigration by Chinese laborers for a twenty-year period. President Arthur vetoed it on grounds similar to those of its Congressional opponents. The length of time violated the "reasonable" requirement of the new treaty and was not in the national interest because unforeseen labor shortages could arise that would necessitate Chinese labor in sooner than twenty years. Congress then easily passed the Exclusion Act of 1882, suspending immigration by Chinese laborers for ten years and also denying entry to this country for wives of current Chinese laborer residents. (The only significant opposition within Congress came from the Northeast.) The act also restricted travel in and out of the U.S. by resident Chinese laborers, mandating that lists be kept of all leaving the country and that special identity cards be issued upon their exit, which cards would be required to be shown for re-entry. And despite the implicit prohibition already in the laws of 1870 and 1875, this Act also specifically forbade naturalization to American citizenship of a Chinese subject. President Arthur signed this bill.[88]

Matters quickly worsened in the elected branches. Over the next dozen years Congress continued to further restrict Chinese immigration. In July, 1884 Congress tightened the language of the sections of the 1882 Act regulating re-entry by Chinese residents and also specified that for non-laborers the only permissible evidence authorizing entry to the U.S. had to be a certificate issued by a Chinese official and visaed by the U.S. Consul in Canton or Hong Kong. Then in quick succession, on September 13 and October 1, 1888, Congress passed laws (the Scott Act) forbidding the return to the U.S. of Chinese *resident* laborers who left the country. The first act was to become valid upon signature by China of a new treaty, but a rumor in a British newspaper that China refused the treaty prompted the second version of the law on October 1. This Act bluntly declared that any Chinese laborer who *had* left the country and was not back on October 1 could never return. Existing return permission

---

87 Ibid., 16–17. Kim 1992-B, 11.

88 Kim, ibid., 11–12; Hune 1982,17–22; Chan 1994, 18-20. *Chew Heong v U.S.*, 112 U.S. 536 (1884). Smith 1997, 370 notes that the reason for explicitly banning Chinese naturalization is that doubts had arisen in some quarters as to whether Chinese should count as "white."

certificates were declared void. The estimate is that this stranded 20,000 Chinese residents outside their U.S. homeland. These acts apparently resulted from the fact that anti-Chinese sentiment was strong enough to sway elections and this was a presidential-election year.[89]

The Scott Act endured, although narrowly amended by treaty with China in 1894. The amendment (the negotiation of which was a rare and minimal act of presidential diplomatic intervention on behalf of the Chinese in this period) exempted from the ban any returning laborer who had a "wife, child or parent" lawfully in the U.S. or property here worth $1,000. The wife had to have been already cohabiting with him in the U.S. for at least a year before the request for the return permit. This exemption had been in the first version of the Scott Act, in the treaty that China delayed ratifying.[90]

The Supreme Court under Chief Justice Waite at first tried to hold the line against such measures. The case of *Chew Heong v. U.S.* (1884),[91] was argued in October of 1884, just prior to the presidential election in which Democrat Grover Cleveland was about to defeat Chester A. Arthur. The Arthur Justice Department took a hard line in the case, arguing that the 1884 exclusion should be applied to keep out a Chinese laborer who had been a lawful U.S. resident at the time of the 1880 Treaty (allowing for "reasonable" regulations of Chinese laborers here), but who had left the country prior to the enactment of the 1882 rule requiring a special identity card for re-entry and who had attempted to re-enter after the July 1884 amendments to the 1882 Act. Because Chew Heong was out of the U.S. (residing in the then-kingdom of Hawaii) from June 1881 to September 1884, there was no procedure available by which he could have obtained the required re-entry ID card.

Justice Harlan authored a seven–two opinion (with dissents from Bradley and from Field, the lone Californian) to the effect that courts were obligated to interpret statutes if at all possible as not conflicting with prior treaties and that so interpreted, various exceptions in the 1882 and 1884 Acts covered Heong and allowed for his re-entry. Dissenting Justice Field insisted to the contrary that it was "impossible from [the statute's] language" (112 U.S., at p. 574) to draw from it the meaning the Court majority claimed it was drawing. He wrote a lengthy dissent, defending the change in China policy from the Burlingame (1868) to the

89 *U.S. v. Chew Heong*, 112 U.S. 536 (1884); *Chae Chan Ping v. U.S.* (aka "The Chinese Exclusion Case"), 130 U.S. 581, 599 (1889); Chan, ibid., 20–22; Odo 2002, 84–6; Smith 1997 363; Park 2004, 81.

90 Salyer 1989, 97; MacMurray 1921; "Scott Act" 1998–1999.

91 *U.S. v. Chew Heong*, 112 U.S. 536 (1884).

1880 Treaty, claiming that the Burlingame Treaty had unfairly offered far more benefit to the Chinese than to Americans, and, if left unaltered, would ruin the U.S:

> Thoughtful persons … exempt from race prejudices saw, in … [easing travel between the two countries], the certainty at no distant day that from the unnumbered millions on the opposite shores of the Pacific, vast hordes would pour in upon us, overrunning our coast and controlling its institutions. A restriction upon their further immigration was felt to be necessary to prevent the degradation of white labor and to preserve to ourselves the inestimable benefits of our Christian civilization (112 U.S., at 569).

Justice Bradley's dissent was both more measured and more to the point than Field's (refraining from political diatribe on China policy). He acknowledged that there was some wording in the 1884 amendments that gave rise to the majority's reading of the Act but he insisted that this language must have been "inadvertent" (at p. 579), because "the whole tenor of the act" went in a different direction and deprived Chew Heong of the entry permission he was seeking.

The Supreme Court under Chief Justice Waite, in *Yick Wo v. Hopkins* (1886), also managed to establish, at least for domestic purposes, the principle, that the Equal Protection Clause of the Fourteenth Amendment rendered void any state law discriminating against a single nationality group (or race), whether the discrimination appeared on the face of the statute or simply in a discriminatory enforcement pattern. A California law restricting the operation of laundries in wooden buildings in San Francisco county or city had been demonstrated by overwhelming proof to have been enforced against Chinese operators of such laundries but not white operators of them. Famously saying that state laws "administered by public authority with an evil eye and an unequal hand" violate the equal protection clause, just as do laws discriminating on their face, the Court struck down the ordinance.[92]

In 1887 Chief Justice Waite wrote an opinion (Harlan dissenting) that was more typical of the Waite Court's middle-ground posture toward racial minorities. Citing the 1883 *Harris* precedent (see discussion above), the Court in *Baldwin v. Franks* refused to allow the federal government to use § 5519 to prosecute mob violence against Chinese residents in California. The Court said that while Congress *could* enact a not-unconstitutional provision for protecting rights that resident foreigners have under treaties, this statute had already been struck down as to its

---

[92] *Yick Wo v. Hopkins*, 118 U.S. 356, 373–4 (1886).

application to Americans within a state, so could no longer be used.[93] Congress was free to act to protect Chinese residents from targeted attacks within states, but had not yet done so.

In its final Asian rights decision, in February of 1888, the Waite Court again restrained administrative excess, as it had in *Chew Heong,* and again ordered the executive branch to allow back into the U.S. a bona fide lawful, resident (laborer) alien, Jung Ah Lung, despite his lacking the required paperwork. Jung Ah Lung had left for a visit to China in 1883, taking with him the proper certificate of identity demanded in the 1882 law. While he was en route, pirates had boarded the ship and stolen his identity paper. Congress revised the law during his absence, legislating that this ID paper was "the only evidence permissible" to establish a re-entry right. Nonetheless, since his physical description matched in every respect the description in his registration papers on record with customs officials, the Court ruled six–three that the substantive proof of his identity outweighed the procedural technicality and he had a right to return to his U.S. home.[94]

In a practical sense, the Scott Act of 1888 amounted to an overruling of the Court's 1884 *Chew Heong* and 1888 *Jung Ah Lung* decisions. Congress left no ambiguity as to its intent. Once it was enacted, irrespective of when a Chinese laborer left the U.S. and irrespective of documentation, none who left could re-enter the U.S.

After Chief Justice Fuller replaced Chief Justice Waite, the U.S. Supreme Court upheld the Scott Act, despite acknowledging that it conflicted with existing treaty law. In *Chae Chan Ping v. U.S.* (aka "The Chinese Exclusion Case") (1889), Justice Field now wrote for the unanimous Court, that Congress is free to abrogate a treaty: "the last expression of the sovereign will must control."[95] In the course of the Court opinion, Justice Field endorsed numerous ethnic slurs against the Chinese en masse (as he had done in dissent in *Chew Heong*), as though to justify Congress's choice.

> They were generally industrious and frugal … their expenses were small; and they were content with the simplest fare, such as would not suffice for our laborers and artisans. The competition between them and our people was for this reason altogether in their favor … . [R]esiding apart by themselves, and

---

[93] *Baldwin v. Franks*, 120 U.S. 678, at 683, 685–686. The Court allowed that the statute would be valid within federal territory, just not within states.

[94] *U.S. v. Jung Ah Lung*, 124 U.S. 621, 627–31 (1888); Kim 1992-B, 13–14.

[95] Odo 2002, 84, 87–8. *Chae Chan Ping*, 130 U.S. 581, 600 (1889). Park 2004, 81.

> adhering to the[ir] customs … It seemed impossible for them to assimilate with our people … [California claims] the presence of Chinese laborers had a baneful effect upon … public morals … [T]heir immigration was … a menace to our civilization. … [The enforcement of the 1880 Act] was attended with great embarrassment … arising from the loose notions entertained by the [Chinese] witnesses of the obligation of an oath [at pp. 594–6].

In two 1891 cases, on Chinese re-entry, *Wan Shing v. U.S.* and *Quock Ting v. U.S.*, the former involving a claim of merchant status and the latter involving a claim of citizenship by birth in the U.S., the Court aligned itself with immigration authorities, ruling that the proof presented for each claim was unpersuasive.[96] In the *Wan Shing* case, the Court specifically said that only the certificate required by the Scott Act could be sufficient to prove merchant status.[97] Nonetheless, the Fuller Court was willing to uphold rights of bonafide non-laborer Chinese residents, even if the U.S. Justice Department was making arguments to the contrary, *and* even when the required certificate was lacking, when the Court itself became convinced that ample proof of merchant status had been presented in court. In March of 1892, the Court upheld the right of a merchant, Lau Ow Bew, longtime resident in the U.S., to re-enter the country.[98] Immigration authorities had detained him for deportation at the port of San Francisco because he lacked a certificate required by the Scott Act for Chinese to enter the U.S., despite his having shown ample proof of his longterm U.S. residence and his merchant status. The district and circuit courts had upheld this executive branch decision but the U.S. Supreme Court reversed, on the grounds that the certificate requirement in the act (properly interpreted) applied only to arrivals by newcomers, not to re-entry by lawful U.S. (non-laborer) residents who could prove their non-laborer status. The Court distinguished the *Wan Shing* case by saying that Wan Shing had in fact been a laborer.

The Fuller Court continued this mixed pattern throughout its tenure. It seemed willing to follow the will of Congress as to the substantive realities—i.e., Asian merchants were wanted and laborers were not—and would be willing to overlook procedural niceties when ample proof of real status was available.

After Congress in 1891 for non-Chinese immigration cases made decisions of the newly created Federal Bureau of Immigration final,

---

96 *Wan Shing v. U.S.*, 140 U.S. 424 (1891); *Quock Ting v. United States*, 140 U.S. 417 (1891).

97 *Wan Shing v. U.S.*, 140 U.S. 424, 428 (1891).

98 *Lau Ow Bew v. U.S.*, 144 U.S. 47 (1892).

eliminating appeals to the judicial branch, the Court acceded to the executive branch's defense of the law: In the matter of second-guessing immigration authorities' judgments on evidence of general eligibility to enter the U.S., the Constitution did not forbid keeping all appeals within the executive branch. Would-be immigrants, such as the Japanese woman Nishimura Ekiu, an alleged pauper, could not claim a due process right to be heard in a judicial branch court on whether she had proof that she would not become a public charge.[99] In 1903, the Court in another case involving a Japanese immigrant ruled differently for situations concerning resident aliens; once in the country, aliens were entitled to due process of law. As to them, this meant that some form of fair hearing of evidence, "an opportunity to be heard," was required before they could be deported as paupers. These hearings did not need, however, all the procedures of a judicial trial, and unfamiliarity with English on the immigrant's part was not enough to disqualify the hearing.[100]

The presidential election year of 1892 brought a re-eruption of national legislative hostility to Asian laborers; Congress produced the 1892 Geary Act, which the President signed on May 5 (one day before the 1882 ban would have expired). This law continued in force all existing prohibitions on Chinese immigration for the next ten years and stipulated, further, that those Chinese laborers still in the U.S. (i.e., permanent residents) now had to come up with proof that their residence since May 5, 1892 had been legal, or else they would be deported. They could do this by obtaining a certificate to that effect within one year from the local revenue office, or prove they were unavoidably unable to obtain such certificate and were entitled to one, to the satisfaction of the Court and with testimony of "at least one credible white witness."[101]

This time the Supreme Court divided six–three over constitutionality, in the case *Fong Yue Ting [and two others] v. U.S.* (1893). Justices Fuller, Field and Brewer wrote lengthy dissents. All three were incensed that the Fifth Amendment, which secures the liberty of all "persons," not merely all citizens, was being flagrantly violated as to lawful, permanent U.S. residents by the U.S. Government. As Justice Brewer noted, "It cannot be due process of law to impose punishment on any person for failing to have that in his possession, the possession of which he can obtain only at

99 *Nishimura Ekiu v. United States*, 142 U.S. 651 (1892); Salyer 1989, 92–3.
100 *Yamatay Kaoru v. Fisher*, 189 U.S. 86 (1903).
101 Kim 1992-B, 21–3; Fiss 1993, 303–11.

the arbitrary and unregulated discretion of any official."[102] The majority opinion relied on a combination of international law on power to deport aliens and on Field's litany of alleged faults of the Chinese from his reasoning in *Chae Chan Ping*.[103]

Again, however, after upholding Congress's plenary authority over deportation policy, the Court showed a willingness to check executive branch excess in applying that policy. In *U.S. v. Gue Lim [et al.]* (1900), a deportation case, President McKinley's Justice Department appealed to have the Supreme Court reverse lower court rulings that interpreted treaties and the Geary Act as not requiring certificates of residence for Chinese wives and minor children of merchants.[104] The Supreme Court upheld the lower courts' interpretation, against the executive branch. And again checking the mistreatment of Chinese merchants by immigration authorities, the Supreme Court in *Tom Hong v. U.S.* (1904) blocked the deportation by an immigration commissioner of three Chinese merchants who had gone out of business (so were now "laborers") but had produced ample proof that they had been merchants in the mid-1890s when they would have had to obtain a residence certificate had they been mere laborers.[105] The Court ruled that since the proof of their having been merchants was ample, including testimony by whites, they could not now be deported as laborers.

Congress proceeded in 1894 in the Chandler Act to extend the ban on appealing to the federal judiciary to those would-be immigrants who were of Chinese descent. Since 1882, the Exclusion Acts, which targeted the Chinese, had been enforced with the assistance of judicial officials, called Commissioners. Customs inspectors interviewed Chinese aspirants while on the ships and recommended to the Port Collector whether each one was qualified to enter as a non-laborer or as a lawful U.S. resident (before 1888), or as a native-born U.S. citizen. The Collector generally followed the advice of the inspector. In substantial percentages of the Chinese cases, the Collector denied permission to land, and thousands of these rejects proceeded to appeal for writs of habeas corpus, to have the

---

102 *Fong Yue Ting [et al.] v. U.S.*, 149 U.S. 698, at 742 (1893). The decision and dissents for this case also addressed the cases originally titled *Wong Quan v. U.S.* and *Lee Joe v. U.S.*

103 *Fong Yue Ting v. U.S.*, 149 U.S. 698, at 706 and 730; Kim 1992-B, 21. In *United States v. Lee Yen Tai*, 185 U.S. 213 (1902), the Court ruled that the 1892 Chinese Exclusion Renewal Act had not been implicitly limited by an 1894 Treaty with China, but that the two were entirely compatible.

104 *U.S. v. Gue Lim [et al.]*, 176 U.S. 459 (1900).

105 *Tom Hong v. U.S.*, 193 U.S. 517 (1904).

Collector's decision reversed. The federal district and circuit courts in Northern California (where most Chinese entered) granted the writs routinely. Then the case would go to the Commissioner, who would hold an evidentiary hearing in order to decide whether to recommend letting the applicant enter the U.S. This Commissioner recommendation was generally followed by the district or circuit court, and in the vast majority of cases the judicial courts overrode the Collector's rejection.[106]

Attempting to halt this judicial "interference" with congressional policy, Congress adopted the Chandler Act, which declared final any decision by the "appropriate immigration or custom[s] officer" to exclude Chinese aliens, subject only to an appeal to the Secretary of the Treasury. (In 1903 the final officer for these appeals was to become the Secretary of Commerce and Labor.)[107]

The Fuller Court upheld this Act,[108] but balked a year later when asked to apply the Geary Act in a way that imposed not only deportation but punishment *within* the U.S. This time, the Supreme Court called a halt when a federal judge, as per the terms of section four of the Geary Act, sentenced to sixty days hard labor (to be followed by deportation) four Chinese residents who could not prove the legality of their presence here. The Supreme Court declared this piece of the Act an unconstitutional violation of the Fifth Amendment rights to grand jury indictment and to due process of law prior to being subjected to an "infamous punishment." The government could deport the men, but it could not subject them, with no chance for a trial by jury, to this additional punishment.[109]

In 1895, a twenty-two year old man named Wong Kim Ark, born to Chinese parents in San Francisco, who had lived all his life in the city, attempted to return from a year-long visit to China, and was denied permission to re-enter the country by customs officials who denied he was a citizen. The lower court ordered him released for entry, but the U.S. Justice Department of the (Republican) McKinley administration

---

106 Between 1882 and 1890, Chinese filed 7,080 petitions against denials of entry, and they achieved judicial reversals in 85–90 percent. Salyer 1989, 92. See also Fritz 1988, 371. Between 1891 and 1904, Chinese turned away by the Collector for the Port of San Francisco filed 2,657 petitions for habeas relief at the district or circuit court, and won the right of entry in the majority of their efforts, some years winning as many as 88 or 89 percent of the appeals, but for 1898–1900 lows of only between 45 and 50 percent each year. Still, they did much better in the federal courts than with the Collector for Customs. Salyer 1989, 100–107, Table 1.

107 Fiss 1993, 316 n.78; Salyer 1989, 111; Act of Aug. 18, 1894, 28 Stat.390.

108 Kim 1992-B, 23–4; *Lem Moon Sing v. U.S.*, 158 U.S. 538 (1895).

109 Kim ibid., 24–5; *Wong Wing v. U.S.*, 163 U.S. 228 (1896).

appealed the case up to the Supreme Court, which handed down its decision in 1898. The Justice Department took the position that the Fourteenth Amendment language, "All persons born in the United States, *and subject to the jurisdiction thereof*" did not include offspring born to persons who were subjects of the Chinese Empire, such as Wong Kim Ark's parents. This reasoning would have cut a huge hole in the Fourteenth Amendment's grant of birth-based citizenship; Congress would be able to specify any immigrant group as unable to be naturalized, and thereby exclude any children born to them on U.S. soil from becoming citizens. The Supreme Court rejected the executive branch argument, and ruled that so long as his parents were here as residents, rather than on a temporary diplomatic mission of the Chinese Government (which, under the reigning legal fiction, would have put them on foreign soil), they were under the jurisdiction of the U.S. Government, and therefore so was he.[110]

This decision was followed by a series of cases (1902–08) where the federal authorities challenged the kind of proof offered to claim birth citizenship by Chinese-descent persons who claimed they were re-entering their homeland. Such person, detained at the port after stays abroad, asked the federal courts for writs of habeas corpus. In December of 1903 the U.S. Attorney General took the position that the decision of the Secretary of Commerce and Labor in rejecting any such appeal should be final, and not susceptible to habeas review.[111] At first the Supreme Court displayed a relatively weak commitment to fair procedures, but over the seven-year period eventually settled on a rule that some sort of fair hearing had to be offered where a person of Chinese descent claiming (birth-right) U.S. citizenship could (and could be required to) offer proof of this status before being kept out of the country or deported. If this fair opportunity were denied (but only then), the administrative refusal of entry could be appealed to the judiciary.[112] Then in 1908, the

---

[110] *Wong Kim Ark v. U.S.*, 169 U.S. 649 (1898).

[111] Salyer 1989, 114.

[112] Kim 1992-B, 34–5; Fiss 1993, 316–21. Recent scholarly investigations confirm that Chinese persons did in fact use fraudulent documents to claim birth-right citizenship, and in massive numbers. Park 2004, 107–8; Salyer 1988, 107. Perhaps this explains the judicial initial willingness to leave matters in the executive branch. The cases in which judicial policy evolved are as follows. The Court, in 1902, in *Chin Bak Kan v. U.S.*, 186 U.S. 193 (also in *Chin Ying v. U.S.*, 186 U.S. 202 (1902)), ruled that federal commissioners, even though they were not Art.III judges, did have authority to judge (and reject) birth-based citizenship claims of Chinese-descent persons attempting to avoid deportation (or to attain

Court extended judicial due process rights even beyond those claiming U.S. citizenship, to a resident Chinese person claiming (lawful) student status and attempting to avoid deportation as a laborer.[113]

At the end of the Spanish American War, in 1898, the U.S. acquired Puerto Rico and the Pacific territories of the Philippines, Hawaii, Samoa, and Guam. The Treaty of Paris ceding Guam, Puerto Rico and the Philippines was ratified in 1899. The Treaty of Berlin in 1899 ceded American Samoa to the U.S. (Also, as a consequence of this war, the U.S. occupied Cuba militarily from December 1898 through May of 1902, and also intervened militarily in Cuba during the 1906–09 period, and leased the naval base in Guantanamo there, but Cuba never became an official U.S. possession.[114]) The Hawaii acquisition came not through war but through diplomatic negotiation with U.S.-descended Hawaiian leaders and a joint Congressional Resolution, signed by President McKinley on July 7, 1898, making Hawaii a part of the U.S.[115] The Hawaiian Organic Act of April 30, 1900 gave U.S. citizenship to all citizens of the Hawaii Republic (i.e., to all native-born Hawaiians, which

---

re-entry), although these would be appealable to a district court, albeit with a ten-day limit, and that it was within Congress's power to put the burden of proof of citizenship on the person of Chinese descent; in *Ah How [et al.] v. U.S.*, 193 U.S. 65 (1904), accepted the Commissioner and District Court ruling against the citizenship of one Lew Guey, even though Lew Guey had shown a written statement from a U.S. Commissioner to the effect that someone named Lew Guey had appeared before him and "was adjudged to have the right to remain in the United States by reason of being a citizen"; in *U.S. v. Sing Tuck*, 194 U.S. 161 (1904) rejected a claim that Chinese descent persons could enter the U.S. from Canada merely by asserting U.S. citizenship by birth: they had to satisfy the immigration inspector as to their citizen status and if inspector were unsatisfied, had to exhaust their appeal to the Secretary of Commerce and Labor before being eligible for a habeas corpus claim; in *Ju Toy v. U.S.*, 198 U.S. 253 (1905) ruled there was no right to habeas corpus to contest a refusal decision on a claim of U.S. birth-right citizenship for entering the U.S., and the appellate decision of the Secretary of Commerce and Labor is final, unless there has been "abuse of discretion"; in *Chin Yow v. U.S.*, 208 U.S. 8 (1908), ruled a fair hearing *is* required on claim of U.S. birth-right citizenship, and if it is denied then habeas may be issued by federal courts; *Liu Hop Fong,* 209 U.S. 453 (1908), extended judicial due process rights even to a Chinese resident claiming student (i.e., non-laborer) status to avoid deportation.

113 *Liu Hop Fong (*ibid.); Fiss 1993, 320–21.

114 OWNO 1998–2014. "History of Cuba."

115 30 Stat. 750.

group included substantial numbers of persons of Chinese or Pacific Islander descent) who chose to accept it, and to U.S. citizens dwelling there.[116]

In a series of decisions over several years at the turn of the twentieth century known as the *Insular Cases*, the U.S. Supreme Court drew a distinction between the new non-Hawaii territories and the rest. The persons dwelling on the islands that Congress did not intend to incorporate into the union of the continental states (irrespective of their individual racial identity) would not receive all the rights listed in the Constitution, purportedly because some of these rights (such as freedom from establishment of religion) were alien to their culture. If they moved to reside in one of the American states, as residents therein, they would be governed by the Constitution.[117]

The Pacific empire complicated Americans' policy of stemming immigration from Asia. Filipinos became U.S. nationals (albeit not citizens) in 1898, and therefore could move freely into the mainland of the U.S. In 1906, Congress legislated permission for those Filipinos who were not racially Asian to become naturalized citizens if they migrated to and resided in one of the states of the Union; this legislation is discussed in more depth in Chapter 5. (As President, Woodrow Wilson supported and signed the Jones Act of 1916, which promised eventual independence to the Philippines; independence was not granted until the end of World War II.[118])

In 1902, Congress indefinitely extended all prior bans on immigration by Chinese laborers and extended the ban to Chinese laborers who might attempt to enter the continental U.S. from our recently acquired "island territories": the Philippines, Guam, Samoa, or Hawaii. Moreover, it required Chinese laborers residing in any of the islands other than Hawaii, to obtain a certificate showing proof of lawful residence within a

---

116 Act of April 30, 1900, 1st Session, 56th Congress; 31 Statutes at Large 141, c.339; *Congressional Record* 1899–1900, 3719; Basson 2008, 110; Hanifin 2002, 27–30.

117 On the *Insular Cases*, see Sparrow 2006. Native-born Puerto Ricans who resided in Puerto Rico were granted birthright U.S. citizenship first in 1917 in the Jones Shafroth Act, and then again in 1941, 8 U.S. Code § 1402. For discussion of the rights of persons of Puerto Rican origin who live on the mainland of the USA, see Chapter 6.

118 Kramer 2006, 354–5.

year or be deported. In 1904, the presidential election year, Congress went through the motion of re-enacting this *already* indefinitely extended law.[119]

Meanwhile, California now developed a labor shortage, due to the absence of Chinese laborers and an unwillingness on the part of other Americans to take menial agricultural jobs. More than 550,000 acres of farmland in the Central Valley was put out of cultivation due to the loss of Chinese labor. California farmers now eagerly sought workers from the Philippines, Mexico and Japan. Between 1898 and 1900 the number of Japanese immigrating to the U.S. annually went from 2,000 to 12,000.[120]

Japanese subjects (while barred by national law from naturalization[121]) did not undergo severe restriction on their immigration until, again provoked by rising anti-Asian sentiment in California that caused diplomatic tensions, the Administration (this time, of Theodore Roosevelt) eventually negotiated an agreement with Japan. Theodore Roosevelt's annual message of December 1905 had in fact endorsed a racially non-discriminatory immigration policy, and when he later learned of a congressional plan to extend Chinese Exclusion to cover the Japanese, he threatened to veto such a bill "even if it passed unanimously."[122]

Matters spun out of his control, however, when the San Francisco school board decided in October, 1906, to place children of Japanese and Korean descent into the segregated school that Chinese children attended. The Japanese Government considered this an insult, and insisted on attendance at the "white" schools. The President negotiated an agreement that responded to Japan's interest in keeping open free intercourse with Hawaii. Japanese subjects who held passports for travel to Hawaii,

---

[119] Odo 2002, 128; Chan 1994, 50, n.49; Act of April 29, 1902, 32 Stat. 176, 641; Act of April 27, 1904, 33 Stat. 394, Chap.1630, Section 5; Takaki 1998, 26 dates the initial exclusion at 1900.

[120] Buell 1922, 606, citing a study published in 1909.

[121] This fact was unbeknownst to occasional local officials who performed naturalization ceremonies for them. In June of 1906, Congress adopted the Naturalization Act (34 Stat. 596), centralizing naturalization decisions into the federal government, and that same year Roosevelt's Attorney General ordered federal courts to deny citizenship to Japanese persons claiming whiteness. In his annual message to Congress in December 1906, Roosevelt urged Congress to legislate to permit Japanese naturalization. Takaki 1998, 207; Pike 2000–2016. The U.S. Supreme Court eliminated any remaining confusion in *Takao Ozawa v. U.S.*, 260 U.S. 178 (1922) and *Takugi Yamashita v. Hinkle*, 260 U.S. 199 (1922); Kim 1992-B, 35–7. These are discussed in Chapter 5.

[122] Buell 1922, 619.

Mexico, or Canada could be barred by executive order from admission to the continental U.S. but Japanese residents of San Francisco would be admitted to its "white" schools. Congress promptly enacted the immigration law of February 20, 1907 authorizing this presidential power and also power to negotiate international agreements to bar immigration of persons excluded from admission to the U.S.; on March 13 the San Francisco School Board rescinded its segregation order; on March 14 President Roosevelt excluded from admission to the continental U.S. laborers holding passports from Japan or Korea (a colony of Japan) that admitted them to Canada, Hawaii, or Mexico; and in 1908 the President's Ambassador concluded a so-called "Gentleman's Agreement" to the effect that Japan and Korea would refrain from issuing passports to the continental U.S. for any laborer except one who previously resided in the U.S., was joining an immediate family member in the U.S., or "possessed an interest in a farming enterprise in the U.S." and would also restrict future immigration to Hawaii. Japanese women, in contrast to Chinese women, were permitted to come to the U.S. to marry a Japanese laborer. Japanese immigration to the U.S. in 1907 numbered 12,888; by 1909 it had dropped to 1,596.[123] As Chapter 5 will document, the situation for Asians in the U.S. was to worsen as the twentieth century moved on.

NATIVE AMERICANS, 1875–1910

The Supreme Court's concern for the equal rights of racial minorities in the final quarter of the nineteenth century extended even more rarely to Native Americans than to Asians, although it did briefly manifest itself in 1883[124] and again in 1905,[125] each time only to be overridden by Congress.

In the matter of late nineteenth-century Indian policy, measures that can be analyzed as rejecting "equal sovereignty" or "equal rights" for Indians were often motivated not by the sentiments of overt hostility or suspicion that can be discerned in matters involving blacks and Asians,

---

[123] Kim 1992-B, 39–40; Kiyama 1999, 140–41; Park 2004, 110–11; Nordyke and Matsumoto 1977, 164. At the time, Korea was a "protectorate" of Japan, to be formally "annexed" in 1910.

[124] *Ex Parte Crow Dog*, 109 U.S. 556 (1883).

[125] *In re Heff*, 197 U.S. 488 (1905).

but rather out of genuine sympathy and concern, however misguided.[126] This is not to deny that innumerable individual Americans engaged in theft, fraud, sexual assault, and even murders toward individual Indians. Nor is it to ignore the enormous carnage perpetrated during the Indian Wars of the last third of the nineteenth century against Indians by the U.S. military, part of the executive branch, notwithstanding that the worst excesses were caused by U.S. soldiers acting in *defiance* of orders from Washington to uphold treaty rights—that is, contrary to official federal policy.[127]

Nonetheless, the broad directions of public policies that did great harm to Indians often proceeded out of benign motives. For instance, reformers in the Bureau of Indian Affairs (BIA), and humanitarian and Christian religious organizations, lobbied Congress starting in 1874 for a bill that would extend the protections of "white man's" criminal law over the reservations as a civilizing influence.[128] As Congress resisted, the BIA attempted to attain its goal via judicial lawmaking; it took the case *Ex Parte Crow Dog* to the Waite Supreme Court in 1883.

Crow Dog was a Sioux who had murdered another Sioux, and the BIA had him prosecuted and convicted in the federal district court. He sued at the Supreme Court for a habeas writ and won his case. The BIA argued that federal jurisdiction was established both by the 1877 statutory assertion that Indians "shall be subject to the laws of the United States,"[129] and by the language of the 1868 treaty with the Sioux:

> if bad men among the Indians shall commit a wrong … upon … any one, white, black, or Indian, subject to the authority of the United States and at peace therewith, the Indians … solemnly agree that they will … deliver up the wrong-doer to the United States, to be tried and punished according to its laws.

In a unanimous opinion, the Supreme Court reasoned that the situation was covered instead by the provision of Rev. Stat. § 2146, which excepts from the general jurisdiction of courts of the U.S. those criminal offenses committed in Indian country by one Indian against the person or property of another Indian and offenses committed in Indian country by an Indian who has been punished by the local law of the tribe. The Court explained

[126] For a detailed account of the sincere, humanitarian arguments that proved persuasive to many elite Americans, see Nackenoff 2006 and Nackenoff 2010, 1–6, 10–18.

[127] Cozzens 2016.

[128] Getches et al. 1993, 184.

[129] Act of February 28th, 1877, c. 72, 19 Stat. 256.

that the "or Indian" language of the Sioux Treaty of 1868 referring to "bad men" who might attack a tribal member was understood on all sides to indicate non-tribal Indians, under the jurisdiction of the U.S. but not under the jurisdiction of the Sioux. Over such persons, as over non-Indians attacking a tribal member, the U.S. had jurisdiction. The Supreme Court emphasized the continuing importance of tribal self-government, while acknowledging the reality that the Indians continued to be a "dependent community" within the United States. By continued local self-government, the tribe "through the discipline of labor and by education, it was hoped[,] might become a self-supporting and self-governed society."[130]

The Secretary of the Interior responded to this defeat by calling on Congress in his Annual Report the following year (1884) to remedy a situation in which murders on Indian reservations would allegedly be punished by the "old Indian custom … of the duty of the next of kin to avenge the death of his relative by either killing the murderer or some one of his kinsmen." In reality, the Crow Dog killing had been satisfied, per tribal rules, by a compensatory property transfer from Crow Dog's family to that of the victim, a fact of which the Secretary of the Interior was well aware. Congress obliged with the Major Crimes Act of 1885, taking away Indian sovereignty over seven serious crimes, even if committed by one tribal member against another.[131]

In *U.S. v. Kagama* (1886) the Supreme Court immediately upheld this extension of federal power over the tribes, even though it contravened numerous prior treaties. Justice Miller carefully reviewed the legal situation of the tribes in doing so. Even before the American Revolution, and continuing since then, wrote Miller, the relation between the tribes and the U.S. has been "anomalous." The United States recognized in the Indians a "possessory right in the soil," over which they roamed, but not "ultimate title" in the sense of a freedom to sell or transfer the soil to a foreign government or nation. They "always have been regarded as having a semi-independent position … not as possessed of the full rights of sovereignty, but as a separate people with the power of regulating their internal and social relations, and thus far not brought under the laws of the Union or of the State within [which they lie]."[132] The Supreme Court reasoned that, because of, essentially, facts on the ground, this law was,

---

130 *Ex Parte Crow Dog*, 109 U.S. 556, 569.

131 Getches et al. 1993, 184–5. *U.S. Statutes at Large*, 23:385; 18 U.S.C. § 1153.

132 *U.S. v. Kagama*, 118 U.S. 375, 381 (1886).

nonetheless, within Congress's competence, despite prior treaty limitations and despite the apparent limitedness of the enumerated power of Congress, "to regulate commerce with the Indian tribes," which did not stretch so far as to cover this Act:[133]

> These Indian tribes are the wards of the nation. They are communities dependent on the United States. Dependent largely for their daily food. Dependent for their political rights. They owe no allegiance to the States, and receive from them no protection. Because of the local ill feeling, the people of the States where they are found are often their deadliest enemies. From their very weakness and helplessness, so largely due to the course of dealing of the Federal Government with them and the treaties in which it has been promised, there arises the duty of protection, and with it the power.
>
> The power of the general government over these remnants of a race once powerful, now weak and diminished in numbers, is necessary to their protection, as well as to the safety of those among whom they dwell. It must exist in that government, because it never has existed anywhere else [and] because the theater of its exercise is within the geographical limits of the United States [at pp. 383–385].

Ultimately Miller concluded for the unanimous Court,

> This power of Congress to organize territorial governments, and make laws for their inhabitants, arises, not so much from the clause in the constitution in regard to disposing of and making rules and regulations concerning the territory and other property of the United States, as from the ownership of the country in which the territories are, and the right of exclusive sovereignty which must exist in the national government, and can be found nowhere else [at p. 380].

In effect Miller is attributing plenary power (of the combined national legislative and executive branches) over the conquered tribes to the category of powers inherent in sovereignty itself. As such, this power over the tribes appeared to be unchecked and uncheckable by either the Constitution or the U.S. Supreme Court.

As for those Indians who voluntarily chose to leave their tribal territory, to live among white men, one might have thought that the Fourteenth Amendment offered them a welcome. It said that: "All persons born or naturalized in the United States, and subject to the jurisdiction thereof, are citizens of the United States and of the state wherein they reside." Framers and ratifiers of the Fourteenth Amendment understood that Indians living on reservations were not completely

---

133 Ibid., at 378.

"subject to the jurisdiction" of the U.S. Government, for in many respects (even after the 1885 Major Crimes Act) the tribes were still self-governing. But it did appear, at least to the Congress that sent the Amendment to the states in 1866, that if Indians *chose* to make themselves "subject to the jurisdiction" of the United States by leaving the reservation for city life, thereby removing themselves from that category, "Indians not taxed," which was excluded in the Fourteenth Amendment's description of the population to be counted for apportioning Representatives, then they would count as U.S. citizens, having been born within the exterior boundaries of the U.S.[134]

So thought one John Elk, who left his tribe for Omaha Nebraska and, after living there long enough to fit the residency requirements for voting, attempted to register to vote and was turned away. He sued the registrar, Wilkins, for denial of his Fifteenth Amendment rights, and appealed his case all the way to the Supreme Court. Justice Gray, writing for the Court, rejected this claim in *Elk v. Wilkins* (1884).[135] Gray cited many treaties with Indians, both before and after the Fourteenth Amendment, that had made explicit provisions for the naturalization of all or some of the tribal members to U.S. citizenship. He also reasoned that although recent Homestead Acts were open to Indians who had left their tribal lands, these Acts did not treat the Indians as ordinary citizens but imposed special regulations on them, such as subjecting them to rules made by the Secretary of the Interior for proving the severing of tribal relations. He inferred from this separate treatment that Indians must go through a naturalization process in order to become American citizens.

Justice Harlan wrote a dissent, joined by Woods (these two of the justices were also relatively protective of black civil rights). Harlan pointed out that the treaty naturalization provisions related to the tribes as a unit, not to individuals separated from their tribes, and accused the majority of reading the Fourteenth Amendment as though it said, "All persons *born subject* to the jurisdiction of, or naturalized in, the United States are citizens of the United States," instead of what it does say.[136]

---

[134] Greenfield and Kates 1975, 663–4 n.9 (Fourteenth Amendment understood by its supporters as entrenching the principles of the 1866 Civil Rights Act); 611, n.40 and 673–4 nn.52–55, citing Cong. Globe 39th Cong., 1st Sess., 599 (re: "every person of color"), 498 (re: "domesticated" Indians who "live in civilized society"), 572 (re: "Indians not taxed"), 573 (discussion of coverage by 1866 Act of non-reservation Indians) (1866).

[135] *Elk v. Wilkins,* 112 U.S. 94 (1884). This was the same year that the Court reached out to protect black voters in *Ex Parte Yarborough.*

[136] Ibid., at 109.

As with Asians, for Native Americans, the situation then went from very bad to even worse. At first the trend was not obvious. In 1887 Congress adopted the Dawes [General Allotment] Act, overriding *Elk v. Wilkins* by granting citizenship to off-reservation Indians, and also setting up a system to encourage Indians to take privately owned land allotments. By all accounts, Republican Senator Henry Dawes of Massachusetts, its prominent sponsor, was a man devoted to "racial equality." According to historian Fred Hoxie, Dawes ended his career in 1892 universally acclaimed as a kind of secular saint and "the Indians' truest friend." Thus was viewed the disastrous Dawes Act in the period up to the early twentieth century.[137]

As a Congressman, Dawes had led the 1870 move to end treaty-making with tribes, mainly as a matter of governmental economizing. In 1881 he joined and became chair of the Senate Indian Affairs Committee. For the next twelve years he spearheaded the governmental policy pushing assimilation on the Indians, motivated by high-minded humanitarian concerns, along with a group of like-minded northeastern Republicans in the House and Senate. The opposition to this group's proposals on Indian policy, typically unsuccessful opposition, came generally from westerners, who wanted to avoid federal meddling in their region, and from southern Democrats. This opposition coalition favored what was in fact the late nineteenth century's politically viable alternative to the assimilation policy: (in Hoxie's euphemistic words) "Open the land to white homesteaders and let nature take its course." This alliance of westerners and southern Democrats appears to have been happy to let Indians simply die out in some sort of Social Darwinist competition. Here is one not untypical sample from their speeches in the House: "If we are going to appropriate every year millions of money for the support of an idle, vagrant, malevolent, malicious race, then let us go to work and take on our hands all the paupers of the United States."[138] One prominent Republican Senator, Henry Teller, who had served as Secretary of the Interior, 1882–1885, did predict the disaster that the law would become, calling it a "pretext to get the Indians' land and occupy them," but his was an uncommon voice of prescience.[139] As the nineteenth century wore on, attitudes toward Indian policy hardened from misguided benevolence

---

137 Hoxie 1984, 30.

138 Ibid., 30–38. Quote is from Rep. James Belford, Colorado in 1885. All of the preceding material in this paragraph is from this section in Hoxie.

139 Otis 1993, 193. Irwin, 1997, 35; "Henry M. Teller"; Hoxie 1984, 58–9. Teller himself, as Secretary of the Interior, had also favored assimilation: he spearheaded the program of federal support for boarding schools for Indian

into more frankly expressed preferences for white ownership of Indian land. Fred Hoxie (1984) locates this shift of rhetoric in the late 1890s (roughly concurrent with *Williams v. Mississippi*, 1898, where the Supreme Court refused to dislodge the white supremacy voting provisions that had begun to taint Southern state constitutions).[140] Discourse within Congress and the federal bureaucracy changed from expressing a desire to convince the Indian to learn to be a productive farmer, to discourse aimed at having the land be more productively employed—i.e., managed by whites, the more capable farmers.[141] Similarly, justifications in federal judicial decisions for the twenty-five year period of governmental supervision of Indian disposition of allotted land changed from talk of the individual Indians' being bound by their tribe's treaty-making commitments concerning the land (1895 decision) to talk of the need "to guard the beneficiaries against … their own improvidence" (in a 1905 decision).[142] But irrespective of motive and rhetoric, from the start the allotment approach in the Dawes Act produced policies harmful to the Indians.

The Allotment Act exemplified a turn in Congress toward support of drastic measures to assimilate the Indians and obliterate tribal ways of life. Earlier the government had made optional individual allotment arrangements with particular tribes, to encourage agriculture, beginning as early as 1853, but before 1887, these totaled only 584,423 acres.[143] Originally, the 1887 Act exempted the Five Civilized Tribes (Cherokee, Choctaw, Chickasaw, Seminole, and Creek), in appreciation of their success as farmers and their settled way of life, but in 1898 the Curtis Act brought them under allotment policy, against the will of the tribal leadership, against extant property law (because the tribes held fee simple titles to their communal lands) and against treaties. Prior to the Curtis Act

children and had promulgated the Indian Religious Crimes Code that had forbidden the practice of Native American religious rites.

140 Hoxie 1984, 30–38. This coincided with a rise of racial Darwinism in the popular and scholarly press. Hoxie at 124–6 cites, for instance, the book by Daniel G. Brinton, *Races and Peoples*, NY: N.D.C. Hodges, 1890, 287, 294–5, to the effect that the Indian race was "indelibly" limited in terms of potential for social progress; left on their own Indians might survive as hunting or simple agricultural peoples, but because of contacts with whites, they were doomed to extinction from "disease and competition." Similar views of the Indians as a race were propounded in William Ripley's *The Races of Europe* (1899); and Madison Grant's *The Passing of the Great Race* (1916). Hoxie 126–7.

141 Hoxie 1984, 30–38.

142 Ibid., 214–15.

143 Getches et al. 1993, 190–91, 194.

the 70,000 members of these tribes had owned the eastern half of the state of Oklahoma, rich in farmland and mineral resources. As to the mineral resources, the Curtis Act paternalistically authorized (in §13) the Secretary of Interior to issue mineral leases on tribal land with monetary proceeds to go to tribal benefit. The Act also took from tribal governments the authority to determine who was a tribal member for purposes of land allotment and delegated this power to the Dawes Commission. These last two provisions were unsuccessfully challenged at the Fuller Court in *Stephens v. Cherokee Nation* (1899) (tribal membership) and *Cherokee Nation v. Hitchcock* (1902) (mineral leases).[144] The allotment system supplemented by viciously unscrupulous practices of the surrounding white population reduced these tribes to eventual poverty.[145]

The accession of Teddy Roosevelt to the White House in 1901 did not end the Dawes Allotment policy, but it brought a more pessimistic tone to expectations of what the Act could accomplish. Roosevelt (along with the westerners with whom he entrusted Indian policy, and also the westerners who tended to dominate Indian policy in Congress during the 1900–1910, many of them Senators from the nine new western states that joined the Union between 1899–1912) favored letting whites of the region dominate policy choices toward a people thought to be racially limited, as he also thought blacks (and Filipinos) were, and therefore doomed to remain for a long period primarily in the menial occupations of society.[146]

The 1890s had first showed a glimmer of hope for support for tribal sovereignty from the Fuller Court, but then a negative turn. In May, 1896 the Court ruled for tribal sovereignty in *Talton v. Mayes*, holding that while the Bill of Rights restricted the U.S. federal government, it did not restrict tribal governments' dealings with their own members.[147] The very next week, however, the Court allowed state-level regulations (of hunting on federally owned land) to undercut treaties Indians had made with the federal government. This ruling, in *Ward v. Racehorse*, broke with two Chase Court precedents to the contrary, *The Kansas Indians* case (1866) and the *New York Indians* case (1866) (see Chapter 3), which had held Indian treaty law supreme over later state law.[148] As Justice Brown pointed out in his lone dissent, the federal law creating the Wyoming

---

144 *Stephens v. Cherokee Nation*, 174 U.S. 445, 485, 488 (1899) (tribal membership); *Cherokee Nation v. Hitchcock*, 187 U.S. 294 (1902).

145 Wilkins 1997, 67.

146 Hoxie 1984, 103–8, 227–8.

147 *Talton v. Mayes*, 163 U.S. 376 (1896).

148 *Ward v. Racehorse*, 163 U.S. 504 (1896).

territory had stated that the rights of persons and property of Indians would continue in the territory "so long as such rights shall remain unextinguished by treaty between the United States and such Indians." The Court majority, by contrast, claimed in *Racehorse* that the later Act conferring statehood on Wyoming "on equal footing with the original states" implicitly abrogated this earlier federal law. Brown's dissent maintained that such a reading violated the rule endorsed in *Kansas Indians* and *New York Indians* and in *Chew Heong* that in doubtful interpretations, treaties are to be construed liberally toward the rights they protect.[149]

The anti-Indian sentiment that seemed to animate the *Racehorse* decision continued through 1903, where the Court refused to block a particularly unsavory transaction under the Dawes Act in the case of *Lone Wolf v. Hitchcock* (1903).[150] A treaty of 1867 between the Kiowa and Comanche, on one side, and the U.S. Government, on the other, had guaranteed that tribal lands in Oklahoma could not be sold off without permission signed by three-fourths of the tribal members. Under the treaty, annuity payments would still be coming to the tribe until 1898, for prior land cessions. Also sharing the reservation were the Apache tribe. A delegation from Washington in 1892 claimed to have obtained the requisite number of signatures for a treaty that sold the tribes' surplus land for $2 million, and allotted the rest of the land to the tribal members, but the chiefs, including Lone Wolf had changed their mind the day after signing and claimed that the translators had deceived the Indians about what they were signing. Lone Wolf and another tribal member testified in Congress against the settlement. The House voted for the agreement, but the Senate requested more information from the Secretary of the Interior. The latter reported that the allotment sizes needed to be doubled because the land was not farmable, that the members of the three tribes were almost unanimously opposed to the sale, that the number of signatures originally gathered did not amount to three-fourths of the current tribal numbers, and that more than three-fourths of the tribal members had now signed a petition against the sale. In 1900, House members slipped the ratification agreement into a bill that dealt with the Fort Hall Reservation in Idaho without indicating in the title of the Fort Hall bill that anything had been added. It passed in the Senate without debate. A lower court denied the tribes' request for a

149 Ibid., at 517, Brown dissenting.
150 *Lone Wolf v. Hitchcock*, 187 U.S. 553 (1903).

preliminary injunction. (Republican) President McKinley issued a proclamation opening the lands for settlement (by non-Indians) on August 6, 1901. In 1903, the Supreme Court recited all of these unsavory facts, and nonetheless ruled that the law was not an unconstitutional taking of the Indians' property without due process. In reasoning that shocks the conscience, the Court said this:

> Plenary authority over the tribal relations of the Indians has been exercised by Congress from the beginning, and the power has always been deemed a political one, not subject to be controlled by the judicial department of the government. Until the year 1871 the policy was pursued of dealing with the Indian tribes by means of treaties, and, of course, a moral obligation rested upon Congress to act in good faith in performing the stipulations entered into on its behalf. But, as with treaties made with foreign nations, the legislative power might pass laws in conflict with treaties made with the Indians [in light of new circumstances] … . In view of the legislative power possessed by Congress over treaties with the Indians and Indian tribal property, *we may not specially consider the contentions pressed upon our notice that the signing by the Indians of the agreement of October 6, 1892, was obtained by fraudulent misrepresentations, and concealment, that the requisite three fourths of adult male Indians had not signed, as required by the twelfth article of the treaty of 1867, and that the treaty as signed had been amended by Congress without submitting such amendments to the action of the Indians since all these matters, in any event, were solely within the domain of the legislative authority, and its action is conclusive upon the courts … . In effect, the action of Congress now complained of was but … a mere change in the form of investment of Indian tribal property, the property of those who, as we have held, were in substantial effect the wards of the government. We must presume that Congress acted in perfect good faith in the dealings with the Indians of which complaint is made, and that the legislative branch of the government exercised its best judgment in the premises. In any event, as Congress possessed full power in the matter, the judiciary cannot question or inquire into the motives which prompted the enactment of this legislation.* If injury was occasioned, which we do not wish to be understood as implying, by the use made by Congress of its power, relief must be sought by an appeal to that body for redress, and not to the courts (187 U.S. 553, 565–8; emphasis added).

Pushed by the administration of Theodore Roosevelt, whose Justice Department twice brought suit on behalf of the Indian treaty rights, the Supreme Court itself did seem by 1905 to abandon the sentiment that animated the *Racehorse* and *Lone Wolf* precedents. That year, in *U.S. v. Winans* (1905), a fishing rights case, the Court turned its back on the anti-Indian-rights logic of the *Racehorse* ruling.[151] A treaty had reserved for Indians fishing rights in the "usual and accustomed places" in common with others. This time the Court majority turned a deaf ear when a private (non-Indian) property owner with a license from the state to make a particular fishing area exclusively his own attempted the argument that the conferral of statehood on Washington "on equal footing with the original states" had given to Washington power to regulate the land bordering its navigable streams—the very argument that had proved decisive in *Racehorse* as to regulating hunting. (White dissented with no opinion.) The majority simply pointed out that federal power is supreme over state power in all the states, and it was the federal power that enacted the treaty. The Court stayed with its *Winans* logic three years later in *Winters v. U.S.* (1908). There it upheld (eight–one), as an implied treaty right, diversion by Indians of river water for navigation purposes, irrespective of Montana state law to the contrary and irrespective of the grant of statehood to Montana "on equal footing with the original states."[152]

The Dawes-sponsored General Allotment Act had not only arranged for individual ownership of heretofore tribal lands, but also bestowed U.S. citizenship on all Indians who received individual land allotments, and upon Indians who had taken up life away from the tribe and adopted "habits of civilized life," thereby legislatively correcting the misguided (1884) *Elk v. Wilkins* ruling. In the same year as the pro-Indian *Winans* decision, 1905, the justices insisted that full citizenship rights meant that equal freedom to buy and sell must belong to Indians. They ruled in *In re Heff* (1905), that the federal law of 1897 banning sale of alcoholic beverages to Indians was unconstitutional as applied to an Indian who had obtained citizenship via allotment.[153]

The decision was widely unpopular,[154] and Congress promptly responded by the 1906 Burke Act.[155] This Act postponed citizenship for future allottees during the twenty-five year period in which the federal government was holding the Indian lands in trust before the Indian would

---

[151] *U.S. v. Winans*, 198 U.S. 371 (1905).

[152] *Winters v. U.S.*, 207 U.S. 564, 577 (1908).

[153] *In re Heff,* 197 U.S. 488 (1905) was later overruled in *U.S. v. Nice,* 241 U.S. 591 (1916), which held that even *after* Indians are granted citizenship, Congress within its discretion may continue a degree of guardianship over them. (This case, too, involved sale of liquor.)

[154] Wilkins 1997, 123.

[155] 34 Stat. 182, 25 U.S.C. 349.

receive the right to sell off the allotted property.[156] For those Indians judged by the government mature enough to have this property right early, the Secretary of the Interior could confer it, and with it would come citizenship. Before the 1924 blanket grant by Congress of citizenship to Native Americans, two-thirds of them had thus attained citizenship.[157]

By 1934, when the Dawes/Curtis Act program was ended, 41 million acres had been allotted to individual Indians, in allotments of differing sizes to, respectively, heads of families, single adults or orphan minors, and depending whether the land suited grazing vs. farming. Most of these allotments were eventually sold off to non-Indians. Indian reservations that totaled 138 million acres in 1887 shrank to 48 million acres by 1934 when the Dawes Act program ended. The non-allotted lost land was sold off for private investment under the fictitious label of "surplus land" with proceeds being held in trust for such things as Indian education. As summed up by John Collier testifying before Congress in 1934, via the allotment system, more than 80 percent of the land value belonging to Indians in 1887 was lost and more than 85 percent of the land value of all the allotted Indians was lost.[158]

CONCLUSIONS

Congress vs. the Court as the Killer of Reconstruction

After Congress in 1894 wiped most of the Reconstruction-era voting rights legislation off the books, in 1895 Chief Justice Fuller (ruling on circuit for the case that reached the Supreme Court as *Mills v. Green*, 1895) signaled the future direction of his Supreme Court by lifting the injunction that Judge Nathan Goff had issued to block the racially discriminatory election process for the South Carolina constitutional convention (which had been called for the purpose of making the voter registration process even more powerfully effective at excluding

---

156 Nackenoff 2006, 388–92. This right was the "patent in fee simple," as distinguished from the "trust patent" during the (twenty-five year or less) probationary period.

157 Getches et al. 1993, 739; Kappler 1929, 1165–6; Bolt 1987, 99–101. According to the Supreme Court of 1916, however, the citizenship conferred on Indians was a watered-down version; see n.134 above.

158 Getches et al. ibid., 191, 195–6.

blacks).[159] The Fuller Court then launched a series of anti-civil-rights decisions, in some instances overruling (albeit *sub silentio*) elements of Waite Court or Chase Court jurisprudence that had upheld rights of black Americans. For instance, *Plessy* v. *Ferguson* (1896) dealt with a state law imposing upon the "colored" race "separate but equal" facilities in passenger cars, plainly a case of "state action," but the Court still upheld the statute, insisting that it did not deny equal protection of the law. The Fuller Court's acceptance (in a seven–one decision) of the argument that a mandate of racial separation *could* be equal as to railroad cars directly contradicted what the Chase Court had announced in *Railroad v. Brown* in 1873, and what only one out of the nine justices on the Waite Court had been willing to endorse (in *L'ville, N.O., & Tex. Ry. v. Mississippi* (1890)).

The popular mind and political tone of the country had moved so far away from interest in the civil rights of blacks, that Charles Warren's Pulitzer-Prize-winning tome, *The Supreme Court in American History*, Vol. III, published in 1922, which covered in detail hundreds of Supreme Court decisions (many of them seemingly minor cases) in the 1856–1918 period, does not even mention *Plessy*. A Google search for mainstream newspaper coverage of the case showed that it received only the most cursory of coverage, in contrast to other (economic issue) cases decided that day.

While these moves were plainly undermining of the rights of blacks, it is not correct to say, as many scholars do, that the U.S. Supreme Court buried Reconstruction.[160] The Waite Court (well before Congress's revocation of Reconstruction legislation in 1894) did strike down a few

---

159 *Mills v. Green*, 67 F. 818 (1895); *Green v. Mills*, 69 F. 852 (1895); *Mills v. Green*, 159 U.S. 651 (1895).

160 E.g., Currie 1985, 402 ("The Court went out of its way to incapacitate the enforcement authorities"), and citations in his n.217; Wiecek 1988, 94 ("Congress assumed the initiative in expanding the rights of blacks, and white southerners together with the Supreme Court maneuvered to negate those rights.... [T]he Supreme Court and Southern Democrats dismantled or enervated these rights so laboriously identified by congressional Republicans."); Bell, 1980, 33 ("Blacks became victims of judicial interpretations of the Fourteenth Amendment and legislation based on it so narrow as to render the promised protection meaningless in virtually all situations."); Howard 1999, 17, 25 (referencing "the Court's systematic destruction of Reconstruction protection for blacks"), 111, and 116 ("The effect of the Court's decisions in *Reese* and *Cruikshank* had been to disarm effective law enforcement relative to antiblack terror"); Brandwein 2011, 1 and extensive citations in n.2 ("[T]he common wisdom since the dawn of the civil right era" has been that "the fatal blow [to Reconstruction] was inflicted

sections of civil rights laws, a very few of the many that Congress had adopted. Any of these might have been refined in a way attentive to the Court's criticism and then re-enacted. Such refinements would not have ended Reconstruction. On the other hand, during the 1874–90 period, when the national voting public manifested indifference to Reconstruction by repeatedly producing divided government, the Supreme Court in 1876 (even as it threw out on technicalities convictions of racist murderers and insisted on a state action/state neglect predicate for Fourteenth Amendment prosecutions) expanded the reach of the Fifteenth Amendment by *eliminating* its state action requirement (suggested by its text), and again handed down pro-civil rights decisions in 1880, 1881, and 1883 (jury rights), 1884 (voting rights) and 1886 (prohibiting racial discrimination in administering facially neutral laws).

Moreover, as the Figure 3.1 illustrates, the sharp decrease in executive branch prosecutions of race-related violence in the South does *not* follow upon the heels of either the 1873 *Slaughterhouse Cases*, or upon the heels of the introduction of the state action doctrine in *Cruikshank* (1876)—both of which get cited by scholars who want to blame the Court for the end of Reconstruction. Rather, the sharp drop off comes between *1874* and 1876. Democrats swept into power in the House of Representatives after the election of November, 1874, taking office in March, 1875. They turned off the spigot of federal funding for prosecutions.[161]

Everette Swinney's book on the subject cites the Circuit Court opinion by Justice Bradley for *Cruikshank* as having swayed Attorney General Williams to order a cessation of enforcement in May of 1875 (even though this order came a full year after the Bradley opinion). Williams wrote, "I am of the opinion that criminal prosecution under these acts ought to be suspended until it is known whether the Supreme Court will hold them unconstitutional or otherwise."[162] But if this memo had been decisive, southern enforcement would have declined to its nadir in 1876 (the first whole year after the memo) and *stayed* there through 1883 (because the Supreme Court opinion of 1876 agreed with the Bradley opinion). Instead, enforcement varied with political sentiment of the U.S. (and somewhat with the incidence of racial violence. See Figure 3.1).

A secondary way in which political change pushed the drop in prosecutions is that once the southern state governments became Democratic, witnesses had more reasons to be fearful about testifying. The

by the Supreme Court," and it "has spread across law, history, and political science.")

161 Swinney 1987, 326.

162 Ibid., 199, 204 n.47.

success rate of convictions went from between 41 percent and 74 percent in the 1871–73 period, to approximately 10 percent in the 1874–94 period, and for this reason the Justice Department had less incentive to prosecute in the latter period.[163]

Reconstruction died because of a century-long campaign of intermittent violent insurgency in the South, launched by whites to subjugate black people. This was accompanied by a sophisticated propaganda campaign, putting out the false story throughout the North that race relations in the South were peaceful, that the southern Negro was better off and happier than blacks elsewhere, and that the vast majority of blacks were too ignorant to be permitted to vote or serve on juries effectively. The propaganda campaign seems to have had three phases.

First the South denied that there was violent terrorism taking place. Obvious racial slaughters, like the Colfax massacre, were explained away by claims that marauding by blacks triggered the rioting. Press releases containing such stories were sent all around the North by the Associated Press, which originated in the South.[164] In this phase fell the assurances by supposed southern moderates like Wade Hampton and Congressman-then-Senator L.Q.C. Lamar to President Hayes that if he would only take federal troops out of the South, state and local authorities would then secure the rights of innocent black people.[165]

In phase two, books and articles in reputable journals, buttressed by the rise of a racially oriented Social Darwinism, put forth the claim that African-Americans were an irredeemably ignorant people suited for farming but not for such difficult tasks as voting.[166] It was on the basis of this claim or belief that southerners in Congress were shameless enough in the 1890s to brag openly about their states' use of fraud and violence to keep blacks from voting and to commit themselves to this policy unless the Fifteenth Amendment were eliminated.[167] And to the degree that northerners swallowed the claim of black ignorance, they accepted

---

[163] Wang 1997, Appendix Seven, 300.

[164] Richardson 2001, 107–8.

[165] Logan 1997, 12–32.

[166] Darwin himself suggested that favored races would be preserved in the "struggle for life," and in 1871 specifically elaborated in *The Descent of Man*: "The civilized races of man will almost certainly exterminate and replace the savage races throughout the world." Schmidt 1984, 737–40. See also Foner 1988, 524–7; Logan 1997, Ch. 13; Klinkner and Smith 1999, 108–9; and n.140 above for some representative publications.

[167] Logan (1997, 62–69) presents numerous examples from the Congressional Record.

the massive southern disfranchisement of blacks via southern state constitutions in the 1890–1910 period. For instance, Republican President Taft told a group of white southerners in 1909 that the Fifteenth Amendment did not conflict with their efforts to avoid "domination by an ignorant electorate."[168]

The third phase of the propaganda was the pretense that the only blacks being deprived of the rights to vote and to serve on juries were the uneducated and the unfit. This pretense was formulated in the versions of statutes adopted to restrict the franchise throughout the South to, for instance, only the literate or only those educated well enough to be able to explain sample provisions of the Constitution. By the time that the systematic maladministration of these laws was publicized outside the South, for instance in challenges at the Supreme Court, many northern voters had become convinced of the general incompetence of the black race from phase two of the campaign.

In sum, significant numbers of northerners either came to agree that the South was justified in these restrictions of black civil rights or gave up opposing the intense resistance to these rights because it was politically and financially costly not to do so. In March, 1875 Congress turned its back on Reconstruction. Elections, violence, propaganda, and the custom of Senate filibusters were the agents of its death.

The post-Reconstruction Presidential Branch and Racial Minorities

Congress's initial burst of enthusiasm for protecting racial minorities after the Civil War had extended to blacks and somewhat to Asians. As to Native Americans, Congress's brief flare-up of support for tribal sovereignty—exhibited by language in the 1866 Civil Rights Act and Fourteenth Amendment that limited birth-right citizenship to those Indians who lived outside the jurisdiction of their tribal authorities and by the 1866 Treaty with the Cherokee—had cooled by 1871 and was utterly extinguished by 1875.

To the extent that between 1875 and 1910 racial minorities continued to receive any help at the national level, it came (albeit to a limited degree) from the President (who has a *national* electoral constituency and an international diplomatic constituency) or from the Supreme Court. This fact suggests that Federalist #10 (with its emphasis on the diversity

---

[168] Brandwein 2011, 212, n. 34; Klinkner and Smith 1999, 109. Nieman 1991, 111, suggests that this prevalence of "scientific racism" is what swayed the northern Republicans on the Fuller Court to accept the South's depriving blacks of their civil rights.

of interest groups that would make up any nation-wide majority) may explain as much as #78 does about what has helped racial minorities in the U.S., since the political momentum for persecutions of these groups was primarily regional, coming from the South as to blacks or, for Asians and Native Americans, from the West.

Moreover, Federalist # 51, with its emphasis on checks and balances among separated powers (letting "ambition counteract ambition") also explains important parts of the story. The President used his veto repeatedly against early attempts by a Democratic Congress to repeal voting rights protections, and also, due to concerns about his *international* diplomatic constituency, vetoed the most extreme of the early efforts to exclude Chinese.

President Theodore Roosevelt during the years 1901–09, to a small but not negligible degree, re-activated prosecutions of southern whites attempting to impose slave-like conditions on blacks; these efforts were blocked by the Fuller Court. This same president, Theodore Roosevelt, rhetorically supported an end to anti-Asian immigration policies, and later intervened to stop California from segregating Japanese children into the "colored" schools, at the behest of the Japanese Government, but did so at the cost of the "Gentlemen's Agreement" that resulted in severe restrictions on immigration by Japanese laborers. Roosevelt also had his Justice Department twice bring (winning) suits on behalf of Indian tribes whose treaty rights to natural resources were invaded by state-level policies. Despite his privately confessed belief that whites were the superior race, Theodore Roosevelt (the president who promised a "square deal" to all) plainly was more committed to protecting rights of racial minorities than were his predecessors of the prior fifteen years, but his efforts were modest in light of the overall policy picture; and even these minimal efforts were in part stymied by the Fuller Court.[169]

---

[169] See paragraphs of text at nn. 42–44. On Roosevelt's private views, see Schmidt 1984, 739; Hoxie 1984, 105–7. Roosevelt also appointed the first black U.S. Attorney, William H. Lewis in 1903, and then promoted him to Assistant Attorney General, where he continued through the administration of President Taft; Klarman 2004, 65; Albright 2005. One commonly cited example of official, racist behavior by TR was his dishonorably discharging three companies of black soldiers after interracial violence in the Brownsville incident of 1906. Roosevelt's position on the matter was that they were being discharged for their en masse refusal to testify, not for their skin color. Klarman 2004, 66–7.

The Court on Rights of Asians and Native Americans, 1875–1910

As with the story of the rights of black Americans, the political branches drove the oppressive policies toward Native Americans and Asians (and were in turn driven by regionally distinctive, local or state-level political forces, as was oppression of blacks in the South). Although the Court would occasionally step in against federal *administrators* for inappropriate mistreatment (e.g., *Crow Dog* (1883), for Indians, and seven cases involving people of Chinese descent—the *Chew Heong* (1884), *Jung Ah Lung* (1888), *Lau Ow Bew* (1892), *Wong Kim Ark* (1895), *Gue Lim* (1900), *Tom Hong* (1904) and *Chin Yow* (1908) cases)—it was loath (perhaps understandably) to interfere with policy that combined the will of Congress with that of the President toward these foreign or quasi-foreign peoples. This contrasts with the situation of the Marshall Court, which had the Supremacy Clause plainly on its side in the early nineteenth century cases where it took stands upholding tribal quasi-sovereignty against individual states in *Johnson v. McIntosh* (1823) and *Worcester v. Georgia* (1832).

There is a notable exception: The Fuller Court did declare unconstitutional one piece of a federal law about Chinese resident aliens in a ruling that endured. In *Wong Wing* (1896), the Court basically found constitutionally intolerable the sentencing of Chinese aliens found here unlawfully to a full year of hard labor prior to deportation. Congress might have authority to deport people like Wong Wing, who had come here lawfully but now could not find the paperwork to prove they had done so, and might make it a crime to stay here knowingly without such proof; but in the latter case, if it wanted to subject someone "to infamous punishment at hard labor," Congress would have to first so legislate, and provide the chance for a jury trial, and meet the burden of proving guilt.[170]

In the postbellum decades, on the two occasions when the Supreme Court attempted to uphold Native American autonomy against national government policy, *Crow Dog* (upholding tribal sovereignty against BIA interference) and *In re Heff* (upholding equal citizen autonomy against national paternalistic legislation for off-reservation Indian citizens), Congress promptly overruled the Court or limited the reach of its decisions by writing new laws: the Major Crimes Act of 1885 and the Burke Act of 1906. At least in a Constitution like that of the U.S. that appears to privilege the authority of the electoral branches over policy toward

[170] *Wong Wing v. United States*, 163 U.S. 228 (1896).

foreign and quasi-foreign relations, judicial review operates with exceptional weakness to protect persons viewed as outside the sovereign body.

By contrast, where the treaty rights of native Americans clashed with state-level law, the Supreme Court in this period more often followed in the footsteps of the Marshall Court (*Worcester v. Georgia*, 1832) and the Chase Court (*Kansas Indians* and *New York Indians*, both 1866) than of Roger Taney (*U.S. v. Rogers,* 1846) in its willingness to construe treaty language liberally in favor of Indian sovereignty and rights of tribal members. Granted, the case of *Ward v. Racehorse* (1896) did uphold state law that restricted Indian hunting rights on federal land that appeared by treaty to have been reserved for these Indians, but it was followed by at least two cases, one in 1905 and one in 1908, that went in a contrary direction with respect to fishing rights and the right to divert river water for irrigation. Thus, the dominant judicial tendency toward the end of this period seems to have been a willingness to uphold tribal rights against state law, albeit not with respect to contrary federal law.

Similarly, the Waite Court acted in 1886 in *Yick Wo v. Hopkins* to constrain state-level mistreatment of Asians, something it almost never tried when the mistreatment came in the form of harsh laws or treaties from the federal government. It could mitigate the harshness by interpretation to guide administrators, as it did in the seven cases listed above, but when federal laws plainly enunciated unjust policies toward non-citizen Asians, as they did in the Scott Act of 1888, judicial options were arguably limited; *Chae Chan Ping v. U.S.* in 1889 unanimously upheld the act. Because the Scott Act restricted (without any claim of individual guilt and in the manner of an *ex post facto* law) the rights of lawful resident aliens, already away from home, to re-enter the U.S. during peacetime, I am confident that if the question arose today, the Court would declare it unconstitutional on Fifth Amendment grounds.[171] At the time, anti-Asian sentiment was so overwhelming that the Supreme Court may well have feared precipitating a constitutional amendment. As it would with respect to Southern blacks in the egregious *Giles v. Harris* (1903) decision, the Court in *Chae Chan Ping* hid behind the political question doctrine:

---

[171] I first wrote these words before the executive order of President Donald Trump in January of 2017 for one or two days did just that. That his Administration withdraw this aspect of the order when it drew political fire, I believe suggests that this is an accurate statement about Supreme Court tendencies in the twenty-first century.

> Whether a proper consideration by our government of its previous laws, or a proper respect for the nation whose subjects are affected by its action, ought to have qualified its inhibition, and made it applicable only to persons departing from the country after the passage of the act, are not questions for judicial determination. If there be any just ground of complaint on the part of China, it must be made to the political department of our government, which is alone competent to act upon the subject (130 U.S. 581, 609).

Finally, although the Fuller Court did defend the citizenship-by-birth rights of Asians under the Fourteenth Amendment (*Wong Kim Ark*, 1898), the Waite Court had faltered in this respect toward citizenship for off-reservation Indians (*Elk v. Wilkins*, November, 1884). The latter was handed down at the time that the Secretary of the Interior was successfully mobilizing Congress to overturn the Supreme Court's refusal to subordinate Indian criminal procedures to U.S. federal courts (cf. *Ex Parte Crow Dog*, 1883, with Major Crimes Act of 1885). By contrast, the *Wong Kim Ark* decision came a decade after Congress had itself in the 1887 Dawes Act corrected the Supreme Court's *Elk v. Wilkins* decision, and now allowed birth-right citizenship for those Indians who took up "habits of civilized life" off the reservation.

Overview

In sum, the Court was not the oppressor of racial minorities in the four decades after the Equal Protection Clause was adopted, nor was it, except on rare occasions, their savior. Once the dominant national electoral coalition turned its attention away from protecting the rights of blacks, starting in 1875, the Court was still willing and able, in limited ways to protect rights of blacks (as in the jury cases and *Ex Parte Yarborough*), as well as, on occasion, of Indians (*Ex Parte Crow Dog*; *U.S. v. Winans*; *In re Heff*; *Winters v. U.S.*) and Asians (*Yick Wo v. Hopkins*; *Chew Heong*; *Lau Ow Bew*; *Wong Kim Ark*; *Gue Lim*; and *Tom Hong*). The years of 1874–1888 were years of frequently divided government, and the Court's willingness to uphold the rights of black Americans in these years against discriminatory state laws or governmental action fits an overall pattern described by scholar Mark Graber: when there is not a mobilized political majority on an issue, the Court has more leeway for intervention.[172]

As to Indians, the few Supreme Court decisions protective of their rights, other than the congressionally overruled *Ex Parte Crow Dog*

---

[172] Graber 1993.

(1883), came long after the Battle of Wounded Knee of 1890 had ended the Indian Wars of the Great Plains tribes of the 1870s and 1880s, and several years after the 1887 Dawes Allotment Act and its extension in the 1898 Curtis Act had taken hold. By 1905, protection of Indian rights on the grounds of federal treaty law, at least against particular *state* laws, was not likely to clash with any powerful federal coalition.

But when Congress with the President plainly mobilized *against* blacks, as it did in the 1894 anti-Reconstruction legislation, or when it legislated to override Supreme Court protections of Indians and Asians, the Court sat on its hands (as in *Williams v. Mississippi,* 1898; and *U.S. v. Kagama*, 1886; and *Chae Chan Ping v. U.S.*, 1889). This aspect of the account in this chapter fits into the analytic framework provided long ago by scholar Robert Dahl: except in brief transition periods, the Supreme Court does not cross a dominant national coalition.[173]

When the two elected branches were not united on policy, the President on important occasions was able to check certain anti-minority policies. This happened on a few occasions with respect to vetoing pending laws restricting Asian immigration or urging amendment to some of their harshest aspects. Unfortunately, checks and balances has cut both ways. When President Theodore Roosevelt used his Justice Department to renew efforts to punish southern white perpetrators of unlawful treatment of blacks, his efforts were almost all blocked by the—one has to say it—racist decisions of the Fuller Court. While this Court repeatedly turned a blind eye to blatant injustices perpetrated upon blacks, however, it was willing, on the other hand, to protect Asian residents and Asian citizens against administrative excess from the executive branch. Not always, but often enough to make a difference in several lives, the Fuller Court's independence from political forces did redound to the benefit of members of the Asian minority.

As a general matter, Mark Graber's account of judicial review in "non-majoritarian" periods within the U.S. fits the Court's role as to minority races during the period 1874–1888. Robert Dahl's fits the 1888–1910 period. The time chart Table 4.1, which follows, offers a visual compilation of these cases for the first four decades following the equal protection clause.

---

[173] Dahl 1957, 285.

Table 4.1 Timechart of interbranch comparison on racial minorities policy 1865–1910

Query: In the first four decades after the Fourteenth Amendment entrenched "equal protection of the laws" for all "persons," what role did each federal branch play in securing equal protection for unpopular racial minorities?

+ = protective policies; – = harmful policies;

Sup.Ct. coded italic; **President bold;** Congress underlined. **Cases coded in bold were brought by Justice Dept. prosecutions on behalf of racial minority (These cases receive a + for executive role).**

I. Asians 1865–75

+/– 1866 Congress enacts Civil Rights Act **over presidential veto**, extending to all persons born in U.S. (excepting "Indians not taxed"—i.e. reservation Indians) American citizenship; U.S.-born Chinese thereby acquire U.S. civil rights.

+ July 28, 1868 **President** + Senate by Burlingame Treaty grant China most favored nation status for its tourists and U.S. residents

++ 1870 in §16 of May 31 Enforcement Act with **Pres. Grant** Congress extends most civil rights from the 1866 law not just to all citizens, but to all persons (within U.S. jurisdiction), and specifically forbids unequal taxation based on country of immigrant origin.

– 1870 Congress with **Pres. Grant** in §16 of May 31 Enforcement Act excludes rights to buy, sell, or lease property, which were guaranteed to citizens in §18 of same Act.

– 1870 Congress with **Pres. Grant** in Naturalization Act, although adding Africans to whites as naturalizable citizens, continues to omit Asians.

–1874 (December) **Pres. Grant** implores Congress to bar immigration of coerced Chinese "coolie" labor and "women imported for shameful purposes."

– 1875 (February) Congress reiterates (by omission) that Asians may not be naturalized.

– 1875 (early March) Congress with **Pres. Grant** adopts Page Act, barring entry from "Oriental countries" of women imported "for lewd and immoral purposes," and barring entry of men under indentured service contract and also men serving sentences for felonies. **Enforced** primarily to bar more than 95% of would-be female Chinese immigrants from U.S.

II. Native Americans 1865–75

+ 1866 **President** + Senate undoes 1846 *U.S. v. Rogers* ruling of Chief Justice Taney by new treaty with Cherokee that makes explicit the tribe's power to extend its exclusive civil and criminal jurisdiction to white men by adopting them into the tribe.

+ 1866 Congress exempts "Indians not taxed" from U.S. citizenship in Civil Rights Act, thereby honoring tribal sovereignty.

+ 1866 Congress sends Fourteenth Amendment to states, exempting those Indians from U.S. citizenship who are "not [fully] subject to the jurisdiction of the U.S.," thereby honoring tribal sovereignty over reservation Indians.

++ 1866 *Sup.Ct.* strikes down state taxes of both Kansas and New York on Indian tribes, on grounds that they conflict with prior treaties.

+ + 1869–80 **Pres. Grant** adopts 2-step "Peace Policy" to eliminate fraud by Indian agents, replacing them with missionaries and appointing a Board of Commissioners, comprised of philanthropists, to supervise these. Goal: avoid extinction of Indians by Christianizing them and teaching them how to survive through farming. Policy also followed by **President Hayes**. **This shifts basic policy from removal to attempted assimilation.**

– March 3, 1871 Congress with **Pres. Grant** forbids treaties with Indian tribes, but continues at first to seek tribal agreement for new policies.

– May 1, 1871 *Sup.Ct.* (*Cherokee Tobacco Tax Case*) upholds **exec. branch** application of a tobacco tax law in way that violates terms of earlier treaty with Cherokee.

> [1866–1890: period of intermittent Indian wars in the West provoked by threat of Indian starvation. 1872–1875: Nine million buffalo killed for skins and left to rot by whites]

III. Black Americans 1865–76

++ March 1865 Congress with **Pres. Lincoln** establish Freedmen's Bureau for freed slaves and war refugees.

+ Dec.1865 Thirteenth Amendment ratified—Congress & states.

+/– 1866 Civil Rights Act –Congress over **Pres. Johnson's** veto.

++ 1866 **President** & Senate in treaty free all the black slaves owned by Cherokee and grant them and their descendants all rights of native Cherokee.

+/– 1866 Congress over **Pres. Johnson's** veto renews Freedmen's Bureau.

+/– 1867 Congress over **Pres. Johnson's** veto enfranchises blacks in D.C. and federal territory.

+/– 1867 Congress over **Pres. Johnson's** veto: Reconstruction Act permitting adult black males to vote in state elections for new state constitutions in South and also under those constitutions (if states are to be re-admitted to Congress).

+ 1868 Fourteenth Amendment ratified—Congress & states.

+ 1870 Fifteenth Amendment ratified—Congress & states.

++ 1870 Congress with **Pres. Grant** in Naturalization Act adds Africans to whites as naturalizable citizens.

++ May 31, 1870 Congress with **Pres. Grant** in Enforcement Act enforces Fifteenth Amendment by punishing political terrorism in the South.

++ April 20, 1871, Ku Klux Klan Act (focuses on acts for which Klan was notorious, such as "going in disguise on a public highway" with intent to deprive of civil rights)—Congress with **Pres. Grant**.

–/+ 1872 *Sup.Ct.* in ***Blyew v. U.S.*** narrowly reads fed. law; avoids removing to federal courts cases where blacks are refused right to serve as witnesses

+ 1873 *Sup.Ct.* in *Railroad Co. v. Brown* broadly reads fed. law desegregating railroad in D.C., rejecting "separate but equal" argument.

– Nov.1874, U.S. public votes overwhelmingly to put Democrats in majority in House of Representatives.

–/+ Jan.1875 Lame duck Republican Congress with **Pres. Grant** adopts (watered down) Civil Rights Act (leaves schools segregated; mandates racial equality in access to public carriers, inns, and theaters, also racial non-discrimination in access to juries).

+ 1871–77 **Exec. Branch** brings hundreds of prosecutions annually of KKK malefactors (see Figure 3.1).

+/– 1876 *Sup.Ct.* twists language of fed. Enforcement Act (***U.S. v. Reese***) to strike down two sections. Also dismisses several murder indictments as lacking proof of required racial motive (***U.S. v. Cruikshank***). But stretches language of Fifteenth Amendment to remove its apparent state action limitation (***U.S. v. Cruikshank***), establishing Fifteenth Amendment voting rights as national rights protectable against private action.

+ 1876 *Sup.Ct.* in *Walker v. Sauvinet* upholds thousand dollar damages award (despite absence of jury trial) against white café owner for violating Louisiana law mandating equal access to public accommodations irrespective of race, when privately owned but state licensed café refused on racial grounds to serve a black man.

IV. Asians 1876–1908

–/+ 1879 bipartisan but more heavily Democrat Congressional majority votes for bill to alter Burlingame Treaty and limit Chinese worker immigration; **Pres. Hayes** (GOP) vetoes it successfully.

– 1880 both major party platforms (plus Greenback Labor Party) pledge to limit Chinese immigration.

– Nov. 1880 China and U.S. sign new treaty endorsing "reasonable" restrictions on immigration–**President** & Senate.

– 1881 **Pres.Chester A. Arthur** (GOP VP who succeeded to the presidency) in annual message endorses restriction of Chinese immigration

–/+ 1881 Congress votes to restrict Chinese immigration for twenty years; **Pres. Arthur** successfully vetoes it as unreasonably extreme.

-- 1882 Chinese Exclusion Act suspends Chinese laborer immigration for ten years; denies entry to U.S. by wives of Chinese laborer residents. Reiterates prohibition on naturalization of Chinese. Specifies that resident laborer Chinese who leave the U.S. must show special federally issued I.D. card in order to re-enter—Congress with **Pres. Arthur.**

– July 1884 Congress with **Pres. Arthur** tightens procedures for ANY Chinese entry to U.S.

+/– Dec.1884 *Sup.Ct.* in *Chew Heong v. U.S.* admits Chew Heong to U.S. on grounds that prior treaties allow his admission, despite **Justice Dept**. argument that 1884 Act bars his re-entry.

+ 1886 *Sup.Ct.* in *Yick Wo v. Hopkins* declares void as violation of equal protection clause a law applied against Chinese but not against similarly situated Anglos.

–/+ 1887 *Sup. Ct.* in *Baldwin v. Franks* refused to allow the U.S. **Justice Dept.** to use §5519 to prosecute mob violence against Chinese residents in California, because it had been struck down already in a case involving violence against American blacks. Said Congress did have authority to enact a (new) law punishing private violence against foreigners residing within U.S.

–/+ Feb.1888 Sup. Ct. in *U.S. v. Jung Ah Lung* overturns Exec. Branch decision to block re-entry of Chinese resident alien laborer despite his lack of required paper because he had ample proof of identity.

– 1888 October 1 Congress with **the President** passes Scott Act forbidding RE-entry to U.S. by lawful Chinese laborer residents out of the country as of Oct.1, 1888 and henceforth.

– 1889 *Sup.Ct.* in *Chae Chan Ping v. U.S.* [*Chinese Exclusion Case*], accepting **Justice Dept**. arguments, upholds Scott Act despite its acknowledged conflict with prior treaty (1871 *Cherokee Tobacco Tax* case).

– 1891 *Sup.Ct.* in *Quock Ting v. U.S.*, agreeing with **immigration officials**, rules that uncontradicted testimony per se is not sufficient to force a court to accept Chinese person's claim of birth-right citizenship, if context makes the testimony appear fraudulent.

– 1891 Sup Ct. in *Wan Shing v. U. S.*, agreeing with **immigration officials,** rules that Chinese person attempting to reenter the U.S. on a claim of merchant status must prove that status by a certificate from the Chinese government, as specified in 1884 law.

– 1892 *Sup.Ct.* in *Nishimura Ekiu v. U.S.*, accepting **Justice Dept**. arguments, refuses to grant review by judges over exclusion of Japanese immigrant on grounds of pauper status by decision of immigration authorities; says law allows immigration appeals (except for Chinese) only to the Secretary of the Treasury. (See also 1903 below.)

+/– 1892 March 14, *Sup.Ct.* in *Lau Ow Bew v. U.S.* rejects **Justice Dept** arguments and reverses decision of collector of the port of San Francisco (upheld at district and circuit court levels). *Sup. Ct.* permits Chinese merchant, long resident in the U.S., to re-enter without certificate from Chinese govt. that port collector wrongly believed 1884 Act required. Court accepts substantive proof in lieu of formally required certificate.

– 1892 May 5, Congress with **the President** in Geary Act §1 extended Chinese laborer exclusion for ten more years; in §§ 2 and 3 said all resident Chinese "and persons of Chinese descent" (my emphasis) who could not satisfy a judge that their residence since May 5, 1892 was legal must be removed from the U.S.

– 1893 *Sup.Ct.* in *Fong Yue Ting v. U.S.*, despite 3 angry dissents, upholds §§ 2 and 3 of Geary Act (requiring that Chinese resident laborers document their right to stay or else be deported), going along with **Executive Branch.**

+ 1894 **President** and Senate by Treaty exempt from Scott Act those Chinese returnees with families or property in the U.S. (Treaty had initially been negotiated in 1888, but China at the time refused to ratify).

– 1894 Congress with **the President** in Appropriations [Chandler] Act removes judicial review over decisions by immigration bureaucrats as to claims of a right of entry by Chinese; appeal against a Chinese exclusion decision is only to Secretary of the Treasury.

– 1895 *Sup.Ct.* in *Lem Moon Sing v. U.S.* upheld 1894 withdrawal of judicial review from individual **executive branch** decisions to exclude an alien.

+/– 1896 *Sup.Ct.* in *Wong Wing v. U.S.*, rejecting **Justice Dept.** arguments, strikes down as violation of due process §4 of Geary Act, which allowed sentencing for up to a year of imprisonment at hard labor prior to deportation of those Chinese who could not prove lawfulness of residency.

+/– 1898 *Sup.Ct.* in *Wong Kim Ark v. U.S.* upheld **against (GOP) Justice Dept**. arguments the citizenship of a Chinese person born in the U.S., implicitly declaring unconstitutional the "and persons of Chinese descent" language of the Geary Act.

+/– 1900 *Sup. Ct.* in *U.S. v. Mrs. Gue Lim* upholds **against (GOP) Justice Dept.** arguments, right of wives and minor children of Chinese merchants to enter and reside in U.S. without certificates.

– 1902 *Sup. Ct.* in *Chin Bak Kan v. U.S.* and in *Chin Ying v. U.S.* accepts judgment by Commissioners over claims to citizenship of U.S.-born persons of Chinese descent, subject to appeals to federal district court; rules Congress entitled to put burden of proof on the Chinese descent person.

– 1902 Congress with **the President** extended all prior bans on Chinese immigration indefinitely.

+ 1903 *Sup. Ct.* slightly modified rule from *Ekiu* case (1892), in case of *Yamatay Kaoru v. Fisher,* another Japanese immigrant alleged to be a pauper. Before deportation as paupers, resident aliens now entitled to some hearing of evidence under due process clause, albeit not a full judicial trial.

– 1904 Congress with **the President** re-enacted the already indefinite 1902 ban on Chinese immigration.

+/– 1904 *Sup.Ct.* in *Tom Hong v. U.S.* blocked deportation by **immigration commissioner** of Chinese merchants who had gone out of business (so were now "laborers").

– 1903 (Dec.) **Justice Dept**. takes position that appellate decisions of Secretary of Labor and Commerce rejecting citizenship claims of Chinese-descent person are final; no judicial court should be allowed to issue habeas writ to review the decision.

–/+ 1904 in *Ah How v. U.S.* (4 consolidated cases) upheld Commissioner and District Court deportation orders despite fact that one appellant (Lew Guey) had a letter from a **U.S. Commissioner** saying he had been adjudged a U.S. citizen.

–/+ 1904 *Sup.Ct.* in *Sing Tuck v. U.S.* only partially agrees with **executive** branch; no *habeas writ* may be issued on appeals of Chinese-descent persons claiming U.S. birth citizenship until after applicant has exhausted appeal remedies through the Secretary of Commerce and Labor.

– 1905 *Sup.Ct.*in *Ju Toy v. U.S.* rules similarly to *Sing Tuck* on **executive branch** discretion over refusing re-entry to Chinese-descent persons claiming U.S. birth citizenship; Secretary of Commerce and Labor decision is final (despite contrary finding on Ju Toy's citizenship by the district court) and not judicially reviewable, except for an allegation that Secretary broke the law or abused discretion.

+ 1905 **Pres. Teddy Roosevelt** in annual message endorses racially non-discriminatory immigration policy, and threatens to veto Congressional exclusion of Japanese.

+ 1906 **Pres. Teddy Roosevelt** in annual message urges Congress to allow Japanese to naturalize.

+/– 1908 *Sup.Ct.* in *Chin Yow v. U.S.* (1908), rejecting **executive branch** arguments, "distinguished" the 1905 *Ju Toy* decision (and related precedents of 1904 and 1902), ruling that a Chinese-descent person claiming citizenship is entitled to a "fair hearing" and if it is denied, can obtain it by judicial review. Chandler Act is thus narrowed.

+/– 1908 *Sup.Ct.* in *Liu Hop Fong v. U.S.* interprets Section 13 of the act of 1888 (25 Stat. 476) to require a full district court hearing ("de novo") on appeal of **Commissioner decision** (rather than mere review of the Commissioner's hearing transcript) before deporting a Chinese adjudged by the Commissioner to have been a laborer despite proper certificate from China affirming status of "student." Ruled that certificate should be given legal effect unless competent evidence to the contrary is presented and that Liu Hop Fong should be permitted to present evidence also.

[1898–1906 labor shortage in California produces sharp increase in Japanese immigration]

+/– 1906–08 **President (T.Roosevelt)** negotiates (prompted by Japanese offense at placement in "colored" schools), and Congress authorizes, a deal with Japan ("Gentleman's agreement"): Japanese resident in San Francisco may attend the "white" school, but Japanese and Korean laborers may not immigrate to the U.S. (unless joining an immediate family member or already owning a U.S. farm or coming to be a wife).

[1907–09 sharp decrease in Japanese immigration].

[– in 1917 Congress bars ALL Asian immigration, including from the Middle East; in 1920s *Sup.Ct.* upholds state prohibitions on landowning by Asians.]

V. Native Americans 1876–1910

–/+ 1883 *Sup.Ct.* in *Ex Parte Crow Dog* rejects effort by **[exec. branch] BIA** to impose U.S. criminal law on Indian reservations

– 1884 **Sec'y of Interior** in annual report lobbies for Major Crimes Act to undo *Ex Parte Crow Dog.*

– 1884 *Sup.Ct.* in *Elk v. Wilkins* ruled that non-reservation Indian (born on reservation within U.S. boundaries, living off reservation) does not have U.S. citizenship unless naturalized (Harlan and Woods dissent).

– 1885 Congress with **the President** enacts Major Crimes Act removing Indian jurisdiction over (and federalizing) seven crimes, even if committed intra-tribally on reservation (undoes *Crow Dog*)

– 1886 *Sup.Ct.* in *U.S. v. Kagama* upheld the Major Crimes Act despite its conflict with prior treaties (*Cherokee Tobacco Tax Case*).

–/++ 1887 Congress with **the President** passes Dawes Act arranging for individual allotments (alienable within 25 years) of heretofore tribal land and also for selling off "surplus" tribal lands [result: by 1934, 80% of land value belonging to Indians lost to them.] Act corrects *Elk v. Wilkins* error: bestows U.S. citizenship on all Indians who take an allotment or take up life away from the tribe, and adopt "habits of civilized life."

+ 1896 *Sup.Ct.* rules in *Talton v. Mayes* that tribal sovereignty exempts tribal governments from restrictions of the Bill of Rights in dealing with tribal members.

–/+ 1896 *Sup.Ct.* in *Ward v. Racehorse* upheld state-level regulations of Indian hunting on federal land that contradicted guarantee in prior Indian treaty; appeared to turn away from the precedents of Kansas and New York Indians cases of 1866. **U.S. Att'y General** is counsel for Racehorse.

– 1898 Congress with **the President** in Curtis Act (June 28) extends Dawes Act to cover the Five Civilized tribes (previously exempted due to agricultural success), contrary to extant treaty and property law. [result: immiseration of previously prosperous tribes]. Also authorizes (in §13) Secretary of Interior to issue mineral leases on tribal land with monetary proceeds to go to tribal benefit.

– 1899 *Sup.Ct.* in *Stephens v. Cherokee Nation* upholds aspect of the Curtis/Dawes Act that lets Dawes Commission determine who is a tribal member for purposes of land allotment.

– 1902 *Sup.Ct.* in *Cherokee Nation v. Hitchcock* upholds legislative grant of authority (in Curtis/Dawes Act) to Secretary of Interior to issue mineral leases on tribal land with monetary proceeds to go to tribal benefit.

– 1903 *Sup.Ct.* in *Lone Wolf v. Hitchcock* upholds selloff and allotment of tribal land in a treaty, which the House favored but slipped through the Senate in 1900 by subterfuge, despite clear conflict with treaty law and massive evidence of fraudulent dealing by the non-Indians and of opposition to the sale by tribal membership. (In 1901 **Pres.McKinley** had already announced that the lands were open for [white] settlement.)

++ 1905 *Sup.Ct.* in ***U.S. v. Winans*** rules that Indian fishing rights preserved in prior federal treaty prevail over later state regulations (turning its back on *Racehorse*, 1896). **U.S. Justice Dept. (of T.R.)** defends Indian treaty rights.

+ 1905 *Sup.Ct.* in *In re Heff* forbids Congress to prohibit sale of liquor to only Indians, saying that they must be treated as equal citizens, having become citizens via the Dawes Act allotment process.

– 1906 Congress with **the President** (provoked by *In re Heff*) in Burke Act postpones Indian citizenship during the 25 years of federal land supervision, with power in Sec'y of Interior to shorten individual supervision periods.

++ 1908 *Sup.Ct.* in ***Winters v. U.S.*** upholds tribal rights to divert streams for navigation on grounds of prior federal treaty in the face of contrary state law (staying with its 1905 *Winans* logic on fishing rights). **U.S. Justice Dept. (of T.R.)** defends Indian treaty against state law.

1910–20, Sup.Ct. language about Indians grows more patronizing; western states keep large numbers of Indians from voting via English literacy requirements, tax requirements, requirements of evidence of being "civilized"; Sup.Ct. overrules *In re Heff* in 1916 *U.S. v. Nice.*

VI. Black Americans 1876–1910

[in 1874 Democrats gain the House and until 1889 Republicans do not again control both branches plus Presidency; closest is 1881-2 when Democrats nonetheless have 50% of Senate with easy filibuster]

+ 1876–85 **Executive branch** prosecutions for electoral terrorism in the South continue in significant numbers but in lower numbers than peak years of 1872–1874

+ + 1877 *Chief Justice Waite* on circuit in ***U.S. v. Butler*** upheld ten indictments of private persons for racially discriminatory vote-discouraging violence.

– 1878 *Sup.Ct.* in *Hall v. DeCuir* invalidates Louisiana statute forbidding race discrimination in common carriers as violation of commerce clause if applied (even within state) to interstate carriers.

+ 1880 *Sup.Ct.* in *Ex Parte Siebold* rejects argument that state officials (of Baltimore MD) may not be held accountable in federal courts for obedience to federal election laws.

+ 1880 *Sup.Ct.* in *Strauder v. W. Virginia* declared unconstitutional state law that restricted jury service to white males.

++ 1880 Sup.Ct. in ***Ex Parte Virginia*** upheld conviction of a state official for federal crime of excluding blacks from jury lists on account of race, under §4 of 1875 Civil Rights Act, which it also upheld.

+ 1881 *Sup.Ct.* in *Neal v. Delaware* rejected as beyond credibility claim of Delaware officials that zero of the 26,000 black residents qualified for jury duty as "sober and judicious persons"; ruled the criminal trial in question unconstitutional.

+ 1883 *Sup.Ct.* in *Bush v. Kentucky* threw out indictment for murder by a black of a white, on grounds that blacks had been excluded from consideration for grand jury service, pursuant to state law in force at time of the indictment.

– 1883 *Sup.Ct.* in ***Civil Rights Cases*** declares unconstitutional the public accommodations provisions of 1875 Civil Rights Act because they fail to specify that unequal treatment by the state or its officials is what is forbidden. Merely private action is ruled not punishable under Fourteenth Amendment.

– 1883 *Sup.Ct.* in *U.S. v. Harris* declares unconstitutional §5519 of the federal code because it allowed punishment of merely private persons (lynch mob), rather than state officials, for denying "equal protection of the laws." Case involved white on white violence but ruling affected black civil rights enforcement.

++ 1884 *Sup.Ct.* in ***Ex Parte Yarborough*** upheld convictions of private persons for violent interference with Fifteenth Amendment rights (i.e., no state action required for conviction.) Also ruled that racial motivation need not be proved for prosecuting federal election interference.

+/– 1887,1888,1889 **Interstate Commerce Commission** interpreted language of the Interstate Commerce Act (1887) forbidding subjecting customers to "unreasonable prejudice or disadvantage" to permit racial separation in railway cars, so long as accommodations were equal but ruled unlawful the specific accommodations because not strictly equal (Schmidt 1984, 749–751, n.61).

+/– 1889–90 The (GOP) House of Representatives passed the Hoar-Lodge bill, which would have sent federal enforcement officials to the South to secure voting rights for blacks. Action in the Senate was blocked by filibuster of Democrats until, during the lame duck session, a handful of GOP Senators voted with the Democrats to bring up a new subject. In 1890 the Democrats again took Congress.

– 1890 *Sup.Ct.* in *L'ville, N.O., & Tex. Ry. v. Mississippi*, upholds Mississippi law requiring separate cars for white and black race in in-state common carriers (despite *Hall v. DeCuir*, 1878), as not undue burden on interstate commerce.

– 1890 *Sup. Ct.* in *Chesapeake & Ohio Ry. v. Kentucky* upholds Kentucky law requiring separate cars for white and black race in in-state common carriers (despite *Hall v. DeCuir*, 1878), as not undue burden on interstate commerce.

– 1891 *Sup.Ct.* in *In re Wood* on procedural grounds (wrong writ, wrong timing) refuses to examine allegation that New York courts have been excluding blacks from juries and thereby denying equal protection.

– 1893–94 both houses of Congress and the **Presidency** were finally controlled by the Democrats. They legislated in 1894 to rescind the federal provisions that enforced voting rights in the South. Republicans had turned their attention away from blacks, to economic issues, and did not filibuster.

– 1895 *Sup.Ct.* in *Mills v. Green* refused to invalidate procedures used in South Carolina to keep blacks from voting for state constitutional convention, ruling that the election was finished, so issue moot.

– 1895 *Sup.Ct.* in *Andrews v. Swartz* (1895) refuses to examine allegation of racial exclusion from jury, claiming procedural error.

– 1896 *Sup.Ct.* in *Gibson v. Mississippi*, *Smith v. Mississippi*, and *Murray v. Louisiana* refuses to examine allegation of racial exclusion from jury, claiming procedural error.

– 1896 *Sup.Ct.* in *Plessy v. Ferguson* permitted a state law that required "separate but equal" accommodations on railway cars for white and non-white races, ignoring "state action" logic of earlier *Civil Rights Cases* (1883).

– 1898 *Sup.Ct.* genuinely turned its back on Reconstruction. In *Williams v. Mississippi* claimed that the Mississippi law, which in application deprived the vast majority of blacks of the vote, and of jury eligibility, was not close enough to the bias in application of *Yick Wo v. Hopkins* to be judged unconstitutional.

– 1899 *Sup.Ct.* ruled in *Cummings v. Bd.* that county did not violate equal protection when it closed the only government-funded black high school but continued to run one for white girls and to subsidize one for white boys, in context where three private high schools were open for blacks.

+/– 1900 *Sup.Ct.* in *Carter v. Texas* remands to state courts to permit convicted murderer to show evidence that selection of the grand juries for many years in his county deliberately excluded qualified blacks on grounds of race; his fate still left to state courts.

– 1900 *Sup.Ct.* in *Wiley v. Sinkler* rejects damages suit from South Carolinian against a voting official who refused to allow him to vote, despite claim he was "in every respect duly qualified" to vote in elections in South Carolina. *Sup.Ct* relied on his neglect to claim in court that he was a registered voter.

+ 1901 **Justice Dept**. under **Pres. Roosevelt** successfully prosecutes Samuel M. Clyatt for forcibly returning two black men into peonage. Clyatt appeal becomes *Clyatt v. U.S.* (1905)

– 1903 *Sup.Ct.* in *Tarrance v. Florida* rejects claim of racial exclusion from jury, saying proof absent.

– 1903 *Sup.Ct.* in *Brownfield v. S.Carolina* rejects claim of racial exclusion from jury, saying proof absent despite allegation that county was 80% black.

– 1903 *Sup.Ct.* in *Giles v. Harris* despite being shown fact pattern as egregious as that of *Yick Wo v. Hopkins* refuses to declare the Alabama voting law unconstitutional either per se or as administered and instead says that only the elected branches are powerful enough to deal with an intransigent state.

– 1903 *Sup.Ct.* in ***James v. Bowman*** ignores rules that have been in place since *Reese* and *Cruikshank* and declares unconstitutional §5507 on grounds that 15th Amendment can be violated only by state, not private, officials.

++ 1903 **President T. Roosevelt's Justice Dept**. indicted two groups of whites for threatening and violently intimidating black workers to leave their jobs [and move away]. The first, ***U.S. v. Morris*** charged eleven whites with intimidating black sharecroppers; the jury did not convict. The second, ***U.S. v. Maples***, charged fifteen white men with intimidating eight black sawmill workers to leave their jobs, and the jury convicted three. The charge was violation of §§ 1977 and 5508, by conspiring to use violence and threats to deprive 8 named black Americans of the 13th Amendment right to contract freely to dispose of their labor. The appeal of this case became the 1906 *U.S. v. Hodges*.

– 1904 *Sup.Ct.* in *Giles v. Teasley* refuses to grant either damages or a writ of mandamus to correct alleged mass violations of the Fifteenth Amendment by Alabama voting registrars.

– 1904 *Sup. Ct.* in *Jones v. Montague* rejects an appeal from blacks denied voting rights by the 1901 Constitution of Virginia on the grounds that the Congressional election of 1902 was completed, so the case was moot.

+/– 1904 *Sup.Ct.* in *Rogers v. Alabama* remands to state courts for proceedings that will allow convicted murderer to present evidence that grand jury was selected in ways that deliberated excluded qualified blacks; defendant's fate still left to state authorities.

–/+ 1905 Sup.Ct. reverses the conviction for peonage in ***Clyatt v. U.S.*** due to wrong wording in the indictment and remands for retrial. Does uphold 1867 federal law against peonage.

++ 1905 Sup. Ct. in ***Riggins v. U.S.*** ruled that federally convicted member of mob that had lynched a black man could not use procedure of writ of habeas corpus.

– 1906 *Sup.Ct.* in *Thomas v. Texas* rejects claim of jury exclusion, claiming evidence absent.

+ 1906 **President T. Roosevelt** calls on Congress to pass anti-lynching bill into law.

+ 1906 **President T. Roosevelt's Justice Dept. indicted** another group of Arkansas whites for violently intimidating a group of black workers to leave their railroad jobs. Case became *Boyett v. U.S.* (1907).

–/+ 1906 *Sup.Ct.* ruled in ***Hodges v. U.S.*** that federal government does not have power under 13th Amendment to punish a private criminal conspiracy to use violence to intimidate blacks (or others) out of freely contracting for a job, and threw out the criminal convictions for having done so.

++ 1906 *Sup.Ct.* ruled in ***U.S. v. Shipp I*** that it had authority to try the members of lynch mob along with compliant sheriff and deputies on charges of criminal contempt for lynching a prisoner after being notified that the Supreme Court had agreed to hear his appeal for a writ of habeas corpus.

–/+ 1907 *Sup.Ct.* relied on *Hodges* to rule per curiam in ***Boyett v. U.S.*** (1907), invalidating the criminal convictions of intimidators of black railroad workers.

–/+ 1908 *Sup. Ct.* in ***Bailey v. Alabama*** disagrees with *amicus* from **Justice Dept.** and refuses to issue pre-trial release on *habeas* of a black man jailed under a peonage law.

– 1908 *Sup. Ct.* in *Berea College v. Kentucky* upheld state law forbidding even private corporations to educate blacks and whites together.

++ 1909 ***U.S. v. Shipp* (II)** (1909) In the only criminal trial ever conducted by the U.S. Supreme Court, Court finds a lynch mob guilty of criminal contempt of court (See ***Shipp I*,** 1906, above for background).

– 1910 *Sup.Ct.* in *Chiles v. Chesapeake & Ohio* rejected claim that refusal by rail company to admit interstate black traveler holding first class ticket into the only first class car, which was whites only, violated his rights to substantially equal accommodations. Court rejected his claim that the colored and smokers car was substantially inferior to the whites only car, despite the former's lack of a toilet and its smoky condition. Court rejected passenger's claim that railway company was acting pursuant to Kentucky law mandating railway segregation rather than its own policy. Court ruled that Congressional silence on racial segregation in interstate travel meant that it was permitted [despite words of 1887 Interstate Commerce Act forbidding common carriers to subject any person to "undue or unreasonable prejudice or disadvantage."]

5. The White and Taft Courts, 1911–30

THE WHITE COURT, 1911–21

The Supreme Court's record on civil rights for black Americans took a sharp turn for the better in 1911, upon the promotion of Justice Edward White to Chief Justiceship in December of 1910. Scholars continue to debate the causes of this change: it may have been due to the departure of pro-slavery Chief Justice Melvin Fuller (who died in 1910), or because of the psychological impact of actually themselves trying guilty parties for a lynching in 1909 (on charges of contempt of court, since the sheriff and deputy co-conspirators involved knew that the appeal of the man they were about to lynch to death had been accepted for a hearing at the U.S. Supreme Court), or because of surrounding socio-political events—or, most likely, some combination of these elements.[1] The cases that comprise the "turn for the better" are described below in the section "Good News for Blacks." In brief, they include two anti-segregation decisions, two anti-peonage-law decisions, and three pro-voting-rights decisions. This turn by the White Court was hardly to be expected. The new Chief Justice White had served as an officer in the Confederate Army and in Louisiana had been a politician who led opposition to Reconstruction.[2] Vanderbilt Law Review presented a symposium on these cases in 1998, and one scholar concluded after reflecting upon the other symposium papers and the cases themselves, "In the end … the[se] Progressive era decisions remain a puzzle."[3]

---

[1] So far as I know, no previous scholar has suggested that presiding on original jurisdiction over a trial for "contempt of court," the federal charge imposed upon this murder by lynching, shaped the Court's jurisdiction in the immediately subsequent decades. See more detailed discussion of the *Shipp* trial below.

[2] Schmidt 1984, 725–6. Schmidt writes that in the twentieth century White Court, "It was the best of times black people had as yet seen." This undervalues contributions of both the Chase and Waite Courts, but there can be no doubt that the White Court proved a dramatic improvement over the Fuller Court. See also, Howard 1999, 161.

[3] Tushnet 1998, 1000.

In the years 1909–12, Brewer, Fuller, Peckham, William Moody, and (pro-civil-rights) Harlan all left the Court. And there was considerable further turnover during the early twentieth century. President Theodore Roosevelt appointed Oliver Wendell Holmes (1902–32); William Day (GOP Ohio, 1903–22; and William Moody (GOP Mass. 1906–10). President Taft (GOP Ohio) appointed Horace Lurton (Dem. Tenn. 1909–14); Charles E. Hughes (GOP NY, 1910–16); Willis Van Devanter (GOP Wyo. 1910–37); Joseph Lamar (Dem. GA. 1910–16); Mahlon Pitney (GOP NJ. 1912–22); and promoted Edward White to Chief Justiceship in 1910. President Wilson (Dem. NJ., who imposed racial segregation on federal civil service jobs and halted the postbellum practice of appointing blacks to patronage jobs)[4] appointed James McReynolds (Dem. Tenn. 1914–41); Louis D. Brandeis (Dem. Mass. 1916–39); and John Clarke (Dem. Ohio, 1916–22). Economic, rather than racially sensitive, concerns seemed to dominate the presidential selection process of those years: Theodore Roosevelt's picks had been dominated, in his words, by a desire to find "a liberal-minded Man, a man with sympathy for the position of labor … a man who is not … scared … from exercising proper control over corporations."[5] Taft, by contrast, sought men with the right sort of conservative "creeds on property."[6] In contrast to the Fuller Court, however, neither the Court under Chief Justice White nor the one under later Chief Justice Taft gave rise to someone like the first Justice John Marshall Harlan who had stood out as the voice for racial justice on the Fuller Court. Although the appointment of Progressive Charles Hughes was particularly important, personnel changes alone cannot fully account for the clearly discernible judicial shift on race, modest though it was.[7]

4 Schmidt 1984, 937–8.

5 Howard 1999, 162; (quotation) Bickel 1984, 5–6.

6 Ibid.

7 Cf. Howard 1999, 160–67. Howard attributes the Court's relatively progressive record of 1911–17 to new personnel, specifically, the presence of Charles Evans Hughes, who had the intellectual heft and commitment to racial justice to outweigh the strong intellectual force of Oliver Wendell Holmes. The latter (despite his reputation as a "liberal") was so strongly committed to deference to local majorities that he frequently voted against black litigants. Howard is no doubt correct as to the direction of Hughes's influence, but Hughes left the Court in 1916, a year prior to the White Court's striking down a segregation ordinance in *Buchanan v. Warley*. See discussion below.

One must consider the changing times as at least part of the equation.[8] Among more educated or affluent whites, and even among some union women, the women's suffrage movement was in full swing, and Progressivism was in flower among white middle class voters. Despite his privately expressed views on inherent racial inequality, (Progressive) President Theodore Roosevelt had used his Justice Department to bring several cases on behalf of minority rights, as was detailed in Chapter 4, although most were blocked by the conservative Fuller Court.[9] In terms of working class life in this period, both industrialization and immigration were at peak levels.

Unfortunately, the latter trend seems to have triggered a rash of northern race riots in the period of 1898–1908 in which mobs of working class whites attacked and even killed random black people, and set fire to black neighborhoods. These northern pogroms had been preceded by a severe outbreak of post-Reconstruction style violence in 1898 in Wilmington, North Carolina, which aimed to discourage black voting and to drive elected black leaders into resigning office and leaving the city. Somewhere between fourteen and sixty blacks were murdered and some 1,400 others moved out of the city.[10]

Then in 1898–1899 racial violence moved north, beginning with a flurry of coal mine riots in three different Illinois towns. Armed union members on strike confronted management's armed guards defending southern blacks who had been recruited as strikebreakers. These clashes produced several deaths of blacks, but (for what it's worth) the mob fury was plainly job related.[11]

The race-based riots of the first decade of the twentieth century were accompanying the increasing stream of black migration into the North.[12]

---

[8] Cf., however, Klarman 2004, 67 ff. Klarman debunks the idea that the "times" were supportive of racial reform: "The political nadir of race relations at the national level may have come in the 1912 presidential election and its aftermath." Presidential candidates Taft and Teddy Roosevelt both endorsed southern home rule on race, and Woodrow Wilson, who won, was a committed southern Democrat, having resided in the South for the first twenty-eight years of his life.

[9] See particularly n.169 and related text, along with section "Free Labor Rights in the Fuller Court," all in Chapter 4.

[10] Klarman 2004, 11, 15, 38; Umfleet 2010.

[11] Lupton 2007.

[12] Black migrants to the North numbered 49,000 in the 1870s; 62,000 in the 1880s, 132,000 in the 1890s and 143,000 in the 1900–1909 decade. Klarman 2004, 12.

Whether these riots were motivated by an underlying sense of competition over jobs,[13] or by cultural clash between rural blacks and staid Midwestern townsfolk,[14] or simply by amorphous racial hostility, their common pattern was an immediate triggering by the formation of a would-be lynch mob, agitated over a black on white crime. The first was in 1900 in New York City, and was set off by the killing of a white plainclothes policeman by a black man acting in self-defense; many blacks were injured to the point of hospitalization.[15] This format of race riot—i.e., one not aimed at disenfranchising blacks or at strikebreakers, but triggered by lynch mob—then recurred in Evansville, Indiana, 1903;[16] Springfield, Ohio, 1904 and 1906;[17] Greensburg, Indiana, 1906;[18] and Springfield, Illinois, 1908.[19] The same pattern spread to the South, occurring in 1900, in New Orleans,[20] in 1904, in Statesboro, Georgia;[21] and in 1906, in Atlanta, Georgia.[22] Then in July of 1910, a new round of race riots broke out in numerous cities in response to the heavyweight championship victory of black boxer Jack Johnson over "great white hope," Jim Jeffries. This wave of riots produced twenty-six deaths.[23]

As can be seen in Table 4.1, apart from the three lynching-related cases of 1905 (*Riggins*), 1906 (*Shipp I*) and 1909 (*Shipp II*), the Fuller Court had produced *no* other decisions truly favorable to black Americans.[24] The Supreme Court under Chief Justice White, by contrast, immediately produced a different outcome in the next peonage case: *Bailey v.*

---

13 This is the thesis of Klarman 2004, 64.

14 This is the thesis of Butler 2000. The account of the Springfield, Illinois riot by Senechal 1996 lends Butler's thesis some support, at 24–5, but ultimately rejects it, at 25. Her conclusion seems to point the finger at amorphous racial hostility, which she phrases in terms of white resentment at black success, harbored not by foreign immigrants or by southern migrants but by natives of Illinois who held secure jobs.

15 Collins 2007, 474–5; Washington 1998.

16 Butler 2000; Blocker 2002.

17 Ohio Historical Society. N.D; Franklin and Moss 1994, 316.

18 Bergman and Bergman 1969, 347; Franklin and Moss 1994, 316.

19 Senechal 1996; Franklin and Moss 1994, 316–19. This riot received extensive press coverage and provoked the formation of the NAACP.

20 Hair 1976, 153, 175-177.

21 Franklin and Moss 1994, 313.

22 Howard 1999, 159; Mixon and Kuhn 2005.

23 "Racism Takes a Blow in Reno"; JP. 2011.

24 To be sure, the Fuller Court in the 1905 *Clyatt* case did at least refrain from declaring unconstitutional the Federal Anti-Peonage Act of 1867, but in that case it ordered a *release* of the man accused of holding a black man in peonage servitude and in 1908 it *resisted* (Teddy Roosevelt's) Justice Department pleas to

Alabama II.[25] This was followed by several pro-civil rights decisions in the ensuing decade.

This timing makes it hard to resist the surmise that the Supreme Court's taking upon itself in 1909 the trial and conviction for contempt of court of the Shipp co-conspirators to lynching was an unusually intense experience for the justices. At no other time has the U.S. Supreme Court conducted a criminal trial. This lynching trial followed by only one year the sizable Springfield, Illinois, race riot, which had received extensive, nation-wide publicity. Then, the year after the lynching trial at the Court, came the national wave of race riots in July 1910 provoked by the victory of black boxer Jack Johnson in the "Fight of the Century." Six months later, in January 1911, the White Court handed down *Bailey v. Alabama II*.

It is thus hard to resist the speculation that a lingering effect from the *Shipp II* decision, exacerbated by judicial awareness of a decade of race rioting that had spread to northern states, pushed the Court's turn toward decisions upholding constitutional rights for black Americans. Lynch law and mob rule directly threatened the very structure of legal order. At some point (one suspects) the justices had to resist. At the time of *Bailey II* (1911), the first time since 1884 that the Court in a non-lynching case supported black rights,[26] five justices remained on the Court who had participated in the (1909) conviction of Shipp and his co-lynchers for contempt of Court: Harlan, McKenna, Holmes, Day, and White. To their ranks had been newly added the progressive on race, Charles Evans Hughes in 1910.

---

issue a pre-trial release of a black man jailed under an Alabama peonage (debt-servitude) law (*Bailey v. Alabama I*). These cases are described in Chapter 4.

25 *Bailey v. Alabama* II, 219 U.S. 219 (1911).

26 There were a couple of jury selection cases in the early 1900s where the Fuller Court went so far as to remand to the state courts to ask them to consider whether the jury selection system had been racially biased, but the Court itself did not find racial bias in any jury case from 1884 through 1922. In 1883, the Waite Court had thrown out a murder indictment on racial bias grounds in *Bush v. Kentucky*. The 1884 case upholding black civil rights was *Ex Parte Yarborough*, See discussion in Chapter 4 and see case list in Table 4.1.

JUDICIAL GOOD NEWS FOR BLACKS ON PEONAGE, SEGREGATION AND VOTING (1911–17), BUT CONGRESSIONAL BAD NEWS

Alonzo Bailey had first brought his case to the U.S. Supreme Court in 1908, the year before the lyncher Shipp's contempt of court trial there.[27] Bailey was the imprisoned victim of an Alabama law that presumed guilt (subject to rebuttal by factual evidence) for the crime of fraudulent larceny from the breaking of a labor contract that paid wages in advance. After having committed himself to work for one year, beginning December 26, 1907, and receiving $15 at signing with the promise of $12 per month pay (from which $1.25 would be deducted to pay back his advance, until it was fully paid off), Bailey walked away from the job in February. The law made such departure *prima facie* evidence of intentional larcenous fraud and did not allow Bailey's testimony for rebuttal as to actual motives. Jailed prior to the criminal trial, Bailey sued for a writ of habeas corpus on the grounds that the law was unconstitutional, violating both the Thirteenth Amendment and the federal Anti-Peonage Law. His plea was rejected by the Alabama courts, and, despite support in an amicus brief from Teddy Roosevelt's Justice Department, his 1908 lawsuit on a writ of error to the Fuller Supreme Court lost in a seven–two decision by Justice Holmes, with a dissent by Justice Harlan (Day concurring).

When the case again reached the Court under Chief Justice White, in 1910–11,[28] the results were diametrically the opposite: a five–two (plus two seats vacant) decision for Bailey, with Holmes, the *Bailey I* opinion author, now in dissent (along with Lurton).[29] By this point, Bailey had been tried, found guilty of fraud and sentenced, for the $13.75 that he still owed his employer, to pay a fine and court costs totaling $76.40, or if unable to pay, which was the situation, to 136 days of imprisonment at hard labor.[30] The Court ruled unconstitutional the law under which Bailey was arrested and imprisoned. It violated the Thirteenth Amendment (as well as federal statute) by virtue of imposing compulsory labor to pay off

---

[27] *Bailey v. Alabama I*, 211 U.S. 252 (1908).

[28] *Bailey v. Alabama II*, 219 U.S. 219 (1911).

[29] Chief Justice White's vacated Associate Justice seat was to be taken by appointee Van Devanter and retired Justice Moody's seat was to be taken by Justice Lamar, but these appointees did not take their seats until the day that *Bailey v. Alabama II* was handed down. Schmidt 1984, 861. The participating justices numbered seven.

[30] Ibid., 860.

a debt, rather than leaving the lender the normal remedy of a lawsuit for damages to recover a debt.

This law was part of a web of southern laws that subjected workers, particularly but not exclusively black workers, to forced labor. One such law made it criminal to fall into the grouping "rogues and vagabonds, idle or dissolute persons," including "persons who neglect their calling" or "all able-bodied male persons over eighteen years of age who are without means of support." This Florida statute (1905) imposed on such "criminals" a $250 fine (which generally they could not pay) or six months on the chain gang. The chain gang system of convict labor was often described by muckraker journalists as worse than chattel slavery. Workers were shackled to one another by chains even during sleep, forced to work vigorously and at pain of frequent and savagely brutal whipping for the state or county or private leaser of the labor, and promptly killed if they attempted escape. Annual death rates of workers under this system were typically 20 percent and in some places reached 50 percent.[31]

Related laws that kept blacks in unofficial bondage included laws forbidding one employer to entice a worker away from an employer who had the worker under a contract. Being without an annual contract subjected laborers to the vagrancy laws just described. Another set of laws in the peonage web, which was to come before the Court in *U.S. v. Reynolds* in 1914, comprised so-called "criminal surety laws."[32] These laws permitted convicts too poor to pay their fines to avoid being put on the chain gang by contracting themselves into servitude for a fixed period to a private person who would pay the fine. Again, combined with dragnet vagrancy laws, this made it possible to trump up charges against blacks and then sentence them to involuntary servitude.[33]

Muckrakers, conscientious southern judges, and the Theodore Roosevelt Administration (assisted from behind the scenes by funding for publicity and litigation from Booker T. Washington and his allies[34]) launched a campaign at the turn of the century against the peonage system, stimulated inter alia by revelations that white immigrants by the hundreds were getting caught up in its snares.[35] Federal Justice Department prosecutions, which numbered more than 100 between 1901 and 1905, ran into something of a brick wall at the Fuller Court. The most

---

31 Ibid, 821–30.
32 *U.S. v. Reynolds*, 235 U.S. 133 (1914).
33 Schmidt 1984, 823.
34 Daniel 1970, 654, 658–65, 667–9.
35 Schmidt 1984, 831–50.

this Court would concede (in the *Clyatt Case*, 1905[36]) was that the 1867 federal Anti-Peonage Law was not unconstitutional. Despite the issuance of scathing Reports from Assistant Attorney General Charles Russell in the 1906–08 period, the Fuller Court found technicalities on which to set free a convicted perpetrator of peonage (Clyatt), to let a victim of an unconstitutional peonage law be held in jail for three years (*Bailey v. Alabama I*) and to set free southern white gangs convicted of violently intimidating blacks into abandoning well-paying jobs.[37]

This pattern changed noticeably under the White Court, with *Bailey v. Alabama II*,[38] for which the Taft Justice Department submitted an amicus brief, and the Taft Administration then continued the pursuit of peonage convictions, succeeding again with *U.S. v. Reynolds* in 1914.[39] (The Taft Justice Department began the prosecution, which became bogged down during the change of administration to Democratic President Woodrow Wilson, no friend of black civil rights. His Justice Department did carry the case to completion, by way of a brief that carefully distinguished between the private criminal surety system and the state-run, chain-gang convict leasing system, which the Wilson Administration wanted to leave in the discretion of the states).

The *Reynolds* case began with the conviction of one Ed Rivers (a black man) in Alabama for the crime of petty larceny. He was fined $15 plus court costs of $43.75, for a total of $58.75. Since he was indigent, he was sentenced to fifty-eight days hard labor to pay the court what he owed. A private individual, J.A. Reynolds paid the $58.75 to the court, for which he received a commitment from Rivers to work for him for nine months and twenty-four days (approximately five times the duration of his hard labor on the chain gang), for which Rivers would additionally receive $6 per month plus room, board and clothing. After a month, Rivers quit the job and was then jailed for failure to perform his "surety contract." This time the judge imposed court costs of $87.05, which resulted in a sentence of 115 days on the chain gang, double his original sentence. To avoid the second sentence, Rivers accepted a second surety contract with an F.W. Broughton for fourteen and a half months labor at $6 per day. At

---

36 *Clyatt v. United States*, 197 U.S. 207 (1905).

37 *U.S. v. Maples*, decided as *Hodges v. U.S.*, 203 U.S. 1 (1906). For further details see Chapter 4, "Free Labor Rights in the Fuller Court."

38 According to Schmidt 1984, 886, the *Bailey II* case produced "an outpouring of commentary."

39 *U.S. v. Reynolds,* 235 U.S. 133 (1914). In 1942, a *Bailey*-type law from Georgia again came before the Court and was struck down unanimously, *Taylor v. Georgia*, 315 U.S. 25 (1942). Wiecek 2006, 643.

this point the case brought Broughton and Reynolds into a group of eleven persons indicted by a federal grand jury convened by the U.S. Attorney. The attorney general of Alabama and the U.S. Attorney General were eager to have a quickly resolved test case to settle the issue of the constitutionality of the criminal surety system, but negotiations for such a test case dragged on amongst them, defendants' counsel, and a Congress Member from Alabama for two years, as Woodrow Wilson came into the Presidency and appointed a new Attorney General. As eventually arranged, Reynolds and Broughton conceded their participation in a criminal surety arrangement but contended that the Alabama system did not violate the Thirteenth Amendment, since it involved servitude as punishment for a crime rather than as payment for a debt (which would be forbidden by the *Bailey II* precedent).[40]

Justice Day wrote the opinion in *U.S. v. Reynolds* for a unanimous Court. The man who served as surety to the state, who received a promise of labor in return, was really receiving the labor of someone who was under compulsion to labor in order to pay off his debt to the private surety person. Therefore the logic of *Bailey II* covered this case and criminal surety systems violated the Thirteenth Amendment. Justice Holmes, who had dissented in *Bailey II* wrote a brief, grudging concurrence that referred to victims of the southern surety system (nearly all of whom were black people, although he did not state this fact) as "impulsive people with little intelligence or foresight" (235 U.S., at p. 150).

While Presidents Theodore Roosevelt and William H. Taft were united with the Supreme Court in opposition to peonage, Congress remained in the grip of the mentality of the worst elements of the South. It refused (Taft) Justice Department requests to broaden the Federal Anti-Peonage Law in 1911, so that indebtedness would not be a required element to prove peonage and so there would be a specified federal penalty for any coercing of labor by a private person, as imposing involuntary servitude.[41]

Similarly, even after the *Shipp* trial at the Supreme Court in 1909, and after active lobbying by the newly formed NAACP, Congress continued in its refusal to pass anti-lynching legislation. Theodore Roosevelt had advocated such legislation as early as 1906, but President Taft, while willing to denounce the lawlessness of lynching, did so from the passive

---

40 Schmidt 1984, 876–86.
41 Ibid., 856.

position that it would be cured only by self-reform at the local level on the part of sheriffs, judges and juries.[42]

Peonage was not the only civil rights problem on which the White Court took a progressive turn. As noted in prior chapters, the Chase Court (of the 1860s–early 1870s) first dealt with a "separate but equal" argument with a level of insight not to be seen again for many decades except in dissents by Justice Harlan. In *Railroad Co. v. Brown* (1873), the Chase Court had ruled that the railroad company's provision of physically *identical* facilities to whites and blacks while forcing them to be separated failed to satisfy the federal law covering D.C.: "No person shall be excluded from the cars on account of color."[43] Justice Davis's opinion for the unanimous court had linked railroad racial segregation to the era of black servitude, thereby implicating enforcement powers under the Thirteenth Amendment.

This sensible insight was lost on the Fuller Court majority, against which Justice Harlan then dissented in *Plessy v. Ferguson* (1896).[44] Even before *Plessy*, as early as 1890, the Fuller Court had already indicated its preference for separate but equal interstate travel decisions (over Harlan dissents) in which it upheld a state mandate of segregated railroad cars against claims that this interfered with the dormant commerce power of Congress.[45] The extreme tokenism of the Fuller Court's understanding of "equal" in "equal protection of the laws" was indicated in an 1899 decision in which the justices upheld the decision of the school board of Richmond County, Georgia to close its only public high school for blacks, while keeping open one for white girls and while continuing to subsidize a church-run high school for white males (in a context where three church-run high schools, not state assisted, were available for blacks to attend).[46]

With the Fuller Court having given its stamp of approval to legally mandated segregation in schools and in public transportation, southern

---

42 Klarman 2004, 67; Dale 2011, 117–18. Roosevelt 1906. "President Taft" 1912.

43 This "law" was a provision in the company's charter that the federal government had issued.

44 *Plessy v. Ferguson*, 163 U.S. 537 (1896).

45 *Louisville, New Orleans, and Texas Ry. v. Mississippi* (1890); *Chesapeake and Ohio Ry. v. Kentucky* (1890); and *Chiles v. Chesapeake and Ohio Ry.* (1910). See also Chapter 4, text at nn. 46–48, and notes themselves. The ICC in the late 1880s was already declaring such discrimination reasonable under the Interstate Commerce Act of 1885. See Table 4.1.

46 *Cummings v. Richmond* (1899).

cities began to enact laws that would segregate residential neighborhoods by race. In December, 1910, Baltimore, Maryland enacted the first. It was followed within a year by three cities: Mooresville and Winston-Salem in North Carolina, and Greenville, South Carolina. In 1913, pursuant to a state law the year before that explicitly permitted such municipal ordinances, five in Virginia followed suit: Richmond, Norfolk, Roanoke, Ashland, and Portsmouth. Also in 1913, Atlanta, Georgia; Madisonville, Kentucky; Birmingham, Alabama; and Asheville, North Carolina joined the trend. In 1914, Louisville, Kentucky followed suit, and by the end of 1916, Dallas, Texas, St. Louis, Missouri, Oklahoma City and New Orleans had also done so.[47] The decade of the 1910s was also the period in which southern legislatures acted to legislate Jim Crow rules for the minutiae of daily life: separate toilets, separate worker entrances and water buckets, separate waiting rooms for trains, separate nurses for white patients and black, etc.[48]

By April of 1916 a constitutional challenge to the Louisville Kentucky neighborhood-segregation ordinance had reached the U.S. Supreme Court for oral argument, but the decision in that case, *Buchanan v. Warley*,[49] was not handed down until November of 1917. Justice Day had been ill during the argument and there was also one seat vacant. In April, 1917 the case was re-argued, with Day now back in his seat and with the formerly vacant seat filled by Justice Brandeis. Justice Hughes had also left the Court, replaced by Justice Clarke. The law at issue in *Buchanan* prohibited blacks from residing on blocks where a majority of the residents were white and vice versa.

Three years earlier the White Court had handed down a transportation precedent which foretold a turn away from Fuller Court pro-segregation decisions. This decision, *McCabe v. Atchison, Topeka, & Santa Fe Railway*,[50] had dealt with an Oklahoma law requiring common carriers (in intrastate travel) to provide separate coaches for "white and negro races" that were equal in "comfort and convenience," but sleeping, dining and parlor cars were permitted to be used "exclusively" by one race and did not have to be provided for the other race if this other race (i.e., blacks) did not use them in high enough numbers to make them profitable for the railroad. The Court in a five–four opinion penned by Justice Hughes had rejected Oklahoma's defense of the law as a

---

47 Schmidt 1984, 791; Meyer 2001, 20–22; Rice 1968, 181–2.

48 Nieman 1991, 109.

49 *Buchanan v. Warley*, 245 U.S. 60 (1917).

50 *McCabe v. Atchison, Topeka, & Santa Fe Railway*, 235 U.S. 151 (1914).

"practical" accommodation to social reality.[51] While the opinion accepted the authority of *Plessy v. Ferguson* as to the constitutionality of a "separate but equal" requirement in law, it rejected the claim of Oklahoma that states were free to legislate in favor of provision of *unequal* facilities because of disproportionate group usage. (In principle, this logic could be deployed against southern states that provided no or very few high schools for black youths. Such a pattern was prevalent all over the South.) Hughes announced for five justices that a constitutional right "cannot depend on the number of persons ... discriminated against ... . [Every] individual is entitled to equal protection of the laws."[52] The *McCabe* decision, however, produced no injunction, because all nine justices agreed that the case was unripe; none of the litigants indicated that he was attempting or about to attempt to travel first class on a train in Oklahoma. They did not yet stand to gain individually and concretely from any Court injunction on the subject.

Buchanan v. Warley (1917) followed in *McCabe*'s segregation-limiting trajectory. With Hughes no longer on the Court, Justice Day wrote the decision. The case arrived at the U.S. Supreme Court for the settlement of a dispute arranged by the Kentucky NAACP. Warley (a black) bought, but did not fully pay for, property on a majority-white block from a friendly realtor, Buchanan, and then refused full payment because of legal incapacity to build a home for himself on the property (being prohibited from residing on a majority-white block). Buchanan sued to get the money (technically, "specific performance of the contract") by a judicial declaration that the segregation law was void. Kentucky courts upheld the ordinance on the grounds that separating the races promotes public welfare (the very ground that had succeeded in *Plessy*).[53] The White Court unanimously declared this residential segregation ordinance unconstitutional.[54]

Both the briefs for Buchanan and the Court's decision emphasize property rights, which were Holy Grail to the majority of the justices of the time. Day's opinion for the Court cited *Holden v. Hardy* for the

---

51 On the case result, however, the justices were unanimous.

52 235 U.S., 161–2.

53 Schmidt 1984, 794.

54 Justice Oliver Wendell Holmes wrote out a dissent that focused on standing problems, but he chose (for reasons never revealed) not to issue it, so the opinion was both published and received as having been unanimous. So far as is known, no others dissented even privately, not even Chief Justice White, who had been part of the Court majority in *Plessy v. Ferguson*. Schmidt 1984, 590–91, 804–10.

principle that under the Fourteenth Amendment, the right to property "includes the right to acquire, use, and dispose of it."[55] This was both a fundamental constitutional right and one that, as a result of the Thirteenth and Fourteenth Amendments and the civil rights laws enacted to implement them, was now protected for both white and black people in the U.S., he continued. The precedent of *Plessy*, the Court insisted, was not to the contrary because that case had not involved deprivation of a property right, but simply called for equal (although separate) accommodations in transportation.[56] Justice Day acknowledged "[t]hat there exists a serious and difficult problem arising from a feeling of race hostility." Then, in language that would be directly quoted four decades later in the only Court opinion ever signed by all nine of the justices,[57] he continued with the following:[58]

> It is urged that this proposed segregation will promote the public peace by preventing race conflicts. Desirable as this is, and important as is the preservation of the public peace, this aim cannot be accomplished by laws or ordinances which deny rights created or protected by the Federal Constitution.

Unlike the Court's pro-civil-rights jury decisions of the early 1880s, *Buchanan v. Warley* had an immediately lasting impact, at least in a *de jure* respect. The wave of residential segregation ordinances petered out. Maryland tried another version right away, but it was struck down by Maryland courts (as also happened with the three such laws in the 1920s in Virginia, Texas, and Indiana), and later ones from Richmond and New Orleans that reached the U.S. Supreme Court were to be given short shrift in *per curiam* rulings in 1930 and 1927, respectively.[59]

Unfortunately, as the legal reasoning of *Buchanan* was grounded in property rights, so its societal impact was limited by property rights. Privately drawn racially restrictive covenants replaced the residential segregation laws, and the former would be ruled enforceable by the Taft Court in *Corrigan v. Buckley* (1926).[60] The promise of *Buchanan v.*

---

55 *Holden v. Hardy,* 169 U.S. 366, 391 (1898); cited at *Buchanan v. Warley*, 245 U.S. 60, 74.

56 *Buchanan*, 245 U.S. at 80.

57 *Cooper v. Aaron*, 358 U.S. 1 (1958).

58 *Buchanan*, 245 U.S. at 80–81, quoted in *Cooper v. Aaron*, 358 U.S., at 16.

59 *Richmond v. Deans*, 281 U.S. 704 (1930) (*per curiam*); *Harmon v. Tyler* 273 U.S. 668 (1927) (*per curiam*); Schmidt 1984, 816–17.

60 *Corrigan v. Buckley*, 271 U.S. 323 (1926).

Warley then lay dormant for another twenty-two years, until the Court overruled *Corrigan* in 1948 in *Shelley v. Kraemer*.[61]

The third topic on which the White Court turned toward promoting civil rights for black Americans was voting. Southern blacks, despite the frequency of KKK-style violence against them, in the immediate post-bellum decades voted in considerable numbers, which fact produced very close elections in the southern states in the 1870s and 1880s. By the end of the 1890s, five southern states had produced statutes or state constitution provisions, which as applied (and as intended) produced almost total disenfranchisement of their black citizens. By 1910, all eleven Confederate states plus Oklahoma had similarly disenfranchised their black citizens. And at the federal level, the majority-Democrat Congress and Presidency of 1893–94 wiped off the books almost all voting rights enforcement laws. Despite the ensuing drastic drop in voting numbers in the South, later Republican Congresses did nothing to apply Section Two of the Fourteenth Amendment to reduce Congressional representation in the South to punish those states for these voting restrictions.[62]

Thus, the elected Congressional representatives of the Northern states appeared to be comfortable in the early decades of the twentieth century with this de facto suspension of the Fifteenth Amendment for Southern blacks. Chapter 4 reviewed the Fuller Court's repeated demonstrations that it was utterly unwilling to uphold voting rights or jury rights (which were often tied to voting rights by statute) for black Americans. In the voting rights arena, too, the White Court provided an unexpected contrast.

Southern state legislatures and constitutional conventions knew that the literacy requirements, "understanding" clauses, and poll taxes they were imposing at the turn of the century would disfranchise numerous white voters, along with blacks. To counteract this impact, the lawmakers adopted a number of workarounds available to whites—for instance registration during a certain narrowly constricted time of year during which registrars would simply turn blacks away, irrespective of qualification, and after which new, absurdly stringent registration requirements would apply forever. Another of these mechanisms was the grandfather clause—e.g., male adult resident citizens would be eligible to vote only if they could read and interpret correctly the most opaque sections of the state constitution OR if they had been themselves eligible to vote before 1867 or their fathers or grandfathers had been eligible to vote then, or if

61 *Shelley v. Kraemer*, 334 U.S. 1 (1948).

62 See Chapter 4 for details about this paragraph.

they were foreign-born naturalized male citizens or their descendants. Such clauses were inserted in voting restriction clauses in the state constitutions of Louisiana (1898), North Carolina (1900), Georgia (1908) and Maryland (1908). Alabama (1901) and Virginia (1902) grandfathered in persons who had fought in the Civil War or prior wars. These two states, and some others in later statutes, concerned to eliminate the mixed-race offspring of white slave-owners, and their descendants, specified in the grandfather clauses the term, "lawful" descendants.[63]

Oklahoma entered the Union in 1907, and was a state with two viable political parties. In a transparent effort to disfranchise the black voters (9 percent of the electorate), because they voted Republican, the Democrats in 1910 pushed through, via a popular referendum prior to the general election, a constitutional amendment that restricted voting registration to two groups: those adult male residents who could "read and write any section" of the state constitution, and those male residents who either themselves prior to 1866 had been entitled to vote or had resided in a foreign country, or else were "lineal descendant[s]" of such a person. The Democratic governor instructed election inspectors to bar blacks from voting; the orders were followed; many thousands of blacks were kept from voting.

Two prominent Oklahoma Republican officials pressed the U.S. Attorney General (under President Taft) to arrest and charge election officials with violation of the remaining U.S. civil rights statutes. These, in general terms with no specific reference to voting, criminalized conspiracy to "injure" the exercise of constitutional rights. With Taft's approval, the U.S. Attorney General refused to prosecute, on the grounds that these provisions dealt with "civil" rights and not with the "political" right of voting. One of the Oklahomans frustrated in his request for federal action, John Embry, was a U.S. Attorney himself, so he went ahead on his own and brought charges against two local election officials, J.J. Beal and Frank Guinn. Taft's Attorney General was furious, but Embry threatened to resign publicly rather than withdraw the charges. The Taft Justice Department [mis]calculated that Oklahoma juries would be unlikely to convict, and wanted to avoid the embarrassment of a public resignation, so let the case proceed in the federal district court. There, for enforcing the combination of literacy test and grandfather

[63] Schmidt 1984, 920–21. The phrase "lawful male descendants" appears in the Maryland clause struck down by the Court in *Myers v. Anderson*, 238 U.S. 368, 377 (1915).

clause, Guinn and Beal were both convicted of conspiring to injure black voters in the exercise of their constitutional rights.[64]

In the process of seeking to hold onto black Republican delegates at the 1912 GOP convention, and to keep them from Progressive candidate, Theodore Roosevelt, Taft quietly shifted his position, and wrote the U.S. Attorney in Oklahoma to go ahead with similar grandfather clause prosecutions. The 1912 election in Oklahoma was fraught with tension because the Democratic governor threatened arrest for any federal official who "interfered" with the election laws of the state. The U.S. Attorney Homer Boardman wrote a much-publicized letter threatening to arrest any (state) election official who kept blacks from voting. Another U.S. Attorney wrote the U.S. Attorney General that "rioting and bloodshed" were probable on election day. The Attorney General sent back word to hold arrests for after the election. Such arrests did transpire and resulted in the *U.S. v. Mosley* case,[65] handed down by the Supreme Court on the same day as *Guinn v. U.S.*[66] Meanwhile, the grandfather clause applied in Annapolis, Maryland had also been ruled unconstitutional in federal district court and was headed to the U.S. Supreme Court as the civil case *Myers v. Anderson*, eventually to be decided with *Guinn*.[67]

Once the openly pro-segregation, raised-in-Virginia, Democrat, Woodrow Wilson, won the presidential election of 1912, the lameduck GOP Justice Department had good reason to fear that the charges would be dropped. It requested an expedited hearing at the U.S. Supreme Court, which it received, but not in time to avoid the Wilson transition into office. The new officials, obdurate segregationist, Attorney General James McReynolds, and Solicitor General, West Virginian, John W. Davis, nonetheless, not only proceeded with the case but even invited amicus briefs from the NAACP and others.[68]

---

64 Schmidt 1984, 928–34.

65 *United States v. Mosley*, 238 U.S. 383 (1915).

66 *Guinn and Beal v. U.S.*, 238 U.S. 347 (1915).

67 *Myers v. Anderson*, 238 U.S. 368 (1915). Material in this paragraph is from Schmidt 1984, 934–45. Maryland's clause combined a property qualification with a grandfather clause exemption from it (along with a naturalized foreign citizens exemption from it). Anderson, along with two others, blacks who would have been entitled to vote in Maryland but for the combination property requirement and grandfather clause, sued Myers and other registration officers, for damages for the act of refusing to allow the three black men to register to vote. Like *Guinn v. U.S.*, the decision struck down Maryland's grandfather clause voting scheme, was unanimous, and was written by (Southerner) Chief Justice White.

68 Schmidt 1984, 936–42.

One reason that McReynolds may have opted to carry on the litigation process is that if Guinn and Beal were simply pardoned, the Oklahoma law would remain unconstitutional. John W. Davis presented able arguments, as did the allied briefs, but there remained the chance that the Supreme Court would follow the egregious Fuller Court precedents of the *Williams* Mississippi case and the two *Giles* cases to reverse the lower court.[69]

Although *Guinn* was argued in October 1913, it was not decided until June 21, 1915. Chief Justice Edward White's opinion for the Court came down as unanimous, and there is no known explanation for this exceptionally long delay. Between the argument and the decision announcement, Justice Lurton, who had been severely ill and in frail health beginning December 3, 1913, died on July 12, 1914. He was replaced by Justice McReynolds who had to recuse himself from participation in the decision because of his earlier role in the case as Attorney General. Scholar Benno Schmidt speculates that both Justice J.R. Lamar and Justice Lurton wanted to dissent in *Guinn* and *Myers*, but has no explanation why they did not (and rejects the suggestion from a son of the attorney who argued for Oklahoma that Chief Justice White purposely waited for Lurton to die so as to attain unanimity).[70] Justice Lamar did live to write a dissent in the third black voting rights case handed down that day, *U.S. v. Mosley* (shortly after which, he too died).[71]

The unanimous decisions in both *Guinn* and *Myers*, not only rejected the grandfather clauses as having no other logical motive than to disfranchise black voters who were otherwise as qualified or unqualified as were the white voters being grandfathered in. The at-issue broadly worded civil rights statutes, for criminal and civil liability, were ruled applicable to Fifteenth Amendment rights, along with other constitutional rights, with the Court referring to the *Mosley* decision of the same day for its statutory interpretation reasoning. In both decisions, the Court not only struck down the grandfather clauses but also struck down the literacy and property qualifications to which they were attached.

Thus, if the two states wanted to disfranchise blacks, they would need to enact new laws. Oklahoma did so promptly, by grandfathering in all persons who had voted in 1914, when the now-unconstitutional grandfather clause had been treated as in effect. All other voters were required to register during twelve days, April 30–May 11, 1916, or, according to

---

[69] See Chapter 4 for discussion of these earlier cases. For explanation how the Court might have followed them, see Schmidt 1984, 958–9.

[70] Ibid., 945–9.

[71] Ibid., 955–8.

scholar Michael Klarman "be forever disfranchised." Without a Justice Department eager to attack such laws, this one stayed in effect until 1939.[72]

Besides eliminating the literacy qualification in Oklahoma and eliminating the property qualification in Annapolis, Maryland, the justices in these 1915 decisions were also to some degree undoing the goal of those congressional Democrats who in 1894 had removed from the federal code those statutes from the Reconstruction era that had explicitly enforced voting rights.[73] This judicial interpretation moved protection of voting rights by the federal government via civil liability into Section 1979 of the Revised Statutes, and via criminal liability into Section 19 of the Criminal Code. The first of these made actionable for civil damages any act under color of law that deprived someone of "rights … secured by the Constitution and laws." The second made it criminal to "conspire to injure, oppress, threaten, or intimidate any citizen in the free exercise or enjoyment of any right or privilege secured to him by the Constitution or laws of the United States." This aspect of the *Guinn* and *Myers* decisions was by implication the target of Justice Lamar's dissent in the case *U.S. v. Mosley*, where he objected at length to the Court's undoing of Congress's known intention of 1894.

Mosley had been a member of a county election board in Oklahoma who, with a fellow board member, had deliberately refused to include in the 1912 vote tally any votes from precincts known to have allowed sizable numbers of blacks to vote (by ignoring the grandfather clause law). The two had done so under instructions of the Democratic governor and State Election Board, and then been prosecuted by the Republican U.S. Attorney. Mosley and his colleague, in contrast to Guinn and Beal, had succeeded in having their demurrer to the indictment upheld in Federal district court, on the grounds that the broadly worded Section 19 of the U.S. Criminal Code did not explicitly apply to voting and should not be inferred to do so. Justice Holmes wrote for the (seven–one) majority in *Mosley,* to the effect that the plain words of the statute (Section 19) can clearly embrace a joint undertaking by two or more persons to interfere with blacks' efforts to vote. Irrespective of past intentions of Congress, "we cannot allow the past [to determine] the present."[74]

---

72 Klarman 2004, 86. The decision to strike it down was *Lane v. Wilson*, 307 U.S. 268 (1939).

73 28 Stat. 36 (1894). See also lengthy discussion thereof in Schmidt 1984, 951–5.

74 *Mosley*, 238 U.S., at 388. See also Schmidt 1984, 953–4.

To anyone familiar with the Fuller Court line of race-related decisions, these progressive moves by the White Court on peonage, residential segregation and voting rights appear as a startling break. The Court's regressive momentum on race certainly was halted in the second decade of the twentieth century. However, the White Court did not have revolutionary ambitions. Other of their race-related decisions disappointed black litigants and provide a sobering reminder of the limits on what the White Court was willing to accomplish.

THE BAD NEWS FOR BLACKS UNDER THE WHITE COURT

The segregation-limiting *McCabe* decision of 1914 and *Buchanan* decision of 1917 were book-ended by two decisions that honored both private and state-mandated segregation practices: *Butts v. Merchants and Miners Transportation Co.* (1913)[75] and *South Covington & Cinc. St. Ry v. Kentucky* (1920).[76] In the first, the Court rejected the claim under the Civil Rights Act of 1875 of Mary Butts, a black woman who bought a first-class ticket for a voyage from Boston to Norfolk, Va., but was relegated (as were other non-whites) to second-class accommodations. The Court ruled unanimously that even though the Act had been declared unconstitutional in 1883 solely on the grounds that it interfered with state authority over in-state commerce, such that the reasoning did not plainly cover areas within the plenary control of Congress, such as travel on the high seas, nonetheless, the Act contained no special language directed at interstate commerce, commerce in the territories or on the high seas, and thus its regulations of commerce all fell as a whole. If Congress wanted to forbid segregated facilities in interstate commerce, it would need to legislate anew.

In the *South Covington* streetcar decision, the Court's six–three majority opined that Kentucky's law requiring common carriers within the state to separate the races by, at a minimum, a "sturdy partition" did not impose an undue burden on interstate commerce. It is difficult to see this claim as plausible in light of the following circumstances: At issue was a single car streetcar that ran only a six-mile distance partly in Kentucky and partly in Ohio, charged only a single price for the whole length of the trip, carried a load of whom 80 percent of the passengers traveled

---

75 *Butts v. Merchants and Miners Transportation Co.*, 230 U.S. 126 (1913).
76 *South Covington & Cinc. St. Ry v. Kentucky*, 252 U.S. 399 (1920).

interstate, and had to cope with the rule of a contrary Ohio law that prohibited racial segregation on streetcars.

The dates of the cases indicate that personnel change does not do a lot to explain the variation in outcomes; racial progressive (and author of the *McCabe* opinion) Justice Hughes was on the Court for the *Butts* 1913 decision and did not dissent.[77] For the 1920 decision upholding Kentucky's segregated streetcar law as applied to an interstate line, Justice Brandeis had already joined Justice Holmes on the Court, and their two votes, if added to the dissent of Justice Day (along with the allied Van Devanter and Pitney), would have changed the outcome. They chose to align with the majority.

OVERVIEW OF THE WHITE COURT ON BLACKS' CASES

It is not obvious to scholars why the White Court broke in the way that it did from the pattern set by the Fuller Court. I have offered a suggestion above that the trauma of actually having tried a lynching case in 1909, shortly before White moved into the Chief Justiceship, and having done so in an era when anti-black race riots had spread into the North, may have triggered a new determination to make clear that there were legal limits in this country on what whites could do to blacks (as in the peonage cases) and on what southern state laws could mandate against blacks (as in the voting rights cases of 1915 and in the limits put on segregation in *McCabe*, 1914, and *Buchanan*, 1917). The White Court, however, made clear in 1913 in *Butts* and in 1920 in *South Covington* that it was not interested in undoing *Plessy v. Ferguson* (1896), nor in pushing racial integration onto interstate transportation without a clear lead from Congress. The furthest the justices were willing to go on the transportation subject was the line drawn in *McCabe* (1914), and it was a highly formal line at that: states could not under the Fourteenth Amendment legislate that it was permissible for common carriers to provide separate and *unequal* facilities for the races (even if usage of first-class facilities was highly disproportionate by race). If the railroad companies did so on their own, however, the Fourteenth Amendment did not limit them; it limited only action by states.

---

[77] Schmidt 1984, 771–2 describes private correspondence to the effect that Holmes cast a dissenting vote in conference, but chose not to write one, so his reasoning is not known. There were no officially recorded dissents to *Butts v. Merchants*.

Outside the Court, support from the executive branch Justice Departments of Taft and Wilson for these civil rights advances was tepid at best; and from a Congress containing a Senate easily filibustered by determined white southern racists, support was not to be found. Among the public at large, the pause in major anti-black race riots endured only from 1910 to 1917.

In 1917 one of the nation's worst anti-black riots took place over a two-month period in East St. Louis, Illinois, triggered by white resentment at black strike breakers, and then re-triggered by blacks' shooting to death two policemen mistaken for white hooligans who had been shooting from a car into black neighborhoods. According to an NAACP investigation, this mob violence resulted in the deaths of 100–200 blacks and the destruction of 300 buildings.[78] This was followed by a summer of violence in 1919, where riots took place in some twenty-five cities, including D.C., Chicago, Omaha, and many all over the South. Partly these were provoked by a new assertiveness of the black community, stemming both from pride in the black servicemen who returned from World War I, and from new economic resources obtained by migration into northern industrial jobs during the war. Whites rioted over perceived threats to their jobs, status and neighborhoods. Blacks fought back, and death rates were high on both sides. In the Chicago riot (of 1919), 178 white deaths were recorded and 342 black.[79] After a couple of years, yet another major race riot/race war burst forth in Tulsa Oklahoma, serious enough that four units of the National Guard were called forth to quell it. This one resulted in the deaths of fifty whites and between 150 and 200 blacks.[80]

The White Court, thus, both began and ended in eras of race rioting. Whether the outbreak of violence on the part of whites antagonistic toward racial integration of neighborhoods and jobs in the summer of 1919 all over the U.S. caused some on the Court to side with the majority in the bizarrely reasoned 1920 *South Covington* decision is impossible to say. Justice Brandeis himself came from Louisville and would have been familiar with the intensity of feelings in his home state on behalf of racial segregation. In sum, the Court did take a few important steps forward in the decade of 1911–21, but stopped far short of unraveling the South's Jim Crow system, its massive denial of voting rights to blacks, or its brutal convict/chain-gang labor system.

---

[78] Franklin and Moss 1994, 344; Gibson 2014.
[79] Franklin and Moss ibid., 349–52.
[80] Gibson 2014.

ASIANS AT THE WHITE COURT

Since the Fuller Court had proved less anti-Asian than anti-Black, there was not so much space for dramatic improvement by the White Court. The Fuller Court had already stood up to the Justice Department in insisting on birthright citizenship for U.S.-born Asians in the *Wong Kim Ark* case (1898); had gradually acceded, by 1908, to the principle that Chinese descent persons claiming birth-right citizenship for purposes of entering the country deserved a fair hearing on the issue, and, if denied one, could appeal to the judiciary; had in seven cases restricted the behavior of overzealous immigration officials on behalf of Chinese or Chinese-Americans; and had even struck down part of a federal law, which punished by hard labor (to be followed by deportation) Chinese residents of the U.S. who could not prove that they were here lawfully (demanding a kind of proof that had not been required at their initial, potentially lawful entry).[81] The White Court did not backtrack on this progress, but neither did it move forward to any noticeable degree in this harshly anti-Asian era.

Resident Aliens

California acted in 1913 to forbid non-naturalizable aliens from purchasing property or from leasing it for any longer than three years, and then in 1920 to forbid them from leasing property at all.[82] The 1920 law closed a number of loopholes that, particularly, Japanese farmers had developed for owning farms (such as owning them in the name of minor children who were American), and a 1923 law went further, forbidding non-naturalizable aliens from even "cultivat[ing]" or "enjoy[ing]" real property.[83] Although Japanese immigrants frequently managed to evade these laws,[84] nonetheless, California's example was to be followed by some eight other states by 1925.[85] The White Court did not get an opportunity to review these specific laws, but it did get a chance to

---

[81] See Chapter 4 for details.

[82] California's law was preceded by a one in Washington State in 1886, adopted in opposition to Chinese immigration. Since few Chinese worked on farms, this one did not attract much notice from other states. Stuen 1992, 604.

[83] Takaki 1998, 203–7.

[84] Higgs 1978; Stuen 1992, 605.

[85] Arizona in 1917; Louisiana, 1921; New Mexico, 1922; Idaho, 1923; Montana, 1923; Oregon, 1923; Kansas, 1925; Utah, 1943. McGovney 1947, 7–8. A few states adopted such laws in the 1940s, but these would have had almost no

review two anti-alien laws of other states; one from Nebraska barring land ownership by *non-resident* aliens, which it upheld quickly and unanimously in *Toop v. Ulysses Land Co.* (1915), and the other, from Arizona, restricting alien employment, which produced a quite different result.[86] In the *Toop* case, only two weeks after oral argument the Court simply dismissed as "frivolous" the claim that such a ban might violate the Fourteenth Amendment's Equal Protection Clause. In *Truax v. Raich* (1915),[87] however, five months later, the Court struck down the law of Arizona that imposed a maximum cap for alien workers of 20 per cent per employer. Writing for the Court, Justice Hughes reasoned that if a state could "deny to lawful inhabitants, because of their race or nationality … the right to work for a living in the common occupations of the community," then the Equal Protection Clause "would be a barren form of words."[88] Moreover, the anti-alien statute arguably conflicted with federal immigration statutes: "The assertion of an authority to deny to aliens the opportunity of earning a livelihood when lawfully admitted to the State would be tantamount to the assertion of the right to deny them entrance and abode, for, in ordinary cases, they cannot live where they cannot work" (at p. 42).

Chinese Claims of Birth-right Citizenship

As *Truax v. Raich* maintained continuity with the Waite Court's insistence in *Yick Wo* that the Equal Protection Clause precluded any laws that derived simply from "hostility to race and nationality,"[89] so the White Court also continued the rules set forth by the Fuller Court to maintain judicial protection of fair procedures in determinations of the validity of claims of birthright citizenship by Chinese-descent persons attempting to re-enter the U.S. The White Court did turn down the claim of one Tang Tun (and his wife, whom he brought from China), but only after a meticulous review of the documentary evidence introduced at prior

---

impact, because by then the vast majority of Asians in the U.S. would have been native-born and therefore citizens.

86 *Toop v. Ulysses Land Co.*, 237 U.S. 580 (1915).

87 *Truax v. Raich*, 239 U.S. 33 (1915).

88 *Truax v. Raich*, 239 U.S., at 41. Although it made no mention of the 1870 Civil Rights Act, the Court's treating the right to earn a living as a more basic right of aliens under the Fourteenth Amendment than the right to own land, followed a distinction Congress had made in that Act itself. See Chapter 3 for details.

89 *Yick Wo v. Hopkins*, 118 U.S. 356, 374 (1886).

hearings. Justice Hughes had the unanimous support of the Court in ruling (in 1912) that the Secretary of Commerce and Labor had not abused his discretion in rejecting the citizenship claim of Tang Tun, and that the Circuit Court's rejection of the writ of habeas corpus issued by the District Court had been correct.[90]

The Court's language insisting on fair procedures in *Tang Tun* was not empty verbiage; in 1920 the Court demonstrated that it took seriously its expressed rule that the Secretary of Labor's decision is conclusive upon the courts only so long as the proceedings are not "manifestly unfair" and do not show "an abuse of discretion."[91] In that year, the Court overturned the Secretary of Labor's ruling that Kwock Jan Fat was not a bonafide native-born U.S. citizen. The Court ruled that the proceedings had been "manifestly unfair," since the Commissioner had rejected Kwock's claim of citizenship without having been apprised of the fact from the record that the three highly respectable white witnesses not only answered questions about their acquaintance with Kwock and their knowing that he was born in the U.S., but also confronted him face-to-face before the Inspector, and all recognized him to be who he claimed. (The Secretary of Labor for the appeal had been apprised of the sheer fact of the recognition but did not receive any record of the testimony from the face-to-face meeting.) The White Court's attitude toward these cases is summed up in the penultimate sentence of Justice Day's unanimous opinion: "It is better that many Chinese immigrants should be improperly admitted than that one natural born citizen of the United States should be permanently excluded from his country."[92]

Entry and Deportation Procedures for Aliens

The Immigration Act of 1907 produced some ambiguity about how and whether the power it was conferring on the Secretary of Commerce and Labor to summarily deport any alien found to be unlawfully residing in the U.S. would apply to Chinese aliens found here. The Supreme Court resolved this ambiguity in a way that at first did extend this power for deporting a Chinese man who had entered the U.S. illegally,[93] but then limited the Secretary's authority in the case of a Chinese merchant claiming a lawful residence here.[94] Both decisions were unanimous

---

90 *Tang Tun v. Edsell*, 223 U.S. 673 (1912).

91 *Kwock Jan Fat v. White*, 253 U.S. 454, 457–8 (1920).

92 253 U.S., at 464.

93 *United States v. Wong You*, 223 U.S. 67 (1912).

94 *U.S. v. Woo Jan*, 245 U.S. 552 (1918).

(nine–zero and eight–zero, respectively). The Court explained that the difference in outcome turned on the fact that the first man had violated general immigration restrictions and the second was alleged to have violated specifically the Chinese Exclusion Laws, which provided more procedural protections and which Congress had specifically exempted from being altered by the 1907 Act.[95]

The White Court showed a willingness to override the Secretary of Labor's "final" decision for Chinese merchants, also, in re-entry cases. In 1920, it reversed the decision of the Commissioner of Immigration and the upholding of it by the Secretary of Labor, to require the admission of Chin Fong, a merchant whose misstatement of his year of entering the country had caused the Commissioner of Immigration to believe he had originally entered the country fraudulently, so should not be allowed re-entry, despite ample documentation of the fact that he had lawfully worked as a merchant in the U.S. for many years.[96]

In *Low Wah Suey v. Backus* (1912), the Court had dealt with a relatively straight-forward application of the statutory rule, "Any woman who might lawfully be naturalized under the existing laws, married, or who shall be married, to a citizen of the United States, shall be deemed and taken to be a citizen."[97] Li A. Sim, a Chinese woman, was the wife of Low Wah Suey, an American-born citizen of Chinese descent and was found entertaining other men in suspicious circumstances. Were Li A. Sim a white female alien, her marriage to Low Wah Suey would have rendered her a U.S. citizen and therefore not deportable as an alien guilty of the crime of prostitution (although such a marriage would have been forbidden by California's anti-miscegenation laws). But since she was racially excluded from being naturalizable, her marriage did not eliminate her alien status, so the Court upheld the order that she be deported under the Secretary of Commerce and Labor's finding that she was guilty of prostitution.

Similarly, in its final decision on Asians,[98] the White Court again applied a relatively straightforward law, again with harsh results. Yee Won had lawfully entered the U.S. as the minor son of a merchant and then accumulated enough property here as an adult that he was statutorily entitled to leave the country and return. After residing in China for three

---

[95] Ibid., at 558–9.

[96] *White v. Chin Fong*, 253 U.S. 90 (1920). It took Chin Fong eleven years and two tries at the U.S. Supreme Court to win re-entry. See *Chin Fong v. Backus*, 241 U.S. 1 (1916) and the circuit court brief, McGowan 1920.

[97] *Low Wah Suey v. Backus*, 225 U.S. 460, 472–5 (1912).

[98] *Yee Won v. White*, 256 U.S. 399 (1921).

years, where he married and had two children, he attempted to re-enter the U.S. with his family. He was allowed in but they were not. The relevant statute said, "The coming, except under the conditions hereinafter specified, of Chinese laborers to the United States shall be absolutely prohibited," but this "shall not apply to the return to the United States of any registered Chinese laborer who has … property therein of the value of one thousand dollars." Yee Won thereby fit into the category of a laborer owning property and returning to his U.S. home, but the wife and children were "coming … to the United States" in the category of "laborer" and were "absolutely prohibited." Justice Clarke did dissent but without written opinion.

Overview of White Court on Asians

In sum, the White Court continued what had been the relatively benign pattern of the Fuller Court toward Asians. The Court accepted that the authority over foreign policy and foreign commerce lay in the hands of the elected branches, but was willing in at least three cases of administrative overreach to rein in the discretion of the executive branch both for Chinese-Americans (Kwock Jan Fat, 1920) and for Chinese resident aliens (Woo Jan in 1918; Chin Fong, 1920), where it could identify procedural unfairness that had not been explicitly sanctioned by law, and also was willing to rein in state laws (as in *Truax v. Raich*, 1915) that in failing to provide equal protection to lawful resident aliens could be viewed as clashing with federal immigration policy.

CONGRESSIONAL ASIAN POLICY, 1911–30

The elected branches during the tenure of the White (1911–21) and Taft (1921–30) Court years became, if anything, even more anti-Asian than they had been prior to 1911. The 1911 Treaty with Japan carefully distinguished, and discriminated against, Japanese farmers. It permitted the Japanese to own buildings for commercial or residential purposes and to *lease* land for commercial or residential purposes. Agricultural purposes were pointedly omitted, as was land ownership in general.[99]

Unfortunately, this discrimination with respect to foreign land ownership, was not a recent innovation. In the 1866 Civil Rights Act, Congress had legislated:

---

[99] *Terrace v. Thompson*, 263 U.S. 197, 198 (1923) citing treaty between the United States and Japan of February 21, 1911, 37 Stat. 1504.

> That all persons born in the United States and not subject to any foreign power, excluding Indians not taxed, are hereby declared to be citizens of the United States; *and such citizens, of every race and color* … shall have the same right, in every State and Territory in the United States, to make and enforce contracts, to sue, be parties, and give evidence, to inherit, purchase, lease, sell, hold, and convey real and personal property … *as is enjoyed by white citizens* [emphasis added].

In 1870, Congress had re-enacted this law, and had provided the following additional section, which:[100]

> further enacted, That *all persons* within the jurisdiction of the United States shall have the same right in every State and Territory in the United States to make and enforce contracts, to sue, be parties, give evidence, and to the full and equal benefit of all laws and proceedings for the security of persons and property *as is enjoyed by white citizens*, and shall be subject to like punishment, pains, penalties, taxes, licenses, and exactions of every kind, and none other, any law, statute, ordinance, regulation, or custom to the contrary notwithstanding … . [emphasis added]

In stark contrast to what the 1866 Act gave to citizens, this one did not accord to non-citizens a right equal to those of white citizens to "inherit, purchase, lease, sell, hold, and convey real … property." In this respect, the refusal in the 1911 Treaty to negotiate land purchase or even land leasing rights for Japanese residents of the U.S. accorded with a pattern set by even a Congress that had been the most racially liberal theretofore.

In 1917, Congress went much further in its anti-Asian trajectory. It enacted the Asiatic Barred Zone Act. This Act had passed Congress in 1915, only to be blocked by veto from President Wilson, but wartime tensions intensified xenophobic sentiment in Congress, and now it passed over Wilson's veto.[101] The law added to the existing restrictions on immigration by Chinese, Japanese, and Korean laborers, all of southeast Asia (including islands down to but excluding New Zealand; also exempting Japan, as covered by the Gentleman's Agreement), all of South Asia (including Afghanistan but excluding Persia), a section of southeast Arabia, the Sultanate of Muscat and Oman, and the southern part of the Russian Empire that was in central Asia.[102] This law, instead of specifying the prohibited group as "laborers," simply banned all persons born within the specified latitudes and longitudes of Asia and then listed the permitted exceptions: government personnel, clergy and

---

100 Section 16 of the Enforcement Act of May 31, 1870, 16 Stat.140, 144.
101 Rodriguez 2007, 143–4.
102 Hull 1992, 405; Cheng 2013.

religious teachers, missionaries, lawyers, doctors, chemists, civil engineers, teachers, students, authors, artists, merchants, and tourists, and the legal wives and children under sixteen of the same.[103] Moreover, the Act eliminated the judicial protection previously accorded to Chinese persons facing deportation as violators of the Exclusion Acts. After 1917, final decision-making authority in a deportation for violating the Chinese Exclusion Acts was now vested in the immigration bureaucracy.[104]

During World War I, Congress wanted to express encouragement and appreciation for enrollment in the armed services by American nationals from the American territories of the Philippines and Puerto Rico, as well as by resident aliens in the U.S. It therefore amended the 1906 naturalization law in 1918 so as to allow an expedited naturalization process to such persons after three years of armed service. Whether the requirement that to become a U.S. citizen one must also be either "white" or of African descent still operated as a [dis]qualifier to these island residents was left unclear in the law. The Court would be resolving the ambiguity in *Toyota v. U.S.* (1925), discussed below.

The ending of World War I did not improve the situation. U.S. immigration law became even more nativist. In 1921, for the first time the U.S. Congress adopted a quota cap in immigration, limiting non-Asian countries to 3 percent of the number of people from that country in the U.S. census of 1910.[105]

In 1924, Congress tightened the immigration cap to 2 percent of comparable residents, and shifted the census date to 1890, thereby privileging northern and western Europe as compared to the eastern and southern European countries of more recent U.S. immigration. The 1924 legislation completely ended Asian immigration, adding Japanese now to the formally excluded group: the only entrants permitted from Asia (excluding New Zealand and Australia) were clergymen, professors, students attending college in the U.S., lawfully resident Asian aliens returning from temporary trips abroad, and the wives and minor children of these categories, "not coming as an immigrant." According to Sucheng Chan, "by implication," tourists, persons in transit, and merchants from Asia also could enter (on the understanding that these groups did not come as immigrants).[106]

This law thus continued the harsh prohibition, illustrated in the *Yee Won* case, against the bringing of a wife from China, even if the man

103 Act of Feb 5, 1917, 39 Stat. 874, chap.29.

104 Ibid.

105 Kim 1992-B, 44.

106 Chan 1994, 33; Hull 1992, 407; 43 Stat. 153, May 26, 1924.

wanting to do the bringing was himself an American citizen of Chinese descent. Once the Supreme Court, under Chief Justice (and former President) Taft, in 1925 made plain this import of the statute,[107] Chinese lobbying for a reform intensified. In 1930, Congress finally carved out a narrow exemption from the 1924 law to permit U.S. citizens to bring in wives from abroad even if the wife were "ineligible for naturalization" (which meant: of Asian extraction), but only if the marriage had taken place prior to the 1924 law![108]

That this harsh judicial interpretation of 1925 accurately captured Congressional intent from the 1917 law is highly probable in light of what Congress had said in the separate Cable Act of 1922.[109] For non-Asians this Act ended automatic naturalization for a woman who married an American, and required that the foreign wife undergo naturalization herself. Also the Act ended the automatic loss of citizenship upon marriage, of an American woman who married a non-Asian foreigner (and permitted former citizens, already in such marriages to regain U.S. citizenship via naturalization). However, a U.S. female citizen (including those of Asian extraction) who married an Asian alien ("alien ineligible to citizenship") would lose her citizenship upon marriage, and any foreign woman, otherwise naturalizable, could not become naturalized as long as she was in a marriage to an Asian alien. Plainly, Congress was going all out to prevent permanent immigration by Asians to the U.S.,[110] including Asian spouses of Americans, male or female. This restriction on a right as basic as the choice of marriage partner, blatantly discriminated against Asian-American citizens; female ones would lose their citizenship if they married within their race to a foreigner, and in many U.S. states were forbidden to marry anyone outside their race. Male American Asians, too, were in many states forbidden to marry outside their race, and if they married within their race to a foreigner, they could not bring their wife to live in the U.S. That the League of Nations had adopted a resolution in 1920, two years before the Cable Act, creating via international law a national obligation to protect "racial, linguistic, or religious minorities"[111] appeared to have been of little consequence to the U.S. Congress.

---

107 *Chang Chan et al. v. Nagle*, 268 U.S. 346 (1925).
108 Chan, 1994, 35.
109 Act of September 22, 1922, 42 U.S. Statutes at Large 571.
110 Except for clergy members and professors.
111 Cover 1982, 1298.

THE TAFT COURT AND ASIANS, 1921–30

In 1921, President Harding appointed former president William Taft to be Chief Justice. Then Justice Sutherland and Justice Butler joined the Taft Court in 1922 (replacing Justices Clarke and Day); Justice Sanford, in 1923 (replacing Pitney); and Justice Stone (a Coolidge appointee), in 1925 (replacing McKenna).[112] Like the White Court before it, the Taft Court produced a mixed record on the rights of Asians.

On the same day in May, 1925, that the Taft Court read U.S. law to forbid allowing U.S. born citizens of Chinese descent (or any other U.S. citizens) to bring into the country their wives if the wives were not eligible for naturalization,[113] the Court produced the contrary result for the situation of wives of Chinese merchants.[114] The Court read prior treaties as establishing the understanding that merchants entered "not as immigrants" but for purposes of commerce, and thus were exempt from exclusion, and so were their wives and minor children. Since the 1924 immigration law did not plainly alter this understanding (but was silent about it), the Court chose to keep it in force by way of inference.

By contrast, the Taft Court in 1923, upheld laws of Western states that prohibited the owning, acquiring or leasing of property by persons unable to become naturalized citizens, i.e., Asians, in apparent contradiction to the principle it had set forth in *Yick Wo*, protecting nationality groups from state-level discrimination under the equal protection clause.[115] (Granted, since Asian-descent persons could be citizens by reason of being born here, and by 1920 more than 50,000 of them were,[116] to restrict alien land ownership did not necessarily discriminate against the entire race/nationality.) The Taft Court chose to view the question in terms of alignment of state policy with federal foreign policy. Since the Treaty of 1911 between the U.S. and Japan itself permitted a prohibition

---

[112] Justice Edward Terry Sanford had been the successful prosecutor of lynch-mob member Sheriff Shipp and his accomplices for contempt of court in Shipp II (1909), the U.S. Supreme Court's only original-jurisdiction criminal trial. "Justice Sanford Deserves Greater Recognition." 2016.

[113] *Chang Chan et al. v. Nagle*, 268 U.S. 346 (1925).

[114] *Cheung Sum Shee v. Nagle*, 268 U.S. 336 (1925).

[115] Kim 1992-B, 41–3; Stuen 1992. *Terrace v. Thompson*, 263 U.S. 197 (1923); *Porterfield v. Webb*, 263 U.S. 225 (1923); *Frick v. Webb*, 263 U.S. 326 (1923); *Webb v. O'Brien*, 263 U.S. 313 (1923); *Cockrill v. People of California*, 268 U.S. 258 (1925).

[116] The 1920 census lists some 54,000 "Asians and Pacific Islanders" as native-born residents. (https://www.census.gov/population/www/documentation/twps0029/tab08.html accessed July 20, 2014).

to Japanese residents on the leasing of land for agricultural purposes and on the purchase of land within the U.S., the Court reasoned that neither the state of Washington nor the state of California was violating the Constitution in forbidding persons ineligible to citizenship from owning land, or controlling the land by way of a lease on it. Because the state police power includes the power to protect public safety, and because control of agriculture amounts to control of the food supply, "each State, in the absence of any treaty provision to the contrary, has power to deny to aliens the right to own land within its borders."[117]

The Treaty of 1911, however, cut both ways. The Taft Court applied it one year later to strike down an anti-alien law of Seattle that prohibited the granting of pawnbroker licenses to aliens, since the treaty imposed no occupational restrictions.[118]

The Taft Court also continued the judicial pattern of restricting administrative excess by immigration authorities. The case of *Ng Fung Ho et al v. White*[119] presented challenges to summary deportation orders issued under the 1917 Immigration Act against a group of four "persons of the Chinese race," as Justice Brandeis described them. Two of them, the Court ruled, could be summarily deported by executive branch officials pursuant to executive branch hearings finding their presence here unlawful, even without judicial process. This followed the long-standing rule: "Congress has power to order at any time the deportation of aliens whose presence in the country it deems hurtful, and may do so by appropriate executive proceedings."[120]

The other two litigants, however, were presenting claims that they were American citizens of Chinese descent. Justice Brandeis wrote for a unanimous Court that someone within the borders of the U.S. and claiming U.S. citizenship, whom the executive branch is attempting to deport as a non-citizen, is entitled to the protections of a full judicial trial for defending the claim of citizenship. The Fifth Amendment requires this as a matter of due process.[121] The Court explicitly refrained, however, from deciding whether the rule to be applied in these deportation cases would be the one from the 1892 Chinese Exclusion Act that imposed the burden of proving citizenship on the Chinese person, rather

117 *Terrace v. Thompson*, 263 U.S. 197, 217 (1923).
118 *Asakura v. City of Seattle*, 265 U.S. 332 (1924).
119 *Ng Fung Ho v. White*, 259 U.S. 276 (1922).
120 Ibid., at 280.
121 Ibid,, at 284–5.

than imposing upon the government, via the Fifth Amendment Due Process Clause, the burden of proving deportability.[122]

The Taft Court also maintained the rule, established in prior cases, that the executive branch, so long as it did not proceed with "manifest" unfairness or in violation of a law, did have final authority to refuse admission at the port of entry to a foreign-born person claiming to be a citizen by virtue of the citizenship of his or her father. It applied this rule in 1927, to refuse to order admission of Quon Quon Poy, a fifteen-year old, claiming to be the son of the U.S. born citizen, Quon Mee Sing, after a detailed examination of the hearing record.[123]

The Court was on firmer ground protecting Asian minorities against state-level, or territorial government-level laws than it would be in an effort to clash with Congress over foreign policy. Thus, in a couple of cases it was able to protect language rights of such minorities. The Philippines passed a law in 1921 that in effect criminalized the keeping of account books in Chinese, in a patent effort to discriminate against Chinese merchants on the islands. In 1926, the U.S. Supreme Court struck it down as a violation of both the equal protection and the due process provisions of the Philippine Constitution.[124]

Also in 1927, the Court extended substantive due process rights of the U.S. Constitution to non-citizen residents of Hawaii.[125] Hawaii had passed a law insisting on its right to prescribe what subjects could and could not be taught and what textbooks could be used in the 163 foreign language schools that operated within Hawaii for its Japanese, Chinese, and Korean residents. The Court said that the fundamental rights protected by the Fourteenth Amendment due process clause against state governmental abridgment in cases like *Meyer v. Nebraska* and *Pierce v. Society of Sisters*, in particular, the right of parents to direct the teaching and learning of their own children, also applied via the Fifth Amendment due process clause to the federal government and "agencies set up by Congress for the government of the territory."[126] Therefore, this drastic restriction of that liberty was unconstitutional.

---

[122] Ibid., at 283.

[123] *Quon Quon Poy v. Johnson*, 273 U.S. 352 (1927).

[124] *Yu Cong Eng v. Trinidad*, 271 U.S. 500 (1926).

[125] *Farrington v. Tokushige*, 273 U.S. 284 (1927).

[126] Ibid., at 299. *Meyer v. Nebraska,* 262 U.S. 390 (1923); *Pierce v. Society of Sisters*, 268 U.S. 510 (1925).

THE TAFT COURT AND THE WHITENESS QUESTION

In 1922 for the first time the U.S. Supreme Court confronted the question of what counts as "white" for purposes of applying the statute that allowed only whites, Africans, and descendants of Africans to become U.S. citizens via naturalization. In *Ozawa v. U.S.* (1922)[127] a Japanese-born but U.S.-educated man who had inhabited the U.S. for twenty years, appealed the lower court denial of his application for naturalization, claiming the status of whiteness. He claimed that when Congress in 1790 specified "white" in the naturalization law, they meant simply all persons who were neither native Indian nor black. He also claimed to be as fair-skinned as many Caucasians. The Court ruled that color was not the criterion but rather the guideline would be the common understanding of whiteness, which meant being of the Caucasian race.

On the same day, in a companion case, *Yamashita v. Hinkle*, the Court actually undid the naturalization of a Japanese-born man who had believed he had been lawfully naturalized sixteen years earlier in a court in Washington State. The U.S. Supreme Court declared this prior naturalization null and void.[128]

The following year the Court had to face a challenge to its one-year old doctrine that Caucasian-ness rather than skin-color determined whiteness for purpose of naturalization law. Bhagat S. Thind, a native of India and what the Court called a "high caste Hindu of full Indian blood," had obtained naturalization in a federal district court, but the federal bureaucrat who examined naturalization cases challenged the decision. At the federal Circuit Court of Appeals certain legal questions were certified over to the Supreme Court. The Supreme Court was unanimous in dropping its commitment to Caucasian racial membership as the mark of whiteness, now that they learned that full-blooded Asian Indians are considered by ethnologists to be Caucasian. They retreated to a kind of average-man test. "White" in "the understanding of the common man" is what was required for naturalization, and this did not fit Thind, or others of South Asian extraction.[129]

In 1906[130] Congress had acted to permit naturalization of those Filipinos, and also Puerto Ricans—the residents of America's island possessions, who chose to move to the mainland U.S. Specific legislation was needed because they did not fit into the category "aliens." So this Act

---

[127] *Ozawa v. U.S.*, 260 U.S. 178 (1922).

[128] *Yamashita v. Hinkle*, 260 U.S. 199 (1922); Kim 1992-B, 35–7.

[129] *U.S. v. Bhagat Singh Thind,* 261 U.S. 204, 209 (1923); Kim 1992-B, 37–8.

[130] Act of June 29, 1906, 34 Stat. 601.

allowed that "persons not citizens who owe permanent allegiance to the United States and who may become residents of any State or organized territory of the United States" could become naturalized if they declared an intent to be naturalized two years prior to doing so *and* followed the other appropriate naturalization laws. Since the other naturalization laws contained racial qualifiers, this seemed to mean that many Filipinos, whether of Japanese, Chinese, Korean or "Malay" extraction, would not qualify as white, whereas persons of Spanish or other European or European-African descent would qualify. Evidently, Congress similarly believed that questions existed about the non-Asian bona fides of some Puerto Rican residents of the U.S. territory of Puerto Rico, because Congress amended the 1906 law in 1918 to express its gratitude and encouragement for the military service of both Filipinos and "Porto Ricans" by extending to them, *irrespective of race*, the chance to become U.S. citizens, and to do so on an expedited basis.[131] As worded, the law extended this benefit to "any native-born Filipino" and "any Porto Rican" and "any alien" who had served in the armed forces for three years and was twenty-one or older. When a Japanese-born ten-year veteran of the U.S. Coast Guard, Hidemitsu Toyota, tried in 1925 to avail himself of the benefits of the "or any alien" language of the 1918 amendment, the Taft Court took the occasion to clarify these words: When it came to "Asiatic" persons this law did not eliminate the racial restrictions on naturalization except as to the specifically mentioned categories of "Porto Rican" and Filipino. And for those persons, the lifting of racial restrictions applied only to veterans of the armed forces. All other racially Asian Filipinos were still barred from naturalization. The Court based this interpretation on legislative history (referencing Congressional debates and Senate and House Reports) and also on the "long … national policy to maintain the distinction of color and race."[132]

Mr. Gong Lum, a Chinese resident of Mississippi, wanted the right to have his daughter attend the public high school that Mississippi reserved "to white children exclusively."[133] The U.S. Supreme Court accepted the view of the Mississippi Supreme Court that it was within the range of the

---

131 Act of May 9, 1918, 40 Stat. 542. Many Chinese laborers had migrated to Puerto Rico at the end of the nineteenth century; they and their descendants would be affected by this law. Puerto Ricans of black or white or mixed black and white descent would already have been eligible for naturalization (African-Americans having been eligible since the end of the Civil War), although not previously under the expedited process.

132 *Toyota v. U.S.*, 268 U.S. 402, 410–12 (1925).

133 *Gong Lum v. Rice,* 275 U.S. 78 (1927).

state's police power to separate school children into two categories, white and non-white ("colored" in the words of the statute). This Mississippi Supreme Court opinion obfuscated the question whether there was only one high school at all geographically accessible to the Gong Lum family, the one for whites only. It simply explained that colored districts and white districts had separate lines, and that every colored resident had a district that contained a common school.[134] The U. S. Supreme Court responded to this murkiness by putting the burden on the Chinese family:[135]

> Had the petition alleged specifically that there was no colored school in Martha Lum's neighborhood to which she could conveniently go, a different question would have been presented, and this, without regard to the State Supreme Court's construction of the State Constitution as limiting the white schools provided for the education of children of the white or Caucasian race. But we do not find the petition to present such a situation.

The U.S. Supreme Court then went along with the fiction presumed by the Supreme Court of Mississippi: "The question here is whether a Chinese citizen of the United States is denied equal protection of the laws when he is classed among the colored races and furnished facilities for education equal to that offered to all, whether white, brown, yellow or black." For that question, the Court simply replied that the precedents since *Plessy* were clear.[136] The Taft Court was not willing to dive into the intense conflict that it would have provoked by undoing *Plessy* in 1927. It had, however, pointed to a potential path for future litigants: a challenge to racial segregation based on documented inequality of the dual school system. Hardly any districts in the South in this period offered high schools for non-whites.

BLACKS DURING THE TAFT COURT YEARS, 1921–30, WITH SEQUELAE OF HUGHES COURT YEARS, 1930–41

While the decade of the 1920s was a time for the flowering of African-American culture in places like Harlem and Paris, litigants at the Supreme Court attained more modest progress on legal and political rights for black Americans.

---

134 *Rice v. Gong Lum*, 139 Miss. 760, 787 (1925).
135 275 U.S. 78., at 84.
136 Ibid. at 85–6.

The hint in the *Gong Lum* case that the Court was open to arguments about situations where "separate" was nowhere close to "equal," in the matter of segregated education did not get addressed until after Justice Hughes, who had left the Court in 1916 to run for President on the Republican and Progressive Party tickets, came back onto the Court, replacing Chief Justice Taft in February, 1930. In the meantime, Hughes was publicly associating himself with opposition to the Ku Klux Klan, to anti-Catholicism and to Anti-Semitism by co-founding the National Conference of Christians and Jews in 1927 (now known as the National Conference for Community and Justice).[137]

Still, the Taft Court did contribute to black civil rights by forbidding southern state laws that limited the Democratic Party primary to white voters. The first signal from the Court on such laws was not propitious. In 1924 a case came up from Texas, *Love v. Griffith*, where, as in most southern states by this time, the intraparty election for the Democratic Party nomination sealed the outcome of the general election, since the Republican Party in the South had been destroyed by a combination of violent intimidation and manipulation of voter eligibility laws and abandonment by the national organization of its earlier commitment to the rights of southern blacks. (The Populist Party faded into insignificance after the 1896 election.) Democrats in Texas wanted to assure the absence of influence from the few remaining black voters. As early as 1905, Texas enacted a law that empowered local officials to shut blacks out of Democratic Party primaries.[138] In January, 1921 the Democratic Executive Committee of Houston published a rule forbidding blacks to vote in the February 9, 1921 primary. Charles Love, a black newspaper publisher and columnist, along with other black Democrats sued for an injunction to block operation of the law.[139] The case did not reach the Supreme Court until 1924, as *Love v. Griffith*. The election was long past, and the Taft Court simply dismissed the case, declaring it moot.

Meanwhile, however, Texas in 1923 had passed a straightforward, no-blacks-may-participate law for the Democratic primaries of Texas, and the *Love* case had attracted the attention of NAACP leaders to the potential for voting rights progress against Texas laws, if the right case could be found.[140] The NAACP located a black Democrat happy to vote in 1924 in order to challenge the law. He was Lawrence Nixon, a physician and drugstore owner, who had voted regularly in Texas primaries of El Paso

137 National Conference for Community and Justice. N.D.
138 Hales 2010; Hine 2003, 84–5.
139 Hines 2003, 100–101.
140 Ibid., 110–13.

prior to the passage of the 1923 law.[141] After he was blocked from voting, pursuant to the law, he sued for ($5,000) damages.[142]

Justice Holmes decided *Nixon v. Herndon* for a unanimous court. He dodged the question whether participation in a party primary was covered by the Fifteenth Amendment reference to "the right to vote," and simply said that participation in a primary, which can determine the final outcome of an election, is an important right and, as such, under the Fourteenth Amendment cannot be taken away from a group of citizens on the basis of race. To do so violates equal protection.[143]

The Taft Court also in *Moore v. Dempsey* (1923) pioneered the use of the Due Process Clause of the Fourteenth Amendment to throw out convictions of Southern blacks for killing a white person when the conviction was attained via mob-dominated procedures. The reasoning in this case, and several that followed from later courts, described the racial background to the case and the particulars of the lynch mob atmosphere, but set forth the due process right in terms that would apply to trials of anyone in the U.S.[144] This conviction followed upon the heels of a multiday white-against-black race riot in 1919 in Helena, Arkansas that produced the death of more than 100 blacks and one white. In the totality of circumstances that proved that a fair trial was not granted, so due process was denied, the Court listed the personal bias in grand jury composition (it contained several men from the posse that had hunted down the suspects); the "systematic" exclusion of blacks from the grand and petit juries; whipping and torture to extract testimony from persons used later as witnesses; the grossly negligent presentation by assigned defense counsel (no request for venue change, no consultation with accused, no calling of witnesses); the dispersal of the lynch mob by official promises that if they permitted a trial, "justice would be done"; the forty-five minute duration of the trial and the less than five minute duration of the time of jury deliberation; and the fear-infused courtroom atmosphere, such that any dissenting juror would need to fear for his life.

The 1931–40 Hughes Court would be producing several similar decisions, again with reasoning that, while including descriptively the presence of racial hostility, was based as a matter of law on the absence of fair trial procedures. These decisions, which undid particular instances of severe

---

141 Ibid., 113.

142 *Nixon v. Herndon*, 273 U.S. 536 (1927).

143 Ibid., at 540–41.

144 Karst 2000; *Moore et al. v. Dempsey*, 261 U.S. 86 (1923). Cover 1982, 1305–6, argues that this case was the beginning of the Supreme Court's "Judicial Activism in the Protection of Minorities."

racial injustice, thus precedentially created rights for all Americans accused of crime, as distinguished from rights of racial minorities as such. Prominent examples would be: *Powell v. Alabama* (1932) (Scottsboro Boys case applying to state's constitutional right to counsel in some cases);[145] *Brown v. Mississippi* (1936) (requiring, via Fourteenth Amendment, exclusion of coerced confessions by states; the defendant had been whipped, but, in the words of the deputy sheriff, "not too much for a Negro");[146] *Chambers v. Florida* (1940) (ruling that murder confessions extracted from four black men for murder of a white man in an atmosphere of mob violence, after police holding of suspects incommunicado for five days of questioning, including an all-night grilling and limited access to food and water, constitute coerced confessions and violate due process).[147] These are treated comprehensively in Chapter 7.

Meanwhile the *Moore v. Dempsey* decision may have combined with anti-lynching activity in the elected branches to promote a sharp decline in the lynchings of blacks. The House of Representatives, in 1922, did adopt a federal anti-lynching bill, the Dyer Bill, but it died in a Senate filibuster.[148] The official failure of that bill may well have produced an impact contrary to appearances. Due to a strong NAACP lobbying campaign, not only Congressman Dyer, but also President Harding, promoted the bill. The bill, if enacted, would have made negligence by public officials in preventing lynchings and in apprehending lynchers a federal felony punishable by up to five years in prison. The fact that the bill progressed as far as it did seems to have functioned as a wake-up call to corrupt or cowardly southern sheriffs. As shown in Table 5.1 below the number of lynchings of blacks dropped from 51 in 1922 (year anti-lynching bill nearly became law) to 29 in 1923 (year of *Moore v. Dempsey*) to 16 in 1924, after which it never rose above 24 in a year, and by 1936 it fell permanently into single digits.[149]

---

145 *Powell v. Alabama*, 287 U.S. 45 (1932).

146 *Brown v. Mississippi*, 297 U.S. 278, 284 (1936).

147 *Chambers v. Florida*, 309 U.S. 227 (1940).

148 "NAACP History: Anti-Lynching Bill." 2009–14.

149 Klarman 2004, 118–20, suggests, "the decline [in lynchings of southern blacks] probably [partly] depended on replacing lynchings with quick trials that could be counted on to produce guilty verdicts, death sentences, and swift executions," but his timing is somewhat off. This explanation can account for the drop after the Dyer Bill's near success, but not for the further decline that followed the Court's condemnation of such lynch-mob-dominated, sham trials in *Moore v. Dempsey* (1923).

Table 5.1 Lynchings: By year and race 1882–1968

Year	Whites	Blacks	Total
1882	64	49	113
1883	77	53	130
1884	160	51	211
1885	110	74	184
1886	64	74	138
1887	50	70	120
1888	68	69	137
1889	76	94	170
1890	11	85	96
1891	71	113	184
1892	69	161	230
1893	34	118	152
1894	58	134	192
1895	66	113	179
1896	45	78	123
1897	35	123	158
1904	7	76	83
1905	5	57	62
1906	3	62	65
1907	3	58	61
1908	8	89	97
1909	13	69	82
1910	9	67	76
1911	7	60	67
1912	2	62	64
1913	1	51	52
1914	4	51	55
1915	13	56	69
1916	4	50	54
1917	2	36	38
1918	4	60	64
1919	7	76	83
1920	8	53	61

Table 5.1 Lynchings (cont.)

Year	Whites	Blacks	Total
1921	5	59	64
1922	6	51	57
1929	3	7	10
1930	1	20	21
1931	1	12	13
1932	2	6	8
1933	2	24	26
1934	0	15	15
1935	2	18	20
1936	0	8	8
1937	0	8	8
1938	0	6	6
1939	1	2	3
1940	1	4	5
1941	0	4	4
1942	0	6	6
1943	0	3	3
1944	0	2	2
1945	0	1	1
1946	0	6	6
1947	0	1	1
1954	0	0	0
1955	0	3	3
1956	0	0	0
1957	1	0	1
1958	0	0	0
1959	0	1	1
1960	0	0	0
1961	0	1	1
1962	0	0	0

Year	Whites	Blacks	Total
1963	0	1	1
1964	2	1	3
1965	0	0	0
1966	0	0	0
1967	0	0	0
1968	0	0	0
Total	1,297	3,445	4,742

Source: Linder 2000-B.

The only other race-related topic to come before the Taft Court produced a twenty-year set-back of the right to be free of racial discrimination in housing. The White Court had struck down state laws imposing such discrimination in *Buchanan v. Warley* (1917), and the Taft Court, to its credit, struck down thinly disguised copycat laws attempted by first New Orleans and then Richmond.[150] The Court decided these *per curiam*, in single sentence decisions, relying simply on *Buchanan v. Warley*. Although it stayed with the letter of *Buchanan v. Warley*, the Taft Court refused in a 1926 case, *Corrigan v. Buckley*, to move beyond it for dealing with privately arranged covenants, attached to deeds, that promised not to sell the property to blacks (the clauses often mentioned other groups as well: Jews, Italians, Asians[151]).

Corrigan v. Buckley, concerned a covenant drawn up in 1921 among twenty-five residents of a D.C. neighborhood, agreeing that their property would "not ever" (for a twenty-one year period) be "sold, leased or given to, any person of the negro race or blood."[152] Buckley initially sued for a Court order enjoining Corrigan from transferring her property to a black woman, Helen Curtis. He obtained the injunction at the District Court, and it was sustained at the Court of Appeals. The U.S. Supreme Court reasoned that the federal law saying "all persons and citizens shall have equal right with white citizens to make contracts and acquire property" was not applicable to the situation of private agreements; these clauses referred to legal rights, as distinguished from actual opportunity. Nor did the Fourteenth Amendment help Corrigan's case, since, said the Court, it restricted only action by states, not by private individuals. Consequently,

150 *Harmon v. Tyler* 273 U.S. 668 (1927) (*per curiam*); *Richmond v. Deans*, 281 U.S. 704 (1930) (*per curiam*).

151 Silva 2009.

152 *Corrigan v. Buckley*, 271 U.S. 323, 327 (1926).

the Court dismissed the appeal as failing to have presented a substantial federal question.

CONCLUSIONS AS TO BLACKS AND ASIANS, 1911–30

The fate of black and Asian-Americans became officially intertwined in 1886 in *Yick Wo v. Hopkins*. In its first crack at interpreting the Fourteenth Amendment Equal Protection Clause, the Supreme Court had announced the following in 1873, in the *Slaughterhouse Cases*: "We doubt very much whether any action of a State not directed by way of discrimination against the negroes as a class, or on account of their race, will ever be held to come within the purview of this provision."[153] (Interestingly, in that same opinion, the Court majority had linked Negro slavery to the Chinese Coolie labor system and the Mexican peonage labor system, indicating that the Thirteenth Amendment would forbid all three,[154] but this was a discussion of labor perceived to be coerced rather than racial categorization as such.) *Yick Wo* then did what the Court had said would not be done. The Waite Court used the Equal Protection Clause to strike down a laundry regulating ordinance, with the explanation that, as applied:[155]

> no reason for it exists except hostility to the [Chinese] race and nationality to which the petitioners belong, and which, in the eye of the law, is not justified. The discrimination is, therefore, ... a denial of the equal protection of the laws and a violation of the Fourteenth Amendment of the Constitution.

The Fuller Court that followed, from 1888 through 1910, however, almost never saw an anti-black discrimination that it did not like, the only exceptions being three decisions against perpetrators of murder by lynching.[156] By contrast, this Court was willing on several occasions to

---

153 *Slaughterhouse Cases*, 83 U.S. 36, 81 (1873).

154 Ibid., at 72.

155 *Yick Wo v. Hopkins*, 118 U.S. 356, 374 (1886).

156 *Riggins v. U.S.* (1905) (ruled that federally convicted member of mob that had murdered a black man via a lynching could not use procedure of writ of habeas corpus); *U.S. v. Shipp I*, (1906) (U.S. Supreme Court had authority to try the members of lynch mob along with compliant sheriff and deputies on charges of criminal contempt for lynching a prisoner after being notified that the Supreme Court had agreed to hear his appeal for a writ of habeas corpus); *U.S. v. Shipp II* (1909) (Shipp and fellow lynch mob members guilty of criminal contempt of court).

check administrative excess in mistreatment of the Chinese or Chinese-Americans (see Chapter 4 for examples).

The two Courts treated in this chapter, that headed by Chief Justice White and that headed by Chief Justice Taft, covering the period of 1911–30, improved markedly upon the dismal record of the Fuller Court as to blacks, and continued in this Court's mixed record pattern as to Asians. Both of these later Courts continued the Fuller Court's commitment to protecting the citizenship rights of Asian persons born within the U.S.; they could not be deported as undesirable aliens prior to having a chance in a full judicial trial to document their citizen birth (*Ng Fung Ho et al v. White* (1922)), and they could not be excluded at the border in an unfair proceeding (*Kwock Jan Fat v. White* (1920)). And like the Fuller Court, these justices also continued the pattern of checking administrative excess both at the border (*White v. Chin Fong* (1920); *Cheung Sum Shee* (1925)) and in alien deportation decisions (*U.S. v. Woo Jan* (1918)). Both the White Court and the Taft Court struck down state laws that unreasonably restricted employment opportunities for aliens (*Truax v. Raich* (1915) and *Asakura v. Seattle* (1924)). And the Taft Court even extended to Japanese residents of Hawaii, the substantive due process rights to have private schools free of unreasonable interference from the government of Hawaii (*Farrington v. Tokushige* (1927)). Ultimately with respect to Asians, however, the justices' options were limited, since the elected branches make foreign policy, and the questions of admitting or expelling aliens appeared to them, as well as to Congress, the President and the U.S. public, to be matters for decision by the elected branches. By contrast, with respect both to Asians and American Indians, the Court could hold state governments or (similarly subordinate) territorial governments to honoring rights under federal treaty law or provisions of the U.S. Constitution (as in the case of Japanese language rights in Hawaii).

The big change after the Fuller Court was in judicial policy toward blacks. Whereas the Fuller Court had used legal technicalities to postpone intervening to halt southern peonage practices,[157] the White Court in one of its earliest decisions (1911) declared debt servitude peonage unlawful and a violation of the Thirteenth Amendment.[158] It then (in *U.S. v. Reynolds* (1914)) proceeded to strike down the criminal surety system

---

157 *Bailey v. Alabama I* (1908) (disagrees with *amicus* from Justice Department and refuses to issue pre-trial release on *habeas* of a black man jailed under a peonage law); *Clyatt v. U.S.* (1905) (despite acknowledging constitutionality of 1867 federal law against peonage, reverses the conviction for peonage due to wrong wording in the indictment and remands for retrial).

158 *Bailey v. Alabama II* (1911).

of debt servitude (but not the working off of fines in convict "chain gang" systems, which would have been more difficult in light of the wording of the Thirteenth Amendment).[159] It went on to declare in dicta that racial segregation of common carriers could not be imposed via state laws that explicitly allowed unequal facilities to be provided to different racial groups based on disproportionate usage (*McCabe v. Atchison, Topeka, & Santa Fe Railway* (1914)). Much more consequentially, it declared unconstitutional the racial residential segregation law of Louisville, a law of which many cities had put into place their own version by the time of the decision (*Buchanan v. Warley* (1917)). And it declared unconstitutional grandfather-clause-linked voting restrictions on blacks in two different states in three 1915 decisions (*U.S. v. Guinn*; *U.S. v, Mosley*; and *Myers v. Anderson*), which, in their reasoning, gave new force to generally worded civil rights statutes that had not before been used to enforce the right to vote.

The Taft Court continued this trajectory: In two decisions it reaffirmed *Buchanan v. Warley*, throwing out residential segregation laws of Richmond and New Orleans (*Richmond v. Deans* (1930) and *Harmon v. Tyler* (1927)). In 1923 it upheld the claim of twelve black men convicted in the South of murdering four white men, throwing out their convictions on the ground that a lynch mob atmosphere, rigged juries, woefully inadequate counsel, and witnesses tortured into producing testimony, added up to a flagrant denial of the fair hearing required for due process, and remanding to federal court for a fresh trial (*Moore v. Dempsey*). And in 1927 (*Nixon v. Herndon*), the Taft Court moved black voting rights forward by striking down a Texas white primary law.

To be sure, the record of both the White and Taft Courts on black civil rights was not without blemishes. The White Court continued judicial permission for state segregation laws and for company practices imposing the regime of "separate but equal" on common carriers (*Butts v. Merchants* (1913) and *South Covington v. Kentucky* (1920)) and the Taft Court did the same for the program of "separate but equal" in public schools (*Gong Lum v. Rice* (1927)). And in *Corrigan v. Buckley* (1926) the Taft Court gave the stamp of "not unconstitutional" to private schemes for achieving racial segregation by attaching restrictive covenants to deeds.

---

[159] Thirteenth Amendment: "Neither slavery nor involuntary servitude, *except as a punishment for crime whereof the party shall have been duly convicted*, shall exist within the United States …" (emphasis added).

Like these Courts' respective records on Asians, the overall picture was mixed. Meanwhile, the executive branch during the Taft Administration (1909–13) did follow through on peonage prosecutions, but not with the enthusiasm that Teddy Roosevelt had brought to the subject. And Taft's Attorney General prosecuted the voting rights (grandfather clause cases) only after embarrassing political pressure was brought to bear. Surprisingly, Woodrow Wilson's Justice Department (1913–17) finished the job on the grandfather clause cases, with success at the Supreme Court, but Wilson undermined black civil rights on other fronts. Wilson racially segregated the federal civil service and drastically cut back on patronage for blacks. Once Teddy Roosevelt left the White House, President Taft returned to supporting Congress's zeal to keep Asians out of the U.S.

Congress throughout this period did nothing to help protect American blacks from voting rights denials or mob violence and repeatedly reiterated hostility to both Asian immigration and naturalization. The imperial ambitions of Presidents William McKinley and Teddy Roosevelt had brought Pacific Island territories into the U.S., but except for native born Hawaiians (who were governed by white elites) Congress did not allow the American nationals of Asian extraction from Guam, the Philippines, Samoa or Puerto Rico who might migrate to the U.S. to be naturalized as citizens with the narrow exception (starting in 1918) of Filipinos or Puerto Ricans who served three years in the U.S. armed forces.[160]

And finally, the 1923 *Moore v. Dempsey* decision initiated two trends that were to become much more prominent during the 1940s and 1950s. First, it signaled the beginning of a longterm Supreme Court crackdown on blatantly rigged, absurdly expedited, southern trials of black suspects—in effect lynchings (or attempted lynchings) dressed up to look like trials. This process included the re-invigoration of the right of blacks to serve on southern juries, a right that had been short-circuited by the Fuller Court, after it had been honored in the early 1880s. Secondly, the *Moore* decision revealed an intertwining or interdependence of black rights and Asian rights, a doctrinal development that was going to become more pronounced in the 1940s and 1950s.

In the nineteenth century, Asian constitutional rights cases accumulated on the foundations of the rights of blacks to the degree that they derived

---

[160] In 1917, the U.S. by purchase from Denmark added the U.S. Virgin Islands to its territorial possessions. Congress legislated to make the residents born in these islands citizens in 1927. As with the other territorial possessions, these citizens are not represented in Congress but can move to the mainland and be treated as any other resident citizens.

from either the Fourteenth or Thirteenth Amendments. *Yick Wo* (1886) expanded the Equal Protection Clause to cover anti-Chinese discrimination in state governmental practices, and the *Wong Wing* decision of 1896 utilized the Thirteenth Amendment (as well as the Fifth Amendment Due Process Clause and the Sixth Amendment trial by jury clause) to strike down the law (backed by the Justice Department, as well as Congress), that resident aliens unable to bear the burden of proving the lawfulness of their stay here could be summarily sentenced to up to a year in prison at "hard labor."[161]

Moore v. Dempsey (1923) for the first time used an Asian rights precedent as a foundation for expanding black rights. The *Moore* majority opinion primarily relied on a dictum from the *Frank v. Mangum* decision[162] that had gone in the opposite direction. This *Moore* mention of the dictum said the following:

> In *Frank v. Mangum*, 237 U.S. 309, 335, it was recognized of course that if in fact a trial is dominated by a mob so that there is an actual interference with the course of justice, there is a departure from due process of law; and that "if the State, supplying no corrective process, carries into execution a judgment of death or imprisonment based upon a verdict thus produced by mob domination, the State deprives the accused of his life or liberty without due process of law."[163]

Justices Holmes and Hughes had dissented in the *Frank* case, pointing out, inter alia, that the courtroom atmosphere was so permeated by lynch mob sentiments that the judge had persuaded Frank's attorney to keep Frank away from the courtroom for the reading of the verdict, because, if it came in as not guilty, the judge could not assure Frank's safety. In arguing that habeas should be granted, Justice Holmes, author of the two-person dissent, cited his own opinion in the Asian case *U.S. v. Sing Tuck* (1904), on the propriety of using the writ to upset a verdict.[164]

---

161 *Wong Wing v. U.S.*, 163 U.S. 228, 238 (1896).

162 *Frank v. Mangum*, 237 U.S. 309, 335 (1915). This was an appeal of a conviction of a Jew for allegedly raping a white, non-Jewish 13-year old in Atlanta, Georgia. Anti-Semitic sentiment largely fueled the hostile mob. The U.S. Supreme Court rejected the appeal in April. The governor then commuted his sentence from execution to life in prison; Leo Frank was lynched on August 17, 1915.

163 *Moore v. Dempsey*, 261 U.S. 86, 90–91 (1923).

164 *Frank v. Mangum*, 237 U.S. 309, at 348 (Holmes, J. dissenting), citing *U.S. v. Sing Tuck,* 194 U.S. 161, 168 (1904).

Holmes then, in deciding *Moore v. Dempsey,* followed the logic of his *Frank* dissent of eight years earlier.

Justice McReynolds (with Sutherland) vehemently dissented in *Moore,* insisting that the longstanding rule restricting the use of habeas, which rule had been followed in the *Frank* case, should, contrary to the majority argument, now be followed:

> It follows as a logical consequence that where, as here, a criminal prosecution has proceeded through all the courts of the state, including the appellate as well as the trial court, the result of the appellate review cannot be ignored when afterwards the prisoner applies for his release on the ground of a deprivation of federal rights sufficient to oust the state of its jurisdiction to proceed to judgment and execution against him. This is not a mere matter of comity, as seems to be supposed. The rule stands upon a much higher plane, for it arises out of the very nature and ground of the inquiry into the proceedings of the state tribunals, and touches closely upon the relations between the state and the federal governments.[165]

It had been precisely on this point that the Holmes dissent in *Frank v. Mangum* had cited the passage from *U.S. v. Sing Tuck,* at 168:

> The first mode of attacking his decision is by taking that appeal. If the appeal fails, it then is time enough to consider whether, upon a petition showing reasonable cause, there ought to be a further trial upon *habeas corpus* … .
>
> If the allegations of a petition for *habeas corpus* setting up want of jurisdiction, whether of an executive officer or of an ordinary court, are true, the petitioner theoretically is entitled to his liberty at once. Yet a summary interruption of the regular order of proceedings, by means of the writ, is not always a matter of right. A familiar illustration is that of a person imprisoned upon criminal process by a state court, under a state law alleged to be unconstitutional. If the law is unconstitutional, the prisoner is wrongfully held. Yet, except under exceptional circumstances, the courts of the United States do not interfere by *habeas corpus*. The prisoner must, in the first place, take his case to the highest court of the state to which he can go, and after that he generally is left to the remedy by writ of error if he wishes to bring the case here.
>
> [see also at 170—not cited by Holmes in *Frank*:] … . We agree with the circuit court of appeals that a petition for habeas corpus ought not to be entertained *unless the court is satisfied that the petitioner can make out at least a prima facie case.* A mere allegation of … [wrongful proceeding] is not enough [emphasis added].

165 *Moore v. Dempsey*, 261 U.S. 86, 95 (1923), McReynolds, J. dissenting.

Holmes, in remanding Moore's case for a new trial in federal court on the question whether habeas was warranted, summarized the Moore majority's conclusion as follows:

> [I]f the case is that the whole proceeding is a mask—that counsel, jury and judge were swept to the fatal end by an irresistible wave of public passion, and that the State Courts failed to correct the wrong, neither perfection in the machinery for correction nor the possibility that the trial court and counsel saw no other way of avoiding an immediate outbreak of the mob can prevent this Court from securing to the petitioners their constitutional rights.[166]

The basic difference between, on the one hand, the Holmes majority opinion in *Moore,* and his dissent in (the earlier) *Frank*, and, on the other hand, the majority in *Frank,* and Sutherland's dissent in *Moore*, which followed *Frank,* was that the majority in *Frank* and dissent in *Moore* took "perfection in the machinery for correction"—i.e., a procedurally adequate appellate process—to be conclusive. If the state supreme court ruled that the trial was fair, the old approach was to accept this as a finding of fact and habeas would be denied. *Moore v. Dempsey* fundamentally took the fate of southern blacks out of the hands of southern state supreme courts.[167] This move (at least in the mind of opinion author

---

[166] Ibid., at 91.

[167] Although the tension between the two case outcomes is obvious, scholars and Supreme Court justices are divided over the extent to which *Moore* broke with *Frank* as a doctrinal matter. An excellent overview is provided by Eric Freedman in "Leo Frank Lives … ." Freedman himself believes that *Frank* was a more "liberal" ruling than is generally perceived—that it called for an "in-depth federal habeas corpus review of state prisoner convictions.:" (at p. 1472.) When Prof. Felix Frankfurter asked Justice Brandeis a few months after the decision why the "Frank case was departed from," Brandeis answered by listing three justices who had left the Court—Pitney (author of the Frank majority opinion), Chief Justice White, and Justice Day. They were replaced respectively by Sanford, Taft, and Butler, but Sanford joined only on the day *Moore* was handed down, so the Court division was six–two (email from Eric Freedman, Aug.18, 2014). Brandeis then alluded to the fact that justices often may disagree with a decision and for various reasons refrain from writing a dissent, suggesting perhaps that the division of opinion in *Frank* was closer than it had looked: ibid., pp. 1535–7. Brandeis did not deny that *Moore* "departed from" *Frank*. In fact, by the time of *Moore*, only three justices remained who had participated in *Frank*—Holmes (who dissented in *Frank*; wrote for the Court in *Moore*) and Van Devanter and McKenna (who both were in both majorities!).

Justice Holmes) had roots traceable back to the Asian rights case, *U.S. v. Sing Tuck*. In the 1931–54 period, the interdependence of black anti-discrimination rights with Asian anti-discrimination rights would become more pronounced.

Overall, in comparison with the other two branches, for the two decades 1911–30, modest as the progress of the Supreme Court was on behalf of the rights of African-Americans and Asian-Americans, the Court nonetheless stands out as the most protective of the three branches at the federal level. To be sure, the executive branch did bring cases to the Court in both the anti-peonage and anti-grandfather-clause cases, but the Court moved ahead of the executive branch both in opposing residential segregation and segregated transportation. And the U.S. Justice Department did not play a role in *Moore v. Dempsey* (1923), the judicial breakthrough decision on due process as applied to accused black persons in the South.

NATIVE AMERICANS, 1911–30

In the post-Fuller-Court period, policy toward Indians continued in the assimilationist vein of the Dawes Act approach, but one modified by the paternalism that emerged from a threeway dialogue among the branches, provoked by the *In Re Heff* (1905) decision. Congress, by the 1906 Burke Act, counteracted the Court's declaration in *Heff* that sales of alcoholic beverages to Indians who had become citizens (via allotment) could not be restricted by the federal government, on the grounds that Indian citizens were entitled to equal protection and equal citizen privileges. This Burke law, in an immediate response to the Court decision, postponed citizenship by up to twenty-five years for Indians who took land allotments (fewer years if the Indian Office bureaucrat deemed the Indian suitably mature).

After the Burke Act, the Indian Office pressed cases in the courts to have the Supreme Court acknowledge that the government's guardian role over Indians should extend beyond protecting improvident land transactions to such matters as limiting alcohol consumption. The first inroad came in a narrowly focused decision of 1908, *Dick v. U.S.*; there the Court upheld a prosecution of a liquor dealer for selling to an Indian citizen on the grounds that this Indian's tribe had signed an agreement with the Indian Office in 1893 to the effect that, on all its reservation land sold off as surplus, selling liquor to Indians would be banned for a twenty-five year period.[168] The Court then in 1909 clarified the import of the Burke Act by ruling that allotted land that was not yet out of the probationary period was still considered "Indian country," subject to federal liquor regulations.[169]

The next inroad came from the White Court in its first year. The case, *Tiger v. Western Investment Co.* (1911), exemplifies the perplexity that faces an analyst attempting to decide whether a case is "pro-Indian" or not. Mr Tiger had sold off some of his allotted land to the Western Investment Company, but had not obtained the permission from the Secretary of the Interior that was mandated in federal law. He, Tiger, now wanted out of the deal and wanted his land back. The U.S. Justice Department argued the case for Tiger, along with his own attorneys, agreeing with his interpretation of the federal law. The Oklahoma Supreme Court had ruled in favor of the investment company, but the U.S. Supreme Court, citing a long line of precedent statements to the effect that Indians were a dependent people and that the federal government functioned as their guardian, ruled unanimously that Congress had put these restrictions into the law to make sure that Indians were receiving a fair price for their lands, and the Congressional restriction had to prevail here. The Court said:

> We agree with the construction contended for by the plaintiff in error, and insisted upon by the Government, ... that the act of April, 1906, while it permitted inherited lands to be conveyed by full-blood Indians, nevertheless *intended to prevent improvident sales by this class of Indians*, and made such conveyance valid only when approved by the Secretary of the Interior.[170]

Even though this paternalistic decision undermined the autonomy of individual Indians in general, it responded favorably to a legal request from the Indian most directly affected by the decision, was applying a federal law that his own tribal government had ratified, and in these circumstances, therefore (I would conclude), was upholding the legal rights of Indians (to be legislatively protected by Congress).

Once the U.S. Supreme Court had bought into the language of Indian incapacity, it was but a small extension to say that even the grant of citizenship to Indians might be restricted or constrained by federal legislation, contradicting what it had stated in 1905 in *Heff*. The Court

---

168 Hoxie 1984, 221–2; *Dick v. U.S.*, 208 U.S. 354 (1908).

169 Hoxie, ibid.; *U.S. v. Celestine*, 215 U.S. 278 (1909); *U.S. v. Sutton*, 215 U.S. 291 (1909).

170 *Tiger v. Western Investment Co.*, 221 U.S. 286, 309–10 (1911) (emphasis added).

soon did so in a 1913 case involving the Santa Clara Pueblos, who held their land in fee simple from Spain, had never themselves had a treaty with the U.S. Government, and had become U.S. *citizens* en masse under the Treaty of Guadalupe Hidalgo in 1848. Despite all these markers of autonomy, the U.S. Supreme Court, in *U.S. v. Sandoval*, upheld the federal government's prohibition on liquor on the Pueblo reservation with the explanation that the Pueblo need governmental supervision because they are "Indians in race … a simple, uninformed, backward people."[171] Similarly, later that year the White Court extended federal criminal jurisdiction over two Dawes-Act-citizens-to-be for a crime committed on allotted land that was still under federal trust supervision, with the maxim, "The fundamental consideration is the protection of a dependent people."[172]

After an accumulation of these decisions affirming federal guardianship to prevent improvident land sales and to permit federal laws restricting the sale of alcoholic beverages to narrowly identified Indians, in 1916, the Supreme Court in *U.S. v. Nice* (another liquor case), finally formally overruled *In re Heff* (1905) in a ruling applying to Indians in general:[173]

> Of course, when the Indians are prepared to exercise the privileges and bear the burdens of one *sui juris*, the tribal relation may be dissolved and the national guardianship brought to an end; but it rests with Congress to determine when and how this shall be done, and whether the emancipation shall at first be complete or only partial. Citizenship is not incompatible with tribal existence or continued guardianship, and so may be conferred without completely emancipating the Indians, or placing them beyond the reach of congressional regulations adopted for their protection … .

The Court (at p. 601) shrugged off the contrary reasoning of *In Re Heff*, saying that it had been undermined by later enactments showing the true intent of Congress.

On the whole, the White Court, which had moved ahead of the political branches on the matter of black civil rights, appeared to move in lockstep with elected branches of the federal government in taking a paternalistic, almost infantilizing, approach to the rights of Native Americans. This is perhaps attributable to Congress's pointed rebuff in

---

171 *U.S. v. Sandoval*, 221 U.S. 39, 45–6 (1913); Hoxie, *Final Promise* 223–4. The case was understood as distinguished from *Heff* because that decision applied to Dawes-Act-granted citizenship.

172 *U.S. v. Pelican*, 232 U.S. 449, 450 (1913).

173 *U.S. v. Nice*, 241 U.S. 591, 598–601 (1916).

the 1906 Burke Act of the Fuller Court's pro-Indian-autonomy decision of 1905, *In Re Heff*, and the subsequent alignment of the U.S. Justice Department with Congress's paternalism, as it brought prosecution after prosecution for such things as selling liquor to Indians, until the Supreme Court finally overruled *Heff* in the *Nice* decision (1916).

In 1918, in an Appropriations Act, the U.S. Congress introduced into federal law a racial purity test in order to qualify for entry into federally funded Indian schools. Persons had to be, at a minimum, one-quarter Indian by birth in order to qualify.[174]

Prior to 1924, a number of statutes granted citizenship to groups of Indians: the Treaty of Guadalupe Hidalgo of 1848, to those settled Indians (mostly Pueblo) who had Mexican citizenship; the Dawes Act of 1887, to allottees; an 1888 law, to Indian women who married U.S. citizens; the Burke Act (1906), to allottees who received their land patent in fee simple (ending federal supervision over their land); a 1919 Act, to American Indians who had served in the military during World War I.[175] Then in 1924 by a blanket grant, Congress accorded it to the remainder, which by this time was only about one-third (125,000) of the approximately 300,000 Native Americans of the United States.[176] The wording of this act left a lacuna: what of Indians born after the 1924 Act? The fate of such Indians was finally clarified in the Nationality Act of 1940, granting citizenship to "all persons born in the United States to members of an Indian … or other aboriginal tribe."[177]

Nonetheless, the rhetoric of Indian "pupilage," emanating from Congress, federal bureaucrats, and the U.S. Supreme Court of this "progressive" period, took its toll at the state level with respect to Indian voting rights. Some state governments in the West (Wyoming, Colorado, South Dakota, Montana) simply relied on the withholding of citizenship that came with the Burke Act of 1906. California deployed an English literacy test. In Minnesota, Wisconsin and North Dakota, voter eligibility turned on having "the language, customs, and habits of civilization." Oklahoma's grandfather clause gave voting rights to descendants of the Five Civilized Tribes; others had to prove English literacy. Living on a tribal reservation according to the Minnesota Supreme Court in 1917 was *ipso*

---

174 Haas 1957, 22; 40 Stat. 561, 564.

175 Bruyneel 2004, 30; Indian Citizenship Act, 2 June 1924, United States Statutes at Large, 43:253; Citizenship for World War I Veterans Act, 6 Nov. 1919, U.S. Statutes at Large, 41:350. Haas 1957, 16.

176 Getches et al. 1993, 739; Kappler 1929, 1165–6; Bolt 1987, 99–101; Haas 1957.

177 Haney-Lopez, 2006, 29–30.

facto evidence of being uncivilized. Idaho, New Mexico, and Washington required taxpayer status for voting, and exempted reservations from state taxes. Finally, Arizona, Nevada, and Utah required that voters live off of reservations (be "state residents"), be taxpayers, and be citizens. Guardianship in the late nineteenth century had been to protect the tribes. By the early twentieth century guardianship enabled the government to supervise individual Indians on the grounds of their "backwardness."[178]

These suffrage restrictions were fueled, no doubt by a combination of anti-Indian bias and the pro-middle-class bias that typified the Progressive era. These laws restricted not only Indians. Hoxie reports, for instance, that Apache County, Arizona, census records for 1910 showed about 2,000 adult residents; half of these, Indians. In the 1912 election, 245 people voted in the county.[179]

The Supreme Court willingness to allow restrictive standards for voting first emerged in cases involving blacks, as detailed in Chapter 4. It was a willingness with roots that go all the way back, however, to Congress's own deliberations on the wording of the Fifteenth Amendment. It was all too compatible, one might say with the original intent of the framers of that amendment. The Amendment's framers rejected arguments that they should give the vote to all adult (male) citizens, but instead simply specified the grounds on which suffrage could not be denied: race or prior servitude. Other statutory qualifications (such as literacy) were understood to be, if not frankly invited, at least permitted. Not until the Voting Rights Act of 1965 with its federal enforcers, were Native Americans protected against the fraud and intimidation used by some states along with poll taxes and literacy tests to reduce voting by them.[180] Even after that, the ACLU reports that reservation Indians were kept from voting in considerable numbers by Colorado until 1970 and by Montana into the 1980s.[181]

Apart from voting rights, the White Court, like most Supreme Courts before it, did exhibit a willingness to check state laws infringing on Indian treaty rights. Oklahoma tried to tax Indian land granted under the Curtis Act (the parallel to the Dawes Act for Choctaw and Cherokee land) but this Act had stipulated that the land would not be taxed by the state as long as it was still owned by the Indian grantee. The Supreme

---

178 Hoxie 1984, 230–37.

179 Ibid., 233–4.

180 "Voters: Native Americans," N.D. For itemization of restrictions from various states that lasted into the 30s, 40s, and late 1950s, see Haas 1957.

181 ACLU Voting Rights Project 2009, 7 *Voting Rights in Indian Country*.

Court blocked Oklahoma's effort, ruling in *Choate v. Trapp* (1912) that the tax exemption was a vested property right under the Curtis Act.[182]

During the tenure of the Taft Court (1921–30), faith that assimilation of the Indians would bring them into the mainstream of American society faltered. A research report on the condition of American Indians (commissioned by the Department of the Interior) written by Lewis Meriam from the Institute for Government Research of the Brookings Institution, funded by the Rockefeller Foundation, (known as the Meriam Report) was submitted to the Secretary of the Interior and published in 1928. It reported that Indian infant mortality was double that of the general population; the death rate from tuberculosis septuple the national average; and an illiteracy rate as high as 67 percent in one state. Two-thirds of Indians earned under $100 per year.[183] President Hoover responded to the report in his first message to Congress, in December, 1929, with an insistence that more needed to be done to raise the standard of living for Indians. Appropriations to the Indian Bureau were promptly increased.

As already noted in Chapter 4, the Dawes Allotment policy proved a disaster, costing Indians by 1934 80 percent of their land value. By 1933, 90,000 American Indians had no land.[184] Spurred by the Coolidge-Administration-contracted Meriam Report, delivered and published during the Hoover Administration of 1928, the FDR Administration in 1934 officially ended the Dawes policy via the Indian Reorganization Act.

---

182 *Choate v. Trapp*, 224 U.S. 665 (1912).

183 Hoxie 1984, 242. Parman and Meriam 1992, 255.

184 Haas 1957, 15.

6. A new "racial" minority: Hispanics, 1800–1992

In a Supreme Court decision of 1954, *Hernandez v. Texas*, the Warren Court recognized persons of "Mexican or Latin American descent" and "persons with Mexican or Latin American surnames" to be the members of a single "class," at least in Jackson County, Texas, warranting equal protection of the laws,[1] because proof had been presented that they faced group discrimination there. The Court left open the question whether Mexican Americans would or should always be judicially viewed as a protected class under this clause—be it in Jackson County, in Texas, in the Southwest generally, or even in the whole United States.[2] Prior to that time, more specifically, prior to the mid-1940s, the histories of Americans of Spanish descent had varied drastically from one part of the U.S. to another.

THE PREQUEL: 1803–1920, SEPARATE HISTORIES

In the nineteenth century, as the Spanish Empire slowly crumbled, the United States acquired vast areas of land containing (in addition to indigenous tribes) Spanish-speaking settlers and residents of Spanish descent. These began in 1803 with the massive area of the Louisiana Purchase (for a long time French-ruled, but for thirty years ruled by Spain); followed by the territory of Florida in 1821; then in 1845 and 1848 a vast area now in the southwestern U.S. which had belonged to

---

1 *Hernandez v. Texas*, 347 U.S. 475, 478–82 (1954), handed down two weeks before the more famous *Brown v. Board of Education*. The protected class may also include native Spanish-speaking persons (irrespective of homeland), because one of the markers of discrimination cited by the Court was the designation on the door of a toilet at the courthouse set aside for Hispanophones; the door had two labels: "Colored Men" and "Hombres Aqui" ("Men Here"). Ibid., 478.

2 "We do not have before us the question whether or not the Court might take judicial notice that persons of Mexican descent are there considered as a separate class." *Hernandez v. Texas*, 347 U.S. 475, 479 n.9.

Mexico, many of whose residents were of mixed Native American/ Spanish descent. Its Mexican settlements were in the future states of Texas, California, Arizona and New Mexico; the rest of it contained unconquered, non-pueblo Indian tribes.[3] The gaining of the Mexican Cession of 1845–48 was followed in 1898 by acquisition of the Philippines (with a population that was a mix of indigenous islanders, descendants of Asians, and also descendants of Spanish-speaking people)[4] and Puerto Rico (mostly Spanish or Afro-Spanish descent, but also containing a sizable population of Chinese laborers by the end of the nineteenth century).[5]

These lands were obtained in a number of ways: Texas successfully rebelled against Mexico in 1836, and after a time of independence, in 1845 negotiated joining the United States. Diplomacy produced the Louisiana Purchase of 1803, and for Florida (diplomacy supplemented by military threats), the Treaty of Adams-Onis of 1819 (ratified in 1821; also called the Transcontinental Treaty).[6] Conquests produced the rest of the Southwest territory, via the Mexican War, settled in the Treaty of Guadalupe Hidalgo of 1848 and its negotiated modification in the Treaty of Gadsden of 1853;[7] and, via the Spanish-American War, the acquisitions of the Philippines and Puerto Rico. (With the ending of the Spanish-American War, the U.S. also acquired Guam from Spain, and in 1900 acquired American Samoa from Germany, but both of these had tiny populations.) State populations of Spanish-speaking Americans first became U.S. citizens in the fullest sense as these territories became

---

[3] "Mexican Americans" N.D.; Noel 2011. This mixed racial heritage was often denied by middle-class, turn-of-the-century (1900) Hispanic-Americans who claimed instead direct and "pure" descent from the Spanish. Noel 2011, 446–8.

[4] From 1899–1902 Filipinos participated in a war of independence against the U.S. The U.S. granted the Philippines independence in 1946. U.S. Department of State Office of the Historian, "... The Philippine-American War, 1899–1902." The treatment of Filipino-Americans who were of Asian extraction appears in Chapter 7.

[5] As of the mid-twentieth century, one-fourth of the population of Puerto Rico was categorized as "Negro." Maslow 1961, 354 n.11.

[6] McKeehan 1997–2001; U.S. Department of State Office of the Historian, "Acquisition of Florida ..." In addition to Florida, this treaty settled that the U.S. owned land immediately along the Gulf coast between Florida and Louisiana that had been disputed between Spain and the U.S.

[7] U.S. Department of State Office of the Historian. "Gadsden Purchase" and "The Annexation of Texas ... and the Treaty of Guadalupe-Hidalgo."

states, beginning with Louisiana in 1812 and Florida in 1845.[8] Prior to statehood but post-acquisition, they were American nationals, who could freely settle anywhere in the U.S. and its territories.

Texas entered the union (also in 1845) with ready-made statehood for its citizenry, including those citizens of Spanish/Mexican descent. The other areas acquired prior to 1850 from the Spanish Empire (Louisiana Purchase and Florida) and from Mexico in 1848 (the American Southwest) entered the U.S. polity with treaties announcing their future "incorporation" into the Union of the United States with a promise of citizenship with all its attendant rights to all the "inhabitants" (Louisiana Purchase Territory and Florida territory) or, for the Southwest, to all the Mexican citizens therein who chose to become Americans.[9] If the former Mexicans stayed in the transferred territory, their property and liberty were said to be secured and they were given one year to announce a preference for retaining Mexican citizenship, without which they would automatically become American citizens. Fewer than 1,000 in the new southwest territory chose to retain Mexican citizenship.[10] The rest, on paper at least, became American citizens, but here the story begins to get complicated. Because this history does not readily fit into the periodization of the other chapters, it is here given its own separate treatment.

What is an Indian? The Pueblo Story

The Pueblo Indians who resided within the Mexican Cession comprised approximately one-tenth of the settled (i.e., non-nomadic) population as of the beginning of the war.[11] As Mexicans, they had been accorded full and equal citizen rights, including the right to vote, since the time of Mexico's having become an independent republic in the 1820s.[12]

---

8 Ultimate History Project N.D. Of course, individual Spanish-speaking migrants may have settled in any of the existing Anglo states, just as any other European may have, and become naturalized.

9 McKeehan 1997–2001; U.S. Department of State Office of the Historian, "Acquisition of Florida," "Gadsden Purchase," and "The Annexation of Texas … and the Treaty of Guadalupe-Hidalgo."

10 Noel 2011, 436 n.9.

11 Rosen 2003, 21–2, n.2.

12 *United States v. Jose Juan Lucero*, 1 N.M. 422 (N.M., 1869), at Section *5.

Citizens without the vote, 1848–77

Following this tradition, the Territory of New Mexico adopted its draft for its Organic Law on May 15, 1850, with wording that seemed to imply that "whiteness" per se was not required of former Mexican citizens for U.S. citizenship; it conferred all rights of U.S. citizenship on "free white" inhabitants, *and* on those citizens of Mexico who had become American citizens under the Treaty of Guadalupe Hidalgo.[13]

The Hispano citizens, who comprised the majority in the territory in 1850, favored immediate statehood and drafted a proposed state constitution; statehood was opposed by the Anglo minority. The military governor, John Monroe, issued a proclamation permitting Pueblos to vote in the June, 1850 referendum on statehood. Statehood won overwhelmingly, but Congress opted to keep New Mexico as a territory.[14] In the course of the election, both sides pressured and intimidated Pueblo voters to a degree that distressed them.[15]

Congress, too, when it produced its own binding version of the Organic Law, on September 9, 1850, which would serve as the constitution of the Territory, distinguished between "free white male" adult residents, who would receive rights to vote and hold office in the first territorial election, on the one hand, and those who became American citizens by virtue of the 1848 Treaty, on the other hand, who *could* be added to the voter and office-holder categories, by provision of the territorial legislature thereafter.[16]

One ominous note for the Pueblo appeared in the Congressional version of the Organic Law. Its Section 5 described the rules for apportioning districts for the state legislature on a population basis but added the tell-tale parentheses "(Indians excepted)."[17] Within the New Mexico territory, the Pueblo, a people who had lived in settled agricultural villages for some three centuries, were widely understood (as were similarly settled other Indians within the Mexican cession) to fall into a

---

[13] Menchaca 1993, 590, citing "New Mexico Organic Law of 1850" in *Laws of the Territory of New Mexico*. 1851.

[14] Many sources assert that the death of President Zachary Taylor had the effect of postponing statehood for New Mexico, but one cannot know what Congress would have done even if Taylor's presidency had not ended prematurely.

[15] Simmons 1979, 209.

[16] Thorpe 1909. "New Mexico—1850," Section 6.

[17] Ibid., Section 5.

different category from the "wild Indians,"[18] and thus were allowed to vote in that first election (apparently for this purpose, being viewed locally as equivalent to "whites").[19] Once elected, the First Legislative Assembly enacted voting regulations in 1851, wherein it continued the Congressional restriction to white male adult citizens.[20] Still, the Pueblo Indians actually did continue to vote, with approval of New Mexico officials (again, being treated for legal purposes as "white").[21] Congress then stepped in on September 5, 1853 and refused to count votes cast by the Pueblo for the Congressional delegate from the New Mexico Territory, and this Congressional decision threw the election to the opposing candidate.[22] Shortly thereafter, the legislature of New Mexico ratified this deprivation of the vote from the Pueblo, in a law of February 16, 1854 that limited the voting rights of Pueblo Indians to the selection of officers for their own local Pueblo institutions, which rule was declared to remain in effect unless Congress were to decide to accord full voting rights to the Pueblos.[23]

In the late 1860s two territorial judges of New Mexico, one at the district court level[24] and the other speaking as the Chief Justice of the Supreme Court of the Territory[25] in cases involving questions of Pueblo rights to control and sell their own land ruled squarely that Pueblo Indians were not embraced in federal legislation about "Indians," because they were not savage and uncivilized, and in fact were citizens of the U.S., by virtue of the Treaty of Guadalupe Hidalgo. That they did not have full voting rights did not mean they were not U.S. citizens.[26] When confronted with a similar issue in 1877, the U.S. Supreme Court agreed,

---

18 *U.S. v. Lucero* 1 N. M. 422 (1869), at Sections *3-*6. The U.S. Supreme Court had in 1854 agreed that references to "Indians" in such U.S. laws as those restricting private purchase of Indian land did not apply to privately owned land of agricultural, "civilized" individual Indians residing in the Mexican Cession, because such persons were accorded full equality of citizenship under Mexican fundamental law. They were not the "savage Indians" contemplated by Congress in such legislation *U.S. v. Ritchie*, 58 U.S. 525, 540 (1854).

19 Menchaca 1993, 590.

20 Section 19 of "Election Laws," July 20, 1851, pp. 196–204 in *Laws of the Territory of New Mexico*, cited by Rosen 2003, 23, n. 14.

21 Menchaca 1993, 590.

22 Larson 1969, 82.

23 Rosen 2003, 8.

24 *U.S. v. Benigno Ortiz* (1867), reprinted in full in *U.S. v. Jose Juan Lucero*, 1 NM 422 (N.M. 1869), available online in pdf format.

25 *U.S. v. Lucero* (1869).

26 Ibid., at Section *10.

as it had done as early as 1854 in a case (*U.S. v. Ritchie*) involving a similar non-Pueblo, settled, Mexican Indian.[27] Even though in 1851 Congress extended to the New Mexico Territory the federal ban on private land purchase of, or non-Indian settlement upon, Indian land, such legislation applied only to the nomadic Indian tribes, not to the civilized, law-abiding, peaceful and intelligent Pueblos, said the Court.[28] The "Indian" territory covered in the 1851 extension act was territory claimed by the nomadic, savage Indian tribes, not that of the Pueblos. As to the matter of whether the Pueblo Indians were U.S. citizens, the U.S. Supreme Court refused to address it in this 1877 case, since it was tangential to the issues at hand.

In sum, at this point the Pueblos remained in a kind of legal limbo: the terms of the 1848 Treaty meant that they were to be treated as citizens of the American New Mexico Territory, and to become fully its citizens, along with the other former Mexicans once New Mexico became a state in the union. But they were citizens only in the sense that they had legal rights to property and to go to court to protect their property and to vote in local Pueblo elections. The Fifteenth Amendment adopted in 1870 should have protected their rights to vote in state and federal elections, once New Mexico attained statehood in 1910, but this issue does not seem to have been raised.

Meanwhile, at the level of the federal bureaucracy, Indian superintendents and Indian agents, from 1848 through the 1870s kept petitioning for the federal government to put the Pueblo more squarely into the category of tribal Indians who would be under federal control and receive protection for their land from the federal government.[29] For the period then of 1848–77, the Pueblo were protected as at least quasi U.S. citizens by the federal courts and were subjected to continual questioning of their citizenship status by the executive branch. Congress refused to accord them voting rights in federal elections, but otherwise stayed out of the controversy until the twentieth century.

Pueblos lose their "white" status

Some scholars mistakenly conclude that in *Elk v. Wilkins* (1884) or *U.S. v. Sandoval* (1913) the U.S. Supreme Court took away the citizenship

---

27 *U.S. v. Joseph*, 94 U.S. 614 (1877); *U.S. v. Ritchie*, 58 U.S. 525, 540 (1854).

28 Ibid., at 616–17 (quoting *U.S. v. Lucero* [1869]).

29 Rosen 2003, 2–8, 11–15.

rights of Pueblo Indians.[30] This seems to be a misreading of those decisions. John Elk, "born a member of one of the Indian tribes within the United States" (as the Court put it)[31] had severed his tribal relationship and lived in Omaha and attempted to vote as a U.S. citizen, per the language of the Fourteenth Amendment, "born in the United States and subject to the jurisdiction thereof." The Supreme Court ruled that he was not free to vote, and that the Fourteenth Amendment language on citizenship by birth did not include tribal Indians, irrespective of their residence. But the Court in the *Elk* case added a sentence with direct import for Pueblos, "Nor is it contended by his counsel that there is any statute or treaty that makes him a citizen."[32] The Pueblos had the Treaty of Guadalupe Hidalgo.

The case of *U.S. v. Sandoval* (1913)[33] is similarly misunderstood as having denied citizenship to the Pueblo people.[34] *Sandoval* concerned a challenge to the federal prohibition on selling alcohol to a Pueblo Indian within "Indian country" in New Mexico. Congress in 1910 (finally persuaded to do so by the federal executive bureaucracy) had inscribed into its Enabling Act, to which New Mexico had to agree in order to attain statehood, a provision that designated all Pueblo lands as thenceforth included in Indian Territory and covered by Congressional legislation dealing with Indians. Thereby the Pueblo people lost their previous special status of being excluded from the general term "Indian." Here is what the Court said about them in *Sandoval*:[35]

> The people of the pueblos, although sedentary rather than nomadic in their inclinations, and disposed to peace and industry, are nevertheless Indians in race, customs, and domestic government. Always living in separate and isolated communities, adhering to primitive modes of life, largely influenced by superstition and fetichism (sic), and chiefly governed according to the crude customs inherited from their ancestors, they are essentially a simple, uninformed, and inferior people. Upon the termination of the Spanish sovereignty they were given enlarged political and civil rights by Mexico, but *it remains an open question whether they have become citizens of the United States*. See treaty of Guadalupe Hidalgo, arts. 8 and 9, 9 Stat. at L. 922, 929;

---

30 Menchaca 1993, 592; Menchaca 2001, 279. Her treatment has been adopted by some later scholars as well, who cite her to establish the claim of fact.

31 *Elk v. Wilkins*, 112 U.S. 94, 99 (1884).

32 Ibid.

33 *U.S. v. Sandoval*, 231 U.S. 28 (1913).

34 E.g., by Menchaca 1993, 592; Menchaca 2001, 279.

35 231 U.S., at 39 (1913). Menchaca 1993, 591 mistakenly attributes this decision (and this quotation) to New Mexico's Supreme Court.

> United States v. Joseph, 94 U.S. 614, 618 ; Elk v. Wilkins, 112 U.S. 94. Be this as it may, they have been regarded and treated by the United States as requiring special consideration and protection, like other Indian communities. Thus, public moneys have been expended in presenting them with farming implements and utensils … . (emphasis added).

Plainly, this is not a rejection of Pueblo claims to citizenship. The Court is simply retreating from its highly unpopular insistence in *U.S. v. Heff* (1905) that once Indians have become U.S. citizens, no special restrictions or protections may be applied to them. In a decision a few months after *Sandoval*, the Court made a similar move; it extended federal criminal jurisdiction (in lieu of state jurisdiction) over the murderer of an Indian who was in the midst of a twenty-five year transition to citizenship under the Dawes Act, as amended in 1906 (to effectively limit the impact of *In re Heff*).[36] Finally, in 1916, the Court in *U.S. v. Nice,*[37] explicitly overruled *In re: Heff* (1905), saying that citizenship for Indians did not place "them beyond the reach of congressional regulations adopted for their protection."[38] This whole set of decisions from *Sandoval* through *Nice* points not to a withdrawal of the treaty-conferred citizenship from the Pueblo people of New Mexico, but rather to a shift by the Court to accommodate Congress's sentiment that even after Indians acquire U.S. citizenship they are racially so different that Congress may continue to protect (and restrict) them.

Meanwhile, at the territorial- and then state-level in New Mexico, as Anglo-American numerical dominance became more firmly entrenched,[39] during the decades of peak racial Darwinism in 1897 the Pueblo were deprived of their right to vote in their own local elections.[40] As prescribed by Congress, in 1911 New Mexico's first state Constitution followed up by designating all Pueblo land holdings to be Indian Territory under federal jurisdiction.[41] The state of New Mexico did not again grant full voting rights to Pueblo Indians until 1948, when forced to do so by a three-judge federal district court.[42]

---

36 *U.S. v. Pelican*, 232 U.S. 449, 450 (1914).

37 *U.S. v. Nice*, 241 U.S. 591 (1916).

38 Ibid., at 598–601.

39 Rosen 2003.

40 Menchaca 1993, 191.

41 Menchaca 1993, 591, citing New Mexico Constitution 1911, Art. XX1, Sec. 8.

42 Simmons 1979, 222. Matthew Martinez 2004–2015. The case was *Trujillo v. Garley*, U.S. Dist. Ct. of N. M. #1353).

The policy changes of 1910–13 moved the Pueblos from the status of quasi-white, entitled to control their own landholdings, to "Indians," warranting federal protection of their landholdings. The *Sandoval* decision threw into limbo the deeds, even the post-1877 (per *U.S. v. Joseph*) legitimately purchased ones, of non-Pueblos residing on Pueblo Territory.

By 1922 Congress came up with a solution for dealing with these non-Pueblo claimants to Pueblo land, of whom there were 4,000 families occupying about 10 percent of Pueblo Territory. The bill, however would have treated illegal squatters just as well as legitimate land-owners, confirming all titles held for ten years prior to 1912 and also submitting all land and water rights litigation to the state courts, which tended to be hostile to the Pueblos. This hostile Bursum Bill, had the support of both President Harding and his Secretary of the Interior, but it provoked organized opposition from sympathetic prominent Anglos in New Mexico and from the General Federation of Women's Clubs and John Collier (discussed in Chapter 7), as well as from an All-Pueblo-Council convened at the urging of John Collier. This pro-Pueblo lobby succeeded in having the bill dropped and replaced by the Pueblo Lands Act of 1924, which set forth strict criteria by which non-Pueblos would have to prove valid title. For all these valid titles, Congress gave compensation to the Pueblos (on the theory that the 1877 Supreme Court decision had been an error and that Congress should have protected the land all along) and for all the non-Pueblos who lost their claims, Congress also gave compensation.[43]

The Non-Pueblo Former Mexicans of the American Southwest

The experience of Hispanic Americans in the Mexican Cession and in Texas varied sharply across state lines. Texas and California entered the Union early, just after predominantly Anglophone Florida did in 1845: Texas, in 1845–46[44] and California, in 1850. State status was delayed for New Mexico and Arizona until 1912, in part because of their heavily Hispanic populations.

---

[43] Simmons 1979, 215.

[44] In December of 1845 Annexation was formally approved by both the Texas Constitutional Convention and the U.S. Congress, but the transfer of governmental authority became effective in February, 1846. De León 2010.

Florida: contrast to the Southwest

Between Florida's acquisition by the U.S. from Spain in 1821 and its becoming a state in 1845, its small Hispanic population became overwhelmed by settlers from Anglo-American states to the north. The early Spanish settlers and their descendants after 1845 became such a small minority that they do not appear in standard histories of the state. Their miniscule numbers, in comparison with the later Anglophone settlers, appear to have made their presence a non-issue. It seems that Anglophones viewed the Hispanophones of Florida (and in Louisiana earlier) as simply one European-descent group among others, and did not legislate any discernible discrimination against them (in sharp contrast to tribal Indians and blacks).

In the 1845 Constitution's list of the first state-level government officials, only one name (out of dozens listed) appears to be potentially of Spanish descent: Mariano D. Papy. Born in Saint Augustine in 1824, only three years after the U.S. officially acquired the territory from Spain, Papy (1824–75) was Clerk to the Supreme Court in 1845, later a state representative in the legislature, and ultimately Attorney General of the State. The Papy/Pappy family in Florida was one of a group of families from Minorca (a Spanish island in the Mediterranean) prominent in the St. Augustine area of Florida. This group included the following surnames: Solana, Reyes, Peso de Burgo, Marin and Oliveros.[45]

The first Constitution of the State of Florida, whose population as of 1845 was about 46 percent slaves, begins with the declaration "That all freemen when they join to form a social compact are equal," followed shortly thereafter by the declaration that "All elections shall be free and equal."[46] Thus, in the beginning years of Florida statehood, free Americans were equal under the law, irrespective of Hispanic background.

Later in the nineteenth century, after civil unrest broke out in Cuba in 1868 (culminating in the Cuban Revolution of 1895), a wave of Cuban immigration to the U.S. ensued. As of the 1870 federal census, New York City held approximately 2,800 Cubans; Key West, Florida, 1,047; and New Orleans, 1,014. The Cubans in Key West comprised 20 percent of the population. By the 1880 census, that fraction was up to 2,400, 24 percent of the population. Naturalized Cubans in the 1870s and 1880s

---

[45] Constitution of Florida 1845; Raney 1876; Thompson 2008.

[46] Florida Department of State. 2015; Constitution of Florida 1845, Art I, Secs. 1, 4.

attained such posts as elected state representative, elected mayor of Key West and appointed county judge.[47]

Between 1887 and 1900, Ybor City, Florida was founded as a cigar-factory town by a wealthy Cuban. By 1890, Ybor City held 6,000 cigar workers, most of them Cuban. They worked side by side with immigrant workers of other nationalities.[48]

Historian de la Cova observed that in more than one city, federal census takers in different years or in different wards would identify that same Cuban individual as variously "white," "mulatto," or "black." The enumerator of the census did not inquire as the individual's self-identification, but simply categorized on the basis of appearance. Thus, when a different enumerator came along, the Cuban's race would be transformed.[49] The laws of Florida did not discriminate against Cubans as Hispanic, but in the postbellum decades, one can safely presume that those who appeared to government officials as blacks, were discriminated against as such.

Hispanics in Florida, like Puerto Ricans in New York City and Chicago, if they had skin so dark that they appeared black or mulatto, would have been subjected to anti-black discrimination. Neither of these groups was subjected to legally imposed discrimination on the basis of being Hispanic per se.

Texas

Texas entered the Union in 1846. The residents of Spanish or Mexican descent in Texas were not covered by the guarantee of the Treaty of Hidalgo, but instead entered the U.S. as ready-made citizens of Texas. In the 1836 Constitution of the Texas Republic, Mexican residents of Texas had been accorded citizenship, and Congressional resolutions in 1845 contemplating the admission of Texas, also had affirmed citizenship therein for Mexican-descent persons.

The first U.S. census to count Texas (in 1850) listed some 15,000 residents of Mexican descent. For decades, Texas, because of the Rio Grande, was the main point of entry for Mexican migrants (later, many migrated within the U.S. to Southern California[50]). By 1930 the

---

[47] De la Cova 2011, 294–5, 297, 307, 317; Florida Memory N.D.

[48] National Park Service. N.D. The town was later annexed by Tampa.

[49] De la Cova 2011, 288.

[50] As of 1900, 80 percent of the approximately 100,000 Mexico-born residents of the U.S. lived in Arizona or Texas; California had only about 8,000. Between 1900 and 1930, however, Mexicans poured into Southern California, mostly from other U.S. states. By 1930, Los Angeles contained about 97,000

Mexican-descent population of Texas is estimated to have been around 700,000.[51]

Alarmed by the growing political power of *Tejanos*, in 1896–97 (the same period when Pueblos were being deprived of territorial voting rights in New Mexico, and blacks were being disenfranchised throughout the South), two political leaders of San Antonio (one a Populist and one a Republican) petitioned in a federal court case, *In Re: Ricardo Rodriguez*, to challenge (unsuccessfully), on strictly racial grounds, the rights of migrants from Mexico, and their descendants, to become naturalized American citizens. Their argument was that persons of Mexican descent were of American-Indian descent, and therefore were neither white nor African-American and could not be eligible for naturalization. They insisted that Senatorial discussion of the Treaty of Guadalupe had never clearly accorded citizenship to Mexicans and that in fact *no* persons of Mexican descent (irrespective of prior naturalization or prior voting or, by a misreading of *Elk v Wilkins*, even irrespective of birth in the U.S.) were legitimately U.S. citizens.[52]

The federal district court judge deciding *In Re: Rodriguez* emphatically rejected their arguments, relying on the precedents of the independent Texas Constitution, the Congressional resolution on Mexican citizenship post-statehood, and the Treaty of Hidalgo, and the earlier treaties regarding persons of Spanish descent in Florida and Louisiana. Moreover, the judge accepted as legally determinative the assertion of Rodriguez, irrespective of his dark complexion, that he was not descended from the Aztecs or other Indian tribes of Mexico, that he was "a pure-blooded Mexican," even though, in the words of the judge, "If the strict scientific classification of the anthropologist should be adopted, he would probably not be classed as white."[53] Because Congress had so often, in documents like these, collectively naturalized "all Mexicans, without discrimination as to color,"[54] and also because at least one treaty between the U.S. and Mexico that had lasted until 1882 referred approvingly to the fact that Mexicans had been individually naturalized as U.S. citizens,[55] the federal

Mexicans, of which five-sixths of the families reported a Mexican-born head of household (in a total L.A. population of 1,240,000). In 1928, Los Angeles had the largest Mexican population of any U.S. city. Sanchez 1993, 13, 19, 70, 90–92.

51 De Leon 2010. By 1990, it was four million.

52 Menchaca 2011, 122–5, 129–33, 152–6.

53 *In Re:Rodriguez*, 81 F. 337, 349(1897) (District Court W.D. Texas).

54 Ibid., at 352.

55 Ibid., at 353–4.

judge reasoned, that for purposes of naturalization, it was the "spirit" of the totality of these laws that Mexicans should count as "white."[56] Moreover, the petitioners' reference to *Elk v. Wilkins* was misplaced; that decision applied only to Indians under tribal jurisdiction, and all citizens of Mexico covered by the Treaty of 1848, and their descendants, lived outside of any tribal jurisdiction.[57]

Despite this clear ruling on citizenship eligibility under federal law, Martha Menchaca has uncovered a very strong bias pattern in the actual acceptance/denial rates by local-level judges in Texas responding to petitions for naturalization. In the 1848–1906 period, in twenty-six counties whose records she examined (where the bulk of Mexicans resided), the percent of Mexicans who succeeded at becoming naturalized ranged from 1.2 to 1.5 percent. By contrast, the success rate of naturalization efforts from Europeans, including Spanish Europeans considered separately, ranged between 38.7 and 47.1 percent.[58] Thus, while the federal law itself was even-handed toward Mexicans—in effect treating them as "white"—its *application* by government officials decidedly was not.

As for Mexican-American voting rights, despite some debate in the Texas legislature on the subject, Texas entered the Union without any formal restriction of the vote to Anglos. Nonetheless, pressure, both violent and otherwise to keep *Tejanos* from voting was brought to bear in certain localities in certain time periods. In others, by contrast, Mexican-descent Texans wielded significant political influence because of population majorities.[59]

In the early twentieth century, before the Supreme Court declared them unconstitutional, the Democratic Party in certain localities in Texas deployed whites-only primary rules against Mexican-Americans as well as against blacks.[60] The exclusion of Mexicans by these laws, however, was far from complete; Martha Menchaca reports that whereas 95 percent of former African-Americans voters were excluded by 1906,

---

56 Ibid., at 354–5.

57 Menchaca 2011, 154–5, citing *Rodriguez*, at 353.

58 Ibid., 256–9. The percentage for immigrants directly from Spain was 40 percent. Other scholars mistakenly read the results numbers (percentage who actually became naturalized) as showing that "few [Mexican] immigrants [of southern Texas] *sought* to become American citizens." (My emphasis.) See e.g., Rodriguez 2007, 133 (discussing a slightly later period, noting that by 1920 90 percent of Mexicans in El Paso remained non-citizens).

59 Acosta 2010; De León 2010.

60 Greenberg 2010.

fewer than half of the Mexican-American voters were (by 1908). The fate of these white primary laws is covered in depth in Chapters 5 and 7. Similarly, per local Texas administrative practices, Mexican-descent children were often placed in segregated schools for non-whites.[61] By the 1930s, Mexican Americans for the first time outnumbered Mexicans in the U.S., and they began efforts in more than one state to contest segregation.[62] These efforts are covered below in the section on segregation and desegregation.

California

California entered the Union in 1850. Prior to the Mexican War, Southern California, then part of Mexico, was settled largely by Mexicans and up through the early 1840s, relations with the tiny Anglophone ("Mexican-ized") minority were amicable.[63]

In Southern California, wealthy owners of the large ranches constituted the socio-political elite. Some few of these wealthy families were of purely Spanish stock, although most in fact were *mestizo* to one or another degree. Nonetheless, the wealthy rancheros and wealthy former Mexican administrators as a group claimed to be of purely Spanish descent and considered this supposed fact to enhance their social status. This elite group amounted to the top 10–20 percent (in wealth and influence) of the Spanish speaking communities in Southern California.[64]

---

[61] De León 2010.

[62] Foley 2007, 299.

[63] Camarillo 1979, 107; Rodriguez 2007, 77–9, 106. In 1846 Hispanic Californians numbered 7,000; U.S.-born immigrants, 1,300; and "Christian Indians" (who had been converted by Spanish or Mexican missions), 64,000. By 1850, the Spanish-speaking population had dwindled to merely 11 percent of the Gold-Rush-booming non-Indian state population; by 1870, 4 percent. These figures are for the state as a whole. Southern California stayed predominantly Mexican until 1870. Ibid., 79, 106.

[64] Camarillo 1979, 10–11, 103; Rodriguez 2007, 63–72, provides evidence that in the late eighteenth century, under Spanish rule, (prior to an independent Mexico) Hispanic-Americans changed their reported racial heritage, whitening it over time, in reports to Spanish census-takers. Incentivizing this practice, within its empire, the Spanish Government openly preferred to give its high-status positions to whites, particularly whites born on the Iberian Peninsula, Menchaca 1993, 584–6; 2001, 154–5. Gomez-Quinones 1994, 194–5, notes that this practice of claiming Spanish (as distinguished from *mestizo*) heritage continued through the nineteenth century throughout the Southwest, and was especially pronounced in New Mexico.

The laboring class and the small-scale, subsistence farmers and ranchers were *mestizo*.[65] Later, in the 1880s and 1890s, after the Spanish-speaking population had experienced massive downward mobility, an elite of 5 percent or so managed to maintain their elite status by claiming to be purely Spanish, and by emphasizing their ties to Spanish culture.[66]

After the Mexican War ended in 1848, Anglos gradually moved into Southern California in greater numbers, but the Mexican population remained dominant there for a couple of decades. Mexicans were also immigrating up from northern Mexico. In addition, a sizable outlaw element moved in from both Anglo and Mexican populations; vigilante violence between the two ethnic communities as well as inter-cultural hostility was common. The vigilante violence in Los Angeles in the mid-1850s was so extensive that Albert Camarillo characterized it as a "race war." The hostility was so pronounced that Anglo juries would refuse to convict Anglos for crimes against Mexicans and vice versa: Mexican juries refused to convict accused Mexicans.[67]

In the 1850s, the conflict played out politically in Santa Barbara over the language of instruction to be used in the public school. With most of the population Mexican, instruction had been in Spanish. In 1855 the state government mandated that all public school instruction must be in English. The local compromise was to add an English language school to the Spanish one, but this proved too expensive. Then a bilingual school was tried, but Anglo parents withdrew their children because the school was two-thirds Mexican. In 1858 the public school again switched over to English instruction. In 1857 a parochial school for Spanish-speakers had been opened, so this arrangement, informally segregating the two groups, became established.[68]

By the 1870s, southern California transitioned from predominantly Mexican to predominantly Anglo.[69] Two forces were at work. Weather developments in the 1860s caused hard times for Hispanic ranchers and farmers, who were losing out to Anglo competition (coupled with some Anglo chicanery). This force pushed out-migration by some of the Spanish speakers. Meanwhile, Anglos increasingly migrated in, attracted by perceived health benefits of life in Southern California.[70]

---

65 Camarillo 1979, 11.
66 Ibid., 68–71.
67 Ibid., 22–4, 108–9.
68 Ibid., 17.
69 Ibid., 41.
70 Ibid., Chapters 2 and 3.

When California first entered the Union, the state constitution, influenced by Mexican political strength at the constitutional convention, granted voting rights to white male U.S. citizens *and* to those "white male citizens of Mexico" who became U.S. citizens under the Treaty of Guadalupe Hidalgo.[71] The racial question had in fact been a contentious issue at the convention. The Convention understanding of which Mexican *mestizos* counted as "white" was expressed as follows: "If an [alleged?] Indian is more than half Indian, he is Indian. If he is more than half white, he is white."[72] To those persons who were exactly one-half of each, the legislature settled this in the laws of 1850: they would count as Indian.[73] Interestingly, the Constitution also assured a degree of bilingualism: all state laws were to be printed in both Spanish and English.[74]

The actual practice of distinguishing between those Mexicans who would count as white and those who would count as Indian appears to have been influenced substantially by class; Don Pablo de la Guerra, one of the Mexican founding fathers of the American state of California, and a very wealthy ranchero, noted at the constitutional convention that even if some citizens have a "very dark skin" they must be understood to be white, so long as they are not of African descent. The actual practice seems to have been that upper class status for Mexicans usually served to assure "white" heritage, irrespective of skin tone.[75]

By 1851, the legislature changed to a rule that one-fourth or more of Indian blood rendered citizens non-white (and therefore ineligible to vote).[76] The Anglo domination of the state legislature, starting in the 1850s, also produced a variety of laws against Mexican cultural practices (such as bear fights and bull fights and the unfenced, free grazing of livestock), an anti-vagrancy act called the "Greaser Law" and also anti-Hispanic gerrymandering of voting districts.[77] Finally, the Constitution of California was amended in 1879, repealing the provision for bilingual laws.[78]

---

[71] California Constitution of 1849, Art. II, Sec.1.

[72] Browne 1850, 63–73 (quote at 73); Gomez-Quinones 1994, 226–7.

[73] Menchaca 2001, citing California Statutes, 1850, Chap.99, Sec.14, p. 230; Chap.142, Sec.306, p. 455.

[74] Gomez-Quinones 1994, 225–8.

[75] Almaguer 1994, 51–60.

[76] Ibid., citing California Statutes, 1851, Sec.394, p. 114.

[77] Camarillo 1979, 108–13; Bedolla 1999, 37.

[78] Gomez-Quinones 1994, 225–8.

By the end of the nineteenth century, most of the land owned by Mexicans was lost to Anglos. The losses were due to a variety of forces: exploitative practices by lawyers charging exorbitant fees for defending land claims, usurious mortgage rates, crooked dealings by Anglos taking advantage of Mexicans' lack of English-language skills, and competitive economic pressures.[79] Some scholars treat the U.S. Supreme Court ruling in *Botiller v. Dominguez*, 130 U.S. 238 (1889), as expressing an anti-Hispanic bias, since Dominguez lost out in her "perfected" claim that her title to land granted by Mexico was valid despite her ancestors' having failed to file a claim during the two-year time limit established by the federal California Land Settlement Act of 1851.[80] This conclusion, however, ignores the fact that the competing successful claim to the land came from a Mexican citizen, Brigido Botiller.[81]

In 1870, the California Supreme Court was confronted with an effort by the executive branch of the state to challenge the citizenship bona fides of the same Don Pablo de la Guerra founding father mentioned above, and implicitly of *every* non-naturalized person of Mexican heritage in California. Attorneys for the state based their challenge on the claim that Congress had never acted specifically to grant citizenship to the former Mexicans of California, despite having allowed the state into the Union, despite the terms of the Treaty of Guadalupe Hidalgo, and even though the state constitution had "generously confer[red] the right of suffrage upon the[m]."[82] These attorneys insisted that no former

---

79 Camarillo 1979, 114; Bedolla 2005, 37–8; Almaguer 1994, 66–8. First-hand Anglo accounts of wasteful extravagance by wealthy rancheros were common.

80 Soltero 2006, 9–16.

81 Del Castillo 2000, 533–4.

82 *People of California v. Pablo de la Guerra*, 40 Cal. 311; 1870 Cal. LEXIS 196 (1870) (Appellant's Brief), at Lexis 18. Menchaca 2001, 220–22, mischaracterizes this case as having been about the racial status of de la Guerra. To the contrary, the attorneys for the state do not contest de la Guerra's race, arguing instead that *none* of the formerly Mexican citizens living in California when the state joined the U.S. thereby acquired U.S. citizenship (1870 Cal. LEXIS 196 at 1–21). His race was not an issue. The first sentence of the California Supreme Court opinion reads: "The respondent … *is admitted to have been a white male citizen of Mexico* at the date of the treaty of Guadalupe Hidalgo." (40 Cal. 311, 339 emphasis added.) The Court gave short shrift to the appellant's argument that the formerly Mexican citizens living in California in 1849 included three racial groups and that the fact that only the whites among them were allowed to vote under the California Constitution proved that the Mexicans were not as a group made U.S. citizens (because then all of them would have had voting privileges).

citizens of Mexico residing in California were U.S. citizens, unless they had individually been naturalized from their foreign status. Since de la Guerra had not been, despite his having held many elected state-level offices and having been part of the state constitutional convention, and despite his recent, otherwise valid election to the office of district judge, they claimed he was debarred from that office because only U.S. citizens could lawfully occupy it.

The California Supreme Court found this a strange argument, considered the terms of the Treaty of Guadalupe Hidalgo to have a plain meaning, and considered their conclusion an obvious one. The formerly Mexican citizens residing in California as of the time of the Treaty became fully U.S. citizens, per the terms of the Treaty, when the U.S. Congress admitted California into the Union. In the period when California was a U.S. territory prior to statehood, they were as much U.S. citizens as were other Americans residing in the territories. The political forces attempting to deprive Mexican Californians of their citizenship in 1870 were thwarted by the California Supreme Court.[83]

Because many Mexicans easily circulated back and forth between California and Mexico, it was not until the twentieth century that California's population of Mexican-descent experienced rapid growth. This was stimulated by many forces: irrigation developments enhanced the agricultural industry there (opening up jobs for laborers); the development of train connections to and from Texas eased travel to California; the tyrannical government in Mexico, and then the Mexican Revolution and civil wars (1910–20) that the tyranny provoked, produced a massive exodus of fleeing Mexicans; the various Asian exclusion acts created a shortage of laborers for both mining and agriculture; and finally, the Immigration Act of 1917 made multiple crossings of the border (the earlier pattern of behavior) more burdensome: one had to prove literacy and pay a head tax each time. Large employers obtained group exemptions for their workers, but even these exemptions required time-consuming paperwork, which pushed migrants into evading the law. The casual circular migration pattern that had prevailed for decades along the border therefore changed: now re-entry after the habitual return to

---

The Court simply pointed out that "possession of all political rights is not essential to citizenship" (40 Cal. 311, 343). This decision was handed down in the October term of the court, after the February national ratification of the Fifteenth Amendment, but it was discussing events of 1849–50, and, of course, even after 1870 female U.S. citizens were kept out of voting booths.

[83] *People of California v. Pablo de la Guerra*, 40 Cal. 311 (1870).

Mexico had been rendered costly, so considerably more Mexicans settled here permanently.[84]

The degree of residential segregation (or "barrioization") of Mexican-descent Californians varied from one period to another. Its nadir was the era of rapid immigration of a variety of ethnic groups in 1900–1940. At no point, however, did the state law segregate Mexicans either residentially or in schools.[85]

Despite, however, the absence of state laws segregating Mexicans, many communities in California did put Mexican-descent persons into separate schools on the alleged grounds of language deficiency.[86] Mexican Americans in the 1930s–1950s attacked these laws successfully in courts, as described below in the section on segregation and desegregation.

New Mexico

Apart from the Pueblo Indians, the other former Mexican citizens in New Mexico were from the start designated by the U.S. Census (1850) as white.[87] They were also from the start given voting rights. Still, while many of them, especially but not exclusively the economic elite, understood themselves to be primarily of Spanish descent (in contrast to those they viewed as *mestizo)* and called themselves "Spanish American, or "Hispano-American," the Anglos instead called them "Mexicans," which they understood to connote some absence of whiteness.[88]

As racism intensified and became more fully dominant in the U.S. Congress toward the end of the nineteenth century, some legislators voiced concern that the large Mexican fraction of the New Mexico population rendered the state unfit for statehood. The dominant response from those who favored statehood was to stress the purity of the Spanish heritage of the non-Indian Mexican population. Even though there was in fact an admixture of Indian blood over the three centuries of Spanish life in the New World, this self-identification of New Mexicans with the heritage of *conquistadores* served as a way both to put themselves above the savage Indian tribes and the more recent peasant arrivals from

---

84 Sanchez 1993, 44–70; Rodriguez 2007, 129–36.

85 Sanchez 1993, 74–8; Foley 2007, 297.

86 Foley 2007, 297. Historian Francisco Balderrama etimates that "more than 80%" of California's school districts did so by 1930. Ruiz 2001, 23, citing Balderrama, *In Defense of La Raza* (University of Arizona Press, 1982).

87 Nieto-Phillips 2004, 47.

88 Ibid., 46–92. The perception of Mexicans as somehow the non-white whites occurred all over the Southwest, according to Greenfield and Kates 1975.

Mexico and also to claim an identity as white, deserving of statehood and U.S. citizenship.[89]

By 1910, the strategy finally succeeded, and President Taft signed Congressional legislation conferring statehood on both Arizona and New Mexico, which was to become effective on January 6, 1912. The Congressional enabling act, however, did impose a burden of language discrimination on Hispanics in both states: public schools would be obliged to teach all primary coursework in English, and all state-level office-holders would have to "speak, write, read, and understand English well."[90] Nonetheless, New Mexico entered the Union with a constitution that (like California's original Constitution) mandated that all public documents be printed in both English and Spanish, and also that both were official languages of the state, that no one be disfranchised on grounds of "race, religion, language or color," that English proficiency could not be a prerequisite for sub-state-level office holding or for jury duty, and that "children of Spanish descent" be guaranteed "perfect equality with other children in all public schools," toward which end, funding would be provided by the state to train all teachers in both Spanish and English.[91]

Arizona

Although Arizona was combined with New Mexico in a single territory before 1863,[92] and entered the Union along with New Mexico, the inter-ethnic politics within the two states provides a study in contrasts. Whereas Mexican Americans were numerous at the New Mexico constitutional convention and pleased with its results, only one Mexican American served as a delegate to the Arizona Constitution and he refused to sign its final product.[93] Before 1900, interest in statehood in the two states had been less than overwhelming. This changed after the U.S. acquired the island territories of Puerto Rico, the Philippines and Hawaii. As longtime Americans, the residents of Arizona and New Mexico now sought to legally entrench a status above that of the non-self-governing territories: to be able to choose their own judges and governor and to share voting rights in the U.S. Congress. Both states then underwent

89 Menchaca 1993; Nieto-Phillips 2004.
90 Noel 2011, 460.
91 Nieto-Phillips 2004, 92; Noel 2011, 460–61.
92 Menchaca 1993, 589.
93 Noel 2011, 430–31.

substantial delays of their quest for statehood due to Congressional hostility to persons of Mexican descent.[94]

New Mexico's population as of 1900 was listed as 195,000 of whom 180,000 were white, about 13,000 Indian, and the rest black or Asian. According to Linda Noel, "various estimates" put the Mexican-heritage population as at least 90,000, within the white group. In contrast to California and Texas, the geography of New Mexico offered only limited opportunities for unskilled wage laborers, so immigration from Mexico or migration from nearby states by such persons remained low. Moreover, New Mexico started out with a large number of Mexican settlers who ran successful ranches. As they lost their properties to competition from (as well as some fraudulent dealing by) Anglos, these long-term residents of Mexican descent took what laboring jobs were available.[95]

Arizona was much more sparsely settled than New Mexico in 1848, and remained so until the federal irrigation projects around the turn of the twentieth century made farming feasible. The Homesteading Act of 1862 and the Dawes Act of 1882 encouraged in-migration by whites by making land available, as did completion of the transcontinental railroads in the 1880s and the surrender of Geronimo in 1886. These developments, along with a boom in mining, brought in corporate ownership of mining and ranching and farming land, which in turn brought in unskilled laborers, mostly of white European descent. By one estimate, the Mexican-descent fraction of Arizona's population fell from 45 percent in 1870 to a mere 20 percent by 1900. Of these, about half had been born in Mexico (another contrast to New Mexico, whose "Mexicans" were almost all U.S.-born in this era).[96]

The extreme numerical dominance of Anglos among the U.S. citizens in Arizona, fortified by Anglo control of the economy and jobs and Anglo efforts to diminish Hispanic political clout, diminished the political power of Mexican-descent Arizonans, almost to the vanishing point at the constitutional convention.[97] In 1909 (pre-statehood) Arizona adopted a requirement of English language literacy for all of its elections, but Congress in the 1910 enabling act waived this requirement both for elections to the state constitutional convention and for the first election to members of the new state government.[98] This Congressional action did

---

94 Ibid., 433–4.

95 Ibid., 436–7.

96 Ibid., 450.

97 Ibid., 450–51, 455–6, 463.

98 Ibid., 459-460. Half of the foreign-born Arizonans were from Mexico. Ibid., 450.

have the effect in the Arizona constitutional convention of dissuading Arizonans from putting an English literacy requirement into their state constitution.[99] Arizona also refrained from legislating school segregation of Mexican-descent children; its legislature did enact school segregation for African-American children in 1913 (along with an ambiguous provision allowing school board discretion to segregate pupils "as they deem advisable").[100] Still, like Texas and California, Arizona ended up with many local communities that established school segregation for children of Mexican descent.[101] Arizona Hispanics began to challenge these policies by 1925.

NATIONAL-LEVEL ELECTED BRANCH POLICIES TOWARD MEXICAN-AMERICANS

After 1912, Congress's attention toward Mexican-Americans moved beyond the issue of state-by-state admission to the Union. The Mexican Revolution and consequent civil wars that lasted into the 1920s prompted both a flow of political refugees and a transborder overflow of violence. These movements then became intertwined with the politics of World War I.

Policing the Border and Immigration Red Tape, 1912–24

In the years 1913–17, a variety of violent skirmishes along Mexico's border with Texas and New Mexico, as well as agitation by anarchist Mexican exiles in California, produced a situation where 80 percent of the U.S. army was either stationed along the border or had invaded parts of Mexico. Texas Rangers peremptorily executed 300 people of Mexican descent. Police in Los Angeles California, fearing sabotage of federal buildings, announced that neither guns nor liquor could be sold to "Mexicans." The L.A. County Board of Supervisors called for deportation of

---

[99] Ibid., 464.

[100] Powers 2008, 470. This re-enacted a 1909 provision from its territorial legislation. The first 1913 enactment was Ariz. Rev. Statutes of 1913 §11-2733; the second was §11-2750. Municipal swimming pools were also segregated against blacks. Ibid., 471, 478 n.6. In 1951, following upon a referendum that upheld black-white school segregation, legislation was adopted authorizing local school boards at their discretion to "segregate groups of pupils" in elementary and secondary schools. Ibid., 470.

[101] Ibid., 470; Noel 2011, 464–5.

those Mexicans likely to become public charges. Further fueling animosity toward Mexico (and by less logical extension, toward Mexican-Americans) was a telegram intercepted from Germany and made public by President Wilson in March 1917 offering generous support to Mexico if it would join Germany's side in World War I.[102] In fact, tens of thousands of Mexican-Americans served honorably in the U.S. armed forces (in the "white" units), and tensions with Mexico eventually eased.[103]

Before 1917, Congress had not limited immigration from the western hemisphere. This 1917 telegram from Germany reinvigorated an immigration initiative that President Wilson had blocked two years earlier, and now, in 1917, it passed over his veto. Although the primary purpose of the law was to keep out Asians, with its creation of the "Asiatic Barred Zone" (see Chapter 5), the fact that it imposed a literacy requirement and an eight-dollar head tax proved prohibitively burdensome to Mexicans. Southwestern agricultural and industrial interests successfully lobbied to get waivers for Mexican laborers, but even then, the related bureaucratic delays for individual migrants produced two unintended consequences. Now, far more Mexicans settled permanently in the U.S. rather than routinely migrate back and forth, and an illicit industry of trafficking non-documented migrants into the U.S. from Mexico was born. The federal imposition in 1924 of a ten-dollar visa fee simply exacerbated both these developments.[104]

Deportation, 1920s–30s

In the aftermath of the revolution in Mexico, and in specific response to its government's confiscation of American property, presidential policy toward Mexican residents of four states: Texas, Arizona, California, and Oklahoma, took a sharp negative turn after the Mexican Revolution turmoil of 1910–20.[105] President Harding in April 1921 initiated a deportation of all indigent or unemployed Mexican resident aliens therein, not in response to domestic policy concerns but as a tool of foreign policy to pressure the President of Mexico to compensate wealthy Americans for certain property of theirs that had been seized during the revolution. By May more than 60,000 Mexicans had been "deported" (of whom many left on their own because when the government moved

---

[102] Rodriguez 2007, 137–43.
[103] Ibid., 153–6.
[104] Ibid., 143–7.
[105] Menchaca 2011, 234, 240–44.

them, it simply stranded them at the border with no additional travel money). Harding's deportation policy created an uproar among farmers and chambers of commerce in the southwest who complained of a pending labor shortage, which would impede harvesting. Reassured that the Mexican Government would permit Americans to recover at least their oil fields, Harding ended the deportation as of July 1.[106]

The deportation by Harding at least focused on aliens, albeit irrespective of the length of their residence in the U.S. Historian Vicki L. Ruiz puts the number of Mexican immigrants *into* the American Southwest and Midwest between 1910 and 1930 at more than one million.[107] During the Great Depression years, beginning in 1931, the Hoover administration, under the leadership of the Secretary of Labor William Doak, aided by the national coordinator of the President's Emergency Committee for Employment, again adopted a deportation policy, this time one that swept up citizens along with resident aliens. Over this period 1929–34 (across two different presidential administrations), more than 400,000 people were "deported," of whom an estimated 60 percent were U.S.-born citizens, primarily the children of departing Mexican parents, but also some orphans parented by Mexicans were sent to homes in Mexico or to orphanages there.[108]

Technically speaking, only a tiny fraction of those repatriated to Mexico were formally deported; actual deportation would have required lengthy formal hearings and proof of illegal entry or else proof of having become a "public charge within five years of their [otherwise lawful] arrival due to causes originating before their arrival in the U.S." Instead the federal government enlisted the help of local governments eager to reduce their relief rolls. The local agencies played upon fears of deportation, fears caused by actual, occasional federal raids that ferreted out undocumented aliens eligible for deportation. Local government played up the fact that federal deportees were simply left stranded at the border, and instead offered to pay the costs of travel to the hometown in Mexico. U.S. cities paid the costs of chartered trainloads of Mexicans,

---

106 Ibid., 242–3.

107 Ruiz 2001, 23.

108 Menchaca 2011, 253–4; Rodriguez 2007, 159–64; Ruiz 2001, 25; Balderrama and Rodriguez 2006, 136. Ruiz estimates as many as half a million; Balderrama and Rodriguez 2006, 148–51, put the figure at a million, acknowledging that the official figure from dispatches sent from the American Consulate General in Mexico City to the U.S. State Department put the total for 1930–40 at 422,831, but assuming that more than this number crossed back over the border unobtrusively and unofficially, as they had come.

along with food and lodging on the trip. Mexican consular authorities assisted in the effort, because they viewed U.S.-trained Mexican workers as a potential boon to their less skilled and less disciplined labor force.[109]

Also a significant political element within the Mexican-American community had long encouraged a sense of Mexican patriotism among the expats, many of whom stayed in the U.S. out of perceived economic necessity, not out of a desire to become American. This group of Mexican-Americans had assisted Mexican authorities in running Spanish language schools and libraries and patriotic Mexican festivals. The group in fact welcomed the offers of financial assistance to enable less well-off Mexicans to return to the homeland.[110]

Census Bureau Politics, 1930–Present

Apart from deportation, the Great Depression also gave rise to a Congressional debate on restricting Mexican immigration. This debate in turn prompted Congress to ask the Census Bureau to find out how many Mexicans resided in the U.S. After the census-takers of 1930 were instructed to list all persons of Mexican parentage as of the "Mexican race" unless they were "definitely white, negro [sic], Indian, Chinese or Japanese," the government received protests from the Mexican Government, the U.S. State Department and Mexican-Americans. The 1940 Census Bureau shifted the policy to count instead "Spanish-speaking persons," and to count Mexicans as white unless they "definitely" appeared to be some non-white race. By 1950, the policy was modified to counting persons with a Spanish surname. The 1970 Census combined both practices, counting "Persons of Spanish Language or Spanish Surname." In 1980 the Census reported on the population of "Spanish Origin." Since 2000, the Census has offered respondents the chance to indicate their ethnicity as either "Spanish/Hispanic/Latino" or "not Spanish/Hispanic/Latino."[111]

---

109 Rodriguez, ibid.; Sanchez 1993, 108–25; Balderrama and Rodriguez 2006, 74–8; Ruiz 2001, 25 adds that "duplicitous social workers ... exaggerated the opportunities" in Mexico to persuade Mexicans to go voluntarily.

110 Sanchez, ibid. Cf. Camarillo 1979, 225–7, who depicts the deportation period of the 1930s as run by "anti-Mexican forces," and omits mention of the complicity of the Mexican government and of many well-off Mexican-Americans who enjoyed their close connection to Mexican consular officials and took pride in their Mexican cultural heritage, even as American citizens.

111 Greenfield and Kates 1975, 671 n.38, 699–700 n. 197, 714 n. 301; Wilson 2005, 207–10; Haney-Lopez 1997, 1144 n.4, 1146, n.15, 1148 n.20; Martinez

While many political activists would like to unify persons of Hispanic heritage into a combined political force, it turns out that the majority of Latinos prefer to identify as members of individual nationalities rather than under a single blanket label. Historian Stephen H. Wilson reported in a 2004 article that three out of every four respondents to the National Latino Political Survey preferred being labeled by a term reflecting their country of origin rather than by aggregative terms such as Hispanic or Latino.[112]

Deportation, Naturalization and Immigration, 1940–65

The Supreme Court in 1934 pointed out in a footnote that many Latino immigrants to the U.S. had genetic admixtures of native Indian heritage, and that the limitation in naturalization law to whites and persons of African descent, potentially excluded such persons from eligibility to U.S. citizenship.[113] After a six-year delay, in 1940, Congress addressed this issue in broader terms, clarifying whether Latinos irrespective of racial designation qualified to become naturalized citizens. It enacted permission for naturalization of "descendants of races indigenous to the Western Hemisphere" along with white persons and persons of African nativity or descent.[114] This new law, of course, covered indigenous people who immigrated from Canada as well as across the southern border.

Deportation of unwanted Mexicans did not cease when involvement in World War II turned around the American economy. Between 1942 and 1964, the U.S. Government cooperated with the Mexican Government, in setting up and running a "bracero" program to enable Mexican workers to labor north of the border for short periods of time and then return home to Mexico.[115] The program accepted only healthy young men, experienced as agricultural workers, who owned no land and who could obtain from a local bureaucrat a certification that their labor was not needed in the hometown.[116] Mexicans who did not qualify for the bracero

---

1998, 177; "The Hispanic Population: Census 2000 Brief," U.S. Census Bureau 2000, 1–2.

[112] Wilson, ibid., 225.

[113] *Morrison v. California*, 291 U.S. 82, n.5 (1934). The case dealt with prosecution of a Japanese resident for leasing and using agricultural land.

[114] Nationality Act of 1940, Act of October 14, 1940, ch. 876, § 303, 54 Stat. 1140.

[115] Hernández 2006, 423.

[116] Ibid., 425–6.

program and were not literate or who could not pay immigration fees could not lawfully migrate to the U.S. in search of work, even though there were no immigration quotas on Western Hemisphere countries per se.[117] The huge wage gap between the U.S. and Mexico and the permeability of the border thus produced a very sizable flow of undocumented Mexican immigrants in the 1940s and '50s.[118]

The Mexican Government tried cracking down on this illegal flow northward in order to stem the losses to its own labor force, but needed U.S. cooperation. In 1942, Mexican officials met in Mexico City with leaders from the U.S. State Department, I.N.S., the U.S. Department of Justice and the U.S. Border patrol, insisting that the cost of the Bracero Program had to include U.S. assistance in both stemming the flow northward and bringing back some of the Mexicans who had entered the U.S. unlawfully. The U.S. doubled the size of its Border Patrol staffing between 1940 and 1943. In December of 1943, the Mexican Embassy, still unhappy at the large flow northward, sent to the State Department threats to cut off the Bracero Program if more was not done by the Americans. The U.S. Border Patrol responded within six months by deploying special deportation teams in both Chicago and Texas, in June of 1944, to round up and deport several thousand undocumented Mexican workers. In 1943, a total of 11,775 were deported; by 1944 the number was 28,173.[119] In 1945 the Mexican Government began actively to support the deportation/repatriation program by arranging with the U.S. Government that Mexico would pay for and operate relocation of the deportees from the border into the deep interior, so that return to the U.S. would be more difficult.[120] As portrayed by historian Kelly Lytle Hernández, the active deportation of undocumented Mexican workers in the U.S. was driven by the desire of the Mexican Government to stem unauthorized migration of laborers to the U.S.: the U.S. Border Patrol efforts in this regard picked up whenever the Bracero Program, desired by the U.S. Government, was working smoothly; when negotiations for renewing the Bracero Program broke down, U.S. authorities backed off from active deportation, causing a perception of labor shortages in Mexico. The latter was experienced by the Mexican Government as an incentive to re-instate the Bracero Program in order to obtain the help of the U.S. in repatriating Mexican workers.[121]

---

117 Ibid., 424.
118 Ibid., 426.
119 Ibid., 427–9.
120 Ibid., 429–34.
121 Ibid., 434–5.

The U.S. Border Patrol arrested and deported 279,379 Mexicans in 1949; 459,289 in 1950 and 501,713 in 1951. Approximately a third of these were repeat offenders, who simply crossed and re-crossed the border to obtain work.[122] The sharp jump in deportations was the product of a program of systemic raids of farming areas throughout the Southwest to round up undocumented workers and transport them by truck, bus, plane and automobile to the border. This program began in February 1950 and by March 2 was dubbed "Operation Wetback."[123] By 1953, the number of apprehensions had reached 827,440.[124] This steep rise in numbers, largely attributable to the enhanced enforcement approach, produced a perception that the U.S. was facing a crisis of undocumented immigration. President Eisenhower appointed retired Army General Swing in the spring of 1954 to head the INS in an effort to improve the efficiency of border control, and in May of that year U.S. Attorney General Brownell announced that "Operation Wetback of 1954" would be launched, as did officials in Mexico, to collaborate in blocking, detaining and deporting undocumented northward migrants with added intensity.[125] The Eisenhower Administration publicized as new and newly efficient, a deportation program that had been going on and growing for a decade. For fiscal year 1954 (which included only two weeks of "Operation Wetback of 1954"), the Administration announced more than one million people deported.[126] Deportations for FY 1955 dropped off sharply, as political attention turned to other matters.[127]

It is difficult to find data on how many Americans with Mexican parents were driven out of the country with them in Operation Wetback or how many families were torn apart by the program, as the parents of American birth-right citizens were compelled to leave the country. Balderrama and Rodriguez (2006) offer many anecdotal cases of painful family disruptions in the earlier 1930s deportation drive, and, of course, also of U.S.-born children being taken with their fleeing parents. John Dillin, writing in the *Christian Science Monitor*, offers an estimate that the 1954 Operation Wetback deportations scared approximately seven to nine times as many Mexican migrants back to Mexico as were actually deported. He cites a figure of "over 50,000 aliens" deported in the first six weeks from Arizona and California, while in that time 488,000 more,

---

122 Ibid., 440.
123 Ibid. 441.
124 Ibid., 442.
125 Ibid., 1, 441–2.
126 Ibid., 444.
127 Ibid., 443–4.

fearing the extremely harsh conditions in the deportation transport vehicles (operated by Mexico) fled on their own. In the first two and a half months of the 1954 program in Texas, 80,000 were seized for deportation while "an estimated 500,000 to 700,000 illegals had left the Lone Star State voluntarily."[128] The Mexican-American civil rights groups, the American G.I. Forum supported the program, on the grounds that undocumented migrant labor harmed working conditions for other workers, but there can be no reasonable doubt that many children with U.S. citizenship, here as a matter of birth, ended up taken from their homes, by fleeing parents, despite their legal right to stay. Although the deportation of these non-adult U.S. citizens was not official policy, it was the foreseeable consequence of Operation Wetback and imposed harsh treatment on a particularly helpless minority.

The U.S. Government imposed no limit specifically on immigration from the Western Hemisphere countries prior to its immigration law of 1965 (the same law that liberalized immigration from Asia).[129] This law imposed a numerical cap of 120,000 immigrants from the Western Hemisphere (not counting family members of U.S. citizens who petitioned for family unification) and 170,000 from the Eastern Hemisphere. But now the emphasis was to be on employment skill quotas rather than nationality quotas. Since most Mexican and other Latino immigrants were laborers, the adoption of this law imposed the status of "illegal" or "undocumented" on what continued to be a steady flow of Latinos across the Mexican border in search of higher wages.[130] Policies toward immigrants continued to fluctuate thereafter, influenced primarily by the U.S. labor market, and not primarily by racial attitudes.[131]

PUERTO RICANS

In 1900 the Foraker Act established a government for the newly acquired Puerto Rican Territory. The territory was given an elected legislature, whose acts would be subject to veto by the U.S. Congress. The governor and judges would be appointed by the U.S. President. The Act made no mention of citizenship. In 1904, the U.S. Supreme Court confronted the citizenship question, after already having ruled in the *Insular Cases* of 1901 that the U.S. Constitution did not necessarily apply in all its

---

128 Dillin 2006. Similar numbers appear in Koestler 2015.
129 79 U.S. Statutes at Large 911.
130 Menchaca 2011, 262–3.
131 For details on the policy fluctuations, see Menchaca 2011, 271–301.

particulars to the new island territories, because they, in contrast to the existing territories, had not been explicitly "incorporated" into the Union as states-in-utero.[132] In other words, the U.S. was now an empire with colonies. Residents in those colonies, such as Guam and Puerto Rico did not acquire the full rights of American citizenship. The Court ruled in *Gonzales v. Williams* (1904) that by the treaty ceding Puerto Rico from Spain to the U.S., Puerto Rico's citizens became U.S. nationals, of American nationality. Whether they would need to become naturalized in order to exercise U.S. citizenship if they became residents of a state was left unclear by the decision. But as U.S. nationals (just like U.S. citizens who had permanent residence in one of the incorporated territories), they could travel freely within the United States and its territories, and take up residence anywhere in the U.S.

Because of the federal government's racial restrictions on both immigration and naturalization, in 1911 the U.S. Immigration Commission published a *Dictionary of Races or Peoples.*[133] According to this dictionary, one could be a Puerto Rican irrespective of race; the term simply meant "any citizen of Porto Rico regardless of race" and it referred readers to the terms Spanish-American, Cuban, and Negro.[134] Since residents were primarily black or white or admixtures thereof, and since both blacks and whites were allowed to become naturalized Americans, the race of Puerto Ricans, for national policy purposes was a non-issue. The small minority of Chinese-descent laborers who had become Puerto Rican citizens were apparently invisible to the Dictionary compilers.

Native-born Puerto Ricans who resided in Puerto Rico were granted birthright U.S. citizenship twice, first in 1917 in the Jones Shafroth Act, and then again in 1941. This meant, starting in 1917, that any Puerto Rican who moved to one of the mainland states would have all the same rights as those accruing to anyone who moved in from one state into another.

The 1917 Act created a detailed Constitution for Puerto Rico which amounted to a modified paraphrase of the U.S. Constitution. One modification was that, although Puerto Rico would have a two-chamber elected legislature, unlike the states it could not select its own governor or judges and its legislation would be subject to Congressional veto. In the Act, Congress "modernized" the versions of the Bill of Rights and the rights listed in Art. I, secs. 9 and 10 of the U.S. Constitution and of

---

132 *De Lima v. Bidwell*, 182 U.S. 1 (1901); *Downes v. Bidwell*, 182 U.S. 244 (1901); *Gonzales v. Williams*, 192 U.S. 1 (1904).

133 Okihiro. 2006. 36, 38 n.41.

134 *Ibid.*, 36.

Supreme Court interpretations of the Fifth and Fourteenth Amendment by adding details forbidding governmental support of church bodies and forbidding child labor, forbidding imprisonment for debt, and also establishing the eight-hour workday and social welfare legislation and establishing Prohibition. It specified that all current Puerto Rico citizens were henceforth citizens of the United States, and that children born in Puerto Rico to foreigners could become U.S. citizens by declaring a wish to do so within one year after reaching adulthood and by residing in Puerto Rico. And, significantly, in its version of the Bill of Rights, the rights to a grand jury indictment and trial by jury before being punished for a crime were both omitted.[135]

The Nationality Act of 1940 took effect in January, 1941. It broadened birth-right citizenship in Puerto Rico by simply granting it to all born in the territory, in language parallel to that in the Fourteenth Amendment for birth within a state.[136]

There is ample evidence that the Congressional and Supreme Court choice to establish Puerto Rico (and Guam and the Philippines) as "unincorporated" (i.e., not destined for statehood) territories was influenced by wariness about their being inhabited by darker, allegedly less civilized, races.[137] By contrast, when the Supreme Court decided in *Balzac v. Porto Rico* (sic) (1922),[138] as when the U.S. Congress chose the same policy option in the Jones Shafroth Act of 1917, to refrain from imposing the rights of grand jury indictment and trial by jury upon the list of criminal due process procedures in the Puerto Rican Constitution, it appears that a concern for granting local autonomy out of respect for a foreign legal/cultural tradition was at least as important as racial bias as a motivator. As Chief Justice Taft expressed this (combined) sentiment in *Balzac*:

---

135 Jones-Shafroth Act, *U.S. Congressional Record*, 64th Congress, Session II, Ch. 145, pp. 951–68. Approved March 2, 1917. On jury trial, see discussion below of the case, *Balzac v. Porto Rico* (sic), 258 U.S. 298 (1922).

136 The Nationality Act. 8 U.S. Code § 1402.

137 For a good general overview, see Sparrow 2006. For specific examples of harsh racial snobbery at the turn of the twentieth century toward the Philippines and Puerto Rico from the Harvard and Yale Law Reviews, see Soltero 2006, 22–3.

138 *Balzac v. Porto Rico*, 258 U.S. 298 (1922). In 1919 Puerto Rico amended its criminal code to allow the right of jury trial for misdemeanors but the trial in question predated this amendment. *Balzac*, at 303. It is possible both here and in *Dorr* (see below) that despite the language of self-determination, some justices were motivated by a lack of respect for the islanders' capacity to be jurors.

> Congress has thought that a people like the Filipinos or the Porto (sic) Ricans, trained to a complete judicial system which knows no juries, living in compact and ancient communities, with definitely formed customs and political conceptions, should be permitted themselves to determine how far they wish to adopt this institution of Anglo-Saxon origin, and when.[139]

In *Balzac v. Porto Rico* the U.S. Supreme Court was upholding both a locally adopted criminal code that secured the right of jury trial for felonies but not misdemeanors and a decision of the Puerto Rico Supreme Court.[140] In its reasoning, the Court specifically relied on its 1904 *Dorr* precedent concerning the Philippines.[141] There, Justice Day had written for a unanimous Court:

> The two rights alleged to be violated in this case [right to trial by jury and presentment by grand jury] are not fundamental in their nature, but concern merely [an alternative to] a method of procedure which sixty years of practice had shown to be suited to the conditions of the islands, and well calculated to conserve the rights of their citizens to their lives, their property and their well being.[142]

He had reasoned further that Congress's plenary power to rule the territories was limited by all those provisions in the Constitution that protect truly fundamental rights, but that the specific procedures of trial by jury and indictment by grand jury are not so fundamental to fairness that they must be applied to Congress's role as local governor of the territories. (Just as these two rights had not been "incorporated" into the due process clause yet to apply to state-level governments, they were not obligatory upon the non-state territories.)

Chief Justice Taft in the 1922 decision simply applied this same reasoning to Puerto Rico. It applied not racially or ethnically but territorially. Anyone in Puerto Rico was subjected to the Puerto Rican legal system, irrespective of ethnicity, and any Puerto Rican traveling or residing in the U.S. was subjected to all the constitutional rights that applied within that locus. Thus, contrary to the reading of some scholars,[143] *Balzac v. Porto Rico* does not appear to be an instance of the

---

139 *Balzac*, at 310.
140 *People v. Balzac*, 28 P.R.R. 139 (1920).
141 *Dorr v. United States,* 195 U.S. 138 (1904).
142 *Dorr*, at 144–5.
143 E.g., Soltero 2006, 17–33.

Supreme Court's denying a right to a racial or ethnic minority. Nor does Congress's 1917 decision omitting jury trials from the Jones Shafroth Act.

In 1947 Congress passed (and President Truman signed) the Elective Governors Act, moving Puerto Rico from a system of U.S.-appointed governors to elected ones. Puerto Rico finally had a fully democratic constitution, with the first election therefor to be held in 1948.[144] Three years later Congress enacted (and Truman signed) "Public Law 81-600," conferring Commonwealth status (rather than protectorate) and allowing Puerto Ricans to draft their own constitution for their own local self-government.[145]

In the two decades 1945–65, Puerto Rico lost one-quarter of its population via migration to the mainland U.S.[146] In 1997, 3.1 million people of PR extraction were living in the U.S. and 3.7 million people were living on the island, for a ratio of almost half and half.[147]

During the World Wars, Puerto Ricans were drafted, along with other Americans. While the island had its own Spanish-speaking unit, Puerto Ricans from the mainland were not segregated by Puerto Rican ethnicity. Instead, those who appeared to be of African descent were assigned to black units, and the rest of Puerto Rican recruits, along with Mexican-descent-Americans, were intermingled among other American (i.e., white) soldiers.[148]

As residents within the U.S., Puerto Ricans, as such, since they gained citizenship in 1917, have not been subjected to explicit *de jure* discrimination, although they have been disproportionately affected (along with many Chicanos) by laws requiring English literacy for voting, by the social practice of refusing to rent or sell privately owned housing (or to finance such purchases) in predominantly "white" neighborhoods to Puerto Ricans, by employment discrimination for higher status jobs, and by unofficial anti-Puerto Rican bias on the part of police officers. As is the situation with black Americans, the civil rights reforms in the mid-twentieth century by Congress and the Supreme Court, have benefited Puerto Ricans by restricting these discriminatory practices. These reforms are discussed in other chapters. Their administration has been problematic for Latinos, as it also has for blacks, but in different ways.

---

144 Rivera 2015, "Puerto Rico's History 1900–49."

145 Rivera 2015, "Puerto Rico's History 1950–2014"; Puerto Rico Report 2012.

146 De Genova and Ana Y. Ramos-Zayas 2003, 24.

147 Ibid.

148 Hernandez 2013, 546–7; Rodriguez 2007, 154–5.

The administrative difficulties faced by Hispanics who sought civil rights reforms are discussed in the next section.

SEGREGATION AND DESEGREGATION OF LATINOS

Mexican-American children in many parts of California, Texas, Arizona, and also Colorado, were systematically separated off into their own schools, known informally as the "Mexican schools."[149] In California, formal statutes authorized school segregation only of Asians, *not* of blacks or Mexicans. In Texas and Arizona, statutes authorized only segregation of blacks.[150] The official segregation of Mexicans, albeit unauthorized by statute, contrasts sharply with children of Puerto Rican or Cuban extraction outside the Southwest, who were officially segregated, if in the South, only if they showed African-American heritage.

The most important of the Mexican-American desegregation lawsuits, however, *Mendez v. Westminster School District* (1946–1947),[151] brought together at the level of personnel involved, a Puerto Rican mother, a

---

149 Sometimes they were placed simply in separate "Mexican classrooms" within the same building as "white classrooms."

150 Greenfield and Kates 1975, 681–2. Technically, the California statutes specified for school segregation, in addition to children who were of "Chinese," "Japanese," or "Mongolian" parentage, those "Indians" who were *neither* wards of the U.S. Government (i.e., on reservations) *nor those* who were "descendants of the original American Indians of the United States." This would seem to mean Indians who might migrate up from Latin America or down from Canada. The Attorney General of California in 1929 and 1930 (Ulysses Webb) had announced that although there was no explicit authority for segregating Mexican children, "Indian Mexicans" comprise "the greater portion of the population of Mexico," so could be put into segregated schools. In 1931, at least one community, Carpinteria, California, did deploy this rationale to justify their Mexican school. Alvarez 1986, text at nn. 38–40 (describing the Carpinteria situation); Brilliant 2010, 65; cf. Greenfield and Kates 1975 n.92 (denying that the clause on Indians was ever applied to Mexican-Americans) and Trisha Martinez 2014, p. 9-5 (citing 1947 *Mendez* decision denying that any California law authorized segregating Mexican-Americans). By 1946 the Attorney General of California, now Robert Kenney, asserted decisively that the statutory silence as to Mexican or Mexican-American children meant that the legislature was directing that separate schools for them not be maintained. Brilliant 2010, 80. See Sections 8003 and 8004 of the California Education Code, quoted in *Mendez v. Westminster*, 64 F. Supp. 544, at 548 n.5.

151 *Mendez v. Westminster School District*, 64 F. Supp 544 (S.D. Cal. 1946) ["*Mendez I*" in references below]; *Westminster Sch. Dist. v. Mendez* 161 F. 2d 774 (1947) ["*Mendez II*" in references below].

Mexican-American father, and the soon-to-become famous, black attorney Thurgood Marshall, later to serve on the U.S. Supreme Court. Moreover, it precipitated an overturning of the California statute that authorized school segregation of "Chinese, Japanese, and Mongolians," thus bringing together at least three of the four minority groups treated in this volume.[152] This important case was preceded by a few other notable Chicano desegregation cases from the Southwest and also by federal involvement, even at the level of the President, to combat anti-Chicano discrimination. School desegregation nation-wide, discussed more fully in Chapter 7, built heavily upon the *Mendez* precedent. Its implementation did not come in a significant way until Congress and the federal executive branch came on board in the mid-1960s. Executive implementation of desegregation of Latinos did not begin until the late 1960s.

The earliest court case, *Romo v. Laird,*[153] arose in Tempe, Arizona, where school authorities in 1912 began sending Mexicans to a separate school after a new school was built for "whites" only. (This was in the same year that Arizona attained statehood.) No Arizona statute, nor any other state-level statute, specifically authorized segregating Mexican-Americans from other Americans; federal law treated Mexican-Americans as "white." Moreover, the Attorney General of Arizona included in his published Biennial Report of 1915–1919 a letter that the Assistant Attorney General wrote in response to an inquiry from a private citizen, which letter stated plainly that Arizona law "does not empower the [public school] trustees to segregate children of the Mexican race unless, of course, children of the Mexican race might also be of African descent, by being intermingled with African blood through birth."[154]

In 1925, Adolfo Romo, after having been refused by both the District Superintendent and the Tempe School Board, sued in Maricopa Superior Court for an order allowing his children to attend the school run for whites. Judge Joseph Jenckes granted the order as to these children, but also observed that Arizona statute did provide blanket permission to school authorities to segregate children "as they may deem advisable."[155]

---

152 The fourth, Indians, were obliquely involved but only in the most minimal sense; the California statute allowed for school segregation of Indians not native to the U.S., and a few authorities used this clause to rationalize segregating Mexican-American children on the assumption that they might be partially Indian. See fuller discussion below.

153 *Romo v. Laird*, No. 21617 (Ariz. Super.) cited in Powers 2008, 480.

154 University of Texas College of Education 2005; Powers 2008, 470.

155 Ariz. Rev. Stat. §1913.

Because of this catch-all statutory authorization, despite his order acceding to the plaintiff, the judge refrained from ordering the Hispanic segregation system dismantled. In the ensuing years, the District authorities allowed Mexican-American children, upon their request, to attend the "white school"; the Mexican-Americans' school stayed 100 percent "Mexican."[156]

Like *Romo v. Laird*, a California court too, in 1931 produced an isolated desegregation decision that affected only one district, although this one reached the entire district, (in contrast to Tempe) not simply individual Chicanos who might request a transfer. The case was *Roberto Alvarez v. Lemon Grove School District*. There in January 1931, 75 Mexican-American children (of whom all but four were American citizens by birth and most of whose parents were Mexican), were blocked from entering their previous school (where they comprised nearly half the student population), and told to take classes henceforth in an old two-room building nearby. The parents contacted the Mexican consul who helped provide attorneys to contest the decision, and the group won a judgment from Judge Claude Chambers of the California Superior Court in San Diego, who declared that there was no legal authority in California to segregate children simply because of Mexican descent and ordered all the children readmitted to their previous school. The board complied without appealing.[157]

In 1929, the same year that the Hoover Administration initiated its plans for large-scale deporting of Mexicans who were "public charges," a group of middle class Mexican-Americans in Texas formed the League of United Latin American Citizens (LULAC), aimed at promoting integration and equal treatment, on the model of the NAACP (which had already started to attain prominent litigation successes on such topics as white primaries, residential segregation laws, and rights of accused persons).[158] Additional LULAC chapters within three years arose in California, New Mexico, Colorado, and Arizona and helped to fund the desegregation lawsuits discussed below.[159]

Texas had begun creating separate schools for Mexicans in 1902. In 1930, when the Del Rio Independent School District announced a project to quadruple the size of the two-room Mexican school, which served Chicano children in grades one through three. Jesus Salvatierra, joined by several other Mexican-descent parents and assisted by an attorney from

---

156 Powers 2008, 472.
157 Alvarez 1986, cited in Powers 475–476.
158 See Chapter 5 for discussion of these NAACP cases.
159 Foley 2007, 300.

the fledgling LULAC, requested an injunction to restrain construction of the school addition and to block school authorities "from segregating the children of plaintiffs and others similarly situated from children of Anglo-Saxon parentage of like ages and educational attainments within the school district." At trial, Judge Joseph Jones granted their injunction.[160]

The Court of Civil Appeals, however, while agreeing with the court below on the principle that Texas law did not permit the arbitrary segregation of schoolchildren from children of the "other white races," "solely because they are Mexican," nonetheless dissolved the injunction. Appellate Judge Smith was persuaded by the superintendent's testimony that Mexican children were receiving special supplemental language instruction in the first three grades to compensate for their deficiencies in English. Judge Smith did not order formal language testing, but was content to rely on administrative discretion, in the understanding that individualized teacher assessment of each student's pedagogical needs would suffice, and made more sense than a blanket court order.[161] The U.S. Supreme Court refused to hear an appeal of the decision. By the early 1940s, 90 percent of Chicano children in Texas, for grades one and two were segregated in school; 50 percent continued in the segregated schools as high as sixth grade.[162]

Public accommodations in Texas in the 1940s were so pervasively segregated that Mexican consuls themselves were refused service at hotels and restaurants in both major cities and small towns. LULAC activists worked with these consuls to bring complaints to the Mexican Embassy in D.C., who then brought pressure on the State Department to intervene. Following up on these complaints, the Foreign Minister of Mexico in 1943 officially blacklisted Texas, refusing to allow guest workers ("braceros") to continue to enter the state. (The *bracero* program had been established just the year before, between the U.S. and Mexican Governments to help with the wartime labor shortage.) A month before this blacklist, the Texas legislature (wanting the guest workers) in an appeasement effort had "resolved" (with no enforcement mechanism) that all Caucasians have the right to "full and equal accommodation" at all

---

[160] Orozco 2010. *Del Rio Ind. Sch. Dist. v. Salvatierra,* 33 S.W.2d 790, 793–4 (Tex. Civ. App. 1930); cert. denied, 284 U.S. 580 (1931).

[161] Ibid., at 794–5.

[162] Haney-Lopez 1997, 1198 n.162, citing Wilson Little, *Spanish-Speaking Children in Texas*, 1944.

"public places of business or amusement." LULAC then lobbied for enforcement measures such as fines, but to no avail.[163]

The legislature's concurrent resolution was not enough to sway a Texas judge faced in the following year (1944) with a request to order a privately owned swimming pool to serve Mexican-Americans. He ruled that, despite passage in both houses and a signature of the governor, only official legislation, not a mere "concurrent resolution" could have that effect.[164]

In the same year (1944), a Chicano group in California had better success using a *Fourteenth Amendment* equal protection argument in *federal* court against a *city* operated swimming pool and playground that were closed to Mexican-American residents.[165] The city, San Bernardino California, was making no claim that it offered "separate but equal" facilities. This was simply an instance of rank inequality, and the judge said that the city presented no health or safety or public welfare reason for the discrimination. He permanently enjoined against any further discrimination in the facilities.[166]

Around this time, in the thick of World War II, the President finally got involved in the issue of anti-Chicano discrimination. Franklin Roosevelt feared that Axis powers would gain a propaganda advantage in countries like Mexico and Argentina, interfering with U.S.-Latin America trade relations in a way that could hurt the war effort. As early as 1940 FDR established the Office of the Coordinator of Inter-American Affairs (OCIAA), an agency headed by Nelson Rockefeller and charged with promoting cultural and economic relations with Latin America. In 1943 this office sent investigators to both Texas and California (the two states, to this day, with the largest numbers of Mexican-Americans) to investigate the numerous complaints of discrimination received by federal agencies. With funding promised from OCIAA and pressure being placed on him by Texas farm interests anxious about the ban on guest workers, Texas Governor Coke Stevenson established the Texas Good Neighbor

---

[163] Foley 2007, 300–301. Green 2010.

[164] *Terrell Wells Swimming Pool v. Rodriguez*, 182 S.W.2d 824 (Tex. Civ. App. 1944), cited in Martinez 1994, n.34.

[165] *Lopez v. Seccombe*, 71 F. Supp. 769 (1944). Foley 2007, 302, notes that the litigant group here [as in the later *Mendez* case discussed below] brought together Mexican-Americans and Puerto Ricans. The judge in the decision described one of the five petitioners as follows: Eugenio Nogueroa is an American citizen of Latin descent, a graduate of Cayey High School, Porto Rico, and of University of Porto Rico … [and current resident of San Bernardino].

[166] Ibid., at 770 (Section X.)

Commission (GNC).[167] The GNC functioned from 1943–45 on federal funding via the OCIAA, and then began operating on Texas funds. Its mission was to improve education, housing, and employment conditions for both guest workers and Latino permanent residents. By 1947, Mexico lifted the Texas ban on *bracero* admission.

(The GNC continued its anti-discrimination work through 1965, after which this side of its task was largely supplanted by the newly created federal Office of Economic Opportunity under President Lyndon Johnson. In 1948 it played a major role in the *Delgado v. Bastrop Indep. Sch. Dist* litigation[168] discussed below. After 1965 its tasks were gradually narrowed to focus on Inter-American relations and migrant workers from Latin America, and it was phased out in 1987.[169])

Meanwhile in California, Mr. and Mrs. Gonzalo Mendez, in 1945 became angry after their three children were turned away from the school nearest their home, when they had gone to register with their more fair-skinned first cousins (who had last names that were not obviously Hispanic and), who were allowed into the "white" school. With the help of the California branch of LULAC, they retained David Marcus, the successful attorney of the San Bernardino 1944 swimming pool case, for challenging California's segregation of Chicano school children. As had the swimming pool case, this case, too, involved litigants who were both of Mexican and Puerto Rican descent, in this instance the Mendez couple. The mother of the three children was Felicita Gomez Mendez, whose own parents had brought her with them from Puerto Rico in 1926, when they had been part of a group of 1,500 Puerto Rican workers imported to Arizona because of a labor shortage caused by recent legislation restricting immigration from Europe. She and Gonzalo Mendez (a Mexican-American) were both U.S. citizens; their three children were fluent in English.[170]

Marcus convinced the Mendez family to join with families from other discriminatory districts, as a way of strengthening their complaint. As the case went to court in 1945, it presented plaintiffs from four different

---

[167] Powers 2008, 301-302.

[168] Final Judgment, *Delgado v. Bastrop Indep. Sch. Dist.*, Civ. No. 388 (W. D. Tex. June 15, 1948, Box 79, Folder 5, George Sanchez Papers, Benson Latin American Collection, University of Texas, Austin.) cited in Powers 2008, 309; Green 2010.

[169] Green 2010.

[170] Foley 2007, 302; Aguirre 2005, 323; Morales 2012; Regua 2007.

school districts in Orange County, who petitioned on behalf of themselves and all the other districts' residents "of Mexican or Latin descent or extraction." One district superintendent testified forthrightly that in his district children were assigned to elementary school based simply on last name, but that occasionally Mexican-descent children would be put into Anglo schools if they had European-sounding names or "looked white."[171]

Another superintendent testified that he believed Mexican children as a group to be dirty, to carry disease and to be slower learners than whites. Such commentary provoked Attorney Marcus to liken his views to those of Hitler. The same superintendent testified in response to Marcus's question that even if a particular Latino child were qualified in every way to compete in an Anglo classroom, he would "never allow" such a child to attend an "all-white" school.[172]

Marcus had some children testify, partly to demonstrate their perfect fluency in English and to talk about what sorts of inequalities in facilities they observed between Anglo and Chicano schools, but also to talk about what sorts of feelings being segregated evoked in them. He also presented a social science expert, the chairman of the UCLA Anthropology Department, who testified that separating Anglo children from Latino children in this way "would stamp the Mexican-American children with a badge of inferiority and the White children with a badge of superiority and that such practice would lead to unproductive Mexican-American citizens," and he likened such practices to those of Nazi Germany. Another expert witness, a former principal in the Los Angeles County schools testified that school segregation engenders harmful feelings of inferiority in the discriminated-against children.[173]

Federal District Court Judge Paul McCormick began with the obvious: "[T]he Education Code of the State [by omitting them from its list of who is to be segregated] prohibits segregation of pupils of Mexican ancestry in the elementary schools from the rest of the school children." He conceded the persuasiveness of the school district claims that the "technical facilities and physical conveniences offered in the schools housing entirely the segregated pupils, the efficiency of the teachers

[171] *Mendez et al. v. Westminster School District et al.*, 64 F. Supp. 544, 545 (1946) [*Mendez I* below]; Aguirre 2005, 324-325.

[172] Ruiz 2001; Aguirre 2005, 174–5.

[173] Ruiz, ibid.; Aguirre, ibid. (the quotation is Aguirre's paraphrase); Foley 2007, 302.

therein and the curricula are identical and in some respects superior to those in the other schools in the respective districts."[174]

This was not going to be a decision calling for upgrading facilities to make them at least "separate but equal." Judge McCormick insisted on the following:[175]

> We think such practices clearly and unmistakably disregard rights secured by the supreme law of the land [Citation omitted.]
>
> The equal protection of the laws pertaining to the public school system in California is not provided by furnishing in separate schools the same technical facilities, text books and courses of instruction to children of Mexican ancestry that are available to the other public school children regardless of their ancestry. A paramount requisite in the American system of public education is social equality. It must be open to all children by unified school association regardless of lineage.
>
> ***
>
> The evidence clearly shows that Spanish-speaking children are retarded in learning English by lack of exposure to its use because of segregation, and that commingling of the entire student body [would] instill[] and develop[] a common cultural attitude among the school children which is imperative for the perpetuation of American institutions and ideals [as schools are required to do by the California Code §10051]. It is also established by the record that the methods of segregation prevalent in the defendant school districts foster antagonisms in the children and suggest inferiority among them where none exists.

If this line of reasoning, in its focus on psychological impact, on fostering interracial communication skills and building up the students' civic faculties, and in directing attention away from the equalizing of physical school facilities and equipment and instructional skills, strikes the reader as similar to reasoning later found in the Supreme Court's 1950 *Sweatt v. Painter* and *McLaurin v. Oklahoma* cases and in its 1954 *Brown v. Board* decision, that would be no coincidence.[176]

The district court decision of Judge McCormick immediately attracted the attention of NAACP attorneys looking for ways to challenge the rule of "separate but equal" head-on. At the time they were working on the law school desegregation case of Heman Sweatt in Texas (*Sweatt v. Painter*). Thurgood Marshall and his co-counsel Robert Carter both took

[174] *Mendez I*, at 546–8.

[175] *Mendez I*, at 549.

[176] *Sweatt v. Painter*, 339 U.S. 629 (1950); *McLaurin v. Oklahoma*, 339 U.S. 637 (1950). *Brown v. Board of Ed.*, 347 U.S. 483 (1954).

direct encouragement from the *Mendez I* opinion for future strategizing and also signed on with the California litigants to write an amicus brief to counter the appeal of the school districts against the *Mendez I* ruling.[177] One of Marshall's two co-authors on the *Mendez II* brief, Robert Carter, has stated that[178]

> [h]e was so impressed by how social science knowledge had been used to criticize segregation in the *Mendez* [I] case that he suggested to Marshall that the "social science approach would be the only way to overturn segregation in the United States." Carter explained that the *amicus curiae* brief he and Marshall filed in the appellate court in support of *Mendez* was a "dry run for the future."

In addition, David Marcus the attorney for *Mendez* ended up supplying Thurgood Marshall with all his files and notes from the *Mendez* cases for Marshall's later desegregation efforts.[179] Robert Carter was one of the two attorneys who then argued the *McLaurin v. Oklahoma* (1950) case at the U.S. Supreme Court, and Thurgood Marshall was one of the two attorneys who, on the same day, argued the *Sweatt v. Painter* (1950) case at the U.S. Supreme Court (and each appears on the list of a half dozen of "assistance of counsel" attorneys for the other case). Robert Carter and Thurgood Marshall were two of the three attorneys for the NAACP Legal Defense Fund who argued the *Brown v. Board* case at the Supreme Court for the 1954 decision.[180]

Moreover, that *Mendez I* had undercut the foundation of *Plessy v. Ferguson*—the premise that separation of the races imposed by law could count as equal protection if the physical facilities were equal, because the social humiliation imposed by the law counted for nothing—was noted in several of the most prominent law journals of the country in the years 1946–48: Columbia, Harvard, Yale, Illinois, Michigan, Southern California and Minnesota.[181] Even the *New York Times* observed after *Mendez I* that the appeal of the case is being "closely watched as a guinea pig case [on school desegregation]."[182] Thus it was highly likely to have come to the attention of Supreme Court law clerks working on the 1950 Supreme Court cases of *Sweatt* and *McLaurin*.

---

177 Powers 2008, 476–7. Ramos 2011, 35–6.
178 Bernstein. 2007, 93.
179 Ibid.
180 There were an additional three from the Kansas NAACP.
181 Valencia 2005; Strum 2010, 146–7.
182 Strum, ibid.

Although the judge in *Mendez II* did not carry forth the specific argument of the district court that the Equal Protection clause required that children be allowed associational, or "social" equality, and that government policies engendering inferiority feelings in one group of children hardly amount to equal protection of the laws, versions of these *Mendez I* arguments show up later in *Brown v. Board* (1954), in the opinion of Chief Justice Earl Warren, who had been governor of California in 1946, during the *Mendez* I trial. During that trial, as governor, Warren had personally assigned the California Attorney General the task of writing a supporting amicus brief from the state government for the *Mendez II* hearing, *against* the school districts of Orange County.[183] Robert Carter (of the *Mendez II* NAACP amicus brief) was one of the NAACP attorneys for Linda Brown in the original federal district court case of *Brown v. Board of Ed. of Topeka Kansas,* 98 F. Supp. 797 (1951). Chief Justice Earl Warren quoted extensively from the judge's opinion for that case in his 1954 *Brown* opinion to make the point that the feelings of inferiority engendered by segregation undermine children's motivation to learn, depriving them of equal educational opportunity.[184] This argument begins in Judge McCormick's opinion for *Mendez I*.[185]

Warren had available to him two lines of argument. He could have followed the "suspect classification" rule made available in *Korematsu v. U.S.* (1944), and applied by the Vinson Court in *Oyama v. California* (1948): the rule that laws discriminating against a single racial/national group are suspect and can be upheld only if proven necessary for a compelling purpose (such as military survival of the U.S.).[186] He had been the state attorney general in California in 1942 and the governor in 1943, carrying out the controversial wartime incarceration of Japanese-Americans, so this line of precedent may have been unattractive to him in

---

183 Aguirre 2005, 329

184 *Brown*, at 494 (1954).

185 *Mendez I* at 549.

186 *Korematsu v. U.S.*, 323 U.S. 214 (1944); *Oyama v. California*, 332 U.S. 633 (1948). These and the other wartime internment cases are discussed in Chapter 7. In fact, the NAACP mentioned the three wartime Japanese internment cases in their amicus brief for *Mendez II*, but only to establish the principle that the federal government too, not only the state governments, is bound by an equal protection principle that forbids ancestry-based discrimination, The brief did not use a strict scrutiny argument, instead affirming, as Chief Justice Warren would later agree in *Bolling v. Sharpe* (1954) that racial segregation promoted no valid purpose, and was in fact arbitrary, or unreasonable. Robinson and Robinson 2003, 178–80. See note 187 below.

1954. Instead, in *Brown* he quoted the arguments set forth in 1950 by Chief Justice Vinson in *Sweatt* and in *McLaurin*, focusing on intangible factors that make segregated education intrinsically unequal. Then, familiar as he was with the *Mendez I* opinion, he underlined the factor identified by Judge McCormick: segregation affects the children's "hearts and minds in a way unlikely ever to be undone."[187] He then (in contrast to *Korematsu*, which had been, granted, technically a due process rather than equal protection case) simply concluded that equal protection had been denied, without engaging in any discussion of whether there might be a governmental interest to justify this unequal treatment.

Moreover, a second dimension of the McCormick (*Mendez I*) opinion had a historic impact *within* California: The opinion quoted verbatim the California Education Code sections 8003 and 8004, which authorized segregating "Chinese, Japanese, and Mongolian children,"[188] and immediately noted that "distinctions among pupils based upon race or ancestry ... have recently been declared by the highest judicial authority of the United States 'by their very nature odious to a free people whose institutions are founded upon the doctrine of equality,' and are said to be 'utterly inconsistent with American traditions and ideals.' *Kiyoshi Hirabayashi v. United States*, 320 U.S. 81 [1943]."[189] This juxtaposition attracted the attention of Governor Earl Warren and/or important members of the California state legislature; while *Mendez II* (the federal circuit court's ultimate disposition of the case) was pending, the legislature was working on eliminating these sections of the education code. The State Assembly voted to abolish the school segregation provisions on April 10, 1947. *Mendez II* was handed down on April 14, 1947. The offending sections of the Code were removed on June 14, 1947, when the State Senate's vote completed legislative approval of Assembly Bill Number 375 and Governor Earl Warren signed it. The Court of Appeals

---

[187] *Brown*, at 493–4. Chief Justice Warren does cite the *Hirabayashi* (1943) and *Korematsu* (1944) wartime cases on curfew and evacuation of Japanese-Americans in the 1954 District of Columbia companion case to *Brown*, *Bolling v. Sharpe*, 347 U.S. 497, but he does so primarily to make the point that there are precedents establishing that the Fifth Amendment due process clause (which restrains the federal government) implicitly contains a rule of equal protection of the laws. See discussion in Chapter 7.

[188] *Mendez I*, at 548 n. 5. In fact, this provision had gone unenforced since 1929, when the Chinese-American school-age population in San Francisco had outgrown the two elementary school buildings for them. Rather than pay the cost of a third building, the authorities opted to let the overflow Chinese-Americans into nearby schools, previously attended only by non-Asians. Kuo 1998, 210.

[189] *Mendez I*, at 548. See Chapter 7 for discussion of *Hirabayashi*.

for *Mendez II* then corrected its (already-issued) decision in a new version issued on August 1, 1947, that noted parenthetically the recent legislative repeal of Education Code sections 8003 and 8004.[190]

Mendez II was actually not as nationally consequential as *Mendez I*: the Circuit Court ordered an end to the Chicano school segregation by straightforward application of California statute; the statutes did not authorize non-Asians to be separated by nationality, so to treat Mexican-Americans this way was to deny them liberty without due process of law and also to deny them equal protection of the law.[191]

The Circuit Court of Appeals hearing of the appeal against Judge McCormick's important *Mendez I* opinion attracted, in addition to the State Attorney General and the NAACP, a wide range of interest groups, all of whom submitted amicus briefs in support of LULAC's David Marcus who was arguing for the Mendezes and the other Latino families. These included the American Jewish Congress,[192] the American Civil Liberties Union, the Japanese-American Citizens League, and the National Lawyers' Guild (a leftwing organization).[193] This was the first time that the Japanese-American Citizenship League (JACL) intervened in a civil rights lawsuit involving another group. While their brief argued for doing away with Sections 8003 and 8004 of the Code, which authorized segregating Asians, they also argued against all segregation in California schools.[194]

Stimulated by the *Mendez II* cooperation with the NAACP, two of the three JACL attorneys (A. L. Wirin and Saburo Kido) went on to present amicus briefs in some important NAACP civil rights cases that reached the U.S. Supreme Court. First was *Hurd v. Hodge* (1948, the District of Columbia companion case to state-level *Shelley v. Kraemer* challenging

---

[190] Strum 2015, 21-22. Trisha Martinez 2014, 9-5 and 9-6; Strum 2010, 168; See, *Westminster et al. v. Mendez et al. (Mendez II),* 161 F. 2d 774 at 780 (1947).

[191] 161 F.2d 774 (1947).

[192] One of the three co-authors of this brief was the African-American woman and civil rights attorney, Pauli Murray, who four years earlier had been one of the four co-founders of CORE, the Congress on Racial Equality. Pauli Murray Project N.D.

[193] Of these, only the National Lawyers Guild and the ACLU had participated as amicus in the district court case (*Mendez I*). They contributed to a combined brief for *Mendez II*, submitted in the name of the Japanese-American Citizenship League, whose attorneys, A.L. Wirin and Saburo Kido (President of the JACL) were the only ones besides David Marcus to present oral arguments against the school districts in the *Mendez II* hearing. Robinson and Robinson 2003, 176; Brilliant 2010, 37.

[194] Foley 2007, 303–4.

racially restrictive real estate covenants), a case that was argued late in 1947. The NAACP returned the favor, presenting an amicus brief for the 1948 JACL litigation in *Takahashi v. Fish and Game Commission.*[195] And this JACL commitment continued up through both *McLaurin v. Oklahoma* (1950)[196] and *Brown v. Board of Education* (1954). For *Brown,* the JACL was the only non-black racial minority organization to present an amicus brief.[197]

Immediately, the *Mendez* precedents were picked up by attorneys for Latinos in Texas and Arizona, and they proved persuasive for obtaining judicial orders ending the legitimacy of school segregation of Chicanos in both states. One of the two co-authors of the amicus brief of the Japanese-American Citizenship League for *Mendez II,* was the attorney A.L. Wirin (a staff attorney for the ACLU of Los Angeles). The next year he then became (by way of his ties to the ACLU, which was also helping finance the lawsuit) one of a group of attorneys in Texas, assisted by LULAC, who brought a lawsuit on behalf of the Delgado family and a group of other Mexican-American families to challenge the segregation policies of the Bastrop Independent School District and four other districts in Texas.[198] They succeeded in obtaining the permanent injunction against Chicano school segregation in Texas that they were seeking (the injunction applied to all five districts and the state level Superintendent of Public Instruction). The court order issued for *Delgado v. Bastrop Indep Sch. Dist.* (1948) cited *Mendez* as a relevant precedent.[199]

In Arizona two years later, A. L. Wirin was again retained (by the lead plaintiff, Gonzales) in a suit to desegregate Chicano school children. He was one of three attorneys who presented the lawsuit. The lawsuit was launched by a group of parents who spoke on behalf of some 300 Mexican-American citizens, parents of children in the Tolleson Arizona school district. Their lawsuit, *Gonzales v. Sheely,*[200] was heard on the day after the U.S. Supreme Court handed down *Sweatt v. Painter* and

---

[195] Robinson and Robinson 2003, 183: *Hurd v. Hodge*, 334 U.S. 24, 25 (1948); *Shelley v. Kraemer*, 334 U.S. 1 (1948); *Takahashi v. Fish and Game Commission*, 334 U.S. 410, 412 (1948). For discussion of *Hurd* and *Shelley*, and *Takahashi*, see Chapter 7.

[196] Strum 2010, 150–51.

[197] Robinson and Robinson 2003, 183.

[198] Powers 2008, 477; Foley 2007, 305–6.

[199] Foley 2007, 304; Final Judgment *Delgado v. Bastrop Indep. Sch. Dist.*, Civ. No. 388 (W.D. Tex. June 15, 1948) (location cited as George I. Sanchez papers in Foley 2007, 309 n.30).

[200] *Gonzales v. Sheely*, 96 F.Supp 1004 (1951).

McLaurin v. Oklahoma. Citing those two Supreme Court precedents, federal district Judge Ling decided with the plaintiffs and drew his decision of this case "almost word for word from McCormick's decision in *Mendez* [*I*]."[201] *Gonzales v. Sheely* (as had McCormick in *Mendez I*) linked the intangible factors argument deployed by the Supreme Court in *Sweatt* and *Painter* to the plight of segregated Latino elementary school children; it took the judicial step in 1951 for the state of Arizona that the U.S. Supreme Court would be taking for African-American children across the U.S. in 1954 in *Brown v. Board of Education*.[202]

After the Texas State Superintendent promptly promulgated orders forbidding the segregation of Latino schoolchildren, these orders appear to have been widely ignored for a long time by local school officials outside of the specific districts covered by the injunction.[203] As with the 1954 *Brown v. Board* decision, attaining each of these judicial pronouncements was winning a major battle, but getting compliance in districts all over the country was a much bigger war.[204]

Effective school desegregation—whether for African-Americans or Latinos—required a legislative push from Congress and executive enforcement led by the President. The political will for these did not come until a decade after *Brown v. Board of Education* (and after a number of horrific events including the murder of black Sunday School children and major urban riots in several cities including Los Angeles). In 1964, Congress passed the Civil Rights Act,[205] which not only forbade racial, religious, or nationality discrimination by public accommodations that operated in interstate commerce (Title II); by state and local governmentally run facilities (Title III); and by employers who did business in interstate commerce (Title VII);[206] but also it prohibited the allocation of federal funds by grant or loan to any governmental program that practiced discrimination on racial or nationality grounds (Title VI). Moreover, Title IV of the 1964 Act ordered the federal Commissioner of Education to survey public school systems from elementary through college level and report within two years to Congress and the President

---

201 Powers 2008, 476.

202 Discussions of *Sweatt, Painter*, and *Brown* are in Chapter 7.

203 Rangel and Alcala 1972, 316.

204 Rosenberg. 2008, Part I; Goldstein 2011-B, 178–9. For a complete narrative of the ups and downs of school desegregation from the 1950s to the present, see Orfield 2015.

205 Civil Rights Act of 1964. Pub.L. 88–352, 78 Stat. 241, enacted July 2, 1964.

206 This Title also prohibited sex discrimination in employment.

whether equal educational opportunity was available irrespective of religion, race, or nationality, and to offer technical and financial assistance to those school systems attempting desegregation who requested help. It also authorized the Attorney General to bring lawsuits for desegregation upon receipt of a meritorious complaint from someone experiencing denial of equal protection from a public school board or experiencing denial of admission to a public college on grounds of race, religion or nationality, when those parties were unable to sue on their own.

The Title VI prohibition took on real teeth for public schools the following year when Congress passed the Elementary and Secondary Education Act of 1965. This law for the first time offered significant financial help to local school districts for educational expenses, particularly those with low income students. Now federal law was offering a large carrot and stick incentive to encourage school districts to desegregate, because if they did not, Title VI the 1964 Act withdrew the generous federal funding that would otherwise be available. School desegregation nationwide finally took place in earnest after these two federal laws were implemented.[207]

At first, however, even these massive federal political initiatives left Hispanics by the wayside. The 1964 Civil Rights Act authorized the Department of Health, Education, and Welfare (HEW) to issue goals and guidelines for school desegregation. However, despite the U.S. Supreme Court's 1954 condemnation of discrimination against Hispanics with which this chapter began, HEW's own Office of Civil Rights, whose job it was to investigate alleged discrimination, initially gathered statistics using only black and white categories. Only after three years, once Hector P. Garcia (at the time U.S. Ambassador to the U.N., later to become the first Mexican-American member of the U.S. Civil Rights Commission)[208] rebuked the Office of Civil Rights for failing to examine Mexican-Americans' complaints, did HEW even begin to collect data on Mexican-Americans. This improved initiative then took the form of publishing data on black, white, and "other." The "others" included "any racial or national origin group for which separate schools have in the past been maintained or which are recognized as significant 'minority groups'

[207] Elementary and Secondary Education Act of 1965, Pub.L. 89–10; 79 Stat. 27. The supplemental funding being offered in some Southern school districts amounted to as much as 20–25 percent of their annual budget. Orfield 2015, 407.

[208] Garcia, a physician, military veteran, and civil rights activist, founded the Latino rights-advocacy organization, American G.I. Forum. Rozeft 2011.

in the community." HEW offered examples: "Indian American, Oriental, Eskimo, Mexican-American, Puerto Rican, Latin, Cuban, etc."[209]

U.S. SUPREME COURT AND LATINOS

Supreme Court decisions, just like policies from the federal elected branches, can shape the lives of Latinos, even when the group is not mentioned in the rulings, statutes or regulations. For instance, once the U.S. Supreme Court ruled in *Shelley v. Kraemer* (1948)[210] that racially restrictive covenants (excluding blacks) could not be enforced by the government without violating the equal protection clause, state appellate courts in both Texas and California promptly did as they were supposed to do with respect to covenants restricting home-sellers against selling to Mexican-Americans. They ruled these covenants, too, unenforceable in state courts.[211]

In other legal contexts, however, the lower courts or local policymakers defied federal laws or judicial rulings that should have been applied to protect Latinos against discrimination. The first of these was the case with which this chapter began, *Hernandez v. Texas* (1954).[212] The Supreme Court had made clear in a long series of cases between 1935 and 1953, more than a couple of which came from Texas, that excluding all or almost all blacks from juries and grand juries violated due process of law and/or equal protection of law, and would cause convictions to be overturned.[213] Nonetheless, communities in Texas were continuing to do the same to Mexican-Americans, defending the practice by the claim that since they were white, and since other whites were put on the jury, the exclusion of one particular ethnicity is not constitutionally problematic. In 1954, in *Hernandez v. Texas*, the U.S. Supreme Court called a halt.

Pete Hernandez was convicted of murder in Jackson County, Texas, which had a Spanish-surnamed population of 14 percent.[214] For the previous twenty-five years, not a single such person had been placed on a jury in Jackson County.[215] And the county showed an unmistakable

---

209 Wilson 2005, 209–10.

210 *Shelley, v. Kraemer*, 334 U.S. 1 (1948).

211 *Clifton v. Puente,* 218 S.W.2d 272 (Tex. Civ. App. 1948); *Matthews v. Andrade*, 198 P.2d 66 (Cal. App. 1948).

212 *Hernandez v. Texas,* 347 U.S. 475 (1954).

213 See Chapter 7, section on equal access to juries.

214 *Hernandez*, at 480.

215 Ibid., at 482.

pattern of discriminating against Mexican-Americans by segregating its public facilities.[216]

The U.S. Supreme Court, in this context, unanimously signed on to Chief Justice Warren's opinion for the case, which said, among other things, "It taxes our credulity to say that mere chance resulted in there being no members of this class among the over six thousand jurors called in the past 25 years. The result bespeaks discrimination … . The judgment of conviction must be reversed."[217] The Court established plainly in *Hernandez* that the Constitution creates a right for an accused person to be tried by "juries selected from among all qualified persons regardless of national origin or descent."[218] Interestingly, Chief Justice Warren quoted the same rule of law from *Hirabayashi*, the Japanese-internment-related case (from his time as Governor of California), that the federal district judge had quoted in *Mendez I*. "Distinctions between citizens solely because of their ancestry are, by their very nature, odious to a free people whose institutions are founded upon the doctrine of equality."[219]

In contrast to the inter-ethnic cooperation of mid-century that this chapter highlighted in the school desegregation cases, the Supreme Court cases dealing with Latinos from the next two decades reveal tensions or potential tensions emerging between Mexican-Americans and Puerto Ricans in the first case and between Mexican-Americans and African-Americans in the next. In the 1965 Voting Rights Act, most of which dealt with southern states that had established records of malfeasance in terms of the systematic use of subterfuges to deny Fifteenth Amendment rights to black citizens, Section 4(e), instead, focused on the situation of Puerto Ricans who have moved to the mainland but been disfranchised due to non-literacy in English. The State of New York, in particular, had a large Puerto Rican population but a state law insisting on literacy in English. If someone considered him- or herself literate in English, but did not want to go through a literacy test, he or she could qualify to register in New York State upon proof of completing sixth grade in an accredited school where *English* had been the language of instruction.[220] Section 4(e) of the federal Voting Rights Act directly countermanded this New York law by permitting the completion of sixth grade in any "school

[216] Ibid., at 479–80.
[217] Ibid., at 482.
[218] Ibid.
[219] Ibid., footnote 4, citing *Hirabayashi v. United States,* 320 U.S. 81, at 100 (1943).
[220] *Katzenbach v. Morgan*, 384 U.S. 641, 644–5 (1966) (Emphasis added).

accredited by, any State or territory, the District of Columbia, or the Commonwealth of Puerto Rico in which the predominant classroom language was *other than* English," to count as evidence of literacy for purposes of the right to vote, anything in state law to the contrary notwithstanding.[221] New York State challenged this federal law as an interference with its power to regulate its own elections, and a Puerto Rican woman, literate in Spanish but not English, Martha Cardona, challenged the New York State regulation itself as a violation of the Equal Protection Clause, arguing that literacy in Spanish, the language in which she was educated in Puerto Rico should suffice for the suffrage. New York City, where she resided had a plethora of Spanish language newspapers and radio broadcasts, and she considered herself well informed on election issues. Her challenge, *Cardona v. Power*,[222] was dealt with by the Supreme Court together with *Katzenbach v. Morgan*, both in 1966.

The Supreme Court majority in opinions by Justice Brennan first rejected New York State's challenge, reasoning that the federal law was a reasonable way to enforce the requirement of equal protection of the law; Puerto Ricans deprived of voting rights by New York would have a hard time securing their equal protection rights to be free of discrimination in "the provision or administration of governmental services, such as public schools, public housing and law enforcement."[223] As for the case of Ms Cardona, the Court majority remanded the decision back down to the court of appeals because her initial challenge had claimed that the New York law itself was unconstitutional, violating the Equal Protection Clause; now that the federal Voting Rights Act had been upheld (superseding the New York law), she might be already entitled to vote in New York (if she graduated from sixth grade in Puerto Rico), so the Supreme Court would not have to decide her constitutional claim.

Justices Fortas and Douglas, dissenting, saw it differently. What of persons who were literate in Spanish but had not lived in Puerto Rico (but instead migrated, say, from Mexico)? Or who were literate in other languages, such as Chinese, and had access within their U.S. communities to news media in which they were literate? Why should they be deprived of a right as important for equal protection of the laws as the right to vote?

---

221 79 Stat. 439, 42 U.S.C. § 1973b (e) (1964 ed., Supp. I). (Emphasis added.)

222 *Cardona v. Power*, 384 U.S. 672 (1966).

223 *Katzenbach*, at 652.

Here one sees a divergence of political interest between a potential naturalized Mexican-American, perhaps educated to sixth grade in Mexico but not Puerto Rico, shut out of the Voting Rights Act.[224] That both groups have Hispanic surnames and Spanish-speaking ancestry does not assure in the U.S. a shared political interest. The combination of Puerto Rican litigants with Mexican-American litigants in the Southwest desegregation cases is not necessarily a typical pattern. Both groups may sometimes share an interest, for instance, bilingual education programs for recent arrivals to the U.S., but particular government policies can also leave them on opposing sides, as with the clause of the Voting Rights Act at issue in *Katzenbach v. Morgan*. Consequently, there currently exist two separate organizations, the Mexican American Legal Defense and Education Fund and the Puerto Rican Legal Defense and Education Fund.

The concerns expressed by the dissenters in the Cardona case did produce reforms in Congress. In 1970 the Voting Rights Act was amended to ban all literacy tests; in 1975, to prohibit discriminatory voting practices that target language minorities and to require provision of foreign language explanations of the ballot in covered areas of the country. As amended in 1992 the Act requires that if 5 percent of the citizens of voting age or more than 10,000 such people in a governmental entity are members of a single language minority and are of limited English proficiency, then the government must provide them with instructions and ballots in their minority language.[225]

The underlying issue of the *Hernandez v. Texas* litigation—the pretense that Mexican-Americans are not being governmentally discriminated against because they belong to the general group, whites—came up again in 1973 in the Supreme Court's next major case dealing with anti-Chicano discrimination, *Keyes v. School District … Denver*.[226] As part of the massive resistance to school desegregation that followed the *Brown v. Board* decision, many school district administrators attempted to avoid

---

[224] In 1964 the President of the Council of Mexican-American Affairs, speaking at a California state convention of LULAC, itemized in a list of urgent "state-level problems" faced by Mexican-Americans "English literacy tests as a bar to voting." Brilliant 2010, 230.

To be sure, the U.S. Naturalization requirements demand "literacy in English." But the test of this is minimal; current U.S. law requires ability to read or write correctly only one sentence out of three. A given state may wish to set higher standards for voter literacy, such as a sixth grade completion or sixth grade reading level.

[225] Soltero 2006, 60.

[226] *Keyes v. School Dist. … Denver*, 414 U.S. 189 (1973).

having to mix Anglo students with blacks and with Mexican-Americans, by simply combining Mexican-descent [legally white] pupils with black pupils, and leaving the Anglo pupils in their own neighborhood schools.[227] Since Chicanos themselves, however, had been victimized by being put into segregated schools, putting them with other victims of segregation was hardly a remedy to the problem of segregated schooling. The U.S. Supreme Court recognized this in 1973, in the *Keyes* case. After noting that the U.S. Commission on Civil Rights had found that in Arizona, California, Colorado, New Mexico, and Texas, both Hispanic and Black students had endured the "same educational inequities" and that the District Court had agreed that the two groups had in common both poverty and victimization by discrimination, the Supreme Court opinion concluded the following:[228]

> This is agreement that, though of different origins, Negroes and Hispanos in Denver suffer identical discrimination in treatment when compared with the treatment afforded Anglo students. In that circumstance, we think petitioners are entitled to have schools with a combined predominance of Negroes and Hispanos included in the category of "segregated" schools.

In addition to pioneering the analysis of desegregation for "tri-ethnic" segregated school systems, the Denver case also was the U.S. Supreme Court's first acknowledgment that northern-style school systems—ones that did not have laws openly mandating segregation of black people—nonetheless were practicing *de jure* (and therefore unlawful) segregation. The Court acknowledged that, even though the segregation was not as open as the anti-Chicano school segregation dealt with by lower courts in the 40s and 50s, where Chicano children were openly (albeit irrespective of statutes) told by officials, "You must attend the Mexican school," still, when school authorities manipulated school district boundaries and selected sites for new schools and for temporary mobile classrooms in ways calculated to maximize racial/ethnic separation in schools, they were imposing *de jure* segregation. Thus the *Keyes* case had reverberations all over the United States; Denver was far from the only city that engaged in these practices. Soon cities all over the North were roiled by controversy over the corrective measure, "forced busing."

For Chicanos and Puerto Ricans and more recently arrived other Latinos, however, a new concern emerged immediately. As the immigration reform of 1965 took hold, ending the overwhelming bias in favor of

---

227 Bowman 2015-B, 35–6; Behnken 2011-B, 66–7.
228 *Keyes*, at 197–8.

immigration from Europe,[229] the issue of English instruction in public schools for children in communities of high-immigrant concentration of Latinos and Asians became prominent on the public agenda.

FEDERAL POLICY AT CROSS-PURPOSES: DESEGREGATION VS. ELL CONCENTRATION, 1964–74

As early as 1964, but more insistently in 1966 and 1967, leaders of Mexican-American interest groups and elected Chicano officials began prioritizing the provision of bilingual education for Chicanos in public schools. In an ironic twist of history (echoing the rationale of anti-Mexican segregationist educators of the 1940s) spokesmen for the Mexican American Political Association (MAPA) and the Mexican American Legal Defense and Education Fund (MALDEF) both in public pronouncements and in speeches to Chicano organizations insisted that obtaining bilingual education for Mexican-Americans who were learning English or had an imperfect grasp of English was their top educational priority.[230]

By 1971, Chinese-American leaders in California, confronting "forced busing plans," took up the same plea. "Forced busing" for racial desegregation would deprive their children of needed bilingual education in school and make much more difficult their attendance at after-school education in Chinese culture. Even before there was a "forced busing" order to complain about, however, Chinese-Americans in San Francisco had gone to federal district court in 1970 to ask for bilingual education as a constitutional right under the equal protection clause, and a statutory right under California law and the 1964 Civil Rights Act Title VI.[231] The case was *Lau v. Nichols*, and they lost in the lower courts, but kept appealing upwards. After unsuccessfully attempting to persuade the litigants to drop their case, out of fear that it would lose at the U.S. Supreme Court, the leading Mexican-American civil rights organizations—LULAC, MALDEF, and the American G.I. Forum (along with the Association of Mexican American Educators) filed a joint amicus brief under the name of MALDEF at the Supreme Court, on

229 See discussion in Chapter 7.
230 Brilliant 2010, 227–56.
231 Ibid.

behalf of the *Lau* litigants.[232] The Puerto Rican Legal Defense and Education Fund submitted one, too.[233]

Federal government policy offered some hope for their position and to some degree had been both driving and supporting the push for bilingual schooling. These pushes came along two fronts, immigration law and education law. The 1965 immigration reform (described in Chapter 7) had a growing cumulative impact. In 1960, 6 percent of immigrants were from Mexico; by 1970 there were 8 percent from Mexico and 5 percent from Cuba, by 1980, 16 percent from Mexico and 5 percent from Cuba. Also by 1980, 4 percent from the Philippines and 2 percent from Korea. Population concentrations in localities were much higher in this time period than these numbers, because the bulk of these new immigrants concentrated themselves within the Southwest, Florida, New York and Chicago.[234]

As students needing bilingual education poured into the country, Congress passed the Bilingual Education Act of 1968, for the first time offering states federal funding if they wished to adopt special programming for students not proficient in English—i.e., English Language Learners, or ELL.[235] Then in 1970, under the Nixon Administration, HEW issued a memo interpreting Title VI of the 1964 Civil Rights Act as protecting ELL students.[236] Part of a wider governmental shift toward requiring affirmative remedies to counteract previous governmental discrimination, this was one of the early federal policies that defined identical treatment of groups that were differently situated as "discrimination" against one of the groups. The regulation said that school districts must "take affirmative steps to rectify the language deficiencies effectively barring children from receiving an education." Nixon's U.S. Commission on Civil Rights in 1972 issued a report to the effect that one half of Chicano first graders "were likely in need of" bilingual educational programming, but that only 2.5 percent of them were receiving it.[237]

---

232 Ibid., 249–50; 345 n.121.

233 *Lau v. Nichols*, 414 US 563, 564 (1974).

234 Bowman 2015-B, 38; de Genova and Ramos-Zayas, 2003 (on Mexican and Puerto Rican concentrations in Chicago). In the twenty-first century, Latino immigrants are spread much more widely around the U.S. Bowman 2015-B, 44.

235 Ibid., 37; Elementary and Secondary Education Amendments of 1967, Public Law 90-247, 81 stat.783, 816-820 (1968) (codified as amended in scattered sections of 20 U.S.C.).

236 Ibid., 39.

237 Ibid.

In 1973, the appeal of *Lau v. Nichols* reached the U.S. Supreme Court. The Nixon Justice Department filed an amicus brief on behalf of the Chinese-American students' families (after having filed a brief in opposition to it at the federal circuit court level!),[238] agreeing with their claim of a federal right to a bilingual education. This brief bolstered the Lau family's lawyer's brief by arguing that failure to counteract a deficiency in English comprehension to a degree sufficient for "meaningful[] participat[ion] in the educational program ... accessible to ... English speaking classmates" violated both the Equal Protection Clause of the Fourteenth Amendment and Title VI of the 1964 Civil Rights Act. The latter point of view, as noted, was already being promoted by the Department of HEW under Nixon. The Supreme Court issued a unanimous opinion in 1974, agreeing with the statutory part of this Justice Department argument.[239]

Justice Douglas relied heavily on the HEW regulations, drawn up to assure that school districts receiving federal funds did not discriminate on the basis of race, color or national origin:

> In 1970 HEW made the guidelines more specific, requiring school districts that were federally funded "to rectify the language deficiency in order to open" the instruction to students who had "linguistic deficiencies," 35 Fed. Reg. 11595. ... Discrimination among students on account of race or national origin that is prohibited includes "discrimination. . . in the availability or use of any academic ... or other facilities of the grantee or other recipient." 45 CFR § 80.5 (b). Discrimination is barred which has that *effect* even though no purposeful design is present: a recipient "may not ... utilize criteria or methods of administration which have the effect of subjecting individuals to discrimination" or have "the effect of defeating or substantially impairing accomplishment of the objectives of the program as respect individuals of a particular race, color, or national origin." *Id.*, § 80.3 (b) (2).[240] (at pp. 567–8)

"It seems obvious," wrote Justice Douglas, that the failure to provide English language training to large numbers of pupils of one nationality who need it in order to effectively participate in the public school curriculum violates this set of federal laws. If California did not want to give up federal funds it was receiving for its schools, it was obliged to now provide special English language instruction to children who needed it, including not only Chinese immigrants but also Mexican immigrants, who dramatically outnumbered them. This case was hailed as a victory

---

238 *Lau v. Nichols*, 483 F.2d 791 (1973).
239 *Lau v. Nichols*, 414 U.S. 563 (1974).
240 Ibid., at 567–8.

in the Mexican American civil rights community but it vastly complicated the logistics of potential desegregation of Latino school children.[241]

Congress acted almost immediately to codify the Supreme Court's ruling in *Lau v. Nichols* (1974). The Court decision came down in January, and by August Congress had adopted the Equal Educational Opportunities Act. This act put into statute form (thereby preserving it against vacillation from future administrations that have authority to alter regulations) the language from HEW regulations and the *Lau* opinion: School districts must "take affirmative steps to rectify the language deficiencies effectively barring children from receiving an education."[242]

It is perhaps not merely coincidence that the late 60s, just when Chicano lobbying for bilingual education became prominent, was also the time that certain African-American leaders began agitating on behalf of Black Power. The book of that title was published in October 1967, written by Stokely Carmichael (later Kwame Ture), then a leader of the Student Nonviolent Coordinating Committee (SNCC) and Charles Hamilton, Professor of Political Science at Columbia University. Almost immediately, certain Chicano leaders, in the late 1960s and early 1970s began organizing as "brown" rather than "white" and agitating for Brown Power.[243] The push for bilingual Spanish-English programming made Anglo-Chicano desegregation more difficult, but many Chicano leaders hoped that the bilingual programming would also be "bicultural," encouraging respect for and pride in Hispanic culture and history (just as the Black Power movement was promoting, inter alia, respect for African-American history and culture).[244]

CONCLUSIONS

After 1820, when the U.S. acquired Florida, for approximately a century, the federal government dealt with Hispanic-Americans primarily in the context of foreign relations. With the acquisition of territory from Spain or Mexico, its citizens were by treaty made U.S. nationals, able to travel and reside freely within the U.S. as Americans, and, once the territory where they resided attained statehood, its people became state citizens, as did American nationals of other European ancestries. When Cubans

241 Brilliant 2010, 253–4; Bowman 2011-B, 40–41.

242 Ibid.; Equal Educational Opportunities Act of 1974, Public Law 903-380, § 259, 88 Stat. 514, 521 (1974) (codified at 20 U.S.C. §1232g (2006).

243 Behnken 2011-B, 66–70.

244 Brilliant 2010, 229–33.

immigrated to the U.S. in large numbers in the early twentieth century, they were treated as other white or black immigrants, free to become naturalized citizens, and many did.

Since Puerto Rico was acquired at the turn of the century in a treaty that did not mention statehood, the Supreme Court had to clarify in 1904 that its permanent residents were American nationals, as had been the permanent residents of other U.S. territories, pre-statehood. Congress removed this anomaly in 1917, legislating citizenship for Puerto Ricans. The only exceptions would have been persons from Asia dwelling in any of these territories, just as they were exempted when dwelling within states.

Within the Southwest territories, the exception to the above generalization about the residents of the Mexican Cession was the former Mexicans who were Indians. Mexico had ruled the Pueblos, tribes of Indians who lived in settled agricultural communities and whom Mexico had Christianized. There were also other such settled, Christianized Indians, not Pueblos, dwelling within the formerly Mexican territory, and all of these settled Mexican Indians had enjoyed equal citizenship under the Mexican Government. Congress prohibited the Pueblo-American citizens from voting in the New Mexico territorial elections.

This situation presented a reversal from a pattern commonly uncovered in this book—oppression by the local majority against its local minority, which sometimes then could acquire protection from one or another branch of the federal government. The denial of rights to the Pueblo was coming from Congress, not the local populace. When federal bureaucrats brought to the federal courts legal issues concerning the Pueblo and similar Mexican Indians, at first the U.S. Supreme Court (as well as lower courts), treated these Indians, who did not live as "wild savages," as not legally Indians, but as "white by law"—or perhaps as semi-white, because Congressional restrictions on voting were kept in place.[245] The federal courts ruled that the Pueblo and other settled Indians were not subjected to the various restrictions on buying and selling land or whiskey that affected other Indians. These U.S. Supreme Court rulings stretched from 1854 through 1877.[246] Indian agents, working in the federal executive branch, disapproved of these court rulings, and during the 1848–77 period, often asked Congress to group these Indians

245 The phrase is borrowed from Haney-Lopez 2006, who uses it to describe Mexican-Americans, not Indians.

246 *U.S. v. Ritchie*, (1854) (a non-Pueblo, but settled, property-owning Indian in the Mexican Cession); *U.S. v. Joseph* (1877) (a Pueblo in New Mexico territory).

explicitly with the others, but Congress stayed its hand until 1910. At this point, it legislated that henceforth Pueblo lands would be considered "Indian Territory" and be ruled by the various regulations of such territory. The U.S. Supreme Court upheld this shift in the 1913 *U.S. v. Sandoval* decision. As more and more Anglos inhabited the formerly Mexican territory, the Pueblo may well have been in need of more protection by federal Indian agents, as the agents were claiming. In any event, by 1897 the now Anglo-dominated government within New Mexico took away Pueblo voting rights even for choosing their own local officials.

In sum, if one defines non-oppression of the Pueblo (and Pueblo-type) Indians of the Mexican Cession as considering them citizens with the same rights to buy and sell freely as other citizens, then the federal courts were protectors of the rights of these Indians, for as long as they could be, which was from 1848 until 1913. If non-oppression means honoring their equal voting rights as Mexico law required and as the treaty of the Mexican Cession seemed to require, then only the original New Mexico Government did this and only until Congress forced it not to, in 1853. And if non-oppression means treating Indians as unable to protect themselves in the commercial world, as the federal agents of the Indian bureaucracy claimed from the start, these Indians' non-oppression did not begin until 1910 when Congress put them under the rules of Indian Territory and stopped allowing them to handle their own business transactions. My own view is that the federal courts did the most to honor the Pueblos' equal citizenship as promised by treaty, and Congress did the least, of the federal branches. And the territorial government of New Mexico deserves credit: for a couple of years it was able to withstand Congressional pressure to deny voting rights to the Pueblo, until in 1853 Congress forced its hand.

The rest of the settled residents of the Mexican Cession were treated by U.S. law as either white or black. Those of Hispanic descent, while almost always to one degree or another biologically *mestizo*, were "white by law," although this fact did not guarantee that their neighbors treated them as equal citizens. As the lands of the Southwest became Anglo-dominated, citizens of Mexican descent were locally subjected to discrimination in non-statutory ways—in the sale of houses by neighborhood, in employment, in school assignment, in the administration of parks and public pools, and in biased law enforcement—including in determining the validity of land titles and selection for juries and in being kept away from the ballot box. Some states were worse than others. New Mexico seems to have been the most comfortable state for Chicanos, where they experienced the least discrimination and had the most effective role in governance. Texas appears to have been the worst, for there even white primary laws were deployed against voting by Mexican-Americans.

To the extent that white primary laws were deployed to keep Chicanos from voting, these were dealt with by the U.S. Supreme Court, as described in Chapters 5 and 7. It was Congress, however, that stepped in on behalf of Puerto Ricans in New York with the 1965 Voting Rights Act. Then in 1970 it intervened to protect all non-English-literate citizens by abolishing literacy tests; and in 1975 and 1992, by requiring ballot explanations in foreign languages wherever sizable groups of minority language citizens reside.

It was the U.S. Supreme Court that moved to guard against blatant exclusion of Chicanos from service on juries in 1954 in the *Hernandez v. Texas* case. The Court has had more trouble dealing with the problem of school segregation. In 1973 the Supreme Court outlawed the ploy of grouping blacks with Chicanos as a way to avoid schools that integrated the three groups together (*Keyes v. School District of Denver*), but was immediately beset with the question of whether Congress had created a legal right to be educated in a way that was language-accessible. Congress had not said anything like this explicitly but had prohibited national-origin discrimination by schools that receive federal funds. The Supreme Court agreed in *Lau v. Nichols* (1974) that pupils did have a right in public schools to have education geared to their degree of English proficiency (or its absence) such that they have an opportunity to learn the curriculum available to English-proficient students. Congress immediately embraced this ruling, in the Equal Education Opportunity Act of 1974. If school districts want to give instruction in English as a second language to Spanish speaking students, the logical step is to concentrate those students together, rather than dispersing them among Anglos. Even before the Supreme Court backed away from enforcing desegregation plans, which it did in the 1990s, its English instruction rulings, backed by both Congress and executive branch regulations in the 1970s put a halt to the desegregation of Latinos, at least those who needed the supplemental instruction.

For the overall situation of Latinos, none of the branches of the federal government stands out as their protector, although each one occasionally rose to the occasion. The Court contributed in the 1950s and 1970s as noted above, and protected the "not wild Indians" status of the Pueblo between 1854 and 1913. The executive branch was generally swayed by international diplomacy imperatives; President Wilson by veto power could stave off Congress's desire to limit immigration from Latin America for two years, until 1917, but then Congress overrode him.

President Harding, as a weapon of diplomacy, deported tens of thousands of Mexican residents. Under the economic pressures of the Depression, and with approval of the Mexican Government, Hoover and then Roosevelt were willing to deport, or to intimidate into exiting the country, hundreds of thousands of Chicano immigrants, along with their U.S. citizen children in the 1930s. On the other hand, the President and his bureaucrats did provide assistance to reduce anti-Chicano discrimination in Texas during the 1940s, as a way of getting Mexican cooperation in the *braceros* program. And the executive branch has enforced Congressional mandates both on English instruction in schools and on language help mandated in the Voting Rights Act.

The fact that Latinos often lived in geographically concentrated areas and had the vote, did give them some voice in Congress, even early on. For a long time, the voice was drowned out by that of hostile Anglo sentiment, but it definitely showed up in the crafting of the Voting Rights provisions on English language literacy and in the 1974 Equal Education Opportunity Act.

7. Branch variation in rights leadership, 1930–late twentieth century

INTRODUCTORY OVERVIEW

During the period 1930–68, protecting the civil rights of racial minorities came into prominence as an active concern of the federal government. But the answer to the question of which branch led the way varied from one minority to another.

In February of 1930, Charles Evans Hughes returned to the Supreme Court as its Chief Justice, to head the Court during a decade in which the Court continued its post-1910 leadership role (as compared to the other two branches) in enhancing the rights of black Americans. Although President Franklin Roosevelt, apparently due to worry about the southern flank of his party, during his first term maintained a relatively low profile on racial justice, he eventually appointed a sufficiently large number of racial liberals or at least moderates to the Justice Department and Supreme Court, to bring noticeable policy changes from the judicial branch. By 1939, a "Note" in the *Harvard Law Review* declared, "The Court seems in recent years to be utilizing its long dormant power to aid the Negro's fight for fair and equal treatment."[1]

The Supreme Court's leadership role on civil rights for African-Americans was to continue until the mid-1960s, modified only by a six-year interlude, from 1947 until January 1953, during which leadership was shared by President Harry Truman. Between 1964 and 1968, as detailed in this book's Introduction and in Chapter 6, the combination of Lyndon Johnson's presidential leadership and Congress's willingness to act finally completed the stalled promise of Reconstruction (most of the laws and constitutional amendments of which had been adopted while the seceded states were excluded from Congress and/or had been forced upon the South as the price of re-entry). The 1960s legislation, with executive branch support, was a major step toward securing effective implementation of equal rights in schools, voting, and the world of

[1] Note 1939, 832.

commerce for black Americans.[2] The further push for equal rights in schooling that came from the U.S. Supreme Court's decisions of the late 1960s and early 1970s (detailed in this book's Introduction), with executive branch implementation, eliminated the vestiges of governmentally imposed school segregation of black children throughout the United States. The post-1960 account of what happened to black civil rights, briefly outlined in this book's Introduction, has been sufficiently detailed by other authors and is not a primary focus of this book.[3]

In setting policy on Asians and Asian-Americans in this (1930–99) period, the elected branches dominated.[4] The economic hardships of the Great Depression intensified Congressional xenophobia. In addition to the measures to deport Mexican residents (including their U.S.-born citizen children) described in Chapter 6, the unemployment crisis stimulated intense opposition to immigration by Filipino laborers, who, by virtue of being American nationals, had been escaping the established ban on Asian immigration. This pressure produced the Tydings-McDuffie Act of 1934, which turned the Philippines into a Commonwealth in a twelve-year transition to independence. Even though independence did not come until 1946, a draconian annual immigration cap of fifty was put on the numbers of Filipinos who could immigrate to the mainland U.S., beginning in 1934.[5]

With respect to Asians, the wartime crisis of World War II brought out both the worst and best from the federal government. During the war, Congress, and the President cooperated in treating innocent Americans with Japanese ancestry as virtual prisoners of war, and the Supreme Court (albeit deceived in significant part by the executive branch) eventually allowed all aspects of this oppressive program excepting only (largely after-the-fact) its long-term imprisonment feature. The correction

---

2 First half of Introduction and in Chapter 6, text at nn. 205 ff.

3 E.g., Rosenberg 2008, Part One and Appendices 1–4.; Klinkner and Smith, 1999, Chapter 9; Tushnet 2010; Balkin 2011; Goldstein 2011-B, 177–9.

4 In the decade of the 1930s the rights of Asians, except for Filipinos, underwent little change. Kim, 1992-B, 47. In keeping with the enhanced concern with the fairness of criminal procedures of the 1930s Supreme Court, the Hughes Court did issue a ruling making it marginally more difficult to prosecute Asians (aliens "ineligible to be naturalized") for a criminal conspiracy leasing land from citizens; in criminal prosecutions, California could not put the burden of proving eligibility to lease or own land on the accused Asian; California would have to both prove the ineligibility and prove that the citizen owner who leased the land knew of the ineligibility—in other words, prove guilt. *Morrison v. California*, 291 U.S. 82 (1934).

5 "Immigration to America" 2015.

of these wartime injustices was a long time coming, but when it did come in the form of apologies and reparations, it came at the hands of Presidents Ford and Carter (i.e., in the 1970s) and, ultimately, from the Congress of 1988.[6]

On the positive side, the World War II pattern of alliances moved President Franklin D. Roosevelt to push Congress to repeal Chinese exclusion from immigration, which it did in December, 1943, in a law that, for the first time in U.S. history, permitted Chinese nationals to become naturalized Americans. It was the President, with an eye to his worldwide diplomatic constituency, who led also in the broader mid-century program of de-racializing our immigration and naturalization laws. Truman, Eisenhower, and Kennedy, all unsuccessfully urged Congress to move more rapidly and more thoroughly to eliminate the anti-Asian racial biases in these laws. Lyndon Johnson eventually persuaded Congress to completely eliminate racial bias from the immigration system by 1965.

The executive branch, in turn, during the decade of the 1930s led the way in persuading Congress to adopt a bold new policy for expanding tribal sovereignty of Native American peoples, in dropping assimilationist pressures upon them, and in attempting to rebuild and reconsolidate tribal land holdings to counter the disastrous impact of the Dawes Act. The elected branches then lost faith with this approach, moving back into an assimilationist direction for the period 1948–60. The government adopted a policy that aimed at terminating both reliance by Indians on federal assistance and terminating tribal structure itself. Even as the Truman Administration moved gradually toward the terminationist policy that was decisively to mark the Eisenhower years, however, it nonetheless pushed to end the disfranchisement of tribal Indians. After the Eisenhower Administration, under President Kennedy and those who followed, the executive branch moved firmly back into the posture of respecting and enhancing tribal sovereignty and respecting tribal culture. Congress followed along with these presidential initiatives, but also enhanced individual rights of Indians vis à vis tribal government with the 1968 Indian Bill of Rights. The enhancement of individual rights produced some Supreme Court decisions, perforce favoring one or another side (tribe vs. Indian individual), but not either pro or anti-Indian as such.

Perhaps coincidentally, during the peak of the termination period, the Supreme Court produced two decisions that have been lambasted by

---

[6] President Reagan opposed the reparation bill of 1988, but in the end did sign it.

advocates for Native Americans: *Tee Hit Ton v. U.S.* (1955) (rejecting a claim to a huge tract of Alaska land under aboriginal title) and *FPC v. Tuscarora Indian Nation*, 361 U.S. 99 (1960) (rejecting an allegation that earlier treaty language rather than later federal law covered a dispute over federal eminent domain power to build a dam). Although Indian tribes did lose both of these cases, it is not obvious to me that Supreme Courts in other eras would have decided them differently. The Court in the modern period, beginning in the 1930s has been willing to check Congressional intrusion on Indian tribal rights by resort to such features of the Constitution as the Just Compensation Clause, but throughout this period, the Court has remained constricted in policy toward Indians, as toward Asians, by the fundamental principle that the elected branches are empowered to control foreign policy, naturalization policy and policy toward the Indian tribes.

LATE 30s HUGHES COURT SHIFT ON BLACKS?

In the late 1930s the Hughes Court took on a dramatically new tilt, due to the appointment of five economically liberal justices by FDR. Hugo L. Black took his seat in 1937; Stanley Reed in 1938; Felix Frankfurter and William O. Douglas in 1939; and Frank Murphy in 1940. With this new constellation, the Court abandoned its Lochnerian hostility to legislative regulation of the economy and turned its attention to the protection of society's less powerful groups, including union members, persons accused of crime, blacks, and practitioners of non-mainstream religions, such as Jehovah Witnesses.[7] The newly emerged Court majority famously signaled this new orientation in Footnote Four of the *U.S. v. Carolene Products* (1938), indicating that it "may" subject to "more exacting judicial scrutiny" not only laws contravening liberties singled out explicitly in the Bill of Rights, but also "legislation which restricts those political processes [such as voting and peaceable assembly] which can ordinarily be expected to bring about repeal of undesirable legislation," and "statutes directed at particular religious, or national, or racial minorities."[8]

Not all of the Court's shift of the late 1930s, however, can be attributed to new personnel. Justices do not, anymore more than elected officials, remain unaware of world political developments. Samples of some justices' thinking about the emerging war in Europe and Asia, and its

---

[7] Bixby 1981.

[8] *United States v. Carolene Products Company*, 304 U.S. 144, 152 (1938).

connection to racism are available. Justice (and later Chief Justice) Stone (a Hoover appointee) wrote privately on the day after he issued the *Carolene Products* decision with its portentous footnote, "I have been deeply concerned about the increasing racial and religious intolerance which seems to bedevil the world, and which I greatly fear may be augmented in this country."[9] Although the famous footnote preceded *Kristallnacht* in Germany by seven months, there is ample evidence that members of the Supreme Court of the late 30s and the World War II years were attentive to the rise of Nazism and its consequences in Europe. Years before he was appointed to the Court, Felix Frankfurter (himself Jewish) wrote to FDR in 1933 warning about the "ferocious anti-semitism and fanatical racism" of Hitlerism.[10] Justice Murphy spoke out publicly in 1940, prior to joining the Court,

> The purveyors of hatred, the provokers of division and strife, the swaggering apostles of force and violence are methodically and with premeditation laboring to bring to the United States the same conditions of group hatred and civil war that have destroyed the peace of Europe.[11]

Whatever inferences individual justices may have drawn from their awareness of the nature of the war raging abroad, it is unreasonable to assume that their thinking on cases before them remained completely uninfluenced by such thoughts.

Whereas the long-term shift of general direction represented in the *Carolene Products* footnote has been the topic of much scholarly discussion, less attention has been paid to the fact that the Hughes Court lent support to the civil rights of black American from its *earliest* years (e.g., *Nixon v. Condon*, 1932; *Powell v. Alabama*, 1932; *Norris v. Alabama*, 1935; *Hollins v. Oklahoma*, 1935; *Brown v. Mississippi*, 1936; *Hale v. Kentucky*, 1938; *Missouri ex rel. Gaines v. U.S.*, 1938; all of these are described below). And the last of these, *Gaines*, was decided eight–one. The Hughes Court of 1938 did not need the two new FDR appointments for its majority supporting the civil rights of black Americans. In fact, it was carrying on a trajectory that began with the White Court of the second decade of the twentieth century.

---

[9] Bixby 1981, 765.
[10] Ibid., 769.
[11] Ibid., 774.

DUE PROCESS REVOLUTION OF HUGHES COURT (1930–41) AND SEQUELAE

The 1930s was the decade in which the 1923 *Moore v. Dempsey* case ripened into a clear cut pattern that then endured through the 40s and 50s; the U.S. Supreme Court would no longer tolerate the sham trials of the South where accused blacks were ramrodded through what were in effect mob-inspired lynchings, thinly disguised by the trappings of judicial procedures. These decisions amounted doctrinally to civil liberties advances for all Americans, but they also gave plain signals to the South that the U.S. Supreme Court would no longer look the other way with respect to blatant injustice toward black defendants.

Denials of Fundamental Fairness under the Hughes (1930–41), Stone (1941–46), and Vinson (1946–53) Courts

Concluding that the Fourteenth Amendment Due Process Clause had been violated, the Hughes Supreme Court as early as 1932 began throwing out convictions that had produced death sentences in a lynch-mob-dominated atmosphere in two decisions involving the (black) Scottsboro Boys—*Powell v. Alabama* (1932)[12] (procedural violation: absence of assistance of counsel to young, impoverished, and uneducated persons facing death penalty in context of lynch mob atmosphere) and *Norris v. Alabama* (1935)[13] (procedural violation: systematic exclusion of blacks from the jury). The justices also threw out on due process violation grounds a third mob-dominated conviction where the main evidence against the three southern black defendants convicted of murdering the man for whom they sharecropped was their confession extracted through torture—*Brown v. Mississippi* (1936).[14] When one deputy during the Brown trial was asked whether he had witnessed the defendant being whipped in order to produce a confession, and after his affirmative reply, was asked how severely he was whipped, the deputy answered, "Not too much for a negro; not as much as I would have done if it were left to me."[15]

This set of precedents then led to several 1940s reversals of convictions of southern blacks on the grounds that they had been based on

---

12 *Powell v. Alabama*, 287 U.S. 45 (1932).
13 *Norris v. Alabama*, 294 U.S. 587 (1935).
14 *Brown v. Mississippi*, 297 U.S. 278 (1936).
15 297 U.S., at 284; Klarman 2004, 129.

coerced confessions: *Chambers v. Florida*, 309 U.S. 227 (1940); *Canty v. Alabama*, 309 U.S. 629 (1940); *White v. Texas*, 310 U.S. 530 (1940); *Lomax v. Texas,* 313 U.S. 544 (1941); *Ward v. Texas* 316 U.S. 547, 552 (1942).[16] All of these decisions were based on the underlying principle that the accused in question had been denied the fundamentally fair hearing required by due process.

If all that southern black arrestees were asking for was a reversal of an unlawful conviction, these precedents proved helpful, but when the federal Justice Department cracked down (finally!) in the 40s and tried prosecuting southern white officials for blatant violations of black civil liberties, success was more elusive. By this time Frank Murphy sat on the Court as an Associate Justice. The Civil Rights Section of the Justice Department, which Murphy had created in 1939 during his year as U.S. Attorney General, brought charges against a southern white sheriff and deputies who beat to death a black arrestee, right after arresting him on a supposed charge of stealing a tire. The charge was violating Section 20 of 18 U.S.C. § 52 (now § 242): willfully depriving their prisoner of a Constitutional right, here, the right not to be deprived of one's life other than by due process of law and to be punished only consequent to conviction in a fair trial.

In *Screws v. U.S.* (1945),[17] the Stone Court majority, in a fractured decision with no majority reasoning, returned the case to Georgia for a new trial on the grounds that the jury instructions had to explain that "willfully" meant with a knowing intent to deprive of due process of law (at 101-6). Local juries refused to convict Screws on the remand (in fact, he continued to serve as sheriff and later was elected to the State Senate[18]), but the legal question posed in the *Screws* case returned to the Vinson Supreme Court in 1951 concerning a different defendant, Police Officer Williams. Williams's jury had received the jury instructions mandated by the *Screws* majority; Williams had brutally beaten four black suspects until they confessed to theft.[19] This time the Court could and did uphold the conviction of the police officer for willful deprivation of a constitutional right (in a five–four vote).

16 Klarman 2004, 528, n.148.
17 *Screws v. U.S.*, 325 U.S. 91 (1945).
18 Wiecek 2006, 657.
19 *Williams v. United States*, 341 U.S. 97 (1951).

Debtor Cases

The Stone Court upheld another conviction of a southern sheriff in one of the cases (*U.S. v. Gaskin*) where it threw out a series of three state-level, phony false-pretenses statutes, similar to the one struck down as peonage in *Bailey v. Alabama* (1911): *Taylor v. Georgia* (1942), *U.S. v. Gaskin* (1944), and *Pollock v. Williams* (1944).[20] These laws presumed the guilt of fraudulent intent when a worker took an advance on pay and then later walked off the job, imposing sentences far in excess of the money owed and then extracting coerced labor to pay for the new debt. Even the Court's most openly racist and pro-segregation member, James Byrnes voted to strike these down.[21] The FDR Justice Department was invoking Congress's 1867 Anti-Peonage Act and bringing prosecutions against sheriffs who applied these laws[22] and the twentieth century post-Fuller Supreme Court did not backtrack in its opposition to such laws.

Right of Equal Access to Juries, 1930–53

The Hughes Court produced a lengthy string of decisions revivifying the right of black access to juries that had lain dormant in the period after the 1883 *Bush v. Kentucky* case,[23] during which time this right had been effectively nullified by the Fuller Court.[24] The Hughes Court finally returned to enforcing this right by reversing convictions obtained in

---

[20] *Taylor v. Georgia*, 15 U.S. 25 (1942), *U.S. v. Gaskin*, 320 U.S. 527 (1944), and *Pollock v. Williams*, 322 U.S. 4 (1944).

[21] Wiecek 2006, 643.

[22] Not all of its prosecutions reached the Supreme Court, but the *Gaskin* case was one that did and the Roosevelt Justice Department filed an amicus brief in the *Taylor* case.

[23] *Bush v. Kentucky* 110 (1883) (ruling unconstitutional the murder conviction and sentence of John Bush, a black man, under a state law that required all-white grand juries). See also *Neal v. Delaware* 370 (1881), which used the drastic disproportion between the local population of blacks (26,000 in a total state population of 150,000) and the number ever called for jury duty—zero—to infer that there must have been discrimination; thereby rendering the black on white murder conviction constitutionally invalid. These were Waite Court decisions.

[24] See Chapter 4 for the string of some dozen jury cases where the Fuller Court either ignored blatantly obvious discrimination or remanded back to the culprit state to decide whether there had been discrimination, thus offering no relief.

systems that had produced obviously rigged jury venires for years.[25] The Hughes Court returned to the practice of the Waite Court of believing its own judgment and common sense in rejecting preposterous claims by southern courts of their inability to find qualified black jurors for years on end. This string began with *Norris v. Alabama*, 294 U.S. 587 (1935) and continued with the reversing of convictions in *Hollins v. Oklahoma*, 295 U.S. 394 (1935); *Hale v. Kentucky*, 303 U.S. 613 (1938); *Pierre v. Louisiana*, 306 U.S. 354 (1939); *Smith v. Texas*, 311 U.S. 128 (1940). These rulings continued to be needed through the Stone Court years (1941–46) and even into the Vinson Court years (1946–53): for instance, *Hill v. Texas*, 316 U.S. 400 (1942) (conviction reversed because no blacks appointed to grand jury for sixteen years); *Patton v. Mississippi*, 332 U.S. 463 (1947) (conviction reversed because no blacks had been appointed to grand or petit juries in the county for thirty years); *Cassell v. Texas*, 339 U.S. 282 (1950) (conviction reversed because jury commissioners chose for grand jury only people they knew and they knew few blacks—the black population was 15.5 percent, and percent of blacks on grand juries over five years was 6.7); and *Avery v. Georgia*, 345 U.S. 559 (1953) (rape conviction thrown out because jury producing the conviction had been selected by drawing names from a container that had white slips for names of white jurors and yellow slips for names of black jurors; jury chosen was all-white; jury commissioners denied purposeful discrimination).[26]

JUDICIARY ON ANTI-BLACK DISCRIMINATION IN NON-CRIMINAL CONTEXT, 1930–53

In the decade of the 1930s, blacks continued to make progress in eliminating white primary laws, but eventually ran into the same road-block that had stymied their efforts against racially restrictive housing covenants:[27] the Court's unwillingness to reach private action that lacked obvious encouragement in official legislation. In 1932, in *Nixon v.*

---

[25] See also *Aldridge v. U.S.*, 283 U.S. 308 (1931), where the Hughes Court reversed a lower court ruling that had forbidden the lawyer for a black defendant to ask jurors during the voir dire whether they harbored prejudice against black people. In doing so, the Court threw out the conviction of a black man for murdering a white police officer in the District of Columbia. Davis and Graham 1995, 74.

[26] Ibid., 74-5, Table 2.3.

[27] See *Corrigan v. Buckley* (1926), discussed in Chapter 5.

Condon,[28] the Hughes Court did strike down a Texas law that empowered the State Executive Committee to set voter qualifications for the primaries (which had resulted in the Committee's banning black participation). Next, however, the state simply eliminated this law, and the Democratic Party itself declared its primaries off limits to non-whites.

Setbacks and Progress on Voting and Housing

The Hughes Court then in *Grovey v. Townsend* (1935)[29] unanimously refused to rule the resulting all-white primary unlawful. It reasoned that the Democratic Party was merely a private association.

On the other hand, the Hughes Court did reiterate the prohibition on grandfather clauses that restricted black voting. In *Lane v. Wilson* (1939), it struck down Oklahoma's law that had been adopted to thwart the *Guinn v. U.S.* (1915 grandfather clause) decision.[30]

In the decade of the 40s the Supreme Court would be changing its mind on both the enforceability of racially restrictive covenants and the legality of the all-white primary. The voting rights change began on the Stone Court with *U.S. v. Classic* (1941).[31] *Classic* involved prosecution of voting officials for ballot tampering and related fraud (under the statutes that are now numbers 18 U.S.C. §241 and 18 U.S.C. §242) with respect to primary voting in Louisiana for Democratic Congressional candidates. The Court did not mention that the frauds were perpetrated against the voters of black precincts![32] Although the Court's reasoning relied pivotally on the rule that the voting in question was for federal officials, and therefore within the purview of Congressional supervisory legislation, it also included the points that the Democratic primary election was an integral part of the procedure for choosing representatives, financed and regulated by the state, and in its practical operation routinely secured the general election victory of the primary nominee.[33]

This latter line of reasoning undermined *Grovey v. Townsend*'s 1935 conclusion that operating the primary election in the South involved only private, not state, action. Not surprisingly, then, in 1944, the Supreme

---

28 *Nixon v. Condon*, 286 U.S. 73 (1932).

29 *Grovey v. Townsend*, 295 U.S. 45 (1935).

30 *Lane v. Wilson*, 307 U.S. 268 (1939). This law had simply given a different date for when one's grandfather needed to have voted in order to make one eligible to vote—1914 instead of 1865.

31 *United States v. Classic*, 313 U.S. 299 (1941).

32 Wiecek 2006, 636.

33 *Classic*, 313, at 311–14.

Court ruled eight–one, in *Smith v. Allwright*,[34] that it had erred in the *Grovey* ruling that had allowed white primaries so long as no state law explicitly authorized the party to prescribe voter qualifications for the primary. Now it ruled that the Fifteenth Amendment prohibits all-white primaries because they are intertwined with the official electoral process.

The Vinson Court continued along this trajectory. When some Texan Democrats fought on for the right to discriminate in choosing Democratic Party candidates by using an organization called the Jaybird Association, which allowed white members only and whose sole purpose was to nominate candidates of the Democratic Party, the Vinson Court saw through the ruse. It declared such procedures unconstitutional in 1953 in *Terry v. Adams*.[35]

Racially restrictive covenants, in turn, were rendered judicially unenforceable by the Vinson Court in the 1948 companion cases, *Shelley v. Kraemer* (covering state jurisdictions) and *Hurd v. Hodge* (covering D.C. and other federal jurisdictions).[36] The Court departed from its 1926 *Corrigan* ruling, to declare that courts are parts of the state apparatus; therefore, when they enforce racial discrimination, this enforcement violates the commands of the equal protection clause. (For *Hurd v. Hodge*, the Court relied on the 1866 Civil Rights Act, since the Fourteenth Amendment is directed at states.) Such private covenants could still be made, as interpersonal promises, but state and local governments could neither enforce nor support them. Because restrictive covenants discriminated against so many minorities, the Supreme Court litigation attracted a number of other minorities to the side of the NAACP, each presenting their own group's angle on opposition to the covenants. These included the American Jewish Congress, the Japanese-American Citizens League (JACL), and the American Indian Citizens League of California.[37]

---

34 *Smith v. Allwright*, 321 U.S. 649 (1944).

35 *Terry v. Adams*, 345 U.S. 461 (1953).

36 *Shelley v. Kraemer*, 334 U.S. 1 (1948); *Hurd v. Hodge*, 334 U.S. 24 (1948). The Hughes Court, confronted with a similar issue eight years earlier, had refused to allow a particular restrictive covenant to be judicially enforced, but did so on a legal technicality; the covenant itself was procedurally flawed. *Hansberry v. Lee*, 311 U.S. 32 (1940). The personal side of the case was made famous by Lorraine Hansberry's play, "Raisin in the Sun." Kamp 1986.

37 Vose 1959, 163–5; *Hurd v. Hodge*, 334 U.S. 24, 30–34 (1948). The JACL continued its support of the NAACP through the *Brown v. Board* litigation. See Chapter 6.

Hughes Court Initiates School Desegregation

The final civil rights advance of the 1930s that, like the others described here, launched a trajectory that continued its advance in the 40s and 50s concerned segregation of publicly supported schools. In 1931, the year that Chief Justice Hughes re-joined the Court, the NAACP assigned a young lawyer, Nathan Margold to develop a litigation strategy for attacking school segregation. Margold disputed the strategy being recommended by other NAACP leaders—a strategy of suing for a writ of mandamus in every school district that provided unequal (per pupil) funding for whites and blacks, to order equalization of expenditures. This strategy, argued Margold, would be counterproductive, because mandamus actions are always retrospective, so new ones would need to be brought every year, and they would need to be brought district by district, having no society-wide, or even state-wide impact. Instead, Margold insisted, *Yick Wo v. Hopkins* (1886)[38] should provide the foundation of the litigation campaign.

One can observe, partly as a result of the evolution of the Margold strategy, a continued intertwining of Asian rights with black rights, in the reasoning of the U.S. Supreme Court. (The deepest roots of this development stretch further back into some of the cases described in Chapter 5.) *Yick Wo v. Hopkins* offered to Margold the inferrable rule of law that:

> [legally imposed] segregation coupled with discrimination resulting from administrative action [e.g., expenditure decisions, decisions to build schools, purchase supplies, hire teachers, etc.] permitted but not required by state statute is just as much a denial of equal protection of the laws as is segregation coupled with discrimination required by express statutory enactment.[39]

Citing *Yick Wo*, he paraphrased the point with the statement that the NAACP should "boldly challenge the constitutionality of school segregation if and when irremediably coupled with discrimination."[40] The outcome of Margold's strategy, if successful, would be that states would have to enforce equalization of facilities (which he believed they would

---

38 *Yick Wo v. Hopkins*, 118 U.S. 356 (1886).
39 Tushnet 1987, 15–16, 26–9.
40 Ibid.

find prohibitively expensive) or else desegregate. The attack would be on "separate but equal" as *practiced*.[41]

In 1933, Margold moved on to a job in the Department of the Interior (where he was to become an important force for the liberalization of U.S. policy toward Indians under Franklin Roosevelt).[42] The specifics of his desegregation strategy were not pursued by the NAACP, but what eventually bore fruit was his inkling that success would lie with proving that segregation is intrinsically discriminatory ("irremediably coupled with discrimination") just as giving unlimited discretion in issuing licenses to prejudiced administrators in San Francisco was found intrinsically discriminatory by the Supreme Court in 1886 in *Yick Wo*.[43] While Margold's report to the NAACP dwelt at length on the *Yick Wo* case, he used *Gong Lum* (1927)[44] (a second Asian rights case) for the capstone of his argument, noting that, "This was precisely what Chief Justice Taft meant in *Gong Lum v. Rice*," where he (Taft) stated, "Had the petition alleged specifically that there was no colored school in Martha Lum's neighborhood to which she could conveniently go, a different question would have been presented … ."[45] The Mississippi Supreme Court had blurred the facts in its *Lum* decision by simply claiming there was a school in every colored district that colored residents could attend.[46] In fact, it is doubtful that Lum's district contained a high school for colored children near enough for her to "conveniently" attend. Colored high schools throughout the South were shockingly sparse in this era.[47] But this segment of Margold's analysis pointed directly to the path that NAACP attorneys later chose to pursue: the claim that states were obligated to provide appropriate higher education to qualified black applicants in every state that provided it to whites.

The NAACP started its attack at the graduate/professional school level, on the grounds that inequality was easiest to prove there. It was not a

---

41 Ibid.

42 Paterson et al, 2005.

43 Tushnet 1987, 15–16, 26–9.

44 *Lum v. Rice*, 275 U.S. 78 (1927).

45 *Gong Lum v. Rice,* 275 U.S. 78, 84 (1927). Margold 1931, 97 (Microfilm, Part 3, Series A Reel 4, Frame 651). I thank Mark Tushnet for referring me to the microfilm collection.

46 *Rice v. Gong Lum*, 139 Miss. 760, 787 (1925).

47 According to Michael Klarman, there were no public high schools for blacks in many Deep South cities until the 1920s and in hundreds of rural counties until after 1945. Klarman 2004, 148. The state of Delaware offered only two "colored" high schools for the entire state. For details on the *Gong Lum* case, see Chapter 5 above.

question of merely unequal funding, as with elementary schools. Rather it was a question of programs existing for whites and NOT existing for blacks. Five southern states, even as late as 1943 (five years after the Supreme Court plainly indicated that this was unconstitutional), had no professional education at all for blacks.[48] Moreover, finding willing litigants against inequities in graduate/professional school availability was likely to be easier than against inequities in children's education; adults wanting to enter graduate school were likely to be more willing to risk facing white efforts at intimidation than parents of elementary students would be to put their children in danger.[49] And finally, the small numbers of blacks ready to enter graduate or professional schools would be far less anger-inducing to white racists than would be the mixing of millions of black school children together with whites.[50]

This approach succeeded in the first case that posed the issue to the Supreme Court, *Missouri ex rel. Gaines v. Canada* (1938).[51] Chief Justice Hughes writing for an eight-justice majority, cited *McCabe v. Atchison, Topeka* (1914) (his own opinion) for the principle that a state may not supply unequal facilities to two different racial groups based on disproportion of usage. In a state that provides law school education for whites, the fact that fewer blacks attend law school is not legitimate grounds for failure to provide law school education within the state for a black individual who does want to attend.[52] And he cited the Chinese rights case *Yick Wo v. Hopkins* (1886) for the principle that "the equal protection of the laws 'is a pledge of the protection of equal laws.'"[53] Laws that say (1) white residents may attend law school at the state-taxpayer-supported University of Missouri but (2) black students, with tuition provided by Missouri, must go out of state if they wish to attend law school, are not "equal laws." Hughes also cited *Gong Lum* but only for its statement that the school facilities furnished must be equal.[54] (He does not cite the specific passage from *Gong Lum* quoted above at n.45 and noted in the Margold report, although this would seem to have been the precise analogue to Gaines's situation.)

For more than twenty years the Fuller Court (1888–1910) had run roughshod over the rights of black Americans, but had shown a measure

---

48 Tushnet 1987, 36.
49 *Ibid.*, 36.
50 Kluger 2004, 136.
51 *Missouri ex rel. Gaines v. Canada*, 305 U.S. 337 (1938).
52 Ibid., 350–52 (1938).
53 Ibid., 350.
54 *Gong Lum*, 275 U.S. 78 at 85 and 86; cited in *Missouri,* 305 U.S. at 344.

of solicitude to the rights of Asians, particularly with respect to administrative abuses (where the Court had the most leeway for corrective actions in the foreign policy realm). When later Supreme Courts turned around with an interest, finally, in requiring equal protection for blacks, and due process for blacks, it should perhaps not surprise readers that the Court ended up citing from its precedents names like Sing Tuck (see Chapter 5) and Yick Wo.

On the civil rights of black Americans, the contrast between the Fuller Court of the 1899 *Cummings v. Board* decision and the Hughes Court of *Gaines* (1938) was stark. In 1899, the *closing* of the only government-operated high school for blacks, where three private schools open to blacks (to which the government did not contribute) were operating and where the state operated a public high school for white girls and subsidized a public high school for white boys, was deemed *not* to violate equal protection of the laws, but in 1930 the Court judged Missouri's provision of full tuition for black students to attend nearby out-of-state government-funded law schools, while actually providing a law school for whites, to violate equal protection.

Desegregation by the Stone (1941–46) and Vinson (1946–53) Courts

The 1940s was a decade in which the first step toward school desegregation that the Hughes Court had taken in the *Missouri ex rel. Gaines* decision was followed with others by succeeding Courts on the topics of interstate transportation and national labor unions, and was also re-affirmed for a law school case in Oklahoma (*Sipuel v. University of Oklahoma*, 332 U.S. 631 (1948)) where the facts were somewhat similar to those faced by Gaines.

The 1940s was also a decade when U.S. national domestic policy stopped treating Asians as comprising a single, indivisible race and started differentiating among Asians by nationality. While U.S. policy toward Asians was bifurcating particularly as between Japanese (whose ancestral homeland was at war with the U.S.) and Chinese (whose ancestral homeland was our wartime ally), at the same time, Supreme Court doctrine was announcing a rule for race discrimination with respect to Japanese-Americans that would later be applied to black Americans. It was first applied in an embryonic version with respect to school desegregation in the District of Columbia (1954), and more fully in the 1960s with respect to anti-miscegenation laws. This rule is still with us. Moreover, the 40s was a decade in which reasoning was used (in a lower federal court) to decide a racial discrimination case involving Mexican-American and Puerto Rican children that would later become the foundation of the reasoning ordering desegregation of black and white schoolchildren across the U.S. in *Brown v. Board* (1954).

Under the Vinson Court (1946–53) two higher education cases were handed down, *McLaurin v. Oklahoma* (1950) and *Sweatt v. Painter* (1950). The reasoning in these, as is detailed below, revealed that racially segregated education was intrinsically unequal and thus could never satisfy equal protection of the laws. This reasoning, as shown in Chapter 6, built upon the reasoning from a federal district court Latino desegregation case in Southern California, *Mendez v. Westminster* (1946). Two NAACP attorneys (the lead attorneys in *Sweatt* and *McLaurin*), Thurgood Marshall and Robert Carter, alerted by Nathan Margold's report to look for ways to show that school segregation was intrinsically discriminatory, had noticed this federal district court opinion and had contacted the attorney on the *Mendez* case to offer to produce an amicus brief to help at the appellate level. (See Chapter 6 for details.) Also under Chief Justice Vinson, the two 1952 public school desegregation cases, *Brown v. Board* and *Bolling v. Sharpe*, were argued. The cases were ordered re-argued the following year and Chief Justice Vinson died before a decision was handed down.

Still, the 1954 *Bolling v. Sharpe* decision, which involved the District of Columbia and therefore the Fifth rather than the Fourteenth Amendment, ended up relying somewhat on reasoning produced by the Stone Court, specifically, in the 1944 Japanese rights case, *Korematsu v. U.S.* This reasoning from *Korematsu* had put into the Fifth Amendment the equal protection concept that categorization by race is a suspect classification in federal law. The reasoning in *Bolling* is more fully explicated later in this chapter. The Stone Court had in a separate case, on the same day of the *Korematsu* decision in 1944, interpreted the Constitution's Fifth Amendment as imposing an "equal protection" principle on the federal legislature with respect to blacks, i.e., as containing the rule that the federal government may not subject blacks to "irrelevant and invidious" discrimination.[55] A decade after ordering school desegregation (both in states and D.C.), the Warren Court would apply the complete rule from *Korematsu* that race is a suspect classification, demanding exacting scrutiny and needing to meet a "very heavy burden of justification," to a

---

[55] *Steele v. Louisville and Nashville Railroad*, 323 U.S. 192, at 202, 203 (1944) (Discussed in the "Labor Union Desegregation" section below).

context involving anti-black discrimination: the justices used the rule to strike down state level anti-miscegenation laws in the mid-1960s.[56]

The transportation cases

In his final year on the Court, Chief Justice Hughes, revivified the language of the 1887 Interstate Commerce Act, just as he had revivified the 1886 *Yick Wo* decision in the *Gaines* case. The 1887 Act had always forbidden subjecting any interstate passenger to "undue or unreasonable prejudice or disadvantage." In decisions in 1887, 1888, and 1889 the Interstate Commerce Commission had ruled that racially separate accommodations on common carriers did not violate the law so long as facilities were *strictly* equal. In these three nineteenth century cases it found them to be *unlawfully unequal*.[57] As time passed, the ICC became lenient, even heedless, about the degree of equality required by the federal statute.[58] Blacks were routinely denied first-class accommodations on many trains in the South, even well after the *McCabe* ruling.[59]

The U.S. Justice Department gradually moved to bring these practices to a halt, beginning with the Hughes Court case of *Mitchell v. U.S.* (April 28, 1941).[60] Mitchell, a black U.S. Congressman, was ousted from his sleeper car accommodation by the Chicago, Rock Island & Pacific Railway Company when the train, heading south, entered Arkansas (the train company did offer a partial refund on the cost of his ticket). Congressman Mitchell tried taking his complaint to the Interstate Commerce Commission, but when they dismissed it, he took it all the way to the U.S. Supreme Court. There FDR's Justice Department filed a memorandum opposing the position of the Interstate Commerce Commission, and siding with Mitchell.[61] The Supreme Court ruled that the ICC erred in thinking that the Arkansas law imposing segregation allowed for frankly unequal treatment and also in thinking that minimal demand by blacks as a group for first-class accommodations constitutionally justified denying them to individual blacks.[62] The Court refrained from forbidding segregation, but insisted that both races must get exact equality of

---

[56] See e.g., *McLaughlin v. Florida,* 379 U.S. 184, 192–3 (1964) and *Loving v. Virginia,* 388 U.S. 1, 9–12 (1967).

[57] See Chapter 4.

[58] Schmidt 1984, 749–51, n.61; Klarman 2004, 217.

[59] *McCabe v. Atchison, Topeka,* 235 U.S. 151 (1914).

[60] Davis and Graham, 83–4; Wiecek 2006, 666–7; *Mitchell v. U.S.*, 313 U.S. 80 (1941).

[61] *Mitchell*, 92.

[62] Ibid., 94, 97.

treatment, irrespective of group frequency of demand for first-class compartments.[63]

In a pair of cases in the late 40s, while still avoiding a direct assault on "separate but equal" the Stone and Vinson Courts produced a pair of decisions that were the inverse of *Hall v. De Cuir* (1877)[64] and *Louisville, New Orleans, and Tex. Ry. v. Mississippi* (1890):[65] These were *Morgan v. Virginia* (1946)[66] and *Bob-Lo Excursion v. Michigan* (1948).[67] The older pair had ruled that a state *desegregation* law burdened the free flow of traffic among the states (so was unconstitutional) and then that a state *segregation* law did not (so was constitutional). The more recent pair ruled that a state law imposing racial segregation on interstate buses burdened the free flow of traffic interstate (so was *unconstitutional* for interstate travel lines), and that a state *desegregation* law did not burden the free flow of foreign commerce (so was constitutional).

In 1950 the Vinson Court handled a case that reprised the issues of *Mitchell v. U.S.* (1941) except that it involved denial of dining car access instead of sleeper car access, *Henderson v. U.S.* (1950).[68] It, too, involved a black, high-level official of the U.S. Government traveling in the South. In *Henderson*, too, (this time under the Truman Administration) the Justice Department parted ways with the ICC; it both submitted a brief for Henderson and presented oral argument against the ICC policy.[69] The ICC had not gotten the message of the *McCabe* (1914) precedent. The Henderson denial of service took place in the same year that Mitchell was handed down, but took nine years to reach the Supreme Court because in the course of hearings and trials, the ICC kept modifying its policies. At the time of Henderson's travel, any white in the dining car

---

63 *Mitchell v. U.S.*

64 95 U.S. 485 (1877).

65 133 U.S. 587 (1890).

66 328 U.S. 373 (1946). *Morgan* was handed down on June 3, 1946, having been argued in March. Chief Justice Stone died on April 22, weeks before the decision. Chief Justice Vinson did not take office until June 21 of 1946. Justice Stone, having heard the arguments in *Morgan* (in March), was perhaps included in the majority vote, but one cannot tell because it is not customary to list those voting in the majority. That majority with his vote would have been five out of eight; without him, it would have been four out of seven. Justice Jackson is listed (at 328 U.S. 373, 386) as not having participated.

67 333 U.S. 28 (1948). These two cases were brought by the NAACP attorneys, without any Justice Department participation as amicus.

68 *Henderson v. U.S.*, 339 U.S. 816 (1950).

69 Thanks to Jonathan Entin of CWRU for alerting me to the fact of oral argument.

got served ahead of any black, so Henderson never got service for the whole length of his trip. By the time the case reached the Supreme Court, the policy of the railway was to partition off one table for travel in the South for the use of black customers and to allow no whites to use it. Since blacks used the dining car only 5 percent of the time and there were a total of eleven tables, the ICC upheld this policy as allotting to blacks even more than their share. Under the rule from *McCabe* against having the law allow unequal treatment of individuals based on racial group proportion of use, this was an easy decision; the Court's vote rejecting the ICC rule was unanimous.

President Truman's Attorney General asked the Court in *Henderson* to overrule *Plessy*, but the Court did not do so explicitly. *McLaurin v. Oklahoma*, handed down the same day, as I argue below, did so implicitly, at least with respect to state-funded education. A year earlier, in 1949, the Truman Administration had asked Congress to specifically forbid racial segregation in interstate transportation. The executive branch was ready for an end to separate but equal.[70] Congress was still handcuffed by southern filibuster. The Supreme Court was ready to act decisively in all three cases (*McLaurin, Sweatt v. Painter*, and *Henderson*) but not in terms as bold as those requested by the Truman Justice Department.

Labor union desegregation

While the Roosevelt Administration was timid about forcing either employers or the military to desegregate, the Stone Court by unanimous vote in 1944 interpretively inserted racial equity into the Railway Labor Act of 1934,[71] in *Steele v. Louisville and Nashville Railroad*.[72] The case was argued not by Justice Department lawyers, but by Charles Houston and Thurgood Marshall of the NAACP.[73] This case was decided on the same day as *Korematsu v. U.S.*, where the Court was reaffirming and strengthening its declaration from *Hirabayashi v. U.S.* from the year before, about equal protection principles that would apply, for the first

---

[70] Wiecek 2006, 670–71; Klarman, 219.

[71] Act of 27 June, 1934, Ch.691, 48 Stat. 1185.

[72] *Steele v. Louisville and Nashville Railroad*, 323 U.S. 192 (1944). See also its companion case that granted relief to the petitioner following the logic of *Steele: Tunstall v. Brotherhood of Locomotive Firemen and Enginemen, Ocean Lodge No. 76 et al.*, 323 U.S. 210 (1944).

[73] Wiecek 2006, 644.

time, to the federal government via the Due Process Clause of the Fifth Amendment:[74]

> Distinctions between citizens solely because of their ancestry are, by their very, nature odious to a free people whose institutions are founded upon the doctrine of equality. For that reason, legislative classification or discrimination based on race alone has often been held to be a denial of equal protection [citing two state-level precedents and one under the Philippines Constitution Equal Protection Clause]. We may assume that these considerations would be controlling here [i.e., as restrictions on the federal government via the Fifth Amendment Due Process Clause] were it not for the fact that the danger of espionage and sabotage, in time of war and of threatened invasion, calls upon the military authorities to scrutinize every relevant fact bearing on the loyalty of populations in the danger areas. ... [R]acial discriminations are in most circumstances irrelevant, and therefore prohibited [in federal, as well as state, legislation].

In *Korematsu* the Court would be announcing the new, clear rule for federal-level law, "[a]ll legal restrictions which curtail the civil rights of a single racial group are immediately suspect" and are to be subjected to "the most rigid scrutiny."[75] The Court, however, chose in the same day's *Steele* case not to cite the brand-new *Korematsu* ruling but to rely on the same three precedents—two state-level and one territorial-level—that it had cited the year before in *Hirabayashi v. U.S.*[76]

The Stone Court in *Steele* cited these precedents for the principle that since federal law had empowered the union to be the exclusive bargaining representative for the black workers (who were excluded by the union from membership), as well as for the white workers (who were the union members), the union had to operate under the same constitutional restrictions as those applying to the federal government (323 U.S., at 198). In order keep the law from clashing with those constitutional restrictions, the Court presumed that Congress had intended to abide by the Constitution, and therefore interpreted the Railway Labor Act as *requiring* the Union to represent equally the interests of all the employees in the bargaining unit, not just the interests of its all-white membership. Thus, the Court enjoined against enforcement of the union-negotiated

---

74 *Hirabayashi v. U.S.* 320 U.S. 81, 100 (1943).

75 *Korematsu v. U.S.*, 323 U.S. 214, 216 (1944).

76 *Steele*, citing at 203 *Yick Wo v. Hopkins,*118 U.S. 356; *Yu Cong Eng v. Trinidad,* 271 U. S. 500; *Missouri ex rel. Gaines v. Canada,* 305 U.S. 337; *Hill v. Texas*, 316 U.S. 400. *Missouri ex rel. Gaines*, a third state-level case, is one that the *Steele* opinion added to the three that had been cited in the extended quotation from *Hirabayashi.*

contract, which would otherwise have excluded blacks from all but the most menial jobs with the Railway, reserving the higher paying jobs for its white membership. December 18, 1944 is the date on which the Supreme Court both ruled clearly in *Korematsu* that any law, whether state or federal, penalizing a single racial group would be "immediately suspect," and ruled, in *Steele*, that strictures against invidious racial discrimination, taken from state law now to regulate federal law, will apply to federal-level discrimination against blacks as well as Asians. It is worth noting that at this time President Franklin Roosevelt was still heading up a civil service where the majority of jobs held by blacks were in menial positions.[77] This Court decision implied that such hiring patterns, if intentional, were unconstitutional.

The Stone Court decided one other labor union discrimination case, *Railway Mail Assn. v. Corsi* (1945).[78] Less innovative than *Steele* and also unanimous as to result, this decision ruled that it did not violate the Fourteenth Amendment for New York to legislate that no labor organization could "deny any person membership by reason of his race, color, or creed, or [] deny any member, by reason of race, color, or creed, equal treatment in designation for employment, promotion, or dismissal by any employer."[79]

Desegregation of restaurants and schools

With the Truman Administration ready for an end to segregation by 1950, the Vinson Court acted against both restaurant segregation and school segregation. For the former, it had a relatively easy case. District of Columbia officials decided in 1950 to start enforcing antidiscrimination statutes of 1872 and 1873 that had lain dormant for several decades.[80] These prohibited public eating establishments to refuse on the basis of race to serve, or to seat in the same room with others, any well-behaved person. The restaurant argued that the laws had been superseded and were no longer in force. The U.S. Supreme Court in 1953 unanimously ruled against the restaurant. Again the Justice Department had presented an amicus brief arguing for action against segregation, but this time it was the Eisenhower Administration, continuing in the presidential path

---

77 Eleanor Roosevelt Papers Project N.D.

78 *Railway Mail Assn. v. Corsi*, 326 U.S. 88 (1945).

79 Section 43, New York Civil Rights Law.

80 *John R. Thompson Co. v. District of Columbia*, 203 F.2d 579, 581 (1953).

set forth during the Truman years.[81] Eisenhower himself, five years later, in his announcement sending federal troops into Little Rock to protect black school children from angry white mobs, said of the 1954 school desegregation decisions, "Our personal opinions about the decision[s] have no bearing on the matter of enforcement," (implicitly suggesting his private opposition to them) but in fact his Justice Department had argued in *Bolling v. Sharpe* (1954) for a declaration that school segregation in the District of Columbia was unconstitutional.[82]

The Vinson Court handed down a total of four decisions on school desegregation, all concerning state university graduate or professional education. The first two both involved the same woman, Ada Sipuel (later Ada Fisher). She applied to the University of Oklahoma Law School in 1945, and was rejected strictly because of race. She was told that Oklahoma would provide a law school for blacks when "enough of them applied." She did not wait around, but went to court. When the Supreme Court decided in her favor in 1948, it did so unanimously and per curiam, in a four paragraph opinion and simply citing *Missouri ex rel. Gaines*,[83] which, as already shown, was based in part on both *Yick Wo v. Hopkins* and *Gong Lum v. Rice*. Oklahoma then rented a few rooms and hired a few part-time attorneys and called it a black law school. Her attorney went back to the U.S. Supreme Court (still in 1948), asking for a writ of mandamus ordering that the University of Oklahoma be ordered to admit her to its law school. This the U.S. Supreme Court refused, citing the fact that the original lawsuit had simply asked for admission to a state law school and had not presented an argument against segregation as such.[84] Both Murphy and Rutledge dissented.

The *Sipuel* decisions clarified the limits of the *Gaines* ruling. Together the two decisions were steps toward desegregation only in the practical sense envisioned by Nathan Margold. If southern states were actually forced to provide two substantially equal school systems, the cost would have become so prohibitive that they would have abandoned officially required segregation (or so Margold believed). The doctrinal foundation about to be adopted in 1950 in *Sweatt* and *McLaurin* was fundamentally

---

[81] *District of Columbia v. John R. Thompson Co.*, 346 U.S. 100 (1953). The government brief was presented by Philip Elman, Assistant Solicitor General of the Roosevelt, Truman, and Eisenhower Administrations. Saxon 1999.

[82] *Bolling v. Sharpe*, 347 U.S. 497, 498 (1954). Farber 1982, (quoting Eisenhower's announcement) 396.

[83] *Sipuel v. Oklahoma*, 332 U.S. 631 (1948). Wiecek 2006, 684.

[84] *Fisher v. Hurst*, 333 U.S. 147 (1948). Fisher was Sipuel's married name.

different. In these cases the Vinson Court was finally concluding that separate *could not* be equal.

On June 5, 1950, the Vinson Court unanimously handed down these two decisions, accompanied by reasoning that tolled the death knell for school segregation in America. The Truman Justice Department had again filed briefs to advocate desegregation,[85] and numerous interest groups, as well as state attorneys general, had filed briefs on both sides. The decisions, *Sweatt v. Painter* and *McLaurin v. Oklahoma*, dealt respectively with a state university law school[86] and a state university graduate program in Educational Psychology.[87] The reasoning delivered in each decision, however, meant that "separate" when applied to racially separate schools in the U.S. was going to always be unequal. These decisions fell into a series by which the Court now made plain that, once faced directly with the question, it would no longer tolerate separate and unequal facilities imposed as governmental mandates.

The pivotal move in the Court's reasoning looked beyond physical inequalities in what the states were offering the two races, to what the Court called "intangible factors." The earliest federal court case to do this was decided in 1946 in California on behalf of desegregation for Latinos, *Mendez v. Westminster*. The NAACP lead attorneys for Sweatt and McLaurin, Thurgood Marshall and Robert Carter, had submitted an amicus brief for the appellate review of this earlier case and had based their respective arguments for these 1950 cases upon this brief. (See Chapter 6 for details.)

Texas claimed that the University of Texas Law School (for whites) was "substantially equivalent" to the new law school that Texas had quickly opened up for blacks after Heman Sweatt had applied to UT Law and been rejected on account of race and then been ordered admitted to a law school by a state court in 1946. This court had allowed the state time to put the new school together. Instead of enrolling in the new law school when it opened in February of 1947, Sweatt appealed on the grounds that the facilities offered were unequal. When the U.S. Supreme Court examined the two schools in 1950, it described the differences as follows (at pp. 632–4):

> The University of Texas Law School, from which petitioner was excluded, was staffed by a faculty of sixteen full-time and three part-time professors, some of whom are nationally recognized authorities in their field. Its student

---

85 Wiecek 2006, 687; Klarman 2004, 210.

86 *Sweatt v. Painter*, 339 U.S. 629 (1950).

87 *McLaurin v. Oklahoma*, 339 U.S. 637 (1950).

> body numbered 850. The library contained over 65,000 volumes. Among the other facilities available to the students were a law review, moot court facilities, scholarship funds, and Order of the Coif affiliation. The school's alumni occupy the most distinguished positions in the private practice of the law and in the public life of the State. It may properly be considered one of the nation's ranking law schools.
>
> The law school for Negroes which was to have opened in February, 1947, would have had no independent faculty or library. The teaching was to be carried on by four members of the University of Texas Law School faculty, who were to maintain their offices at the University of Texas while teaching at both institutions. Few of the 10,000 volumes ordered for the library had arrived, nor was there any full-time librarian. The school lacked accreditation.
>
> Since the trial of this case, respondents report the opening of a law school at the Texas State University for Negroes. It is apparently on the road to full accreditation. It has a faculty of five full-time professors; a student body of 23; a library of some 16,500 volumes serviced by a full-time staff; a practice court and legal aid association, and one alumnus who has become a member of the Texas Bar.
>
> Whether the University of Texas Law School is compared with the original or the new law school for Negroes, we cannot find substantial equality in the educational opportunities offered white and Negro law students by the State. In terms of number of the faculty, variety of courses and opportunity for specialization, size of the student body, scope of the library, availability of law review and similar activities, the University of Texas Law School is superior.

These differences are so extreme that it is hard to believe that the lower courts ruled the schools "substantially equivalent." But these are the sorts of differences that can be corrected by money if the state is intensely enough committed to segregation. What the Court said next could not be corrected by money, and this consideration meant that "separate" would henceforth always be found unequal (and therefore unconstitutional) in the realm of schooling.

> What is more important, the University of Texas Law School possesses to a far greater degree those qualities which are incapable of objective measurement but which make for greatness in a law school. Such qualities, to name but a few, include reputation of the faculty, experience of the administration, position and influence of the alumni, standing in the community, traditions and prestige. It is difficult to believe that one who had a free choice between these law schools would consider the question close. (at p. 634).

In a white-dominated and racist society, these sorts of reputational factors would almost inevitably stay unequal in a dual school system. An outstanding black school might someday become the "black Harvard" but it would not be Harvard. And even more decisively, the Court turned to another sort of intangible factor—education in the ability to communicate effectively with the dominant race.

> The law school, the proving ground for legal learning and practice, cannot be effective in isolation from the individuals and institutions with which the law interacts. Few students and no one who has practiced law would choose to study in an academic vacuum, removed from the interplay of ideas and the exchange of views with which the law is concerned. The law school to which Texas is willing to admit petitioner excludes from its student body members of the racial groups which number 85% of the population of the State and include most of the lawyers, witnesses, jurors, judges and other officials with whom petitioner will inevitably be dealing when he becomes a member of the Texas Bar. With such a substantial and significant segment of society excluded, we cannot conclude that the education offered petitioner is substantially equal to that which he would receive if admitted to the University of Texas Law School. (at p. 634).

George McLaurin had similarly been refused admission to the University of Oklahoma graduate school's Ph.D. program in Education strictly on the grounds of race. When he obtained a court ruling that Oklahoma must offer him the graduate education that it offers to whites, the Oklahoma legislature responded by enacting a rule that blacks could be admitted to the University but on a segregated basis. McLaurin was admitted, and provided with a desk labeled "colored" "in an anteroom adjoining the classroom;" a desk so labeled in the library; and a seat in the cafeteria also so labeled. He was ordered to eat at a special time when other students would not be there.[88] The Court's reasoning in the *Sweatt v. Painter* case on the importance of learning how to communicate with members of the dominant race makes it easy to predict the outcome in *McLaurin v. Oklahoma*. There the Court said, in relevant part, the following: "The result is that appellant is handicapped in his pursuit of effective graduate instruction. Such restrictions impair and inhibit his ability to study, to engage in discussions and exchange views with other students, and, in general, to learn his profession."[89]

These unequal reputational factors and communicative factors would always be present in a dual school system. The Supreme Court had laid its doctrinal cards on the table. That the Supreme Court would mandate

---

88 *McLaurin v. Oklahoma*, 339 U.S. 637, 640 (1950).
89 Ibid., at 641.

desegregation of public schools in *Brown v. Board of Education I* (1954) and *II* (1955) was now just a matter of time.[90]

EXECUTIVE BRANCH AND BLACK AMERICANS, 1933–52

Franklin Delano Roosevelt, 1933–45

Beyond its judicial appointments, the FDR executive branch beginning in its second term, in 1937, instituted prosecutions in the South against white farmers for violations of anti-peonage laws with respect to their black tenant farmers,[91] and continued these during the years 1938 and 1941.[92] FDR followed up on the (1938) *Carolene Products* footnote from the Court by appointing Frank Murphy to head the Justice Department in 1939, where the latter established a Civil Liberties Unit, whose title changed soon to the Civil Rights Section (and eventually became the Civil Rights Division).[93] Murphy had already established a reputation as a defender of racial justice through his career as local judge, mayor, and governor, in Michigan.[94] The Civil Rights Unit prepared a memo in 1939 on existing civil rights laws that could be used to bring prosecutions and circulated it to U.S. Attorneys around the country as a way of stimulating litigation to correct violations of the civil rights of African-Americans.[95] And FDR's Justice Department brought charges against a southern white policeman in 1940 for torturing a black prisoner to extract a confession,

---

90 *Brown v. Bd. I*, 347 U.S. 483 (1954); *Brown v. Bd. II*, 349 U.S. 349 U.S. 294 (1955). The Court followed *Brown I* with a series of by then unsurprising *per curiam* decisions to admit black litigants to additional state universities and state colleges. University of Florida: *Florida ex rel. Hawkins v. Bd.*, 347 U.S. 971 (1954); Louisiana State University: *Tureaud v. Bd.*, 347 U.S. 971 (1954); University of Alabama: *Lucy v. Adams*, 350 U.S. 1 (1955); University of North Carolina: *Bd. v. Frazier*, 350 U.S. 979 (1956). Davis and Graham 1995, 118.

91 Bixby 1981, 781.

92 Ibid. These prosecutions did not reach the U.S. Supreme Court, but the FDR Justice Department did file an amicus brief in the first of the two 1940s decisions by the Supreme Court that threw out state-level, phony false-pretenses statutes, similar to the one struck down in *Bailey v. Alabama* (1911): *Taylor v. Georgia* (1942) and *Pollock v. Williams* (1944). For a Roosevelt era peonage prosecution that did reach the Supreme Court, see *U.S. v. Gaskin* (1944).

93 Wiecek 2006, 650; Bixby 1981, 781.

94 Bixby, ibid., 770–71, n.179.

95 Ibid., 781–2.

utilizing the same civil rights statute that the Supreme Court would struggle with in *Screws v. U.S.* (1945).[96]

In December, 1941, the Roosevelt Administration, fearful of how our wartime enemies might gain propaganda value from the true racial situation here, developed a new tactic for prosecuting coerced labor situations in the deep South. The basic and widespread practice finally being confronted by the federal government, a practice which ensnared hundreds of thousands of blacks, was to round up blacks on flimsy charges, such as vagrancy or leaving a labor contract, then issuing an unpayable fine, then letting the fine be paid by a private contractor, who then imposed increasingly lengthy periods of servitude in ostensible "payment" for the fine. The servitude was enforced at gunpoint, and with whippings and nightly shackles.[97] Journalist/historian Douglas Blackmon recounts that one of every nineteen black males over the age of twelve in Alabama "was captured in some form of involuntary servitude."[98]

For these blacks who were simply tyrannized into forced labor situations, without the recourse of presumed evasion of a debt (so not technically in peonage), FDR's Attorney General, Francis Biddle issued Circular No.3591 five days after the Pearl Harbor attack, urging prosecutions that went after southerners for simply re-imposing slavery and that used existing civil rights laws, some dating back to before the Civil War. For some forty years the Justice Department had been declining to prosecute these widespread practices, despite ample documentation of them, leaving them to local jurisdictions that ignored them. These prosecutions now produced convictions throughout World War II.[99] Moreover, the Justice Department attorneys under Attorney General Biddle along with U.S. Attorneys in the South engaged in a widespread educational effort during this decade aimed at southern legislators and law enforcement personnel, urging the rescinding and the non-enforcement of laws aimed at curtailing the mobility of black workers in

96 *U.S. v. Sutherland*, 37 F. Supp. 344 (1940). The federal prosecution proceeded up through two mistrials, but obtained no conviction. Shimsky 2009, 129.

97 Blackmon 2008-A, unfortunately, is not entirely clear on how widespread this practice was. Early in the book he states the number of victims at 100,000–200,000, p. 7. Toward the end of the book he gives a figure as "almost certainly" in the millions, p. 375.

98 Ibid., 375.

99 Ibid., 377–82; Blackmon 2008-B; Goluboff 2009, 1457–9.

the South, since such laws promoted the involuntariness of labor, broadly speaking.[100]

On the other hand, FDR withstood black pressure to adopt the more controversial measure of desegregating the military during World War II, and did not aggressively enforce desegregation of defense industries. In order to stave off a large March on Washington, he did issue Executive Order 8802 of June 25, 1941, ordering non-discrimination in the federal civil service and creating a Fair Employment Practices Committee. The latter had power to investigate and publicize claims of unfair job discrimination in defense industries, and also to negotiate quietly in order to work out plans for hiring blacks in ways that would minimize upsetting white employees. This committee had no power to impose a penalty on resistant employers. In May, 1943, he issued a second executive order, Number 9346, establishing a second FEPC, the first having ceased operations; this one had much greater staffing and funding, and reported substantially greater success.[101] His administration also tripled the hiring of blacks into the federal civil service but continued the pattern of placing the majority of these into menial positions.[102]

The FEPC in its second version, according to a recent careful economic analysis, did produce a measurable and enduring improvement in the quantity and quality of black employment *outside the South*. The FEPC, by its own acknowledgment, did not have success in reducing employment discrimination in the South (where most blacks still resided) and the Roosevelt Administration, attentive to the southern wing of the party and to the volatility of the issue in that region, was not inclined to force change there.[103]

It was also disinclined to promote voting rights for southern blacks. FDR's Justice Department did successfully prosecute *U.S. v. Classic* (1941), which ruling, by legitimating Congressional control over primaries where federal offices are at stake, paved the way for the demise of the all-white primary in *Smith v. Allwright* (1944). However, neither the Justice Department brief for *Classic* nor the Court opinions for it mentioned that the primary ballots alleged to have been tampered with were those of southern blacks![104] And when the NAACP's Thurgood Marshall approached the Justice Department for a helpful amicus brief to challenge all-white primaries for the 1944 *Smith v. Allwright* litigation,

[100] Goluboff ibid., 1463–4.
[101] Collins 2001, 273-4.
[102] Eleanor Roosevelt Papers Project N.D.
[103] Ibid., 283–4.
[104] Wiecek 2006, 636; Bixby 1981, 793–7.

both Attorney General Francis Biddle and Solicitor General Herbert Wechsler turned him down on the grounds that they wanted to avoid alienating the southern Senators who controlled the Judiciary Committee.[105]

FDR was walking a fine line; now that there were northern black voters in significant numbers, he did need to make some gestures in support of civil rights for blacks. Upholding federal anti-peonage laws and prosecuting police who murdered or tortured suspects were relatively non-controversial measures by the 1940s.[106] FDR's Justice Department also supported the right of (more affluent) blacks to purchase and receive first-class accommodations within interstate travel. In the early 1940s this right would likely not directly affect massive numbers of black persons. His administration's pro-civil rights gestures were limited, probably because white southern Democrats were a significant portion of FDR's electoral coalition.

Nonetheless, Roosevelt had another constituency besides U.S. voters. He was U.S. commander-in-chief and, after 1941, leader of the Allied forces against the Axis powers. When the latter, in an attempt to demonstrate to people of color that they would be better off under Axis powers, publicized to the world the fact that one Cleo Wright, a black man, was lynched in 1942 in Sikeston Missouri, the FDR Administration did an about-face on lynchings. Previously, it had avoided prosecuting *even* those that were incontrovertibly within federal jurisdiction because they had interstate dimensions; now, it would actively investigate every lynching (and would attempt to prosecute Wright's killers) because lynchings had become a threat to national defense: they provided propaganda fodder to our enemies.[107]

President Harry S. Truman and Blacks, 1945–52

When Harry Truman acceded to the presidency upon the death of FDR, he immediately appointed Tom Clark to head the Justice Department as Attorney General. The very next year, Truman asked Clark to develop a more comprehensive Justice Department policy for preventing lynchings.[108] Attorney General Clark proceeded to organize the President's

---

105 Wiecek ibid., 637. For colloquy between Biddle and FDR on the issue, see Bixby 1981, 794, n.342.

106 Klarman 2004, 218, 235, 288.

107 Ibid., 176–7.

108 Ibid., 185, suggests that a 1946 flare-up of particularly brutal racial violence triggered this move by Truman. There was a race riot in Tennessee, a

Committee on Civil Rights, which by 1947 published a nearly 200-page-long report, *To Secure these Rights*; this report denounced the pervasive Jim Crow system with terms like "moral havoc" and "moral decay," and "moral dry rot."[109] It pointed to massive economic costs from segregation and to serious diplomatic costs that weakened our Cold War efforts. It called for a vigorous federal program to end racial discrimination in the military, voting, education, interstate transportation, and in employment, by beefing up the Civil Rights Section of the Justice Department, creating a Civil Rights protection section in the FBI, pro-actively pursuing both civil and criminal violations of civil rights, adopting an anti-lynching law and strengthening and broadening the Anti-Peonage Law. It also advocated creating a permanent Commission on Civil Rights to monitor and enforce these changes. And it advocated a review of the World War II program that had incarcerated people on the basis of [Japanese] ancestry and urged development of policies to prevent such occurrence in the future.[110] In the 1948 recodification of the federal criminal code, Congress adopted many of these proposals, particularly those bearing on involuntary servitude.[111]

Also in 1947, Attorney General Clark supervised the drafting of the brief for the *Shelley v. Kraemer* (1948) case, for which he then presented oral argument at the U.S. Supreme Court the following year. After his arguments persuaded the Supreme Court to declare racially restrictive covenants legally unenforceable, he then arranged to have his legal brief published under the title *Prejudice and Property: An Historic Brief Against Racial Covenants*.[112]

In July of 1948, with Executive Orders 9980 and 9981, Truman followed up on his Civil Rights Committee's recommendation to desegregate the U.S. Armed Forces and the federal civil service, moves which caused Dixiecrats to bolt the party. (The presidential Dixiecrat candidate that November carried four states of the deep South: Louisiana,

---

quadruple lynching in Monroe, Georgia (of two African-American war veterans and their wives), and a sheriff's beating of a black veteran, Isaac Woodard, that blinded him. These may indeed have triggered the assignment to the committee, but similar violence had been going on intermittently since the Civil War. Truman acted against it more forcefully than earlier presidents.

109 President's Committee on Civil Rights 1947, 140 and 139.

110 Ibid., "Chapter IV A Program of Action: The Committee's Recommendations," pp. 137 ff.

111 Blackmon 2008-A, 381; Act of June 25, 1948, ch. 645, 62 Stat. 683 (codified at 18 U.S.C.).

112 Wiecek 2006, 431.

Mississippi, Alabama, and South Carolina.) Ultimate supervision of the desegregation of the civil service was lodged in a Fair Employment Practices Board within the Civil Service Commission.[113]

Desegregation of the military began with a vote in the Democratic Party Convention, earlier in July of 1948. White southern delegates lost the vote and left the Convention. This vote overrode initial resistance to this desegregation plank by the advisers of Truman and by the Platform Committee. Once the platform plank was adopted, however, Truman jumped fully onboard; he issued the two Executive Orders on July 26.[114] The Air Force and Navy complied by the end of the year, and the Army stalled up through the early 1950s, but did integrate by the end of Truman's term.[115]

In 1949 Truman nominated Clark to the Supreme Court, but his Justice Department remained on the pro-civil rights path that Clark had established. It continued bringing criminal charges against southern police officials for brutalizing suspects.[116] It continued the break with the ICC in insisting that first class accommodations be made available to blacks—a break initiated by the Roosevelt Administration—but went further by arguing in 1950 that *Plessy v. Ferguson* should be overruled and that separation by race should not be permitted in interstate transportation.[117] President Truman himself in 1949 asked Congress to outlaw segregation in interstate transportation.[118]

In 1950 the Truman Justice Department presented amicus briefs arguing for the desegregation of higher education in both *McLaurin* and *Sweatt*. And during the three final years of his presidency, Truman pushed the U.S. Army steadily, in order to overcome resistance by the top brass to his executive order to desegregate.[119]

Assessment of Executive Branch on Desegregation, 1933–53

Despite the public reputation of Eleanor Roosevelt as an advocate of rights for black people, the hesitancy of her husband to use the

---

[113] Truman 1948.

[114] "Desegregation of the Armed Forces: Chronology."

[115] *Ibid.*; Jensen 2005.

[116] *Screws v. U.S.*, 325 U.S. 91 (1945) (started under FDR; completed under Truman) and *Williams v. United States*, 341 U.S. 97 (1951) (Truman).

[117] *Henderson v. U.S.*, 339 U.S. 816 (1950); Wiecek 2006, 670–71; Klarman 2004, 219.

[118] Klarman, *ibid.*

[119] "Desegregation of the Armed Forces: Chronology."

Presidency to promote these rights is beyond dispute. Although, in June of 1941, to stave off a march on Washington by militant blacks protesting unemployment during World War II, he agreed to create a Fair Employment Practices Committee, the committee had no coercive powers and did virtually nothing to improve the segregated employment picture in the southern U.S. Its conciliation powers did facilitate some black hiring in the North, where opposition was less intense. His Justice Department tread warily in arguing Supreme Court cases, so as to avoid alienating southern members of the Judiciary Committee in the Senate. It is true that FDR did appoint racial liberals or moderates to the Supreme Court; this caused the Supreme Court to move well ahead of his Justice Department on issues of racial justice. His Justice Department refused, for instance, to offer an amicus brief against the white primary in the very case (*Smith v. Allwright*, 1944) where the Court was to declare such primaries unconstitutional, and did not participate in the lawsuit to desegregate railway unions in the 1940s. On the other hand, in part to counter accurate anti-American propaganda during the war, and also perhaps because of growing black voting clout in northern cities, his wife's influence, or even out of personal conviction, FDR did have his Justice Department act against some of the most egregious southern racist excesses: peonage in the late 1930s and the 40s, police torture of black suspects in the 1940s, and refusals to offer elite accommodations to blacks (who happened to be, specifically, high-level U.S. government officials) in interstate travel in the 1940s. During World War II, when Axis powers used anti-black southern violence against blacks for propaganda value, the FDR Administration then cracked down on anti-black lynchings, but not before then. Similarly, it cracked down on the non-debt-related coerced servitude of blacks in the deep South, which it had earlier ignored.

As early as 1946, Harry Truman, who acceded to office from the vice-presidency in 1945, asked Attorney General Tom Clark to develop a comprehensive civil rights policy with particular attention to preventing lynchings. This resulted in the creation of a Committee on Civil Rights and a massive report in 1947 with wide-ranging policy-recommendations. By the presidential campaign of 1948, Truman's advisers decided that the potential importance of the black vote for swinging large northern states with their sizable numbers of electoral votes outweighed the potential cost of southern support, and Truman gave his support to the plank of the platform that called for desegregating the military and civil service. His Justice Department actively promoted desegregation in federal court, continuing FDR's litigation efforts against segregation in interstate travel and the bringing of criminal charges against southern police officials for brutalizing suspects. Truman's administration expanded upon these by proposing to Congress that segregation in travel be explicitly outlawed; and by presenting briefs for the *Shelley v. Kraemer* restrictive residential covenants case and its D.C. companion case, *Hurd v. Hodge*; and by asking the Supreme Court, as a matter of constitutional law, to end the rule of "separate but equal" from *Plessy v. Ferguson* (1896). It also presented amicus briefs in the law school and graduate school desegregation cases (1950) that resulted in rulings forecasting an end to all school segregation.

From 1911 until the time of the Truman Administration, the Supreme Court had been in the lead, however modestly, in promoting justice and civil rights for black Americans. Between 1947 and the end of Truman's term in January 1953, though, the executive branch was playing at least a co-equal leadership role with the Vinson Court. Congress, shackled by southern filibusters, was the laggard, and continued to be so until 1964.[120] At this point, as detailed in the book's Introduction and in Chapter 6,[121] Lyndon Johnson, who like Truman had acceded to the presidency from the office of vice-president, successfully pushed through Congress in the years 1964–68 the most successful civil rights agenda seen in this country to date. From 1969 until the early 1990s, the U.S. Supreme Court again moved into a leadership role on civil rights for black Americans, although from time to time, in contrast to the early twentieth century, Congress would produce important civil rights legislation, such as periodic renewals of the Voting Rights Act.

WORLD WAR II, THE BIFURCATION OF ASIAN RIGHTS, AND THE FINAL LINKAGE TO BLACK CIVIL RIGHTS

As already adumbrated above, the school desegregation decision, *Missouri ex rel. Gaines* (in 1938), of the Hughes Court; the 1943 *Hirabayashi;* and the 1944 *Korematsu* and *Steele v. Louisville and Nashville RR.* decisions of the Stone Court, drew together (and also federalized) the constitutional requirements for treatment of Asian-American and African-American minorities. This development had been foreseen in *Yick Wo v. Hopkins* (1886), forestalled by the Fuller Court,

---

[120] For Congress's role, led by a strong push from President Lyndon Johnson, from 1964 on, see this book's Introduction and Chapter 6, text at nn.205 ff.

[121] Text at nn. 205 ff.

and then grasped conceptually in Nathan Margold's strategy planning for the NAACP.

Fragmentation of U.S. Policy toward Asians, 1941–99

At the same time, and in a kind of ironic reversal, World War II caused a bifurcation in the treatment of Asian-Americans. Due to the war, the official policy toward Asians now no longer treated them as a single bloc, a *race* not allowed to be naturalized. Instead Asians were divisible into separate *nationalities*. The Chinese were our wartime allies. The Japanese were our mortal enemies, having attacked U.S. territory at Pearl Harbor. Not surprisingly, this news had consequences in U.S. domestic policy.

The political branches and the Japanese, 1941–45

Seventy-five days after Japan's December 7, 1941 bombing of Pearl Harbor, President Franklin Roosevelt issued Executive Order 9066, authorizing the Secretary of War, Henry Stimson, to designate Military Commanders who would be authorized, according to their own judgments "to prescribe military areas … from which any or all persons may be excluded" and to impose restrictions on "the right of any person to enter, remain in, or leave" said area.[122] From here, events moved rapidly. The next day, Stimson appointed Lt. General John DeWitt Military Commander of the eight westernmost mainland states. DeWitt in turn issued a proclamation on March 2 establishing six military areas.[123] Of these, Military Area 1 was the western halves of Washington State, Oregon, and California, all of California south of Los Angeles, and the southern half of Arizona.[124] Roughly two weeks later, on March 18, FDR issued Exec. Order 9102, establishing a War Relocation Authority, a civilian agency, to provide for the removal from designated areas of such people as may be required by the interest in national security, and for the "relocation, maintenance, and supervision" of these people; in practice the WRA then built and maintained barbed-wire-enclosed relocation camps in which people were held.[125]

Three days later Congress passed Public Law 77-503, 56 Stat.173 (1942), which imposed criminal penalties for violation of the military orders authorized in Executive Order 9066.[126] The federal government

[122] Bannai and Minami 1992, 757.
[123] Ibid.
[124] Niiya 2014.
[125] Wiecek 2006, 345.
[126] Bannai and Minami 1992, 757.

was united on this policy. Lurking in the background of these events was national awareness that (months prior to Pearl Harbor) in March 1941 a Japanese espionage ring was discovered, and in the aftermath of Pearl Harbor, Japanese submarines were identified off of our West Coast.[127]

On March 24 (1942) General DeWitt issued a curfew upon all German nationals, Italian nationals, Japanese nationals (approximately 30,000), and American *citizens* who were of Japanese descent (approximately 85,000) that extended through all of Military Zone 1. Three days later, DeWitt prohibited the Japanese *and* Japanese-Americans from leaving the area, effective March 29.[128] In a series of orders between March and May, the Japanese and Japanese-Americans in Military Area 1 were evacuated from their homes, moved first to Civilian Control Centers, then to Assembly Centers, then to Relocation Centers. In the latter, each family was assigned one room with cots, a table and chairs. Toilets, showers and kitchen areas were communal. Families had been given a week to arrange for disposition of property and businesses.[129] Internees could leave the camp to enroll in the armed services in the European theater. In 1943, some of the internees were permitted by the WRA to move to the interior U.S. so long as they stayed out of the military area.[130] Most remained in the camps throughout the war. Only on January 2, 1945 did the Department of War rescind its exclusion order for the west coast.[131]

Meanwhile, in June, 1942, eight German nationals, two of whom were naturalized U.S. citizens of whom one had forfeited this citizenship by joining the Wehrmacht, invaded the U.S. east coast intent on committing sabotage. After their prompt arrest and public pronouncements by both the President and members of Congress that they should be executed, the Supreme Court gave its "not unconstitutional" seal of approval to some questionable proceedings. Six of the eight were executed by early August; two imprisoned.[132] There were, in addition, some 14,400 people who were either Germans, German-Americans, Italians, or Italian-Americans whom the FBI investigated and considered suspicious enough that they too were held during the war. This fact is little publicized, but there were no mass roundups of these nationality groups as a whole.[133]

---

127 Wiecek 2006, 341.
128 Bannai and Minami 1992, 757; Wiecek 2006, 345.
129 Wiecek 2006, 345.
130 Bannai and Minami 1992, 758.
131 Brilliant 2010, 39.
132 Wiecek 2006, 306–21.
133 Ibid., 343.

The wartime Japanese cases at the Supreme Court

The wartime curfew, evacuation, and relocation orders, as applied to Americans of Japanese ancestry, all were challenged at the U.S. Supreme Court, where all the orders were defended by the U.S. Justice Department. The Court upheld the first two under a doctrine of wartime emergency and in a context where, unbeknownst to the Court at the time, government briefs were knowingly falsified to make the evidence for Japanese disloyalty look more solid than it was.[134] The "relocation" and the detention or incarceration implied by the term was actually declared in large part *un*constitutional, in the little-discussed *Ex Parte Endo* case,[135] on the day that *Korematsu* was decided. Thus, bad as they are, these cases together stand for the proposition that, in a wartime emergency where danger of invasion appears imminent, American citizens can be temporarily put under curfew on the basis of ancestry,[136] and can even be temporarily evacuated from their homes and workplaces if these are in areas with high concentrations of military bases,[137] *but* they may *not* be locked up and detained indefinitely.[138] At worst, they may be detained temporarily as part of the need for evacuation, but must be unconditionally released as soon as loyalty is determined, *and* the government is obligated to make such determinations expeditiously.[139] In terms of impact on judicial doctrine, the Court's reasoning has turned out to be at least as important as these particular rulings.

In the first of the cases, *Hirabayashi* (1943), the Court posed the question it faced as follows:

> our inquiry must be whether, in the light of all the facts and circumstances, there was any substantial basis for the conclusion, in which Congress and the military commander united, that the curfew as applied was a protective measure necessary to meet the threat of sabotage and espionage which would substantially affect the war effort and which might reasonably be expected to aid a threatened enemy invasion.[140]

---

134 Wiecek, 348–9 details these efforts.

135 *Ex Parte Endo*, 323 U.S. 283 (1944).

136 *Hirabayashi v. U.S.*, 320 U.S. 81 (1943) and *Yasui v. U.S.*, 320 U.S. 115 (1943). *Yasui* was a companion case to *Hirabayashi* and in terms of doctrinal contributions, simply followed it.

137 *Korematsu v. U.S.*, 323 U.S. 214 (1944).

138 *Ex Parte Endo*, 323 U.S. 283 (1944).

139 *Endo*, 323 U.S., at 301–4.

140 *Hirabayashi v. U.S.*, 320 U.S. 81, 95 (1943).

On the basis of significantly falsified briefs, the Court concluded, "Yes." In the process, it said the following about constitutional rules on discrimination:

> The Fifth Amendment contains no equal protection clause, and it restrains only such discriminatory legislation by Congress as amounts to a denial of due process … . *Distinctions between citizens solely because of their ancestry are, by their very, nature odious to a free people whose institutions are founded upon the doctrine of equality*. For that reason, legislative classification or discrimination based on race alone has often been held to be a denial of equal protection. [Here the Court cited three precedents: (1) *Yick Wo* (a state case), (2) a case interpreting the equal protection clause of the Philippines Constitution, and (3) a state-level equal protection case invalidating a verdict by a racially-rigged jury.] *We may assume that these considerations would be controlling here* were it not for the fact that the danger of espionage and sabotage, in time of war and of threatened invasion, calls upon the military authorities to scrutinize every relevant fact bearing on the loyalty of populations in the danger areas. Because *racial discriminations are in most circumstances irrelevant, and therefore prohibited*, it by no means follows that, in dealing with the perils of war, Congress and the Executive are wholly precluded from taking into account those facts and circumstances which are relevant to measures for our national defense and for the successful prosecution of the war, and which may, in fact, place citizens of one ancestry in a different category from others[141] (emphasis added).

As noted earlier, in *Hirabayashi*, the unanimous Court hereby suggested, but did not in so many words rule, that the Fifth Amendment due process clause restraining the federal government contains an equal protection mandate. The explicit statement was to wait for the *Korematsu* decision, the one that produced a far more divided Court because it upheld a more extreme wartime measure, evacuation of American citizens on an ancestry basis from their homes and workplaces, on the rationale of wartime exigency.

In *Korematsu*,[142] the Supreme Court famously said:[143]

---

[141] Ibid., at 100.

[142] The Court delayed handing down *Korematsu* until December 1944, two years and seven months after the initial evacuation order, more than ample time to investigate people's loyalty and release them. The military conceded in the companion *Ex Parte Endo* case (at 293–6) that much of the detention program was because of community hostility in the rest of the U.S. toward letting the Japanese-Americans move in. The Court emphasized in *Korematsu* that it was dealing only with evacuation and not with detention.

[143] *Korematsu v. U.S.*, 323 U.S. 214, 216 (1944).

> [a]ll legal restrictions which curtail the civil rights of a single racial group are immediately suspect. That is not to say that all such restrictions are unconstitutional. It is to say that courts must subject them to the most rigid scrutiny. Pressing public necessity may sometimes justify the existence of such restrictions; racial antagonism never can.

Characterizing the situation as one of "military urgency" (at p. 223), Justice Black writing for the majority upheld the evacuation program. It was Justice Murphy who wrote in dissent, "Being an obvious racial discrimination, the order deprives all those within its scope of *the equal protection of the laws guaranteed by the Fifth Amendment*"[144] (emphasis added). The italicized portion of his sentence was his interpretation of the passage from Justice Black, and it has generally prevailed. From the time of *Korematsu* on, then, two rules of its constitutional law have doctrinally endured: (1) The Fifth Amendment restrains the federal government in the same way that the Fourteenth Amendment restrains the states, i.e., as though it contained an equal protection clause;[145] (2) racial classification in laws are "suspect"; they are unconstitutional unless shown to be justified by "pressing public necessity" (or, in the words of later cases, shown "necessary for a compelling government interest")[146]—i.e., unless they pass the test of "strict scrutiny," or as Justice Black put it in *Korematsu*, "most rigid scrutiny."

---

[144] Ibid., at 234–5.

[145] *Richmond v. Croson*, 488 U.S. 469 (1989) in the context of governmental affirmative action programs and attentive to the language that gives Congress power to enforce the equal protection clause *upon* the states, resisted this equation of the Fifth Amendment's equal protection implications with the rules of the Fourteenth Amendment equal protection clause (distinguishing *Richmond*'s invalidating a local affirmative action program from the Court's upholding a federal one in *Fullilove v. Klutznick*, 448 U.S. 448 (1980)); but *Adarand Constructors v. Pena*, 515 U.S. 200 (1995), accepted the equation of federal with state equal protection rules, and the *Adarand* approach has endured. Sometimes, nonetheless, affirmative action does survive strict scrutiny. See *North Carolina v. Swann*, 402 U.S. 43 (1971) (declaring unconstitutional North Carolina law that "forbids assignment of any student on account of race or for the purpose of creating a racial balance or ratio in the schools" on grounds that such a law interferes with remedies for unconstitutional residual de jure segregation) and *Grutter v. Bollinger*, 539 U.S. 306 (2003) (upholding under strict scrutiny, as suitably carefully tailored, affirmative action admissions program of the University of Michigan Law School).

[146] *Oyama v. California*, 332 U.S. 633, at 640 (1948) (a Japanese land ownership case) introduced the phrase "compelling justification." See discussion below.

Reversal on Japanese-Americans, 1946–99

Nearly fifty years after Pearl Harbor, Congress apologized and arranged for reparation payments to the Japanese-American internees and their descendants. This was the peak of a long period of intermittent governmental penance. Although the Supreme Court had declared the blanket, long-term incarceration program unconstitutional in the *Endo* case in December of 1944 (on the same day that it upheld "evacuation" of Japanese-Americans in *Korematsu*), the camps were not finally closed until 1946. Then, in 1948 Congress authorized token compensation payments under the Congressional Japanese-American Evacuation Claims Act, which allocated up to $37 million for proven property loss due to evacuation. This amounted to about one-tenth of the actual cost of property losses.

In the 1970s, the Japanese-American Citizens League began lobbying for an investigation of the injustices of the internment program, and for prevention of such injustice in the future. The league attained legislative success when Congress in 1971 adopted the Non-Detention Act of 1971, which prohibits executive action to lock up groups of people without specific prior legislative authorization. Their first executive branch success came with an official apology from President Gerald Ford in 1976. Then in 1980 President Jimmy Carter established the Commission on Wartime Relocation and Internment to investigate potential governmental wrongdoing on the subject. In the 1984–87 time period, federal courts issued orders vacating the convictions of Hirabayashi, Yasui, and Korematsu, the three civil disobedients who had been imprisoned in their efforts to challenge the curfew (Hirabayashi and Yasui) and evacuation orders (Korematsu) that the Supreme Court had initially upheld. The Commission reported its final findings in 1988 and, under the leadership of a handful of Japanese-Americans serving in Congress by then, Congress issued its official apology and authorized payments of up to $20,000 per survivor (112,000 people had been evacuated) or for the heir of the survivor. Payments went out over an eleven-year period, and by the end, in 1999, $1.6 billion had been disbursed.[147]

---

[147] *Korematsu v. U.S.*, 584 F. Supp. 1406 (1984); *Yasui v. U.S.*, 772 F. 2d 1496 (1985); *Hirabayashi v. U.S.*, 828 F. 2d 591 (1987); Wiecek 2006, 361–3; "WWII Reparations"; Stone 2004, 305; Qureshi 2013; Molotsky 1988; Longaker, 1974 401-6; email from Daniel Levin of the Political Science Department, University of Utah to the <Lawcourt-1@legal.umass.edu> list on November 11, 2016, 1:44 p.m; Non-Detention Act of 1971, Public Law 92-128, 85 Stat. 347 (1971), 18 U.S.C. § 4001(a).

Postwar Supreme Court on anti-Japanese legislation

With the end of World War II, and with the rest of the federal government reducing its hostility to Japanese-Americans by 1946, it was easy for the U.S. Supreme Court to return to its more customary role of protecting Asians against discriminatory state laws or potential abuse by administrators. In fact, between 1946 and 1952, eleven states retained anti-Asian laws that prohibited land ownership by "aliens not eligible for citizenship." Because of changes in naturalization law in the 1940s,[148] the central target of such laws was basically Japanese residents (more than 48,000), along with fewer than 1,000 residents from Korea, Japan's former colony.[149] The Japanese-American Citizens League brought a lawsuit to the Supreme Court in 1947–48 to challenge such laws on behalf of the Oyama family of California. The Court produced a highly divided opinion for *Oyama v. California* (1948) that refrained from striking down the law but rendered it virtually unenforceable.[150]

Chief Justice Vinson wrote an opinion ostensibly "for the Court," but seven justices expressed other viewpoints. Vinson's Court opinion focused on the enforcement procedure in California: the state was confiscating Oyama's property because he had engaged in the subterfuge of buying the land that he was ineligible to own and then giving it as a gift to his minor son, a U.S. citizen by birth (as a way of evading the prohibition on the father's ownership). The Vinson opinion (against three dissents) treated this confiscation as flagrantly unequal treatment of U.S. citizens. A son of an immigrant British father, for instance, could receive such a gift of land from his father, but the son of a Japanese immigrant father could not. As Vinson wrote: "The discrimination is based solely on his parents' country of origin; and there is absent the compelling justification which would be needed to sustain discrimination of that nature."[151] For the first time, the Supreme Court was invoking the suspect classification (discrimination by ancestry)/compelling justification test to declare void a state law.[152]

This aspect of the Alien Land Law violated the Equal Protection Clause and was therefore void. The Vinson provision left intact the core provision against land ownership by persons "ineligible for citizenship."

---

148 These are detailed in the next section.

149 Brilliant 2010, 30 and n.14 pp. 282–3, citing McGovney 1947, 7–11.

150 *Oyama v. California*, 332 U.S. 633 (1948).

151 Ibid., at 640.

152 This test originated in the federal cases of *Korematsu* and *Hirabayashi* detailed above. The Supreme Court did not again apply the full version of this test until 1964. See discussion of *Mclaughlin v. Florida* (1964) below.

Four justices wrote concurrences in which they argued that the core provision, too, violated equal protection of the laws and should be declared unconstitutional. In any event, the Supreme Court decision had rendered the California law virtually unenforceable. Of the seventy-five pending land seizure enforcement cases 90 percent involved Japanese parents who had gifted real property to their citizen children. The state promptly dropped all seventy-five of these prosecutions.[153]

The same World War II anti-Japanese hysteria that had propelled internment and had motivated California to step up its enforcement of the Alien Land Law in the early 1940s also moved the California legislature to adopt a new restriction against Japanese residents in 1943, amending the Fish and Game Code to prohibit granting a commercial fishing license to any "alien Japanese." This new law lacked the historically deep and wide roots that alien land laws had.[154] Until this time no ethnicity or citizenship restrictions were in the Code. In 1945, as Japanese internees were released from their incarceration, the legislature amended the language of the law in fear that courts would strike it down if it were too explicitly anti-Japanese. The prohibition of fishing licenses to the Japanese became a prohibition on granting them to "alien[s] ineligible to citizenship." Governor Earl Warren signed it into law in May. Tarao Takahashi had received such a license annually from 1915 until his internment in 1942. In 1946 he went to court to challenge the new prohibition. He won the case locally, lost at the California Supreme Court and then appealed to the U.S. Supreme Court, which handed down its decision in 1948, the same year as *Hurd v. Hodge* and *Shelley v. Kraemer*, and the same year in which Congress was making payments to Japanese-American families under the Evacuation Claims Act. The NAACP submitted a friend of the court brief on the side of Takahashi, as did the American Jewish Congress, other interest groups, and, perhaps most consequentially, Truman's Justice Department.[155]

Justice Black wrote for the Court majority of seven, and zeroed in on the discrimination against aliens, rather than attempt to assess the evidence cited by attorneys for their claim that this was a particularly vicious legislative attack on Japanese residents as such. Black's opinion agreed that the law violated the Equal Protection Clause, noting that once the federal government has decided that any given group or person may immigrate here, individual states do not have authority to legislate against

---

153 Brilliant 2010, 43–9.

154 See discussion in Chapter 5.

155 *Takahashi v. Fish and Game Commission*, 334 U.S. 410 (1948).

aliens *per se* in an attempt to keep them from residing within that state. The Equal Protection Clause protects all persons, not merely citizens; this law violated it.

Wartime China policy and post-war Asia policy

Meanwhile, as the Japanese-Americans were being treated as though they were prisoners of war, Chinese residents finally received full civil rights here. The imperative of wartime alliances pushed Franklin Roosevelt to push Congress, in turn, to adopt the Magnuson Act, which became law on December 17, 1943.[156] It ended the sixty-year old ban on immigration by Chinese people. *And it allowed naturalization of Chinese resident aliens for the first time in U.S. history.*[157] In the same year, the Luce-Celler Act was proposed in Congress. It would give *immigration rights and naturalization rights to person of South Asian extraction coming from India, and also to Filipinos of Pacific Island racial background.* Supported first by President Roosevelt and then Truman, it became law in 1946.[158]

At this point, persons of Japanese, Korean, and other Asian extraction were still not permitted to be naturalized in the U.S.[159] This situation did not change until the 1952 McCarran Walters Act.[160] Even though this act was a historic move, completely eliminating racial bans on naturalization for the first time, nonetheless, the law retained an anti-Asian-race animus because people of such race were counted in the (very low) immigration quota of the Asian ancestral home, rather than the country of residence. For instance, a person of Japanese extraction or Thai extraction who lived, say, in Paris as a permanent resident would be counted under Japan or Thailand's immigration quota rather than France's. This racial discrimination aspect of the law brought a veto by President Truman, but Congress retained this clause and passed the measure over his veto.[161] President Eisenhower, with an eye to America's influence in the world,

---

156 Leong 2003.

157 Chesley 2009; "1946."

158 Pusey 2014.

159 Asian "war brides" and their children were permitted to immigrate as of December 28, 1945, and all spouses of U.S. citizens were given immigration rights irrespective of race as of July 22, 1947. Kim and Kim 1977, 390.

160 Ibid.

161 "The Immigration and Nationality Act of 1952" N.D.; Singh 2006. Under the 1952 Act, Guam was added to those territories whose inhabitants acquire birth-right U.S. citizenship. The Northern Mariana Islands were added in 1986 legislation. The only remaining possession where residents are U.S. nationals rather than U.S. birth-right citizens is American Samoa. *Tuaua v. U.S.*, 788 F.3d

similarly pushed without success for further liberalizing immigration law to remove its racial elements.[162] These elements, which geared national quotas to race, were not removed from U.S. immigration law until the Immigration and Nationality Act of 1965, or Hart-Celler Act, promoted first (unsuccessfully) by John Kennedy and then (with success) by Lyndon Johnson.[163]

Racial Discrimination is Racial Discrimination

The joining together of federal judicial doctrine condemning domestic anti-Asian discrimination with judicial doctrine condemning anti-black discrimination, which had advanced significantly in cases of the 1930s and 1940s, culminated on May 17, 1954, when *Brown v. Board of Education*[164] and *Bolling v. Sharpe*[165] were handed down as companion cases. Moreover, in deciding these two cases, the Supreme Court continued the building upon reasoning from the Latino desegregation case, *Mendez v. Westminster I* (1946) that it had begun in *Sweatt* and *McLaurin.* By this time Earl Warren had replaced Vinson as Chief Justice. Warren served as chief justice from 1954 through June 1969. Warren had been governor of California during the *Mendez* case, and, as documented in Chapter 6, was familiar with it. In these two 1954 desegregation cases, *Brown* and *Bolling*, groundwork that had been laid in litigation by Asian-Americans and Mexican-Americans became the foundation of rulings that eventually inspired Congress to legislate in ways that profoundly changed the place of African-Americans in the life of this country.

Brown v. Board of Education

In the school desegregation cases, the core principle of *Yick Wo v. Hopkins* (1886) identified by the NAACP's Nathan Margold as having

300 (D.C. Cir. June 5, 2015); "Acquisition of U.S. Nationality in U.S. Territories and Possessions," N.D.

162 Le, C.N. 2014.

163 Ibid. The non-discrimination principle in the act had been endorsed by Truman and Eisenhower, too, before Kennedy. Center for Immigration Studies 1995, "Three Decades of Mass Immigration: The Legacy of the 1965 Immigration Act." The 1965 Act was not a panacea. For a critique that points to its uneven impact, which created much greater backlogs of immigration applicants from the Philippines, Korea, China, and India than from other countries, see Tamayo 1992.

164 *Brown v. Board of Ed.*, 347 U.S. 483 (1954).

165 *Bolling v. Sharpe*, 347 U.S. 497 (1954).

the potential to be a successful weapon against school segregation, was finally applied to do just that. This core principle was that when a state law race-neutral in its terms, such as "separate but equal," can be shown in its *application* to do disproportionate harm to one race, then that law is an unconstitutional violation of the equal protection clause. The post-Margold judicial discovery, first explicated in the federal district court opinion for *Mendez v. Westminster*,[166] of the idea of "intangible factors" that affect the quality of education (such as psychological harm), strengthened this *Yick Wo* principle; now lawyers and judges could argue that in education, racial segregation would *inevitably* produce unequal education (or as Nathan Margold would have said "irremediably" would do so) even if money was spent to produce physically equal educational facilities. When the Supreme Court described the force of "intangible factors" of school reputation and interracial communication in *Sweatt* and *McLaurin*, the Court had in effect announced that separate in schooling would always be unequal. By keeping blacks apart from whites, the dominant racial group in U.S. society, segregation inevitably hampered black children's ability to learn effective intergroup communication with whites and vice versa. (This is not to say that individual smart people could not overcome the barrier and learn to deal effectively with people of other races, but the dual school system was hampering this educational process.) Because of white dominance over valued resources in U.S. society, this inevitably hurt black children more than white children.

The Supreme Court in *Brown* added yet another intangible factor, the harm that segregation imposed on black children's self-esteem, undermining their motivation to excel in learning. This factor originated in the federal district court judge's opinion for the Mexican-American school desegregation case, *Mendez v. Westminster*, a decision unmentioned in *Brown*, but handed down in California during Earl Warren's tenure there as governor.[167] This factor buttressed the argument already available from *Sweatt* and *McLaurin* that segregation deprived black children of the intangible element of learning effective interracial communication; therefore, no amount of money spent to upgrade buildings and curricular resources could make segregated education equal. Only desegregation could do that. Thus, school desegregation was ordered in *Brown*, fulfilling the promise Margold had seen in *Yick Wo v. Hopkins*.

---

[166] *Mendez et al. v. Westminster School District et al.*, 64 F. Supp. 544 (1946) (*Mendez I*).

[167] For details see discussion of "*Mendez I*" in Chapter 6.

***Bolling v. Sharpe* and the *Hirabayashi*, *Korematsu*, and *Steele* cases**

A separate legal development produced judicial doctrine eventually used to decide the *Bolling v. Sharpe* (1954) companion case to *Brown v. Board* (1954). This doctrinal line placed the rules of the Fourteenth Amendment equal protection clause into the Fifth Amendment due process clause, which constrains *federal* domestic policy. *Bolling* dealt with schools in Washington, D.C. With this new rule in place, the Court could declare racial segregation unconstitutional in D.C. schools, once it showed in *Brown* that such segregation was a violation of the equal protection clause.

For *Bolling*, Chief Justice Warren drew upon three Stone Court precedents: he announced the rule from *Korematsu* and *Hirabayashi*: "Classifications based solely upon race must be scrutinized with particular care, since they are contrary to our traditions, and hence constitutionally suspect."[168] And, as the Stone Court had done in the *Steele* case of 1944, Warren applied this constitutional rule of disapproval against ancestry-based discrimination in federal law, not only to anti-Asian discrimination, but also to anti-black discrimination.[169] Warren concluded that scrutiny of the school segregation law showed, "Segregation in public education is not reasonably related to any proper governmental objective."[170] Race-based segregation was so irrational that it did not even meet the test of ordinary scrutiny. Public school segregation was therefore unconstitutional in federal territory as well as in the states.

The litigation strategy culminating in the *Brown v. Board* (1954) school desegregation decision was inspired by two much earlier cases brought by Chinese people: the *Yick Wo v. Hopkins* and *Gong Lum v. Rice* precedents. Moreover, both the arguments by NAACP lawyers for the

---

[168] *Bolling v. Sharpe*, 347 U.S. 497, 499 (1954). This version of the rule omits mention of the second half of the test—search for justification by a compelling government interest, akin to military urgency (without which the law is unconstitutional). See also discussion of *Oyama v. California* (1948) above for application of the full-blown version (mention of suspect classification combined with compelling governmental interest test) to protect Japanese-American citizens against discriminatory laws. See also discussion of *Mendez I* in Chapter 6 for discussion of Chief Justice Warren's apparent disinclination to deploy the strict scrutiny rule from the *Korematsu* line of cases in *Brown v. Board*. The Warren Court did not apply the full-blown strict scrutiny test to any case concerning blacks until 1964, to deal with a law prohibiting interracial co-habitation. See above n.56.

[169] *Steele v. Louisville and Nashville Railroad*, 323 U.S. 192, at 202, 203 (1944).

[170] *Bolling*, 347 U.S., at 500.

Brown v. Board decision and Chief Justice Warren's decision in that case itself derived from the reasoning in the federal district court case rejecting school segregation of Latino school children, *Mendez v. Westminster I* (1946). The reasoning in the *Bolling v. Sharpe* (1954) D.C. desegregation case, in turn, built upon precedents that addressed anti-Japanese discrimination. By mid-twentieth century the U.S. Supreme Court was using the power of judicial review to protect a wide array of racial minorities, and the racial minority groups had begun to cooperate in seeking anti-discrimination decisions. Chapter 6 detailed cooperation during this period among blacks, Latinos, and Japanese-Americans.

INDIAN POLICY, 1933–90s

As indicated at the end of Chapter 5, The Meriam Report publication in 1928 (which report had been commissioned by the Department of Interior) stimulated the federal political branches to take seriously the need to help American Indians. The Hoover Administration, substantially increased appropriations for food, health, and irrigation projects, while softening hard-line assimilationist policies in Indian education. Hoover's Co-Commissioners for Indian Affairs, Rhoads and Scattergood, injected into official policies respect for traditional Indian culture. Beginning in 1931, under the leadership of their appointed director of Indian Education, Carson Ryan, who continued in his post well into the Roosevelt Administration (until 1936), it became an officially announced goal of Indian education to "protect[] and preserv[e] as much of their own ways of living as possible."[171]

Plainly, even before FDR took office, the electoral branches now realized that Indians no longer posed a military threat and had become a desperately needy segment of American society. Still, the more ambitious goals set forth in the Meriam Report for reversing the harm done by Dawes Act allotment policies were being blocked both by old guard civil servants in the federal bureaucracy and by assimilationists in Congress.[172]

The Elected Branches

Upon entering office, Franklin Roosevelt appointed as Commissioner of Indian Affairs John Collier of the American Indian Defense Association, who had for a decade been a nationally prominent advocate for Indians.

171 Prucha 1986, 313–15.
172 Ibid.

Collier came in with the backing of Harold Ickes, Secretary of the Interior. Collier took office in April 1933 with an ambitious program, one that immediately aroused controversy, not only in Congress and among missionaries to the Indians, but, more importantly, among Indians themselves. Uncontroversial was his immediate advocacy, one quickly approved, of establishment of a Civilian Conservation Corps that would be separate for the Indians. The Indian CCC accomplished much immediate good promoting conservation, alleviating economic suffering, and providing industrial training.[173] Also non-controversial and beneficial were the Pueblo Relief Act of 1933 and the Johnson-O'Malley Act of 1934. The former set up a Pueblo Land Claims Board to ameliorate inequities in compensation provided by the Pueblo Lands Board. The latter, the Johnson-O'Malley Act, from 1934–58, was basically a federal aid program aimed at helping public school districts educate Indian children from reservations and from other Indian-owned, tax-exempt land areas, because such children did not pay taxes to their local school districts.[174] In 1958, it became a program for funding special supplemental education to Indian children, and since 1975 has required Indian parental input in guiding this supplemental education.[175]

Much more bold and controversial was Collier's proposal for an Indian Reorganization Act (Wheeler-Howard Act of 1934). It was an effort to reverse the half-century old Dawes Allotment Act, not only immediately ceasing the allotment process, but undoing its effects by restoring existing "surplus" land back to the tribes, appropriating two million dollars annually for purchasing new lands to add to tribal holdings, authorizing the Secretary of the Interior to transfer individually owned lands to the tribe if such transfer be judged "necessary for the proper consolidation of Indian lands," and taking allotted lands back to the tribe whenever their owner died, rather than letting the owner pass the property on to heirs. The Act had other important elements (described in next paragraph), but the ones taking property for the tribe back from control of individual allottees aroused the most heated controversy. Collier removed these from the bill, and he added a provision allowing any tribe that so wished to hold a referendum to decide whether to opt out of the bill's rules.

Franklin Roosevelt lobbied actively for the amended version of the bill, and Congress adopted it in 1934. This final version excluded the Indians

---

173 Ibid., 318–19.

174 Ibid.; National Johnson-O'Malley Association. N.D., 15–16.

175 Ibid., 16.

of Oklahoma, who had so thoroughly taken advantage of allotment that they wanted to retain the condition of being integrated among white Oklahomans. In 1936, at Collier's urging, Congress adopted the Indian Welfare Act (or Thomas-Rogers Act) which took the non-allotment-related provisions of the Indian Reorganization Act and applied them to the Oklahoma Indians. These additional pieces of both laws provided that Indian tribes within two years from the moment that the Reorganization Act took place could vote, by tribal majority, to organize a tribal government with its own constitution, subject to approval of, and after consultation with, the Secretary of the Interior. The tribal government would then have power to hire attorneys to work on the tribe's behalf, to prevent the sale of tribal assets, and to negotiate with other governments, whether local, state or federal. Moreover, each tribe was empowered to incorporate itself for business purposes, via a charter obtained from the Secretary of Interior, and in this way manage the tribe's property, selling or leasing mineral rights and so forth. The law created a revolving fund of ten million dollars to be lent to these corporations for economic development projects. The law provided that the Bureau of Indian Affairs would have to give hiring preference to qualified Indians; also, that the Secretary of Interior would have to draw up rules and regulations to provide for appropriate conservation of Indian land and forest resources. After the two-year voting period, 195 tribes accepted the Reorganization Act, and seventy-seven rejected it. Within ten years ninety-three tribes had adopted constitutions and seventy-three had formed corporate charters.[176]

The Indian Reorganization Act profoundly re-oriented the U.S. Government's posture toward American Indians, from one that favored obliterating tribal ways and making Indians fit the mold of American individualism into a posture that respected tribal quasi-sovereignty and traditional Indian culture (albeit in ways that attempted to adapt tribal sovereignty to the corporate legal structure already dominant in the U.S.). In a further expression of cultural respect, Collier also pushed through Congress in 1935 the Indian Arts and Crafts Act. The law created a five-member government agency, appointed by the Secretary of the Interior to provide technical marketing research assistance, establish standards of quality and marks of genuineness—all for the purpose of promoting the sales of Native American arts and crafts.[177] This plank in

---

[176] Prucha 1986, 316–25.
[177] Ibid., 327–8.

Collier's platform for Indians triggered renewed criticism from missionaries.[178] Moreover economic-conservative elements and pro-assimilationists, both Indian and non-Indian, continued their criticisms of him, eventually pushing him to resign in 1945. His backer, Secretary Harold Ickes did so in 1946.[179]

Although these Collier reforms had their critics, especially among Indians, who pointed to their top-down quality and the imposition of Euro-American political forms upon Indians, they caught on and, except for a brief hiatus, basically during the Eisenhower Administration, have endured.[180] They have become the framework of a modern bipartisan consensus on enlightened federal policy toward Indians.

In the late 1940s, one of the reforms for which Collier had long advocated, the creation of an Indian Claims Commission to handle Indian complaints about broken treaties or violated contracts or even dishonorable dealings, was finally enacted as the Indian Claims Commission Act of August 13, 1946.[181] Prior to this time, a tribe's judicial claims that the federal government had taken its lands in violation of treaties had generally been blocked by the doctrine of sovereign immunity. The establishment of a Court of Claims in 1855 partially waived sovereign immunity as to American citizens, but Congress at the time understood this Court to exclude Indians' claims. On 142 separate occasions, prior to the 1946 Act, Congress (in response to lobbying by one or another aggrieved tribe) had enacted special laws allowing for a particular tribal claim to go to the Court of Claims, to settle this tribe's claim of land taken in violation of treaty rights, for which just compensation had been absent.[182]

As the Indian Claims Commission's work extended over the years (until 1978, when its remaining caseload was legislatively turned over to the U.S. Court of Claims),[183] the Indian response to its deliberations and conclusions was often negative; Commission awards of financial compensation tended to be smaller than Indians had hoped for and, increasingly in the 1960s and 1970s, the tribes wanted their lands restored rather than a monetary award. The Commission provided only monetary remedies.[184] Sometimes the Commission even "awarded" the

[178] Ibid., 333.
[179] Ibid., 336, 340.
[180] Ibid., 338–9.
[181] Ibid., 341.
[182] Getches et al. 1993, 311.
[183] Hoxie 1996, 247; Wildenthal 2003, 62.
[184] Prucha 1986, 343.

money to be used to pay charges owed by the tribe for government services, such that the tribe did not actually receive the money; in a particularly bad example, hundreds of thousands of dollars of money for the Menominee were used to finance the termination of the tribe.[185]

In 1948 both the federal legislative and executive branches turned away from promoting tribal sovereignty and back toward active promotion of assimilation, eventually culminating in a policy called "termination"—both because it aimed to terminate Indian reliance on federal governmental assistance and to terminate the tribal structure itself. This reversal of policy direction occurred as a consequence of the successful inclusion of large numbers of Indians in both the armed forces and defense industries for World War II. After the war, the economic boom experienced by whites, appeared to leave Indians behind, and this glaring fact pushed officials in Washington to swing back behind the idea of assimilation, phrased in terms of liberating Indians from governmental dependency and enabling them to join the world of industrial urbanization, which seemed to be benefitting millions of other Americans.[186] This time the assimilation policy was called "termination."

This development was not consciously anti-Indian; it coincided with renewed concern for Indian civil rights. A blistering 1947 Report from President Truman's Committee on Civil Rights condemning the denial of the vote even to Indian war veterans prompted New Mexico and Arizona in 1948 to drop their ban on voting by reservation Indians. By 1957 Utah became the last state to eliminate the ban on voting by reservation Indians. Similarly, 1953 brought an end to longstanding restrictions on the sale of liquor to Indians and also on the sale of guns and ammunition to them.[187]

Under the Eisenhower Administration, Congress established two important pieces of the termination program: House Concurrent Resolution 108 (HCR 108) announced the "sense of Congress" (on August 1, 1953) that a named group of relatively prosperous tribes should be "freed from federal supervision" in the near future. Public Law 280, with *unanimous* approval, two weeks later turned over to state government both civil and criminal jurisdiction on virtually all Indian reservations in the states of California, Minnesota, Nebraska, Oregon, and Wisconsin (and in the territory, later state, of Alaska), and permitted other states to assume such jurisdiction with or without tribal permission. Most of the

---

185 Hoxie 1996, 248.

186 Ibid., 236–41.

187 Pub.L. 83–280, August 15, 1953, codified as 18 U.S.C. § 1162, 28 U.S.C. § 1360, and 25 U.S.C. §§ 1321–1326. Ibid., 240. Prucha 1986, 347.

handful of states that later took jurisdiction did so only with tribal approval.[188] Then, in 1954, Congress established procedures for ending federal protection of the Klamath tribe in Oregon, the Menominee in Wisconsin, and a group of much smaller tribes in Utah, Oregon and Texas. The Alabama Coushatta, with only 450 members, were the first tribe actually to be terminated, in 1955. The Menominees, in 1961, were the last sizable tribe (3,270 members) to do so.[189]

Thus, the peak period of terminating tribes lasted basically seven years. The years of legislating numerous terminations ran from 1954 through 1956.[190]

The phenomenon of termination involved lengthy negotiations between the Department of Interior and the tribe (sometimes forced upon the tribe; sometimes genuinely voluntarily adopted)[191] to arrange an end to federal tax benefits for Indians, to place tribal members into the same relation to state governments that other Americans had, and to distribute tribal assets out of the federal trust. Usually the trust was taken over by a corporation set up by the tribe, but some were run by private banks and sometimes the funds or property were distributed on a per capita basis.[192]

The termination process was widely and quickly recognized to have been unsuccessful; the Klamath and Menominee Indians after termination became much poorer than they had been when prospering under tribal status.[193] In the end, only 3 percent of tribal Indians underwent termination, and the land holdings affected also totaled only about 3 percent of Indian land.[194] Before leaving office John Collier had prompted his Indian employees in the Bureau of Indian Affairs to stimulate the formation of a nation-wide representative organization of the American Indians. In 1944 the first National Congress of American Indians met and

---

[188] Getches, et al. 1993, 481–2 lists the states that did and did not solicit tribal approval. No state assumed jurisdiction after the 1968 Civil Rights Act required tribal approval.

[189] Hoxie 1996, 241–2; Prucha 1986, 346-50. Getches, et al. 1993, 479 lists the three exempted reservations within the five states. According to Prucha, *ibid.*, Congress as a whole displayed little interest in the subject, and simply bowed to the wishes of certain Congress members who represented Western districts.

[190] In 1958, 1959 and 1962, Congress legislated to terminate, respectively, thirty small groups of Indians scattered on Rancherias across California, the Catawba tribe of 631 in South Carolina, and the 442-member Ponca tribe in Nebraska. Prucha 1986, 347–8. Wilkinson and Biggs 1977, 151.

[191] Washburn 1996, 429.

[192] Hoxie 1996, 241–2; Prucha 1986, 347–50.

[193] Washburn 1996, 429.

[194] Prucha 1986, 351.

proceeded to become an active lobbying organization. The group fought hard against termination policy, and can be credited with having brought the legislation of termination (of unwilling tribes) to a halt by 1959. In 1973–76 the Menominee were able to restore their tribal status, and the Klamath did so in 1983. Some smaller tribes that had been terminated did not succeed in undoing their termination.[195]

During the period of 1948–60, in the same assimilationist spirit that motivated termination, the federal government also actively promoted the migration of individual Indians from reservations to cities by providing funds to assist the move and to help with job placement. It set up urban relocation offices for this purpose, and these evolved by 1960 into Indian Centers in several major cities that provided a range of social services and served as Indian gathering points for Indian cultural events.[196]

By 1958, the Secretary of the Interior (Fred Seaton) publicly stated that no termination act would thereafter pass without the full consent of the Indians affected.[197] In 1959, the Eisenhower Administration quietly ceased pursuit of termination for any unwilling tribe.[198] In 1960, President [to-be] John F. Kennedy successfully campaigned for office with a promise to break no contractual promise or treaty with any tribe against its consent, and to respect the cultural heritage of every group. A variety of study groups and commissions, public and private, issued reports in the early 1960s condemning the termination policy.[199] The administration of Lyndon Johnson, too, embraced respect for tribal autonomy, but primarily emphasized economic assistance, as part of its War on Poverty.

After 1960, the federal government did not turn back. John Collier's legacy of rejecting assimilationism took hold for good. Richard Nixon in July, 1970 addressed Congress on the matter of Indian Affairs expressly condemning the termination program and calling for Congress to issue a concurrent resolution doing the same.[200] The announcement occurred in the political context of a few highly publicized militant actions by the

---

[195] Hoxie 1996, 251–4. Prucha 1986, 354–6, 371–3. The two tribes whose termination was legislated the last (in 1959 and 1962) did manage to regain their tribal status; in 1993 the Catawba of South Carolina, termination completed in 1962, regained federal tribal status; and in 1990, the Ponca of Nebraska, termination completed in 1966, regained theirs. SCIWAY 2015; Ponca Tribe of Nebraska, 2015.

[196] Hoxie 1996, 242–3.

[197] Wilkins, 1997, 237.

[198] Wildenthal 2003, 31.

[199] Prucha 1986, 357–9.

[200] Ibid., 364–5.

American Indian Movement (AIM) of Russell Means and Dennis Banks, along with their allies, which took place between 1969 and 1973.[201] Since 1970, both Congress and the Presidency have officially favored tribal self-determination and [quasi]sovereignty and the preservation of Indian culture.[202] In December, 1970 the federal government returned to the Taos Pueblo 48,000 acres around the sacred Blue Lake, land seized under the Theodore Roosevelt administration in 1906 for the Carson National Forest. The tribe had persistently rejected a U.S. offer of monetary compensation for these lands.[203] Not all land restoration claims of Indians have been satisfied. The value of the monetary compensation package (brought about by the *U.S. v. Sioux Nation* [1980] case described in the Supreme Court section below), still being rejected by the Sioux for the Black Hills of South Dakota, currently exceeds $1.3 billion. But the money remains on offer.[204]

Several pieces of Congressional legislation in the 1970s expressed this new posture supportive of tribal sovereignty. One was the Indian Self-Determination and Education Assistance Act of January 1, 1975 (P.L. 93-638). This Act amended the Johnson-O'Malley Act of 1934, to assure that when tribal governments made contracts (using the granted federal funds from the Department of Interior or from HEW) with state and local agencies for educational and health services, Indian people would have a say in choosing the programs they wanted to use and in determining the shape of the programs being delivered.[205] In 1978, Congress adopted Senate Joint Resolution 102 announcing it to be federal policy to "protect and preserve" the right to exercise the traditional religions of American Indians, Eskimos, Aleuts, and Native Hawaiians.[206] In the same year,

---

201 Ibid., 365–7.

202 Ibid., 364–5. Washburn 1996.

203 Prucha, ibid., 368.

204 Uenuma and Fritz 2011.

205 Prucha 1986, 379–80; Wilkins 1997, 187; Washburn 1996, 408. Washburn, ibid., notes that this Act let tribes operate Indian Health Service programs in their communities and also lists the Indian Health Care Improvement Act (P.L. 94-437) of 1976, and the amendment thereto in P.L.96-537 of 1980 as setting the admirable goal of bringing Indian health to parity with that of other Americans by 1987. By 1987 the Indian Health Service was the health provider for over a million Indians and Alaska Natives and had massively improved the average health statistics of American Indians.

206 Prucha 1986, 368–9. This law is also known as the American Indian Religious Freeedom Act. Public Law No. 95-341, 92 Stat. 469 (Aug. 11, 1978) (commonly abbreviated to AIRFA), codified at 42 U.S.C. § 1996. Wildenthal 2003, 31.

Congress enacted the Indian Child Welfare Act, which enhanced tribal control over the adoption of Indian children, in order to keep them from being placed outside the tribe.[207]

In 1968, Congress crafted a Civil Rights Bill for American Indians, because, since they are not "subject to the jurisdiction of the United States" on reservations, the Fourteenth Amendment does not apply the Bill of Rights to tribal governments, as it does to the state governments.[208] Importantly, this Act restored to any tribe that wanted it, the state criminal and civil jurisdiction over reservation Indians that had been taken away by Public Law 280 during the termination era. It also exempted tribal governments from the Bill of Rights ban on governmental establishment of religion.[209]

This 1968 Act did grant individual Indians the civil liberties prized by other Americans such as the right against unreasonable search and seizure, rights of free speech and press, right against compelled incrimination, right to counsel, and so forth. On this score it was criticized by advocates of total tribal sovereignty, but it can hardly be viewed as anti-Indian. This law in turn produced more than one case that went all the way to the U.S. Supreme Court presenting conflicts between a tribal government and individual Indians asserting their federal legal rights against said government. Some of these are described below.

Meanwhile, the War on Poverty programs of the Johnson Administration of the 1960s, along with follow-up anti-poverty programs in the 1970s, naturally had a major impact on this most impoverished segment of the American population, its Native Americans.[210] By the 1980s, Congress was appropriating three billion dollars annually for various services to Indians, and in a 1985 published report, it took six pages to list all the titles of federal programs for Indian assistance.[211]

These programs, coupled with the post-1960 respect for tribal governments and cultures, have made a difference. Long the laggard among all minorities in statistics on health, income, education, and longevity, Indians have since surpassed African-Americans on these measures. In

---

[207] Pub.L. 95–608, 92 Stat. 3069, enacted November 8, 1978, codified at 25 U.S.C. §§ 1901–1963; Wildenthal 2003, 32.

[208] Technically, not all of the rights itemized in the Bill of Rights apply to state governments, but all the ones that people care about have by now been applied to them by the U.S. Supreme Court, including most recently (for better or worse) the right to bear arms.

[209] Prucha 1986, 363–4.

[210] Washburn 1996, 430–32; Prucha, ibid., 359–60.

[211] Washburn, ibid., 408, 432.

1980, life expectancy for Indians exceeded that for African-Americans, and was only four years shorter than that of Euro-Americans. In 1941, Indian life expectancy was fifty-one. By 1980, it was 71.1.[212] The incidence of death from homicide among Indians in 1955 was five times higher than that of the U.S. as a whole. By 1988, it was down to a ratio of 1.6:1.[213] Wilcomb E. Washburn of the Smithsonian Institute terms the period of 1960–90 an "Indian renaissance," and cites an extensive range of similar statistics across education, employment and earnings to support the label.[214]

Belatedly, only in 1988 did Congress announce explicitly that it "repudiates and rejects House Concurrent resolution 108 ... and any policy of unilateral termination of federal relations with any Indian nation."[215] But Congressional concern for respecting tribal traditions nonetheless continues: a more recent example is the Native American Graves Protection and Repatriation Act of 1990, which expands tribal authority over Indian burial remains and other religious and cultural artifacts.[216]

Congress also acted in the post-1970 period to improve tribal involvement in the management of their forest resources and of the mineral development. It was legislating as late as 1991 to expand the Indian land base, in a continuing effort to undo the damaging impact of the 1887 Dawes Act.[217]

The respect for tribal sovereignty expressed in Congressional statutes also continued to show up in the executive branch of the 1980s and 1990s. President Reagan's Environmental Protection Agency in 1984 adopted a government-to-government relationship with tribes, in effect treating them as equivalent to state governments. Thus, in 1987 after

---

212 Ibid., 404, 464.

213 Ibid., 463.

214 Ibid., 464–6.

215 It did so within the Comprehensive Elementary and Secondary Education Act, 102 Stat. 130 (1988). Wilkins, 1997, 237, 334.

216 Wildenthal 2003, 32. 104 Stat. 3048, Public Law 101-601 (Nov. 16, 1990). And beyond the time period covered by this chapter, in 1994 Congress amended federal law to provide protection against any prosecution of religious use of peyote by Native Americans. Public Law No. 103-344, 108 Stat. 3125 (1994).

217 National Indian Forest Resources Management Act of 1990, 25 U.S.C.A. §§ 3101–3120; Indian Mineral Development Act of 1982, 25 U.S.C.A. §§ 2101–2108; Indian Land Consolidation Act of 1991 25 U.S.C.A. §§ 2201–2211; Getches, et al. 1993, 256–9 catalogs additional national laws enacted to help the tribes in this period.

Congress authorized the EPA to delegate certain of its enforcement powers under the Clean Water Act to qualified tribes (as the EPA also does to state governments), the EPA did so. This produced a clash in the 1990s, in which the Isleta Pueblo ordered the city of Albuquerque to clean up its water. Albuquerque fought it in court from 1992–97, ultimately losing in the Tenth Circuit, with the Supreme Court refusing to hear the appeal in 1997.[218] Similarly, President William (Bill) Clinton issued a number of orders and memos during the 1990s urging respect for the "government-to-government relationship with federally recognized Native American tribes."[219]

Modern U.S. Supreme Court on Indians

The U.S. Supreme Court in recent decades has wrestled with the conflict between the protection for individual rights indicated in the (1968) Indian Civil Rights Act described above, and the respect for tribal sovereignty expressed by now in many other pieces of federal legislation. Two much-discussed examples are *Santa Clara Pueblo v. Martinez* (1978) and *Mississippi Band of Choctaw Indians v. Holyfield* (1989).[220] *Martinez* pitted the individual equal protection right to be free of gender bias, against the tribe's right to set its own membership rules. Had Martinez been male, her daughter would have been a tribal member entitled to emergency services from the Indian Health Services. Because she was not, her daughter died. The lawsuit was on behalf of Martinez's other children, still living on the reservation with her, to extend to them rights of tribal membership. The U.S. Supreme Court sided with tribal sovereignty and against Martinez, invoking the doctrine of sovereign immunity to protect the tribe from private lawsuits.

The *Holyfield* case involved the Indian Child Welfare Act of 1978, which said that when Indian children are being placed for adoption, absent "good cause," the first preference must be other family members, second preference other tribal members and third preference other Indians. It also gave tribal courts exclusive jurisdiction over placements of children domiciled on a reservation, and it gave tribes and their members the right to petition for tribal jurisdiction over foster care and adoption placements, which jurisdiction they would receive absent a "good cause" objection. The Supreme Court interpreted this law as

---

218 Wildenthal 2003, 126; Lenderman 1998.

219 Wildenthal 2003, 125–6.

220 *Santa Clara Pueblo v. Martinez*, 436 U.S. 49 (1978) and *Mississippi Band of Choctaw Indians v. Holyfield*, 490 U.S. 30 (1989).

denying parental choice of adoptive family for their newborn twins to two parents who moved off the reservation for ten days, specifically in order to place their children, once born, with a (state-court-approved) non-Indian family. Other Court decisions had seemed to establish that this liberty belongs as a fundamental due process right to non-Indian parents under the Constitution,[221] but the Court ruled here that it does not belong to reservation Indians.

Sometimes, however, Indian rights created by the 1968 Bill of Rights do prevail against tribal authority. It had been very longstanding U.S. practice to allow tribal authority to punish offenses committed by Indians on Indian territory, except where Congress has carved out explicit exceptions to this aspect of primeval indigenous sovereignty (as Congress did in the Major Crimes Act of 1885).[222] In the Indian Country Crimes Act, dating back as far as 1790, Congress had extended federal criminal law into Indian country, for purposes of both punishing and protecting non-Indian criminals and non-Indian crime victims there.[223] But for Indian-on-Indian crime, traditionally (although not on every reservation, depending on treaty wording[224]), this jurisdiction under tribal sovereignty extended to Indian non-members of the tribe as well as to members. Congress over the centuries had generally been content to extend U.S.

---

[221] E.g., *Caban v. Mohammed*, 441 US 380 (1979) (father who has participated in the raising of his child cannot lose custody rights by unilateral act of the mother wishing to give adoptive father's rights to her current husband); *Stanley v. Illinois*, 405 U.S. 645 (1972) (father has fundamental right to care and custody of child he has sired and raised).

[222] Some of this history is traced by the Court in *Oliphant v. Squamish Indian Tribes*, 435 U.S. 191, 197–212 (1978). Justice Marshall, joined by Chief Justice Burger, dissented but offered no precedents to support their position that tribal sovereignty over tribal territory included jurisdiction to try non-Indians.

[223] Rev.Stat., sec. 629, cl. 20, sec. 2145, sec. 5339, cl. 1., cited in *United States v. McBratney*, 104 U.S. 621, 621–2 (1882). Wildenthal 2003, 71. This 1882 decision allowed state courts to handle crimes between a non-Indian culprit and a non-Indian victim, even if on Indian Territory within the state *if*, as was the case in Colorado, the federal government neglected to reserve federal jurisdiction in its 1875 Act creating the state (it had inserted such reservation for some other states, e.g., Kansas). After 1882 Congress wrote such reservation clauses into laws creating all later states except Hawaii's. Wilkins and Lomawaima 2001, 192.

[224] The 1868 Ute Treaty involved in the 1882 *McBratney* case explicitly included non-Ute Indians, extending the protections of federal law to "any one, white, black, or Indian, subject to the authority of the United States" against crimes committed on the Ute Territory, even if by a Ute. *U.S. v. McBratney,* 104 U.S., at 622.

jurisdiction over whites, leaving Indians to be dealt with by Indians. In 1990, however, an Indian being tried for a crime he was accused of committing on the property of a tribe not his own, by the court of this not-his-own tribe, relied on the claim that the 1968 Civil Rights Act did confer "equal protection of the laws" upon Indians. To offer the protection of due process as understood in U.S. Courts only to whites accused of committing crimes on tribal land, but not to non-tribal-member Indians accused of the same, amounted to the kind of race-based discrimination frowned upon under equal protection principles. In *Duro v. Reina* (1990)[225] the Supreme Court ruled that inherent tribal sovereignty under conditions of dependency on the U.S. Government with respect to external relations, and as limited by extant federal law, meant that tribes retained criminal jurisdiction over tribal members for offenses committed on the tribe's territory, but *not* over non-members of the tribe on tribal territory, irrespective of the race of the non-member. The Supreme Court majority did not emphasize equal protection issues, although the federal district court that first decided the case had done so. Justices Brennan and Marshall dissented, arguing that the residual tribal sovereignty was territorial and therefore did extend to all persons and acts not explicitly exempted from it by Congress. The dissent was silent as to a potential equal protection problem under the Fifth Amendment that might stem from Congress's according whites, but not non-tribal Indians, due process protections for accusations of crime on Indian territory.

One problem created by the *Duro* decision was that now on reservations such as that of the Ute in Colorado, while the state had jurisdiction over white-on-white crime, the tribe had jurisdiction over intratribal crime and the federal government had jurisdiction both over any crime listed in the Major Crimes Act and over any crime committed between a white and an Indian, *no* governmental body had jurisdiction over a crime committed by a non-Ute Indian on Ute land against a Ute or vice versa. Congress quickly stepped in to address this void: It amended the Indian Civil Rights Act in 1991 by creating a tribal power on its own territory to "exercise criminal jurisdiction over all Indians" as one of elements of tribal self-government (overriding the *Duro* decision).[226] As with some of the Court decisions indicated, one has trouble categorizing this move by Congress as pro-Indian or anti-Indian: it boosted tribal governing powers

---

225 In *Duro v. Reina*, 495 U.S. 676 (1990).

226 25 U.S.C. § 1301 (4). Wildenthal 2003, 80–85; Getches, et al. 1993, 417–19.

at the expense of saying that even though whites are protected by federal due process on tribal lands, non-member Indians are not.

By contrast, the modern Supreme Court has been clear and unvacillating on the principle that in matters of civil law, business regulations, taxing, and so forth, Indian territory is ruled by tribal courts, not by state (or federal) courts (in the large majority of states that have not assumed jurisdiction under Public Law 280). This principle has been upheld in several modern cases, e.g., *Williams v. Lee* (1959) (affirming exclusive power in tribal courts to judge civil lawsuit brought by a small business operated by a non-Indian on the reservation); *Fisher v. District Court* (1976) (rejecting claim of state court jurisdiction for an adoption dispute where all parties lived on reservation); and *New Mexico v. Mescalero Apache Tribe* (1978) (rejecting state regulatory authority over fishing and hunting on tribal territory).[227] The Court has carved out a narrow exception. Non-Indians who bought land in fee simple within the bounds of a reservation during the Allotment era and later non-Indian owners of this land may hunt or fish on their own property under state laws rather than under tribal laws (at least in situations where there is no allegation that such activity imperils the tribe or its well-being).[228]

Conflict between statutorily created federal rights of individual Indians and tribal governing rights is a relatively modern judicial issue. More enduring, and perhaps more problematic because of its greater sweep, is the issue of Congressional deviation from its treaty commitments. Sometimes cases posing this conflict came about because the federal government decided that it wanted back land that earlier governments had ceded in treaties.

The particularly egregious, early twentieth century Fuller Court decision of *Lone Wolf v. Hitchcock* (1903) showed a Court unsympathetic to Indian claims of this type, even where ample evidence of corrupt dealings had been presented both in Congress before the fact and in court after the fact. In this case, the Court relied on the traditional rule that a later Congress may reject earlier treaty commitments in light of new circumstances; granted Congress the benefit of the doubt in presuming that Congress was acting as a trustee for the benefit of the Indians; and ruled that it was inappropriate for courts to be second-guessing legislative judgments as to which policies best promoted Indian well-being.[229]

---

[227] *Williams v. Lee*, 358 U.S. 217 (1959); *Fisher v. District Court*, 424 U.S.382 (1976); *New Mexico v. Mescalero Apache Tribe*, 462 U.S. 324 (1978); Wildenthal 2003, 85–6.

[228] *Montana v. U.S.*, 450 U.S. 544 (1981).

[229] *Lone Wolf* is discussed in Chapter 4.

Cases in the later twentieth century present a stark contrast to *Lone Wolf*, as does Congress's behavior toward the cases. The very lengthy Sioux litigation over the Black Hills offers a glimpse of both branches' evolving pattern of behavior in the twentieth century. From early on, the Sioux had been contesting an 1877 Act that abrogated an earlier treaty and seized the Black Hills from them in order to allow in white settlers. In 1922 Sioux lobbying of Congress produced a special jurisdictional act (waiving its relevant sovereign immunity) to let the Sioux take their case to the Court of Claims. The Sioux then petitioned this court promptly in 1923 to order just compensation to the tribe, as required by the Fifth Amendment. Not until 1942, however, did this court dispose of the claim, finally ruling that the petition be dismissed because the jurisdictional statute did not authorize it to assess whether the compensation paid had been "just" or not. The Supreme Court at the time refused to grant cert.[230]

After Congress passed the 1946 Indian Claims Commission Act, the Sioux went to the Indian Claims Commission with the same claim. After a lengthy period of decisions and counter decisions, the Indian Claims Commission ruled in favor of the Sioux, but was then overruled by the Court of Claims on appeal in 1975. The latter cited the legal doctrine of *res judicata* to block about 84 percent of the damages awarded by the Claims Commission. At the time, the full Claims Commission award would have been $107.55 million, but the Claims Court was allowing only $17.55 million. Here, in 1978, Congress stepped in, after successful lobbying by representatives of the Sioux Nation, to offer a nudge to the judicial branch to look more favorably on the Sioux claims. The 1978 law allowed the Court of Claims to review its earlier decision and disallowed the U.S. Government the defenses of *res judicata* and collateral estoppel.[231]

After this Congressional nudge, the Court of Claims reversed its earlier judgment, now awarding the full amount of damages plus interest. The U.S. Supreme Court affirmed eight–one in *U.S. v. Sioux Nation* (1980). In explaining its decision the Supreme Court embraced a ruling from the Court of Claims in the 1968 *Fort Berthold v. U.S.* case, which, the Court explained, reconciled two potentially competing precedents:[232] *Lone Wolf* (1903) stood for the proposition that Congress has plenary power over Indian land because of its trustee role as guardian of the Indians and can

230 *U.S. v. Sioux Nation*, 448 U.S. 371, 384 (1980).

231 Ibid., 384–9.

232 *Three Tribes of Fort Berthold Reservation v. United States*, 182 Ct.Cl. 543; 390 F.2d 686 (1968).

therefore act toward Indians in a way that might look like a violation of a treaty obligation. By contrast, *Shoshone Tribe v. U.S.*, (1937) established that Congress's power over the tribes does not allow the federal government either to give tribal land to others or to take tribal land for public purposes in violation of the Just Compensation Clause of the Fifth Amendment.[233] When Congress takes the land away from a tribe, it must give the Indians just compensation. The (1968 Court of Claims) *Berthold* decision ruled that the powers of Congressional trusteeship over Indians and their property, on the one hand, and of eminent domain, on the other hand, were mutually exclusive. When Congress exercises the latter power, it is constrained by the Fifth Amendment. The test whether the trustee power is being exercised or not, is to ask whether Congress was making a good faith effort at the time of the sale of Indian land to afford just compensation. If it was, then "there was not taking"; it was acting as a trustee. The Supreme Court, in the 1980 *Sioux* case, now having embraced this guideline for future cases, then agreed with the Court of Claims award.[234]

The modern U.S. Supreme Court has not always sided with Native American land claims. A 1955 case *Tee Hit Ton Indians v. U.S.* presented the question whether the surviving sixty to seventy members of a clan of the Tlingit tribe were entitled to compensation for resources sold by the federal government from 350,000 acres of land and 150 square miles of water claimed by the group under aboriginal title, i.e., not from title stemming from any native tribal treaty with the U.S. Government.[235] The dispute turned on interpretation of the following passages from two Congressional acts, the 1884 Organic Act for Alaska (cited in footnote 10 of the Court opinion) and the 1900 Act to provide civil government for Alaska (cited in footnote 11):

> [cited in footnote 10 of the opinion] … [T]he Indians or other persons in said district shall not be disturbed in the possession of any lands actually in their use or occupation or now claimed by them but the terms under which such persons may acquire title to such lands is reserved for future legislation by Congress … .
>
> [cited in footenote 11] The Indians or persons conducting schools or missions in the district shall not be disturbed in the possession of any lands now actually in their use or occupation.

---

233 *Shoshone Tribe v. U.S.*, 299 U.S. 476 (1937).
234 *U.S. v. Sioux Nation*, 448 U.S., at 407–16 (1980).
235 *Tee Hit Ton Indians v. U.S.*, 348 U.S. 272 (1955).

The three dissenters took these passages, along with the absence of any passages explicitly granting rights to others to settle in Alaska or to purchase land there, and also along with Congressional testimony from the debates on the Organic Act, to show that Congress in 1884 "recognized the claims of these Indians to their Alaskan lands," and fully intended to "let them keep what they had prior to the new act."[236] These dissenters would have left it to the Court of Claims to determine whether this tribe in fact had used the forests in 1884 in such a way as to establish a later claim for the timber. The six justice majority, by contrast, took the same language to show the Congress was allowing the aboriginal tribes only rights of occupancy and use but not such "title" to the land as would require compensation if its resources were ever sold off to other parties. In terms of the big picture, the kind of wholly uncompensated taking permitted by the Supreme Court in the Alaska situation involving the Tee Hit Ton clan has been a rare exception in the history of American Indian law. The general historical picture has been that the vast majority of the takings of Indian land ("practically all of the real estate acquired by the United States since 1776," in the words of legal scholar Felix Cohen, writing prior to *Tee Hit Ton*) was accompanied by compensation paid to Indians either via negotiated treaties or agreements, or by special legislation permitting tribal claims, or by claims brought pursuant to the Indian Claims Commission Act of 1946.[237]

Beyond the matters of tribal sovereignty and specific land claims, the modern Supreme Court has shown a friendliness to Indian claims in other respects, as well. In 1974, when the Court was gearing up to cast a critical eye at race-based affirmative action policies in general,[238] it rejected a claim that the longstanding (since the Reorganization Act of 1934) federal legislative preference for hiring Indians into civil service positions of those agencies that regulate Indians conflicted with the 1974 Equal Employment Act provision forbidding the federal government from doing race-based hiring or promotions. Nor, the Court ruled, did it conflict with equal protection of the laws. Despite the late twentieth century Supreme Court's skepticism toward affirmative action, in *Morton v. Mancari* (1974)[239] it upheld the longstanding hiring preference for

---

236 *Tee Hit Ton Indians v. U.S.*, 348 U.S. 272, at 292-4 (1955) (Justice Douglas with Chief Justice Warren and Justice Frankfurter, dissenting).

237 Getches, et al. 1993, 308.

238 Compare *DeFunis v. Odegard*, 416 U.S. 312 (1974) (dismissed as moot) with *Regents v. Bakke*, 438 U.S. 265 (declaring the race-based affirmative action admissions program of U.C Davis unlawful).

239 *Morton v. Mancari*, 417 U.S. 535 (1974).

Indians, explaining that the category was a political rather than a merely racial one. These agencies, to one or another degree governed Indian life, so the preference was a way to enhance self-government of Indians. As of 1993, 80 percent of employees of the Bureau of Indian Affairs were Native Americans.[240]

Although more than one Congressional statute has carved out special respect for Indian religious life,[241] the modern Supreme Court has not always opted to honor that preference. For instance, *Lyng v. Northwest Indian Cemetery Protective Ass'n* (1988) pitted the (First Amendment) religious exercise rights of certain members of three tribes to meditate in a peaceful and undisturbed setting against the authority of the U.S. Government to build a logging road within the National Forest. During the litigation, Congress did ban the practice of logging itself within the area that concerned the Indians. But Congress did not choose to block the road. Neither did the U.S. Supreme Court. Justice O'Connor's opinion for the majority observed that the existence of the road would make the particular religious practice only marginally more difficult, but would not have the effect of blocking or preventing it or bringing coercive pressure against it.[242] Consequently, the Court chose not to apply the strict scrutiny that would have been required at the time under *Sherbert v. Verner* (1963) against laws coercively pressuring people to abandon religious practices.[243]

Apart from religious exercise, U.S. laws of general applicability may also present problems due to infringements of longstanding treaty rights apart from efforts at outright taking back of land. There is a general rule that later laws may depart from earlier treaties (whether treaties with foreign powers or with Indians) as a result of changed conditions (just as current legislatures may change laws adopted by earlier legislatures). Ever since the time of John Marshall, the guiding principle (sometimes honored in the breach) has been that Congressional intent for a later statute to be upheld in a way that transgresses a treaty must be explicit or otherwise clear in order for the deviation from the treaty to be upheld by

240 Getches, et al. 1993, 265.

241 For instance, The Bald Eagle Protection Act bans the capturing of bald or golden eagles but specifically exempts their taking by Indians for religious purposes as authorized by the Secretary of the Interior. 54 Stat. 250, 16 U.S.C. 668 et seq. (Eagle Protection Act), 16 U.S.C. 668a. This section of the 1940 statute was added to it in 1962. Wisch 2002. See also text at n.209 above.

242 *Lyng v. Northwest Indian Cemetery Protective Ass'n*, 485 U.S. 439, 450–52 (1988).

243 *Sherbert v. Verner*, 374 U.S. 398 (1963); See Bogen and Goldstein 2010.

a court. Thus, in modern cases, debate within the Supreme Court has often turned on whether such intent (to deviate from the earlier treaty) was made sufficiently clear by Congress in the legislation at issue.

For instance, in *Menominee Tribe v. U.S.* (1968), the Court addressed an effort by the state of Wisconsin, beginning in 1962, to enforce its hunting and fishing regulations on Indians within tribal land. The state claimed that the federal termination of the tribe in 1954 had given Wisconsin this authority. The federal Court of Claims ruled, contrary to the Wisconsin Supreme Court, that the Wolf River Treaty of 1854 establishing the reservation prevailed despite tribal termination and awarded the tribe compensation for the loss of its hunting and fishing rights. Despite the case title, the U.S. Justice Department argued on the side of the tribe for upholding the Court of Claims award, and Wisconsin argued the contrary via an amicus brief. The specific termination Act had been silent as to hunting and fishing rights. However, Public Law 280 (effective as of 1954), which gave Wisconsin civil and criminal jurisdiction over Indians in Indian territory, specifically said that rights and privileges of Indians secured via federal treaty with respect to hunting, trapping, and fishing were to be maintained. The Court chose to abide by this latter language as guiding the sense of the nearly coterminous Termination Act of 1954 and awarded the claim to the tribe.[244] The justices took guidance from the longstanding principle that "the intention to abrogate or modify a treaty is not to be lightly imputed to Congress."

By contrast, where abrogation of a former treaty was quite explicit, the modern Supreme Court continues to follow the rule that Congress may deliberately violate a past treaty. In 1901, the Oregon Klamath Tribe ceded some land with an agreement that relinquished "all their claims, right, title and interest" in these lands. When the tribe in 1985 attempted to assert that they still maintained an earlier treaty-honored right to hunt and fish there without limitation by state law, the Supreme Court rejected their claim.[245]

The following year, the Court handed down a decision (*U.S. v. Dion*) based not on such explicit language but on reasonable inference from other parts of a statute. A current federal ban on hunting eagles permitted a religion-based exemption to be accorded to Indians. This narrowly drawn exemption, the Court ruled, implied that other exemptions—such

---

[244] *Menominee Tribe v. U.S.*, 391 U.S. 404 (1968).

[245] *Oregon Dept of Fish & Wildlife v. Klamath Indian Tribe*, 473 U.S. 751 (1985).

as an Indian right to unlimited hunting of eagles for commercial purposes—was not properly inferrable, despite prior treaties.[246]

One can also point to additional cases that went against Indian tribal claims while applying this interpretive principle, for instance *South Dakota v. Bourland* (1993), holding that Congress had clearly implied, albeit not expressly stated, that federal law opened up land in question for hunting and fishing by non-Indians.[247] One can also mention *FPC v. Tuscarora Indian Nation* (1960), holding that the eminent domain power of the FPC to take land for the purpose of a dam project did apply to Tuscarora land that had been purchased as fee simple in 1804 (not held as result of treaty provision) because the relevant Federal Power Act exempted land reserved to tribes by virtue of treaties but not fee land purchased by them.[248] Casebook authors Getches, Williams, and Wilkinson suggest that the result in FPC "probably would not obtain today" because eminent domain power over Indian fee land was not explicitly granted by Congress.[249] Indian law scholar Wildenthal chimes in similarly, claiming that the Supreme Court became more liberal on Indian issues after the *Tee Hit Ton* (1955) and *FPC v. Tuscarora* (1960) decisions by the time it decided *Menominee v. U.S.* (1968).[250]

What appears clear is that even before 1960, the modern Court has been attempting to follow the will of Congress, as best it can, with the general guidance that benefit of the doubt goes with upholding treaty provisions unless Congress clearly specifies otherwise. Individual justices naturally vary in interpreting the sense of this guideline, but the currently guiding principle of Supreme Court Indian law jurisprudence leans toward upholding the tribal claim to the degree feasible under the will of Congress. This qualifiedly pro-tribal principle has been since 1937, at least, buttressed by the principle that the U.S. Government is bound by the Just Compensation Clause when it takes or sells off Indian land that was theretofore protected by treaty.[251]

Post-1932 Interbranch Comparison on Indians

The modern era has been one in which on Indian matters, as with Asians, the legislative branch and the executive branch moved largely (albeit not

---

246 *U.S. v. Dion*, 476 U.S. 734 (1986).
247 *South Dakota v. Bourland*, 508 U.S. 679 (1993).
248 *FPC v. Tuscarora Indian Nation*, 361 U.S. 99 (1960).
249 Getches, et al. 1993, 346–8.
250 Wildenthal 2003, 64–5. See discussion of *Menominee* above at note 244.
251 *Shoshone Tribe v. U.S.*, 299 U.S. 476 (1937).

perfectly) in tandem. And except for the Eisenhower Administration (1953–60) and its now thoroughly discredited termination policy, the movement has been toward respect for tribal quasi-sovereignty (under the umbrella of U.S. sovereignty as to external tribal relations and as to "major" crimes) and tribal cultural heritage, and even toward some degree of land restoration. To be sure, no branch of the three has advocated a retreat by Euro-Americans back to Europe—that is, for anything anywhere near full land restoration—but there has been even within Congress more respect for attempting to honor extant treaty commitments and for fostering Indian health and well-being. As the elected branches during the modern period have moved on Indian policy, so has the Supreme Court in general, with the qualification that the Court has the responsibility for figuring out how to reconcile conflicting federal laws in particular instances of clash—for instance, adjusting the mutually conflicting claims of a mandate to respect tribal religion and a mandate to develop federal land in a way that might clash incidentally with a particular Native American tribal tradition.

CONCLUSIONS

This chapter has highlighted a number of respects in which the modern period of Supreme Court policymaking, which I am dating from the beginning of the FDR Administration (January, 1933) until the early 1990s, differed from prior ones. First, the Supreme Court, in the matter of policy toward black Americans, moved from a position slightly out in front of (i.e., better than) the elected branches, as it had been beginning with the post-Fuller Courts led by White and Taft, respectively, and was at the beginning of the 1930s Hughes Court, to a position most of the time decisively ahead of the elected branches under the later Hughes Court (beginning with its attack on segregation in the 1938 *Missouri ex rel. Gaines* decision) and both the Vinson and Warren Courts. The Court's role of leadership on the civil rights of blacks was noticed by law-attentive journalists as early as the 1930s. Harry Truman (1945–52) and Lyndon Johnson (1963–68, covered in this book's Introduction), notably, both presidents who had ascended to office via a death of their predecessor, rather than by being directly elected to it, took on a mantle of dramatic civil rights leadership that equaled the one donned by the Court, but their administrations were the exceptions. Over the stretch of time from 1911 to the early '90s, the Court stood out for its leadership, until it turned its back on black civil rights in 1991, when it began the process of declaring the period of school desegregation at an end.

The other noteworthy development uncovered in this chapter was the degree of interdependence, at the Supreme Court level, of rights developments between blacks and Asians, just as Chapter 6 uncovered a degree of interdependence among Hispanic-, Asian- and African-American civil rights. For contesting school segregation, African-American litigants took encouragement from certain Asian rights cases and the Supreme Court chose to build upon doctrine developed in those cases, just as Justice Earl Warren chose to build upon reasoning from the obscure *Mendez v. Westminster* case in his *Brown v. Board* reasoning.

On issues concerning Asians and American Indians, the elected branches finally did a meaningful about-face. They chose to make citizenship with all its attendant rights available to all Asians by the post-war period (in the case of Japanese and Koreans, the final major groups, by 1952), and to open immigration on a non-racial basis in 1965. Also, starting in the 1930s, the elected branches finally turned away from the policy of pushing assimilation upon American Indians, and despite a relapse in the 1948–59 period, have since 1960 permanently abandoned that direction as ill-advised and harmful. In both of these moves, momentum has come from the Presidency, and, in fact, Presidents were well ahead of Congress in the move to place immigration reform onto a non-racial foundation. The Supreme Court made only marginal improvements in the period to policies toward these groups, checking (in principle) the ethnicity-based, longterm incarceration of innocent Japanese-Americans (*Endo*) but not the exclusion from their homes (*Korematsu*). Similarly, the Court bounded Congress's failures to protect Indian treaty-granted lands by the Just Compensation Clause[252] but continued (as ever) to allow Congress to deviate from past treaties in new legislation.[253] Because of the Constitution's terms and structure, the Supreme Court is obliged to tread lightly on matters of foreign policy, naturalization, and Indian policy; it can check state-level abuses or administrative overreach, but is obliged to carry out the basic contours of policy set by the national political branches.

---

[252] *U.S. v. Sioux Nation*, 448 U.S. 371 (1980); *Shoshone Tribe v. U.S.*, 299 U.S. 476 (1937).

[253] *South Dakota v. Bourland*, 508 U.S. 679 (1993); *FPC v. Tuscarora Indian Nation*, 361 U.S. 99 (1960).

8. Overview and conclusions

OVERVIEW

This book began, in a sense, at the end. From the mid-twentieth century until its last decade, the U.S. Supreme Court, at least with respect to the African-American minority, stood out as leading the charge to protect minority rights in comparison with the elected branches.

It is true that in the twentieth century a couple of presidents, Harry Truman (who desegregated the military) and Lyndon Johnson, each of whom had ascended to office via the death of his predecessor, took firm and consequential civil rights stands.[1] Johnson in particular was highly effective at mobilizing Congress to act. Assisted first by Congressional sympathy from the Kennedy assassination and then by a heavily Democratic Congress swept in by opposition to the Goldwater candidacy, he ushered through Congress important civil rights legislation, and he ably deployed his Justice Department to enforce those laws. The face of America changed. It is doubtful that without the effects of the Civil Rights Act of 1964, and its enforcement via the funding of the Elementary and Secondary Education Act of 1965, and the Voting Rights Act of 1965, Barack Obama could have risen to become President of the United States in 2008. Of course, not only his life, but hundreds of thousands, nay millions, of other lives were altered as well.

Still, the Supreme Court led the way. In the mid-1950s it ordered school desegregation and desegregation of other government-run facilities, while Congress was still tied in knots by southern filibusters. In the 60s, it declared poll taxes unconstitutional in state and local elections.[2] It upheld judicial busing orders in the decade of the 70s, despite opposition among the public and in Congress, and foot-dragging by the Nixon

[1] President Theodore Roosevelt (another ascendant via the vice-presidency) also took a firm stand, authorizing vigorous prosecutions of white southern malefactors. The Fuller Supreme Court, however, brought those prosecutions to naught.

[2] *Harper v. Virginia Board of Elections*, 383 U.S. 663 (1966). The states and Congress had acted in 1964 in the Twenty-Fourth Amendment to ban them in federal elections.

Administration. Only at the end of the 1980s did the Court give way, applying strict scrutiny for the first time to race-based affirmative action programs (*Richmond v. Croson* (1989)) and producing two decisions that made it more difficult for plaintiffs to win job discrimination claims (*Price Waterhouse v. Hopkins* and *Wards Cove Packing Co. v. Antonio*[3]—decisions reversed by Congress in the Civil Rights Act of 1991), and then in the 1990s removing federal judicial supervision from several school districts that had desegregated and thereafter strongly discouraging race-based affirmative action.

This book has examined the question whether those four decades of Supreme Court leadership (1950–89) in protecting the rights of the African-American minority has been typical across the Court's first two centuries. And not only whether other time periods were similar with respect to African Americans, but also whether the pattern was similar with respect to other racial minorities: Native Americans, Asians, Latino Americans. As a general matter, with respect to guarding the rights of racial minorities, groups perhaps the most harshly treated by our majority-elected legislatures, did the Supreme Court, protected with lifetime tenure against retaliation by a voting majority, do any better than the elected branches?

To be sure, the Court's actual power to effect change is limited; the Court has, as Alexander Hamilton noted from the start, in Federalist #78, only the power of judgment, no coercive ability. If Congress and the President agree to provide it with U.S. Marshals to carry out its judgment, then enforcement can come. But in fact the enforcement is coming from the other branches. This is not news. On actual power to effect change, no branch can hold a candle to Abraham Lincoln's executive branch action freeing almost all the slaves within the geographic bounds of the country in which he was elected. Of course, it did take winning the war to make his proclamation matter, and Congressional action was needed to pursue the war. This inquiry has been focused not on the Court's ability singlehandedly to enforce change but more on its willingness to defy electoral majority opinion in support of minority rights. The chapter-by-chapter answers were something of a surprise to me (and also painful to research, because so many oppressive policies were carried out by the U.S. Government against blacks, Asians and Indians). Often (although regrettably, not always), the oppressive policy was simply to refrain from acting to correct violent acts of lawless

---

[3] *Price Waterhouse v. Hopkins,* 490 U.S. 228 (1989) and *Wards Cove Packing Co. v. Antonio,* 490 U.S. 642 (1989).

individuals and lawless acts perpetrated by state and local officials acting in violation of legal duties.

As early as the first chapter, a pattern emerged. The Supreme Court, in principle, can check abuses of power at the state level (by deploying the Supremacy Clause) (and similarly can check abuses by territorial-level legislatures, parallel to those of states) and can check abuses of power by administrative officials (on the grounds that these officials exceeded their powers under existing legislation). The Court has hardly ever declared an act of Congress unconstitutional on the grounds that it infringed on the rights of a racial minority. Two exceptions to this blanket assertion are ones that, in a sense, "prove the rule." The Supreme Court in *Bolling v. Sharpe* (1954) declared unconstitutional laws that segregated schools in D.C., but these were laws of only local reach, similar in function to those of a state or local legislature.[4] The other such exception is *In re: Heff* (1905), declaring unconstitutional a law that restricted the equal liberty of Native American citizens; the Court overruled itself on this point within eleven years (*U.S. v. Nice*, 1916), following upon a clear political rebuke from Congress.

I should acknowledge that I also did find a third exception to this generalization, and it seems to be a genuine exception. In *Wong Wing v. U.S.* [1896] the Court struck down the part of the Geary Act that subjected unlawfully present Chinese to a year of hard labor before deportation, without any requirement of a jury trial and proof of guilt. One year's hard labor amounted to a classically criminal penalty and thereby went beyond Congress's plenary power over foreign commerce, trespassing into the protected domestic realm of due process. In contrast to the rarity of these exceptions, this book has demonstrated that the Court has declared unconstitutional many, many state actions that discriminated on the basis of race.[5]

---

4 Act of May 20, 1862 (§ 35, 12 Stat. 394); Act of May 21, 1862 (12 Stat. 407); Act of June 25, 1864 (13 Stat. 187); Act of July 23, 1866 (14 Stat. 216); Revised Statutes Relating to the District of Columbia, Act of June 22, 1874, (§§ 281, 282, 294, 304, 18 Stat. pt. 2). Congressional Research Service, Library of Congress. 2013. "Acts of Congress Held Unconstitutional in Whole or in Part." https://www.gpo.gov/fdsys/pkg/GPO-CONAN-2013/pdf/GPO-CONAN-2013-11.pdf I am indebted to Daniel Hoffman, Mark Graber, Matthew Hall, and Daniel Guenther for these references. Emails of January 13, 2016.

5 The very modern Court, when it turned against even federal level affirmative action in *Adarand v. Pena* (1995) did so to protect whites, not any racial minority (and *Adarand* itself was finally settled in the lower courts). I should add that my point here on judicial review's having been far more efficacious against state-level laws than against national ones provides support

This pattern first showed up during the Marshall Court years with particular respect to Indians. In its first major Indian case, *Johnson v. McIntosh* (1823), the Court established the principle that only the federal government, where the treaty-making power lay, not individual state governments, could sell off Indian land. In the famous *Worcester v. Georgia* (1832), Marshall made clear that Georgia laws oppressing the Cherokee had to give way to the federal treaty. The Court was about to enforce this decision by use of U.S. Marshals, when President Jackson smoothed over the situation by convincing the governor of Georgia to release Worcester via pardon (instead of at the hands of marshals). Checking a state prison official was one thing; checking the combined power of the President and Senate as treaty makers, or of Congress and the President wielding their power as controllers of "commerce with the Indian tribes," was another. The terms of the Constitution have prevented such action, except in the limited sense that the Court may narrow the harmful reach of a statute/treaty by interpreting it more narrowly than an administrator who is claiming to act under it.

With respect to black slaves, the Marshall Court years do not show a branch that stood out in any respect. Two of the Marshall Court justices (Johnson and Marshall) did refuse to uphold South Carolina's egregious treatment of *free* black sailors, but they did so in their role as Circuit Court judges. As to slaves, the elected branches led the way. Congress outlawed the foreign slave trade, as of literally the minute (12:01 a.m., January 1, 1808) that the Constitution permitted doing so. The Attorney General, which is to say the executive branch, was in the forefront as prosecutor of various violators of the slave trade prohibitions and the Attorney General of President John Quincy Adams requested setting free more slaves from the captured *Antelope* (1825–26) than the Court actually did. Moreover, it was Congress who in 1819 altered the punishments for the illegal slave trade, to set free and return to Africa the contraband slaves, ending the practice of allowing states to auction them off for a profit.

The Supreme Court was genuinely helpless in the face of Indian Removal once it became official federal policy. Prior to that, the Marshall Court did take a stand more than once to condemn and block (to the best of its ability) *state-level* violations of the treaty rights of Native Americans. And even President Andrew Jackson, contrary to his deserved image as an Indian fighter and four years before he was to end up

for a generalization that I first heard from Martin Shapiro of the University of California at Berkeley: *viz.*, Judicial review works best in federal systems.

sending federal troops to fight against the Creeks of Alabama in the Indian Removal Policy, ordered federal troops twice into Alabama to protect the Creeks, as per the terms of their treaty, against unauthorized white intrusion onto their lands. The white squatters were backed up by state laws and state officials, and the federal troops attempted to help the Creeks during the summers of 1832 and 1833; Jackson ordered them to withdraw only after being warned that if he did not, five more Southern states would rise up in arms against the U.S. military.

Chapter 2 found a differing pattern in Court behavior between the 1836–45 years of Joseph Story's leadership, and the next fifteen antebellum years of what might be called the unmoderated Taney Court. As to the Indians, the Story-led Court handed down no major decisions during 1836–45, but we do know from Justice Story's private correspondence that he, at least, was deeply sympathetic to their cause and critical of federal policy. Congress and the President, by contrast were carrying out the Indian Removal policy, including the Trail of Tears.

The Court under Story's leadership handed down two major slavery cases, the *Amistad* (1841) and *Prigg v. Pennsylvania* (1842). In both it showed itself to be starkly more pro-freedom than the elected branches of the time; *Amistad* (1841) set free the slaves from the ship engaged in unlawful slave trade instead of sending them to Spain as the Buchanan Administration wanted, and *Prigg* (1842), albeit without a declaration of unconstitutionality, rendered the 1793 Fugitive Slave Act unworkable by, contrary to its terms, allowing states to refuse to enforce it. During this same period, Congress was enforcing, contrary to the First Amendment, a gag rule on anti-slavery petitions, while the President kept the Post Office closed to criticism of slavery directed into southern states.

For the period that ran from 1830 to 1845, then, one can say that the Court stood out from the elected branches as a protector of unpopular racial minorities: Between 1830 and 1832 it issued a number of pronouncements in defense of Indian treaty rights against state-level violations, and in the early 1840s it clearly surpassed the elected branches in its support for freedom of both foreign and runaway slaves.

Once Joseph Story left the Court in 1845, however, *no* branch of the federal government offered protection to Indians or blacks prior to the Civil War.[6] Chief Justice Taney (in *U.S. v. Rogers* (1846)) added insult to the injury of Indian Removal by interpreting an Indian Treaty in terms

---

[6] This Taney Court did, however, make an exception for the (Hispanic) settled agricultural Indians of the Mexican cession, in effect categorizing them as white for legal purposes in *U.S. v. Ritchie* (1854).

less respectful of tribal sovereignty than the wording of the treaty allowed. Congress stepped in with the Fugitive Slave Act of 1850 to repair the large breach that *Prigg* had torn in the enforcement machinery of the Fugitive Slave Act of 1793. The Court then, with its *Dred Scott* decision (1857), outdid Congress's move to spread slavery to the territories north of the Missouri Compromise line in the Kansas-Nebraska Act (1854). The *Scott* decision outlawed *any* restriction of the spread of slavery by the federal government. Meanwhile, the federal executive in 1856 took the trouble to restrict the rights of even free blacks by refusing to let them participate in the program that gave purchasing priority for western lands to anyone who had settled those lands. And in 1858 the President urged Congressional adoption of the already-voted-down-at-the-state-level, proslavery Lecompton Constitution.

The extremist political "moment" of 1854–59 begot a counter-reaction in the election of Abraham Lincoln, against which the South had promised it would secede. Secession and civil war temporarily undid the Constitutional compromise with slavery, thereby permitting a free-states-based Congress and President to free the slaves and adopt far-ranging constitutional amendments and civil rights laws meant to protect the former slaves, who now comprised a sizable minority of the American citizenry.

These pro-black policies, however, could be effected only with the southern states no longer in Congress or in the federal electoral process, due to their own secession. Essentially at gunpoint, Congress forced the South to accept freeing of the slaves, equal citizenship rights for the former slaves, and black suffrage. As the southern states returned to Democratic Party control, after considerable white mob violence and intimidation targeting both black voters and white Republicans, a Republican Congress that had just been voted out of office, nonetheless enacted—largely by the votes of lame duck members—the Civil Rights Act of 1875, providing for non-discrimination in public accommodations and in jury rights. The Supreme Court struck down the former in 1883 but upheld the latter in 1880 and repeatedly through the early 1880s.

The postbellum Supreme Court until the accession to chief justiceship of Melville Fuller in 1888, charted a moderately pro-civil rights course. Under Chief Justice Samuel Chase, it kept pace with the Reconstruction Congress, rejecting the policy of "separate but [strictly] equal" in 1873 to insist on integration in interpreting a D.C. charter for railroads (despite *Congress*'s maintenance of racially separate but equally funded schools for the District). Under Chief Justice Waite, it removed the state action limitation from the Fifteenth Amendment, despite the more restrictive wording of the amendment, and it upheld jury rights in the early 1880s.

The latter decisions included ones that rejected hollow state-level claims that the laws themselves allowed jury service to all upstanding citizens but that administrators could not find such citizens among blacks. On the other hand, the Waite Court did let perpetrators of anti-black violence go free on the grounds of improperly drawn indictments, or sloppily worded parts of federal law. It proceeded cautiously, but definitely was acting to protect black jury rights at the state level, in a way that kept up with part of the 1875 Civil Rights Act, even though that Act had been adopted by a Congress already voted out of office by the American public. As to the public accommodations portion of that act, the Waite Court did declare that section unconstitutional, but in a manner that, at least in my reading of it, would have allowed a future Congress to word the law more carefully and re-enact it, so long as it explicitly stated that the law applied in areas of state neglect of equal protection by race. These jury decisions were handed down during a Republican Administration that was bringing prosecutions of civil rights violators, so, as during the Chase Court years, the Court was operating with, rather than ahead of other federal branches of government on issues related to black Americans.

When the federal executive branch attempted to enlist the help of the judiciary to cut back on tribal sovereignty over Indian-on-Indian crime in 1883, the Waite Court stood firm against the move in *Ex Parte Crow Dog*, ruling in favor of the full measure of tribal sovereignty permitted in extant Congressional statutes. Congress quickly overruled the Court by adopting the Major Crimes Act of 1885.

Congress also turned against the Chinese by adopting the Exclusion Act of 1882 (after similar efforts were vetoed first by President Hayes and next by President Arthur), which closed off future immigration by Chinese workers and which discriminated against current Chinese residents by forbidding immigration by their wives and tightly regulating their own exits and return into the country. Congress tightened these regulations on return in 1884 and outlawed it altogether in 1888. As with American Indians, the Waite Court resisted on behalf of the Chinese minority, at first, in 1884, and then again in 1888; the justices interpreted the relevant legislation in as rights-friendly a way possible, so as to let Chew Heong and Jung Ah Lung, resident aliens back into the United States, their home. Congress retaliated by re-enacting the exclusion law with even tighter language, such that the Court could not maintain this generous interpretation for other Chinese resident aliens who might leave the U.S. and attempt to re-enter. By contrast, the same Court successfully maintained, on constitutional grounds, a ban on state-level anti-Chinese discrimination: In 1886, in *Yick Wo v. Hopkins*, it struck down a

California statute that, while facially neutral, permitted administrative discretion in a way that produced blatant anti-Chinese discrimination.

The Waite Court was succeeded by the Fuller Court; Chief Justice Melville Fuller served from 1888–1910. This Court was the most egregiously anti-black Court since the unmoderated Taney Court of the antebellum years. The Fuller Court (although its reasoning did not say this in so many words) ruled as if there were no Fifteenth Amendment and no precedents giving blacks equal legal access to juries. For most of the Fuller Court period, the Congress and Presidency were equally hostile to the rights of black Americans; in 1894 Congress enacted a repeal of virtually all the voting rights enforcement laws of previous administrations. Even when a president, Theodore Roosevelt, who acceded to office from the vice-presidency in September 1901, actually used his Justice Department to attempt to protect the still extant rights of southern blacks, for instance, rights not to be murdered by organized lynch mobs, rights not to be forced into peonage, rights not to be coerced by racially-motivated gang violence to give up well-paying jobs, the Fuller Court thwarted these prosecutions and decided against the amicus briefs, with the lone exception of murder-by-lynching cases.

On the other hand, the Fuller Court did on several occasions support the rights of Chinese residents against unfair actions by executive officials. It stood up to the Justice Department in insisting on birthright citizenship for U.S.-born Asians in the *Wong Kim Ark* case (1898); gradually acceded, by 1908, to the principle that Chinese descent persons claiming birth-right citizenship for purposes of entering the country deserved a fair hearing on the issue, and, if denied one, could appeal to the judiciary; in seven cases restricted the behavior of overzealous immigration officials on behalf of Chinese or Chinese-Americans; and even (in *Wong Wing v. U.S.*, 1896) struck down part of a federal law, which punished by hard labor (to be followed by deportation) Chinese residents of the U.S. who could not prove that they were here lawfully (demanding a kind of proof that had not been required at their initial, potentially lawful entry).[7]

As to tribal rights, granted, the Fuller Court did fail to stop some egregious actions by Congress and the President against them; nonetheless, by 1905 it began upholding tribal rights (assisted by the executive branch) against state-level violations (in *U.S. v. Winans*). The Fuller Court also upheld rights of individual, non-reservation Indian citizens even to the degree of declaring unconstitutional a federal statute, in *In re: Heff*

---

[7] See Chapter 4 for details.

(1905). Congress found a way to limit the latter ruling by new laws that slowed the acquisition of Indian citizenship, but *In re: Heff* did have a somewhat enduring impact for those Indians who were already citizens. Unfortunately, the Court overruled *In re: Heff* in a series of decisions that culminated in *U.S. v. Nice* in 1916.

In sum, during a period when Congress and the President were more harsh toward African-Americans than any other time after the Civil War, the Fuller Court matched them in harshness. When Teddy Roosevelt's Justice Department started to offer some protection to southern blacks, the Fuller Court thwarted those efforts. On the other hand, the Fuller Court offered occasional protections to Chinese residents and to Native Americans, when none were being offered by the political branches. These mainly took the format of either checking administrative excess or striking down state laws, although one decision (*In Re: Heff,* 1905) did go so far as to declare a federal law unconstitutionally discriminatory against Indians, and another went so far as to check a piece of a federal immigration law that imposed harsh punishment against Chinese within the U.S. without due process (*Wong Wing v. U.S.* (1896)).

The second decade of the twentieth century brought a discernible shift. Despite the southern and pro-Confederacy background of the new Chief Justice, Edward White, the U.S. Supreme Court during his tenure began protecting the rights of African-Americans to a degree not before seen, with the possible exception of the ten years of Justice Story's (unofficial) leadership of the Court. Whereas the Chase Court and the Waite Court had handed down a number of decisions protective of the rights of blacks, they did so in periods when the legislative and executive branches were doing the same (skewed as they were toward Republican dominance by the facts of secession and postbellum exclusion of southern states from Congress, contingent on their ratifying the Thirteenth and Fourteenth Amendments and on their letting blacks vote in new state constitutions). The Fuller Court, 1888–1910, was unremittingly harsh toward blacks, as was what I have called the post-Story "unmoderated Taney Court" of 1845–60, but each of these periods coincided with hostility toward blacks' rights, or at least complacency toward southern denial of such rights, across the entire federal government. This hostility in the executive branch ended by September, 1901. The Supreme Court, for better and for worse, in the period of 1865–1901 was roughly similar to Congress and the President in degree of support for the rights of black Americans.

In the first decade of the twentieth century, the Theodore Roosevelt Administration (1901–09) produced supportive briefs for complainants against peonage and also prosecuted perpetrators of it, and also prosecuted mob violence that aimed at intimidating blacks into abandoning well-paying jobs. These efforts were stymied by the Fuller Court. Only its prosecutions of murderers by lynching were not blocked by this Court.

Suddenly, in the second decade of the century, under Chief Justice Edward White, the Court now began upholding convictions for peonage, being prosecuted under the Taft and Wilson Administrations (the latter with less enthusiasm than under Theodore Roosevelt), and throwing out debt servitude statutes. Moreover, the White Court struck down laws that imposed residential segregation and struck down "grandfather clauses" that clearly targeted blacks for disenfranchisement. The grandfather clause cases were in large part prosecuted by the Taft and then Wilson Administrations (albeit with both of these presidents lacking TR's enthusiasm). These administrations were not, on the whole, supportive of black rights. Wilson re-segregated the federal civil service. The White Court, by contrast, was more supportive than the elected branches on rights of blacks; it supported not only these prosecutions but also produced pro-civil rights rulings in cases not brought by the Administration, such as the one striking down race-based residential zoning laws. Although its distance from the elected branches was not extreme, the Supreme Court beginning in 1911 for the first time was moving ahead of the elected branches in a sustained way to protect the rights of African-Americans.[8] It stayed there until the end of the 1980s.

Moreover, the White Court produced reasoning that could be deployed in future cases to strike at separate but in fact unequal accommodations in interstate transportation. Notably, this dramatic shift away from the Fuller Court's treatment of African-American rights by the White Court was preceded by a decade that brought race riots to the North and that confronted the justices with a murder via lynch mob that directly and *deliberately* interfered with the Court's hearing a specific pending appeal. Now, apparently, the justices finally realized that racially motivated violence and the racial tyranny that it sustained were not simply about allowing the South—that is, white southerners—to maintain their customary way of life, but in fact undermined the rule of law itself. In the second and third decades of the twentieth century, the White and then Taft Courts, respectively, moved out in front of the elected branches as protectors of America's black minority.

---

[8] A possible exception to this "first-time" claim would be the 1836–45 period of Story's intellectual leadership on the Taney Court, but the argument for this exception is based on only two decisions: the *Amistad* case of 1841 and *Prigg v. Pennsylvania* in 1842.

The Court headed by Chief Justice Taft in the decade of the 1920s, maintained and furthered the advances put in place by the White Court in the rights of American blacks. The U.S. Supreme Court in 1927 (*Nixon v. Herndon*) declared unconstitutional a Texas law of 1923 that forbade non-whites from voting in the Democratic primaries of that state. In 1923 (*Moore v. Dempsey*) the Court ruled, for the first time and in a case that shaped many later decisions, that mob-dominated, sham trials—all too frequent in cases where the accused was a black in the South—where witnesses had been whipped into false testimony and no significant assistance of counsel had been allowed, could not count as due process of law. Also the Taft Court twice (in 1927 and 1930) reaffirmed against contrary state laws the ruling from the White Court that states and municipalities may not pass laws requiring residential segregation (although it did not go so far as to extend these rulings to condemn *private* discriminatory agreements to refuse to sell property to racial or ethnic groups in certain neighborhoods).

In 1922, while President Harding did call for a federal anti-lynching law, and the House passed it, the Senate blocked it by filibuster. This Congressional activity, however short-circuited, buttressed by the *Moore v. Dempsey* decision the following year with its related publicity, apparently caused a sharp reduction in the rate of lynchings of blacks in the U.S. These had been horrifically frequent from 1882 through 1922. The rate dropped off sharply between 1922 and 1924.[9] Apart from this abortive Dyer anti-lynching bill, the elected national branches produced no other noticeable attempts to support the rights of black Americans in the decade of the 20s.

Because the Fuller Court had already been moderately protective of Asians and Indians, the White Court's record on these groups did not contrast so sharply as it does on African-Americans. Still, the White Court acted at the margins to protect Asians and Indians during a period when neither elected branch was doing so. Although it upheld state-level restrictions on land ownership by non-resident aliens, the White Court justices struck down a state-level restriction on employing aliens, on the grounds that such laws interfered with Congress's own power over immigration policy (*Truax v. Raich* (1915)). Like its predecessor, the White Court also checked overzealous immigration officials, even one as high as the Secretary of Labor, when the hearing procedures for barring

[9] Lynchings of whites were also frequent in the years 1882–96, dropping off after that. Proportionate to population, far greater numbers of blacks were lynching victims. See Table 5.1.

re-entry of a Chinese-descent person claiming U.S. citizenship did not measure up to the Court's due process standards (1920). Similarly, the Court checked the Secretary of Labor in cases involving summary deportation of Chinese merchants (1918) and re-entry by them (1920). For the most part, to be sure, the Court accepted Congressional plenary power to shape immigration law. However, where the Court saw overreaching by executive branch officialdom or by states, it did check these moves in ways that assisted particular Asians. During this period, Congress displayed extreme hostility to Asians. President Wilson vetoed the Asiatic Barred Zone Act in 1915, but it passed over his veto in 1917. The immigration bureaucracy often dealt harshly with Asians. The situation in these elected branches only worsened in the 1921–1930 period.

During the years 1908–16, the Supreme Court retreated from its vanguard (1905) *In re: Heff* decision, which had declared that once American Indians attained U.S. citizenship, federal law could not restrict their freedoms more drastically than the freedoms of other Americans. The elected branches had rebuffed that decision by amending the Dawes Act to postpone its granting of citizenship to Indians and by bringing a series of cases to the Court arguing for the legitimacy of paternalism toward the Indians. The Court got the message. Over the course of several decisions, the Court gradually undermined the holding and reasoning of *In re: Heff*, until finally overruling it in 1916 in *U.S. v. Nice*. Basically, during the 1911–21 years of Chief Justice White, the Court bowed to the federal elected branches on this matter, backing away from defending an Indian citizen right against discrimination. On the other hand, this Court (in 1912) continued to act on the established judicial tradition of striking down *state* infringements on Indian rights that federal treaty law had protected.

The anti-Asian animus in the elected branches was so strong in the early twentieth century that Congress added enormous areas to the zone from which Asian laborer immigration would now be prohibited. The Asiatic Barred Zone Act, which Wilson's veto failed to block in 1917, categorized Southeast Asia (except New Zealand) and South Asia and some parts of Arab Asia and the southern portion of the Soviet Union as areas from which common working people could not immigrate to the U.S. Within five years of this massive prohibition the Supreme Court had to address a new question: once in the U.S., who could count as a white person for purposes of naturalization? The Court shifted its answer as each case arrived, in the end, forgoing clear rules and virtually admitting that this was a "we know it when we see it" situation. In 1922 the Court ruled that Japanese people, not being Causcasian, no matter how pale in complexion, may not be naturalized as "whites"; in 1923 it ruled that people of East Indian descent could not be lawfully considered white for this purpose, no matter how many anthropologists or ethnologists testified that such persons were of the Caucasian race. When Chinese persons wanted to be counted as "white" for purposes of attending the white high school in Mississippi, the Court said in *Gong Lum v. Rice* (1927) that this was a matter for state law to determine.

The Taft Court, like the White and Fuller Courts, did offer some protection to Asian-descent persons. In two respects it followed the White Court pattern: in 1924 it struck down state-level employment restriction on them once they were living here, although it refused to strike down state-level restrictions on land ownership by Asian aliens. It also cracked down against executive branch officials who denied full and fair judicial hearings to Asian-descent persons claiming U.S. birth-based citizenship. Moreover, it checked territorial legislatures, such as that of Hawaii, that discriminated against particular resident Asian minorities. On the other hand, the Court remained powerless to check increasingly anti-Asian U.S. immigration policies adopted by Congress in the decade of the 1920s.

The Taft Court (1921–30) issued no major decision protective of the rights of American Indians. On the other hand, policy in the elected branches toward Indians started to soften. In 1924 Congress granted U.S. citizenship to all remaining Indians who did not yet have it. In 1928–29, the executive branch commissioned a report that revealed the disastrous impact of the Dawes Act, persuading Congress in 1930 to increase appropriations for assistance to American Indians. This change of policy direction was to grow much stronger during the Franklin Roosevelt Administration.

The 1920s also brought forth the beginning of a judicial intertwining of precedents on the rights of Asians with those of African-Americans. In deciding the germinal *Moore v. Dempsey* case, protecting criminal due process rights of a black defendant, Justice Holmes relied in large part on his own dissent from *Frank v. Mangum* (1915), a case involving a southern mob-dominated trial of a Jew, where Holmes had in turn relied in significant part on his own *U.S. v. Sing Tuck* (1904) decision concerning due process rights of a Chinese national. This intertwining was to become more consequential in the 1940s and 1950s.

Until the 1930s, the federal government, with a single exception, did not adopt domestic policies toward Latinos (Mexican-Americans, Puerto Ricans, Cuban-Americans); they were dealt with as incidental to foreign policy concerns. The one exception was the subject of Pueblo Indians and other agricultural or "settled" Indians of the Mexican cession, who came into the U.S. as Mexican citizens with U.S. citizenship promised to them. In 1853 the New Mexico territory was forced by Congress to deny voting rights to the Pueblo in the election for choosing a delegate to Congress from the New Mexico territory. Congress refused to count votes cast by Pueblo. This situation contrasts with the general pattern uncovered in this book, which is that local majorities tended to oppress local minorities, who then got protection, if at all, from one or another branch of the federal government. In the sole case of the Pueblo, particularly but not exclusively in New Mexico, they were accepted legally as equals by fellow former Mexicans (who had become Americans by the Mexican Cession of 1848), but forced into a subjugated status by the Congress of the United States.

The Supreme Court did not overturn this Congressional policy on voting but did rule twice, 1854 and 1877, that the settled agricultural Indians of the Mexican Cession (such as the Pueblo) would not be covered by legislation that restricted commercial rights of "Indians," because these people, in contrast to those called "Indians," were not wild savages. In effect, they were "white by law," although the matter of who could vote in the territories was still regulatable by Congress.[10] Not until 1913 did the Supreme Court officially accept the Congressional preference to reduce the Pueblo and similar Indians to the subject status of Indians in general, removing from them their earlier quasi-white legal status. In a final twist on this federal-state relationship, in 1948, it was a federal district court that forced the state of New Mexico to grant full voting rights to Pueblo Indians.

During the Great Depression, under the Hoover and Roosevelt Administration those Mexican residents in the U.S. who were viewed as "public charges" or as threatening the jobs of Americans were "deported" in large numbers, numbers amounting to hundreds of thousands. More than half of this group are estimated to have been children who were U.S. citizens by birth. In fact, most of those who left did so without formal deportation hearings, because in contrast to formal deportation, if they left without formal coercion they could get free transportation to their hometowns.

The discrimination faced by American Latinos generally came not by explicit, official statutes but by informal discrimination at the local level. The Supreme Court decision that struck down Texas's whites-only primary law in 1927 had the incidental effect of protecting voting rights of those Latinos whose local community treated them as non-white

---

[10] Here I borrow the phrase from Ian Haney-Lopez 2006.

despite their official legal status. Mexico in 1943 cut Texas out of the *braceros* foreign worker program because discrimination in that state was so pervasive. The President in 1943–45 via his Office of the Coordinator of InterAmerican Affairs (OCIAA), in order to improve relations with Mexico, gave funding to assist Texas to crack down against private discrimination (in public accommodations) against Latinos. Texas continued the crackdown with its own funds for years afterward, and Mexico in 1947 responded favorably by reinstating the *braceros* program. Officials in many local communities in the southwest, despite an absence of statutory authorization, put Mexican-Americans into schools separate from those of Anglos. In Texas local communities kept people of Mexican descent off of juries. The latter practice was corrected by the U.S. Supreme Court only in 1954.

The school situation was more complicated. A local school desegregation case in California in 1944–47 successfully opened up all California schools to Latinos, at least in principle, in a case that contributed mightily to the major school desegregation precedents of the 1950s, *Sweatt, McLaurin*, and *Brown*. Effective actual desegregation of Latino school children was complicated not only by problems of residential segregation but also by the fact that Latinos by law were "white," and, eventually, by the widespread need in many areas for bilingual education. In the 1970s, all three branches of the federal government recognized bilingual education, where needed, as a legal right, and this fact often made desegregation, both for recent Latino immigrants and for East Asian immigrants logistically difficult.

Congress did act in 1965 to open up voting rights to those citizens, irrespective of English literacy, who had at least a sixth-grade education in a Puerto Rican school, but did not do so for other citizens (such as those from Mexico) who might not be literate in English. In 1970, Congress extended the act to other non-English-proficient voters.

On the whole, for Hispanic Americans, no single branch of the federal government stands out as their protector. Discrimination against them only rarely reached the U.S. Supreme Court, and policies focusing on them got adopted occasionally in the legislative or executive branches based on politics of a given moment, sometimes against them, as with deportation, and sometimes to protect them, as in Texas of the 1940s; on the policy of offering support for English Language Learners in the 1960s and 1970s, all three branches came together.

The enforced legal rights of black Americans continued to be strengthened by the Supreme Court of the 1930s, 40s and 50s. The federal judiciary led the way, after 1910, to the improvement in civil rights for blacks that culminated in the 1960s and early 70s. While it is widely known that the Supreme Court became markedly more liberal on economic policy as of 1937, the Court's liberal turn on civil rights for black Americans actually came much sooner, beginning with the White Court in 1911. In 1950 that turn intensified with the decisions rejecting "separate but equal" for higher education. And Supreme Court leadership on this policy lasted until 1989.

In two brief periods, Presidents shared this leadership role. From 1947 through 1952 President Truman, who had first gained the Presidency from the position of Vice-President, produced important civil rights policy changes, and then from 1964–68 President Lyndon Johnson, who also had come into office via the vice-presidency, by extraordinarily effective leadership of Congress produced even more momentous advances.

The Supreme Court under the leadership of Chief Justice Hughes (1930–41) doubled down on the due process protections of persons accused of crime that had been initiated by the Taft Court in *Moore v. Dempsey* (1923), overturning as procedurally unfair the convictions of Southern blacks in two Scottsboro Boys decisions (*Powell v. Alabama*, 1932: *Norris v. Alabama*, 1935) and also the conviction of a Mississippi black man who had been whipped into confessing (*Brown v. Mississippi*, 1936). The Hughes Court followed through on its insistence on black access to jury pools announced in the *Norris* case by handing down, on similar grounds, several more reversals of convictions of blacks in the South: *Hollins v. Oklahoma*, 1935; *Hale v. Kentucky*, 1938; *Pierre v. Louisiana*, 1939; *Smith v. Texas*, 1940. Under Chief Justice Hughes, the Court again threw out a grandfather clause voting law that had been adopted in defiance of the Court's ban on such laws from 1915 (*Lane v. Wilson*, 1939). In 1932 (*Nixon v. Condon*) this court struck down a Texas law that had empowered the State Executive Committee of the Democratic Party to set eligibility rules for participation in primary elections (and had thereby insured whites-only primaries). The Supreme Court in 1935, however, refused to strike down a whites-only primary where no obvious *governmental* support for the racial exclusion could be shown (*Grovey v. Townsend*).

Perhaps most momentously, the Court in 1938 took its first step toward wading into the turbulent waters of school desegregation, by ruling (in *Missouri ex rel. Gaines v. Canada*) that Missouri's providing a law school education to whites but only offering tuition to Missouri blacks to attend nearby state law schools *outside* Missouri did not satisfy the "substantially equal" treatment requirement of the equal protection clause. While the decision did not overturn the reigning "separate but equal" doctrine, its contrast with the Fuller Court's turn-of-the-century

Cummings v Board (1899) decision was dramatic. There the Court had upheld a decision by the school board of Richmond County, Georgia, to close its black high school while continuing to operate a highschool for white girls and to subsidize a private highschool for white boys, in an area where three private highschools were open to black children (but not subsidized by the state at all). The Hughes Court had not now abandoned "separate but equal" doctrine but was investing real bite into the standard of substantial equality being demanded.[11] The Supreme Court under both Chief Justice Stone (1941–46) and Chief Justice Vinson (1946–53) continued to lead the federal government in the direction of increased protections of the civil rights of black Americans. The Stone Court in three 1940s decisions continued the crack-down on debt-peonage cases begun by the White Court in the post-1910 years,[12] and also continued to take seriously blacks' rights to serve on grand and petit juries, which had experienced a renaissance under the Hughes Court.[13] The Vinson Court, too, continued to insist on this jury access.[14]

Moreover, the Stone Court outdid the Hughes Court by overturning *Grovey v. Townsend* (1935), to rule in *Smith v. Allwright* (1944) that whites-only primaries are unconstitutional, whether or not explicitly facilitated by state laws. Encouraged to do so by Truman's Justice Department, the Vinson Court in 1948 similarly outdid the 1920s Taft Court by overturning *Corrigan v. Buckley* (1926), to rule that private racially-restrictive housing covenants were non-enforceable under the law.[15] The Vinson Court also continued the Stone Court's strong policy disallowing whites-only primaries by ruling in 1953 that even when the

---

11 The term "bite" is borrowed from the late Gerald Gunther. Gunther 1972, 18–19.

12 *Taylor v. Georgia* (1942), *U.S. v. Gaskin* (1944), and *Pollock v. Williams* (1944).

13 *Hill v. Texas* (1942) (conviction reversed because no blacks appointed to grand jury for sixteen years).

14 *Patton v. Mississippi* (1947) (conviction reversed because no blacks had been appointed to grand or petit juries in the county for thirty years); *Cassell v. Texas* (1950) (conviction reversed because jury commissioners chose for grand jury only people they knew and they knew few blacks—the black population was 15.5 percent, and percent of blacks on grand juries over five years was 6.7 percent); and *Avery v. Georgia* (1953) (rape conviction thrown out because jury producing the conviction had been selected by drawing names from a container that had white slips for names of white jurors and yellow slips for names of black jurors; jury chosen was all-white; jury commissioners denied purposeful discrimination).

15 *Shelley v. Kraemer* (1948); *Hurd v. Hodge* (1948).

Democratic party informally allowed its candidates to be selected by a private whites-only club, the Jaybird Association, such practices violated the Fifteenth Amendment and Congress's 1870 Voting Rights Enforcement Act.[16]

Probably of greatest impact, however, in the 40s and 50s, was the movement toward desegregation by the Hughes, Stone and Vinson courts. Before desegregation was to be made an explicit requirement by the Vinson Court in 1950, the Supreme Court moved toward it on two non-school-related topics: nation-wide labor unions (that were highly regulated by federal law) and interstate transportation cases. Both *Mitchell v. U.S.* (1941) and *Henderson v. U.S.* (1950) declared insufficiently "equal" the accommodations being provided by interstate carriers, despite the ICC's having signed off on them. For both these cases the Justice Department (under FDR and Truman, respectively) had broken with the ICC and was supporting the black complainant.

In the 1944 *Steele v. Railroad* labor case, the Stone Court unanimously moved out ahead of the Roosevelt administration in ruling that because the federal government had made the National Railway Union the exclusive bargaining agent for railway workers, this union, despite limiting its membership to whites, had to produce labor agreements that *equally* benefitted both black workers and white workers. Its labor agreements could not constitutionally restrict black workers to menial jobs with the railroad company.

Moreover, both the Stone and Vinson courts, reversing judicial practice of several decades, presumed that desegregation rather than segregation was the reigning rule in interstate and foreign travel, such that state requirements for segregation would (finally) be treated as burdens on the free flow of interstate or foreign commerce.[17] As with the *Steele* decision, these were handed down in the absence of supportive amicus briefs from the Justice Department.

Under Chief Justice Vinson in 1950, this time supported by amicus briefs from the Truman Administration that were asking for *Plessy v. Ferguson* to be overruled, the Supreme Court declared in *Sweatt v.*

---

[16] *Terry v. Adams*, 345 U.S., at 468–9 (1953).

[17] *Morgan v. Virginia* (1946); *Bob-Lo Excursion v. Michigan* (1948). Cf. *Hall v. De Cuir* (1877) and *Louisville, New Orleans, and Tex. Ry. v. Mississippi* (1890). But see also the earliest of the federal segregated transportation cases: *Railroad v. Brown* (1873), *rejecting* the railroad's argument that exactly equal but racially separate accommodations sufficed to comply with Congress's mandate that the company (chartered to run a train between D.C. and Virginia) not discriminate among passengers on the grounds of race.

Painter and *McLaurin v. Oklahoma* that the segregated higher education systems of Texas and Oklahoma violated the Equal Protection Clause. The reasoning in those decisions made plain to any lawyer with an open mind that race-based *de jure* school segregation was about to be declared unconstitutional. The intangible elements of inequality in education that were produced by such systems included the absence of training in interracial communication (far more costly to the non-dominant race than vice versa) and the production of diplomas from less respected schools in the community for the non-dominant race.

All these judicial developments contributed to the civil rights revolution for African-Americans that is generally recognized as having been launched by the Warren Court decisions of *Brown v. Board of Education* and *Bolling v. Sharpe* in 1954. Moreover, the Court built upon the steps it had taken in its reasoning on Japanese-Americans for the *Hirabayashi* and *Korematsu* decisions, with respect to race being a suspect classification that demands compelling justification and with respect to the Fifth Amendment's implying a rule of equal protection that must guide the federal government. These played a role in the 1948 *Oyama* case to protect Japanese-Americans' right to acquire real estate, in the *Bolling* case to strike down school segregation in D.C., and in the striking down of anti-miscegenation laws of the 1960s.

By the time of the 1954 desegregation decisions, the executive branch of President Eisenhower, which did submit supportive briefs in those cases, retreated into a quieter, secondary role, back from the overt co-leadership stance of the Truman Administration in the 1947–Jan. 1953 years.

President Truman had gone well beyond having his Justice Department bring cases to the Supreme Court in support of protecting the civil rights of black Americans. In his second year in office (1946), Truman asked his Attorney General Tom Clark to develop a more comprehensive Justice Department policy to prevent lynchings. Clark then organized the President's Committee on Civil Rights, which in 1947 published a massive report, *To Secure these Rights*. This report denounced Jim Crow in strong terms, documenting its economic and diplomatic costs and calling for vigorous federal efforts to end racial discrimination in the military, voting, education, interstate transportation, and in employment. It called for the following: beefing up the Civil Rights Section of the Justice Department, creating a Civil Rights protection section in the FBI, pro-actively pursuing both civil and criminal violations of civil rights, adopting an anti-lynching law, and strengthening and broadening the Anti-Peonage Law. It also advocated creating a permanent Commission on Civil Rights for monitoring and enforcement. In the 1948 recodification of the federal criminal code, Congress adopted many of these proposals, particularly those bearing on involuntary servitude.

On July 6, 1948, with Executive Orders 9980 and 9981, Truman followed up on his Civil Rights Committee's recommendation to desegregate the U.S. Armed Forces and the federal civil service, moves which caused Dixiecrats temporarily to bolt the party. The Air Force and Navy complied promptly, whereas the Army resisted for a few years. By the end of the Korean War, however, the U.S. military was fully integrated.

Apart from the six years when Truman allied with the Supreme Court to play, in effect, a co-leadership role, the Supreme Court stood out in the decades of the 30s, 40s, and 50s, as a defender of the rights of African-Americans. While the Court continued through the decade of the 20s to stand up on occasion for due process rights of Asians against federal administrative excess or against oppressive state laws, by the 1930s the elected branches dominated this policy area. When it came to the rights of American Indians this shift took place a decade sooner; in the twenties the Supreme Court gave way to the elected branches for leadership on Indian rights.

On American Indians, the president in the modern period generally led the way, with Congress usually lining up behind him, and with the Supreme Court mostly in an acquiescent role, i.e. acquiescent to the national political branches, not to the local oppressive majorities. On the matter of rights for Asians, too, the President led the way, but Congress played a more (negatively) assertive role, for extended periods refusing to cooperate in the President's calls for reform.

In 1924 Congress granted citizenship to all American Indians who had not already received it by the treaty or allotment process. The 1928 Meriam Report on the condition of American Indians, which the government had commissioned, stimulated the Hoover Administration to act by the early 30s, obtaining from Congress substantial increases in appropriations for Indian well-being. More significantly, the Hoover executive branch broke sharply with longstanding assimilationist policies, injecting respect for traditional Indian culture into both Indian education and pronouncements from the Commissioners of the Bureau of Indian Affairs. However, Congress and some career civil servants in that bureau balked at outright reversal of the Dawes Act initiatives.

Not until the FDR Administration were major policy changes adopted. In 1933 and 1934, with Harold Ickes as Secretary of Interior, and John Collier, longtime pro-Indian activist, as head of the BIA, Congress adopted an Indian Civilian Conservation Corps (1933), the Pueblo Relief Act (1933), and the Johnson-O'Malley Act (1934). The latter provided federal funding for public school education for reservation Indians (since reservations did not pay local taxes).

Most important was the Wheeler-Howard (Indian Reorganization) Act of 1934. This Act created the public policy goal of undoing the massive harm now documented as having resulted from the Dawes Act; it aimed to restore lost lands back to Indian tribes by appropriating millions of dollars each year to purchase land that could be restored to the tribes. It also created procedures by which tribes could form self-governing bodies under their own constitutions in consultation with the Secretary of the Interior, could hire an attorney on behalf of the tribe, and could form a corporation for managing tribal assets. It created a revolving fund of ten million (1934 value) dollars to be lent to tribes for investments in development; it arranged for the Interior Department to promote conservation of natural resources in Indian Territory; and it mandated a hiring preference for Indians in the Bureau of Indian Affairs. The Wheeler-Howard Act represented a seismic shift in U.S. policy toward American Indians. In 1935, Collier followed through by persuading Congress to adopt the Indian Arts and Crafts Act. This law aimed to promote the sale of Indian crafts by creating a government agency that would provide Indians with technical assistance in marketing their work and also would set quality standards and provide marks of authenticity.

Although Collier resigned under pressure from critics in 1945 and Ickes did the same in 1946, their final success was the adoption of the Indian Claims Commission Act of August 13, 1946. Prior to this act, U.S. treatment of Indian complaints that their land was taken in violation of a treaty followed a zigzag pattern: the default position was that such claims were barred from court by the doctrine of sovereign immunity, but Congress often became persuaded that particular claims were compelling so would waive sovereign immunity for that claim, on a case-by-case basis. This happened 142 times before the Indian Claims Commission was set up to deal with such claims under the Just Compensation Clause. The Claims Commission dealt with these cases until 1978, in which year Congress turned the remaining caseload over to the regular U.S. Court of Claims.

The Truman and Eisenhower Administrations brought a temporary halt to the anti-assimilationist approach of Collier and Ickes. The Truman Administration focused particularly on the civil rights of individual Indians, bringing pressure on states to cease their practice of denying the vote to reservation Indians. New Mexico and Arizona dropped these bans in 1948. In 1953 Congress legislated an end to the bans on selling alcohol or guns to Indians. In 1957 Utah became the last state to drop its ban on voting by reservation Indians.

As Indians noticeably lagged behind other Americans during the postwar economic boom, doubts grew about the direction of the Collier and Ickes policies. Early in the Eisenhower Administration, August 1, 1953, Congress issued Concurrent Resolution 108 (HCR 108) itemizing a list of relatively prosperous tribes who were to be freed from federal supervision in the near future. This process was known as tribal termination. Two weeks later Congress unanimously voted to have state governments take over civil and criminal jurisdiction on the Indian reservations in California, Minnesota, Nebraska, Oregon, Wisconsin, and Alaska, and to allow other states to do so if they wanted, irrespective of tribal desires. Congress set forth procedures for tribal terminations in 1954, began doing terminations in 1955, and stopped terminating any sizable tribe after 1961. The Secretary of the Interior announced in 1958 that no tribe would be terminated therafter without its consent. By 1959, the policy of terminating any unwilling tribe ended, with the policy widely recognized as having failed to bring prosperity. Basically, termination either divided up tribal assets among the members or else set up a corporation to hold the tribal assets with the members as the shareholders. Only 3 percent of tribes underwent the process and they ended up generally poorer rather than better off.

The pendulum swung back against assimilation by the time of the presidential campaign of 1960, with Kennedy promising to honor Indian cultural traditions and to violate no treaty or contractual promise with tribes. U.S. policy has remained anti-assimilationist—or more positively stated, respectful of tribal quasi-sovereignty and tribal culture—ever since. Starting with the Kennedy Administration and continuing through the early 1990s, a variety of measures have been passed by Congress and supported by the president that express support for alleviating the economic suffering of Indians (e.g., via extensive anti-poverty programs that began under the LBJ Administration), for land restoration to the tribes (e.g., in 1970 restoring 48,000 acres to the Taos Pueblo), for respecting tribal sovereignty (e.g., the Indian Self-Determination and Education Assistance Act of 1975), and for respecting tribal religious traditions (e.g., the 1978 Senate Joint Resolution 102 expressing this respect and the 1990 Native American Graves Protection and Repatriation Act). A number of tribes have undergone the legal process of restoration of tribal sovereignty after having been terminated. Congress enacted the Indian Civil Rights Act of 1968, guaranteeing many of the Bill of Rights provisions to reservation Indians (who are governed by their tribes), but not including the religion clauses.

Many tribes continue to have grievances about lost land and still bring cases to court when state governments infringe on federal treaty rights.

The Supreme Court generally upholds federal treaty rights against state-level infringements. It wrestles also with conflicts between individual Indian civil rights (produced by the Indian Civil Rights Act of 1968) and tribal sovereignty, and with apparent conflicts between competing federal policies (e.g., federal law establishing respect for Indian religion and federal law allowing economic development of some natural resource near the reservation). In these cases the Supreme Court has seemed in the 1930–90 period to follow what it perceives to be Congress's chosen policy, mindful that whatever it decides concerning tribal Indians, Congress has the power to override if unsatisfied (e.g., by amending the Indian Civil Rights Act). The only exception to this generalization is that the Supreme Court does treat the federal government as bound by the Just Compensation Clause with respect to takings of Indian land. Congress may have power to regulate commerce with the tribes but it may not override the U.S. Constitution.

The treatment of Asians by the U.S. Government in the 1930–90 period has followed a pattern similar to that of American Indians, in the sense that the elected branches led the way in altering their earlier oppressive policies, rather than having those policies corrected by the Supreme Court. In the 1930s, the elected branches initiated a transition period toward independence for the Filipinos, motivated by the ignoble desire to limit Filipino immigration to the continental United States. The fundamental transformation that took place on policies toward Asians is that under the pressures of World War II Congress stopped treating Asians as a matter of domestic policy wherein they were viewed simply as an unassimilable race, one that had to be kept out of the U.S. as much as possible and not allowed to naturalize to citizenship. Instead, Asians suddenly came into view through the lens of foreign policy: the Chinese now were America's friends: the Japanese, our mortal enemies.

Americans of Japanese descent were subjected to horrific treatment, some 85,000 of them incarcerated as virtual prisoners of war. The Supreme Court refused to protect them against the policies—adopted in the elected branches—of curfews and being expelled from their homes and ordered into collection centers. Only after more than two years of their imprisonment, did the Supreme Court finally declare, in the *Ex Parte Endo* (1944) case, that extended imprisonment of persons based solely on ethnic heritage, where evidence of loyalty was clear, violates the U.S. Constitution.

By contrast, in 1943, it was Congress that legislated an end to Chinese exclusion and permission for Chinese to become naturalized American citizens, pressed to do so by President Franklin Roosevelt. Only in 1952 did Congress finally act to remove the remaining exclusion from American naturalization for Japanese and Koreans, and also allow them to immigrate here. And not until 1965 did the U.S. remove racial categorizations from U.S. immigration law, having been pushed to do so, for a long time unsuccessfully, by presidents Truman, Kennedy and Lyndon Johnson, all conscious of their diplomatic agendas, in contrast to the more locally-focused Congress. The 1965 Hart Celler Act fundamentally altered U.S. immigration policy so that nationality quotas for immigrating here are no longer geared to race. Instead, job skills are now the emphasis.

CONCLUSIONS

This book produced a number of (at least to me, its author) unanticipated conclusions. The first is the sad conclusion that H. Rap Brown was correct when he opined during the turbulent 1960s, "Violence is as American as cherry pie."[18] It was deployed not only in the formative Revolutionary War and Civil War and in the Mexican and Spanish American wars of expansion, but also by civilians in the Whiskey Rebellion, by pro-slavery forces to destroy abolitionist printing presses, by abolitionist mobs in the North to free captured fugitive slaves, by racist whites to intimidate and murder blacks from the time of the Civil War through the twentieth century, in the postbellum South to murder white Republican voters, in the Western states to ethnically cleanse cities of Chinese inhabitants, in the anti-Indian Wars, and from the 1960s to the present by black Americans (and sometimes their white allies) outraged at racial injustice.

In terms of the concerns of this volume, the United States has produced four presidents who took a strong leadership role, as judged by the political context of their day, on behalf of black Americans. They were Abraham Lincoln, Theodore Roosevelt, Harry Truman, and Lyndon Johnson. The latter three all came to power as vice-presidents, succeeding a president who had died. Lincoln, the fourth, was elected in a multiparty race and won with a mere plurality of the vote. This fact is not particularly encouraging about the capacity of electoral majorities in the U.S. to produce leaders interested in protecting unpopular minorities.

A third conclusion that more or less jumped out unexpectedly, is that the President, because of his role as what the late Clinton Rossiter called

[18] Esterbrook 2002.

"Chief Diplomat"[19] not infrequently acted to protect minorities of color in the U.S. Responsible for making treaties with their related trade deals and for receiving ambassadors and sending them, the President was positioned to view the domestic treatment of Asians and Latinos as having important diplomatic consequences for the U.S. as a whole, whereas Congress members and Senators, who had far more localized constituencies, were much more inclined to adopt policies that reflected regional white hostilities to these groups (on the West Coast or along the Southwest border). Too often, the hostility in Congress became so overwhelming that even presidential lobbying and/or the presidential veto could not prevail, but that the veto did succeed sometimes, and that reform of immigration and naturalization laws (promoted by several presidents) eventually prevailed is a tribute to the wisdom of Federalist #51. The checks and balances system as a whole, not just the institution of judicial review defended in Federalist #78, has significantly contributed to the protection of minority liberties in the United States.

Further support for the importance of this insight of Federalist # 51 is that even Congress, on at least two occasions (outside of the distorted Civil War context), stepped up against another branch to protect a beleaguered racial minority; in 1830 Congress insisted that President Jackson include in the Indian Removal Act a passage prohibiting the violation of any extant treaty with the Indians, and in the 1991 Civil Rights Act, Congress overturned two 1989 Supreme Court decisions that had restricted the ability of plaintiffs to win claims of racial discrimination in employment.

Moreover, the fact that the Supreme Court exercised its power to protect members of all four groups against oppressive measures at the state level far, far more often than it did against Congressional measures is, in some sense, a vindication of the arguments in Federalist #10 for a large national system to replace the state-dominated system of the Confederation. Justices appointed by a nationally elected president and confirmed by the federal Senate are likely to have political sympathies with the dominant national political coalition. But this coalition often differs from particular state-level majorities, and these local majorities more often than not showed themselves in regional patterns to be more inclined to oppress Asian-Americans, American Indians, Latino-Americans, and African-Americans than the national government was. Indeed, even President Jackson, perhaps the most sincerely anti-Indian president ever to hold the office, was willing to use federal troops in both

[19] Rossiter 1956.

1832 and 1833 to protect the Creeks of Alabama, as per our treaty agreement, when state level officials not only refused to do so, but actively assisted the white settlers who were unlawfully seizing Indian land.

The basic, and perhaps unsatisfying, answer to the query that drove this book, is that whether the Court was more protective of a given minority than the elected branches turns out to have varied according to historical period and particular personnel. And which minority would get judicial protection also varied across periods and across branches. The Marshall Court did less than the elected branches did to check slavery or the slave trade: the elected branches took relatively firm stands against the international trade in slaves, and the John Quincy Adams Administration wanted more slaves freed from the *Antelope* than the Court would agree to. On the other hand, the Marshall Court offered more protection to Native Americans than any other contemporaneous federal branch. Also members of the Marshall Court in Circuit-level cases granted legal protections to *free* blacks against imprisonment under the southern Black Seamen Laws. The Taney Court during the years when Joseph Story provided its intellectual leadership (1835–46) showed itself to be more anti-slavery than the elected branches; once Story left, however, the Taney Court protected no racial minorities (with the partial exception of Hispanic agricultural Indians) and the elected branches were equally bad on the subject.

Similarly, during the years of the Fuller Court (1888–1910), all three branches behaved truly disgracefully toward the rights of black Americans, except for Teddy Roosevelt's presidential tenure. His repeated efforts to enforce black legal rights were blocked by the Fuller Court. By contrast, the Fuller Court did offer some protections to Asians and Asian-Americans, particularly against administrative overreach, and included the important ruling in the *Wong Kim Ark* case that Chinese-descent persons have birth-right citizenship if born within U.S. confines. This court also (eventually) stood up for American Indian treaty rights against state-level violations.

During the years of the Chase Court (1865–73) and Waite Court (1873–88), the policy making pattern was something of a mirror image of the Taney and Fuller Court years. All three branches immediately after the Civil War,[20] when the southern States had removed themselves from legislative power, acted, to some degree, to protect blacks, Asians, and

---

[20] President Andrew Johnson, the least so, but he did insist that southern states abolish slavery and ratify the Thirteenth Amendment.

both Indians and Indian tribes (the last, in the sense of respecting their quasi-sovereign status in the Fourteenth Amendment, but also legislating birth-right citizenship for those individual Indians who were taxpayers and lived off the reservation). Then the southern States re-entered Congress (by 1870) and the northern Congressional electorate by the end of 1874 lost its zeal for protecting former slaves.

Nonetheless, after 1875, Republican Presidential Administrations continued (through 1885) to offer a moderate degree of protection to blacks by prosecuting southern civil rights violators, vetoing Congressional efforts to repeal voting rights enforcement laws (until they succeeded in 1894), and enforcing strict equality of treatment in interstate commerce (through the late 1880s). Likewise, the Waite Court offered a moderate degree of protection: while throwing out several indictments for racial violence on the grounds of procedural inadequacies, nonetheless, the Court expanded the Fifteenth Amendment beyond its state-action-limited wording and upheld the rights of blacks to be tried only in systems that did not bar them from jury service. It also expanded rights of Asians against state-level (legislative or administrative) discrimination in the *Yick Wo* decision of 1886, protected a number of Asians against overzealous immigration agents, and in *Ex Parte Crow Dog* (1883) blocked executive efforts to seize jurisdiction over major crimes in Indian Territory (prior to Congressional action doing so).

Until the twentieth century, the pattern during the post-Story Taney Court, the Chase Court, the Waite Court and the Fuller Court is the dominant one: the Supreme Court is more or less similar to the elected branches both for better and for worse, with periods of exceptions both for Indians and for Asians. Except for the post-Story Taney Court years, the U.S. Supreme Court prior to 1920 was consistently more protective of American Indians than the elected branches were, although the protection came only occasionally. The lone important exception to this statement is that the Congress that sent the Fourteenth Amendment to the states meant for non-reservation Indians to be covered by the birthright citizenship terms, but in 1884 (*Elk v. Wilkins*) the Supreme Court rejected this interpretation. Congress corrected this judicial move in the 1887 Dawes Act.

Similarly, from 1882, the time of the first Chinese Exclusion Act, until World War II, the Supreme Court was more protective of Asians than the elected branches were. Judicial power to protect American Indians or Asians or Asian-Americans, however, was sharply circumscribed by Congress's ability to override the Supreme Court's legislative interpretations and to alter its jurisdiction.

In the twentieth century this basic picture shifted. Perhaps influenced by having just experienced its *only* original jurisdiction hearing for criminal contempt—contempt of itself in a racially inspired murder-by-lynching case—the post-Fuller twentieth century Supreme Court moved out ahead of the political branches on the matter of the rights of black Americans. It moved slightly but consistently ahead from the years 1911 until 1930. Then from 1930 until 1989 it was clearly ahead of the elected branches, with two exceptions: President Truman provided co-leadership in the years 1947–52; and during the 1964–68 LBJ years, all three branches moved together to complete the unfulfilled promise of Reconstruction. This pattern of Supreme Court leadership on the civil rights of black Americans for eight decades, with strong leadership during the six later decades was not typical of the nineteenth century.

The twentieth century Supreme Court also offered occasional protection to Hispanics against state-level discrimination, as did presidents when diplomatic pressures made it expedient, and as Congress did in the 1965 Voting Rights Act and later amendments to it. There has been no clear institutional pattern on Hispanic Americans.

The treatment of American Indians changed fundamentally in the post-1920 period. Starting in 1928, both elected branches with the exception of the period of 1948–59, moved decisively into the role of respecting traditional tribal culture and respecting tribal sovereignty, albeit with (as of 1968) protection for many civil rights of individual Indians with respect to their tribal government.

Similarly, the treatment of Asian-Americans changed fundamentally in the mid-twentieth century. World War II moved the elected branches, led particularly by Presidents Truman through Johnson, to distinguish *among* Asians in a way that prioritized national identity over racial identity. Starting in 1943 with permission for the Chinese to become naturalized citizens and completed finally by 1965, U.S. immigration and naturalization laws were cleansed of their longstanding racial bias.

The fact that this study examined together the civil rights history of four different racial minority groups brought to light one final conclusion: to the degree that the judiciary has been an agent for establishing constitutional rights of racial minorities (not to mention women[21] and people of minority sexual orientation), there has been significant interdependence of minority rights from one group to another. Because of the American common law system, when appellate courts decide cases, they explain their reasoning in opinions that deduce general rules from prior

---

21 Throughout the nineteenth century in the U.S., women were a minority.

cases and explain how these rules apply to the case at hand. Precedents build on one another. Thus, in the 1920s, when Justice Holmes wrote an opinion that began to establish the right to due process in criminal procedure of (even) black defendants in the South, he reached back indirectly to a due process precedent concerning an Asian, Sing Tuck. In the 1930s, when striking down as inadequate Missouri's approach to "separate but equal" in higher education for black residents, the Supreme Court cited its own Chinese anti-discrimination decision, *Yick Wo v. Hopkins* (1886) and also the judicial guideline provided in the failed challenge by a Chinese-American to school segregation in Mississippi, the *Gong Lum v. Rice* (1927) case. The federal district court opinion for the school-desegregation challenge brought by Mexican and Puerto Rican parents as *Mendez v. Westminster* (1946) provided the logic that undergirded the Supreme Court decisions on African-American desegregation of *Sweatt v. Painter* (1950), *McLaurin v. Oklahoma* (1950), and *Brown v. Board* (1954). The World War II cases brought by Japanese-Americans to challenge their mistreatment produced reasoning later deployed by the Supreme Court in deciding *Bolling v. Sharpe* (1954), and in the 1960s striking down of anti-miscegenation laws. Minority group attorneys tend to be aware of this interdependence, but the general, educated public may not be. A more widespread awareness of it may help to foster intergroup political alliances.

All this said, one can conclude that for most periods in the Court's first 200 years, the answer to my basic query, with important qualifications, is that "Yes, the Court has, within strictures created by the Constitution, acted to protect rights of one or another racial minority group to a greater degree than elected branches have been willing to do." Even the Taney Court during its low point (on race) after Story exited (1846–64), issued a decision in 1854 to the effect that the settled agricultural (Pueblo-style) Indians of the Mexican cession could not be treated as "Indians" in being denied rights to buy and sell property or buy whiskey, because they were not "wild savages."

The qualifications to this broad conclusion are not small ones. For one thing, the Court was not so prominently out in front most of the time as it was from 1930–89. Although it began protecting blacks more than the political branches in 1911, its distance from policies set by the elected branches was not large. Also, the Court's willingness to protect one group did not necessarily extend to others. Indians received some protection of treaty rights under the Marshall, Waite, Fuller and White Courts; Asians, from the Supreme Courts of 1882–1934. Presidents, too, on more than a few occasions played important protective roles, as has been shown. And in at least three instances, even Congress checked the executive or judicial branch on behalf of a racial minority. (In 1991 Congress checked Court, expressly strengthening anti-discrimination laws; in the late nineteenth and early twentieth century it overrode the Supreme Court's *Elk v Wilkins*, to give birthright citizenship to Indians who live off of reservations as assimilated Americans; and in the 1830s Congress constrained President Jackson's Indian Removal Policy, insisting that it abide by treaties with the Indians).

The institution of lifetime tenure for federal judges, who have power to strike down executive actions as unauthorized by law and power to strike down state laws (and constitutions) as in violation of the Supremacy Clause (as well as power to declare federal laws unconstitutional, a power that has been little used in the context of this study) has obviously not been able to prevent majority oppressions of racial minorities in the democratic republic created by the Constitution. It has, however, provided the Supreme Court with enough protection that the Court has in fact helped to some degree, some of the time, to check such oppression. The hopes expressed in Hamilton's Federalist #78 have not been in vain.

References

"14th Amendment." 2005. *Blue and Gray Trail.* http://blueandgraytrail.com/event/14th_Amendment (accessed 12/3/2011).

"1946." N.D. Asian American History http://www.dartmouth.edu/~hist32/History/20th%20Century%20-%20post%20WWII.htm (accessed Aug.20, 2014).

"A Whole State Enjoined." 1895. *New York Times* May 8. http://query.nytimes.com/mem/archive-free/pdf?res=FA0715FF3B5D15738DDDA00894DD405B8585F0D3 (accessed May 17, 2013).

Abraham, Henry. 1992. *Justices and Presidents.* 3rd ed. New York: Oxford University Press.

Abrams, Kerry. 2005. "Polygamy, Prostitution, and the Federalization of Immigration Law," *Columbia Law Review* 105(3): 641–716.

ACLU Voting Rights Project. 2009, *Voting Rights in Indian Country*, Atlanta: ACLU (available online as pdf, accessed October 18, 2014).

Acosta, Teresa Palomo. 2010. "IN RE RICARDO RODRIGUEZ," *Handbook of Texas Online* (http://www.tshaonline.org/handbook/online/articles/pqitw). Published by the Texas State Historical Association (accessed May 08, 2015).

"Acquisition of U.S. Nationality in U.S. Territories and Possessions," N.D. 7 FAM 1120: 7 FAM 1121.4-2 "Under the Immigration and Nationality Act of 1952 (INA)," U.S. Department of State (accessed Dec.9, 2016) https://fam.state.gov/FAM/07FAM/07FAM1120.html#M1121_4_2.

Aguirre, Frederick P. 2005. "*Mendez v. Westminster School District*: How It Affected *Brown v. Board of Education*," *Journal of Hispanic Higher Education* 4: 321–32.

Albright, Evan J. 2005. "William Henry Lewis: Brief Life of a Football Pioneer, 1868–1949," *Harvard Magazine* (Nov.-Dec.). http://harvardmagazine.com/2005/11/william-henry-lewis-html (accessed March 26, 2014.)

Allen, Austin. 2006. *Origins of the Dred Scott Case.* Athens, GA: University of Georgia Press.

Almaguer, Tomas. 1994. *Racial Fault Lines: The Historical Origins of White Supremacy in California.* Berkeley: University of California Press.

Alvarez, Roberto, Jr. 1986. "The Lemon Grove Incident: The Nation's First Successful Desegregation Court Case," *The Journal of San Diego History, San Diego Historical Society Quarterly* 32(2). Available online as http://www.sandiegohistory.org/journal/86spring/lemongrove.htm (accessed July 27, 2015).

Balderrama, Francisco and Raymond Rodriguez. 2006. *Decade of Betrayal: Mexican Repatriation in the 1930s* (rev.ed.). Albuquerque: University of New Mexico Press.

Balkin, Jack M. 2011. *Constitutional Redemption: Political Faith In An Unjust World.* Cambridge, MA.: Harvard Univ. Press.

Bannai, Lorraine K. and Dale Minami. 1992. "Internment during World War II and Litigations," in H.-C. Kim, ed. *Asian Americans and the Supreme Court*, 755–88.

Basson, Lauren. 2008. *White Enough to Be American? Indigenous People and the Boundaries of State and Nation.* Chapel Hill: UNC Press.

Bedolla, Lisa Garcia. 1999. *Fluid Borders.* Berkeley: University of California Press.

Behnken, Brian, ed. 2011-A. ed. *The Struggle in Black and Brown.* Lincoln: University of Nebraska Press.

Behnken, Brian, 2011-B, "The Movement in the Mirror," in Behnken 2011-A, 49–77.

Bell, Derrick. 1980. *Race, Racism, and American Law.* 2d ed. Boston.

Benedict, Michael Les. 1978. "Preserving Federalism: Reconstruction and the Waite Court," 1978 *Supreme Court Review* 39–79.

Bergman, Peter M. and Mort N. Bergman. 1969. *The Chronological History of the Negro in America.* NY: Mentor.

Bernstein, Shana. 2007. "WHA Roundtable Essay: From California to the Nation: Rethinking the History of 20th Century U.S. Civil Rights Struggles Through a Mexican American and Multiracial Lens," *Berkeley La Raza Law Journal* 18: 87–95.

Bickel, Alexander. 1984. *Part One of The Judiciary and Responsible Government 1910–1921.* Vol. IX of Oliver Wendell Holmes Devise History of the Supreme Court of the United States. New York: Macmillan.

Bixby, David M. 1981. "The Roosevelt Court, Democratic Ideology, and Minority Rights: Another Look at *United States v. Classic*," *Yale Law Journal* 90(4): 741–815.

"Black Voting Rights: The Creation of the Fifteenth Amendment, Ratification." 1998–2005. http://15thamendment.harpweek.com/HubPages/CommentaryPage.asp?Commentary=03Ratification (accessed Aug. 13, 2011).

Blackmon, Douglas A. 2008-A. *Slavery by Another Name*. NY: Doubleday.

Blackmon, Douglas A. 2008-B. "The World War II Effect," *Wall Street Journal, March 29.* http://www.wsj.com/articles/SB120674498432473091 (accessed Aug. 23, 2015).

Blocker, Jack. 2002. "Vice and Violence," Review of Butler, Brian, *An Undergrowth of Folly: Public Order, Race Anxiety, and the 1903 Evansville, Indiana Riot*. H-Net Reviews. http://www.h-net.org/reviews/showrev.php?id=5848 (accessed March 29, 2014).

Bogen, David. 2007. "Why the Supreme Court Lied in *Plessy*," *Villanova Law Review* 52: 411–70.

Bogen, David and Leslie F. Goldstein. 2010. "Culture, Religion and Indigenous People," *Maryland Law Review* (winter) 69: 101–17.

Bolt, Christine. 1987. *American Indian Policy and American Reform*. London: Allen & Unwin.

Bowman, Kristi, ed. 2015-A. *The Pursuit of Racial and Ethnic Equality in American Public Schools:* Mendez, Brown, *and Beyond*. Lansing: Michigan State University Press.

Bowman, Kristi. 2015-B. "Pursuing Equity at the Intersection of School Desegregation, English-Language Instruction and Immigration," in Bowman, ed. 2015-A, 31–54.

Boyer, Paul et al. 2008. *The Enduring Vision, A History of the American People*. Boston: Houghton Mifflin.

Brandwein, Pamela. 2011. *Rethinking the Judicial Settlement of Reconstruction*. New York: Cambridge University Press.

Brilliant, Mark. 2010. *The Color of America Has Changed; How Racial Diversity Shaped Civil Rights Reform in California 1941–1978*. NY: Oxford University Press.

Browne, J. Ross. 1850. *Report of the Debates in the Convention of California on the Formation of the State Constitution in September and October, 1849*. Washington, D.C.: John T. Tower.

Bruyneel, Kevin. 2004. "Challenging American Boundaries: Indigenous People and the 'Gift' of U.S. Citizenship," *Studies in American Political Development* 18 (Spring): 30–43.

Buell, Raymond L. 1922. "The Development of Anti-Japanese Agitation in the United States," *Political Science Quarterly* 37: 605–38.

Burke, Joseph C. 1969. "The Cherokee Cases: A Study in Law, Politics, and Morality," *Stanford Law Review* 21: 500–31.

Butler, Brian. 2000. *An Undergrowth of Folly: Public Order, Race Anxiety, and the 1903 Evansville, Indiana Riot*. NY: Routledge.

Calhoun, John C. 1851. *Disquisition on Government and a Discourse on the Constitution and Government of the United States*. (Columbia, S.C.: A.S. Johnston.

Camarillo, Albert. 1979. *Chicanos in a Changing Society: From Mexican Pueblos to American Barrios in Santa Barbara and Southern California, 1848–1930*. Cambridge: Harvard University Press.

Carson, Jamie L. and Jason Matthew Roberts. 2011. "Ambition, Competition, and Electoral Reform: The Politics of Congressional Elections Across Time," http://www.duke.edu/~mcb20/carson_roberts_duke.pdf (accessed 12/20/2011).

Chan, Sucheng. 1994. "Exclusion of Chinese Women," in McClain, ed. *Asian Americans and the Law, Vol. 1 Chinese Immigrants and American Law,* 2–54.

Cheng, John. 2013. "The 'Asiatic Barred Zone.'" The Mongo Project, http://planet-mongo.com/2013/01/the-asiatic-barred-zone/ (accessed Feb. 06, 2017).

Chesley, Frank. 2009. "Chinese Exclusion Repeal Act, aka the Magnuson Act, is signed on December 17, 1943." *HistoryLink.org* (2009) http://www.historylink.org/index.cfm?DisplayPage=output.cfm&file_id=8993 (accessed Aug. 20, 2014).

"Civil Rights." 2012. Oxford African American Studies Center. www2.oxfordaasc.com/article/opr/t0004/e0114 (accessed March 4, 2012).

Cizauskas, Albert C. 1986. "The Unusual Story of Thaddeus Kosciusko," *Litianus: Lithuanian Quarterly Journal of Arts and Sciences* 32(1). http://www.cizauskas.net/acc/thaddeus_kosciusko.html (accessed Nov. 24, 2006).

Cohen, Felix. 1947. "Original Indian Title," *Minnesota Law Review* 32: 29–58.

Collins, Ann V. 2007. "New York City Riot of 1900," in Rucker, and Upton, eds, *Encyclopedia of American Race Riots,* Vol. 2, 474–6.

Collins, William J. 2001. "Race, Roosevelt, and Wartime Production: Fair Employment in World War II Labor Markets," *The American Economic Review* 91(1): 272–86.

"Congressional Anti-Busing Sentiment Mounts in 1972." 1973. 11-119-11-120 in *CQ Almanac 1972*, 28th ed., Washington, DC: Congressional Quarterly. http://library.cqpress.com/cqalmanac/cqal72-1250143 (accessed Dec. 23, 2015).

Constitution of Florida. 1845. "Acts and Resolutions of the General Assembly of the State of Florida (Laws of Florida)," State Library and Archives of Florida Public Documents Collection. http://edocs.dlis.state.fl.us/fldocs/leg/actsflorida/index.htm (accessed May 14, 2015).

Cottrol, Robert J. and Raymond T. Diamond. 1991. "The Second Amendment: Toward an Afro-Americanist Reconsideration," *Georgetown Law Journal* 80: 309–61.

Cover, Robert. 1975. *Justice Accused.* New Haven: Yale University Press.

Cover, Robert. 1982. "The Origins of Judicial Activism in the Protection of Minorities," *Yale Law Journal* 91: 1287–316.

Cozzens, Peter. 2016. *The Earth Is Weeping*. New York: Alfred A. Knopf.

Curriden, Mark. 2009. "A Supreme Case of Contempt," *ABA Journal* (June) http://www.abajournal.com/magazine/article/a_supreme_case_of_contempt/ (accessed Dec. 19, 2013).

Currie, David. 1985. *The Constitution in the Supreme Court.* Chicago: University of Chicago Press.

Currie, David. 1990. *The Constitution in the Supreme Court: The Second Century 1888–1986*. Chicago: University of Chicago Press.

Curtis, Michael Kent. 1986. *No State Shall Abridge: The Fourteenth Amendment and the Bill of Rights*. Durham: Duke University Press.

Curtis, Michael Kent. 2000. *Free Speech, "The People's Darling Privilege," Struggles for Freedom of Expression in American History*. Durham: Duke University Press.

Curtis, Michael Kent. 2009. "The Klan, the Congress, and the Court: Congressional Enforcement of the Fourteenth and Fifteenth Amendments and the State Action Syllogism, A Brief Historical Overview," *University of Pennsylvania Journal of Constitutional Law* 11: 1381–430.

Dahl, Robert. 1957. "Decision making in a Democracy; The Supreme Court as a National Policy-Maker," *Journal of Public Law* (now *Emory Law Review*) 6: 279–95.

Dale, Elizabeth. 2011. *Criminal Justice in the United States, 1789–1939*. New York: Cambridge University Press.

Daniel, Pete. 1970. "Up from Slavery and Down to Peonage: The Alonzo Bailey Case," *Journal of American History* 57 (Dec.): 654–70.

Davis, David B. 2003. *Challenging the Boundaries of Slavery*. Cambridge: Harvard University Press.

Davis, Abraham L. and Barbara Luck Graham. 1995. *The Supreme Court, Race, and Civil Rights*. Thousand Oaks, CA: Sage.

De Genova, Nicholas and Ana Y. Ramos-Zayas. 2003. "Debating American Identity: Southwestern Statehood and Mexican Immigration," *The Journal of Latin American Anthropology* 8(2): 18–57.

De la Cova, Antonio R. 2011. "Cuban Exiles in Key West during the Ten Years War, 1868–1878," *Florida Historical Quarterly* 89: 287–319.

De León, Arnoldo. 2010. "MEXICAN AMERICANS," *Handbook of Texas Online*. Texas State Historical Association. http://www.tshaonline.org/handbook/online/articles/pqmue (accessed May 08, 2015).

De Loria, Vine. 1996. "American Indians in Historical Perspective," in John Wunder, ed. *Native American Law and Colonialism, Before 1777 to 1903*. New York. Garland, 123–34.

Del Castillo, Richard Griswold. 2000. "Unfulfilled Promises: The Legal and Historical Issues in the Treaty of Guadalupe-Hidalgo," in Gordon M. Bakken, ed. *Law in the Western United States*. Norman: University of Oklahoma Press, 529–38.

"Desegregation of the Armed Forces: Chronology." N.D. Harry S. Truman Library and Museum. http://www.trumanlibrary.org/whistlestop/study_collections/desegregation/large/index.php?action=chronology (accessed December 13, 2014).

Dillin, John. 2006 "How Eisenhower Solved Illegal Border Crossings from Mexico," *Christian Science Monitor* July 6. http://www.csmonitor.com/2006/0706/p09s01-coop.html (accessed December 12, 2015).

Easterbrook, Frank H. 1983. "The Most Insignificant Justice: Further Evidence," 50 *University of Chicago Law Review* 50: 481–503.

Eleanor Roosevelt Papers Project. N.D. "Fair Employment Practices Committee," https://www.gwu.edu/~erpapers/teachinger/glossary/fepc.cfm (accessed May 19, 2016).

Epp, Charles. 1998. *The Rights Revolution: Lawyers, Activists, and Supreme Courts in Comparative Perspective*. University of Chicago Press.

Esterbrook, John. 2002. "Life for '60s Radical H. Rap Brown," CBS News.com, March 13 http://www.cbsnews.com/news/life-for-60s-radical-h-rap-brown/ (accessed Dec. 20, 2016).

Fairman, Charles. 1971, 1987. *History of the U.S. Supreme Court (Oliver Wendell Holmes Devise) Vol. VI, VII: Reconstruction and Reunion 1864–1888*. New York: Macmillan.

Farber, Dan. 1982. "The Supreme Court and the Rule of Law: *Cooper v. Aaron* Revisited," *University of Illinois Law Review* 387–412.

Farrand, Max, ed. 1911. *Records of the Federal Convention of 1787*. 3 Volumes. New Haven: Yale University Press.

Federal Judicial Center. N.D. "U.S. Circuit Courts and the Federal Judiciary," http://www.fjc.gov/public/home.nsf/hisc] accessed Jan. 27, 2008.

Fehrenbacher, Don E. 1978. *The Dred Scott Case*. NY: Oxford University Press.

Finkelman, Paul. 1986. *The Law of Freedom and Bondage*. New York: Oceana Press.

Finkelman, Paul. 1994. "Story Telling on the Supreme Court: *Prigg v Pennsylvania* and Justice Joseph Story's Judicial Nationalism," *The Supreme Court Review*, Vol. 1994: 247–94.

Finkelman, Paul. 2002. "The Proslavery Origins of the Electoral College," *Cardozo Law Review* 23: 1147–57.

Finkelman, Paul. 2005. "Civil Rights in Historical Context: In Defense of *Brown"* (Book Review), 118 *Harvard Law Review* 118: 973–1029.

Fisher, Louis. 2002. *Religious Liberty in America: Political Safeguards.* Lawrence, University Press of Kansas.

Fiss, Owen. 1993. *Troubled Beginnings of the Modern State, 1888–1910.* Vol. VIII Oliver Wendell Holmes Devise History of the Supreme Court of the United States. New York: Macmillan.

Flores, Juan and Renato Rosaldo, eds. 2007. *A Companion to Latina/Latino Studies*. Malden, MA: Blackwell.

Florida Department of State. 2015. "Statehood," and "Territorial Period," *A Brief History*. http://dos.myflorida.com/florida-facts/florida-history/a-brief-history/ (accessed May 14, 2015).

Florida Memory, State Library & Archives of Florida. N.D. "The Cuban Experience in Florida." https://www.floridamemory.com/online classroom/cuban-revolution/photos/ (accessed July 8, 2015).

Foley, Neil. 2007. "'God Bless the Law, He is White': Legal, Local and International Politics of Latina/o and Black Desegregation Cases in Post-World-War II California and Texas," in Flores and Rosaldo *A Companion to Latina/Latino Studies*, Ch. 27.

Foner, Eric. 1988. *Reconstruction*. NY: Harper Collins.

Foreman, George. 1953 (and 1932). *Indian Removal: The Emigration of the Five Civilized Tribes of Indians.* Norman OK: University of Oklahoma Press.

"Fort Sumter." N.D. www.us-civilwar.com/sumter.htm (accessed June 7, 2010).

Franklin, John Hope and Alfred A. Moss, Jr. 1994. *From Slavery to Freedom; A History of African Americans*. 7th ed. NY: Alfred A. Knopf.

Frantz, Laurent. 1964. "Congressional Power to Enforce the Fourteenth Amendment against Private Acts," *Yale Law Journal* 73: 1353–84.

Freedman, Eric. 2000. "Leo Frank Lives: Untangling the Historical Roots of Meaningful Federal Habeas Corpus Review of State Convictions," *Alabama Law Review* 51: 1467–540.

Friedman, Barry. 2009. *The Will of the People*. NY: Farrar, Straus and Giroux.

Fritz, Christian. 1988. "A Nineteenth Century 'Habeas Corpus Mill': The Chinese Before the Federal Courts in California," *American Journal of Legal History* 32: 347–72.

Gales and Seaton's *Register of Debates in Congress* in *A Century of Lawmaking for a New Nation: U.S. Congressional Documents and Debates, 1774–1875.* N.D. http://memory.loc.gov/ammem/amlaw/lawhome.html (accessed Jan. 3, 2010).

Getches, David, Charles Wilkinson, and Robert Williams, Jr. 1993. *Cases and Materials on Federal Indian Law*. 3rd ed. St. Paul: West.

Gibson, Robert A. 2014 (written 1979). *The Negro Holocaust: Lynching and Race Riots in the United States, 1880–1950*. New Haven: Yale-New Haven Teachers Institute http://www.yale.edu/ynhti/curriculum/units/1979/2/79.02.04.x.html (accessed June 16, 2014).

Goldman, Robert M. 2001. *Reconstruction and Black Suffrage: Losing the Vote in Reese & Cruikshank*. Lawrence: University Press of Kansas.

Goldstein, Leslie F. 2001. *Constituting Federal Sovereignty: The European Union in Comparative Context*. Baltimore: Johns Hopkins University Press.

Goldstein, Leslie F. 2007. "The Specter of the Second Amendment: Re-reading *Slaughterhouse* and *Cruikshank*," *Studies in American Political Development* 21: 131–48.

Goldstein, Leslie F. 2011-A. "A 'Triumph of Freedom' After All? *Prigg v. Pennsylvania* Re-Examined," *Law and History Review* 29: 763–96.

Goldstein, Leslie F. 2011-B. "Constituting Politics and the Political Constitution," Review Essay, *Tulsa Law Review* 47: 177–83.

Goluboff, Risa. 2009. "The Thirteenth Amendment in Historical Perspective," *University of Pennsylvania Journal of Constitutional Law* 11: 1451–73.

Gomez-Quinones, Juan. 1994. *Roots of Chicano Politics 1600–1940*. Albuquerque: University of New Mexico Press.

Graber, Mark. 1993. "The Nonmajoritarian Difficulty: Legislative Deference to the Judiciary," *Studies in American Political Development* 7: 35–73.

Graber, Mark. 2006. *Dred Scott and the Problem of Constitutional Evil*. New York: Cambridge University Press.

Graham, Hugh Davis. 2002. *Collision Course: The Strange Convergence of Affirmative Action and Immigration Policy in America*. New York: Oxford University Press.

Green, George N. 2010. "GOOD NEIGHBOR COMMISSION," *Handbook of Texas Online*. Texas State Historical Association http://www.tshaonline.org/handbook/online/articles/mdg02 (accessed July 26, 2015).

Green, Michael. 1996, "The Expansion of European Colonization to the Mississippi Valley, 1780–1880," in Trigger and Washburn. eds, *The Cambridge History of the Native American Peoples of the Americas, Vol. I North America, Pt.1*, 461–538.

Greenberg, Sanford N. 2010. "WHITE PRIMARY," *Handbook of Texas Online*. Texas State Historical Association. http://www.tshaonline.org/handbook/online/articles/wdw01 (accessed May 08, 2015).

Greenfield, Gary A. and Don B. Kates, Jr. 1975. "Mexican Americans, Racial Discrimination, and the Civil Rights Act of 1866," *California Law Review* 63: 662–731.

Gunther, Gerald. 1972. "The Supreme Court, 1971 Term—Foreword: In Search of Evolving Doctrine on a Changing Court: A Model for a Newer Equal Protection," *Harvard Law Review* 86: 1–306.

Haas, Theodore H. 1957. "The Legal Aspects of Indian Affairs from 1887 to 1957," *Annals of the American Academy of Political and Social Science* 311 (May): 12–22.

Hair, William. 1976. *Carnival of Fury: Robert Charles and the New Orleans Race Riot of 1900.* Baton Rouge: Louisiana State University Press.

Hales, Douglas. 2010. "LOVE, CHARLES N.," *Handbook of Texas Online*, http://www.tshaonline.org/handbook/online/articles/floac (accessed March 10, 2017).

Hamer, Philip M. 1935. "Great Britain, the United States, and the Negro Seamen Acts, 1822–1848," *The Journal of Southern History* 1 (Feb.): 3–28.

Hamilton, Daniel W. 2004. "Militia Act (1862)." *Major Acts of Congress*, ed. Brian K. Landsberg. Vol. 2. Gale Cengage. *eNotes.com.* http://www.enotes.com/militia-act-1862-reference/ (accessed Dec 22, 2011).

Haney-Lopez, Ian. 1997. "Race, Ethnicity, Erasure: The Salience of Race to LatCrit Theory," *California Law Review* 85: 1143-1211

Haney-Lopez, Ian. 2006. *White by Law*. New York: NYU Press.

Hanifin, Patrick W. 2002. "To Dwell on the Earth in Unity: Rice, Arakaki, and the Growth of Citizenship and Voting Rights in Hawai'i," *Hawaii Bar Journal* V: 15–44.

Harper, Douglas. 2003. "Slavery in the North." http://www.slavenorth.com (accessed Nov. 30, 2006).

Harris, Cheryl. 1993. "Whiteness as Property," *Harvard Law Review* 106: 1707–91.

Henkin, Louis. 1987. "The Constitution and United States Sovereignty: A Century of 'Chinese Exclusion' and Its Progeny," *Harvard Law Review* 100: 853–86.

"Henry M. Teller." N.D. http://www.senate.gov/artandhistory/history/common/generic/Featured_Bio_Teller.htm (accessed May 7, 2011).

Hernández, Kelly Lytle. 2006. "The Crimes and Consequences of Illegal Immigration: A Cross-border Examination of Operation Wetback, 1943 to 1954." *The Western Historical Quarterly* 37(4): 421–44.

Hernandez, Prisco. 2013. "Puerto Ricans—World War II," in Alexander M. Bielakowski, ed. *Ethnic and Racial Minorities in the U.S. Military*. Santa Barbara: ABC-CLIO, 546–50.

Hershberger, Mary. 1999. "Mobilizing Women, Anticipating Abolition: The Struggle Against Indian Removal in the 1830s," *Journal of American History* 86: 15–40.

Hershberger, Mary. 2006, "Review of Portnoy, Their Right to Speak," *Journal of American History* 93: 528–9.

Higginbotham, A. Leon. 1978. *In the Matter of Color: Race and the American Legal Processs: The Colonial Period.* New York: Oxford University Press.

Higgs, Robert. 1978. "Landless by Law: Japanese Immigrants in California Agriculture to 1941," *Journal of Economic History* 38: 205–25.

Hine, Darlene Clark. 2003. *Black Victory: The Rise and Fall of the White Primary in Texas.* 2d ed. Columbia, MO: University of Missouri Press.

"*Hodges v. U.S.*" 2006. *Encyclopedia of Arkansas History and Culture.* http://www.encyclopediaofarkansas.net/encyclopedia/entry-detail.aspx?entryID=7404 (accessed Feb. 19, 2013).

Holden-Smith, Barbara. 1993. "Lords of Lash, Loom, and Law: Justice Story, Slavery, and *Prigg v. Pennsylvania*," *Cornell Law Review* 78: 1086–151.

Hoover, Herbert. 1930. "Statement on Indian Affairs" (Jan.3) Online by Gerhard Peters and John T. Woolley, *The American Presidency Project.* http://www.presidency.ucsb.edu/ws/?pid=22510 (accessed Aug. 27, 2015).

Howard, Benjamin Chew. 2008. *West's Encyclopedia of American Law*, 2d ed. The Gale Group. http://legal-dictionary.thefreedictionary.com/benjamin+chew+howard (accessed Sept. 1, 2015).

Howard, John. 1999. *The Shifting Wind: The Supreme Court and Civil Rights from Reconstruction to Brown.* Albany: SUNY Press.

Hoxie, Frederick E. 1984. *A Final Promise: The Campaign to Assimilate the Indians 1880–1920.* Lincoln: U of Nebraska Press.

Hoxie, Frederick E. 1996. "The Reservation Period, 1880–1960," in Trigger and Washburn. eds, *The Cambridge History of the Native Peoples of the Americas*, 183–258.

Hoxie, Frederick E. 2007. "What was Taney Thinking? American Indian Citizenship in the Era of Dred Scott," *Chicago-Kent Law Review* 82: 329–59.

Hull, Elizabeth. 1992. "Naturalization and Denaturalization," in Kim, *Asian Americans and the Supreme Court*, 403–24.

Hune, Shirley. 1982. "Politics of Chinese Exclusion: Legislative-Executive Conflict 1876–1882," AMERASIA 9: 5–27, reprinted in McClain 1994-A.

Hylton, J. Gordon. 1991. "The Judge Who Abstained in *Plessy v. Ferguson*: Justice David Brewer and the Problem of Race," *Mississippi Law Review* 61: 315–64.

Hyman, Harold, ed. 1966. *New Frontiers of the American Reconstruction.* Urbana: University of Illinois Press.

"Immigration to America: Tydings-McDuffie Act (United States) (1934)." 2015. http://immigrationtous.net/299-tydings-mcduffie-act-united-states-1934.html (accessed Sept. 21, 2015).

"The Immigration and Nationality Act of 1952." N.D. Department of State website https://history.state.gov/milestones/1945-1952/immigration-act (accessed Dec.2, 2014).

Irwin, Lee. 1997. "Freedom, Law, and Prophecy: a Brief History of Native American Religious Resistance," *American Indian Quarterly* 21: 35–55.

Jack, Theodore H. 1916. "Alabama and the Federal Government: The Creek Indian Controversy," *The Mississippi Valley Historical Review* 3: 301–17.

"James D. Cameron," in "Biographical Directory of the U.S. Congress." N.D. http://bioguide.congress.gov/scripts/biodisplay.pl?index=c000065 (accessed Aug.14, 2011).

Jensen, Ron. 2005. "Army Was Pushed to Desegregate by Escalation of Korean War," *Stars and Stripes.* February 13 Issue. http://www.stripes.com/military-life/army-was-pushed-to-desegregate-by-escalation-of-korean-war-1.33183 (accessed May 31, 2016).

Jones, Reinette and the University of Kentucky Libraries. 2015. "Bush v. Kentucky (John Bush vs The Commonwealth of Kentucky)," *Notable Kentucky African Americans Database.* http://nkaa.uky.edu/record.php?note_id=3002 (accessed April 14, 2015).

Jordan, Winthrop. 1968. *White Over Black: American Attitudes Toward the Negro 1550–1812.* New York: Norton.

Joy, Natalie Irene. 2008. Hydra's Head: Fighting Slavery and Indian Removal in Antebellum America, Ph.D. dissertation, University of California, Los Angeles.

JP. 2011. "A Boxer's Unforgivable Brashness: The Champ Who Dared To Be Black" http://selvedgeyard.com/2011/01/09/a-boxers-unforgivable-brashness-the-champ-who-dared-to-be-black/ (accessed May 22, 2014).

"Judge Goff Is Overruled." 1895. *New York Times*, June 12.

"Judicial Selection in the States – History of Reform Efforts." 2016. National Center for State Courts. http://www.judicialselection.us/judicial_selection/reform_efforts/formal_changes_since_inception.cfm?state= (accessed Jan.12, 2016).

"Justice Sanford Deserves Greater Recognition." 2016. Knoxville (Tennessee) News Sentinel, December 27. http://www.knoxnews.com/story/opinion/editorials/2016/12/27/justice-sanford-deserves-greater-recognition/95850332/ (accessed Feb. 22, 2017).

Kamp, Allen R. 1986. "The History Behind *Hansberry v. Lee*," *U.C. Davis Law Review* 20: 481–99.

Kappler, Charles J., ed. 1929. *Indian Affairs: Laws and Treaties, Vol. IV, Laws* (Compiled to March 4, 1927) Washington: Government Printing Office.

Karlan, Pamela S. 2005. "Contracting the Thirteenth Amendment: *Hodges v. United States*," *Boston University Law Review* 85 (June): 783–809.

Karst, Kenneth. 2000. "Moore v. Dempsey," in Leonard W. Levy and Kenneth L. Karst. Eds, *Encyclopedia of the American Constitution*. Vol. 4. 2nd ed. Detroit: Macmillan Reference USA, 1757–8.

Kelly, Alfred H. 1959. "The Congressional Controversy over School Segregation, 1867-1875," *American Historical Review* 64: 537–63.

Kelly, Alfred H., Winfred Harbison, and Herman Belz. 1983. *The American Constitution, Its Origins and Development*. 6th ed. New York: W.W. Norton.

Kent, James. 1826. *Commentaries on American Law*. New York: O. Halsted.

Kerber, Linda. 1975. "The Abolitionist Perception of the Indian," *Journal of American History* 62: 271–95.

Kernell, Samuel and Gary C. Jacobson. 2000. *The Logic of American Politics*. Washington DC: CQ Press.

Kim, Chin and Bok Lim C. Kim. 1977. "Asian Immigrants in American Law: A Look at the Past and the Challenge Which Remains," *American University Law Review* 26: 373–407 (reprinted in McClain 1994-B).

Kim, Hyung-Chan, ed. 1992-A. *Asian Americans and the Supreme Court*. NY: Greenwood Press.

Kim, Hyung-Chan. 1992-B. "An Overview," in Kim, 1992-A, 1–76.

Kiyama, Henry. 1999. (Frederick L. Shodt, trans.) *The Four Immigrants Manga*. Berkeley: Stone Bridge Press.

Klarman, Michael. 2004. *From Jim Crow to Civil Rights: The Supreme Court and the Struggle for Racial Equality*. New York: Oxford.

Klein, Christine, 1996. "Treaties of Conquest: Property Rights, Indian Treaties, and the Treaty of Guadalupe Hidalgo," *New Mexico Law Review* 26: 201.

Klinkner, Philip A. and Rogers M. Smith. 1999. *The Unsteady March: The Rise and Decline of Racial Equality in America*. Chicago: University of Chicago Press.

Kluger, Richard. 2004. *Simple Justice: The History of Brown v. Board of Education and Black America*. 2d ed. NY: Vintage Books.

Koestler, Fred L. 2015. "Operation Wetback," *Handbook of Texas Online*. Texas State Historical Association https://tshaonline.org/handbook/online/articles/pqo01 (accessed December 12, 2015).

Kolchin, Peter. 1993. *American Slavery 1619–1877.* New York: Hill and Wang.

Kousser, J. Morgan. 1974. *The Shaping of Southern Politics: Suffrage Restrictions and the Establishment of the One-Party South, 1888–1910.* New Haven: Yale University Press.

Kousser, J. Morgan. 1992. "The Voting Rights Act and the Two Reconstructions," http://www.hss.caltech.edu/~kousser/racial%20 discrimination/Brook.pdf (accessed 2/18/12). Reprinted, 135–76 in Chandler Davidson and Bernard Grofman, eds., 1992. *Controversies in Minority Voting: A Twenty-Five Year Perspective on the Voting Rights Act of 1965.* Washington: Brookings Institution.

Kramer, Paul A. 2006. *The Blood of Government: Race, Empire, the United States and the Philippines.* Chapel Hill: University of North Carolina Press.

Kuo, Joyce. 1998. "Excluded, Segregated and Forgotten: A Historical View of the Discrimination of Chinese Americans in Public Schools," *Asian American Law Journal* 5: 181–212 http://scholarship.law.berkeley.edu/aalj/vol5/iss1/7 (accessed Sept. 21, 2015).

Larson, Robert. 1968. *New Mexico's Quest for Statehood.* Albuquerque: University of New Mexico Press.

Lasser, William. 1988. *The Limits of Judicial Power.* Chapel Hill: University of North Carolina Press.

Laws of the Territory of New Mexico Passed by the First Legislative Assembly in the City of Santa Fe. 1851. Santa Fe: James Collins & Co.

Le, C.N. 2014. "The 1965 Immigration Act" *Asian-Nation: The Landscape of Asian America.* <http://www.asian-nation.org/1965-immigration-act.shtml> (accessed August 22, 2014).

Lee, Erika. 2003. *At America's Gates: Chinese Migration during the Exclusion Era, 1882–1943.* Chapel Hill: University of North Carolina Press.

Leip, David. 2008. "1860 Presidential General Election Results," *Atlas of U.S. Presidential Elections* http://www.uselectionatlas.org/RESULTS/national.php?off=0&year=1860 (accessed April 12, 2010).

Lenderman, Jason. 1998. "A Tiny Tribe Wins Big on Clean Water." *High Country News* (Feb.2) https://www.hcn.org/issues/123/3922 (accessed October 31, 2015).

Leong, Karen J. 2003. "Foreign Policy, National Identity, and Citizenship: The Roosevelt White House and the Expediency of Repeal," *Journal of American Ethnic History* 22: 3–30.

Lewis, H.H. Walker. 1976. "The Maryland Constitution—1776," *Archives of Maryland Documents for the Classroom.* http://msa.maryland.gov/megafile/msa/speccol/sc2200/sc2221/000004/000000/html/00000005.html#walk (accessed Dec. 27, 2015).

"Lincoln's First Inaugural Address March 4, 1861." N.D. http://www.gutenberg.org/dirs/etext90/linc111h.htm (accessed June 7, 2010).
Linder, Douglas. 2000-A. "The Amistad Case" http://www.law.umkc.edu/faculty/projects/ftrials/amistad/adamsarg.html (accessed March 12, 2007).
Linder, Douglas. 2000-B. "Lynchings by Year and Race." Shipp Trial Home Page. http://law2.umkc.edu/faculty/projects/ftrials/shipp/lynchingyear.html (accessed Dec. 2, 2016).
Linder, Douglas. 2000-C. "The Shipp Trial, An Account" http://law2.umkc.edu/faculty/projects/ftrials/shipp/shipp.html (accessed June 5, 2013).
Litwack, Leon. 1961. *North of Slavery*. Chicago: University of Chicago Press.
Logan, Rayford W. 1997. *The Betrayal of the Negro*. New York: Da Capo Press (reprint of 1965).
Longaker, Richard P. 1956. "Andrew Jackson and the Judiciary," *Political Science Quarterly* 71: 341–64.
Longaker, Richard P. 1974. "Emergency Detention: The Generation Gap, 1950–1971," *Western Political Quarterly* 27(3): 395–408.
"Louisiana Purchase." 2008. Avalon Project, Lillian Goldman Law Library, Yale University. http://avalon.law.yale.edu/19th_century/louis1.asp (accessed April 19, 2015).
Lupton, John. 2007. "Virden, Pana and Carterville (Illinois) Mine Riots, 1898–1899," in Rucker and Upton, eds., *Encyclopedia of American Race Riots, Volume 2*. 671–5.
"Lynchings by Year and Race." N.D. Shipp Trial Home Page. http://law2.umkc.edu/faculty/projects/ftrials/shipp/lynchingyear.html (accessed Dec. 2, 2016).
Lyman, Sanford. 1991. "The Race Question and Liberalism: Casuistries in American Constitutional Law," *International Journal of Politics, Culture, and Society* 5: 183–247.
MacMurray, John V.A., ed. 1921. "Convention Regulating Chinese Immigration," –11 in *Treaties and Agreements with and Concerning China 1894–1919*. New York: Oxford University Press.
Magliocca, Gerard. 2003. "The Cherokee Removal and the Fourteenth Amendment," *Duke Law Journal* 53: 875–965.
Maltz, Earl. 2009. *Slavery and the Supreme Court, 1825–1861*. Lawrence, KS: University Press of Kansas.
Margold, Nathan. 1931. The Margold Report. *NAACP Papers*, Microfilm. Part 3, Series A, Reel 4, frames 0559-0772.
Marks, Carole. 2009. *Moses and the Monster and Miss Anne*. Urbana: University of Illinois Press.

Martinez, George A. 1994. "Legal Indeterminacy, Judicial Discretion and the Mexican-American Litigation Experience: 1930–1980." *U.C. Davis Law Review* 27: 555–618.

Martinez, George A. 1998. "Mexican Americans and Whiteness," in *The Latino/a Condition: A Critical Reader*, eds. Richard Delgado and Jean Stefanic. New York: NYU Press, Ch.25.

Martinez, Matthew. 2004–2015. "Pueblo People Win the Right to Vote-1948," New Mexico Office of the State Historian. New Mexico State Record Center and Archives. http://dev.newmexicohistory.org/filedetails.php?fileID=415 (accessed Aug. 15, 2015)

Martinez, Trisha, ed. 2014. "Students in Public Schools." Legal Services Department, Orange County, California http://www.ocde.us/LegalServices/Documents/Chapter-IX-Students-in-Public-Schools-July-2014.pdf (accessed Aug 2, 2015).

Maslow, Will. 1961. "De Facto Public School Segregation," *Villanova Law Review* 6: 353–76.

McBride, David. 1986. "Mid-Atlantic State Courts and the Struggle with the 'Separate but Equal' Doctrine: 1880–1939," *Rutgers Law Journal* 17: 569–89.

McClain, Charles Jr. 1985: "The Chinese Struggle for Civil Rights in Nineteenth Century America: The Unusual Case of *Baldwin v. Franks*," *Law and History Review* 3: 349–73.

McClain, Charles Jr. ed. 1994-A. *Asian Americans and the Law, Vol. 1 Chinese Immigrants and American Law.* NY: Garland.

McClain, Charles Jr. ed. 1994-B. *Asian Americans and the Law, Vol. 4 Asian Indians, Filipinos, Other Asian Communities and the Law.* NY: Garland.

McClain, Charles Jr. 1999. "The Chinese Struggle for Civil Rights in Nineteenth Century America: The First Phase, 1850–1870," *California Law Review* 72: 529-568.

McConnell, Michael. 1994. "The Forgotten Constitutional Moment," *Constitutional Commentary* 11: 115–44.

McDonald, Forrest. 1982. *A Constitutional History of the United States.* New York: Franklin Watts.

McGovney, Dudley O. 1947. "The Anti-Japanese Land Laws of California and Ten Other States," *Caifornia Law Review* 35: 7–60.

McKeehan, Wallace L. 1997–2001. "The Adams-Onis Treaty," *New Spain Index* http://www.tamu.edu/faculty/ccbn/dewitt/adamonis.htm (accessed April 19, 2015).

Menchaca, Martha. 1993. "Chicano Indianism: A Historical Account of Racial Repression in the United States," *American Ethnologist* 20: 583–603.

Menchaca, Martha. 2001. *Recovering History, Constructing Race*. Austin: University of Texas Press.

Menchaca, Martha. 2011. *Naturalizing Mexican Immigrants, A Texas History*. Austin: University of Texas Press.

"Mexican Americans," N.D. *Handbook of Texas Online*. Texas State Historical Association https://tshaonline.org/handbook/online/articles/pqmue (accessed April 21, 2015).

Meyer, Stephen G. 2001. *As Long as They Don't Move Next Door*. Lanham, MD: Rowman and Littlefield.

Miles, Edwin A. 1973 "After John Marshall's Decision: Worcester v. Georgia and the Nullification Crisis," *The Journal of Southern History*: 519–44.

Mixon, Gregory and Clifford Kuhn. 2005. "The Atlanta Race Riot of 1906," *New Georgia Encyclopedia*. http://www.georgiaencyclopedia.org/articles/history-archaeology/atlanta-race-riot-1906 (accessed Mar. 29, 2014).

Molotsky, Irvin. 1988. "Senate Votes to Compensate Japanese-American Internees," *New York Times*, April 21 http://www.nytimes.com/1988/04/21/us/senate-votes-to-compensate-japanese-american-internees.html (accessed Sept. 6, 2015).

Morales, Ed. 2012. "The school desegregation case you don't know." http://inamerica.blogs.cnn.com/2012/02/03/an-important-latino-civil-rights-victory-born-from-a-mexican-puerto-rican-alliance/ (accessed July 7, 2015).

Morris, Thomas D. 1974. *Free Men All: The Personal Liberty Laws of the North 1780–1861*. Baltimore: Johns Hopkins University Press.

NAACP. 1919. *Thirty Years of Lynching in the United States, 1889–1918*. NY: NAACP (reprnt 2012. Clark NJ: Lawbook Exchange).

"NAACP History: Anti-Lynching Bill." 2009-2014. National Association for the Advancement of Colored People http://www.naacp.org/pages/naacp-history-anti-lynching-bill (accessed Aug.1, 2014).

National Conference for Community and Justice. N.D. "Our Story," https://www.nccj.org/our-story (accessed Aug.3, 2014.)

National Park Service. N. D. "Ybor City Historic District Tampa, Florida" http://www.nps.gov/nr/travel/american_latino_heritage/Ybor_City_Historic_District.html (accessed July 8, 2015).

Nackenoff, Carol. 2006. "Constitutionalizing Terms of Inclusion: Friends of the Indian and Citizenship for Native Americans, 1880s–1930s," in Ronald Kahn and Ken Kersch, eds, *The Supreme Court and American Political Development*. Lawrence: University Press of Kansas, 366–413.

Nackenoff, Carol. 2010, "Sovereignty and Governing the Self: Native American Governance during the Dawes Act Era," paper presented at

Workshop on Sovereignty and Constitutionalism, University of Wisconsin Law School, Madison, October 15–16, 2010.
"Nathan Goff, Jr." N.D. http://en.wikipedia.org/wiki/Nathan_Goff,_Jr. (accessed May 17, 2013).
National Johnson-O'Malley Association. N.D. JOM Program Handbook. Link at http://www.aps.edu/indian-education/johnson-omalley-program-jom/johnson-omalley-program-jom (accessed Sept. 8, 2015).
National Portrait Gallery. N.D. "The Amistad Case," http://www.npg.si.edu/col/amistad/index.htm Accessed March 12, 2007
Nelson, Robert. 1995. *Public Land and Private Rights*. Lanham, Maryland: Rowman and Littlefield.
Newmyer, Kent. 1969. "On Assessing the Court in History: Some Comments on the Roper and Burke Articles," *Stanford Law Review* 21: 540-547.
Newmyer, Kent. 2001. *John Marshall and the Heroic Age of the Supreme Court*. Baton Rouge: Louisiana State University Press.
Nieman, Donald G. 1991 *Promises to Keep: African-Americans and the Constitutional Order, 1776 to the Present*. New York: Oxford University Press.
Nieto-Phillips, John. 2004. *The Language of Blood: The Making of Spanish American Identity in New Mexico, 1880s–1930s*. Albuquerque: University of New Mexico Press.
Niiya, Brian. 2014. "Military Areas 1 and 2" *Densho Encyclopedia* http://encyclopedia.densho.org/Military_Areas_1_and_2/ (accessed Aug. 20, 2014.)
"19th Century U.S. Immigration Statistics." N.D. http://www.latinamericanstudies.org/immigration.htm (accessed July 12, 2014).
Noel, Linda C. 2011. " 'I am an American': Anglos, Mexicans, *Nativos*, and the National Debate over Arizona and New Mexico Statehood," *Pacific Historical Review*: 80: 430–67.
Noel, Linda C. 2014. *Debating American Identity: Southwestern Statehood and Mexican Immigration*. Tucson: University of Arizona Press.
Noonan, John T. 1977. *The Antelope: The Ordeal of the Recaptured Africans in the Administrations of James Monroe and John Quincy Adams*. Berkeley: University of California Press.
Nordyke, Eleanor C. and Y. Scott Matsumoto. 1977. "Japanese in Hawaii: a Historical and Demographic Perspective," *Hawaiian Journal of History* 11: 162–74. https://evols.library.manoa.**hawaii**.edu/bitstream/handle/.../JL11174.pdf? (accessed July 17, 2014).
Norgren, Jill. 2004. *The Cherokee Cases*. Norman: University of Oklahoma Press.
Note. 1939. "The Negro Citizen in the Supreme Court," *Harvard Law Review* 52: 823–32.

Odo, Franklin, ed. 2002. *The Columbia Documentary History of the Asian American Experience.* NY: Columbia U Press.

Ohio Historical Society. N.D. "Springfield Ohio, Racial Conflicts." http://www.ohiohistorycentral.org/w/Springfield,_Ohio,_Racial_Conflicts?rec=2100 (accessed March 29, 2014).

Okihiro, Gary. 2006. "Colonial Vision, Racial Visibility: Racializations in Puerto Rico and the Philippines during the Initial Period of U.S. Colonization," in *Racial Transformations: Latinos and Asians Remaking the United States*. de Genova, Nicholas and Ana Y. Ramos-Zayas. eds, Durham: Duke University Press.

Orfield, Gary. 2015. "Education and Civil Rights: Lessons of Six Decades and Challenges of a Changed Society," in Bowman, ed. 2015-A, 405–30.

Orozco, Cynthia E. 2010. "Del Rio ISD v. Salvatierra," *Handbook of Texas Online*. Texas State Historical Association http://www.tshaonline.org/handbook/online/articles/jrd02 (accessed July 25, 2015).

Otis, Delos Sacket. 1993. "History of the Allotment Policy," 1934 H.R.7902 Committee Hearings, 191–195 in Getches et al. 1993.

OWNO. 1998–2014. "History of Cuba," Nations Online Project. http://www.nationsonline.org/oneworld/History/Cuba-history.htm (accessed April 20, 2015).

Park, John S. 2004. *Elusive Citizenship.* NY: NYU Press.

Parman, Donald L. and Lewis Meriam. 1992. "Lewis Meriam's Letters during the Survey of Indian Affairs 1926-1927 (Part 1)." *Arizona and the West* 24: 253–80.

Paterson, Eva et al. 2005. "Equal Justice–Same Vision in a New Day," *Yale Law Journal.* http://yalelawjournal.org/forum/equal-justicea8212same-vision-in-a-new-day (November 20, 2014).

Pauli Murray Project. N.D. "Biography," http://paulimurrayproject.org/pauli-murray/biography/ (accessed August 1, 2015).

Pike, John. 2000-2016. "Japan War Scare of 1906–1907." http://www.globalsecurity.org/military/ops/japan1906.htm (accessed Dec. 6, 2016)

Pildes, Richard H. 2000. "The Canon(s) of Constitutional Law: Democracy, Anti-Democracy, and the Canon" *Constitutional Commentary* 17: 295–319.

Pommersheim, Frank. 2009. *Broken Landscape: Indians, Indian Tribes and the Constitution.* NY: Oxford University Press.

Ponca Tribe of Nebraska. 2015. "History." http://www.poncatribe-ne.org/History (accessed Sept.10, 2015).

Potter, David M. 1976. *The Impending Crisis 1848–1861,* ed. Don E. Fehrenbacher. New York: Harper and Row.

Portnoy, Alysse. 2005. *Their Right to Speak: Women's Activism in the Indian and Slave Debates.* Cambridge: Harvard University Press.

Powers, Jeanne M. 2008. "Forgotten History: Mexican American School Segregation in Arizona from 1900–1951," *Equity & Excellence in Education*, 41: 467–81.

President's Committee on Civil Rights. 1947. *To Secure These Rights.* Harry Truman Library and Museum http://www.trumanlibrary.org/civilrights/srights4.htm#139 (accessed December 13, 2014).

"President Taft on Lynching." 1912. *Boston Evening Transcript*, p. 10, col.6, April 12.

Prucha, Francis P. 1986. *The Great Father: The United States Government and the American Indians.* Abridged Ed. Lincoln: University of Nebraska Press.

Puerto Rico Report. 2012. "The Origin of the 'Commonwealth' Label." http://www.puertoricoreport.com/the-origin-of-the-commonwealth-label/#.VUeRZPAYP06 (accessed May 4, 2015).

Pusey, Grace. 2014. "Today in History: Luce-Celler Act Signed in 1946," *South Asian American Digital Archive* http://www.saadigitalarchive.org/news/20140702-3609 (accessed August 20, 2014).

Qureshi, Bilal. 2013. "From Wrong To Right: A U.S. Apology For Japanese Internment," *NPR*, April 9. http://www.npr.org/sections/codeswitch/2013/08/09/210138278/japanese-internment-redress (accessed Sept. 6, 2015).

"Racism Takes a Blow in Reno." 1997–2000. *International Boxing Hall of Fame.* http://www.ibhof.com/pages/archives/johnsonjeffries.html (accessed May 22, 2014).

Ramos, Lisa, 2011. "Not Similar Enough: Mexican American and African American Civil Rights Struggles in the 1940s," 19–48 in Behnken 2011-A.

Ramos-Zayas, Ana Y. and Nicholas de Genova. 2003. *Latino Crossings.* NY: Routledge.

Raney, George P. 1876. "In Memoriam … of M. D. Papy." *Florida Reports* (*Reports of Cases Argued and Adjudged in the Supreme Court of Florida*) 15: XI-XIII. Tallahassee: Office of the Floridian.

Rangel, Jorge and Carlos Alcala. 1972. "Project Report: De Jure Segregation of Chicanos in Texas Schools," *Harvard Civil Rights-Civil Liberties Law Review* 7: 314–91.

"Readmission to Representation in Congress." N.D. *Reconstruction Era.* http://en.wikipedia.org/wiki/Reconstruction_Era_of_the_United_States#cite_ref-89 (accessed Dec. 19, 2011).

Regua, Nanette. 2007. "*Mendez v. Westminster* Case." Blog. http://mendezwestminstercase.blogspot.com/2007/08/mendez-v-westminster-case.html (accessed July 28, 2015).

"Results from the 1860 census." N.D. *The Civil War Home Page* http://www.civil-war.net/pages/1860_census.html (accessed Dec.4, 2016).

Rice, Roger L. 1968. "Residential Segregation by Law," *Journal of Southern History* 34: 179–99.

Richardson, Heather C. 2001. *The Death of Reconstruction.* Cambridge: Harvard University Press.

Rivera, Megaly. 2015. "Puerto Rico's History 1900–1949," and "Puerto Rico's History 1950–2014," in *Welcome to Puerto Rico*. http://www.topuertorico.org/history5.shtml (May 3, 2015).

Robinson, Toni and Greg Robinson. 2003. "*Mendez v. Westminster*: Asian-Latino Coalition Triumphant?" *Asian Law Journal* 10: 161–83.

Rodriguez, Gregory. 2007. *Mongrels, Bastards, Orphans, and Vagabonds: Mexican Immigration and the Future of Race in America*. NY: Pantheon Books.

Roper, Daniel. 1969. "In Quest of Judicial Objectivity: The Marshall Court and the Legitimation of Slavery," *Stanford Law Review* 21: 532–9.

Roosevelt, Theodore. 1906. State of the Union Address. http://www.infoplease.com/t/hist/state-of-the-union/118.html (accessed June 2, 2014).

Rosen, Deborah. 2003. "Pueblo Indians and Citizenship in Territorial New Mexico," *New Mexico Historical Review* 78: 1–28.

Rosenberg, Gerald. 2008. *The Hollow Hope: Can Courts Bring About Social Change?* 2nd ed. Chicago: University of Chicago Press.

Rossiter, Clinton. 1956. *The American Presidency*. New York: Harcourt Brace and World.

Rozeft, Norman. 2011. "Garcia, Hector Perez," *Handbook of Texas Online* Texas State Historical Association http://www.tshaonline.org/handbook/online/articles/pqitw (accessed July 30, 2015).

Rucker, Walter C. and James N. Upton, eds. 2007. *Encyclopedia of American Race Riots, Volume 2*. Westport, CT: Greenwood Press.

Rudko, Frances Howell. 2001. "Pause at the Rubicon, John Marshall and Emancipation: Reparations in the Early National Period?" *John Marshall Law Review* 35: 75–89.

Ruiz, Vicki L. 2001. "South by Southwest: Mexican Americans and Segregated Schooling, 1900–1950," *OAH Magazine of History* 15: 23–7.

Rutherglen, George. 2013. *Civil Rights in the Shadow of Slavery*. NY: Oxford University Press.

Salyer, Lucy. 1989. "Captives of Law: Judicial Enforcement of the Chinese Exclusion Laws, 1891-1905," *Journal of American History* 76: 91–117.

Sanchez, George J. 1993. *Becoming Mexican American*. NY: Oxford University Press.

Saunt, Claudio. 2015. "Creek Indians." *New Georgia Encyclopedia*. http://www.georgiaencyclopedia.org/articles/history-archaeology/creek-indians (accessed Jan. 7, 2016).

Saxon, Wolfgang. 1999. "Philip Elman, 81, Government Lawyer in 1954 Desegregation Case" *NY Times*, Dec. 5. http://www.nytimes.com/1999/12/05/us/philip-elman-81-government-lawyer-in-1954-desegregation-case.html (accessed Aug. 20, 2014).

Schlup, Leonard and James G. Ryan. 2003. "Vance Zebulon Baird" at 511 in *Historical Dictionary of the Gilded Age*. Google e-book: M.E. Sharpe.

Schmidt, Benno. 1984. *Part Two of The Judiciary and Responsible Government 1910–1921*. Vol. IX of Oliver Wendell Holmes Devise History of the Supreme Court of the United States. New York: Macmillan.

Schmitt, Jeffrey. 2007. "Rethinking *Ableman v. Booth* and States' Rights in Wisconsin," *Virginia Law Review* 93: 1315–54.

Schmitt, Jeffrey. 2011. "The Antislavery Judge Reconsidered," *Law and History Review* 29: 797–834.

Schoeppner, Michael A. 2010. *Navigating the Dangerous Atlantic: Racial Quarantines, Black Sailors and United States Constitutionalism*, Ph.D. Diss. University of Florida, 2010. etd.fcla.edu/UF/UFE0042328/schoeppner_m.pdf (accessed Oct. 3, 2014)

SCIWAY. 2015. "South Carolina—Indians, Native Americans—Catawba" http://www.sciway.net/hist/indians/catawba.html (accessed Sept. 10, 2015).

"Scott Act." 1998–1999. *The Chinese-American Experience 1857–1892*. Harp Week. http://immigrants.harpweek.com/ChineseAmericans/2KeyIssues/ScottAct.htm (accessed Aug.15, 2014).

"Senate Apologizes for Not Passing Anti-Lynching Laws." June 13, 2005. Associated Press. http://www.foxnews.com/story/2005/06/13/senate-apologizes-for-not-passing-anti-lynching-laws/ (accessed June 2, 2014.)

Senechal, Roberta. 1996. "The Springfield Race Riot of 1908," *Illinois History Teacher* III (2): 22-27, from Illinois Periodicals Online http://www.lib.niu.edu/1996/iht329622.html (Accessed Mar.29, 2014).

Shay, Alison. 2012. "Remembering Executive Order 9981" in *This Day in Civil Rights History*.

Shimsky, MaryJane. 2009. "Hesitating between Two Worlds": The Civil Rights Odyssey of Robert H. Jackson. Dissertation in History, City University of New York. UMI Microform.

Silva, Catherine. 2009. "Racial Restrictive Covenants: Enforcing Neighborhood Segregation in Seattle," Seattle Civil Rights & Labor History Project http://depts.washington.edu/civilr/covenants_report.htm (accessed Dec. 3, 2016).

Simmons, Marc. 1979. "History of the Pueblos Since 1821," in "Southwest," Alfonso Ortiz. ed. *Handbook of North American Indians*. William Sturtevant. Washington, D.C.: Smithsonian Institution, Vol. 9, 206–23.

Singh, Inder. 2006. "Struggle of Indians for US Citizenship," *Guyana Journal*, July 2006 http://www.guyanajournal.com/immigration_indians.html (accessed Aug. 20, 2014).

Smith, Jean Edward. 2000. "Marshall Misconstrued: Activist? Partisan? Reactionary?" *John Marshall Law Rev*iew 33: 1109–29.

Smith, Rogers M. 1997. *Civic Ideals: Conflicting Visions of Citizenship in U.S. History*. New Haven: Yale University Press.

Soltero, Carlos R. 2006. *Latinos and American Law Landmark Supreme Court Cases*. Austin: University of Texas Press.

Sparrow, Bartholomew H. 2006. *The* Insular Cases *and the Emergence of American Empire*, Lawrence: University Press of Kansas.

Staples, Brent. 2016. "A 'Most Dangerous' Newspaper," *New York Times Book Review Section*. Jan.10, 2016. (Review of *The Defender* by Ethan Mitchell.)

Stone, Geoffrey R. 2004. *Perilous Times*. NY: W.W. Norton.

Story, Joseph. 1987. *Commentaries on the Constitution of the United States*. Durham: Carolina Academic Press, repr. of 1833.

Story, William Wetmore. 1851. *Life and Letters of Joseph Story*, in two volumes. Boston: Little and Brown.

Strum, Philippa. 2010. *Mendez v. Westminster: School Desegregation and Mexican-American Rights*. Lawrence, University Press of Kansas.

Strum, Philippa. 2015. "Our Children Are Americans: *Mendez v. Westminster* and Mexican American Rights," in Bowman, ed. 2015-A, 9–30.

Stuen, Thomas E. 1992. "Asian Americans and their Rights for Land Ownership," in Kim. 1992-A, 603–30.

Sturgis, Amy. 2007. *The Trail of Tears and Indian Removal*. Westport, CT: Greenwood Press.

Swinney, Everette. 1987. *Suppressing the Ku Klux Klan: The Enforcement of the Reconstruction Amendments 1870–1877*. New York: Garland.

Swisher, Carl. 1974. *The Taney Period 1836–1864*. Vol. V of the Oliver Wendell Holmes Devise History of the Supreme Court of the United States. New York: Macmillan.

Takaki, Ronald. 1998. *Strangers from a Different Shore*. Boston: Little, Brown.

Tamayo, William. 1992. "Asian Americans and Present U.S. Immigration Policies: A Legacy of Asian Exclusion," in Kim 1992-A, 1105–30.

"The Border—History: Timeline—1948–American G.I. Forum." 1999. http://www.pbs.org/kpbs/theborder/history/timeline/19.html (accessed April 21, 2015).

"The Great Slavery Case." 1842. *N.Y. Tribune*, Mar. 14, at 1.

"The Surrender." N.D. www.nps.gov/apco/surrend.htm (accessed June 7, 2010).

"The Thirteenth Amendment Ratification and Results," 1998–2008. *Harp Week*. http://13thamendment.harpweek.com/HubPages/CommentaryPage.asp?Commentary=05Results (accessed 12/3/2011).

Thompson, Lorraine. 2008. "Saga of the Pappy Family," *The St. Augustine Record*, September 14. http://staugustine.com/stories/091408/community_0914_007.shtml#.WO9xEoWcG3Q (accessed April, 1, 2017).

Thorpe, Francis N. ed. 1909. *The Federal and State Constitutions, Colonial Charters, and Other* ... "New Mexico—1850" in *Vol. 5. New Jersey–Philippines*. Washington: Government Printing Office. Digitized by Google. (accessed April 29, 2015).

Tillery, Alvin. 2009. "Tocqueville as a Critical Race Theorist," *Political Research Quarterly* 62: 639–52.

Trigger, Bruce and Wilcomb E. Washburn, eds. 1996. *The Cambridge History of the Native Peoples of the Americas*, Vol. I, Pt. 2. NY: Cambridge University Press.

Truman, Harry S. 1948. "Executive Order 9980 – Regulations Governing Fair Employment Practices within the Federal Establishment." July 26. Online by Gerhard Peters and John T. Woolley, *The American Presidency Project*. http://www.presidency.ucsb.edu/ws/?pid=78208 (accessed December 13, 2014).

Tushnet, Mark. 1987. *The NAACP's Legal Strategy against Segregated Education, 1925–1950*. Chapel Hill: University of North Carolina Press.

Tushnet, Mark. 1998. "Progressive Era Race Related Cases in their 'Traditional' Context," *Vanderbilt Law Review* 51: 993–1002

Tushnet, Mark. 2010. *Why The Constitution Matters*. Yale University Press.

Uenuma, Francine and Mike Fritz. 2011. "Why the Sioux Are Refusing $1.3 Billion." PBS Newshour WLIW21 http://www.pbs.org/newshour/updates/north_america-july-dec11-blackhills_08-23/ (accessed Oct 29, 2015).

Ultimate History Project Staff. N.D. "La Leyenda Negra: Old Views of the New World" http://www.ultimatehistoryproject.com/la-leyenda-negra.html (accessed April 30, 2015).

Umfleet, LeRae. 2010. "The Wilmington Race riot – 1898" NC Office of Archives and History www.history.ncdr.gov/ (accessed March 29, 2014 via http://ncpedia.org/history/cw-1900/wilmington-race-riot).

U.S. Census Bureau, "Table 55. South Carolina – Race and Origin: 1790–1990." N.D. http://www.census.gov/population/www/documentation/twps0056/tab55.pdf (accessed May 17, 2013).

U.S. Citizenship and Immigration Services. N.D. "Study Materials for the English Test," www.uscis.gov/citizenship/learners/study-test/study-materials-english-test (accessed Aug. 2, 2015).

U.S. Department of State Office of the Historian. N.D. "Milestones: 1801–1829 'Acquisition of Florida'" https://history.state.gov/milestones/1801-1829/florida (accessed April 17, 2015).

U.S. Department of State Office of the Historian. N.D. "Milestones: 1830–1860 'The Annexation of Texas, the Mexican-American War, and the Treaty of Guadalupe-Hidalgo, 1845–1848'" https://history.state.gov/milestones/1830-1860/texas-annexation (accessed April 17, 2015).

U.S. Department of State Office of the Historian. N.D. "Milestones: 1830–1860 'Gadsden Purchase, 1853–1854' " https://history.state.gov/milestones/1830-1860/gadsden-purchase (accessed April 17, 2015).

U.S. Department of State Office of the Historian. N.D. "Milestones: 1899–1913, 'The Philippine-American War, 1899–1902.'" https://history.state.gov/milestones/1899-1913/war (accessed April 21, 2015)

United States Statutes at Large, Vol. 18, Pt.2. 1875. (1st Session 43rd Congress, 1873–1874). Washington D.C.: Government Printing Office.

University of Texas College of Education. 2005. "Other Artifacts [Letter to Mrs. Luther Stover, dated December 22, 1915]" http://www.edb.utexas.edu/faculty/salinas/students/student_sites/Fall2005/Latino_Segregation_in_Public_Schools/Other_Artifacts.html (accessed July 25, 2015).

Valencia, Richard R. 2005. "The Mexican-American Struggle for Equal Educational Opportunity in *Mendez v. Westminster*," *Teachers College Record* 107: 389–423. Available online www.tcrecord.org/library (accessed Aug. 3, 2015).

Vose, Clement. 1959. *Caucasians Only*. Berkeley: University of California Press.

"Voters: Native Americans," N.D. Library of Congress. http://www.lcweb.loc.gov/teachers/classroommaterials/presentationsandactivities/presentations/elections/voters9.html (accessed Dec. 9, 2016).

Wallace, D.D. 1896. "The South Carolina Constitutional Convention of 1895," *The Sewanee Review*, 4: 348–60.

Walter, Yvonne. 2007. "Asian Americans and American Immigration and Naturalization Policy," *American Studies Journal*. No.49. Special Edition. http://www.asjournal.org/archive/49/15.html#11 (accessed Aug. 14, 2014).

Wang, Xi. 1997. *The Trial of Democracy: Black Suffrage and Northern Republicans, 1860–1910*. Athens: U of Georgia Press.

Warren, Charles. 1922. *The Supreme Court in U.S. History*, Vols. II and III. Boston: Little, Brown.

Washburn, Wilcomb E. 1996. "The Native American Renaissance, 1960–1995," in Trigger and Washburn, 401–73.

Washington, Margaret. 1998. "The New York City Riot," (interview in) *America 1900*. Boston: WGBH Educational Foundation, David Grubin Productions http://www.pbs.org/wgbh/amex/1900/filmmore/reference/interview/washing_nycityriot.html0 (accessed March 29, 2014).

Weinberg, Louise. 2007. "Dred Scott and the Crisis of 1860," *Chicago-Kent Law Review*, 82: 97–139.

Wiecek, William. 1978. "Slavery and Abolition before the U.S. Supreme Court 1820–1860," *Journal of American History* 65: 34–59.

Wiecek, William. 1988. *Liberty under Law: The Supreme Court in American Life* Baltimore: Johns Hopkins University Press.

Wiecek, William 2006. *The Birth of the Modern Constitution: The United States Supreme Court, 1941–1953*, Volume XII of The Oliver Wendell Holmes Devise History of the Supreme Court of the United States. NY: Cambridge University Press.

Wildenthal, Bryan. 2003. *Native American Sovereignty On Trial: A Handbook With Cases, Laws, and Documents.* Santa Barbara, CA: ABC-CLIO.

Wilkins, David E. 1997. *American Indian Sovereignty and the U.S. Supreme Court, The Masking of Justice.* Austin: U of Texas Press.

Wilkins, David E 1998. "Book Review of *Blue Clark,* Lone Wolf v. Hitchcock*: Treaty Rights and Indian Law at the End of the Nineteenth Century*," *American Indian Quarterly* 22: 528–32.

Wilkins, David E. and K. Tsianina Lomawaima. 2001. *Uneven Ground: American Indian Sovereignty and Federal Law*. University of Oklahoma Press.

Wilkinson, Charles F. 1987. *American Indians, Time, and the Law*. New Haven: Yale University Press.

Wilkinson, Charles F. and Eric R. Biggs. 1977. "Evolution of the Termination Policy," *American Indian Law Review* 5: 139–54.

"William Drew Washburn" in "Biographical Directory of the U.S. Congress" N.D. http://bioguide.congress.gov/scripts/biodisplay.pl?index=c000065 (accessed Aug.14, 2011).

"William D. Washburn," N.D. http://en.wikipedia.org/wiki/William_D._Washburn (accessed Aug.14, 2011).

Williams, Lou Falkner. 1996. *The Great South Carolina Ku Klux Klan Trials, 1871–1872*. Athens, GA: University of Georgia Press.

Wilson, Carol. 1994. *Freedom at Risk: The Kidnapping of Free Blacks in America 1776–1865*. Lexington: University Press of Kentucky.

Wilson, Steven H. 2005. "Some Are Born White, Some Achieve Whiteness, and Some Have Whiteness Thrust upon Them: Mexican Americans and the Politics of Racial Classification in the Federal Judicial Bureaucracy, Twenty-five Years after *Hernandez v. Texas*" *Chicano-Latino Law Review* 25: 201–25.

Wisch, Rebecca. 2002. "Detailed Discussion of the Bald and Golden Eagle Protection Act," Animal Law Legal and Historical Center of Michigan State University College of Law. https://www.animallaw.info/article/detailed-discussion-bald-and-golden-eagle-protection-act (accessed November 8, 2015.)

Wolff, Jeremy. 2014. "A Timeline of Boston School Desegregation, 1961–1985," link found in Peter Balonon-Rosen, "Boston School Desegregation and Busing: A Timeline Of Events," September 5, 2014 WBUR "Learning Lab." http://learninglab.wbur.org/2014/09/05/boston-school-desegregation-and-busing-a-timeline-of-events/ (accessed September 5, 2015).

Woodward, C. Vann. 1966. "Seeds of Failure in Radical Race Policy," in Hyman, 125–56.

Woolley, John and Peters, Gerhard. 1999–2017. "Election of 1860," *The American Presidency Project* http://www.presidency.ucsb.edu/showelection.php?year=1860 (accessed Dec. 4, 2016).

"WWII Reparations: Japanese-American Internees." 1999. *Democracy Now*, February 18 http://www.democracynow.org/1999/2/18/wwii_reparations_japanese_american_internees (accessed Sept. 6, 2015).

Index

All pages for court cases are to be found in Table of cases